LEARNING FROM SIX PHILOSOPHERS

Learning from Six Philosophers

Descartes, Spinoza, Leibniz, Locke, Berkeley, Hume

JONATHAN BENNETT

VOLUME 1

CLARENDON PRESS · OXFORD

2001

OXFORD

UNIVERSITY PRESS

Great Clarendon Street, Oxford OX2 6DP

Oxford University Press is a department of the University of Oxford.
It furthers the University's objective of excellence in research, scholarship,
and education by publishing worldwide in

Oxford New York

Athens Auckland Bangkok Bogotá Buenos Aires Cape Town
Chennai Dar es Salaam Delhi Florence Hong Kong Istanbul Karachi
Kolkata Kuala Lumpur Madrid Melbourne Mexico City Mumbai
Nairobi Paris São Paulo Shanghai Singapore Taipei Tokyo Toronto Warsaw

and associated companies in Berlin Ibadan

Oxford is a registered trade mark of Oxford University Press
in the UK and in certain other countries

Published in the United States
by Oxford University Press Inc., New York

British Library Cataloguing in Publication Data

Data available

Library of Congress Cataloging in Publication Data

Data available

ISBN 0–19–825091–6

1 3 5 7 9 10 8 6 4 2

Typeset by Hope Services (Abingdon) Ltd.
Printed in Great Britain
on acid-free paper by
T.J. International Ltd.
Padstow, Cornwall

Preface to Volume 1

This half of my two-volume work is devoted mainly to themes in the works of Descartes, Spinoza, and Leibniz. The second volume is primarily addressed to Locke, Berkeley, and Hume, though Leibniz will come in a good deal in his role as a commentator on Locke and (in Chapters 23 and 40) in other ways as well. Chapter 24 will be wholly devoted to a theory of Descartes's which I prefer to expound only after presenting related work by Locke and Leibniz.

Chapters 6–11 overlap my *Study of Spinoza's Ethics* (Hackett, 1984), especially on themes treated in Parts 1 and 2 of the *Ethics*. But the work is deepened, sharpened, and clarified; I also do more than I did in the earlier book to relate Spinoza's work to the thought of Descartes before him and Leibniz after.

I respond to some criticisms of my earlier work, where it seems profitable to do so. But my main concern is to present what I now have to say in as clear and uncluttered a manner as possible.

Each volume contains the Contents and Abbreviations for the entire work. The Bibliography and Indexes have been divided, with each volume containing only what is relevant to it. Each Index of Topics includes references to the 'six philosophers'; all other personal references are in the Index of Persons. In the Bibliography for this volume I do not list works by Leibniz to which I refer only briefly and infrequently.

A comprehensive treatment of my six philosophers, even on the topics within their work which I discuss, could not be achieved by one person or presented in a mere forty chapters. I have chosen topics which I find interesting and nourishing to wrestle with. A reader who stays with me will at the end have some sense of the overall shape of each of the six, though providing this has not been my chief aim.

The title *Learning from Six Philosophers* declares my attitude in this work: I want to learn from these men, which I do by arguing with them. Whether this is worthwhile is the topic of the Introduction.

Where I can, I refer to French and Latin texts through inexpensive English translations, because I want the work to be useful to students with small libraries. I often modify the translations a little, without notice. For Leibniz translations, I refer in the text to Francks and Woolhouse, failing which the less accurate Ariew and Garber, failing which the more expensive Loemker, failing which the less widely available Morris and Parkinson.

This work arises out of teaching across forty years at several universities— Cambridge, Cornell, Michigan, Princeton, British Columbia, Syracuse. My intellectual debts to colleagues and students at those institutions are too numerous, and not clearly enough remembered, for me to acknowledge them in detail; but

I place on record my gratitude for the doctoral programme at Syracuse University and for my eighteen happy years of contact with its students and faculty.

Further opportunities to interact with able and dedicated philosophers were provided by two Summer Seminars for College Teachers which I conducted in Syracuse in 1995 and 1996. These did much to push along my thinking about Descartes, Spinoza, and Leibniz.

I was also helped by sabbatical leaves in which I was supported by Syracuse University and (in two) by the National Endowment for the Humanities and (in a third) by the John Simon Guggenheim Foundation. To all three organizations I am grateful.

At a late stage in its life, the entire manuscript was read for Oxford University Press by Don Garrett, who provided several dozen comments and suggestions for its improvement. I have availed myself of many of these, and thank Garrett for the generosity and thoughtfulness of his help.

Readers who have comments, suggestions, or corrections to offer are invited to send them to me at jfb@mail.com.

J.F.B.

Bowen Island, BC
May 2000

Contents

VOLUME 2

Abbreviations and Other Conventions used in Text and Bibliography

The symbol '§' refers only to sections of this book. Unadorned occurrences of the form '§n' mean '[Some aspect of] this was discussed in §n above' or '. . . will be more fully discussed in §n below'.

An asterisk after a reference to a translation means that the translation contains a significant error which I have corrected in quoting.

All references are by page number unless otherwise indicated here.

In quotations from Descartes, material in <angle brackets> is not in the original, and comes from a later translation which Descartes is thought to have approved.

Individual works by the 'six philosophers' that are listed here are characterized more fully in the Bibliography.

A	German Academy of Science, ed., *Gottfried Wilhelm Leibniz: Sämtliche Schriften und Briefe* (Darmstadt, and Berlin: Akademie Verlag, 1926–); reference by series, volume, and page.
Abstract	Abstract of Hume's *Treatise of Human Nature*; reference by paragraph.
AG	R. Ariew and D. Garber (eds.), *G. W. Leibniz: Philosophical Essays* (Indianapolis: Hackett, 1989).
Alexander	*The Leibniz–Clarke Correspondence*, ed. H. G. Alexander (Manchester University Press, 1956).
AT	C. Adam and P. Tannery (eds.), *Œuvres de Descartes*, nouvelle présentation (Paris: Vrin, 1964–76); reference by volume and page.
Comments	Leibniz, Comments on Spinoza's Philosophy (1707).
Couturat	Louis Couturat (ed.), *Opuscules et fragments inédits de Leibniz* (Hildesheim: Olms, 1988).
Critique	Immanuel Kant, *Critique of Pure Reason* (1781); reference by A and B numbers given in the margin of the Kemp Smith (Macmillan) edition.
CS	E. Curley (ed.), *The Collected Works of Spinoza*, vol. 1 (Princeton University Press, 1985).
CSM	J. Cottingham, R. Stoothoff, and D. Murdoch (eds.), *The Philosophical Writings of Descartes*, vols. 1 and 2 (Cambridge University Press, 1984–5); reference by volume and page.
CSMK	J. Cottingham, R. Stoothoff, D. Murdoch, and A. Kenny (eds.), *The Philosophical Writings of Descartes*, vol. 3 (Cambridge University Press, 1991).

CT	Leibniz, Critical Thoughts on the General Part of the *Principles* of Descartes (1692).
Dia 1	The first of Berkeley's *Three Dialogues between Hylas and Philonous* (1713); similarly 'Dia 2' and 'Dia 3'; reference by page in LJ 3.
DM	Leibniz, *Discourse on Metaphysics* (1686*a*); reference by section.
DP	Spinoza, *Parts I and II of Descartes's 'Principles of Philosophy'* (1663).
Enquiry	Hume, *Enquiry Concerning the Human Understanding* (1748); reference by section and part, and by marginal number in the Selby-Bigge (OUP) edition.
Essay	Locke, *An Essay Concerning Human Understanding* (1690); reference by book, chapter, section, or by page and line in the Nidditch (OUP) edition.
Ethics	Spinoza, *Ethics Demonstrated in Geometrical Order* (1675?); reference by part and axiom (a), definition (d), proposition (p), corollary (c), demonstration (d), and scholium (s) (thus 1d4 is the fourth definition in part 1, and '2p13,d' refers to part 2's 13th proposition *and its* demonstration), or by page in *CS*.
F. de C.	Foucher de Careil (ed.), *Nouvelles lettres et opuscules inédits de Leibniz* (Paris, 1857).
FW	G. W. Leibniz, *Philosophical Texts*, trans. and ed. R. S. Woolhouse and R. Francks (Oxford University Press, 1998).
G	C. I. Gerhardt (ed.), *Die philosophischen Schriften von Gottfried Wilhelm Leibniz* (Berlin, 1875–90); reference by volume and page.
GH	R. Gennaro and C. Huenemann (eds.), *New Essays on the Rationalists* (Oxford University Press, 1999).
GM	C. I. Gerhardt (ed.), *Leibnizens mathematische Schriften* (Berlin, 1875–90); reference by volume and page.
Grua	G. W. Leibniz, *Textes inédits*, ed. Gaston Grua (New York: Garland, 1985).
LBH	Jonathan Bennett, *Locke, Berkeley, Hume: Central Themes* (Oxford University Press, 1971).
L	Gottfried Wilhelm Leibniz, *Philosophical Papers and Letters*, ed. L. E. Loemker (Dordrecht: Reidel, 1969).
LJ	A. A. Luce and T. E. Jessop (eds.), *The Works of George Berkeley* (London: Nelson, 1949); reference by volume and page.
Mason	H. T. Mason (ed.), *The Leibniz–Arnauld Correspondence* (Manchester University Press, 1967).
Med 1	The first of Descartes's *Meditations on First Philosophy* (1641); similarly 'Med 2', etc.
Method	Descartes, *Discourse on the Method of Rightly Conducting One's Reason and Seeking the Truth in the Sciences* (1637*a*).
MM	Descartes, *Principles of Philosophy*, ed. V. R. Miller and R. P. Miller (Dordrecht: Reidel, 1983).
Mon	Leibniz, 'Monadology' (1714*a*); reference by section.

NE	G. W. Leibniz, *New Essays on Human Understanding* (1705); reference by book, chapter, section, or by page in the Remnant–Bennett edition (which has the same pagination as the French text in A 6:6).
NI	Leibniz, 'On Nature Itself' (1698); reference by section.
NS	Leibniz, 'New System of Nature' (1695).
NT	Berkeley, *An Essay Towards a New Theory of Vision*, reference by section.
Obj 1	The first set of Objections to Descartes's Meditations; similarly 'Obj 2', etc.
OED	*Oxford English Dictionary*.
PAB	Leibniz, 'A Physicist against Barbarism' (1716).
Passions	Descartes, *Passions of the Soul* (1649); reference by section.
PC	Berkeley, *Philosophical Commentaries* (1708); reference by number of entry.
PHK	Berkeley, *A Treatise Concerning the Principles of Human Knowledge* (1710); reference by section.
PHKI	Ibid., introduction; reference by section.
PM	G. W. Leibniz, *Philosophical Writings*, ed. M. Morris and G. H. R. Parkinson (London: Dent, 1973).
PNG	Leibniz, 'Principles of Nature and of Grace' (1714).
PP	Descartes, *Principles of Philosophy* (1644); reference by part and section.
PT	Leibniz, 'Primary Truths' (1686).
Rep 1	The first set of Descartes's Replies to Objections to the Meditations; similarly 'Rep 2', etc.
Rules	Descartes, *Rules for the Direction of the Mind* (1628).
SD	Leibniz, 'Specimen of Dynamics' (1695*b*).
Study	Jonathan Bennett, *A Study of Spinoza's Ethics* (Indianapolis: Hackett, 1984).
Treatise	Hume, *A Treatise of Human Nature* (1739); reference by part and section (always of book I except where otherwise noted), and by pages in the Selby-Bigge (OUP) edition.
UO	Leibniz, 'On the Ultimate Origin of Things' (1697*b*).
W	Descartes, *The World* (1633).
Wolf	A. Wolf (ed.), *The Correspondence of Spinoza* (London: Allen & Unwin, 1928).

Introduction

Collegial early modern studies

This book is an exercise in the collegial approach to early modern philosophy, in which one studies the texts in the spirit of a colleague, an antagonist, a student, a teacher—aiming to learn as much philosophy as one can from studying them. I 'treat those who are great but dead as if they were great and living, as persons who have something to say to us *now*' (Grice 1986: 66).

Good collegial work on early modern philosophy requires care for, and knowledge of, the historical settings of the texts under study. A philosophical encounter with one of the greats can hardly be profitable by accident. Its chance of fruitfulness lies in its engaging with what the philosopher actually thought; and to establish this, one needs knowledge of the historical setting—what philosophers this one had been reading, which of them influenced him, what problems worried him, what a given word meant at the time he used it.

There is a doubly sliding scale of opinions as to how much of this is needed for how much gain in philosophical understanding. It is always true that some further item of historical knowledge might make a difference, but eventually one must stop digging in the background and turn back to the main project. Philosophers differ in how they calibrate the cost and benefit scales; Michael Ayers's scales, for example, are quite unlike mine. I believe that a certain way of distributing my energies between (for short) scholarship and analytic philosophy gives me my best chance of casting light on certain philosophers and problems; Ayers no doubt thinks that his markedly different distribution makes the best use of his talents. We are probably both right.

Historical knowledge carries danger for the project, just as does the corresponding ignorance. At the most general level, one risks treating one's subject philosopher too much as a passive node in a network of influences, and not enough as an active genius who is thinking for himself. To someone with a hammer, everything looks like a nail; to someone learned about the influences to which a past philosopher could have been subject, every facet of his thought may look like an effect of such influences.

As well as the placing of a work in its setting of other works by that author and his near-contemporaries, there is the placing of a segment in the context of the work as a whole. There are risks in taking passages chopped out of context, and not relating them to the subject author's purposes. But there are also risks in the other direction. A scholar whose thought is continuously informed by a clear,

strong view about a work's overall purposes may overlook textual episodes that
do not fit the pattern. When that happens, something is lost. Such a misfit passage can be the philosopher's fragmentary response to a half-recognized
difficulty in his position, or his expression of a half-conscious insight that he
hasn't turned into doctrine. One can learn from exploring a great philosopher's
subliminal sensitivities as well as from studying his declared doctrinal programme. Certainly there is value in knowing all about the studied work's unity
of purpose, but there is value of a different kind—less sedate and often more
interesting—in approaching a masterpiece more openly and vulnerably, more
ready to be surprised by it, never comfortable with it.

Adams and Sleigh

In their ground-breaking recent Leibniz books, Robert Adams and Robert Sleigh
have both written about how to approach early modern philosophy. Adams: 'I
believe that historical accuracy and careful attention to the historical context are
important to the philosophical as well as the historical value of a work in the history of philosophy and, conversely, that philosophical argument and critique are
important for historical understanding in philosophy' (1994: 5). I have endorsed
the first half of this, though I cannot match the depth and detail of scholarly
knowledge that Adams brings to his *philosophical* work on Leibniz. I now turn to
the converse thesis.

   Much historically motivated work on early modern philosophy is philosophically lax, superficial, and uninformed. Some throw the word 'teleological'
around without, apparently, having worked on teleology in its own right (§108).
People write about causation in early modern philosophy without understanding the issues concerning event- versus fact- versus agent-causation; about dispositions without having worked on counterfactuals; about 'ideas' without
having struggled independently with the concept of meaning; and so on. Early
modern studies would be healthier, more muscular, if every practitioner also
sometimes did work that was purely philosophical and in no way historical.

   Of all this, Adams is innocent. So is Sleigh. In his much-discussed account of
why he is not a collegial early modernist (1990a: 2–6), Sleigh describes his own
'exegetical' approach as having two components: (1) the fact-finding one, establishing a 'surface account' of what the subject author thought about this topic at
that time; (2) the explanatory component, exploring the author's reasons for his
views, digging down to find 'the rational basis' that underlies them. This second
component, Sleigh says, is 'a more difficult, and surely more exciting, task', and
he adds that the collegial approach at its best contributes to this.

   Yet Sleigh rejects the collegial approach because in the hands of less than excellent practitioners it 'allows the author a front for probing philosophical problems, presenting arguments, even reaching conclusions, without being held to

current standards of rigor'. True; however, any serious line of endeavour risks being done badly; yet Sleigh says nothing about what *non*-collegial early modern studies degenerate into when done less than excellently. He seems to hold that in the collegial approach the fall-off in quality is notably steep, basing this not on any epidemiological study but on reasoning about the odds against success in collegial history of philosophy.

The reasoning starts from the premiss that although 'philosophy is not related to its history in the way physics is to its history', still 'there *is* progress in philosophy'. From this Sleigh infers that if you want to understand personal identity, reading Shoemaker is 'more important' than reading Locke, on whose shoulders he stands; and that for students of the metaphysics of modality, Kripke is 'more to the point' than Leibniz.

Anticipating the reply that properly to engage with the problems of Shoemaker and Kripke you must frame them in their history, Sleigh gives it the lie direct. 'It is not necessary to study the history of a philosophical problem', he writes, 'in order to make a fundamental contribution toward the understanding, perhaps even the solution, of that problem.' When his opponents on this point protest, he could reply that the onus of proof is upon them, and that it has not been discharged. I think that Sleigh is right about this. For evidence look at the work of David Lewis, who is reckoned by many of us to be the most fruitful philosopher alive, and whose work is not visibly influenced by any knowledge of the history of philosophy.

Sleigh's other claim—that in working philosophically on any problem which engaged early modern philosophers and engages us today, studying the best contemporary work is more important or pointful than studying the early moderns—is worth pondering. Standing on the shoulders of our masters, we can sometimes see further, and the examples of Shoemaker and Kripke are persuasive.

For progress with currently live philosophical problems, then, historical studies are neither *necessary* nor *more important* than studying our contemporaries. Like most collegial early modernists (I should think), I can calmly accept this, having never thought otherwise. What I have found is that collegial early modern studies are *helpful* to me in my grasp of some philosophical problems that still engage me.

Learning from successes

On some topics, indeed, we have not made significant progress: for example, we have not advanced much beyond Hume in our understanding of causation. Without accepting his whole theory of meaning, we can get from him—as has been brought out in fine works by Pears (1990) and by Blackburn (1990)—a profound sequence of thoughts about the demand for intellectual security regarding the future. There is an irony here. The recent fashion for taking Hume to be a shallowly commonsensical fellow who is content to be a 'sceptical realist' about causation has arisen from, among other things, a failure to *learn from Hume* what he has to teach on this topic.

Descartes saw, as perhaps nobody had before him, what a vast array of behavioural conditionals must be true of someone who is competent in some language and is thus disposed 'to give an appropriately meaningful answer to whatever is said in his presence' (§49). He tacitly granted that such a set of conditionals could be grounded in a purely material system, but he said explicitly that it is not thus grounded in actual human beings, because their heads are too small to hold the required mechanisms. It is a non-trivial exercise, when one has fully taken in Descartes's profoundly insightful premiss, to see how to avoid his conclusion.

On other topics, too, we are not yet at the end of learning from great philosophers of the past: Kant on the dangers of rational psychology and on the interplay between concepts and sensory intake, Hume on nature versus reason; Leibniz on the counting of substances, Spinoza on the counting of substances, Descartes on space and place, Locke and Leibniz on determinism and moral responsibility; and so on.

A philosopher of the past can also help by teaching us smaller nuggets of demonstrated philosophical truth. Kant's Refutation of Idealism contains a wretchedly worded presentation of a splendid argument about how to remember the order in which events occurred—an argument with a true conclusion, which I did not know to be true until I dug it out of Kant's text (Bennett 1966).

Sometimes no digging is needed. Leibniz writes in his *New Essays* that if there were a spatial vacuum, we could in principle measure it, but that 'if space were only a line and if bodies were immovable', no stretch of empty space could be measured. Think about how we can in fact measure a vacuum: we can triangulate on a pair of points on its edge from a point outside it (space is not a line), and we can lay a measuring device through the vacuum and then remove it (bodies are movable). One could realize this without help from Leibniz; but it came to me through my thinking about Leibniz's half-sentence on this topic.

Examples abound. But the philosophical help we can get from early modern studies does not consist mainly in learning truths which the subject philosophers also thought were truths. The collegial approach is criticized on the assumption that help in philosophy must consist in the delivery of true doctrine. A decent teacher does not shovel in truths; rather, he or she offers warnings and pointers and suggestions—notice that x is different from y; consider whether z has something in common with w; ask whether you can solve problem P without having a tenable view about problem Q; and so on. I get countless things like this from my early modern studies, and they are obtainable from that source only through the collegial approach. Even the strenuously philosophical work of Sleigh does not, and is not meant to, yield many benefits of this kind; *a fortiori* no such help can be expected from historically oriented early modern studies that do not go beyond the first of Sleigh's two stages—the kind he rightly characterizes as superficial, easy, and relatively boring.

Sleigh is right: there is progress in philosophy. But even on a topic on which we have progressed beyond the point where a past philosopher was stuck, we can get a better grasp of where we are, and why, by understanding where he was, and why. How could it not be instructive to hang around a great philosopher, attending carefully to what he has to say as he struggles with problems? We have our own stock of reasons for the positions we adopt, statable in terms drawn from our contemporaries; but some of us find that these reasons can be deepened and clarified by being related to early modern endeavours. This is not about pastness as such; it concerns the invigorating effect of testing one's ideas against the work of philosophers whose thought is original, deep, broad, and brave.

Learning from struggles and failures

J. L. Austin once said to me, of a philosophical opinion that he thought was Leibniz's, that 'It is a very great mistake, and only a very great philosopher could have made it'. In that paradoxical remark there is this much truth: a philosopher can be led into error by the very power of his thought, making serious mistakes that he might not have made if he had seen less and probed less deeply. Studying those mistakes can help one to dig deeper into what is true. I now sketch a few examples of that kind of help—cases where I have learned from the struggles and failures of the philosophers who are addressed in this book.

Any philosopher today wanting to give a psychological analysis of the concept of personal identity would require that the different temporal stages of a person be causally related to one another. That can be argued for on its own merits, without reference to earlier centuries; but our grasp of why it is right, and of how important it is, can be improved by seeing in detail what goes wrong with Locke's own account of personal identity, in which causation plays no part (§298).

It is today commonly and rightly thought that to make good sense of the concepts of belief and desire, one must bring them within a single explanation which also relates them to both sensory intake and physical behaviour. I have a better sense of why this is right from having looked at Hobbes's and Spinoza's attempts to understand desire separately from belief (§85).

Most of us think that on the meanings of natural-kind terms Putnam and Kripke are basically right (as was Leibniz before them). One's grasp of the reasons for this can be gleaned from studying Locke's great attempt to describe the meanings of classificatory words without help from existential quantifiers—that is, without help from '. . . having a real essence or chemical constitution which . . .' (§198).

There are philosophical as well as physical obstacles to the idea of instantaneous causal propagation across a distance. One way of starting to get hold of them is to follow Descartes's view that the propagation of light is instantaneous and his apparent failure to integrate this with his physics of collisions (§20).

Sometimes it has taken a good deal of digging to expose the learnable lesson. Here is an example.

Spinoza held that so-called error is really a species of ignorance. In trying to find out why, working not on the surface where doctrinal counters are pushed around but at the deeper level where real reasons must be sought, I came across things that helped me in my philosophical thinking about error. Spinoza's starting-point, I came to think, was this: a belief is a natural object or event, so a belief cannot be outright false; for how could a real, natural object contain falsity? I worked out how I think this difficulty can be overcome, and then considered what elements in that solution were unavailable to Spinoza, and why. This project gave me a much firmer grasp on, and clearer view of, the conceptual elements that go into the concept of belief as I understand it (§77).

Learning from contrasts

Hume's account of personal identity is evidently modelled on Locke's chapter on identity. There are many differences of detail, and one large programmatic one: Locke steers mainly by thought-experiments about particular cases, whereas Hume is guided rather by his principled views about what must be going on when any diachronic identity-judgements are made. This difference between them, and its upshots in their detailed treatments of personal identity, have refreshed and vivified my own thinking about personal identity—and indeed about philosophical analysis generally. The difference between those two approaches could have been thought of, and instantiated, in other contexts as well; but I was alerted to it by the work of these two philosophers.

Why can a pebble not be a substance? One of Leibniz's answers: it is too large. One of Spinoza's: it is too small. There is philosophy to be learned from brooding on that contrast.

Berkeley and Leibniz both held that all reality is fundamentally mental, which leads some scholars to label both as 'idealists'. Despite the similarity, however, there is also a great difference. Berkeley's immaterialism proceeds from first-person, present-tense, psychological foundationalism; it accepts the problem Descartes gives himself in the First Meditation, and rejects his attempted solution of it in the Sixth. Leibniz's basis for his comparable position is nothing like this. My own thinking about immaterialism has been nourished by pondering this similarity and difference between these two philosophers.

Locke worried about the concept of an enduring thing, which he saw as requiring, but defying, analysis; Berkeley helped himself to that concept, and did not worry about it as he should have; Leibniz used the concept, and gave an analysis of it; Hume denied that there are enduring things, but his account of what leads us to think there are has much in common with Leibniz's analysis.

How could one attend carefully and intelligently to all this without being helped in one's own philosophical thinking?

It has traditionally been held that reason, when used properly, is infallible. This was a problem for Spinoza and and for Hume, each of whom regarded human reason as a natural feature of a natural object, and thus prima facie no more eligible for infallibility than a thermometer or a chisel is. Spinoza dealt with this through a theory according to which error is a species of ignorance, of which reason, by definition, is incapable. Hume took the other route, and denied the traditional view of reason's infallibility. I have chewed at length on this contrast, to my benefit.

Criteria for interpretation

In trying to decide how best to understand some part of a philosopher's work, should we look for the interpretation which (1) fits best with his intentions at the time of writing? (2) comes closest to making what he says true? (3) makes what he wrote most philosophically interesting and instructive?

Even if one's chief interest is in 3, one must start with 1. It could happen that the study of an early modern text brought philosophical illumination by accident, the insights gained having no relation to the actual thoughts of the philosopher in question; but it is enormously unlikely. One's best chance of getting help from a great philosopher of the past is to plug into his mind, rather than dancing around in its vicinity waiting for lightning to strike.

The primary way to plug into his mind is of course to establish what he consciously wanted to communicate when he wrote. As a sole objective, however, that is in one way too broad and in another too narrow.

It is too broad for my purposes, because some questions about what a great philosopher was up to are not philosophically interesting. For example, Descartes had a theory of motion according to which it is literally true that the earth does not move; this enabled him to part company with Galileo, who had been in trouble with the Roman Church for saying that it does move. How far was Descartes drawn to this theory by that consequence of it? This question seems to be of interest only to intellectual biographers. The answer to it has no evident effect on the workings of the rest of Descartes's philosophy, implying nothing about the intelligible reasons there are in favour of the theory or about its drawbacks.

The objective is too narrow, because some of what is most instructive and revealing in the thought of a great philosopher is to be found not in his consciously intended and openly proclaimed doctrines, but rather in the margins, between the lines, just beneath the surface. Like all of us, the great philosophers were subject to intellectual pressures that they did not fully recognize and so could not turn into outright doctrine; and discovering and exploring these can be richly rewarding. The present work gives many examples of this, and some are sketched in this Introduction.

Sometimes, I contend, a philosopher's proclaimed doctrine may be better understood as a misformulation of something different, more interesting, and closer to the truth. Consider, for example, Locke's thesis that ideas of primary qualities do, whereas those of secondary qualities do not, resemble material objects. This, as it stands, is untenable—there are no square ideas—and if we are confined to the literal meaning of what Locke wrote, there's an end of it. But we can reasonably take Locke to be groping for the thesis that the language in which we characterize our primary-quality ideas ('idea of square') is also needed in physics ('square'), while that in which we characterize our secondary-quality ideas ('idea of green') is not. This stays close to the concept of resemblance; it is philosophically respectable and in Locke's day would seem to be true; and it fits with Locke's central thesis that secondary qualities are dispositions to cause certain 'ideas' in suitably placed observers (§193).

A much more radical transformation is the one I offer for Hume's thesis that every simple idea is caused by a similar impression, which officially means that every feeble 'perception' is caused by a similar vivid one (§244). Taken as it stands, this is of no philosophical interest. I subject it to a triple transformation which brings it to life, connecting it with the uses that meaning-empiricists have made of Hume's work through two centuries, and giving the thesis a coherent fit with Hume's own uses of it.

As this last point implies, I do not think it is a coincidence that Hume's handling of his thesis makes good sense in, and only in, the triply transformed version of it. It seems to me certain that the transform was in some way at work in his thought, guiding his uses of his sterile thesis that feeble perceptions are copied from vivid ones; so that when one works on Hume's texts with the aid of the transform, one is still plugged into his mind.

Attributing error

I presented three possible goals for an interpreter of a philosopher of the past: (1) the interpretation that fits best with his intentions at the time of writing, (2) the one that comes closest to making what he says true, and (3) the one that makes what he wrote most philosophically interesting and instructive.

Ultimately I shoot for 3. It often conflicts with 2: an interpretation under which a philosopher has gone wrong is often more interesting than one which makes what he said come out true—but also obvious, boring, and safe, like the thesis that when Berkeley said that sensible things are ideas, he meant *only* that we perceive them.

Of course (3) the most philosophically nourishing interpretation of a piece of work can also be the one that (2) makes it true; and so 2 and 3 can work together.

What I object to is making 'What the great philosopher said is true' an axiom, or even a dominant guiding principle.

Mistakes, tangles, and the like can reflect credit on their authors. With the really great philosophers, in my opinion, the trouble they get into often comes from how much they have noticed: they have subliminally felt conceptual pressures of various kinds, and have subtly responded to them, without always managing to bring them into the open to be dealt with theoretically. That is why my kind of interpretation, in which error and contradiction and confusion are often alleged, is more respectful towards the studied philosopher than the kind which makes him right but trite.

Some scholars demand that we *mean well* in our dealings with the great philosophers of the past—politely find their writings sensible, consistent, and commendable; not be fiercely demanding; become comfortable with each text and with its author. I contend that this gives to the author, in a phrase of Strawson's, 'the wrong kind of respect'. The right kind will lead us to interrogate our philosopher's text closely, worry away at discrepancies and anomalies, and cleanse our minds of soothing approximations. When we have become uncomfortable with it, we can start to learn from what it gets right and what it gets wrong. This approach does the philosopher more honour than one driven by an insistence that he did not make bad mistakes.

Chapter 1

Cartesian and Aristotelian Physics

1. Aristotelian physics: a quick sketch

Much of Descartes's work was not 'philosophical' in any narrow sense; without his non-philosophical works, it might be hard to understand how tall he stood among his own contemporaries and immediate successors. He theorized about music. He wrote on meteorology, with what success I do not know. He addressed himself to optics, and discovered Snell's law, which some European textbooks still call 'the Descartes–Snell law' (Taton 1958). It relates the angle at which light meets a translucent medium to the angle at which it penetrates it, and is crucial to the theory and practice of magnifying glasses. Descartes made and published revolutionary discoveries in mathematics, taking the important first steps towards the algebraic treatment of geometry. (I would have said that he invented that treatment, but believable warnings against that have been issued by Emily Grosholz (1980), though I am not equipped to evaluate them.) He wrestled constantly with problems in theoretical general physics.

In physics he was an early follower and important developer of the scientific revolution that Galileo had started. We need to know something about this if we are to engage with some of Descartes's work in philosophy, more narrowly conceived; it also has a bearing on the work of Locke, Spinoza, and Leibniz. To get a handle on it, we must contrast it with what went before. For centuries up to the time of Galileo, what passed for physics was dominated by Aristotle, or by what the medievals made of him; and what was crucially new in Descartes's thought is best understood against this background. I shall present these matters in open reliance on the secondary literature.

Aristotle's explanations of events in the physical world were rooted in biology. The crucial explanatory fact about an organism is its 'form'. This is not a subset of the properties that the organism has, but rather a set of those that are *proper* to it, and towards which it strives or tends. Why does an acorn develop into an oak rather than a pig? Because of its special relation to the form that defines *oak*: it develops as it does because, while still an acorn, it lacks some of the properties that oaks have, and is somehow drawn towards instantiating that form more fully.

This inserts a kind of teleology right into the middle of biology. The most sober, basic, respectable biological explanations will have the form 'x did A in order that it might become the case that P'. Aristotle postulated four kinds of 'cause', or explanation: material, formal, efficient, and final. But he says that two or more of these may coincide in a particular case, and that for organisms the formal cause is also always final—which is to say that the normal development of an organism can be explained as occurring *so that* the organism may more thoroughly exhibit or participate in or be informed by its proper form. (See his *Physics* 2:7.) I find this summary helpful:

According to Aristotle, all natural motion is directed towards an end. What is the end that is sought in nature? It is the development from a state of potentiality to one of actuality, the embodiment of form in matter. With Aristotle . . . the teleological view of nature prevails over the mechanical. . . . The teleology is not, however, all-pervasive and all-conquering, since matter sometimes obstructs the action of teleology (as, for instance, in the production of monsters, which must be ascribed to defective matter). Thus the working of teleology in any particular instance may suffer the occurrence of an event which does not serve the end in question. (Copleston 1946: 325)

Notice Copleston's use of 'natural'. In Aristotle's scheme of things, 'natural' motion contrasts with 'violent' or unnatural motion: when you throw a stone into the air, its upward movement is unnatural, the downward one natural.

Copleston here uses 'motion' in the sense which it often bears in translations from Aristotle, to cover change of all kinds. Descartes comments disapprovingly on this use of *motus*. In one place, having mentioned 'shape, motion, position, duration, number and so on', he adds: 'By "motion" I mean local motion [that is, change of place]: philosophers have imagined that there are other kinds of motion distinct from local motion, thereby only making the nature of motion less intelligible to themselves' (*PP* 1:69, CSM 1:217; see n. 2 on that page). Descartes writes as though there were something substantive at stake here, but to my eye it looks verbal.

As Copleston implies, Aristotle also invokes teleology outside the biological realm: '*All* natural motion is directed towards an end.' It is obviously plausible to bring teleology into one's thoughts about organisms; for the non-organic realm it is less so, but Aristotle is helped in this by his doctrine about basic kinds of stuff and the kinds of movement that are 'natural' to them. He held that material stuff is of four basic kinds—the four elements—traditionally called air, earth, fire, and water. Each was supposed to have its own natural kind of movement and natural position: earth at 'the centre', water above it, air above that, and fire rising above all the rest; and Aristotelian physicists thought they could explain non-biological phenomena partly in terms of the forces that stuff is subjected to, but partly, also, in terms of stuff's moving so as to get into the relative position that is natural to it, where 'so as to' is teleological. (For a brief introduction by Aristotle himself to the themes of these two paragraphs, see his *On the Heavens*, bk. I, ch. 2.)

I shall highlight six features of this Aristotelian scheme of things, comparing them with Cartesian physics and the physics that is accepted today. Through all of this, I use 'physics' to cover biology as well.

2. Aristotle and Descartes: how many fundamental kinds?

Aristotle's physics contains many basic or irreducible terms for use in classifying things and explaining phenomena. There are only four elements, but Aristotle postulates thousands of forms, to which he gives an explanatory role.

In stark contrast with this, Descartes held that there are no basic differences between portions of matter: at the deepest physical level, there is just *matter*. So none of the variety that we find in the material world is basic; all qualitative variation derives from differences in how portions of homogeneous matter are structurally organized. For Descartes the concept of structure is a little peculiar; but that can wait until §18.

Descartes saw this as a fundamental issue of intelligibility. He wrote:

When flame burns wood . . . we can see with the naked eye that it sets the minute parts of the wood in motion and separates them from one another . . . Others may, if they wish, imagine the form of fire, the quality of heat, and the process of burning to be completely different things in the wood. For my part, I am afraid of mistakenly supposing there is anything more in the wood than what I see must necessarily be in it, and so I am content to limit my conception to the motion of its parts. (W 2, CSM 1:83)

By 'what must necessarily be in it' Descartes means 'what is essential to it just *qua* matter'. It is risky and unwarranted, he holds, to credit wood with any basic, irreducible properties except determinates of extension, which he thinks is the essence of matter, and he proposes therefore to confine himself to features of it that concern only its material layout—the relations of its parts to one another, including their relative motions. In this doctrine, he points out, he is only extending to the microscopic level something that one can see with the naked eye to be happening on the larger scale.

A similar impulse can be felt behind something Descartes says about Aristotle's four 'elements', or basic kinds of stuff—earth, air, fire, and water. These were supposed, rather fancifully, to result from the four combinations of the polarities hot/cold and wet/dry. Descartes, having announced that he distinguishes them in terms of the structures and microscopic motions that each involves, continues:

If you find it strange that, to explain these elements, I do not use the qualities they call heat, cold, moisture and dryness, as the philosophers do, I shall tell you that these qualities seem to me to stand in need of explanation themselves. Unless I am deceived, not only these four qualities, but also all the others, and even all the forms of inanimate bodies, can be explained without there being any need to suppose anything else in their matter except the motion, size, shape and arrangement of its parts. (W 5, CSM 1:89)

In these passages Descartes employs the primary qualities in setting a standard of intelligibility, a criterion for what counts as something's being firmly grasped, for what explains as against what needs to be explained. Gilson has written:

There are hardly any broad avenues into metaphysical speculation other than those of Plato and of Aristotle. We can have a metaphysics of the intelligible, disregarding the sensible, using mathematical methods and extending to a science which measures; or a metaphysics of the concrete, disregarding the intelligible, using biological methods and extending to a science which classifies. One ends up in mechanism, the other in animism. Since he had just abandoned the Aristotelianism in which his masters had tried to engage him, Descartes had to return to Platonism. (Gilson 1951: 199)

That seems to me just right, except that 'disregarding the sensible' is too strong: Descartes regarded his physics as answerable to empirical findings (Garber 1993a).

He shared his view of physics in its broad outlines with Galileo before him, contemporaries such as Gassendi, and Locke and others after him, and also with the ancient atomists Democritus and Leucippus. All these thinkers held that there is only one fundamental kind of matter, so that the basic repertoire of physics must be confined to concepts that apply to all matter—concepts of shape, size, position, relative velocity, and so on—and out of this arises the view that all other qualitative differences in material things must arise from differences of micro-structure. The privileged concepts are those of things' shapes and sizes, which Boyle called their 'primary qualities' (§188).

It is fairly easy to see how some facts about a thing might be explained in terms of its primary qualities. That sugar dissolves in water while lead does not is a fact that one can easily imagine arising from structural differences; similarly that iron is harder than cork, that mercury flows less freely than water and more freely than glass, and so on. We can see how in principle those effects might come from facts about micro-structures combined with the laws about how portions of homogeneous matter interact, so that the difference between (say) water and hydrochloric acid would resemble that between a ladder and a ramp, or a key and a corkscrew.

Not so for things' colours, tastes, and smells—their 'secondary qualities'. There seems to be no prospect of explaining structurally the difference between red and green, or sweet and sour. For the entire programme to survive, therefore, the secondary qualities must somehow be de-fanged, set aside, shown to be irrelevant or harmless to the Galilean ideal for physics. Descartes himself argues in this manner in PP 4:198 (CSM 1:284–5). The Galileo–Descartes–Locke de-fanging procedure will be the topic of Chapter 25, where I shall focus on Locke's version of it.

As one of my quotations indicates, Descartes held that the basic repertoire of physics is confined to concepts of determinables which belong to the essence of matter as such. No concept C, he held, belongs in fundamental physics unless it is absolutely impossible that there should be matter to which C is not applicable.[1] This may have been the view of most of the Galileans, but the problem about secondary qualities could arise from something weaker than that. In fact, a physics

---

[1] In my seventeenth-century usage, to call something 'absolutely impossible' is to say that it is impossible in the strongest way. Various weaker sorts of modality are relative: something may be impossible relative to the causal laws of the actual world, or to the law of the land, or to the technical means now available. The proper antonym of 'relative' is 'absolute': so absolute necessity is just necessity, as distinct from necessity-relative-to-x for some x.

might be richer than Descartes's in either of two ways while still being essentially Galilean and thus still confronting a problem over secondary qualities.

One enrichment yields a physics whose basic repertoire includes concepts of determinables which are not all essential to matter as such, though all are in fact possessed by all portions of matter. That is still Galilean in spirit; it still yields a picture of basically homogeneous matter, and so it raises the question of how to fit in the secondary qualities, even though it stops short of saying that the only basic properties of matter are absolutely essential to it.

Now take a further step to a system of physics S—a theoretically unified one, susceptible of mathematical handling—whose basic repertoire includes not only concepts that are applicable to all matter, but also ones that differentiate some matter from the rest. According to S, some matter is F, and some is not, and this is a fundamental difference between them. The facts about whether given bodies are F or not will perform in the same causal arena as do facts about shapes, sizes, and positions, making differences to how bodies behave in collisions, how strongly cohesive they are, how fast they move under various conditions, or the like. Now, secondary qualities will still be a problem for system S. Colours, tastes, and smells show no better prospect of being reducible to the basic concepts of S than they do to those of Descartes's leaner system.

I have mentioned this in order to bring contemporary physical theories into the picture. They postulate basically different kinds of matter (or ingredients of matter), but they still belong to the tradition of Galileo and Descartes; in the fundamental issue between Aristotle and them, Galileo and Descartes have won. A contemporary physicist is free to say that there are countless sorts of things and stuff—acorns, water, planks, fire, pigs, and so on—but he will say that what ultimately explain the physical properties of such items are facts about their structures combined with facts about the behaviour of their basic constituents. So the secondary qualities are prima facie as much a problem for contemporary science as they were for Descartes.

3. Aristotle and Descartes: four more differences

(1) Because he does not confine himself to a few basic kinds of thing, Aristotle has to admit many fundamental causal or explanatory principles. For him each form is a law unto itself. No amount of knowledge of other biological forms could enable one to understand what happens when an acorn grows, let alone to predict how an acorn will grow. The Galileans, with their smaller repertoire of fundamental concepts, have at least the possibility of devising a physics containing only a few underived causal laws. In general, they availed themselves of that possibility, as do physicists today.

Descartes offered a small set of laws which he took to constitute a complete physics. There are three 'laws of nature' (*PP* 2:37–40, CSM 1:240–2) regarding how bodies move when they do not collide and when they do, and seven 'rules' which present a more detailed physics of impact (*PP* 2:46–52, MM 64–9). This is supposed to be a complete physics, I believe, in the sense that these laws and rules—when conjoined with structural descriptions of particular bits of the world—will explain any events in the material world that can be explained in materialistic terms. The structural descriptions are needed: according to Descartes, the behaviour of a magnet, for example, depends in part on the peculiar shape of certain invisible pores that the magnet contains and the shapes of various particles that brush up against it (*PP* 4:144, MM 249).

One naturally thinks of a complete physics—at least before quantum indeterminacy arrived—as having the means to predict the outcome of any fully described physical set-up. One measure of the completeness of an explanation after the fact, we think, is that it could have yielded a prediction in advance. Descartes's 'laws of nature' are not determinate enough for that, however, because they are not quantitatively precise. He was not greatly influenced by the predictive model of what a good explanation is, and was content with something less demanding. I have found only one place in his writings where scientific prediction, as we understand it, is mentioned:

The only experiment I ever made on this question was one I made about five years ago. I had a glass cut from a design drawn by M. Mydorge. When the experiment was made, the rays of the sun which passed through the glass all gathered exactly at the point beyond the glass which I had predicted. This convinced me that either the craftsman had made a fortunate blunder or my reasoning was not false. (CSMK 36)

One anecdote does not a programme make! Descartes writes of 'deducing an account of effects from their causes' (*PP* 3:4); he says that a causal hypothesis is almost certain to be true if it 'allows all the phenomena to be clearly deduced from it' (3:43; see also 44); and he writes proudly:

Consider how amazing are the properties of magnets and of fire, and how different they are from the properties we commonly observe in other bodies: how a huge flame can be kindled from a tiny spark in a moment, and how great its power is; or how the fixed stars radiate their light ⟨instantly⟩ in every direction over such an enormous distance. In this book I have deduced the causes—which I believe to be quite evident—of these and many other phenomena from principles which are known to all and admitted by all, namely the shape, size, position and motion of particles of matter. (*PP* 4:187, CSM 1:278–9)

In none of this, I submit, do we see a physicist pursuing explanatory hypotheses that will generate precise predictions which can then be tested against observations. In this respect, Descartes is unlike Leibniz, who worked with the idea of a successful physics as predictive.

(2) Aristotle divided movements into two kinds—natural movements (downwards for solids) and violent movements (upwards for solids). Descartes flatly rejected this. 'The term "violent" refers only to our will, which is said to suffer violence when something happens which goes against it. In nature, however,

nothing is violent: it is equally natural for bodies to collide with each other, and perhaps to disintegrate, as it is for them to be still' (CSMK 381).[2]

(3) In all its luxuriant richness of basic laws and principles, Aristotelian physics distinguishes—at a basic level in the theory—some places from others. Indeed, it does this in two ways. Aristotle says that sublunary bodies naturally move in straight lines, superlunary ones in circles. Also, in his doctrine that earth and water naturally move down, while fire and air naturally move up, he takes *up* and *down* not as relative, but as absolute terms—that is, to say that fire moves up is to name the place towards which it moves.

Particular places are not distinguished in contemporary theoretical physics, or in the physics of Descartes. According to him, some parts of the heavens are unlike others, and he seeks to explain some astronomical facts by postulating great masses of fluid matter whirling around the sun. But this is mere large-scale geography, so to speak; none of Descartes's basic laws pick out any particular places, and none is said to hold sway only in certain places.

(4) Aristotle's explanations are qualitative rather than quantitative: his physics does not lend itself to development through mathematics. The contrast with today's physics could hardly be greater. It also contrasts with the physics of Descartes, though less strikingly. Garber (1992: 206) reports that in his first writings on physics Descartes speaks of conservation of motion, but shows no interest in getting anything quantitative into his physics. But 'as early as 1639' this changes, and quantities become central. Still, Garber also comments (230) on how much less quantitative Cartesian physics was than Newtonian. For his laws of motion and of impact to *predict* the outcomes of various physical events, they would have to become more precise than they are. Still, Descartes's physics is a science which can in principle be handled quantitatively, whereas Aristotelian physics is not.

4. Aristotle and Descartes: teleology

In sketching Aristotle's system, I mentioned its liberal use of teleological explanations. Descartes is famous for rejecting teleology outright. He said to Burman:

This rule—that we must never argue from ends—should be carefully heeded. For . . . the knowledge of a thing's purpose never leads us to knowledge of the thing itself; its nature remains just as obscure to us. Indeed, this constant practice of arguing from ends was Aristotle's greatest fault. (CSMK 341)

In this respect, too, contemporary physics has come down on Descartes's side. Teleology has a role in biology; but most biologists would—and I think that all should—agree that this is not *basic* teleology. In my 1991a I discuss how it can be anything else.

Teleology and Descartes's rejection of it are complex matters, which we should explore a little right away. What Descartes says against teleology largely

[2] See also CSMK 79: 'I do not regard anything in nature as violent.' For more on this topic, see Hall 1954: ch. 3.

concerns the divine sort, as employed in such explanations as 'The acorn develops as it does because God wants it to become an oak'. Descartes vigorously
rejects all that:

> When dealing with natural things we will . . . never derive any explanations from the pur-
> poses which God or nature may have had in view when creating them. For we should not
> be so arrogant as to suppose that we can share in God's plans. We should, instead, con-
> sider him as the efficient cause of all things. (PP 1:28, CSM 1:202)[3]

Descartes thinks that God is 'willing that we should have some knowledge' of
efficient causes (PP 1:28). That knowledge, he presumably thinks, concerns *what
happens*, whereas a knowledge of God's purposes would concern *why it happens*,
and that lies beyond our reach.

A sincere Christian such as Descartes evidently was might be expected to have
views about God's purposes, given some premiss saying that God is good, benev-
olent, or the like. Descartes, however, accepts no such premiss, maintaining that
there are no standards of reasonableness or value independent of God's will
(§182). Rather than saying that God chose to create this world because it is good,
we should say that this world is good because God chose to create it. We shall see
Locke taking this view about value (§170). It has had many adherents down the
centuries, and many opponents. To some theists, it demeans God to suppose that
standards of value and morality exist independently of him. Others think that
there must be such standards, because if God's will is the source of all value, then
the all-important doctrine that he is perfectly good degenerates into the tame
news that he is perfectly satisfied with himself. This is a serious problem for theists in the Christian tradition; I offer no opinion on how they should solve it.

Descartes's rejection of teleology goes beyond the issue of God's purposes. He
suggests this when he speaks of 'the purposes which God *or nature* may have had
in view'; he implies it when he rejects Aristotle's teleological explanations, which
are not about God's purposes; and the whole tenor of Descartes's scientific work
shows him to be turning his back on all teleological explanations, whether God-
involving or not.

5. Descartes and two predecessors

Descartes was not the first philosopher to think that the physical world is to be
understood purely in terms of structure. In ancient times, the atomists, led by
Leucippus and Democritus, thought so too. Democritus said that there are only
atoms and space, and whatever happens in the world is to be explained in terms
of how the atoms relate to, and bump into, one another. There is no 'finality' or
purpose in all of this—'The concourse of atoms is fortuitous'—and there are no

---

[3] See also Fifth Replies, CSM 2:258, and the paragraph on CSM 2:38–9. In the quoted passage 'God or
[*aut*] nature' means 'God or else nature'; unlike Spinoza's 'God or [*sive*] nature', which means 'God, i.e.
nature'.

special, restricted causal laws, and no *fundamental* qualitative differences except that between matter and space.

Like most of the great philosophers—an exception being the usually generous and always eclectic Leibniz—Descartes disliked being compared to his predecessors. We shall see this in his reply to the suggestion that the *Cogito* argument had been anticipated by Augustine (§143). He is especially strenuous in distancing himself from Democritus. Granting that 'Democritus also imagined certain small bodies having various sizes, shapes and motions, and supposed that all bodies that can be perceived by the senses arose from the conglomeration and mutual interaction of these corpuscles', Descartes claims to differ from him in four crucial ways. There are indeed three differences; but they do not justify Descartes's astonishing claim that 'The philosophy of Democritus differs from my own just as much as it does from the standard view ⟨of Aristotle and others⟩' (*PP* 4:202, CSM 1:287).

First, 'Democritus supposed his corpuscles to be indivisible—a notion which leads me to join those who reject his philosophy.' That is a real difference: Democritus believed in causally unsplittable bodies, and Descartes did not. In this respect the subsequent course of physics has favoured Democritus. Without saying that the material world consists of little hard balls, physics does have the concept of fundamental particles—discrete things, not continuous stuff—and assumes that ultimately a level is reached at which the things are no longer divisible.

'Secondly, [Democritus] imagined there to be a vacuum around the corpuscles, whereas I demonstrate the impossibility of a vacuum.' Except for the claim of success, this is right too. Democritus said that there are only 'atoms and the void', and Descartes rejected not only atoms but also the void (§§10–11). The later development of physics has not been kind to Descartes in this respect either.

'Thirdly, he attributed gravity to these corpuscles, whereas my understanding is that there is no such thing as gravity in any body taken on its own, but that it exists only as a function of, and in relation to, the position and motion of other bodies.' In this context 'gravity' (*gravitas*) means weight or heaviness, not a universal attractive force in the manner of Newton. The idea is that bodies move towards the earth because they have an intrinsic property of heaviness which results in their tending to go in a particular direction that is natural for heavy bodies. This associates *gravitas* with the idea of a privileged place or direction for bodies of a certain kind, whereas Cartesian physics allows no such privilege. According to Descartes, bodies fall to the earth because they are pushed by other bodies (§24). I do not know of anyone before Newton who believed that the 'natural' downward movement of matter might be due to a universal attractive force operating between any two bodies.

On the matter of 'gravity', understood in terms of a privileged downward direction or bottom place, science after Newton has sided with Descartes (though not with his way of explaining the phenomena). This partial success of his, however, does not mark a failure by Democritus, because Democritus did not believe in the kind of gravity that Descartes is talking about (Lloyd 1963: 450a; Copleston 1946: 73).

Fourthly:

Democritus did not show in detail how all things arose merely from the interaction of corpuscles; or rather, if he did show this in some cases, the reasons he gave for them did not hang together sufficiently to show that the whole of nature could be explained in the same way (at least one could not learn this from such of his opinions as have come down to us). But I leave it to the reader to judge whether the reasons I have offered in this treatise are interconnected enough, and if one can deduce enough things from them. (PP 4:202, CSM 1:287*)

Nobody today would give Descartes the judgement that he hopes for. His explanations of physical phenomena in terms of micro-structure are many and ingenious; he makes some show of interlocking them into a system, and repeatedly claims to be showing how the whole of nature *could* be explained; whereas Democritus seems to have offered nothing so ambitious. But this apparent difference is hardly a triumph for Descartes, because all his detailed microstructural explanations are wrong.

They were bound to be, because most of the relevant facts about small-scale structure and movement involve chemistry, which did not exist in Descartes's day. The English word 'chemistry' has a history that tracks the development of the science. Well before and during Descartes's time, 'chemistry' was in use as a name for alchemy and (in a different sense) for one school of medical theory. Carrying anything like its present meaning, the OED starts at 1646, only four years before Descartes died; and this has to do with 'chemistry considered as an art'—the art of boiling, dissolving, etc., in order to separate a complex material into two or more simpler ones. For chemistry 'considered as a science', the OED starts with Priestley in 1788. Only in the late eighteenth century did there come to be some understanding of what the individual chemical 'elements' are and of how they combine to make compounds. These discoveries brought in forces of attraction, which Descartes, Locke, and Leibniz all rejected (§23). These three philosophers, like most of their contemporaries, were confident that bodies can interact only by impact—bumping and pushing—involving forces of repulsion rather than attraction; and this confidence impeded a breakthrough to the fundamentals of chemistry that were needed if the Democritus–Descartes programme was to be properly launched.

Summing up: Descartes is dead right to say that Democritus believed in atoms and the void whereas he (Descartes) rejected both. On 'gravity' Descartes differed importantly from some of the ancient atomists, though not from Democritus. The fourth point does not amount to much, as I have tried to show. These contrasts leave room for a great deal of overlap of metaphysical and scientific view between Descartes and his atomist forebears, who are more alike than either is to Aristotle.

Closer to Descartes's own time was Galileo. (Descartes was 37 years old when the elderly Galileo was tried and condemned in Rome. See Method 6, CSM 1:141–2.) Galileo's physics broke decisively with what went before it, in two major respects.

First, it offered promise of a quantitative physics; some of Galileo's immediate predecessors had seen this as desirable, but the prevailing Aristotelian physics could not be quantified. Secondly, it rejected the descriptions of the phenomena that had been handed down from Aristotle, and especially the division of movements into two fundamentally different kinds—natural and violent or unnatural.

However, Galileo explicitly declined to assert, as Descartes did, that there is a universal physics which holds throughout the material realm; and the ancient atomists had no real physics, only the hope of one. So it is basically true to say that 'While nearly all of Descartes's physics is wrong in detail, his grand attempt is the beginning of theory in the modern sense' (Truesdell 1955: 6). 'Critical as both Newton and Leibniz were of the details of Descartes's sloppy natural philosophy, they were at one in accepting his view of nature as a great machine, the workings of which could be explained by sufficiently adroit mathematical reasoning applied to mathematical representations of observed facts' (Truesdell 1978: 90; see also 181, 278 in that same volume). It is pleasant to be able to add this: 'That Newton's primary indoctrination in the principles of terrestrial and celestial motion came initially through his study of Descartes—rather than, as was once thought, from reading Galileo and Kepler—is now firmly documented. In late 1664, on taking up the bulky *Principia Philosophiae* in which the Cartesian world-view had first been publicly presented twenty years before, he had rapidly absorbed . . .' etc. (Whiteside 1974: 3–4; see also the excellent Dijksterhuis 1961: 403–21).

6. Aristotle, Descartes, and the manifest image

This section is named for something Turnbull says about Aristotle's science:

It is reasonably effective for organizing bodies of knowledge. From the perspective of modern physical and biological science, however, it is severely crippled by its close linkage with what Wilfrid Sellars calls 'the manifest image', i.e. what is available to us by means of our very limited sense organs. . . . The tie to entities known through perception prevents access to—much less the discoveries of—modern physics (and, consequently, chemistry and biology). (Turnbull 1988: 120)

This could mean either of two things. Taken one way, it draws a line separating Aristotle from Descartes and contemporary physics; taken in another, it puts Aristotle and Descartes together in contrast with the physics of today.

We can distinguish Aristotle's physics from that of Democritus or Descartes by saying that his proceeds entirely in terms of what can be found on the surface of things through gross observation, while theirs does not. To explain how an acorn develops, say Democritus and Descartes, you must dig down to its microstructure; whereas Aristotle holds that the whole theory of acorns can be given in terms of the kind *acorn*—those big, visible, recognizable, organic lumps. In so far as his science thinks in terms of facts that are not available to unaided sensory observation, they are facts about the elements, which are aspects of matter, rather than tiny particles of it; and the move towards them is not thought of as a move towards ever more complete causal explanation.

Or so I am given to understand; but in *PP* 4:202, where Descartes contrasts himself with Democritus, his rage for intellectual isolation leads him to imply that this is mostly wrong. Discussing why Democritus' physics had been generally rejected, Descartes says: 'This rejection has never been based on the fact that his philosophy deals with certain particles so minute as to elude the senses, and assigns various sizes, shapes and motions to them; for no one can doubt that there are in fact many such particles.' Later in the section: 'As for the consideration of shapes, sizes and motions, this is something that has been adopted not only by Democritus but also by Aristotle and all the other philosophers.' This is evasive. No doubt every philosopher has thought that material things have parts which are too small to see or feel, and has thought that all material things have shapes, sizes, and motions. But not all philosophers have thought that whatever happens in the material realm can be explained in terms of collisions amongst the invisibly small parts of bodies. This was the position of Democritus and Descartes, but not of many who came between—Aristotle, for instance.

Aristotle is tied to 'the manifest image' in another way as well. In his science, there is no need for any classificatory terms that could not be learned from examples given through ordinary sense perception. His explanations of how the world works employ some technical terms—'form' and 'matter', 'act' and 'potential'—but their basic classificatory vocabulary is one that any child might have—'oak', 'earth', and so on. Aristotelian science shares this feature, unlike the preceding one, with the science of Democritus, whose only basic term is 'material particle that cannot be cut', and with that of Descartes, whose only basic term is 'portion of matter'.

Did it occur to anyone before the nineteenth century that the fundamental *kinds* of things might be other than those that present themselves to our senses? Apparently it did, for Descartes takes the trouble to deny it: 'There is nothing more in keeping with reason than that we judge about those things which we do not perceive, because of their small size, on the model of and by comparison with those we do see' (CSMK 65). Leibniz goes even further, asserting that 'In small particles everything is proportional to what can occur in large ones', and that 'difference between large and small, between sensible and insensible' is not accompanied by any other significant difference (*NE* 440, 474). Leibniz held that matter is only an appearance of an underlying system of sizeless 'monads', which are nothing like what we encounter through our senses (§89). But that is irrelevant to our present topic. Although he holds that some features of his physics are to be explained in terms of the underlying monads, those explanations—like the monads themselves—lie outside the bounds of the physics.

C. D. Broad wrote somewhere that philosophers and scientists, in this confidence that the small differs from the large only in size, were writing a blank cheque which Nature's bank honoured for a remarkably long time. The cheque has finally bounced: the perhaps fundamental particles that physicists now believe in could not have been envisaged by either Democritus or Descartes.

Chapter 2

Matter and Space

7. 'Material = extended': why Descartes wanted this doctrine

Descartes had a firm view about the nature of his one basic kind of stuff, which he called 'matter'. Being material (or being a body), he said, is being extended. Extension is the *whole* essence of matter: not only is 'material and unextended' self-contradictory, but so also is 'extended and immaterial'. Let us ask four questions about this.

(1) Apart from any evidence Descartes may have had for his doctrine about matter, he wanted it to be true, thinking that it brought benefit to his physics and metaphysics. Why? (2) He also *argued* that the concept of matter contains nothing but the concept of extension. How? (3) He denied that there could be vacuum or empty space, for reasons involving his thesis about the essence of matter. How do they involve it? You may think: 'It's simple. Space is by definition extended and immaterial, and Descartes holds that anything extended must be material, therefore . . . etc.' Though plausible, that has almost nothing to do with what Descartes wrote; so the question still stands. (4) His view of matter, when combined with his rejection of vacuum and certain other doctrines of his, has troublesome implications for his metaphysics and his physics. What are they?

Here is a short answer to the first question. By equating materiality with extension, Descartes could convince himself that he had a peculiarly firm conceptual hold on the world of matter. Like everyone else up to about 150 years ago, he thought he perfectly understood extension because Euclidean geometry—a complete and secure science—gave the whole truth about it.

(Or nearly so. From Euclid's time onwards, mathematicians uneasily realized that the parallel postulate was neither self-evident nor, apparently, deducible from the other axioms and postulates; but only in 1823 did they begin to grasp that coherent geometries can come from conjoining Euclid's other premisses with some contrary of the parallel postulate. Ironically, Saccheri had done just that a century earlier, when he unknowingly developed a non-Euclidean geometry which he thought was a proof by *reductio ad absurdum* of the parallel postulate. He published this in a book entitled *Euclid Freed of Every Flaw* (see Hofstadter 1979: 91–2). I have no evidence of Descartes's worrying about the parallel postulate.)

Then did Descartes hold that physics (the study of matter) can be reduced to geometry (the study of extension), so that its results can all be established a priori, as he thought those of geometry can? Sometimes he wrote as though he did, most notably here: 'The only principles which I accept or require in physics are those of geometry and pure mathematics; these principles explain all natural phenomena, and enable us to provide quite certain demonstrations regarding them' (*PP* 2:64, CSM 1:247). That plainly makes physics a part or a consequence of mathematics: not only does mathematics provide physics with 'certain demonstrations', but it also gives it 'the only principles' that it needs.

Later in the same section Descartes writes that physics treats only of 'what the geometers call quantity, and take as the object of their demonstrations, i.e. that to which every kind of division, shape and motion is applicable'. That might seem also to make physics a branch of mathematics, but really it does not, because of how motion comes into it. Even if all movable things have properties that geometers study, it does not follow that geometers study motion; and they do not. Given the whole story about how this particle has been moving for the past two seconds, and about all the bodies in its environment, how will it be moving one second from now? Geometry ignores such questions, but it would be a miserable physics that did so. Could Descartes have overlooked this fairly obvious point? Although not dominated by the ideal of a richly predictive physics, he must have credited his physics with *some* power to connect events at one time with events later; so he must have seen that the needs of physics go beyond what geometry can supply. How could he regard physics as being entailed by pure geometry?

He could not, and did not. After the passage last quoted, he continues:

My consideration of such matter involves absolutely nothing apart from these divisions, shapes and motions; and even with regard to these, I will admit as true only what has been deduced from indubitable common notions so evidently that it is fit to be considered as a mathematical demonstration. . . . All natural phenomena can be explained in this way.

While still claiming that physics can be done a priori, this does not represent it as a branch of mathematics. Its premisses are 'indubitable', Descartes says; and in calling them 'common notions' he implies that they can be known a priori by anyone whose mind is not cluttered with false prejudices (*PP* 1:50). His examples of common notions, however, are not mathematical:

'Things that are the same as a third thing are the same as each other' (*Rules* 12, CSM 1:45).
'Things that cannot be related in the same way to a third thing are different in some respect' (ibid.).
'It is impossible for the same thing to be and not to be at the same time' (*PP* 1:49, CSM 1:209).
'What is done cannot be undone' (ibid.).
'He who thinks cannot but exist while he thinks' (ibid.).

In a letter to Dinet, indeed, Descartes explicitly links common notions with metaphysics, and separates them from 'the province of the mathematicians'

(CSM 2:391). The appeal to 'common notions', then, claims an a priori but not a mathematical status for physics. This goes with what Descartes said earlier: 'The fundamental principles of my physics . . . are almost all so evident that they need only to be understood to be believed, and . . . I think I can demonstrate all of them' (*Method* 6, CSM 1:145–6). And in *PP* 2:64 he says that anything derived from common notions is 'fit to be considered as a mathematical demonstration'—which stops short of saying that it is one.

Descartes's physics consists primarily of three 'laws of nature', which appeared first in *The World* and then in slightly different form in the *Principles of Philosophy*:

(1) 'Every thing, in so far as it can, always continues in the same state; and thus what is once in motion always continues to move' (*PP* 2:37, CSM 1:240).

(2) 'All motion is in itself rectilinear; and hence any body moving in a circle always tends to move away from the centre of the circle which it describes' (39).

(3) 'If a body collides with another body that is stronger than itself, it loses none of its motion; but if it collides with a weaker body, it loses a quantity of motion equal to that which it imparts to the other body' (40).

Descartes adds details in seven 'rules' about impact (*PP* 2:46–52, MM 64–9). All of this material links times with other times; none falls purely within mathematics as Descartes understood it; and he insists that God makes it all true by choosing to make bodies move thus rather than so. Garber puts this nicely: 'While the objects of physics are the objects of geometry made real, in [becoming] real they take on properties that they did not have in Euclid. Because they are created and sustained by God . . . they satisfy laws of motion that are entirely foreign to the objects of pure mathematics' (Garber 1992: 292–3).

Descartes cannot distinguish cleanly between 'warranted by mathematics' and 'chosen by God', because he held that even mathematical and logical truths are made such through God's will. When I explain this in Chapter 24, it will turn out to be irrelevant to our present concerns, and no impediment to Garber's view that for Descartes physics does not belong to mathematics.

Here is why Descartes thinks he can establish the basic principles of his physics a priori. (1) When one body collides with another, and one or both change direction or speed of motion, neither body causally acts on the other—according to Descartes. This is 'occasionalism' about the seeming action of bodies on bodies: the white ball's hitting the stationary red ball does not cause the latter to start moving, but serves as God's occasion for starting it to move. The facts about collisions—which for Descartes exhaust the whole of physics—result from God's activities in swatting bodies around, changing how fast or in what direction each one moves, in the light of (on the occasion of) changes in how it relates to other bodies. (2) Descartes thinks he has an a priori proof of the existence of a God with all perfections, one of which is unchangingness. And a God who does not change will act in regular ways: 'God's perfection involves not only his being unchanging in himself but also his operating in a manner that is always utterly constant and unchanging' (PP 2:36, CSM 1:240).[1]

I use 'unchanging' here to translate the French *immuable*, standardly rendered by 'immutable'. The latter unambiguously means 'unchangeable', and *immuable* can mean that too; but often it means merely 'unchanging', and Descartes usually gives it that sense. I can find no dictionary backing for the suggestion that the Latin *immutabilis* offers the same choice; but in Descartes's writings it does. He often uses it to mean 'unchanging', as here: 'Since they are always the same, it is right to call them *immutabiles* and eternal' (CSM 2:262). He frequently explains why something is *immutabilis*, or draws conclusions from something's being *immutabilis*, and, except at CSM 1:297, lines 9–8 up, they never contain a necessity operator, nor does one need to be supposed for the passage to make good Cartesian sense. I shall use 'immutable' when it seems reasonable to think that a modal notion may be involved; otherwise, 'unchanging'.

I shall not discuss Descartes's a priori argument for God's existence, or the concept of perfection which it involves, or the assumption that unchangingness falls under that concept. As for the supposed derivation of Cartesian physics from the premises that God makes bodies move and that he operates in a 'constant and unchanging' manner: that does not hold. Descartes's occasionalism about body–body relations, and his doctrine of God's unchangingness, do perhaps jointly entail that bodies move in conformity with unchanging laws, so that *some physics* is true; but we cannot wrestle them into yielding that *Cartesian physics* is true. Descartes might reasonably have said this: 'Granted, God's unchangingness might have manifested itself in a different physics from the actual one. Still, the physics that we find our world to have is the work of an unchanging God, it manifests the constancy of his operations, and to that extent his unchangingness explains it.' But that is weaker than what he does say, and it does not imply that he could demonstrate his physics a priori. (For more about this, see Garber 1992: 282–4.)

Why did Descartes think it important that extension should be the whole essence of matter, if not so that his physics would be a branch of geometry? I suppose it was because he thought that a physics whose only basic concepts were *those of geometry plus the concept of time* would be cleaner, simpler, more graspable, and more likely to be completable, than one which also included some independent concept such as that of force, mass, inertia, or the like. If the behaviour of bodies depended upon principles involving the geometrical concepts, time, and (say) *mass*, we could not know in advance what mass is. The concept of mass needed for physics, having to grow out of experimental results, would be a permanent hostage to fortune: at any stage we might find that we had got it wrong. No such threat, Descartes must have thought, attends the use of the geometrical and temporal concepts.

---

[1] See also W 7, CSM 1:96. Descartes omits unchangingness from his two lists of God's attributes in the Third Meditation, then adds it each time in the French version (CSM 2:28, 31). I do not know why.

Consider what happens in the Second Meditation when he discusses the piece of wax, concluding that its whole essence is extension. (He describes the wax as extended, flexible, and changeable; but the first of the trio is all he needs.) He infers that 'The nature of this piece of wax is in no way revealed by my imagination, but is perceived by the mind alone' (CSM 2:21). He here uses 'the mind' to mean 'the intellect', as distinct from the imagination and the senses; and when he speaks of how we 'perceive' matter, he might as well have said 'conceive'. His point, that is, concerns how we think about matter rather than how we know about it. A little later he speaks of how one 'conceives' the wax, with no hint of changing the subject; he also speaks of 'what gives me my grasp of the wax', which again suggests conception. The main point concerns concepts rather than knowledge. (For good help with Descartes on the role of the senses in our knowledge of material things, see M. D. Wilson 1993b.)

Why does Descartes conclude that the concept of extension is not sense-based? His reason comes from this: 'The extension of the wax . . . increases if the wax melts, increases again if it boils, . . . etc. The wax . . . is capable of being extended in many more different ways than I will ever encompass in my imagination' (CSM 2:21). Before this he says the same thing about flexibility. He is rejecting concept-empiricism—the view that everything in the understanding was first in the senses. The concepts of extension, etc., cannot be intellectual possessions derived from our senses, he holds. On the contrary, what we *understand* about extension, etc., far outruns anything that the senses could give us, because it includes the possibility of an infinity of shapes and sizes. This fits with what I take to be Descartes's chief reason for wanting extension to be the whole essence of matter.

The essence of matter, or of wax, or of this one piece of wax? Part of the charm of the passage comes from how immediately and specifically Descartes confronts us with his fresh sweet-smelling piece of wax: he wants us imaginatively to feel it, smell it, taste it, and so on; and as he recites the changes it could undergo, he keeps emphasizing that it would still be 'the same wax', apparently meaning the same individual portion of matter. Yet he cannot mean to be exploring what makes something be *the same piece of wax* as one encountered before: if he were, he would say something about spatio-temporal continuity. In fact, he does not even gesture towards the obvious fact that if the wax I hold at T_2 is the wax that you held at T_1, then there must be a continuously waxen spatio-temporal track between those two zones.

Furthermore, his conclusion regarding 'this particular piece of wax' is, he says, 'even clearer with regard to wax in general'. This shows, albeit obscurely, that individual identity or continuity is not his topic. Nor is it wax in general. If it were, he would be saying that the whole essence of *wax* is extension, implying that bread and water and prison bars are all wax. The real topic is the concept of *matter* or *body* (which for present purposes we can equate): Descartes is discussing not the essence of a particular body, or of wax as a kind of body, but rather the essence of body, or the concept of corporeality. This is confirmed when he alludes to this same thought-experiment in *PP* 2:4, and ties it to the notion of matter as such.

As well as his point about the concepts under which we bring the wax, Descartes makes a point about our knowledge of it. It appears when he anticipates this objection (I am not quoting): 'We say that we see the wax itself, if it is there before us, not that we judge it to be there from its colour or shape; and this might lead me to conclude without more ado that knowledge of the wax comes from what the eye sees, and not from the scrutiny of the mind alone.' He responds that what we call seeing the wax involves intellectual judgement:

If I look out of the window and see men crossing the square . . . I normally say that I see the men themselves, just as I say that I see the wax. Yet do I see any more than hats and coats which could conceal automata? I *judge* that they are men. And so something which I thought I was seeing with my eyes is in fact grasped solely by the faculty of judgment which is in my mind. (Med 2, CSM 2:21)

This episode does not succeed. For one thing, the judgement of which Descartes speaks occurs not in seeing the wax but in thinking that what one sees is wax. Furthermore, the operation in question involves visual intake as well, and is not a matter solely of the faculty of judgement.

I should add that Descartes has no doctrinal reason for putting this in the Second Meditation. It interrupts the treatment of scepticism that dominates the first three Meditations, and adumbrates a doctrine of matter which he develops fully in the scepticism-free atmosphere of *PP* 2. The discussion of the wax owes nothing to the treatment of scepticism: it makes normal assumptions about what the material world contains. Descartes's only attempt to fit the wax discussion in with the rest in an organic way occurs in the final paragraph of the Second Meditation. Consider it for yourself.[2]

8. 'Material = extended': how Descartes defended this

My second question was: How did Descartes argue that extension is the whole essence of matter? Well, he considers the various features that our sensory engagement with the wax leads us to attribute to it—hardness, taste, smell, colour—and says that it could lose any of these while still being 'the same wax'. From this he concludes that none of those properties is essential to the wax. All that remains that could constitute its essence, he says, is the bare trio—the wax is 'merely something extended, flexible and changeable'—of which I focus on 'extended'.

---

[2] Bernard Williams (1978: 227) thinks that the wax passage contributes to the scepticism material because (he says) Descartes relies on it in his remark, at the start of the Fifth Meditation, that his ideas of material things are true and unchanging natures rather than conceptual fictions. I disagree.

The argument is not careful or thorough. For one thing, although it shows that no one colour is essential to the wax, it does not rule out the possibility that *being coloured* is essential to it. Also, what about solidity? At each moment the wax occupies a region of space, perhaps a disconnected one, to the exclusion of other portions of matter; and Descartes does not mention this. Locke made that point against him: 'Solidity is so inseparable an idea from body that upon that depends its filling of space, its contact, impulse and communication of motion upon impulse', whereas 'Extension includes no solidity, nor resistance to the motion of body, as body does' (*Essay* II.xiii.11, 12).[3]

As a start on solidity, let us distinguish it from hardness. Locke does it for us: 'Solidity consists in . . . an utter exclusion of other bodies out of the space [the solid body] possesses; but hardness [consists] in a firm cohesion of the parts of matter . . . so that the whole does not easily change its figure' (*Essay* II.iv.4). That is mainly right, as is this by Leibniz: 'If two bodies were simultaneously inserted into the two open ends of a tube into which each of them fitted tightly, the matter which was already in the tube, however fluid [or soft] it might be, would resist just because of its sheer impenetrability' (*NE* 124). Also:

Those who find the essence of body in antitypy or impenetrability derive the concept of it, not from our hands or from any senses, but from the fact that a body does not give place to another body homogeneous to it unless it can move elsewhere. [He gives an example.] From this we may understand what the difference is between hardness, which is a property of some bodies only, and impenetrability, which belongs to all. Descartes should have considered the latter as well as hardness.[4]

The remark about our hands may be a response to this by Descartes:

As regards hardness, our sensation tells us no more than that the parts of a hard body resist the motion of our hands when they come into contact with them. If, whenever our hands moved in a given direction, all the bodies in that area were to move away at the same speed as that of our approaching hands, we should never have any sensation of hardness. And since it is quite unintelligible to suppose that if bodies did move away in this fashion they would thereby lose their bodily nature, it follows that this nature cannot consist in hardness. (*PP* 2:4, CSM 1:224)

This seems to rest on the madly verificationist idea that bodies would not be hard if we did not detect their hardness; but perhaps we can rescue it. One section earlier Descartes had written that 'sensory perception does not show us what really exists in things', which suggests that in section 4 he means that in the envisaged situation we would be sure we were seeing bodies, while having no evidence for their hardness; which proves that hardness does not enter into our concept of body. The argument remains bad, though, for we could keep our hands in our pockets, yet still observe bodies to be hard by seeing how they interact.

---

[3] The whole of II.iv and xiii.11–17, 21–6 is worth reading in our present context.

[4] 'Critical Thoughts', L 392. 'Antitypy' scans like 'humility'. Its four syllables are preferable to the seven of its synonym 'impenetrability'.

Why is Descartes arguing about this? Does he envisage opponents who think that hardness (as against softness) is of the essence of matter, so that 'soft matter' is a contradiction in terms? I hesitate to credit him with bothering to aim at such an enormous target, yet he seems to do so in *PP* 2:4, and he clearly does in 2:11: 'We will first of all exclude hardness [from the essence of matter], since if the stone is melted or pulverized it will lose its hardness without thereby ceasing to be a body.' I suspect that when he announced that the concept of matter does not include hardness Descartes was thinking unclearly about solidity.

9. Solidity

We have seen Locke urging solidity—not hardness—as an important component in the concept of matter, and accusing Descartes of omitting it. Let us look into this, starting with two paragraphs on a preliminary point.

I have quoted Locke as implying that every body 'utterly excludes' every other body from its location. In this he differs from Leibniz, who writes that although everyone would agree that 'bodies are reluctant jointly to occupy a single place . . . yet some people are not convinced that this reluctance is unconquerable' (*NE* 122–3): so unless those folk are muddled, their concept of body does not include absolute impenetrability. If we ask Locke to prove that bodies must be absolutely impenetrable, he cannot answer us convincingly. He rightly treats impenetrability as an upshot of an underlying property. Characterizing solidity as 'that which hinders the approach of two bodies when they are moving towards one another', he contrasts it with 'impenetrability, which is negative, and is perhaps more a consequence of solidity than solidity itself' (*Essay* II.iv.1). Locke here introduces the concept of solidity as a theoretical one: solidity is that property—whatever it may be—the possession of which makes a body impenetrable. He wants to replace this by something more direct and specific, but does not make a good job of it: 'If anyone asks me what this solidity is, I send him to his senses to inform him: Let him put a flint or a football between his hands and then endeavour to join them, and he will know' (*Essay* II.iv.6). I need hardly say that this will not do. Our concept of solidity has nothing to do with tactual sensations. Thus Locke assigns to our hands the primacy with solidity that Descartes accorded them with hardness. And—returning to my earlier point—the feel of a flint tells us nothing which implies that matter must be absolutely impenetrable.

A better account of solidity arises obliquely in Kant: 'We are acquainted with substance in space', he writes, 'only through forces which are active in this and that space, either bringing other objects to it . . . or preventing them from penetrating into it' (*Critique* B 321). And in another work (1786: 50) he discusses the theory that a minimal body does not have a size itself, but 'fills a space by mere repulsive force'. This does not contradict anything in Locke's philosophy, but it provides no basis for his absolutism. Bodies may be invested with repulsive powers that can with difficulty be overcome. Enough about this! From now on I shall, for convenience's sake, write as though solidity had to involve absolute impenetrability.

When Locke accuses Descartes of omitting solidity from the essence of matter, one wants to agree: something seems to be missing from Descartes's account, and 'solidity' strikes us as a good name for it. When we try to justify our complaint, however, it turns out to be tricky. If Cartesian matter does not have to be solid or, therefore, impenetrable, then it follows that two portions of such matter could be *co-located*—that is, could be at the same place at the same time. If this does not follow, I do not know what 'solid' means. If it does follow, then we should ask for evidence that matter as Descartes conceives it admits of co-location.

Descartes himself certainly thought it does not, and in one place, writing to More, he argues for this:

It is impossible to conceive of one part of an extended thing penetrating another equal part except by understanding that half of that extension is taken away or annihilated; but what is annihilated does not penetrate anything else; and so, in my opinion, it is established that impenetrability belongs to the essence of extension and not to that of anything else. (CSMK 372)

Garber reconstructs this 'simple and ingenious' argument thus: 'If a body is an extended thing, in the sense in which Descartes understands it, then take away extension and you take away body. But if two bodies could penetrate one another, then the total volume, and thus some amount of body itself, would be eliminated' (Garber 1992: 147). This helpfully clears the air, enabling us to see that the argument should not convert anybody. It assumes that the physical fusion of a body with volume V_1 and a body with volume V_2 must be a body with volume $(V_1 + V_2)$; but that is equivalent to the conclusion that the bodies cannot share any space. If they could interpenetrate, then one body might have V_1 and the other V_2, though the two together have less than $(V_1 + V_2)$; in which case neither has lost any volume. Analogously, let the volume of a sound be that of the region throughout which it is audible; then it can happen that a fire alarm has a volume of 550,000 cubic yards, and an explosion one of 780,000 cubic yards, although their combined volume measures less than a million cubic yards because throughout much of the city people can hear both.

With that circular argument set aside, we still have to ask whether Descartes's fundamental views imply that bodies can be co-located, or that they cannot. To get a handle on this, look at some more things Locke says about the ingredient missing from Descartes's account of the concept of matter. Speaking of a body's solidity as 'This resistance, whereby it keeps other bodies out of the space which it possesses', Locke contrasts it with 'pure space without solidity, whereinto another body may enter without either resistance or protrusion of any thing' (*Essay* II.iv.3). Considered as explanations of what differentiates bodies from space, these passages may seem circular: a body is marked off by its keeping other *bodies* out of its location. This feature appears almost every time Locke broaches this topic, most notably in *Essay* II.xiii.11–17, in the course of which he distinguishes 'body' from 'extension' or from 'pure space' thus: 'Extension includes no solidity, nor resistance to the motion of body, as body does' (12).

The circularity can be eliminated, however, by explaining 'body' through 'pair of bodies', like explaining 'twin'. Thus, a body is a thing of a kind such that no two things of that kind can be co-located.

Given this partial account of what a body is, Locke's objection to Descartes fails: a region of space is a thing of a kind such that no two things of that kind can be co-located. We will all sense that this does not really meet the objection. Spatial regions cannot interpenetrate, because they cannot move—we want to say— whereas bodies can move, changing their locations, but two of them cannot simultaneously have the same location. If that is the real complaint, then we have to dig deeper. For a start, we must look into what Descartes says about space.

10. Space as extended nothing

In this famous passage Descartes denies that there can be vacuum, or empty space:

It is a contradiction to suppose there is such a thing as a vacuum, i.e. that in which there is nothing whatsoever. The impossibility of a vacuum, in the philosophical sense of that in which there is no substance whatsoever, is clear. . . . A body's being extended in length, breadth and depth in itself warrants the conclusion that it is a substance, since it is a complete contradiction that a particular extension should belong to nothing; and the same conclusion must be drawn with respect to a space that is supposed to be a vacuum, namely that since there is extension in it, there must necessarily be substance in it as well. (*PP* 2:16, CSM 1:229–30)

Two things are going on here: one straightforward, the other not.

The former rejects 'vacuum' understood as *extended nothing*, an instance of extension that does not consist in some thing's being extended. The idea of vacuum as bulky nothing is a good one to reject, but who has ever had it? Is not Descartes here poking at a straw man? He thinks not. He writes, of something believed to be 'an empty space', that 'almost everyone is convinced that this amounts to nothing at all' (*PP* 2:5). Elsewhere he makes a more fine-grained accusation: 'People judge that so-called empty space is nothing; all the same they conceive it as a positive reality' (CSMK 194). I like the subtle distinction between what people judge and how they conceive or represent things, but I shall not linger with it now. Let us consider the allegedly common view of space as extended nothing.

Surprisingly, this allegation has a basis. I learn from Copleston that Leucippus, while holding space to be as real as body, referred to it as 'what is not' and to body

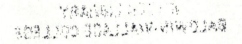

as 'what is' (Copleston 1946: 73). Aristotle and a number of medieval philosophers said similar things. (For examples, see Grant 1981: ch. 2.) Under their influence, I suppose, Leibniz wrote to Clarke that 'the perfection of matter is to that of a vacuum as something to nothing' (L 691).

Even today, echoes linger of this way of thinking. After discussing early ideas about space purely in terms of 'emptiness', Daniel Garber abruptly says: 'Aristotle, of course, would have none of this nothingness' (Garber 1992: 127). This unheralded intrusion of nothingness into the discussion presumably happens under prodding from the ancients and medievals whom Descartes attacked. Again, a theoretical physicist recently said, 'There's a lot we don't know about nothing' (*New York Times*, 7 December 1999), commenting on recently acquired evidence that space is granular. Some nothing!

So Descartes may have needed to refute the thesis that space is a bulky nothing; but that refutation does not suffice to establish his own position. Locke seems to have a viable alternative to Descartes's position, and it does not commit him to regarding space as an extended nothing.

11. Container space

I now present a metaphysic of space which may be Locke's, and is certainly a rival to Descartes's. According to it, space is a container, an extended substance whose parts (regions) can be co-located with extended substances of a different kind, namely bodies. If there is a body at a certain place, according to this metaphysic, there are two things there: the body and a portion or region of container space.

(Do not confuse this with the peculiar kind of co-location that is said to obtain between an object and the stuff composing it. The new ring on my finger now coincides in space with an old portion of gold, so perhaps they are two co-located things. But when a body is co-located with a region of container space, the two can part company: the body can move, while the region stays. My ring, however, could not thus separate from its constituent gold.)

This metaphysic regards space as an enormous thing or substance. All I mean by 'substance' here—and all that anyone has ever *clearly* meant by the word—is something like 'item that is properly treated substantivally in a basic account of the world'. If in your scheme of things some item figures irreducibly as an *it*, a *thing*, something to be quantified over, then you are treating it as a substance. The question of whether you are right to do so is the question of whether some other treatment of it would be better, as it is better in philosophical contexts to replace talk of 'shortages' by talk in which no such noun appears.

When Locke faces the question of whether space is a substance, he fumbles it: 'If it be demanded (as usually it is) whether this space, void of body, be substance or accident; I shall readily answer, I know not; nor shall be ashamed to own my ignorance, till they that ask show me a clear distinct idea of substance' (*Essay*

II.xiii.17). Then he swings off into a dismissive treatment of the 'idea of substance in general' (§203). He would have done better to take the question to concern whether, at the deepest metaphysical level, space has to be treated in a thing-like manner or whether, instead, it can be treated as adjectival on other things. With the issue thus understood, Locke appears to take space to be substantial:

> 'The extension of space [consists in] the continuity of unsolid, inseparable, and
>   immovable parts' (*Essay* 126:12).
> 'Pure space without solidity, whereinto another body may enter, without
>   either resistance or protrusion of any thing' (124:24).
> 'Pure space between is sufficient to take away the necessity of mutual contact;
>   but bare space in the way is not sufficient to stop motion' (176:16).

These passages present space as having parts, as a container, as stretching between things. Also, in II.xvii.4 the notion of space as something 'actually existing' is busily at work. Using Descartes's good distinction, we can say that Locke conceives space as substantial, but declines to judge it to be so.

Descartes does not say what he has against container space; indeed, he never mentions it. Whenever he reaches a point where it would be appropriate to discuss it, he instead rails against the view of empty space as extended nothing. Still, perhaps his basic views make a difficulty for accepting container space. I shall consider three candidate obstacles: one is wrong, the second shallow, and the third just right.

(1) The first is the argument against co-location in the letter to More. It concludes that no extended item can be co-located with any other—no 'part of an extended thing' can penetrate another part of such a thing. If the argument—which does not explicitly mention bodies or matter—were sound, it would hold against the penetration not only of body by body but also of space by body; which means that it would hold against container space. Indeed, a little later, Descartes uses it to rule out More's strange suggestion that two parts of space might be co-located. (See also CSMK 252.) I cannot find him explicitly applying it to a space–body pair, but he should be willing to do so; if the argument held in the other cases, it would also hold there. Still, that is merely a bad argument that Descartes uses once; it reveals nothing structural in his thought that rules out container space.

(2) Such space might be thought to be condemned by Descartes's doctrine that whatever is extended must be corporeal. I shall call this doctrine 'Extension', for short. Descartes seems to claim that he has argued against container space—or at least against empty container space—in just that manner: 'In *Principles* 2:18 I said expressly that I think the existence of a vacuum involves a contradiction, because we have the same idea of matter as we have of space' (CSMK 275). In *PP* 2:11 he explicitly says that we have the same idea of matter as we have of space; perhaps there and in 2:18 he can be seen as inferring from this that the existence of a vacuum involves a contradiction, though the argument is muffled. Anyway, let us consider the strength of this argument, whatever its status in Descartes's text.

Extension does rule out container space considered as something extended and incorporeal. But must it be considered like that? 'Portions of container space could not be bodies'—to your ears and mine that sounds right, but only because we do not accept Extension. If we did, we could cheerfully accept container space as one kind of matter or body. We would have no reason to shrink from calling it 'body' if we meant by that only that it is extended. So Extension, all by itself, poses no threat to container space.

(3) So as to make peace with Extension, let us call container space 'matter', and call portions of it 'bodies'. Then, in admitting it into our ontology, we concede that some bodies can be co-located with others—diamonds, for instance, with regions of container space. Must that be false? Aristotle thought so. If two bodies could be co-located, he said, then all bodies could be co-located, which would shrink the entire world of matter to the size of a grain of wheat. He offered this argument to show that *no* two extended items could be co-located, and in that form it was destroyed in the sixth century by John Philoponus who pointed out that bodies might be co-locatable with regions though not with other bodies (Grant 1981: 19–22). This rebuttal relies on the idea that extended items are of two basic kinds, co-location being possible between the kinds but not within either. If Descartes were to admit container space, it would presumably have to be in that version, the alternative being to allow co-location to run riot as threatened by Aristotle. You and I might state the position like this:

> Extended items are of two kinds, bodies and regions of container space. There can be co-location between the kinds, but not within either.

Descartes, however, would have to put it thus:

> Extended items (bodies) are of two kinds. There can be co-location between the kinds, but not within either.

Now at last we approach the real trouble—the serious Cartesian objection to container space. If Descartes admitted these two kinds of matter, he would need to declare whether the difference between them is fundamental or derived; and each answer would be abhorrent to him. If the difference is basic, he loses the unity and conceptual spareness of his physics, which will now need not only geometrical and temporal concepts but also the concept of the differentia between the two kinds of body. If, on the other hand, the difference is derivative, supervening on something that involves only geometrical and temporal concepts, Descartes has to tell us *how* it supervenes—analogous to his accounts of fluidity, solubility, softness, etc.—and he has no chance of succeeding in doing so.

12. Spaces and places

If there is container space, it might all be full, so that nature is a plenum; or some might be empty, so that there are stretches of vacuum. Which of those obtains

would be a contingent matter. Now, Descartes holds that there is matter everywhere, and sometimes he speaks of 'spaces' as 'full' rather than 'empty', and as
having bodies 'in' them. He cannot mean these terms in their container-space
senses, so how does he mean them?

He has no clear meaning for them. His talk about things being *in* spaces is not
controlled by any firm underlying theory. Here again is the core of *PP* 2:16:

A body's being extended in length, breadth and depth in itself warrants the conclusion
that it is a substance. [Similarly for] a space that is supposed to be a vacuum: since there
is extension in it, there must necessarily be substance in it as well.

This argument is odder than is generally recognized. Look at it:

> Whatever is extended is a substance.
> Every region of space has extension in it.
> So every region of space has a substance in it.

Taking the first premiss of that to mean 'Wherever there is extension there is a
substance', the argument looks valid; but its second premiss is mysterious. What
can it be for something to have extension *in* it? Descartes might mean that any
region of space has extension in it-as-subject, which is just to describe it as
extended. That is a recognized way of speaking (see CSM 1:294–5). We do say
that properties are 'in' the things that have them; and the second premiss on that
reading of it is true. But that makes his argument invalid, for it now runs like this:

> Whatever is extended is a substance.
> Every region of space is extended.
> So every region of space has a substance in it.

What actually follows is that every region of space is a substance. So Descartes
reaches the conclusion that every region of space contains a substance through
an argument which is plainly invalid or else has a perfectly obscure second premiss.

I cannot rescue him from this tangle, but I can explain his general tendency to
use the language of containment. It arises from his not always verbally distinguishing *(regions of) space* from *places* or *locations*. A place is abstract: it is a complex relational property, and thus differs *toto coelo* from a region of space. It is in
fact a relational property that a region can have, just as a body can. If a body is
co-located with a region of container space, then those two items have the very
same place—that is, they are related in the same way to (other) bodies. When I
use the word 'place', it will be only to express the concept of the *where* of a
thing—its set of spatial relations to other things. That is one proper use of 'place';
I do not care whether it can also be acceptably used to mean the same as 'region'.

When Descartes writes: 'The subtle matter around a candle . . . moves in a
circle, and tends to spread out from there and to leave an empty space, that is to
say, a space which contains only what might come into it from elsewhere' (CSMK
138), one cannot believe that he means to tolerate container space, though that

is what his words imply. What he does mean, I propose, is that when the subtle matter moves, it ceases to have certain relational properties, and matter from elsewhere comes to have them; it leaves a certain place, and other matter enters it. Everything Descartes says about 'spaces' as 'full' or 'empty'—the entire language of 'containment' between spaces and bodies—should probably be understood in this innocent way.

At the start of *PP* 2:17 he uses the phrase 'place or space', and then equates it with 'place'. In 2:19 he alludes disparagingly to the common view that (parts of) 'space' can be 'empty', and then in 2:33 he reports that in 2:18–19 he has said 'that every place is full of bodies'. These turns of phrase support my conjecture if—but only if—Descartes in them means 'place' in my sense.

The best fairly direct evidence that he does so mean it occurs in *PP* 2:10–15, where he runs 'place' and 'space' in a single harness. Of the several things he says about how they differ, the most revealing is this:

There is no real distinction between space, or internal place, and the corporeal substance contained in it; the only difference lies in how we are accustomed to conceive of them. For the extension in length, breadth and depth which constitutes a space is in reality exactly the same as that which constitutes a body. The difference arises as follows: in the case of a body, we regard the extension as something particular, and thus think of it as changing whenever there is a new body; but in the case of a space, we attribute to the extension only a generic unity, so that when a new body comes to occupy the space, the extension of the space is reckoned not to change but to remain one and the same, so long as it retains the same size and shape and keeps the same position relative to certain external bodies which we use to determine the space in question. (*PP* 2:10, CSM 1:227)

The best I can do with this obscure passage is to suppose that Descartes's label 'space, or internal place' applies to a complex relational property that may be possessed first by one body, then by another. Then it can be true that first one body and then a different one is 'in' a certain place, without there having to be some thing which literally contains first one and then the other.

For two reasons, I doubt that Descartes had this thought in a clear, explicit and controlled manner. (1) He thought of places as being extended; but places (in my sense) are not; complex relational properties do not have length, breadth, and depth. Objection: 'If it lacks length etc., how can it contain bodies?' Answer: It does not, strictly speaking, contain anything. When we say that a body is 'in' a place, we should mean only that it has a certain relational property; we should not be using 'in' to stand for containment, any more than we do when we say 'He is in a bad mood'. It is safer to avoid 'in', and to say that things are 'at' places. (2) Descartes says that 'there is no real difference' between a body and the place that it is 'in'. Well, we can agree that *it is not the case that the body is one thing and the place is another thing*; but Descartes seems to mean more strongly that *the body is one thing and the place is the same thing*. In my sense of 'place', this is not true, for places are abstract, they are relational properties—not things but 'modes' of things.

Anyway, whether or not we can rescue what Descartes says about spaces as 'full' and 'empty', he certainly does not believe of any item that it can literally

contain bodies. (The humdrum sense in which a flask can contain myrrh is irrelevant to our topic. It involves one body's surrounding another body; Descartes
would never say about the flask and the contained myrrh, as he does about the
space or place and the body 'in' it, that 'there is no real distinction' between
them.)

13. Space as a system of relations

Descartes gave short shrift to container space, but he dismissed another time-hal-
lowed metaphysic of space as though he had never heard of it. I shall approach it
through his attempt to 'correct our preconceived opinion about absolute vacuum' by means of this argument:

> If someone asks what would happen if God were to take away every single body con-
> tained in a jar, without allowing any other body to take the place of what had been
> removed, the answer must be that the sides of the jar would in that case have to be in con-
> tact. For when there is nothing between two bodies they must necessarily touch each
> other. And it is a manifest contradiction for them to be apart, or to have a distance
> between them, when the distance in question is nothing; for every distance is a mode of
> extension, and therefore cannot exist without an extended substance. (*PP* 2:18, CSM
> 1:231)

This argument deserves patient scrutiny. Descartes challenges us with the question: 'What is there between the opposite sides of the jar?' He warns us against
answering: 'Only a distance.' Distances are modes, he says, meaning that they are
adjectival upon things. You cannot have a sheer five inches between two things:
it must be some third thing that measures five inches along one of its dimensions.
'It is a complete contradiction that a particular extension should belong to nothing,' we have seen him saying; and he is right. This belongs to his just denial that
space could be a bulky nothing.

What is there between the sides of the jar after the air has been removed? Here
is another possible answer: 'Before God took action, there were two jar-shaped
and -sized things in there—a portion of matter and a region of space—and after
he had removed the matter the space remained.' That is the container-space
answer, and Descartes here offers no reason to reject it (as Locke complains in
Essay II.xiii.16).

Descartes also ignores a third answer. If when God removes the matter from
the jar, it does not collapse, then it follows that the opposite sides of the jar are
apart; that much is uncontroversial. Now, Descartes assumes that if

(1) Side S_1 is apart from side S_2,

that must be because

(2) Some thing is between S_1 and S_2

—the seemingly dyadic fact about apartness must be an upshot of a triadic fact about betweenness. That snubs the possibility that 1 is a *basic* fact about how the two things are related, not one made true by an underlying fact about how the two relate to a third thing. That view was later endorsed by Leibniz in his famous correspondence with Clarke (§141); some earlier theories of space also implied it, but perhaps not clearly enough. At any rate, Descartes does not even hint at it.

He might challenge the Leibnizian: '*If there is nothing between two things, they are contiguous.* That is so trivially obvious that someone who denies it ought not to be heard. And it entails, by contraposition, that if two things are not contiguous, there is something between them.' The Leibnizian should reply that the 'trivially obvious' thesis is false when taken strictly and philosophically, and that it seems undeniable only when taken in a loose, colloquial fashion in which 'There is nothing between them' merely means that they are contiguous.

The (S) relational view of space, which Descartes ignored and Leibniz defended, should not be confused with a (P) relational view of *place*. Locke espoused P: our notion of where a body is, he held, must be a notion of how it relates spatially to other bodies. It cannot be the sheer notion of what region of space the body is in, because space is all 'uniform'. He does not regard that as a down payment on the theory that spatial concepts generally must be reduced to relational ones, so that space is a structure of relations. About that he is carefully agnostic (*Essay* II.xiii.10, 26). He is entitled to be, for one can consistently affirm (P) that our only concept of place is a relational one while denying (S) that space is a system of relations. This is illustrated not only by Locke, but also by Descartes, who accepted a version of P and silently turned his back on S (§15).

14. The fourth view: space as a separator

We have looked at Descartes's treatment or neglect of three views of space: as a **bulky nothing**, as a **substantial container**, and as a **structure of relations**. He puts energy into denying the first; his rejection of the second is silent, but there are reasons for it in his work; and he seems to ignore the third without having good reasons for or against it.

There remains one other possible view of space: namely, as a **separator**, relating to bodies as water does to fish swimming in it. Water does not relate to fish in the 'container' manner: no fish is co-located with any water; rather, a fish swims among the portions of water, pushing them aside as it moves; fish and water compete for places. The portions of water, rather than 'containing' the fish in my sense, separate fish from fish. The separator metaphysic is analogous to that: there are regions of space and there are bodies, and the two kinds jointly exhaust all the locations there are; but no two particulars have the same position at the same time. Where body starts, space stops; just as where fish starts, water stops.

Portions of separator space would be, in Descartes's terminology, portions of *matter*; they would be *bodies*. He distinguishes portions of matter as more or less 'subtle', less or more 'dense'; and the items I have been calling regions of separator space are what he would call portions of *absolutely subtle matter*—bodies which can be divided and brushed aside by fish, bullets, feathers, and so on without these being deflected, slowed down, or otherwise impeded. To avoid verbal tangles, I shall follow Descartes in this usage, reserving the label '*dense matter*' for the extended things that satisfy the plain person's ideas about matter.

Portions of subtle matter can move, just as portions of dense matter can. They are also like dense matter in this: they cannot be co-located with anything else, so are perfectly impenetrable, so are solid. Unlike dense matter, however, they have no inertial resistance to being moved, so that no force is needed for them to be brushed aside to make way for a portion of dense matter. They are not tangible as water is when you swish your hand through it: you feel the water because it resists as it moves away, which absolutely subtle matter does not. Still, if we could arrange for your hand to be a piston moving into a cylinder containing subtle matter, with your hand fitting so snugly that the matter could not escape between your hand and the cylinder wall; and if we could also ensure that neither the cylinder wall nor your hand had fissures through which the subtle matter could leak away; then that subtle matter would be tangible to you, obdurately stopping your hand's motion into the cylinder and feeling like steel.

Does Descartes allow that there is—or even that there might be—absolutely subtle matter? Sometimes he seems to stop short of that, apparently suggesting that any portion of subtle matter would, if studied minutely enough, be found to have properties of dense matter. He speaks of our careless tendency to think we have found empty space when confronted by regions in which 'we do not perceive anything by sight, touch or any other sense', and criticizes the supposition 'that a space we call empty contains not just nothing perceivable by the senses but nothing whatsoever'.[5] If Descartes is here referring strictly to the unaided senses, and excluding what might be learned through artifice, he may be assuming that each apparently empty region would show up as granulated, striated, or the like through powerful enough microscopes, or would impede the movement of other bodies by an amount that could be detected by sensitive enough measuring instruments.

He does not say this explicitly, however, and sometimes he denies it. He says that there may be 'nothing in a given place but extension in length, breadth and depth' (PP 2:5); he declares to be intelligible the idea of 'bodies which in no way hinder or assist the motion of other bodies' (PP 4:21); he makes assertions about what happens when 'a body moves through a space containing only matter which neither speeds it up nor slows it down' (AT 2:442); and he writes that 'what

---

[5] These are from *Rules* 12, CSM 1:48, and *PP* 2:17, CSM 1:230, respectively. See also *W* 4, CSM 1:87, and Med 6, CSM 2:56.

is commonly called empty space is . . . a real body deprived of all its accidents', which he explains to More as meaning that the body is deprived of every property except determinates of extension (CSMK 381). In passages like these, Descartes seems to countenance extended items which will not affect sense-organs or scientific instruments—ones whose existence as things depends purely upon their geometrical properties together with abstract metaphysical argument against the notion of extended nothing. (For an acute and historically rich exploration of Descartes's dealings with separator space, see Palmer 1999.)

15. Descartes's 'neighbour' account of motion

Having mentioned Descartes's relational view of place, I append a section on the relational view of motion which he associates with it. He accepts the generic doctrine that facts about how bodies move are really facts about how their spatial interrelationships alter; the interest is in what species of this he adopts. Extreme relationalism says that there is never any absolute fact of the matter about whether or how a thing is moving; any change in how any two things are spatially related entitles us to describe either of them as 'moving'. At first Descartes seems to accept that:

To determine the position [of a body], we have to look at various other bodies which we regard as immobile; and in relation to different bodies we may say that the same thing is both changing and not changing its place at the same time. For example, when a ship is under way a man sitting on the stern remains in one place relative to the other parts of the ship; . . . but he is constantly changing his place relative to the neighbouring shores. . . . Then again, if we believe the earth moves, and suppose that it advances the same distance from west to east as the ship travels from east to west in the corresponding period of time, we shall again say that the man sitting on the stern is not changing his place; for we are now determining the place by means of certain fixed points in the heavens. (PP 2:13, CSM 1:228)

It turns out later, though, that Descartes here meant only to be describing how plain folk usually think and talk about motion. His own view is what I shall call *neighbour* relationalism about motion. According to this, motion 'is the transfer of one piece of matter, or one body, from the vicinity of the other bodies which are in immediate contact with it, and which are regarded as being at rest, to the vicinity of other bodies' (PP 2:25, CSM 1:233). On this view, a thing counts as moving only if a change is occurring in its spatial relations to its immediate neighbours; so the ship is moving because of its changing relation to the water, but not because of its changing relation to the shore.

There is still a subjective or 'take your pick' element, embodied in Descartes's clause 'which *are regarded as* being at rest'. I shall explain. The plain person's idea of motion can be put like this:

The fundamental concept of motion is a dyadic one, it is the concept of a *relatively moving pair*, a pair of bodies whose spatial relations to one another are altering. *This concept applies to every pair of bodies except ones whose members are not changing in their spatial inter-relations.* Given any relatively moving pair, there is no objective fact about which is at rest and which moving; that is to be settled pragmatically or conventionally. If there were such a fact, then we would after all have a monadic rather than a dyadic concept of motion.

Descartes's account is the same, except that it replaces the italicized sentence by this:

This concept applies to every pair of bodies except (1) ones whose members are not changing in their spatial inter-relations and (2) ones whose members are not contiguous.

The rest of the story is the same. The concept is still dyadic, and the application of the monadic 'is at rest' and 'is in motion' to the separate members of a relatively moving pair is still to be settled by convention or convenience. The only difference lies in which pairs are eligible, and there is nothing subjective or conventional about that.

That difference has the effect of reducing our range of choice over what to say about a given body's movements. As Descartes points out in *PP* 2:28, the plain person's concept allows us to say that a given body is at rest or moving thus or moving so, whereas his concept—though it may offer a choice between 'It moves' and 'It is still'—does not offer a choice of different kinds of movement that can be attributed to a particular body at a particular time.

The point is nicely put in some 'notes on the *Principles* that Descartes seems to have written some time after the publication of the Latin *Principles* in 1644' (Garber 1992: 167), where Descartes writes:

When I said that motion and rest are contrary, I understood this with respect to a single body, which is in contrary modes when its surface is separated from another body and when it is not. . . . Motion and rest differ truly and *modaliter* if by motion is understood the mutual separation of two bodies and by rest the negation of this separation. However, when one of the two bodies which are separating mutually is said to move, and the other to be at rest, in this sense motion and rest differ only *ratione*.

To say that they 'differ *modaliter*' is to say that they are genuinely different states; to say that they 'differ only *ratione*' is to say that they are two ways of thinking about a single state.

Garber shows (1992: 171) that Descartes cannot do physics with his concept of motion. That is a complicated question, however, and I recommend Slowik 1999 for an acute discussion of the issues and the literature.

Given that Descartes's concept of motion does not fit easily into his physics, one wonders what drew him to it in the first place. Perhaps he wanted to reduce the amount of subjectivity, of pragmatic choice, in our use of 'It moves' and its cognates. Or he may have been moved by a political reason. He holds that the earth is embedded in a 'vortex' of fluid matter whirling around the sun, like flotsam carried around in a whirlpool (*PP* 4:24–30). So, according to his 'immediate neighbour' analysis of the concept of motion, Descartes points out in *PP* 4:28, 'strictly speaking, the earth does not move'! Perhaps he adopted the 'immediate neighbour' analysis so as to get this result, thereby protecting himself from the trouble that Galileo encountered from the Church of Rome because of his assertion that the earth does move. Like Garber (on whom I am relying here), I doubt that; but I have nothing to say about it, nor is it philosophically interesting.

Chapter 3

Descartes's Physics

16. Smallness of parts

We have seen that Descartes seems sometimes to countenance separator space—that is, portions of absolutely subtle matter, 'bodies' lacking density, inertia, resistance, and any other properties through which they could be detected other than their merely geometrical ones of size, shape, and location. He cannot accept a *basic* difference between absolutely subtle and dense matter. If he did, his physics would lose its prized unity and conceptual parsimony. However, Descartes openly holds that some bodies are subtler than others, ranging all portions of matter along a subtler/denser continuum; but for him this difference is not basic but derivative, like that between warmer and colder or hard and soft. Let us see how he derives it.

In his *Optics* he contrasts 'some very subtle and very fluid matter' with 'the less fluid or coarser parts of the air'; this opposition between 'subtle' and 'coarse' indicates that subtleness depends on size of parts (1637*b*, CSM 1:154). Again, having introduced the spherical particles of matter which are his 'second element', Descartes introduces his 'first element', which he characterizes in Latin as 'other more subtle matter' and in French as 'other more tiny particles' (*PP* 3:49). The link between subtleness and smallness of parts is made explicit in many places. Sometimes Descartes describes subtle matter as 'a continuous liquid', implying that it is indefinitely or infinitely finely divided (CSMK 123).

To explain how bodies might differ in the smallness of their parts, Descartes must tread delicately. Every portion of matter can be split into sub-portions, which can be split in their turn, he insists; so all matter has parts that are indefinitely small, if 'part of x' means 'portion of x that could be isolated by splitting x'. For a theory in which bodies can differ in the size of their parts, therefore, he needs a different concept of 'part'. I shall call it '*actual* part', taking my lead from Descartes: 'All the bodies in the universe are composed of one and the same matter, which is divisible into indefinitely many parts, and is actually divided into a large number of parts which move in different directions' (*PP* 3:46, CSM 1:256). So it can happen that a body is divisible into parts into which it is not actually divided. What can Descartes mean by this?

For many metaphysicians, an actual part would be a physical part surrounded by separator space or by some empty container space, but Descartes knows that he cannot say this. In his early work *The World* he characterizes matter of the first element as 'the most subtle and penetrating liquid that the world contains', and continues: 'I imagine that its parts are much smaller and faster moving than those of other bodies. Or rather, so as not to be forced to admit any vacuum in nature, . . .' (AT 11:24). This is a response to the problem that actual parts must not be portions of matter surrounded by space, and that Descartes needs to explain what else they can be. The unquoted remainder of the sentence seems irrelevant to the problem; but Descartes then connects part-hood with differences in movement, at first rather obscurely, but then in his next chapter with great clarity:

Let us suppose that God really divides matter into many parts, some larger and some smaller . . . however we care to imagine them. It is not that God separates these parts from one another so that there is some void between them: rather, let us regard the differences he creates within this matter as consisting wholly in the diversity of the motions he gives to its parts. (W 6, CSM 1:91)

In later works Descartes presents this idea less tentatively, and generalizes it, contending that *all* qualitative variety in the extended realm comes from differences in how portions of matter move:

The matter existing in the entire universe is . . . one and the same, and it is always recognized as matter simply in virtue of its being extended. All the properties which we clearly perceive in it are reducible to the sole fact that it is divisible [*partibilis*] and that its parts can be moved, and its resulting capacity to be affected in all the ways which we perceive as being derivable from the movement of the parts. . . . Any variation in matter or diversity in its many forms depends on motion. (PP 2:23, CSM 1:232)

So differences in how portions of matter move must beget, among other things, the concept of actual part which we are pursuing. In writing about subtle matter, Descartes frequently conjoins the fine division of its parts with the speed of their relative motions. Whatever else he makes of the concept of high speed, the mere fact that these particles are moving relative to one another is necessary and also sufficient for their being actual parts.

Here is how Descartes must get the concept of *actual part* out of relative motions of mere portions, or *geometrical parts*. Let us say that a portion of matter is *internally static* if no relative motion occurs within it, all its sub-portions being in motion (or at rest) together in a block. Then a geometrical part P of a body is an actual part of it just in case:

P is internally static, and
P is not a geometrical part of any larger internally static portion of matter.

So the actual parts of any portion are its largest internally static geometrical parts. A portion is 'actually divided' if some physical parts of it are moving relative to others; if all its physical parts are moving together it is undivided but—like all matter—divisible. That is pretty much how Spinoza understood Descartes: 'Matter that moves in various ways has at least as many parts into which it is actually divided as the different degrees of speed that are observed in it at the same time' (CS 266).

With that account of 'actual part' in hand, Descartes could say that the subtleness of any portion of matter depends solely on how small its actual parts
are—that is, on the size of its largest internally static geometrical parts. Then
'Matter can be subtler without limit' is equivalent to 'The largest internally static geometrical parts of a portion of matter can be smaller without limit'.
Descartes seems to accept this when he writes in *PP* 3:52 that matter of the first
element 'is divided into particles of indefinite smallness'. Given the proposed
account of subtleness, this commits him to admitting separator space—that is,
matter which does not resist being pushed around by other matter.

Whether this really is Descartes's view about what subtleness consists in is
unclear. Some texts favour Yes, others No, and I cannot settle the issue. Nor can
I get properly clear about what he *ought* to say about this. Can he, by his own
lights, explain matter's being subtle by appealing only to how finely it is 'actually
divided'? Having wrestled inconclusively with this question, I spare you the
details. One deep source of my difficulties will come to the surface in §20.

17. Subtleness and speed

When writing about subtle matter, Descartes often alludes not only to the smallness of its actual parts, but also to how fast they move relative to one another,
apparently treating smallness and rapidity as natural companions. 'The first element surpasses all other bodies in speed', he says at CSM 1:323. Speed might
enter the story in any of three ways. (1) Though required for some purposes to
which Descartes puts first-element matter, speed might not be relevant to subtleness—that is, to some matter's lack of resistance to other matter that brushes
it aside. (2) Speed might help to explain matter's subtleness only by helping to
explain the fineness of its division. (3) The speed of the particles of subtle matter
contributes directly to its subtleness.

If 1 is right, then we can drop the topic of speed right away. If 2 is right, then
speed has no independent place in the explanation of subtleness. It is probably
not right, though Descartes does think that speed helps to explain fineness of
division: fast-moving particles bump into one another often and hard, he
explains, thus knocking bits off one another and generally becoming ever smaller
(*PP* 3:52). This, of course, presupposes some grasp of cohesion and of the forces
needed to overcome it (§23).

Now let us consider whether (3) Descartes can invoke the speed of particles
directly—not through size—in explaining subtleness of matter. He tries here:

The parts of fluid bodies easily move out of their places, and consequently do not resist
the movement of our hands into those places; whereas the parts of solid bodies adhere to
one another in such a way that, without sufficient force to overcome their cohesion, they
cannot be separated. [The reason for this difference is that] a body already in motion does
not prevent another body's occupying the place which it is leaving of its own accord,

whereas a body at rest cannot be expelled from its place except by some force ⟨coming from outside⟩. (PP 2:54, MM 69–70)

This is a feckless explanation. When I try to move my hand eastwards, I am shoving it towards a multitude of little places: let us grant that some of these are just then independently being vacated by particles of subtle or fluid matter moving further eastward; but most are moving into other little places which are still in the path of my hand, some indeed moving westward, directly against it. Even particles that are independently heading east, furthermore, may be moving more slowly than my hand.

In a letter to Mersenne, Descartes seems blind to the difficulty:

When I conceive of a body moving in a medium which does not resist it at all, I am supposing that all the parts of the surrounding liquid body are disposed to move at the same speed as the original body, both in giving place to it and in entering the place that it is leaving. Thus, every liquid is such as to offer no resistance to *some* movement . . . (CSMK 132*; my emphasis here and below)

There is no reason to believe this. Take a single uniform linear motion of a hard sphere into a region full of subtle matter: short of a miracle, why should exactly the right amount of subtle matter be independently moving at just the right speed in just the right direction?

Descartes sees a need for a miracle, but not in his account of how some matter can be subtle or non-resistant relative to some particular movement of a dense body. He invokes miracles only in explaining how matter can be monadically subtle—that is, unresistant to *any* movement into its region by *any* dense body. His account continues:

. . . but to imagine some matter which did not resist *any* of the different movements of any body, you would have to pretend that God or an angel was moving its parts at various speeds to correspond with the speed of the movements of the body they surround.

This implies that there is no monadically subtle (= non-resistant) matter, because that would require a miraculously *ad hoc* internal dynamics, with—I would add—the miracle affecting directions as well as speeds. I do not understand Descartes's offering, in explanation of why speed produces subtleness, something that is wrong absent a miracle. Even with that miracle, I shall show in §20, the explanation fails.

It does have a certain formal virtue. We have been concerned not only with subtleness in general, but with the special problem of separator space, to which I now return for a moment. The only prima-facie possible way of getting subtleness from smallness of actual parts was through the principle *the smaller, the subtler*; and that opened the way for Descartes to believe in absolutely subtle matter—that is, separator space. The speed analogue of this is not available to him. If the principle *the faster, the subtler*, were his whole account of subtleness, then separator space would involve particles that move infinitely quickly; and Descartes firmly rejects that. 'No motion takes place in a single instant of time.'

'In order to conceive . . . any possible motion, it is necessary to consider at least two of its instants . . . and the relation between them.' 'No movement can happen in an instant' (*PP* 2:39; *W7*, CSM 1:96–7; AT 2:215).[1] So we can commend Descartes's attempting to get subtleness out of speed without relying on that principle. What he requires for absolute subtleness is not infinite speed but, rather, a speed and direction which are just right for the given intruder.

I conclude that Descartes has no half-way coherent means of explaining degrees of subtleness in terms of speed, let alone explaining separator space. Before leaving these matters, I shall devote a section to the doctrinal framework within which the subtleness problem arises.

18. Qualitative variety

According to a doctrine that I call Supervenience, all qualitative differences within the world of matter supervene on differences in how portions of matter move. This is not forced upon Descartes by Extension (his thesis that extension is the whole essence of matter). Extension is consistent with bodies' differing from one another in certain basic, underived, non-essential properties. But Supervenience and Extension are linked by an underlying intellectual ambition: each arises from the desire for a physics whose only basic concepts are those of geometry plus the concept of time.

Many followers of Galileo held that all qualitative variety in the physical world supervenes on differences in micro-structure. Though it has turned out to be false, because there are different *basic* kinds of material particle, Supervenience is a prima-facie reasonable view. For Descartes, however, it was problematic, as I shall now explain.

The problem is that the concept of structure *presupposes* variety. Suppose we explain a body's being brittle through some structural feature of it: the matter composing it is arranged thus:◆◆◆, rather than like this: ❖❖❖, which would have made it flexible. Those two structures differ only because we can distinguish the bits shown in black from the bits shown in white, and this involves qualitative difference. This might supervene on still smaller-scale structure, but the problem would re-arise on the smaller scale. Nobody would think that this could go on for ever, with structure all the way down.

This poses no problem for a theorist who believes in container space, or allows one basic difference, such as that between dense matter and separator space. So Galileo and Locke were in the clear, but not Descartes.

In *Rules* 12 he apparently tries to use structure as the explanatory underlay for all qualitative variety. At that point he may be on firm ground, because in that work he seems to distinguish bodies basically from space. By 'extension',

---

[1] I gathered these references from Garber 1992: 174.

he writes there, 'we mean whatever has length, breadth and depth, leaving aside the question whether it is a real body or merely a space' (*Rules* 14, CSM 1:59). With bodies distinguished from space, there can be structure, upon which all *other* qualitative variety can supervene. The later works provide no such rescue.

Descartes tries to escape from the impasse by assigning to *patterns of movement* the role that others would give to *structure*. Here, quoted more fully than before, is his version of Supervenience:

All the variety in matter, all the diversity of its forms, depends on motion. The matter existing in the entire universe is thus one and the same, and it is always recognized as matter simply in virtue of its being extended. All the properties which we clearly perceive in it are reducible to the sole fact that it is divisible [*partibilis*] and that its parts can be moved, and its resulting capacity to be affected in all the ways which we perceive as being derivable from the movement of the parts. If the division into parts occurs simply in our thought, there is no resulting change; any variation in matter or diversity in its many forms depends on motion. (*PP* 2:23, CSM 1:232)

Descartes seriously tries to employ this idea that qualitative variety supervenes on *motion* alone. We have looked a little at his attempt to get the subtle/dense continuum out of nothing but motion; but I now argue that within his framework mere motion cannot support any qualitative variation whatsoever. There are three reasons for this.

(1) From the Cartesian point of view, what is the material world like at an instant? Does its state contain any marks of the fact that different bits of matter are moving in different ways? One might say Yes to this, as Leibniz did: he held that at each instant a moving thing is the subject of a tendency or 'conatus' or urge to move, this being a real property of the thing at that instant. Descartes, however, actively opposed such notions, and held that all the facts about how a thing moves—and the bare fact *that* it moves—are captured in the facts about where it is located at different times. For him, then, the fact that x is moving thus and y is moving so is *essentially* a fact about how things are through a period of time; no trace of it can exist at any instant within that period. This, conjoined with his view about the basis for qualitative variety, entails that at any instant the world of matter is qualitatively uniform: since an instant contains no traces of movement, it cannot contain traces of anything that supervenes on movement. A photograph that registered a strictly instantaneous state of the material world should, on this account, come out blank.

Leibniz makes this point against Descartes's view of motion. Defending his own view that 'In the present moment of its motion, a body . . . has a tendency or urge toward changing its place', he warns against denying it:

Otherwise the body A which is in motion would not be different at the present moment (or, therefore, at any moment whatever) from the body B which is at rest, and it would follow from the opinion of this distinguished man [the Cartesian J. C. Sturm], if it is opposed to mine at this point, that there would be no way whatever of distinguishing between bodies, since there is no basis for such a distinction in a plenum or mass that is not varied unless motion varies it. (NI 13, FW 218–19*)

This is a serious objection to Supervenience in Descartes's scheme of things. It does not rule out diachronic variety (the world's being F at one time and not-F at another), but it rules out synchronic variety (the world's being F in one place and at the same time not-F in another).

Descartes might respond by rejecting the very notion of 'how the world is at an instant', maintaining that anything real in the material world lasts through time: 'We can consider shorter and shorter periods of time,' he might say, 'but we cannot consider a durationless instant. In pretending to do so, you opt out of the real world altogether; your ending with a blank shows the absurdity of your procedure, not the wrongness of my metaphysic.' This is plausible, but Descartes is not in a position to say it. A view of his about how God enables things to last through time entails that states of the world that are instantaneous, far from being unreal idealizations, are the fundamental reality (§37).

Leibniz's attack relies on Descartes's holding that motion is purely change of place, so that facts about motion are not registered on things at an instant. One doctrine of Descartes's might seem to go against this. He is explaining why a moving body 'always has a tendency to go in a straight line', and says that if it has another trajectory, such as a circle, it does so 'only under constraint':

This depends solely on God's preserving each thing . . . not as it may have been some time earlier but precisely as it is at the very instant that he preserves it. Now, of all motions it is certain that only *motion in a straight line* is entirely simple and *has a nature which may be wholly grasped in an instant*. For in order to conceive such motion it suffices to think that a body is in the process of moving in a certain direction, and that this is the case at each determinable instant during the time it is moving. By contrast, in order to conceive circular motion, or any other possible motion, it is necessary to consider at least two of its instants, or rather two of its parts, and the relation between them. (W 7, CSM 1:96–7*)

The clause I have italicized might seem to undercut Leibniz's attack, but it does not. Descartes does not hold that a body's being in motion is registered in the body itself at an instant; he grants a body an instantaneous tendency or disposition to move, but this is not intrinsic to the body, but rather a fact about how God is disposed to affect it. And he thinks that a sequence of momentary dispositions in God can, *ceteris paribus*, yield only rectilinear motion. His elaboration of the point in PP 2:39, though not transparent, pretty clearly shows that Descartes is not saying anything that would help him against Leibniz's attack.

(2) Leibniz expands his criticism:

From this view it would also follow, finally, that absolutely nothing would change in bodies, and that everything would always remain the same. For if no portion of matter whatsoever were to differ from equal and congruent portions of matter . . . and if one momentary state were to differ from another only in virtue of the transposition of equal and interchangeable portions of matter, . . . then, on account of this perpetual substitution of indistinguishables, it obviously follows that in the corporeal world there can be no way of distinguishing different momentary states from one another.

This argues that Cartesian Supervenience rules out not only synchronic but also diachronic variety. The argument is too obviously successful to need comment. (For an expanded treatment of Leibniz's attack on Descartes's doctrine of body, see Hartz 1989.)

(3) The third and deepest objection to Supervenience comes from the premiss, accepted by many philosophers, that the very concept of motion pre-requires qualitative variety, so that there is no difference between 'the disc is rotating' and 'the disc is still' for an absolutely homogeneous disc. (See Armstrong 1980.) If that is right, then Descartes's project fails: you cannot base all variety on motion if the latter presupposes the former.

The premiss is controversial: although David Lewis accepts it, for example, Saul Kripke does not. I am inclined to accept it, but I do not know how to argue for it, except to demand: What contentful sense can we attach to the idea that one portion of matter moves relative to its surroundings, at a level where the portions are qualitatively exactly alike? Don't think of this in terms of texture, or of grain or nap as in a carpet; at the foundational level where we are working, our supposedly moving portions of matter must be absolutely homogeneous.

19. Compression

In his argument against co-location (§11), Descartes assumes that an essentially extended item must always have the same extent. This assumption also enters into other lines of his thought, for he firmly believed that there can be no compression or expansion of matter. He envisaged this being used against him:

> [One] possible reason for doubting that the true nature of body consists solely in extension . . . is the widespread belief that many bodies can be rarefied and condensed in such a way that when rarefied they possess more extension than when condensed. Indeed, some people . . . distinguish the substance of a body from its quantity, and even its quantity from its extension. (PP 2:5, CSM 1:225)[2]

The phrase 'the substance of a body' contains a hint of trouble. We know what it means to call a body 'a substance', but what is the substance of a body? Descartes quite often uses 'substance' in this way, to denote something that an item may possess, but he never explains the usage; his official account of 'substance' in PP 1:51 does not provide for it. It seems to represent a loose, unconsidered element in his thinking (§207). Setting this aside, we have him criticizing others for distinguishing a body's quantity from its extension. The only clear sense I can find for this is 'distinguishing the fact that a body has such and such a

---

[2] See also W, CMS 1:88. For discussion of this topic, filling in some of the Aristotelian background, see Woolhouse 1993: 84–5.

size from the mere fact that it is extended', but there is nothing wrong with that distinction.

Never mind Descartes's diagnosis of his opponents' errors. His own positive view is demonstrably wrong. The thesis I call Extension says: *For any portion of stuff to be matter, it is both necessary and sufficient that it be extended.* The denial of compression and expansion is equivalent to this: *The extent that a particular portion of matter has at one time must be the extent that it has at every time.* The second of these makes essential use of the concepts of quantity (extent, amount of extension) and temporal duration. These concepts are both absent from Extension, which thus falls doubly short of implying the other.

Anyway, Descartes *does* regard compression and expansion as impossible, and wants to reconcile this with certain phenomena which 'some people' will adduce to cast doubt on his account of the essence of matter. He writes as though he had a unitary target, but his description of it is ambiguous. He might be trying to explain either (1) how a single body can seem to become larger or (2) how a single body can seem to enlarge while not gaining in weight, or while losing density or inertial resistance. Try to choose between those in the following passage:

Rarefied bodies . . . are those which have many gaps between their parts—gaps which are occupied by other bodies; and they become denser simply in virtue of the parts coming together and reducing or completely closing the gaps. In this last eventuality a body becomes so dense that it would be a contradiction to suppose that it could be made any denser. Now in this condition, the extension of a body is no less than when it occupies more space in virtue of the mutual separation of its parts; for whatever extension is comprised in the pores or gaps left between the parts must be attributed not to the body itself but to the various other bodies which fill the gaps. (*PP* 2:6, CSM 1:225)

Descartes compares this with pouring water into a sponge. This explains well enough the fact (1) that a single body can seem to become larger: it does this by becoming mixed with other matter in such a way that its skin seems to remain intact. Clear, correct, and boring.

But the announced topic is 'rarefaction', not mere 'expansion'. Apparently Descartes means to be explaining (2) the fact that a body can seem to enlarge while becoming less dense—that is, while becoming 'rarer', cubic inch for cubic inch. If so, he fails. Suppose that a few pounds of mercury penetrate the boundaries of a portion of hydrogen: the latter will seem to enlarge, but it will not seem to 'rarefy'. For the explanation to work, it must say that when a body seems to become more rarefied, its boundaries are penetrated by extra matter which is more rarefied than the body itself. So the explanation of 'x seems to become rarer than it was' presupposes that we already have a grasp of 'y is rarer than z is'.

20. The integration problem

When I try to clarify and deepen my thoughts about these issues, I slam into the brick wall of something I call 'the integration problem'. It is the problem of bringing into a single coherent picture two Cartesian theories about events in the material world. They are not mutually inconsistent. Perhaps, indeed, they are too far from any risk of that: they operate on different planes, with no points in common; and while this may keep them from harming one another, it also prevents us from telling a clear, detailed, unitary story incorporating both. Though crucial for the evaluation of Descartes's work, the integration problem has been little attended to in the secondary literature.

(1) *Movement-loop theory*   Descartes is firm in what we might call his triple-C denial: he rejects container space, compression, and co-location. Triple-C denial entails that no portion of matter can travel unless other matter travels at the same time. An arrow's flight must be associated with two sets of other movements. (a) Its place must be taken by some matter, which must in turn be replaced by other matter, and so on. (b) The arrow must displace some matter, which must move away, and thus displace other matter, and so on. Set *a* is required by the denials of container space and of compression, set *b* by those and the denial of the co-location. To meet these two needs, Descartes supposes that the two sets of movements intersect not only at the arrow but also at another place, creating a finite loop of moving matter: the arrow is replaced by air, which is replaced by air, which is replaced by . . . air, which replaces the arrow.[3] The dependencies amongst movements within the loop are absolute, logical, conceptual; so they do not involve any lapse of time; a body in a loop is required to move as it does throughout interval I by the movement *throughout* I of another body on the opposite side of the loop. 'The body at the end of the sequence enters the place left by the first body at the precise moment when the first body is leaving it' (*PP* 2:33). Descartes has to say this, given his opinion that empty space would have to be 'extended nothing': because this is absolutely, conceptually nonsensical, it cannot obtain for even a split second.

(2) *Collision theory*   Descartes presents some 'rules' governing collisions between pairs of bodies (*PP* 2:46–52, MM 64–9). This theory has predictive power: from the fact that two bodies are related *thus* and moving *so* a moment before they collide, Descartes's 'rules' purport to let us infer where they will be, and how they will be moving, a few seconds later. In short, his physics of collisions aims to be time-spanning, fertile with predictions, as one would expect of any branch of natural science.

In contrast to this, loop theory cannot predict anything; it can only tell us that if a particle is moving throughout I then such and such other things must be

---

[3] Descartes says that he is pushed into movement loops by his rejection of compression and container space (PP 2.33), overlooking the denial of co-location. For more on movement-loop theory, see *W* 4, CSM 1:86.

happening throughout I. The two theories differ in other ways as well. Collision theory can be used to explain why a body starts moving, whereas loop theory cannot. Collision theory embodies a direction from cause to effect, whereas loop theory has only the symmetrical dependence of every part of the loop on every other.

Descartes does physics sometimes in terms of fluids and sometimes in terms of discrete, relatively hard bodies, but that split is not my topic. The features of collision theory which concern me could be had by a theory about the movements of, and collisions between, portions of fluid; and, on the other hand, movement-loop theory can be stated in terms of hard bodies, with a loop being likened to the rim of a turning wheel. Also, Descartes explains that fluids are aggregates of extremely small discrete bodies; and he could instead say, conversely, that a discrete body is a portion of fluid that coheres in a certain way. Though each explanation has problems, each is at least plausible; whereas it would be a hopeless project to try to get collision theory out of loop theory, or vice versa.

Now, Descartes needs to solve the integration problem: his collision and loop theories need to be integrated into a single coherent physics. That would involve describing a collision between two balls in such a way as to include, in detail, the fact that each ball is involved in a synchronous movement loop before, during, and after the collision. Presumably at and just after the instant of collision, the white and red balls belong to a single loop; but up to that instant the white ball belonged to a loop that did not involve the red ball. The integration problem may come down to the question of how at the instant of a collision a moving body switches loops.

In trying to drive deeper into my exploration of whether Descartes's collision theory permits separator space, I keep running into loop theory. To get further, I need to solve the integration problem, by learning how to keep both theories in play at once or showing that it cannot be done; but I have failed to do either. Descartes seems to have been oblivious to this problem in his physics—he certainly does not try to solve it—but it makes itself felt in his writings.

A small, shining example occurs in a passage already quoted (§17): 'A body already in motion does not prevent another body's occupying the place which it is leaving of its own accord [Latin: *sponte*].' Descartes is not here attributing a will to the body. He means only that when I put my finger into water, it is not impeded by particles of water which are moving away from it *anyway*, moving away for some reason other than that my finger is pushing them aside. I let it pass back there, where I had other fish to fry; but in fact this safe-looking part of that explanation of Descartes's is toxic. It distinguishes matter that my finger pushes aside from matter that gives way to my finger for other reasons. In the latter case, one body has the role of place-taker, while another serves as expeller; my finger easily plays the place-taker role, because something else is doing the expelling. There is no sound basis for a separation of these two roles in Descartes's physics or metaphysics, and his failure to see this is part of his blindness to the integration problem. The place-taker belongs to loop theory, the expeller to collision theory.

21. Light and movement loops

Most of Descartes's physics is collision theory. When you push him hard on various aspects of it, asking the deepest questions about how they are supposed to work, you will find loop theory demanding your attention also. That was the case with the passage about a body's 'leaving of its own accord': it is not Descartes who brings in loop theory there; we do so as his students and critics. Sometimes, however, he brings it to the fore himself, using it to explain particular physical phenomena such as the speed of light.

The propagation of light is instantaneous, Descartes thought, but he likened it not to a projectile that travels infinitely fast, but rather to the supposedly instantaneous production of an effect at one end of a stick—'however long'—by pushing on the other end (*Rules* 9, CSM 1:34). He likens the action of light to 'the actions or movements transmitted by a stick', and draws the conclusion: 'Although the movement does not take place instantaneously, each of its parts can be felt at one end of the stick at the very moment . . . that it is produced at the other end' (CSMK 100).[4] Descartes was wrong about the stick: your push on one end of it produces a hole in the mud at the other end only because shock waves pass down the stick, taking time to do so. But that is by the way.

In a letter of Descartes to Beeckman, two remarkable things happen. First, Descartes describes an experiment which he says shows that light's effects travel instantaneously (CSMK 46). You might ask: 'How could he think he could discover that light travels instantaneously rather than, say, at a speed of a trillion miles a second?' He doesn't. He conducts the debate on the basis of a stipulation, to which Beeckman evidently agreed, about the maximum speed at which light-particles might travel—a speed which light cannot exceed if its propagation is like the movement of a bullet (Beeckman) rather than a thrusting stick (Descartes). The maximum is stated in terms of heartbeats; a rate of ninety beats per minute seems about right for sedentary meat-eating gentlemen; and that yields an agreed maximum speed for light-particles of eighteen miles per second, which is just ten thousand times too slow.

Second, Descartes writes that if he turned out to be wrong about the velocity of the propagation of light's effects, 'I would be prepared to admit that I knew absolutely nothing in philosophy'. Why? Well, he sees his view about the speed of light's effects as part of loop theory; and this may explain his dramatic conditional concession. But it does not justify it. For one thing, loop theory might be false without Descartes's entire system falling into ruins. Perhaps he could not

---

⁴ Richard Field called my attention to this passage, and gave me other help. See also 1637*b*, CSM 1:154.

admit container space or the co-location of matter with matter; but if he merely allowed that matter could be compressed and expanded, most of his physics would remain intact, though loop theory would fall away.

More important: suppose that the effects of light could not be handled in terms of loop theory, why would it follow that the theory itself was false? Descartes does allow that some physical effects are propagated through the movement of particles through space—for example, sound (CSMK 52). Even without textual evidence, we could be sure that he was familiar with the delay between seeing a hammer-blow and hearing the thud. If the propagation of sound can be handled in terms of projectiles, rather than of synchronous movement loops, then the same could hold for the propagation of light if the evidence demanded it.

This, however, does not bring us to the bottom of Descartes's troubles in this area of his work. Although he does not use loop theory to explain the speed of sound, he must *apply it to* sound; as basic metaphysics, it must apply to everything in the material world. In one place Descartes himself remarks to Mersenne that the motion involved in sound 'is circular' (CSMK 10). When a sound starts to be emitted from a hammer fifty yards away, a complete movement loop comes into existence instantaneously. Does it run through our ears? If it does, then why do we not hear the blow at the moment when we see it? If it does not, why not? Perhaps Descartes would say that the instantaneous loop is smaller than this, and does not extend fifty yards in any direction. But then he should explain why we *never* hear sound instantaneously, and *never* see light after a perceptible delay.

A stronger challenge was suggested to me by Richard Manning. If we hear the hammer-blow, Descartes has to say that the hammer disturbs air, which pushes air, which . . . has an effect on our ears. But how can this be if the initially disturbed air was part of a movement-loop which did not stretch as far as our ears? Why does the smaller synchronous movement loop not *use up* all the effects that those disturbances can have on the material world? This seemingly unanswerable question is at the heart of the integration problem.

Descartes could abolish the problem by giving up loop theory, as I have pointed out. What about the other horn of the dilemma? I do not envisage his denying that bodies collide, but merely his having a physics which ignores collisions. That would be a physics in which movement loops carry the entire causal weight instead of only part of it—an instantaneous physics, according to which no time ever elapses between cause and effect. Hume thought this would imply that the world has no history, but he was wrong about that (§258). The instantaneous physicist can allow that some movements occur at T_1 and others at T_2; what he cannot allow is that any of the former cause any of the latter. So he can have a picture of a world in motion, with its history strung out through time, but causation enters the picture only synchronically: the effects of matter upon matter show up across the extent of any world stage, but not along the time line from stage to stage. This, however, is too far from Descartes's actual physics to be worth following further.

Ironically, if he did relinquish collision theory, Descartes would lose most of his optics. Apart from that single proposition about the speed of light, loop theory does little if any work in his theorizing about light. This is strikingly true of his 'proof' of Snell's Law, about how, when light passes between media, the angle of incidence relates to the angle of refraction (§107). Without saying how he arrived at this, Descartes offers to explain in terms of his physics why it should be true (1637b, CSM 1:156–62). This bizarre explanation has defeated me, but I can see that its core concerns how long it takes a light-particle to get from one place to another—that is, it belongs entirely to collision theory.

22. Other work for loop theory

Evidently, the speed of neural transmission within the animal body impressed Descartes as the speed of light did; for he invokes loop theory for that too. Concerning a part of the human body known as the 'common sense'—a supposed system, invented by Aristotle, which integrates inputs from all the senses—he writes:

When an external sense organ is stimulated by an object, the figure which it receives is conveyed at the very same moment to the common sense, without any real passage of an entity from the one to the other. [Similarly,] while I am writing, at the very moment when individual letters are traced on the paper, not only does the point of the pen move, but the slightest motion of this part cannot but be transmitted simultaneously to the whole pen. (*Rules* 12, CSM 1:41)

This plainly brings neural transmission under loop, rather than collision, theory.
    Descartes also invokes loop theory to explain certain phenomena such as that of the wine barrel:

I want now to adduce another observation in order to show that no motion ever occurs that is not circular. When the wine in a cask does not flow from the bottom opening because the top is completely closed, it is improper to say . . . that this takes place through 'fear of a vacuum'. We are well aware that the wine has no mind to fear anything . . . Instead we must say that the wine cannot leave the cask because outside everything is as full as can be, and the part of the air whose place the wine would occupy if it were to flow out can find no other place to occupy in all the rest of the universe unless we make an opening in the top of the cask through which the air can rise by a circular path into its place. (*W* 4, CSM 1:87)

On Descartes's own showing, this is a bad explanation. To protect loop theory from some phenomena that seem to clash with it—for example, our ability to pump air out of a flask, apparently admitting nothing in its place—he postulates very finely divided matter and crevices for it to get through. When we pump air out of a flask, he contends, much subtler matter flows in through invisible crevices in the glass. Descartes *needs* subtle matter and tiny crevices; and once his world contains them, what is to stop them from ruining his explanation of the wine barrel phenomenon? Anyway, he does not have the facts right. An amended story about the wine barrel would make it equivalent to Torricelli's tube, which Descartes also handles through loop theory, and which we should consider.

Take a long tube full of mercury and up-end it with its open end in a pool of mercury, and, Torricelli found, some but not all of the mercury flows out of the tube. The friends and enemies of container space—the enemies and friends of loop theory—energetically debated about this. When some of the mercury in the tube falls, what lies above it? Pascal came to think that the upper end of the tube contains a vacuum, a portion of empty container space. Descartes held that it is subtle matter which has seeped in through pores in the glass.

Why, given that some mercury falls out of the long tube, does some remain? When discussing the topic in the 1640s, Descartes does not address this question. Milhaud in his classic work says confidently that if Descartes had done so, it would have been along the lines of his 1631 letter to Reneri:

Because the tube is closed at the upper end, air cannot get into it to replace the mercury when it falls. You will say that ether could get in through pores in the tube. I agree; but bear in mind that ether entering the tube must come from the sky, for although there is ether everywhere in the pores of the air, there is sometimes only enough to fill those pores; and so if there comes to be a new place to be filled (the one in the tube), that will require ether that comes from above the air up in the sky, in which case air will have to be raised to take its place.[5]

Never mind the last part, about the difficulty of hoisting enough air to replace the needed ether. Focus on Descartes's claim that the mercury stays put because of a local shortage of matter that is subtle enough to seep in and replace it. If this were right, the mercury columns in two adjacent long tubes would be higher than a single one in isolation; and the height of the mercury would be greater in a wide tube than in a narrow one. Descartes presumably did not check either of those obvious consequences of his conjecture. Also, this explanation of why only some of the mercury leaves the long tube cannot also explain why none leaves the short one. Perhaps in the years since 1631 Descartes had come to see that the local-shortage-of-ether explanation would not do, but what other could he offer?

Garber and others think he would have appealed to the pressure of air holding up the mercury (Garber 1992: 136–43). Why does some mercury fall out of the tube? Because it is heavier than the air into which it falls. Why does not more of it fall out? Because the pressure of the air at the bottom of the tube is great enough to hold up the rest of the mercury in the tube. This also purports to explain why no mercury falls out of a shorter tube. And it is supposed to explain the altitude phenomenon: when Torricelli's experiment is tried out high on a mountain, a shorter column of mercury remains in the tube than at sea-level.

---

[5] AT 1:206–7. In translating the passage I have simplified its rhetoric, but not its content. I found it in Milhaud 1921: 209.

The altitude phenomenon was discovered in Descartes's day, and Pascal plausibly claimed it as support for his position. Descartes declared that it refuted Pascal's view, evidently because he had misunderstood the latter; and Garber has helpfully explained what the misunderstanding seems to have been. However, Descartes also asserted that the outcome of the mountain experiment—which he later claimed to have proposed in the first place—positively confirmed *his* position; and Garber lets him get away with this. The Torricellian data, he thinks, created a stand-off between Descartes and Pascal—each could explain them in terms of his own system. I disagree. The explanation of Torricelli's tube which Garber attributes to Descartes, apparently rightly, is a tissue of confusions, loose ends, and inconsistencies. The mere fact that Descartes brings the weight or pressure of air into it has led some to regard him as a pioneer of the correct understanding of barometric pressure; but Milhaud (1921: 210) rightly declares such praise to be unwarranted, given why and how Descartes brings the weight of air into the story and, underlying that, given his account of what weight is. Before saying a little about that (§24), I should explain why Descartes has such a stubborn problem about weight.

23. Traction

Descartes denied that there are any attractive forces in nature. He used the Latin word *gravitas* to mean 'weight', the phenomenon in which most bodies, if released, tend to fall to the earth, but insisted that this had to be explained in terms of bodies' being pushed from above. He did not vigorously oppose this to the view that weight comes from bodies' being pulled downwards by impersonal attractive forces, but the latter come under fire in other contexts, especially magnetism.

The denial of traction made the cohesion problem insoluble. This is the problem of explaining how bodies hold together—the question, as Leibniz put it, 'Why doesn't the wind carry off our heads instead of our hats?' (quoted in C. Wilson 1989: 50 n.). It is no wonder that Descartes, Leibniz, and others rejected atomism, insisting that every portion of matter can be split into two. For them, the hard problem was to explain how there could be such a thing as a unified portion of matter—a cohesive body—in the first place. As Descartes said in *PP* 2:55, bodies cannot be made to cohere by anything like glue, because glue could do that work only if *it* held together, and that is part what was to be explained. Hooks and strings are no better.

We have already glimpsed how Descartes plans to explain cohesion in what he says about hardness, explaining why you can poke a finger into water, but not into rock:

If we go on to inquire how it comes about that some bodies readily abandon their place to other bodies while others do not, we can easily see that a body already in motion does not prevent another body from occupying the place which it is leaving of its own accord;

a body at rest, on the other hand, cannot be expelled from its place except by some force. (*PP* 2:54, CSM 1:245)

He goes straight on to connect this view about hard bodies with the problem of cohesion. Because cohesion of hard bodies cannot be explained by any substantial 'glue', it must be explained by a mode, Descartes says, because 'we recognize no other categories of things apart from substances and their modes'. And the mode that holds the parts of hard bodies together 'cannot be any mode distinct from their being at rest. For what mode could be more contrary to motion that separates them than their being at rest?' There you have it: what explains the pebble's holding together when the knife descends on it is the fact that its parts do not move! I agree with the commentators who wrote: 'This is not, of course, an explanation of solidity but a *description* of the fact that the parts of a solid do not move relative to one another' (MM 70 n. 65). But Descartes thinks it has explanatory power.

We now know that the cohesion problem can be solved only with help from attractive forces. Several early modern philosophers came within an inch of seeing this, yet the resistance to traction continued. Why? Leibniz wrote that there is no 'attraction' because there is none that can 'be explained from primitive solidity' (SD 51, FW 174). Also, 'A body is never moved naturally except by another body which touches it and pushes it . . . Any other kind of operation on bodies is either miraculous or imaginary' (L 702). Such remarks reflect this line of thought:

Necessarily every material thing occupies space, exclusively or nearly so. It makes no sense to associate a body with a region unless its being there strongly tends to exclude any other body. So when body B_1 moves to a location at which body B_2 now is, it *must* be that when the two meet something happens: B_1 is stopped or diverted, or B_2 moves away. This does not yield a complete impact mechanics, but it captures a fundamental feature of such a mechanics: namely, that when two bodies collide *something has to give*. This comes from the very notion of body. If there were attractive forces, that would be a brute-force addition to the nature of bodies.

That seems to have been what initially led Locke to believe that physics must be all about impact, judging from his renunciation of this (Locke 1698: 467–8), in which he says that 'the judicious Mr Newton's incomparable book' has convinced him that 'God can if he pleases put into bodies powers and ways of operation above what can be derived from our idea of body'. The last six words are crucial. They point to what Leibniz insisted on, deploring Locke's recantation because it credited God with behaving in an arbitrary manner, making things behave in ways that do not arise explicably from their intrinsic natures (§103).

Descartes placed no limits on how God might be expected to behave; he was not driven as Leibniz was by the conviction that for every *Why?* there is a *Because*. He presented the collision part of his physics as an outcome not of the nature of matter, but rather of God's actions. Why, then, should God not have acted in a different way which would make bodies conform to something like Newton's gravitational law, this being a fact about them that was basic within physics, though grounded outside physics in theology? I cannot see that Descartes could answer this.

Nor can I find that he ever makes a case against traction. He repeatedly denies that there is any such force, as here: 'A magnet attracts iron; or rather a magnet and a piece of iron approach each other; for in fact there is no attraction there' (PP 4:171). But if he has any reason for his confidence in this regard, he does not announce it. Perhaps this is a case of guilt by association. Before Newton, the proponents of attractive forces also had a lot of rubbish on sale, and Descartes rejected it all at one blow—for example, when at the end of his lengthy treatment of magnets he boasts of having explained 'all the remarkable effects usually attributed to occult qualities' (PP 4:187).

I now drop this cloudy topic. I am puzzled by how weakly motivated Descartes's denial of attractive forces seems to be, given the price he paid for it.

24. Weight

Unpleasant as the task is, I should sketch Descartes's struggle to find a tolerable account of weight or 'gravity', given that he would not allow himself to explain it through traction.

Early on, he regarded weight as intrinsic to the body that has it, but did not explain how this could be so. We see this in letters to Mersenne (CSMK 8, 15). At about the same time, however, Descartes was writing The World, in which he offered a theory according to which a body's weight is not intrinsic to it, but rather results from its circumstances. In this, he relies on a theory about matter of the second element—globules of matter that are larger than the actual parts of first-element ether but smaller than third-element or 'terrestrial' bodies such as particles of air, grains of dust, and boulders. Second-element matter is prevalent throughout the universe: for example, each planet is swept around the sun by a whirling river of 'heavenly matter' made up of globules of the second element and the even tinier particles of the first. The second-element globules are also abundant down here in the atmosphere. The explanation of weight has three pre-misses (W 11, AT 11:72–80, esp. 73; or see CSMK 135).

(1) One is a thesis about centrifugal force which Descartes has introduced ear-lier in the work. Anything moving in a circle, he holds, tends to fly out in a straight line away from the centre of the circle; he offers empirical evidence to support this, and a theological explanation for it (W 7, CSM 1:96; also PP 2:39, CSM 1:241–2).

(2) The celestial particles 'are turning faster than the earth itself is around its centre, thus having a strong tendency to move away from it'.

(3) When the celestial particles fly upward, they push down the terrestrial ones. This postulates an action/reaction phenomenon. If we think of descending

heavy matter as like a horizontal spoke of a vertical wheel, the spoke moves earthward because a jumper has just kicked off from it.

This downward tendency is, or is the source of, the weight of the earth and thus of all terrestrial matter. Descartes sees himself as explaining not only weight, but also the earth's cohesion, its holding together rather than flying apart in all directions.

Some years later, in the *Principles of Philosophy*, he has yet another account of weight. He still treats it as circumstantial, but differently now. The heavenly globules are disposed to move equally in all directions, Descartes now says, adducing this to explain several phenomena, such as the (supposed) roundness of raindrops (*PP* 4:20). Of all the possible directions, however, one is less open to the globules than the others: that is the earthward direction, which is less freely available because it is blocked by the earth. Thus, down near the earth, the overall net direction of the celestial globules is away from the earth, 'and this is what their lightness consists in' (*PP* 4:22, CSM 1:269). But these light globules can enact their tendency to fly upwards only if their movement is part of a suitable loop of matter; and Descartes gives reasons why the descending part of this loop must consist in terrestrial matter of the third element, which therefore has weight, or a permanent tendency to move towards the earth (*PP* 4:23).

This account of weight omits action/reaction and brings movement loops to the fore. In this treatment, if descending heavy matter is likened again to a spoke of a wheel, the spoke moves earthward because of how the wheel is revolving. This, we must presume, is Descartes's final view about what weight is.

With that as background, let us return to the barometer, Torricelli's tube. For Descartes to have any chance of explaining why some mercury flows from the tube, he must explain why mercury is heavier (volume for volume) than air or ether. The reason for this, he says, is that a greater proportion of the latter than of the former consists in matter of the first and second elements, which has no tendency to move downwards. He spells this out in *PP* 4:24f., from which I shall quote with a few interpolations which may help:

How much heaviness there is in each body. [If we are correctly to calculate the weight of body B] we must observe that in the pores of this body B there is also some heavenly matter, and that this is opposed to ⟨and has as much force as⟩ an equal quantity of similar heavenly matter contained in the mass of air which is to take B's place; and this renders that quantity of heavenly matter in body B useless so that it is only the remainder [of the matter in B] that should be counted [toward B's weight]. Similarly, there are some terrestrial parts in the mass of air, which are opposed to an equal number of the other terrestrial parts of body B, and have no effect on them. However, when these things have been subtracted on both sides, what remains of the matter of the heaven in this mass of air acts against what remains of the terrestrial parts in body B; and B's weight consists in this alone. (*PP* 4:24, MM 192*)

Obscure as it is, this passage is at least clear enough to be flatly in conflict with Descartes's final account of what weight is, which has to do with volumes and nothing else. A terrestrial body tends downwards because something of equal volume tends upwards; the role of a portion of matter in a movement loop depends purely on its volume, regardless of how much of it is subtle and how much terrestrial. In short, Descartes has here drifted from his later circumstantial account of weight back to his earlier one of that type, or even further back to his first one in which a body's weight is intrinsic to it. In this part of his work, one senses, Descartes is not just failing but flailing.

He needs several other things for a complete explanation of Torricelli's tube, but I shall discuss just one, namely an account of why air pressure is greater at lower altitudes. In a letter to Mersenne in 1638 Descartes discusses actual and possible empirical evidence to settle 'the question whether a body weighs more or less when close to the centre of the earth than it does when far from it', approaching this through a sketch of three views about what weight is, and continuing:

My conception of the nature of heaviness is quite different from that of the three views just described. But to set out my view I would have to go into many other things which I do not intend to discuss here. All I can say about [the nature of heaviness] is that it has nothing to teach me regarding the present question [of whether bodies are heavier when nearer the centre of the earth], and that the latter is a purely factual question, that is, one that men can decisively answer only to the extent that they can put it to the test. (CSMK 112*)

No doubt the question of whether things weigh more low down than high up is a factual one which cannot be answered by general theories about the nature of weight; but in saying this, Descartes evades the pressing question of whether his theories *could possibly* explain an affirmative answer to the factual question.

25. Was Descartes a 'new Stoic'?

Before leaving issues arising specifically out of Descartes's physics, I shall touch on one last topic, arising out of an accusation that Leibniz levels against him more than once. In one place Leibniz rails against 'the new Stoics' for a number of intellectual crimes which he lists; and he says that Descartes has laid himself open to the suspicion of belonging to this breed by several aspects of his thought, also listed. The first charge in the indictment of the 'new Stoics' is: 'They believe that all possible things happen one after the other, following all the variations of which matter is capable.' The last item in the list of Descartes's suspect activities is this: '. . . and finally, by letting slip (though in passing) that all the possible variations of matter happen successively, one after another' (1677, AG 282).

Leibniz brings this up elsewhere too, writing to Molanus: 'Descartes's God is something approaching the God of Spinoza, namely, the principle of things and a certain supreme power or primitive nature that sets everything going and does everything that can be done. Descartes's God has neither will nor understanding'

(AG 242). My focus is on 'does everything that can be done'. It is not obvious why Leibniz should object so strongly to this. He seems to take it as meaning that every causally possible configuration of particles occurs at some time, with this construed as enlarging our ideas about what occurs, not as narrowing our ideas about what is causally possible; and I suppose he thinks that this leaves no room for God's choices to make an imprint on the world. This is a complex matter, which I shall not explore here.

Did Descartes accept this 'all possible variations' doctrine that Leibniz attributes to him? And if he did, why? The only prima-facie evidence that he did is this: 'By the operation of these laws, matter must successively assume all the forms of which it is capable; and if we consider these forms in order we will eventually be able to arrive at the form which is this world's' (*PP* 3:47, CSM 1:258). Before rushing to judgement on this, let us look at its context. In the background lies Descartes's thesis that any portion of matter could be polished or buffeted into any shape, as he wrote to Mersenne: 'There is no matter in the universe which could not take on all the forms one after the other' (CSMK 133). This has been taken to express the 'all possible variations' doctrine, but that seems wrong. Descartes is saying merely that any portion of matter could have any shape.

With help from that innocent thesis, he persuaded himself of the truth of something rather odd: namely, that God has selected laws of physics such that the world was bound to end up in its present condition, whatever its initial state was. Descartes says this several times, early and late:

God has established these laws in such a marvellous way that even if we suppose he creates nothing but . . . a chaos, the laws of nature suffice to bring it about that the parts of this chaos disentangle themselves and come to be arranged in such good order that they will have the form of a quite perfect world—a world in which we shall be able to see not only light but also all the other things, general as well as particular, which appear in the real world. (*W* 6, CSM 1:91)[6]

Call this the 'from chaos to here' doctrine. In deciding what doctrine it is, we have two main questions to settle:

(1) Is Descartes saying (strongly) that the world's present state *must* or *inevitably would* arise from any initial state by the actual laws of nature or only (weakly) that it *could* do so?

(2) Either way, how are we to take 'all the things, general as well as particular, which appear in the real world' and (phrases in passages I listed, but did not quote) 'material things just as we now see them', and 'that same order now to be found in things'? Is Descartes speaking of the route from any starting-point to (strongly) precisely the world as we have it, or merely to (weakly) a world state sharing certain general features with ours?

Give both questions strong answers, and you get an enormously strong claim about the inevitability—not just through actual time, but across a large range of

---

[6] See also *Method* 5, CSM 1:133–4; *PP* 3:47, CSM 1:257–8.

possible worlds—of exactly the world state we have, including every word you spoke today, and so on. The passage I have quoted suggests the weak answer to question 1, but the following does not: 'By the operation of these laws matter *must* successively assume all the forms of which it is capable' (*PP* 3:47, my emphasis). This implies the strong answer to question 1. But I am inclined to credit Descartes with offering only a weak answer to 2. He continues: '. . . of which it is capable; and, if we consider these forms in order, we will eventually be able to arrive at the form which is this world's.' It all depends on what he means by that final phrase. I conjecture that in this and like passages he is talking only about the world's present actual inventory of shapes and sizes of particles. Our Cartesian understanding of how the material world works depends crucially on our having first- and second- and third-element matter. God might have begun the world with those three; but even if he had not, some particles would have collided with others and smashed them into smaller bits; others would have coalesced into bigger bits; and eventually the world would have contained something like its present inventory. The relevant passages look like that, and it is all that Descartes had any reason to assert. I do not think that he 'let slip' any more radical doctrine. But I would be surer of this interpretation if he had written: 'If we consider these forms in order, we will eventually be able to arrive at the *forms* which are this world's.'

Chapter 4

Descartes's Dualisms

26. Property-dualism

Descartes's work is permeated by a severe dichotomy between mind and matter. He is a property-dualist: the properties that things can have (he thinks) naturally fall into two non-overlapping, sharply demarcated groups, pertaining to mentality and materiality respectively, with nothing in either group being in any way reducible to the other. This seems to have taken root in his mind, as also in the minds of followers such as Locke and Spinoza, at a level too deep for argument. Here is his most explicit treatment of the question:

Can I show my critics . . . that it is self-contradictory that our thought should be reduced to corporeal motions? By 'reduced' I take it that they mean that our thought and corporeal motions are one and the same. My reply is that I am very certain of this point, but I cannot guarantee that others can be convinced of it, however attentive they may be, and however keen they may judge their powers of perception to be. I cannot guarantee that they will be persuaded, at least so long as they focus their attention not on things which are objects of pure understanding but only on things which can be imagined. (Rep 6, CSM 2:286–7)

Descartes here admits to having no arguments to offer.

What, according to him, is there on each side of the line? Well, we have seen him equating what is material with what is extended; and I have no more to say about that. As for mentality—which Descartes calls 'thought'—his only explanation is this:

By the term 'thought' I understand everything which we are aware of as happening within us, in so far as we have awareness of it. Hence, thinking is to be identified here not merely with understanding, willing and imagining, but also with sensory awareness. (PP 1:9, CSM 1:195)

This is narrow, confining mentality or 'thought' not only to what we *can be* but also to what we *are* aware of in ourselves. Leibniz thought that we have many mental states of which we are not actually aware; most of his contemporaries disagreed, sharing Descartes's view of minds as perfectly open to their owners; but Descartes has to reject Leibniz's position in an extreme way, because for him it is self-contradictory.

Descartes identifies items as mental—as instances of 'thought'—not through what they are like, but through how we know about them. Whether or not this is a seriously considered theoretical proposal, it certainly reflects how Descartes proceeds in his thinking about mentality. He characteristically thinks of minds in terms of *his* mind, and of that in terms of what he can know about it through immediate self-awareness. This, as we shall see, imports a certain thinness to everything that he says about the mind. His practice of going it alone, studying the mind from the inside, goes with his stance of 'methodological solipsism', the procedure of philosophizing as though one initially believed that nothing but oneself existed (Carnap 1967: sect. 64).

He also accepts substance-dualism, which says of the two sharply demarcated sets of properties that no one substance has properties from each set. Humans may seem to be thinking animals, Descartes held, but really each of us is a pair of things: an extended unthinking animal and an unextended thinking mind. This could be false even if property-dualism were true: even if you are not a pair, but a unitary animal that thinks, your material and thinking natures might be differentiated from one another in the way Descartes thinks they are.

27. The indivisibility argument for the 'real distinction'

Although he admits to having no argument for his property-dualism, Descartes earnestly defends substance-dualism, 'the real distinction between the mind and the body', the thesis that his mind and his body are distinct substances, rather than different aspects of a single substance.[1] If substance-dualism conjoins property-dualism with a further proposition P, Descartes assumes property-dualism in defending P.

Because he holds that all matter is extended, the doctrine of the 'real distinction' between mind and body can be expressed as 'Minds are not extended' or as 'Matter does not think'. Take your pick; in the context of seventeenth-century thought they come to the same thing.

Descartes offers two arguments for the real distinctness of mind from body. In one, and in one version of the other, he argues that *his* mind and body are distinct substances, from which he immediately infers that no body can be identified with any mind. Nobody has ever suggested that some but not all creaturely thinking is done by material things, so Descartes's move from his own case to the general claim may be innocuous.

The two arguments occur in the Sixth Meditation, in which one of them looms large. The other gets a single paragraph at CSM 2:59, even less space in the Synopsis to the *Meditations* at 9–10, and one paragraph in *Passions* 30 (CSM 1:339–40). It boils down to this: Every material thing is divisible into parts, no mind is thus divisible, so no mind is material. This 'indivisibility argument' deserves more attention than it usually gets. As well as being inherently interesting, it helps us to relate Descartes to Spinoza, and even more dramatically to Kant.

---

[1] For the terminology of 'real distinction' see *PP* 1:60, CSM 1:213. The crux is that 'real' comes from *res* = thing; the contrast is with 'modal distinction', where 'modal' comes from mode = property.

The argument is obviously valid. Then what about the premisses? One says that all bodies are weakly divisible, meaning that it is not absolutely or logically impossible—though it may be causally so—for any portion of matter to be split into smaller ones. For now, take this on trust (§87). The other premiss has to be that minds are strongly indivisible, meaning that the splitting of a mind is not merely causally, but absolutely or logically, impossible.

Descartes gives one reason for this in the Synopsis: 'We cannot understand a mind except as being indivisible. For we cannot conceive of half of a mind' (CSM 2:9). What lies behind this? If Descartes tried and failed to conceive a 'half of a mind', how did he go about it? What was he looking for?

He does not tell us; but I conjecture that he thought of a half-mind as having to be mind-like, just as half a body is corporeal. What he could not conceive, then, is how two minds could unite to compose a single mind. This ignores the possibility that mentality comes from appropriately assembling various elements which are not mental when taken separately. Descartes assumes, in short, that mentality is basic, rather than being the complex upshot of interactions amongst simpler and more basic items. This is a substantive thesis.

If you bisect a rabbit, you get two items that are animal-like in some ways, but differ from normal animals in others: they do not hunt, graze, flee, copulate, sleep, grow, reproduce, or metabolize. If you divide a rabbit finely enough, you reach constituents that are not animal-like at all; yet we believe that at any given moment there is nothing more to an animal than an assemblage of molecules. Descartes believed this too; but he would say that mentality or 'thought' is unlike animality in this respect. According to him, 'thinking' is metaphysically on a par with 'extended', so that if a thinking thing had parts, they would be thinking, just as the parts of any extended thing are extended. With no supporting reasons, he simply assumes that mentality is basic, and is comparable with materiality rather than with (say) animality.

Even with that assumption granted, this version of the indivisibility argument still has a problem; for we *can* conceive of a half-mind that is mind-like. Since the 1950s evidence has been growing that the functioning of any human mind results from the interplay of two *mind-like* subsystems, each associated with one cerebral hemisphere. Descartes might declare himself to be untroubled by this development, maintaining that his view about the mind's 'simplicity'—that is, its not having parts—rests ultimately on what he can know 'from the inside' about his own mind. When he implied that it is inconceivable that there should be half of a mind, what he really meant (I conjecture he would say) is that no sense can be made of the idea of *being* half a mind or *having* half a mind and knowing, from one's direct experience of it, that it is half a mind. This is the response of a methodological solipsist.

Of the two major philosophers who are most easily seen as kicking off from Descartes, Locke had nothing to say about the simplicity of minds, and Spinoza denied that minds are simple or lacking in parts (*Ethics* 2p15). I trace the latter fact to two underlying differences between him and Descartes. One is that

Spinoza was not a methodological solipsist: he did not come at philosophical problems from the first-person stance adopted by Descartes early in the *Meditations*. The other is that Spinoza did not regard mind-likeness as basic. He would say that 'half of a mind' is strictly analogous to 'half of an animal': just as an animal is a resultant complex of a lot of molecules, so the mind of a whole animal is also a resultant complex of items that correspond to the molecules (§§48, 118).

28. 'I am unable to distinguish parts in myself'

The Sixth Meditation version of the indivisibility argument starts differently: 'When I consider the mind, or myself in so far as I am merely a thinking thing, I am unable to distinguish parts in myself; I understand myself to be something quite single and complete' (CSM 2:59).

Some readers have misunderstood what Descartes says next. Let us get it straight before returning to the main argument. He continues:

Although the whole mind seems to be united to the whole body, I recognize that if a foot or arm or any other part of the body is cut off, nothing has thereby been taken away from the mind. . . . The faculties of willing, of understanding, or sensory perception and so on . . . cannot be termed parts of the mind, because it is the same mind that wills, and understands, and has sensory perceptions.

Descartes is not here arguing that his mind is indivisible, but merely responding to two objections that might be made. (1) 'Your mind is associated with the whole of a spread-out material thing, your body; so it is divisible in a derived way.' This fails, Descartes holds, because it needs a mind–body association where a lessening of the body brings with it a lessening of the mind, which is in fact not the case. Actually, some removals of body parts could cause lessenings of one's mind—the removal of brain tissue can extinguish memories, for example. Descartes would have been on firmer ground if, instead of saying that an amputation does not bring with it any reduction in the mind, he had said something like this: 'If in losing some cerebral tissue I also lost some memories, that would not be because the brain tissue took them with it, with the lost tissue remembering the things I had forgotten.' (2) 'It is well known that every mind has parts—the will, the understanding, the imagination, and so on.' Descartes replies that these are *properties* of the mind, not *parts* of it. He is not question-beggingly arguing that the mind is indivisible, but merely making the point that the mind can lack parts even though it has many faculties.

Now let us see how Descartes can positively support the initial claim: 'I understand myself to be something single and complete.'

Kant grasped what Descartes was up to here. In his treatment of the so-called Paralogisms of Pure Reason, Kant discusses errors that he thinks may be made by a 'rational psychologist'—one who thinks he can discover a priori what minds are like. Descartes could be the main target. Some of the supposed errors are obscure; but light shines brightly in Kant's diagnosis of the Second Paralogism's error of thinking one has established a priori that minds are 'simple' (*Critique* A 351–61). His treatment of this is beautiful and deep and true. Briefly, he contends that if I start where Descartes does, with myself and my inner states, my basic notion of a complex or divisible thing, a thing with parts, must be the notion of a number of items (the parts) that *I* draw together in my thought. It is outright impossible, then, to see one's own mind as composite; any such thought needs oneself, one's mind, sitting outside the scope of the thought and doing the unifying. (For a fuller exposition, see my 1974: 82–92.)

This is profoundly sensitive to the passage at CSM 2:59. Descartes does start with an intensely first-person stance; it is in character that he should explore minds by thinking about his own; there is a deep reason why one cannot *see* one's own mind as composite; and the indivisibility argument in its Sixth Meditation version becomes intelligible if we suppose that Descartes half-saw that he could not do that, and drew a conclusion about the nature of his mind. He does not offer the 'deep reason' to which I have referred, but I think it made itself felt in this thought, increasing his confidence that his own mind must be simple.

It is true that one cannot, unaided, see one's own mind as composite. Consider a person whose cerebral hemispheres are not neurally linked in the ordinary way, so that their inputs and outputs are not as closely integrated as are most people's. We can get evidence that this person has two half-minds, but how could *he* come to that conclusion? Only by getting all the evidence that we have, and thinking about it theoretically; but that is not to approach the question purely from the inside in the Cartesian manner. Rather, he would be stepping outside himself and interpreting himself as he might someone else. Similarly, after studying a person of this sort, you might conclude that you too have a pair of mind-like half-minds that differ from his only in being in closer touch. (Thus Nagel 1971. More discussion and a bibliography can be found in Marks 1981.) Descartes's procedure in the *Meditations* differs greatly in spirit from this. He seeks results that he can get without knowing how he might appear to others.

In the Cartesian methodological solipsist stance, it seems, one could not possibly come to think that one's mind has parts. The internal life of this whole mind will have to be experienced either by part A, which is conscious of various entrances on to and exits from its stage, or by part B, which is conscious of corresponding exits and entrances. A consciousness of the whole mind as a whole mind cannot be had: a purely first-person standpoint makes no room for the thought of one's own mind as having parts.

It does not follow, however, that minds cannot have mind-like parts. That was Kant's point: the restriction which Descartes has found on how he can think introspectively about his own mind does not limit what his mind can be like. He could find himself forced to conclude, from his knowledge of how he behaves in psychological experiments, that his mind results from the working together of several sub-minds. The Kantian criticism is, above all, a rejection of confinement to the first-person stance.

29. From conception to possibility

Descartes's other argument for the real distinction between mind and body—the 'separability argument', as I call it—runs thus:

First, I know that everything which I clearly and distinctly understand is capable of being created by God so as to correspond exactly with my understanding of it. Hence the fact that I can clearly and distinctly understand one thing apart from another is enough to make me certain that the two things are distinct, since they are capable of being separated, at least by God. . . . Thus, simply by knowing that I exist and seeing at the same time that absolutely nothing else belongs to my nature or essence except that I am a thinking thing, I can infer correctly that my essence consists solely in the fact that I am a thinking thing. It is true that I . . . have a body that is very closely joined to me. But nevertheless, on the one hand I have a clear and distinct idea of myself in so far as I am simply a thinking, non-extended thing; and on the other hand I have a distinct idea of body in so far as this is simply an extended, non-thinking thing. And accordingly, it is certain that I am really distinct from my body, and can exist without it. (Med 6, CSM 2:54)

Few English-speaking philosophers these days think that the argument is sound, because few accept its conclusion; but we still debate what the argument is and where it goes wrong. I shall offer an understanding of these matters; they involve a lot of philosophy.

In the *Meditations* Descartes engages in an intellectual drama having to do with the possibility of error. It will be my topic in Chapter 19. All I need from it here is that at a certain point he claims to be perfectly assured that he exists, while not being sure whether there are any bodies. At this moment, he contends, he is in no way muddled or unclear in his thought: in perfect clarity of mind he is assured of his own existence and unsure about whether any bodies exist. From this he infers that it is possible that he should exist when no bodies do, and from that he infers further that he is in fact not a body.

We have, then, two steps to examine: from 'I distinctly conceived myself as immaterial' to 'I could be immaterial', and from 'I could be immaterial' to 'I am immaterial'. We shall examine these in turn. I have nothing useful to say about the generalizing move from 'I am immaterial' to 'All thinking things are immaterial' or 'No matter thinks'.

In the separability argument Descartes infers from 'the fact that I can clearly and distinctly understand one thing apart from another' that 'they are capable of being separated'. He says only that the former proposition makes him certain of the latter, but he means this to be a valid inference, not a mere fact about his psychology. That inference is my present topic.

It rests on this rule for establishing possibilities: *If I distinctly conceive or understand P, it is possible that P.* Writing to Gibieuf, Descartes justifies this rule, or something like it, first theologically: 'for otherwise God would be a deceiver', and then pragmatically: 'and we would have no rule to make us certain of the truth' (CSMK 203). That last clause implies that Descartes accepts the rule because without it he has no procedure for establishing modal truths. Similarly today, when philosophers are asked, 'Why should your modal intuitions be informative about modal truth?', their answer is that this is their only basis for modal claims. As we shall see in Chapter 24, Descartes has another card in his hand; but for most purposes he is content with the pragmatic defence of the inference of modal conclusions from thought-experiments. He writes to Arnauld that a simple thought-experiment would suffice, by normal standards, to establish the distinctness of mind from body, and that the need to appeal to God's veracity came only from the threat posed by radical scepticism (Rep 4, CSM 2:159).

Granting Descartes's right to infer *Possibly P* from some premiss about his having conceived P, we should ask what premiss it is. What sort of conception demonstrates possibility? He answers that it has to be distinct, but too often we have only his word for it that the conception in question *was* distinct in the required way. There are two separate points here.

First, we do not know enough—indeed, we know almost nothing—about what went on in Descartes's mind when he conceived P. There is something too private about all this, as Leibniz complained in a different context. Having noted that Descartes's a priori argument for God's existence requires the premiss that there *can* be a being with all perfections, Leibniz continues: 'It is not enough for Descartes to appeal to experience and allege that he experiences this very concept in himself, clearly and distinctly. This is not to complete the demonstration but to break it off, unless he shows a way in which others can also arrive at an experience of this kind' (L 168). Descartes's best response to this would be to move from thought to language as his basis for modal conclusions. Someone who appeals to a 'modal intuition', which is a thought-experiment of the Cartesian kind, should be prepared to back it up by a *description* of the state of affairs which he declares to be possible. That gets it out into the open, thus meeting Leibniz's objection.

The second point was made by Arnauld, who probingly challenged Descartes's move from conception to possibility (Obj 4, CSM 2:140–3). When he claims to have established that he could exist while nothing is extended, says Arnauld, Descartes may have achieved this apparent result only through unthoroughness in his thinking, like an apprentice geometer who clearly grasps some properties of a triangle while questioning whether it has certain others which do in fact belong to it also. For Descartes's thought-experiment to do its work, Arnauld concludes, it must involve a thought that is not only *distinct* but also *adequate*—by which he means 'complete' or 'complete enough'.

Arnauld's point against Descartes is a needed warning that we should be modest in our use of thought-experiments, and indeed of descriptions, to establish possibilities. I still like what I wrote about this years ago:

One cannot imagine anything which is elementarily logically impossible—such as a four-sided triangle; and it is arguable that any logical impossibility, if spelled out in enough detail, involves simple impossibilities of this 'inconceivable' kind. . . . I can imagine someone working at his desk, shouting 'I have found a fraction equal to $\sqrt{2}$!', receiving the plaudits of an admiring world, and so on; but I cannot imagine the fraction he has discovered together with the correct calculation which shows it to equal $\sqrt{2}$.

This view about detail—which seems to me right—would be better expressed in terms not of imagining or 'conceiving' but of *describing*. It comes to this: if S is a logically impossible story, then it entails obvious logical impossibilities—or it implies both the answers 'Yes' and 'No' to certain questions. The impossibility may not be manifest in S as stated, but it can always be *displayed* by asking the right questions. (*LBH* 273–4)

'If there is an impossibility, it can be displayed'—that is a substantive claim. I have no proof of it, but if it is wrong, we are (as Descartes said) in big trouble. The procedure described above, incidentally, implies that although we can prove P to be impossible, we cannot show definitively that P is possible unless we can show it to be true. We can tell the story, or conceive the possibility, or summon up the intuition, with enough clarity and pertinent detail to convince ourselves and others that any lurking contradiction would have shown up by now; but we can never prove that this is so.

Arnauld and I both ask: Did Descartes conduct his thought-experiment 'adequately'—that is, in enough detail to be entitled to confidence that he could exist even if there were no bodies? Early in his reply to Arnauld, when still manœuvring himself into position for the battle, Descartes writes:

It may be that there is much within me of which I am not yet aware . . . Yet since that of which I am aware is sufficient to enable me to subsist with it and it alone, I am certain that I could have been created by God without having these other attributes of which I am unaware, and hence that these other attributes do not belong to the essence of the mind. (Rep 4, CSM 2:154–5)

That sounds modest: There is much about the mind that Descartes did not know when conducting his thought-experiment. Still, he makes an unqualified possibility-claim: namely, that while in that frame of mind he discovered that he could have existed even if there were no bodies. That requires that his thought-experiment presented to him the supposedly possible state of affairs—Descartes exists while no bodies exist—in enough detail for it to make an impossibility manifest if there were one. I question whether he was entitled to this.

In his Second Replies, Descartes in effect rejects this demand for detail. Mersenne has said that because of God's infinity, Descartes can have only an 'utterly inadequate' idea of him, which implies that he cannot know his idea of God to be a logically consistent one, thus depriving him of his a priori argument for God's existence. Descartes replies:

Even if we conceive of God only in an . . . utterly inadequate way, this does not prevent its being certain that his nature is possible . . . or our being able truly to assert that we have examined his nature with sufficient clarity . . . to know that his nature is possible and also to know that necessary existence belongs to [it]. All self-contradictoriness or impossibility resides solely in our thought, when we make the mistake of joining together mutually inconsistent ideas; it cannot occur in anything which is outside the intellect. . . . Self-contradictoriness in our concepts arises merely from their obscurity and confusion; there can be none in the case of clear and distinct concepts. Hence, in the case of the few attributes of God which we do perceive, it is enough that we understand them clearly and distinctly, even though our understanding is in no way adequate. (Rep 2, CSM 2:108)

This seems to claim quite generally, and not just with respect to the a priori argument for God's existence, that adequacy or completeness does not matter so long as the ideas in question are distinct. However incomplete or undetailed my conception of P is, I can justly claim that it is distinct—free of obscurity and confusion—because this can be immediately obvious to me.

Let us apply this to Goldbach's conjecture that every even number is the sum of two prime numbers. I can conceive this to be so, with no obscurity or confusion in my thought: I have the sharpest possible notions of 'every' and 'even' and 'number' and 'prime' and so on. Descartes would have to say that really I *don't*, and that I am deceiving myself if I think otherwise. But he would have to base this on the complaint that I have not conceived the conjecture's truth in sufficient detail; and that brings us back to the demand for what Arnauld calls 'adequacy'. Descartes erred in thinking he had a useful notion of 'clear and distinct, although in no way adequate'. So the question still stands: Has he conceived the crucial state of affairs—of his existing while no bodies exist—in a manner that entitles him to claim that it is possible?

In direct response to Arnauld's challenge on this point, Descartes says three things at CSM 2:158. The second and third are thin quibbles about disanalogies between Arnauld's geometrical example and Descartes's argument; the first may have more to it, though I am not sure what. It turns on the fact that the geometrical example concerned the separability of *properties*, while Descartes's argument concerns the distinctness not of properties but of *things*. That, he seems to hold, enables him to have the kind of completeness of conception that he needs for his argument without having to get over the hurdles that lie in the geometrician's path. I do not understand this line of thought.[2]

30. From possibility to actuality: essences

Accepting for purposes of argument that I could exist and think while no bodies exist, I am invited by Descartes to infer that I am not a thinking body. He does not make clear why this follows. I shall give a section to each of the two routes he might take from that premiss to that conclusion.

---

[2] A passage in a letter to Gibieuf, CSMK 202, may be relevant. For a detailed discussion of Descartes's notions of 'adequate' and 'complete' ideas, see Yablo 1990: 162–77.

Suppose that the premiss is true and the conclusion false: I *could* exist without being material, but I *am* a thinking material thing. In that case, something can be material (or extended) without being essentially so; that is, a thing's extension might be merely one of its 'accidents' rather than part of its essential nature, the nature that it has at any possible world where it exists. I am here using 'essence' in the standard sense in which F-ness belongs to the essence of x just in case *it is absolutely impossible that x should exist and not be F.* Descartes thought of extension as essential, in this sense, to whatever has it; so he could have argued in this manner from 'I could be immaterial' to 'I am immaterial'. But what entitles him to the premiss that whatever is extended is essentially so?

I cannot find that anything does. The only argument he would be likely to use, so far as I can see, is invalid; but still it is worth looking at. It has two premisses.

One is the thesis that extension is a basic property of anything that has it:

Each substance has one principal property which constitutes its nature . . . and to which all its other properties are referred. Thus extension in length, breadth and depth constitutes the nature of corporeal substance . . . Everything else which can be attributed to body presupposes extension, and is merely a mode of an extended thing. (*PP* 1:53, CSM 1:210)

According to this, the materialistic properties of any extended thing are hierarchically organized, with the property of extendedness being fundamental: every other materialistic property is a 'mode' of extension or anyway something that presupposes it. (Being in motion is not a way of being extended, but Descartes thinks that it presupposes extension, because only extended things can move.) Although he does not ever *argue* that extension is a basic way that things can be, rather than being grounded in or explained by or a special case of some deeper-lying property, we should not be surprised at his believing this. Perhaps we can reject it now, on the grounds that mass can be converted into energy, but Descartes could not be expected to have envisaged such a possibility.

(I did not quote the part where Descartes says that *thought* is also a basic property of whatever has it. That is more vulnerable. Some theories of mentality hold that *thought* is not basic, but is rather a species of the genus *responsiveness to the environment*; and Descartes does not confront such theories—behaviourism, functionalism, and the like—and argue that they should be rejected. His own explanation of 'thought' in terms of self-awareness might seem to imply that it is basic, but I question that. Here is a rival possibility. (I am here guided by Van Gulick 1988, an important paper.) Even quite primitive organisms, to which nobody would attribute thought, must be informed about themselves: an organism has to respond to its environment in ways that will bring it advantage; what ways those are depends upon the organism's condition at the moment; so the organism has to be informed about its own condition. Now, the introspective self-awareness that impresses Descartes may be just a special case of this more general phenomenon, marked off within the genus by a link with language and/or with abstract conceptualization and/or . . . who knows what? This is a live, unrefuted possibility. It probably connects with the §27 question of whether a half-mind must be recognizably mental.

The second premiss comes from this:

> We cannot initially become aware of a substance merely through its being an existing thing, since this alone does not of itself have any effect on us. We can, however, easily come to know a substance by one of its attributes, in virtue of the common notion that nothingness possesses no attributes . . . Thus, if we perceive the presence of some attribute, we can infer that there must also be present an existing thing or substance to which it may be attributed. (PP 1:52)[3]

I take Descartes to be using 'perception' here (as he often does) to cover conception as well, and thus to be rightly saying that one cannot even think about a particular thing except through some of its features.

On the strength of this, he can argue that whatever is basic must also be essential. Consider the thought that x, which is actually F, *might not have been F*. This thought must latch on to x through properties that it has that do not entail its being F. If F is a basic property of x, however, there are no such other properties of it; all the others are subsumed under F, and thus entail F; so we cannot carry the thought of x across from Fx to not-Fx. So what is basic in a thing is also essential to it. QED.

Try it out on an example. I say of a spherical piece of wax, 'This could have been cubic rather than spherical'. You can think of this piece of stuff as being differently shaped: features of it other than its shape enable you to keep your mental hold on it through the envisaged difference in shape. But if I say, 'This could have been unextended', I take away everything through which your thought could grip the stuff. If you try to think of this very bit of stuff as possibly not being extended, you must try to make your thought drop down through *all* the properties of the stuff and latch on to the sheer thing, independently of any of its properties. Descartes rightly says that this cannot be done: any thought about a thing must be about the thing *qua* F for some predicate F.

So now we have him all set to move from his plausible thesis that extension is basic in anything that has it to the conclusion that whatever is extended is essentially so. That then generates a version of the separability argument:

> If I am actually extended, then I am necessarily so; that is, I am extended at every world at which I exist. Now, my distinct conception showed me that there is a possible world at which I exist and am not extended. So, running the chain of thoughts back contrapositively, we get the conclusion that I am not actually extended. QED.

But this argument is cankered at the outset. When Descartes announces that thought and extension are basic in everything that has them, he implies that no substance can have both: each thing has 'one principal property' under which 'everything else which can be attributed to the thing' can be subsumed. This

---

[3] See also Rep 4, CSM 2:156–7.

comes not from the concept of basicness, but rather from Descartes's confidence in the real distinction; he is not entitled to it in any premiss of an argument for the latter. We can sift it out from his account of basicness by generalizing the latter in a natural way:

> All of a thing's properties can be split into groups which do not overlap and each of which contains some property P and modes of P and nothing else.

This still lets thought and extension be 'basic' in a strong sense, while allowing that there could be a thinking animal—a substance that is basically extended and basically self-aware. When assembling premisses for an argument for the real distinction, *that* is the form of basicness doctrine which Descartes should espouse: one which is compatible with, but does not entail, the thesis that each thing has only one basic property.

But then the argument from basicness to essentialness fails. If a given thing has two basic natures F and G, we can have the thought of its losing F, because we have G to carry our thought of the thing itself. We can have the thought, for instance, of a thinking extended thing which ceases to be extended: this requires us to have the thought of tracking a mind through time in the absence of an associated body; and Descartes should agree that this can be done by adopting the first-person stance and thinking of this possibility for oneself. I am a self-aware being; if I believe that I am also an animal—and am thus extended—can I not make sense of the idea that I might lose my animal nature?

I conclude that if the separability argument relies on the premiss that whatever is extended is necessarily so, this needs support which Descartes apparently cannot provide. It does not follow from the thesis that extension is a basic property of whatever has it, and I can find no other source for it.

31. From possibility to actuality: individual identity

Descartes's other possible route from possibility to actuality involves essences too, but in a different way. When he asks, 'Am I an extended thinking thing?', he is asking, 'Is my mind [identical with] my body?' Or, more long-windedly, 'Is the thing that has these thoughts the very same thing that has these arms and legs, this paunch, and so on?' Denying the 'real distinction' between my mind and my body is answering Yes to that question, on a par with affirming any other identity statement, such as 'Mary Ann Evans is George Eliot'. Descartes sometimes sees himself as simply denying an identity statement: 'If one substance can exist apart from another, they are really distinct. The mind and the body are substances which can exist apart from each other. Therefore the mind is really distinct from the body' (Rep 2, CSM 2:120).[4]

---

[4] What Descartes wrote is strictly trivial, because if one substance has any relation R to *another*, then two substances are involved. CSM makes it slightly worse by putting 'the two are' instead of 'they are'.

Now, Descartes may be entitled to infer that my mind and my body are two things from the premiss that it is possible for my mind and my body to be two things. Although truth does not in general follow from possibility, it does seem to follow where identity statements are concerned; or, to put the point contra-positively, it seems that every true identity statement is necessarily true. The reasons for this are now well known, but I shall briefly rehearse them before exploring whether this can help Descartes with the separability argument.

Several philosophers—perhaps including Descartes—have thought that true identity statements are necessarily true; but the reasons for this were not widely appreciated until work by Ruth Barcan Marcus was developed, deepened, and popularized by Saul Kripke in his famous 'Naming and Necessity' (1972).

Recalling that New Zealand is the winner of the America's Cup in 2000, consider this counterfactual:

> If the New Zealand sailors had been drunk throughout all the races, and the Italian crew had sailed well, the winner of the America's Cup in 2000 would not have been New Zealand.

That has a good chance of being true. Imagine someone saying this: 'But "the winner of the America's Cup in 2000" refers to New Zealand, doesn't it? So the counterfactual is saying that if things had been different in certain ways, New Zealand would not have been New Zealand!' It is obvious that something is wrong with this, but we have not always been clear about exactly what the trouble is. Kripke invented the distinction between *rigid* and *non-rigid* designators. A definite description such as 'the winner of the America's Cup in 2000' is non-rigid, which means that it does not refer to the very same item at every possible world. When we consider certain possible worlds where the New Zealanders are drunk and the Italians are not, we apply this definite description to something other than what we apply it to at the actual world. *This has nothing to do with what expressions are used at the possible world in question.* In the given example, it is no doubt true that at that world the description would be applied to Italy and not to New Zealand, but that is not the Kripkean point I am making. My point is that when *we* designate various items at that possible world, *we* do not use the definite description 'the winner . . .' etc. to designate what it designates at the actual world. Kripke rightly maintains that definite descriptions are ordinarily used as non-rigid designators.

The counterfactual which I have presented remains true if in it we replace 'New Zealand' by 'Aotearoa', which is just another name for the same country. But now consider this:

> If the Maoris had never had a name for New Zealand, the winner of the America's Cup in 2000 would not have been Aotearoa.

It is doubtless true that if the Maoris had never had a name for New Zealand, it would never have been called 'Aotearoa' by anybody. But the above counterfactual is wrong: at those worlds New Zealand is not *called* 'Aotearoa', but *we* can and do still use that name to refer to that country, even at those worlds. This is in general how proper names work: we use them as rigid designators—for us they name at other possible worlds the things that they designate at the actual world.

Mary Ann Evans took the *nom de plume* 'George Eliot'. These are both proper names, and thus rigid designators. There are plenty of worlds at which that person is not called 'George Eliot', and we can put this by saying that if such-and-such had been the case, George Eliot would not have been called 'George Eliot'. What we cannot say is that if such-and-such had been the case, Mary Ann Evans would not have been George Eliot. We use both names to refer at every world to what they refer to at the actual world, and at the latter they refer to a single person.

In this terminology, then, Kripke holds that *Any true identity statement using only rigid designators is necessarily true*, which is equivalent to *Any possibly true identity statement using only rigid designators is true*. That is almost trivially true; what was not trivial is getting clear about how the two sorts of designators differ, and using this clarity to clear up philosophical muddles.

Now, Descartes takes his thought-experiment to have shown him that it could be the case that his mind exists and his body does not exist (because no body exists). At a world where that is the case, his mind is not his body; and so at the actual world also his mind is not his body. QED. Analogously, if there is a possible world at which Ernest Shackleton exists and Robert Scott does not, then Shackleton is not Scott. Descartes is thinking along these lines in this version of the separability argument:

From the mere fact that each of us understands himself to be a thinking thing and is capable, in thought, of excluding from himself every other substance, whether thinking or extended, it is certain that each of us, regarded in this way, is really distinct from every other thinking substance and from every corporeal substance. (PP 1:60, CSM 1:213)

Descartes here argues that because I *could be*, therefore I *am*, distinct from every corporeal substance. (Ignore the trivializing 'every *other* substance'.) Similarly, here:

The fact that we often see two things joined together does not license the inference that they are one and the same; but the fact that we sometimes observe one apart from the other entirely justifies the inference that they are different. . . . It is a contradiction to suppose that what we clearly perceive as two different things should become one and the same (intrinsically one and the same, not merely combined); this is no less a contradiction than to suppose that what are in no way distinct should be separated. (Rep 6, CSM 2:299*)

I understand 'observe' as used here to refer not (only) to what we perceptually observe at the actual world, but (also) to what we conceptually encounter at other possible worlds. Only then does the passage connect with Descartes's separability thought-experiment.

Thus construed, is the argument helped by the Kripkean thesis about the necessity of true identity statements? Kripke thinks so:

Descartes . . . argued that a person or mind is distinct from his body, since the mind could exist without the body. He might equally well have argued for the same conclusion from the premise that the body could have existed without the mind. Now the one response which I regard as plainly inadmissible is the response which cheerfully accepts the Cartesian premise while denying the Cartesian conclusion. Let 'Descartes' be a . . . rigid designator of a certain person, and let 'B' be a rigid designator of his body. Then if Descartes were indeed identical to B, the supposed identity . . . would be necessary, and Descartes could not exist without B and B could not exist without Descartes. . . . A philosopher who wishes to refute the Cartesian conclusion must refute the Cartesian premise, and the latter task is not trivial. (Kripke 1972: 334–5)

This challenge has not been sufficiently attended to. Most English-language philosophers these days regard substance-dualism as a non-starter; but Descartes's argument for it involves a move from conception to possibility (widely accepted), followed by a move from possibility to actuality (accepted by Kripke and many others, apparently rightly). This is disturbing, but there are two defences against it.

One defence blocks the first move in the argument with which we are threatened:

> (1) Descartes conceives his existing at a time when there are no bodies. So (2) it could be that he exists when there are no bodies. So (3) it is possible that he is not identical with his body. So (4) he is not identical with his body.

The move from 1 to 2—with the 'conceiving' done thoroughly enough—is to be based on the commonplace that possibilities are established by conceptual thought-experiments, there being no other way to establish them. But that is wrong. The move from thorough conceivability to possibility is all right in connection with modal truths which can show up in conceptual thought-experiments and thus be learned a priori. But the work of Kripke—which is needed for the move from 3 to 4—implies that not all modal truths can be learned in this way. It is necessary that Mary Ann Evans is George Eliot, but you could not discover this by thought alone. Suppose you embark on a world description according to which GE exists and MAE does not, this being a controlled way of 'distinctly conceiving' the world in question. Tell the story in as much detail as you like, and let it assert clearly and explicitly that GE exists and MAE does not; the description need not contain any lurking inconsistency of the sort that mere description or distinct conception can bring to the surface. Yet the description does not fit any possible world because *at the actual world* GE is MAE. In short, there is a kind of possibility that licenses the move from 1 to 2, and a kind that licenses the move from 3 to 4; but the kinds are different, with no overlap. For no kind of possibility, therefore, does the argument go through.

The second defence against the threatening argument challenges the move from 2 to 3. I shall not expound it here, beyond giving this pointer. A world at which there are no bodies may be a world at which my body exists but is not a body. Descartes needs to plug this gap.

Note, finally, Kripke's remark that Descartes could as well have argued 'from the premise that the body could have existed without the mind'. That premiss is so easily available that our suspicions should be aroused, as Curley's were when he remarked drily that 'Kripke's argument promises a high return from a very small investment' (Curley 1978: 202). Descartes himself implies that his argument is not symmetrical in this way, when responding to Arnauld's remark that the real distinction does not follow from the premiss—which any materialist will grant—that there could be bodies at a world with no minds (Obj 4, CSM 2:141; Rep 4, CSM 2:157). Descartes replies, in effect, that his argument needs the premiss that you can conceive of mind without body, and not that you can conceive of body without mind; which shows that he means to be offering an argument that is mind–body asymmetrical. But the Kripkean argument based on an identity statement is perfectly symmetrical. Since Descartes evidently does see the argument as Kripkean, he has replied wrongly to Arnauld; if the intended argument succeeds, then so does the 'high return' argument which infers the real distinction from a premiss which any materialist would accept.

32. The Cartesian concept of man

Any philosopher who holds that a mind is one thing and a body another should consider whether and how a body and a mind can be so interrelated as to constitute a single thing. The present section will lean on a paper by Stephen Voss (1994), who discusses this matter more thoroughly than anyone else I know of; his 1999 paper is a dramatic and richly interesting further development of his thoughts on the topic.

Descartes often answers the whether-question affirmatively: Yes, the two can compose a single thing, 'a man'. I shall follow him in using 'man' as shorthand for 'man, woman or child'. Although he holds that no *substance* can have both thought and extension, he does allow that an entity of a certain kind may do so:

A subject in which we understand only extension and the various modes of extension is a simple entity; so too is a subject in which we recognize only thought and the various modes of thought. But that which we regard as having at the same time both extension and thought is something composite, namely a man, consisting of a soul and a body. (1648a, CSM 1:299)

How do substances differ from other entities? The only clear guidance Descartes gives us is that if something thinks and is extended, it is not a substance.

Now, if a man is the ontological upshot of a suitably related mind and animal body, what are the suitable relations? What does it take for a thinking and an extended substance to 'compose' a single entity? What—to borrow Donne's phrase—are the 'fingers' which 'knit the subtle knot that makes us man'?

Descartes holds that my mind acts on my body when I voluntarily move, and perhaps also that my body acts on my mind in sense perception (§41). But this yields only a part of his answer to our question. The causal flow one way enables my mind to control my body; and the contrary flow enables my mind to be informed about various states of affairs that affect my brain; but, Descartes says, the union of mind with body goes further than this. Mental control is not the whole story: 'It is not sufficient for the soul to be lodged in the human body like a helmsman in his ship, except perhaps to move its limbs. It must be more closely joined and united with the body in order to have, besides this power of move-ment, feelings and appetites like ours and so compose a real man' (*Method* 5, CSM 1:141). Nor, in the other direction, is information the whole story:

By these sensations of pain, hunger, thirst and so on, nature teaches me that I am not merely present in my body as a sailor is present in a ship, but that I am very closely joined and, as it were, intermingled with it, so that I and the body form a unit. If this were not so, I, who am nothing but a thinking thing, would not feel pain when the body was hurt, but would perceive the damage purely by the intellect, just as a sailor perceives by sight if anything in his ship is broken. . . . For these sensations of . . . pain and so on are nothing but confused modes of thinking which arise from the union and, as it were, intermingling of the mind with the body. (Med 6, CSM 2:56)

This is insightful. Knowing of the damage is not feeling pain, and (another of Descartes's examples) knowing of the drought is not feeling thirst—a humdrum point, but it was an achievement to see its significance in an understanding of the human condition.

Conceding that Descartes is 'quite right' to highlight the difference between pain and mere knowledge of harm, Gassendi complains that he has made a bad job of saying what the source of the difference is. Here are excerpts from the splendid passage in which he develops this complaint:

You still have to explain how that 'joining and, as it were, intermingling' . . . can apply to you if you are incorporeal, unextended and indivisible. If you are no larger than a point, how are you joined to the entire body, which is so large? . . . If you wholly lack parts, how are you intermingled or 'as it were intermingled' with the particles of this region? For there can be no intermingling between things unless the parts of each of them can be intermingled. And if you are something separate, how are you compounded with matter so as to make up a unity? Moreover, since all compounding, conjunction or union takes place between the component parts, must there not be some relation between these parts? Yet what relation can possibly be understood to exist between corporeal and incor-poreal parts? (Obj 5, CSM 2:238)

In digging into the question of what it takes for two things to compose a single thing, Gassendi perhaps relies unduly on his own kind of materialism; but his challenge to Descartes is legitimate.

Descartes has no answer to it, as he admits in several places. Here is a striking one, written to Princess Elisabeth in 1643:

The soul is conceived only by the pure intellect; body . . . can likewise be known by the intellect alone, but much better by the intellect aided by the imagination; and finally what belongs to the union of the soul and the body is known only obscurely by the intellect alone or even by the intellect aided by the imagination, but it is known very clearly by the senses. That is why people who never philosophize and use only their senses have no doubt that the soul moves the body and that the body acts on the soul. . . . It is the ordinary course of life and conversation, and abstention from meditation and from the study of the things which exercise the imagination, that teaches us how to conceive the union of the soul and the body. (CSMK 227)

Voss contends that by about 1642 Descartes had stopped worrying about what a composite entity is, and omitted such entities from his metaphysic. This was 'the end of anthropology' for him, meaning that *men* stopped having a role in his serious ontology. The evidence Voss offers for this is persuasive. For a rival view see Baier 1981; for an even stronger dissent see Hoffman 1986.

One of the questions that arises—and Voss raises it—is 'So what?' How does Descartes's serious philosophical work need the concept of a man? That question brings into the limelight his understanding of 'I'. In the *Meditations* he identifies *himself* with a mind, which he eventually comes to think is intimately *associated* with an animal body. If he can stick to this through thick and thin, perhaps he can dispense with the concept of a man, but it is easy to see one price he must pay. He will have to write off as not strictly accurate hosts of things that we ordinarily think are true. 'I remember when I was two inches taller than I am now.' That seems all right, but Descartes must say that it is not strictly true: what remembers is a mind; what has a height is a body; and the statement can be rescued only by taking its 'I was' and 'I am' as a vulgar shorthand for 'my body was (is)'. Though uncomfortable, this is not fatal unless Descartes absolutely needs *men* in his metaphysic—which I suspect he does not.

Now for a few words at the meta-level about the nature of issues surrounding composition. I contend for a sort of conceptual pragmatism. It is legitimate to postulate an entity E, composed out of substances M and B, if:

(1) We know how M and B are interrelated;
(2) We know how any predication on E could in principle be reduced to predications on M and/or on B.
(3) We find it convenient to think and talk as though E existed.

Conditions 1 and 2 join forces to ensure that in postulating E we do not add to our account of the world's *basic* inventory; and on my pragmatic view, 3 justifies our having E in some serious inventory, though not the basic one. Some philosophers hold that those three conditions are not enough. They believe:

Given that we understand how the postulation of E relates to the facts about M and B, and that its postulation is linguistically convenient to us, there is still a further question as to whether M and B *really do* compose a further entity.

I cannot locate that 'further question'. To do so, I need someone to tell me what would count for or against an affirmative answer to it.

Chapter 5

Descartes on Causation

33. Causation and similarity

This chapter will consider Descartes's views on (1) the nature of causation, and (2) the scope of the causal relation—that is, what pairs of items can be related as cause and effect. We shall find 1 to be thin gruel: Descartes had no considered views about the nature of causation; and his views about scope had to come from other sources. Topic 2 is well expounded by Garber (1992, and more conveniently in his 1993*b*). My own treatment, starting in §38, is indebted to him.

Textbooks often say that Cartesians had a problem regarding how minds could act on bodies, or vice versa, given how unalike they are. This is presumably meant to arise from the idea that causing is giving: minds do not have what matter acquires causally (motion), nor do bodies have what minds acquire (thoughts). 'Nothing can give what it does not have', as Arnauld said (CSM: 2:148). Berkeley, much later, refers to this as an 'old known axiom', using it to argue that even if matter existed, it would be thoughtless, and so could not cause thoughts (Dia 3, 236). This popular way of looking at causation seems not to have been scrutinized carefully enough. The truism that what you do not have you cannot give is matched by the platitude that what you give you lose; but when we press a coin on to soft wax, it 'gives' circularity without losing any.

Anyway, whatever the source of the trouble is supposed to be, Descartes was untroubled by it. Confronting the challenge 'How can the soul move the body if it is in no way material, and how can it receive the forms of corporeal objects?', he writes to Clerselier that the question 'arises simply from a supposition that is false, . . . namely that . . . two substances whose nature is different are thereby rendered unable to act on each other' (CSM 2:275). The most natural way to take this is as implying that causes need not resemble their effects. (For a rival reading see Gorham 1999: 302–3.) Still, although this rejection of the thesis that causes must resemble their effects was Descartes's basic and most usual position, a few texts point the other way.

Three years earlier, when Princess Elisabeth expressed the worry about the dissimilarity of mind and body, Descartes did not try to reassure her by explaining that the unlikeness of mind and matter is no barrier to their interaction (CSMK 228). Similarly, when young Burman asked: 'How can the soul be affected by the body and vice versa, when their natures are completely different?', Descartes acknowledged the difficulty by openly evading it: 'This is very difficult to explain; but here our experience is sufficient, since it is so clear on this point that it cannot be gainsaid' (CSMK 346).

I can only guess that Descartes was inhibited by his awareness that, although he did not hold that causes must resemble their effects, he had no alternative theory of causation either. Leibniz, recounting his own failed endeavours to explain how there can be causation between different created things, whether minds or bodies, adds: 'As far as we can see from his writings, Descartes had given up the game on this topic' (NS, FW 149). This suggests that Descartes at least entered the game, trying to develop an account of the nature of causation; but I shall argue later that he did not. His lack of any general theory of causation may have deterred him from coming more openly to the aid of the princess and the graduate student.

None of this, however, explains a protracted episode in the *Meditations*, an argument for God's existence in which Descartes employs a thesis requiring that all causation satisfy a constraint which is close to 'Causes must resemble their effects', and which involves the idea that causing is giving. This argument precedes Descartes's acceptance of his theology, his physics, and most of his metaphysics; so it cannot come from any of those. The only remaining possible source for its causal premiss is the concept of cause; so Descartes is behaving here somewhat as though he had a general analytic view about what causation must be.

The premiss is Descartes's *causal resources principle*, which he introduces here:

There must be at least as much ⟨reality⟩ in the efficient and total cause as in the effect of that cause. For where, I ask, could the effect get its reality from, if not from the cause? And how could the cause give it to the effect unless it possessed it? It follows from this both that something cannot arise from nothing, and also that what is more perfect—that is, contains in itself more reality—cannot arise from what is less perfect. (Med 3, CSM 2:28)

For Descartes 'perfect(ion)' is not a value term: a perfection is just a way of being real. When in his other argument for God's existence he says that God has 'all perfections', he means only that God is real in every possible way, or has every positive property or quality.

The quoted passage starts and finishes with a quantitative thesis: that there must be *as much* perfection or reality in the cause as in the effect; a thing cannot be caused by something *less* perfect. In between, Descartes asserts something qualitative, implying that the cause must have not merely *as much* but *the same* perfection or reality as the effect acquires through the interaction. Descartes's argument for the existence of God employs this qualitative version of the principle, which virtually says that causes must resemble their effects. He recapitulates the argument here:

Nothing that we attribute to God can have been derived from external objects as a copy is derived from its original, since nothing in God resembles what is to be found in external, that is corporeal, things. Now any elements in our thought which do not resemble external objects manifestly cannot have originated in external objects, but must have come from the cause which produced this diversity in our thought. (Rep 3, CSM 2:132)

This assumes that causing is giving, which does not square with Descartes's forthright denial that causes must resemble their effects.

His only attempt to defend his causal resources principle takes the form of a threat: reject that principle, he writes, and you are left defenceless against the thesis that something could be produced by nothing. 'The only reason why nothing cannot be the cause of a thing is that such a cause would not contain the same features as are found in the effect' (Rep 2, CSM 2:97*). The phrase 'such a cause' shows Descartes treating 'nothing' as the name of a thing. The causal resources principle is in bad shape indeed if its best defence is that it is needed to support the idea that 'nothing' names an item which is too metaphysically feeble to be able to cause anything! I am not convinced by the ingenious attempt of Gorham (1999) to defend Descartes at this point.

34. Varying the causal resources principle

Descartes deforms the principle in two ways, which make it worse still—one weakening it enough to make it trivially true, the other strengthening it to the point where it is incredible.

Like any Christian, he would credit God with causing snails and otters to be as they are; but he did not think that God himself is spiral or playful. Discussing this with Burman, he held to the requirement that causes resemble their effects, pleading in mitigation that the resemblance can be thin and remote. Burman: 'But in that case even stones and the like are going to be in God's image.' Descartes: 'Even these things do have the image and likeness of God, but it is very remote, minute, and indistinct' (CSMK 340). Perhaps he had forgotten his original way of handling this matter, to which I now turn.

It invokes the scholastic distinction between having a feature straightforwardly (*formaliter*) and having it 'eminently' (*eminenter*). To possess a quality 'eminently' is to have it 'in a higher manner' (*OED*), which frees one from the limitations that come from having it straightforwardly. For example, a thing that has a shape is limited in a certain way, yet God causes things' shapes, though he has no limits; so he has 'eminently' the feature of being shaped, but his knowledge and power he has straightforwardly. (See Rep 2, CSM 2:98–9.)

The 'eminent' concept can be used to weaken the causal resources principle so that it says only:

If x causes y to be F, then x is straightforwardly *or eminently* F.

Descartes probably connects eminent containment with degrees of reality or perfection, holding that if x eminently contains y, then x is more perfect than y.

But that does not take us far. For a firm grip on this weakening of the causal resources principle, it is not enough to be told that the eminent possessor is more perfect than the possessed, and that eminence involves having a property 'in a higher manner'. But all Descartes offers us in addition is this:

Whatever exists in the objects of our ideas in a way which exactly corresponds to our perceptions of it is said to exist straightforwardly in those objects. Something is said to exist eminently in an object when, although it does not exactly correspond to our perception of it, its greatness is such that it can fill the role of that which does so correspond. (Rep 2, CSM 2:114)

The only 'role' I can find is: causing our ideas to be as they are. But that trivializes the causal resources principle: to have F eminently is *to be able to cause something else to have F straightforwardly*; which, as Cottingham has pointed out (1976: 83), makes it quite trivial that any feature of an effect must be possessed either straightforwardly or eminently by the cause.

As well as twisting it towards triviality, Descartes also stretches his causal resources principle towards wild extravagance. Before expounding it, I should comment on the adverb *formaliter*. For a ball to possess roundness *formaliter* is for it to be

straightforwardly round, in contrast to an uncircular thing which is eminently (*eminenter*) round, meaning that it has some grander property which enables it to cause things to be round; and

intrinsically round, in contrast to an uncircular thing which is representatively (*objectivè*) round, meaning that it represents roundness or some round thing.

Formaliter is used by Descartes only in those two contrasts. In my discussion of the former contrast, I have translated *formaliter* by 'straightforwardly'; in discussing the latter contrast, I shall translate it by 'intrinsically'. There is no excuse, for anyone who purports to be writing contemporary English, for rendering it by 'formally', or *objectivè* by 'objectively'.

The wild extravagance which I mentioned occurs here:

There must be at least as much ⟨reality⟩ in the cause as in the effect. . . . This holds not only for the intrinsic reality of effects but also for the representative reality of ideas. Not only can a stone not begin to exist unless it is produced by something which intrinsically contains everything *that is in the stone*, . . . but also the idea of a stone cannot exist in me unless it is put there by some cause which contains at least as much reality as *I conceive to be in the stone*. . . . My idea requires no intrinsic reality except what it derives from my thought, of which it is a mode. But in order for it to contain such and such representative reality it must derive it from some cause containing at least as much intrinsic reality as there is representative reality in the idea. For if we suppose that an idea contains something that was not in its cause, it must have got this from nothing; yet the mode of being by which a thing exists representatively in the intellect by way of an idea, imperfect though it may be, is certainly not nothing and so it cannot come from nothing.[1]

---

[1] Med 3, CSM 2:28–9, with amendments to the translation and a little streamlining.

Nobody has succeeded in making this look reasonable. Descartes needs it for his argument for God's existence, which relies on the thesis that an actually infinite being must have caused my idea of such a being. The sketchy semblance of a reason that he offers above trades on a trick of language which Descartes had also played a paragraph earlier:

The ideas which represent substances to me amount to something more and, so to speak, contain within themselves more representative reality than the ideas which merely represent modes or accidents. Again, the idea that gives me my understanding of a supreme God, eternal, infinite [etc.], certainly has in it more representative reality than the ideas that represent finite substances.

It happens under our very eyes: Descartes moves from 'amount to something more and, so to speak, contain within themselves more representative reality' to 'has in it more representative reality', from which the cautious 'so to speak' has been dropped. From there on the language of representative containment governs the argument: the contained infinity must have come from something; then the rest of the machinery starts up, and out clanks the conclusion.

Gassendi makes a shrewd start on a challenge to this talk about representative containment:

The reality belonging to my idea of x is, according to your distinction, of two kinds. Its intrinsic reality is . . . [etc.]. The representative reality, on the other hand, can be nothing but the representation or likeness of x which the idea carries, or at any rate the pattern according to which the parts of the idea are fitted together so as to represent x. Either way, it seems to be nothing real, since it is merely a relation amongst the various parts, and between the parts and x; in other words, it is merely a mode of the idea's intrinsic reality, in virtue of which it has taken on this particular form. (Obj 5, CSM 2:202; my 'x')

This could launch a solid challenge to Descartes's talk of ideas as 'containing representative reality'; but Gassendi leaves it undeveloped, and Descartes ignores it (CSM 2:252–3).

Even granted his language of containment, Descartes still needs reasons for holding that the cause of a representatively contained perfection must have that perfection. Caterus challenges that thesis (Obj 1, CSM 2:66–7), and Descartes's reply rests ultimately on the trivially weak version of the causal resources principle. He considers the example of 'someone who possesses in his intellect the idea of a machine of a highly intricate design'. Taking Caterus to have implied that since the intricacy is only conceived, it need not be caused, Descartes reasonably says: 'It is perfectly fair to ask what is the cause of this idea' (CSM 2:75). Then he goes a step further, with a clear hint of causing as giving: 'In order for the idea of the machine to contain such and such representative intricacy, it must derive it from some cause.' Half a page later he goes the whole hog: 'If someone possesses the idea of a machine containing every imaginable intricacy of design, then the correct inference is plainly that this idea originally came from some cause in which every imaginable intricacy really did exist, even though the intricacy now has only representative existence in the idea.' He approaches this extravagance along a ramp of triviality: 'Admittedly there could be various causes of the intricacy contained in the idea of the machine. . . . Perhaps a very subtle intelligence enabled the man to invent the idea without any previous knowledge. But all the intricacy which is to be found merely representatively in the idea must necessarily be found, either straightforwardly or eminently, in its cause, whatever this turns out to be.'

The authors of the Second Objections are also puzzled by Descartes's adherence to the thesis (CSM 2:88), and Descartes responds with a put-down: 'There may be some whose natural light is so meagre that they do not see that it is a primary notion that every perfection that is present representatively in an idea must really exist in some cause of the idea' (CSM 2:97–8). Later, he offers an argument:

We have to accept this axiom, because on it depends our knowledge of all things, whether perceivable through the senses or not. How do we know, for example, that the sky exists? Because we see it? But this 'seeing' does not affect the mind except in so far as it is an idea . . . Now the only reason why we can use this idea as a basis for the judgment that the sky exists is that every idea must have a really existing cause of its representative reality; and in this case we judge that the cause is the sky itself. We make similar judgments in other cases. (Rep 2, CSM 2:116–17; see also 97)

He has a point. In common with many early modern philosophers, Descartes held the following plausible position: (1) I can know what my ideas or sensory states are, independently of any opinions I have about the world around me; and my only route to such opinions is by causal inference from my sensory states. Suppose we add to this a view of Hume's: (2) To consider the matter a priori, any thing may produce any thing (*Treatise* 247). The conjunction of those seems to cut me off from the opinion that there is a sky, or indeed that I have any environment at all. So Descartes, given that he accepts both parts of 1, can reasonably deny 2 and insist that there must be a priori knowable constraints on the causal relation. But this does not show that the constraints must involve the causal resources principle.

Let us stop searching for arguments to support that principle, and admit that we know it to be false. After decades of intermittently brooding on this part of Descartes's work, and reading some of the secondary literature on it, I reluctantly conclude that it is without value. To say that an item which represents a property somehow *contains* it is to play with words; and the assumption that causes must resemble effects and/or that causing is giving is unsupported.

This argument of Descartes's seems not to reflect any deeply considered views about the nature of causation. He is acting here less as a real philosopher than as a theistic opportunist. Wanting to work up an argument for God's existence, he advances the causal resources principle because he thinks it will do the job, then weakens most of it to triviality in the face of counter-examples—some spawned by his own theology—while also endorsing a madly strong variant of it which he needs to reach his conclusion. No doubt he in some fashion believed what he wrote; but mere sincerity is not the same as being driven by philosophical interests, concerns, and problems.

35. Tropes

To proceed, I must first devote a section to a concept that will be active throughout the present work. It is the concept of a property instance, or individual accident, or *trope*—the last term being introduced in this sense by Donald Williams (1953). An important precursor is G. F. Stout (1921), and a useful successor is K. Campbell (1981). A trope is a case or instance of a property: this hammer is a concrete particular which has hardness and other properties; hardness is an abstract universal which is possessed by this hammer and other particulars; and *the hardness of this hammer* is a trope, an abstract particular. (I use 'abstract' in the good, Lockean sense of something not saturated with detail, rather than in any of the *mélange* of contemporary senses—existing necessarily, being out of space-time, lacking causal power, etc.) This trope is unlike the hammer in that all there is to it is hardness, and it is unlike hardness in that it pertains only to this hammer. Many questions arise about tropes: How many can one thing possess at one time? Can one include another? Are the tropes which a thing has at a given time arranged hierarchically, with some basic and the rest dependent? To all of this I reply: Ask the analogous question about (universal) properties, settle on answers, and then give the analogues of those answers to the original questions.

Whether there are any such items as tropes is controversial, but they were widely believed in throughout late medieval and early modern times, and in the past few decades they have regained popularity. To get them clearly before us, I now sketch five theories in which they have a role.

(1) Locke and Leibniz held that events are tropes: when Locke spoke of 'modes', he was usually referring to tropes; and he and Leibniz both included events among the modes (*Essay* and *NE* III.vi.42). On this view, the fall of a sparrow is a particular instance of *falling*—that is, it is a trope; the fall of a different object, or a subsequent fall of the same sparrow, is a different trope, though the universal of which it is an instance is the same. Some contemporary philosophers, including Jaegwon Kim and myself, accept this theory: all the main formal properties of events are ones that tropes—if there are any—must also have. (For a detailed defence see my 1996.) The theory does no visible work in the rest of Locke's or Leibniz's thought, so I shall not pursue it; but it helps to show why philosophers today can accept tropes without blushing.

(2) Many philosophers, in our century and earlier, have held that a thing or substance is a 'bundle of qualities', which in its most plausible form means a bundle not of universals but of instances, abstract particulars, tropes. (For recent discussion, see Simons 1994 and Denkel 1997. On things as bundles of universals, see O'Leary-Hawthorne 1995.) Locke had a famous problem about the concept of substance, which he might have escaped by adopting the 'bundle' view (§205). Hume did adopt it, and Leibniz had an account of substance which at least reminds us of it (§312).

(3) Some metaphysicians go beyond the 'bundle' theory of things, maintaining that basically there are only tropes: a concrete particular is one kind of collection of them, an abstract universal is a collection of another kind. This yields an elegant account of property instantiation: for a particular thing to have a certain property is for a single trope to belong to collections of both kinds; for this pebble to be ovoid is for a trope to belong to both the this-pebble and the ovoidness collections. I have no reason to discuss this further.

(4) In the early modern period the trope concept was active in the view that causation involves the transfer of a trope from one thing to another: a red-hot poker gives an instance of hotness to the water in a bucket, a cue-ball gives an instance of motion to a ball that it strikes. Leibniz, who reasonably thought that Locke had committed himself to this view of collisions, agreed that that's what it would be for one created thing to act on another—from which he inferred that no thing other than God ever acts upon anything else, because the transfer of tropes is metaphysical nonsense (§94). Although this view of causation is no longer with us, one is reminded of it by some recent theories of causation, such as Castañeda's view (1984) that causation is basically the transfer of 'causity'.

(5) Some medieval philosophers held that in sense perception tropes go from the object to the percipient. None of my six philosophers accepted this, but some went to the trouble of denying it. For this and other reasons, I need to expound it in some detail. This theory of sense perception was widely accepted in and after the thirteenth century, perhaps on the strength of some remarks by Aristotle, who says—as a comment on 'all perception'—that 'a sense is what has the power of receiving into itself the sensible forms of things without the matter, in the way in which a piece of wax takes on the impress of a signet-ring without the iron or gold' (*On the Soul* II.12, 424ª17). If a thing's 'sensible form' is a trope which it owns, this expresses the theory that sense perception involves trope transfer: when I see a round thing, its roundness is somehow launched from the thing into my mind. From conversation with John Robertson, and the negative evidence of Wedin (1988), I gather that Aristotle scholars today do not read him in this way. They see him not as theorizing about how perception works, but only as describing the surface facts: When I perceive a round thing, its 'sensible form' gets into my visual sense, in that I come to have a visual representation of roundness—my state of mind comes to involve roundness *somehow*.

Yet many of Aristotle's followers did hold that perception involves the transfer of tropes. In this context the word 'species', especially in the phrases 'sensible species' and 'intentional species', came into play in a family of theories whose main progenitor was Roger Bacon, though there was also influence from several Arab philosophers, including Avicenna. (Georgette Sinkler taught me all I know about this, and led me to the secondary works from which I shall quote.) The theory says that when you see an external object, it sends out 'visible species', which reach you through your eyes:

According to this theory, a visible object generates or 'multiplies' species of light and color in the adjacent, transparent medium. These species, which Bacon also calls 'virtues' or powers, 'forms', 'images', 'similitudes', 'phantasms', and 'intentions', generate further species in the medium continuous to them, which results in a continuous multiplication of species along rays proceeding in all unobstructed directions from all points on the object's surface. These visible species convey the object's accidents through the intervening medium, which serves as their substance, to the eye of the viewer, upon which they are, loosely speaking, 'impressed'. (Tachau 1988: 8)

Notice that a second theory has quietly sidled into our picture. In addition to the view that the 'species' that are transferred in vision are tropes ('forms'), we now have the view that they are items that resemble the seen object ('similitudes'). What is transmitted to me when I see a ball is on one theory *an instance of roundness*, and on the other *something round*. Perhaps some of these philosophers conflated these two theories, assuming that an instance of roundness must be round; but some did not. Here is a report of a fourteenth-century Italian philosopher stating the alternatives, and preferring tropes:

Blasius argues that there is no contradiction in maintaining either that species are true substances (so that 'when I see . . . an ass, that ass multiplies asses from itself through the medium to the eye') or that species are qualities rather than substances; however, he prefers the latter alternative. (Lindberg 1976: 130–1)

The theory that mainly concerns me here is the one that Blasius favoured, according to which vision—or, more generally, sense perception—involves the transfer of tropes.

If it is hard to believe that a single property-instance could migrate from one substance to another, it is perhaps harder to swallow the idea that it could travel through space without having any substance to inhere in. Some of the friends of tropes, perhaps encouraged by Aristotle's *On the Soul* II.7, maintained that the transferred tropes move through an intervening 'medium' which, as Tachau puts it, 'serves as their substance'. This, however, takes them out of the frying pan into the fire. If a roundness trope is transferred from a coin to my eye through an instantiating substantial medium, there must be a pathway of real circles between the coin and my eye; or, in another case, a string of asses. This is even less digestible than unowned tropes.

Furthermore, once the trope reaches the mind, it must be unowned; for otherwise a mind that perceives heat would be hot, one that perceives triangles would be triangular, and so on. The notion of (5) representative ideas as unowned tropes can be helped along by (3) the 'bundle' theory of thinghood, according to which a particular thing is an aggregate of tropes whose members are interrelated in a particular-constituting manner (PC for short). On this theory, an individual mind is a PC-related aggregate of tropes. None of those tropes counts as unowned: because they are PC-related, each is an instance of some property which, as we would ordinarily say, that mind *has*. But there might be further tropes that do not belong to that aggregate, and so are not possessed by that mind, but which have to the aggregate or to some of its members a relation which makes it the case that those tropes are 'in the mind' in a representative way.

Start with the plausible view that sense perception involves an object's acting causally on a mind, add (4) the theory that all causation is trope transfer, and you get as a theorem (5) the trope-transfer account of perception. That was how Bacon saw the situation. Tachau reports that 'For Bacon . . . the visible species are only one instance of a general multiplication of species by all objects and powers in the universe', and she quotes Bacon:

Every efficient cause acts through its own power, which it exercises on the adjacent matter. . . . This power is called 'likeness', 'image' and 'species', and is designated by many other names, and it is produced both by substance and by accident, spiritual and corporeal. . . . This species produces every action in the world, for it acts on sense, on the intellect, and on all matter of the world for the generation of things. (Tachau 1988: 7–8)

On this complex of views, when a round thing puts an instance of roundness into my mind, this is an example of what happens in causation generally. When one thing hits another and makes it move, it passes some of its movement to the other; when a hot poker is plunged into cold water and warms it, a warmth-instance is transferred.

Actually, in moving out from perception to causation generally, one encounters a bump. A rock rolls down a hillside, as a result of which I see it moving, and it hits another rock and starts it moving. In the collision a trope is passed from one rock to another, which then instantiates it; but in my seeing the rock, a trope passes from it to my mind without my mind's coming to instantiate it—my mind does not move, although movingness is represented in it. Most effects involve owned tropes, while sensory effects involve unowned ones; and that is a disunity in this theoretic package.

36. Descartes against tropes

The only respectable metaphysical underlay for Descartes's causal resources principle, and for the associated 'causing is giving' metaphor, is the thesis that causation is the transfer of tropes. Descartes, however, rejects tropes in all their roles. He calls them 'real accidents'—that is, accidents which are thing-like.

Arnauld invokes them in the Fourth Objections, in connection with the doctrine of the Eucharist, according to which the communion bread and wine (1) become the body and blood of the Christ while (2) retaining the accidents of bread and wine, so that there is (1) a change in what substances the priest holds in his hand, but (2) no empirical evidence of its occurring. Arnauld, like many before him, takes this to mean that certain tropes—the whiteness of that bread, the thinness of that wine—come to be possessed by different substances, namely the body and blood of the Christ. Skipping some complications, the basic issue is whether trope transfer is intelligible; Descartes holds that it is not.

So, as an obedient Catholic, he needs to free the doctrine of the Eucharist from requiring the transfer of tropes. In the first edition of the *Meditations* he fast-stepped defensively around this topic, protesting that he had not outright denied the existence of 'real accidents'. But he later added seven paragraphs (CSM 2:176–8) in which he takes the fight to his critic, denying that the doctrine of the Eucharist needs 'real accidents'. All it requires, he writes, is that God turn the wine and bread into blood and flesh which exactly resemble wine and bread. Some philosophical theologians had speculated that the blood and flesh acquire the very same particular instances of the relevant properties that used to be had by the wine and bread; but this, Descartes says, is an otiose addition which they rashly blundered into, finding tropes to be convenient and wrongly thinking them to be philosophically safe.

According to Descartes, the concept of 'real accident' is inherently contradictory: he sees it as the notion of thing-like property—something that is accorded a kind of independence or self-subsistence which requires that it be not an accident but a substance:

If something real is understood to remain it must be thought of as something which subsists; and though the word 'accident' may be used to describe it, it must nonetheless be conceived of as a substance. Hence the supposition that real accidents remain is in fact just like saying that the whole substance of the bread changes but nevertheless a part of that substance called a 'real accident' remains. (Rep 4, CSM 2:176)

His focus is always on the idea that a 'real accident' might be *unowned*; but he must object equally to a trope's *migrating* between substances, even if it is owned all the way. On the next page he denies that there can be 'real accidents existing apart from the substance of the bread in such a way that they do not thereby themselves become substances'. In the Sixth Replies he puts the point even more forthrightly: 'It is completely contradictory that there should be real accidents, since whatever is real can exist separately from any other subject; yet anything that can exist separately in this way is a substance, not an accident' (CSM 2:293). He has a point. If there are tropes, it is hard to avoid supposing that so-called substances are bundles of them; and in that case it looks as though the real substances—the most basic items that the universe contains—are not the bundles, but rather the individual tropes (§306). Still, one can believe in tropes and employ the concept of them in theories without going as far as that.

What did Descartes think that tropes were supposed to do? Writing about the theologians who spoiled the doctrine of the Eucharist, he speaks of their bland confidence that 'the accidents which stimulate our senses were something real and distinct from a substance' (CSM 2:176). This suggestion that he sees tropes primarily as ingredients in a theory of perception is confirmed later: 'The only reason why people have thought that accidents exist is that they have supposed that they are perceived by the senses' (Rep 6, CSM 2:293). I shall come to Descartes's own views on perception in §41.

The trope-transfer theory of causation in general is not an identified target anywhere in Descartes's writings. He does sometimes connect causal issues with 'real qualities'; but the issues do not concern the nature of causation as such, and 'real qualities' are not the tropes or 'real accidents' that I have been discussing, though they are objectionable for the same reason:

> I used to conceive of heaviness as if it were some sort of real quality which inhered in solid bodies; and although I called it a 'quality', thereby referring it to the bodies in which it inhered, by adding that it was 'real' I was in fact thinking that it was a substance . . . Later on I [became clear about] the ideas of body and corporeal motion, and I found that all my previous ideas of 'real qualities' or 'substantial forms' were ones which I had put together or constructed from those basic ideas. (Rep 6, CSM 2:297–8)

Elsewhere Descartes brackets 'real qualities' with 'substantial forms', or treats them as a scholastic technicality (PP 4:198; W 7, CSM 1:94). These 'real qualities' seem to be universals rather than particulars; and they are supposed to have and exercise power, but not themselves to be transferred from one substance to another in a causal transaction. So these passages are at two removes from any trope-transfer account of the nature of causation.[2]

Beware of certain turns of phrase that sound like endorsements of trope transfer. For example, 'The motion which God preserves is not something permanently fixed in given pieces of matter, but something which is mutually transferred when collisions occur' (PP 2:42). This does not mean that in collisions tropes are transferred; Descartes, as he explains at CSMK 382, means only that God maintains the same 'quantity of motion' in the universe.[3]

37. Descartes's non-endurance doctrine

Apart from trope transfer, one other possibly coherent theory of causation had some currency in Descartes's time, namely the thesis that causal necessity is absolute necessity. The flowing of effects from causes, on this view, is as necessary as the following of conclusions from premises in a logically valid argument. That was Spinoza's view; but Descartes never hints that it is his, and for a special reason it could not be. Someone who identifies causal necessity with absolute necessity must hold that modal truths are not always discoverable a priori; the necessities of basic physics, such a person must hold, cannot be displayed through a demonstration that their contradictory is evidently impossible or inconceivable. Hume's attack on this view of causation assumes that what is

---

[2] Descartes writes to Clerselier (CSM 2:275) about 'real accidents like heat, weight, and so on' which are supposed to 'act on the body'. I suppose that 'accidents' was a slip, and that he meant 'qualities'.

[3] See also CSM 1:96, 240, 256. The phrase 'transfer of motion' at CSM 1:234 is a mistranslation; it should be simply 'transfer'. The topic is the transfer of a body between places, not of motion between bodies.

impossible is inconceivable (§262), and on that assumption the attack succeeds. Well, Descartes firmly believed that we have conceptual access to all modal truths: he infers possibility from distinct conceivability (§29); this implies that if something is impossible, a thought-experiment could show it to be so. So he cannot hold that causal laws, with their wholly conceivable contradictories, are of the same kind as the laws of mathematics and logic.

We now approach Descartes's *non-endurance doctrine*, as I call it. This connects with what I have just been saying; and we need it as a background to my next main topic: Descartes's views about what kinds of items cause what other kinds.

The non-endurance doctrine says that a created thing cannot last through time without divine aid. This was a common enough opinion; we find it, for example, in Leibniz (§96) and Locke (*Essay* 204:26). Descartes, however, takes it further than most, explicitly equating that divine aid with continuous re-creation:

A lifespan can be divided into countless parts, each completely independent of the others, so that it does not follow from the fact that I existed a little while ago that I must exist now, unless there is some cause which as it were creates me afresh at this moment—that is, which preserves me. For it is clear to anyone who attentively considers the nature of time that the same power and action are needed to preserve anything at each individual moment of its duration as would be required to create that thing anew if it were not yet in existence. Hence all there is between preservation and creation is a distinction of reason. (Med 3, CSM 2:33)

Bringing something into existence, on this view, is all of a piece with keeping it in existence; they differ only *ratione*, by reason; more bluntly, they are a single activity described in two ways.

Challenged by Gassendi to justify this, Descartes does not give reasons, but describes his doctrine of 'the continual action of the original cause' as 'something which all metaphysicians affirm as a manifest truth' (Rep 5, CSM 2:254). Although it was indeed a commonplace that the created world remains in existence only with God's concurrence, I do not think it was so widely believed that this concurrence is metaphysically on a par with creation *ex nihilo*; and I doubt if any previous philosopher claimed to base this on an insight into 'the nature of time'. Descartes keeps saying this, evidently feeling a metaphysical push as well as a theological pull towards the view that created things have to be kept in existence. The push is what is philosophically interesting. Descartes writes:

The nature of time is such that its parts are not mutually dependent, and never coexist. Thus, from the fact that we now exist it does not follow that we shall exist a moment from now, unless there is some cause—the same cause that originally produced us—which continually reproduces us, as it were, i.e. which keeps us in existence. (PP 1:21)[4]

Responding to Gassendi's protest that the parts of time are paradigms of inseparability and thus mutual dependence, Descartes writes:

----

[4] See also Rep 2, CSM 2:116 (axiom 2); Rep 1, CSM 2:78–9.

The issue does not concern the necessary connection which exists between the divisions of time considered in the abstract. We are considering the time or duration of the thing which endures, and here you would not deny that the individual moments can be separated from those immediately preceding and succeeding them, which implies that the thing which endures may cease to be at any given moment. (Rep 5, CSM 2:255)

This fits with Descartes's use in *PP* 1:21 of the phrase 'the nature of time or of the duration of things'. His premiss, it seems, does not concern time as such.

Rather, he is inviting us to think about some one object—it could be a mind or a body—considered as existing at T_1, and about that same object considered as existing at a later time T_2. We need not suppose that the object has distinct temporal parts; we merely think about x-as-it-is-at-T_1 as a reality (call it Early), and x-as-it-is-at-T_2 as a reality (call it Late). Then we are invited to conceive (if we can) of Early's existing and Late's not doing so—that is, to conceive of the body's existing at T_1 and not at T_2. This turns out to be easy to do; as Hume was to see later, it is always conceivable that any story about how the world develops should swerve or even be cut off altogether (§265).

However, to infer from this that Early does not cause Late, one would need the premiss that causal necessity is absolute (logical) necessity; and there is no evidence that Descartes accepted this. So we need to look further if we are to understand his acceptance of his non-endurance principle.

In an instructive paper, Jorge Secada (1990: 45–52) contends that the principle comes from the thesis that causal influence cannot stretch across time, because there cannot be action at a temporal distance: if e_1 occurs at T_1, and if e_2 occurs at a different time T_2, then the two events are separated in time, so that one could not cause the other. This was fairly common property; Aquinas and other scholastic philosophers accepted it, for example, and so did Descartes: 'The concept of a cause is, strictly speaking, applicable only for as long as the cause is producing its effect, and so it is not prior to it' (Rep 1, CSM 2:78). This, Secada proposes, could be a general thesis of which a special case is that a thing's existing at one time could not cause its existing at another.

This interpretation has two drawbacks. One is that it ignores the theme of separateness or independence that pervades these texts. 'Time's parts are not mutually dependent and never coexist'; 'There is no dependence between the present time and the immediately preceding time'; 'The divisions of time are separable from each other'; 'The individual moments can be separated from those immediately preceding and succeeding them'. Hammering at this theme is an odd way to make a point about action at a temporal distance. Secondly, on Secada's interpretation the non-endurance doctrine concerns causation in general; yet Descartes states it always and only in terms of things' *existence*. The doctrine does (we shall see) imply things about causation generally; but Descartes never mentions those, and was evidently unaware of them.

Conversations with Michael Murray and James Petrik have helped me to a possibly better understanding of the non-endurance doctrine. Without knowing exactly what the status is of Early and Late, we discover by attending to 'the

nature of time' that Early could exist without Late's doing so. From this
Descartes would infer, using the logic that underlies the separability argument
(§31), that Early and Late are *distinct things*, *distinct realities*, one of which starts
to exist at T_2. So the occurrence of Late is the coming into existence of something substantial that is distinct from anything that existed previously. What we
think of as the continual preservation of things through time, therefore, is really
the continual creation of successors to them; and Descartes presumably thought
that only God has the power needed for such work. This rationale for the non-
endurance doctrine has neither of the drawbacks of Secada's.

From the doctrine as thus understood it follows that, strictly speaking, God is
the only enduring substance; and Descartes ought to hold that what we call a single enduring mind or body is really a series of ontologically distinct things which
compose a kind of pseudo-substance because of their qualitative and spatio-
temporal continuity. I accept this, and affirm that Descartes ought to have
accepted it. Probably he did not, though we should recall his saying in *PP* 1:51
that 'The term "substance" does not apply univocally to God and to other things;
that is, there is no clearly intelligible meaning of the term which is common to
God and his creatures'. His reason for this was not the one I find in the non-
endurance doctrine; still, it shows him as willing to agree that created things are
'substances' only in some second-grade sense of the word.

It is tempting—and it used to be common—to associate Descartes's non-
endurance doctrine with the view that time is granular. My seventy years are
composed of a finite number of temporal atoms, each with an extent, but not
made up of shorter intervals; and my existence through that period is really the
successive existence of a finite number of things each of which lasts for one atom
of time. That view of time is not needed for the non-endurance doctrine, however, and Secada argues convincingly that Descartes did not accept it.

The non-endurance doctrine has a sting in its tail. Although it initially concerns the cause of things' continued *existence*—thus the texts, thus our interpretation—it seems to imply that the cause of *any* fact about how a thing is at time
T must exist or occur at T. Descartes's contemporary Louis de La Forge
explained why:

There is no creature, spiritual or corporeal, that can change [the position of a body] or
that of any of its parts in the second instant of its creation if the creator does not do it himself, since it is he who had produced this part of matter in place A. For example, not only
is it necessary that he continue to produce it if he wants it to continue to exist, but also,
since he cannot create it everywhere, nor can he create it outside of every place, he must
himself put it in place B, if he wants it there, for if he were to have put it somewhere else,
there is no force capable of removing it from there. (Quoted in Garber 1992: 300–1)

Garber comments: 'The argument goes from the doctrine of continual recreation, authentically Cartesian, to the conclusion that only God can be the cause
of motion in the world. When God sustains a body, he must sustain it *somewhere*,
and in sustaining it where he does, he causes it to move or be at rest.' The argu-

ment seems cogent. I am also convinced by (Kemp) Smith's version of it, including this: 'Even though bodies could act on one another, as they do not persist they cannot be the effects of other things, save as these are recognized by God in their recreation' (Smith 1902: 73–4; he switched to 'Kemp Smith' when he married Miss Kemp).

So Descartes has unknowingly implied that no event causes anything to obtain at any later time, and that genuine causation operates not horizontally along the time line but vertically from God down to the world at each moment. Thus Kemp Smith (1952: 218): 'God, in His recreation of things, has to be regarded as continuously modifying them in an orderly fashion—the fixed, though for our understanding arbitrary modes in which He acts, in the realization of this order, being what we entitle the laws of nature.'

38. Body on body

This combines smoothly with Descartes's physics. The loop theory part of it, if it is causal at all, involves synchronous causation, so the non-endurance doctrine is irrelevant to it. As for diachronic causation—that is, collision theory—Descartes's position is purely occasionalist: the appearance of causal action of bodies on other bodies is due solely to the continuing intervention of God. Collisions follow dependably regular patterns, which are characterized in the 'laws of nature'; but these 'laws' are not causally explanatory, Descartes holds, because the pairs of events which they connect are not strictly cause–effect ones. Descartes often describes collisions as 'causes' of subsequent events; but he means this as (Humean) vernacular, not serious metaphysics. In such a case, he holds, the whole truth of the matter is this: two bodies collided, then the second one began to move, and this pair of events conforms to a regularity which God established throughout the corporeal world. He ought really to say that the collision merely 'quasi-causes' the body to move, meaning that it seems to cause it, but does not really.

Leave God out of it, and the picture resembles Hume's (§270). But where Hume usually seems content to accept the given regularities as basic, thus founding his picture of the world on a great brute fact, Descartes seeks to explain them by invoking the God in whom Hume did not believe; only then, for Descartes, does real causality within the material world begin.

And end! Descartes has no account of what God's causality consists in, or how he exercises it. We should expect this, however: philosophical theologians normally excuse God's activities from rigorous conceptual inquiry, and do not ask what goes on when he causes something to happen. When God does something according to a Christian philosopher, he just *does* it—'without ways or means', as Leibniz said in a different context. So the attribution of causal power to God throws no Cartesian light on the nature of causation as such.

I have been presenting a view of Descartes's position on body–body causation which I share with Garber and others, but not with every Descartes scholar. Some have been dissuaded from accepting this occasionalist reading of Descartes by his never openly announcing that bodies do not really act upon bodies, and by his frequent use of language suggesting that they do. Neither fact carries much weight, however, given the patent fact that Descartes had no convinced, grounded thoughts about what causation is—a fact which impoverishes the debates over what scope he accords the causal relation.

If he did have a theory about the nature of causation, it might give him grounds for thinking that bodies *cannot* act upon one another, which would force him into occasionalism about inter-body transactions. Someone influenced by the Aristotelian idea that form/matter aligns with active/passive might conclude that all material things are passive, and thus incapable of affecting anything else. Or this conclusion might be reached from the premiss, accepted by Reid and Berkeley, that only a thinking agent could possibly be a cause (§221). Descartes, however, never said that (1) bodies are not metaphysically up to the job of acting on other bodies, let alone that (2) they could not have powers to affect anything. Garber credits him with 1 and criticizes him for stopping short of 2 by allowing that bodies can act on minds (1993b: 20). He asserts that 2 'follows from' 1, but does not explain or defend this. Anyway, Garber seems to be wrong about 1. He does not cite, and I cannot find, any evidence of Descartes holding that bodies *cannot* act upon other bodies; he merely holds that they do not.

But why? One might think that Descartes accepts occasionalism about the interactions of bodies because he wants, as a matter of theology or piety, to maintain that God ultimately brings about whatever happens in the world of matter. But could he not buy that at a cheaper price? Many philosophers have given God the ultimate credit for whatever happens, while also allowing real causal power to bodies. They credit God with giving bodies the power to affect other bodies: God brings it about that F collisions have G upshots *by* bringing it about that F collisions have an intrinsic power to cause G movements. According to this metaphysic, it is a third item, God, that makes the relation hold between the two, but the relation itself is truly dyadic, not a disguised triadic one.

At the end of a long footnote, Hume comments elegantly on the difference between that metaphysic and Descartes's:

I must confess that there is something in the fate of opinions a little extraordinary. Descartes insinuated that doctrine of the universal and sole efficacy of the Deity, without insisting on it. Malebranche and other Cartesians made it the foundation of all their philosophy. It had, however, no authority in England. Locke, Clarke and Cudworth never so much as take notice of it, but suppose all along that matter has a real though subordinate and derived power. By what means has it become so prevalent among our modern metaphysicians? (*Enquiry* vii.1, 57n.)

This is a wry comment on the link between metaphysical fashion and geography. Hume might also have remarked on the instability of the concept of 'a real though subordinate and derived power'—the problem of making clear how it is subordinate while still making it real. Friends of this concept must say that although God conferred the power in the first place and could strip it off at will, its reality consists in the fact that the owner of the power would cause its effect even if there were no God. Can theistic philosophers in the Christian tradition accept this?

If Descartes wants the ultimate agency to be God's, therefore, it might be better for him to resort to occasionalism rather than postulating real derived powers. I have no evidence, though, that this was his operative reason.

His occasionalism seems to be merely an opportunistic improvisation, devised to let him ground his physics in his theology. (The transparency of this motivation is the main evidence that he was indeed an occasionalist about interrelations among bodies.) Descartes wants his physics to come from deeper theses which stand to reason and can be known a priori; not making the physics itself a priori knowable, but making it traceable in an intelligible manner to a demonstrated foundation—the existence of an unchanging God. This entails that there is some true physics which reports the material world as highly and dependably regular, and Descartes thinks that it also entails some of its content. Now, the regularity of God's conduct cannot yield a regular material world unless what happens in that world is God's work. So:

God, who is unchanging, always acts in the same way. . . . I shall set out two or three of the principal rules according to which it must be thought that God causes the nature of this new world to operate. These will suffice to acquaint you with all the others. (W 7, CSM 1:93)

These two rules follow manifestly from the mere fact that God is unchanging and that, acting always in the same way, he always produces the same effect. For, supposing that God placed a certain quantity of motion in all matter in general from the first instant he created it, we must either admit that he always preserves the same amount of motion in it, or not believe that he always acts in the same way. (CSM 1:96)

If Descartes resorted instead to real, though derived, powers, God's unchangingness would not be helpful. He would instead have to claim to know that God *likes* regularity and can be depended upon to endow bodies with powers whose exercise will produce regularities. But Descartes is passionately agnostic about God's preferences and values, and thinks it impertinent and intrusive even to speculate about them. So he needs outright occasionalism if he is to anchor physics in theology. (For a dissenting view see Della Rocca 1999.)

39. Mind on body

Descartes's only attempt to explain what it is for God to cause something is by comparing it with the action of our minds on our bodies:

Although I do not think that any mode of action belongs univocally to both God and his creatures, still I avow that I can find no idea in my mind to represent how God or an angel can move matter except the one which shows me how I am conscious that I can move my body by my thought. (CSMK 375)

This tells us nothing about God's causality, because Descartes does not explain how I can move my body by my thought. When asked about that, he bristles: 'This is one of those self-evident things which we only make obscure when we try to explain them in terms of other things' (CSMK 358). So he invites us to think about God's causality by comparing it with something that is not explained at all, only experienced. Worse, Descartes tells us that this comparison is not literally correct! The word 'univocally' belongs to semantics, and means 'unambiguously'; so when Descartes says that no mode of action belongs *univoce* to God and his creatures, he had better mean that no *description of* modes of action does so—in the spirit of the Thomist maxim that nothing can be predicated univocally of God and man.

Still, that comparison with the actions of our minds on our bodies, though it throws no light on divine activity, does ram home the lesson that Descartes regards the former as the real thing and not as mere quasi-causation. As he wrote to Arnauld: 'That the mind, which is incorporeal, can set the body in motion is something which is shown to us not by any reasoning or comparison with other matters, but by the surest and plainest everyday experience. It is one of those self-evident things' etc. (CSMK 358).

Descartes admits that he has nothing to say about how minds move bodies. I shall briefly explain a theory of his which some have wrongly thought to contribute to this topic. According to him, interaction takes place in the pineal gland, and involves some matter called 'animal spirits'. For example, 'The parts of the blood which penetrate as far as the brain serve . . . primarily to produce in it . . . a very lively and pure flame, which is called the "animal spirits"' (1633, CSM 1:100). 'These parts of the blood make up a kind of air or very fine wind which is called the "animal spirits". These dilate the brain and make it ready to receive impressions both from external objects and from the soul; and in receiving these impressions the brain acts as the organ or seat of the common sense, the imagination and the memory. Next, this same air or these same spirits flow from the brain through the nerves into all the muscles' (1648c, CSM 1:316; see also *Passions* 102).

The 'animal spirits' are portions of matter which enter into quasi-causal relations with other portions of matter in accordance with the laws of physics. The animal spirits 'dilate the brain'; a certain thought 'forms an impression in the brain which directs the animal spirits through the nerves', and so on. Descartes describes a conflict which can occur because 'the little gland in the middle of the brain can be pushed to one side by the soul and to the other side by the animal spirits (which, as I said above, are nothing but bodies), and these two impulses often happen to be opposed' (*Passions* 47). Through all these passages the animal spirits serve as the body's hydraulic system, in Bernard Williams's phrase. This is how Spinoza understood them (see *Ethics* 5, preface). Thus understood, the 'animal spirits' concept goes back at least to the fourteenth century. (See *OED*, 'spirit', sense 16.)

I emphasize this because a dualist worried about how minds and bodies can interact might assign to animal spirits a different role: namely, that of *intermediary*. They can mediate between mind and body because (so the thought goes) although they are matter, they hover on the edge of being non-matter because they are so fine, rarefied, ethereal. This discreditable view has been attributed to Descartes:

How is this utterly insubstantial 'thinking substance' to have any influence on ponderous matter? How can two such very different things be in causal contact? Descartes proposed a very subtle material substance—'animal spirits'—to convey the mind's influence to the body in general. But this does not provide us with a solution. (Churchland 1984: 9)

Nor did Descartes think that it does. Indeed, I have not found any philosopher assenting to this disgraceful view, yet it was sometimes mentioned as though it had adherents. Boyle (1666: 56) attributes something like it to the Peripatetics, accusing them of postulating a process of 'refining or subtiliating some parts of matter into form', which is at least *like* subtiliating them into mind. And Locke, writing about dividing up of a portion of matter 'into as minute parts as you will', says that 'we are apt to imagine [this to be] a sort of spiritualizing, or making a thinking thing of it' (*Essay* 632:33). Also in Donne's great poem 'The Ecstasy' we find:

> As blood labours to beget
> Spirits as like souls as it can,
> Because such fingers need to knit
> The subtle knot that makes us man . . .

This alludes to animal spirits, and understands them as intended to be, though material, more like minds than most matter is, and thus as fitted to mediate causally between matter and mind. Who held this view, I do not know; but Descartes did not.

40. Psychology's invasion of physics

It is often remarked that if Descartes allows minds to move bodies, this compromises the integrity or the completeness of his physics. If an act of my will can affect how a body moves, then either I can cause an infringement of a law of physics, or the laws of physics do not cover all the territory—they leave predictive gaps, or their antecedents are tacitly qualified by a rider of the form 'unless some mind can influence the bodies in question'.

Plausible thought: 'Descartes should shrink from this consequence, and thus be scared off from allowing real action of mind on body.' Plausible, but twice wrong. The consequence does not come from the premiss that there is *real* causal action of mind on body; it would follow just as well if there were *quasi*-causation. Suppose the latter were the case: how a certain body moves depends upon what happens in my mind, because God sees to it that certain bodily events correlate in various ways with certain mental events. Physics is still compromised. The trouble for physics comes from the existence of the pattern in events, whatever its metaphysical underlay is.

Also, rather than shrinking from the consequence, Descartes trumpets it, using it to solve his version of the other minds problem. A perfect physical replica of a mentally endowed human being, he maintains, if left to conduct itself purely in accordance with the laws of physics, will replicate only some of the behaviour of its original. It will not be able to match the complexity of our whole range of behaviour, especially our linguistic behaviour, which requires input from the mind; and that is how each of us can know that other humans have minds. In §49 I shall examine his reason for this; what matters now is just the fact. (See Rep 4, CSM 2:161; *Passions* 6, 16.) Descartes knew he was allowing psychology to intrude into physics:

God's perfection involves not only his being unchanging in himself but also his operating in a manner that is always utterly constant and unchanging. Now there are some changes whose occurrence is guaranteed either by our own plain experience or by divine revelation, and either our perception or our faith shows us that these take place without any change in the creator; but apart from these we should not suppose that any other changes occur in God's works, in case this suggests some inconstancy in God. (PP 2:36, CSM 1:240)

The crucial phrases are 'our own plain experience or . . . divine revelation' and 'our perception or our faith'—each referring to our experience of our mental control over our bodily movements and to miracles which religion requires us to believe in. Without calling the action of mind on body 'miraculous', Descartes rightly sees it as relating to physics as miracles do. He is oddly serene about this, given how he values the supposed purity, unity, and conceptual parsimony of his physics. This is a fact about him which we must simply accept.

A view about psychology and physics which Descartes never expressed has often been attributed to him on the credit of Leibniz:

Descartes recognized that souls can never give force to bodies because there is always the same quantity of force in matter. He believed, though, that the soul could change the directions of bodies. But that was because in his day the law of nature which maintains the conservation of the same total direction in matter was unknown. (Mon 80, FW 279)

Leibniz wrote something similar to Arnauld. At *NE* 224, on the other hand, he attributes this view not to Descartes but—perhaps correctly—to 'the Cartesians'. He envisages Cartesian physics as containing a gap; its conservation laws leave open questions about the future direction of a moving body, so without interfering with those laws a mind could step in and alter the direction. Any physicist who knew that his system was like this would want to fix it, rather than complacently leaving such a gap to be filled mentalistically! Remnant (1979) reports that there is no evidence that Descartes was such a one.

41. Body on mind: sense perception

After body-on-body and mind-on-body, there remains body-on-mind. After colli-sions and gestures, there is perception. Sometimes, at least, Descartes thought of this as involving the action of body on mind. Twice in the *Rules* and once in the *Meditations* he says that in sense perception the mind is at least partly 'passive', which should be a causal term;[5] and in a passage in the Second Replies, quoted in §34, he insists that we can draw conclusions about our material environment from premises about our sensory states only by relying on the principle that 'every idea must have a really existing cause of its representative reality'. Garber (1993b) argues that Descartes tried in his later years to avoid implying that bod-ies influence the mind. Perhaps he did, though he never hints that general con-ditionals running from body to mind are kept true by the uniformity of God's operations, which is what he repeatedly says about conditionals from body to body. Anyway, it matters little. Because Descartes had no considered general the-ory about what causation is, there is little at stake when he considers whether this or that conjunction of events is causal.

In his treatments of sense perception, mainly in *Rules* 12 and *Optics* 4, Descartes's language is causal, but the energy goes elsewhere. He is fending off trope transfer, whether within the physical part of the story or between that and the mental part; but he is not thinking urgently about whether bodies can act on minds or, if they can, how. His position fits what Leibniz wrote about 'the new Cartesians' in his fifth letter to Clarke:

I do not assent to the vulgar notions that the images of things are conveyed by the organs of sense to the soul. For it is not conceivable by what passage, or by what means of con-veyance, these images can be carried from the organ to the soul. This vulgar notion in philosophy is not intelligible, as the new Cartesians have sufficiently shown. It cannot be explained how immaterial substance is affected by matter, and to maintain an unintelli-gible notion about this is having recourse to the scholastic notion of I know not what inexplicable 'intentional species' passing from the organs to the soul. Those Cartesians saw the difficulty, but they could not explain it. (L 710)

Leibniz's famous metaphor about shut windows was anticipated in Descartes's remark to Burman: 'The difference between perception and imagination is . . . that in perception the images are imprinted by external objects which are actu-ally present, whilst in imagination the images are imprinted by the mind without any external objects, and with the windows shut, as it were' (CSMK 345). But

---

[5] *Rules* 12, CSM 1:40, 42; Med 6, CSM 2:55. Perhaps, though, it was not sternly causal for Descartes. See his 1641 letter to Regius, CSMK 199.

when the 'windows' are 'open', that is not so that species or tropes can enter; Descartes is firm about that, as we shall see. (I have been helped with Descartes's treatment of sense perception by Wolf-Devine 1993: 1–26.)

The best place to start is *Rules* 12, where Descartes first wrote down his views about what happens when we sense things outside us. It contains strange and puzzling doctrine, but some themes emerge clearly.

First, there is no trope transfer. In sense perception the perceived body affects the sentient's mind by affecting his body, doing so through touch. What touches the perceiver's body in vision is not the perceived body but rather particles belonging to a loop to which the body also belongs. Still, the core transaction between what is perceived and the perceiver's body is one of impact:

Sense-perception occurs in the same way in which wax takes on an impression from a seal. This is not a mere analogy: The external shape of the perceiver's body is really changed by the object in exactly the way that the shape of the wax's surface is altered by the seal. This holds not only when we feel some body as having a shape, as being hard or rough to the touch etc., but also when we have a tactile perception of heat or cold and the like. (*Rules* 12, CSM 1:40, slightly streamlined)

The impress of a seal on wax is a special kind of collision, which some would understand in terms of trope transfer; but Descartes is laying the groundwork for an account of sense perception in which trope transfer has no place.

In his main other short discussion of these matters (1637*b*, CSM 1:164–6), written perhaps a decade later, Descartes denies that when something is perceived, there must be something *like* it in the brain. (He does not relate this resemblance story to the trope one.) The resemblance assumption is made, Descartes says, by 'the philosophers', who hold that thoughts about things involve images which resemble things:

Their sole reason for positing such images was that they saw how easily a picture can stimulate our mind to conceive the objects depicted in it, and so it seemed to them that in the same way the mind must be stimulated by little pictures formed in our head to conceive the objects that affect our senses. We should, however, recall that our mind can be stimulated by many things other than images—by signs and words, for example, which in no way resemble the things they signify. (CSM 1:165)

The 'images' to which Descartes refers occur in the corporeal imagination; we are not yet talking about how *ideas*—which are mental—can represent things outside us. Descartes has little if any theory about that. Not infrequently he writes as though he equated an idea's veridicality with its resemblance to its object (CSM 2:25–7, 56–7), but I agree with Margaret Wilson (1994) that these passages reflect verbal habits, not considered doctrine. They are signs of Descartes's having no considered view about what makes mental representation possible. Do not be misled by the above remark about 'signs and words' or this: 'Although everyone is commonly convinced that the ideas we have in our mind are wholly similar to the objects from which they proceed, . . . I note many observations which should make us doubt this. Words . . . bear no resemblance to the things they signify, and yet they make us think of these things' (*W* 1, CSM 1:81). Descartes is making an excellent negative point: the word *carré* is not square, so why must an of-a-square idea be square? It is overloading the text to see him, as does Gaukroger (1995: 284), as announcing a positive theory of mental representation in which it is likened to linguistic meaning.

Although mental items are essential in Descartes's account of perception, he says little about how they fit. He writes:

The power through which we know things in the strict sense is purely spiritual, and is no less distinct from the whole body than blood is from bone, or the hand from the eye. It is one single power, whether it receives figures from the common sense at the same time as does the corporeal imagination, or applies itself to those which are preserved in the memory, or forms new ones . . . In all these functions the cognitive power is sometimes passive, sometimes active; sometimes resembling the seal, sometimes the wax. But this should be understood merely as an analogy, for nothing quite like this power is to be found in corporeal things. (CSM 1:42)

So the mind is sometimes active (the seal) and sometimes passive (the wax). Either way, its intercourse with the brain cannot be illustrated by examples from the material world, where 'nothing quite like this' can be found. Descartes is strikingly incurious about this last stage in the causal or quasi-causal chain from the outer object to my sensory awareness of it. Locke inherited all this from him, except for the apparent complacency about the final stage, which 'I can resolve only into the good pleasure of God, whose ways are past finding out' (§192). This is no advance on Descartes, but it does at least acknowledge a problem. Locke would have been made aware of the latter through having some interest in the nature of causation as such, whereas Descartes evidently had none.

42. Mind on mind

One might have expected Descartes to say that the signals from the various senses have their separate effects on the immaterial mind, and that the mind then integrates them into a coherent, unified world picture; but that is not what he says. As Cottingham points out (1993: 38), Descartes postulates a *material* 'common sense', located in the pineal gland, thus assigning the co-ordinating and unifying aspects of the life of the mind to the underlying brain events. For all the later emphasis on the mind, Descartes seems in his detailed theory of perception to let the mind function as little more than a passive taker-in and recorder of information that has been assembled and organized by the brain. The mind's role in this seems to be less complex even than the role of a mirror in reflection. With a mirror there can at least be variations depending on whether the mirror is scratched, or curved, or at an angle to the line of sight, and so on; but Descartes mentions nothing analogous to that for the mind's part in sense perception.

A vivid illustration of this aspect of his thought occurs in a letter to Mersenne. In a preceding letter he has written of *The World* as in progress and nearly complete: 'It only remains for me to add something concerning the nature of man.' Now he returns to this: 'My discussion of man in *The World* will be a little fuller than I had intended, for I have undertaken to explain all the main functions in man. I have already written of the vital functions . . . and the five senses. I am now dissecting the heads of various animals, so that I can explain what imagination, memory etc. consist in' (CSMK 40). There is not a word here about the rational soul. It is not surprising that *The World* was planned as a work about matter and not mind; but it is surprising that Descartes believed that without bringing in thought he could do so much psychology.

This is part of a wider intellectual Gestalt. Up until now I have gone along with Descartes in handling issues about the scope of causation in three parts: collisions, gestures, and perception. But dualism gives us four pairs: the topic that we have omitted is the action of the mind on the mind—the causality that is involved when an individual mind goes through changes of state. Descartes's relative silence about this is evidence that he did not take seriously enough his own doctrine that a mind is a substance, which should mean that it is a richly qualitied thing whose powers and activities are causal upshots of what it does and of what happens to it. He would say that lead is malleable and stone frangible because of their inner natures; these surface differences are ultimately explicable, he holds, by the application of causal laws to the micro-structures of these materials. But he says nothing analogous to this about the powers of minds. His conception of the mind as a substance is metaphysically thin: it does not include any working thought of an inner nature governed by causal laws.

He may have been discouraged from taking seriously the idea of the mind's intrinsic nature by his view that minds are simple, lack parts (§27). This is not in fact an obstacle, however. All he needs is for the mind to be qualitatively complex in ways that bring it under various laws of mental unfolding; one could get this through the kind of structure that requires parts, but it could be had in other ways instead. Leibniz believed in minds that are simple (in the part/whole sense) yet qualitatively extremely rich, and also law-governed; and no one has thought this to be an inconsistency.

Descartes does write about dramatic happenings in the mind:

Although probable conjectures may pull me in one direction, the mere knowledge that they are simply conjectures, and not certain and indubitable reasons, is itself quite enough to push my assent the other way. . . . The mere fact that I [recently] found that all my previous beliefs were in some sense open to doubt was enough to turn my absolutely confident belief in their truth into the supposition that they were wholly false. (Med 4, CSM 2:41)

But this drama is not accompanied by any pointer to there being some backstage reality, some intrinsic nature, which makes it happen.

Descartes's picture of the mind is thin because his thoughts about minds are wedded to his thoughts about himself as known introspectively. For him, the whole mind is on-stage. We have seen him define mentality in terms of self-awareness, and have noted his bent for methodological solipsism—the stance in which he does most of his philosophy of mind. It prevents him from confronting himself as a studiable object: because he is the frame of his picture, he cannot be *in* it. This may be what Bréhier means when he writes (1937: 56): 'Condillac censured Descartes for knowing neither the origin of our ideas nor how they are generated. They did not concern Descartes, and the *intellectus* was to him not a reality to be explained but a point of departure and a fulcrum.' This, so far as I understand it, seems to me right.

Consider, for example, Descartes's doctrine that each mind is infallible and omniscient about its own current activities. If this self-knowledge were a kind of introspection—a looking inward—it would have to involve some kind of mental device or mechanism; there would have to be a *how* regarding it; and that would open the door to the possibility of malfunction, and thus of a mind's being wrong or ignorant about some event that is now occurring in it. Even without knowing what the mental mechanism is, the mere admission that there is one would force Descartes to admit that it could break down, resulting in my being ignorant or in error about something that is happening in my mind. In ruling out such mishaps, he takes self-knowledge out of any comparison with the outer senses, treating it as magic rather than as the exercise of powers that supervene on structure.

When he tries to explain self-knowledge, it is in terms not of causation, but of identity. Speaking of 'willing something' and 'the perception of such willing', he says that 'this perception is really one and the same thing as the volition' (*Passions* 19, CSM 1:335–6; see also CSMK 172). This keeps malfunction at bay by denying that there is any function: when a volition occurs, there is a perception of it; and this is guaranteed in the same way as the great truth that where Ulysses is found, there is Odysseus. This indefensible account of self-awareness shows Descartes keeping at bay any rich thought about the mind's nature and supervening powers.

Objection: 'This is unfair. Descartes does not say what minds are intrinsically like because he knows that he does not know what they are like. In not pretending to have a causal theory of the mind, he is merely being honest.' Not so. Descartes affirms that he knows his mind better than he does any body: 'Our knowledge of our thought is prior to, and more certain than, our knowledge of any corporeal thing; for we have already perceived it, although we are still in doubt about other things,' and he offers this as the key to 'discovering the nature of the mind' (*PP* 1:8). He does not make clear how it can be the key to that; and when he returns to the topic three sections later, he throws little light on it.

However, we get a glimmering when we read this part of a reply to Gassendi: 'I am surprised that you should say that all my considerations about the wax demonstrate that I distinctly know that I exist, but not that I know what I am or what my nature is; for one thing cannot be demonstrated without the other' (Rep 5, CSM 2:248–9). This is odd. I can know that my computer exists without knowing what its 'nature' is in any but the most superficial sense; similarly with knowing that my brain exists, and that quasars do. Why should Descartes think otherwise about the mind?

He continues with a different claim: namely, that my knowledge of the nature of my own mind is guaranteed by my knowledge not of my mind's existence but rather of the nature of wax! We can know that the wax is white, hard, and meltable, he writes:

And there are correspondingly many attributes in the mind: one, that it has the power of knowing the whiteness of the wax; two, that it has the power of knowing its hardness; three, that it has the power of knowing that it can lose its hardness (i.e. melt), and so on. . . . [So] we know more attributes in the case of our mind than we do in the case of anything else. For no matter how many attributes we recognize in any given thing, we can always list a corresponding number of attributes in the mind which it has in virtue of knowing the attributes of the thing; and hence the nature of the mind is the one we know best of all. (Rep 5, CSM 2:249)

This, the strongest claim Descartes makes about the known nature of the mind, is doubly weak. These discoveries are only of particular facts: my mind was able at that moment to know the whiteness of that wax. No basis is laid for attributing to the mind durable 'powers' or durable structures that would support them. Also, even if we did know such general conditionals about our minds, they would concern only how the mind can relate to other things. No heaping up of them can inform us about the mind's intrinsic nature. Compare learning of a rubber ball that it can bounce on concrete, on wood, on iron, on glass, etc. Adding to the list will not enrich our knowledge of the ball, because it will not tell us what is going on, at the microscopic level where the real causes operate, in any one bounce. That Descartes could be satisfied with his account of our knowledge of our minds' powers is evidence of how poor a conception he has of the substantial mind. This is the writing of a man for whom the mind is all surface.

In the fine passage to which Descartes is replying, Gassendi has made it quite clear that his topic is not the random amassing of particular surface conditionals about the mind, but rather an inquiry into its intrinsic nature:

You should carefully scrutinize yourself and subject yourself to a kind of chemical investigation, so to speak [labore quodam quasi chymico], if you are to succeed in uncovering and explaining to us your internal substance. If you provide such an explanation, we shall ourselves be doubtless able to investigate whether you are better known than [a human] body, whose nature we know so much about through anatomy, chemistry, and so many other sciences, so many senses and so many experiments. (Obj 5, CSM 2:193*)

Faced with this, how could Descartes so comprehensively miss the point? Here is how. A little before the remarks I have quoted, he writes:

Nor do I see what more you expect here, unless it is to be told what colour or smell or taste the human mind has, or the proportions of salt, sulphur and mercury from which it is compounded. You want us, you say, to conduct 'a kind of chemical investigation' [labore quodam chymico] of the mind, as we would of wine. This is worthy . . . of all those who have only a very confused conception of everything, and so do not know the proper questions to ask about each thing.

With his phrase 'a kind of chemical investigation, so to speak' Gassendi sought to express the idea of a mostly hidden structure which is there to be explored. Descartes evades the point by taking Gassendi to have implied that the mind is, literally, a chemical compound. To this end he omits Gassendi's word *quasi* ('so to speak'), which served to introduce chemistry analogically rather than literally. This malpractice is hidden in CSM, which ignores *quasi* in its rendering of what Gassendi originally wrote. Descartes performs so poorly here, I suggest, because he is so far from thinking of the mind as something with an intrinsic nature that might be investigated scientifically.

Chapter 6

Preparing to Approach Spinoza

43. How to read the *Ethics*

Most of what I have to say about Spinoza will be based upon his one indisputable masterpiece, the *Ethics*. This work has five parts, of which I shall concentrate on part 1, concerning general metaphysics, with an emphasis on the extended world; and on part 2, dealing with mentality—which Spinoza calls 'thought'. The early stages of part 3, which investigates the conative side of the human condition, will be my topic in Chapter 11.

The *Ethics* is said to be 'demonstrated in geometrical order', and is indeed presented as a system of axioms and definitions from which theorems are deduced. What did Spinoza expect to achieve by this procedure? And what do his expectations imply for how we should approach the work?

He was evidently trying to evoke Euclid's *Elements*, the most successful axiomatized body of theory that the world had ever seen. A popular and persuasive view of this is that it operates as a 'direct convincer'—something through which one comes to accept a body of doctrine by finding the axioms unassailable and the proofs cogent. But it would be astonishing if Spinoza intended the *Ethics* to work like that upon the reader. Adapting a famous anecdote about Hobbes's discovery of Euclid, imagine someone who, seeing the *Ethics* on a library table, reads Proposition 47 of the Third Book: 'p47: Affects of Hope and Fear cannot be good of themselves.' By God, says he, this is impossible! So he reads the demonstration, which takes him back to 3p27, then back to 2p16, and from there to 1a4: 'The knowledge of an effect depends on and involves the knowledge of the cause.' This, together with the rest of the demonstrative input into 3p47, will not convert him to a belief in the badness of hope, especially if he notices how few of the 'demonstrations' are valid. Spinoza had to know this; he had to be aiming at something different.

Bergson characterized Spinoza's 'geometrical' procedure as 'that complication of machinery, that power to crush which causes the beginner in the presence of the *Ethics* to be struck with admiration and terror' (quoted in Shmueli 1978: 197). Nietzsche, though in a general way an admirer of Spinoza, went even further, alleging personal pathology:

Not to speak of that hocus-pocus of mathematical form in which, as if in iron, Spinoza encased and masked his philosophy . . . so as to strike terror into the heart of any assailant who should happen to glance at that invincible maiden and Pallas Athene—how much personal timidity and vulnerability this masquerade of a sick recluse betrays! (1886: sect 5)

If you think that to be wholly unfair, read Spinoza's correspondence, and observe how he resists opening himself up to criticism and learning from it. To my eye, his surly dismissiveness looks like timidity. Still, his 'demonstrations' are not merely a protective carapace. Although almost none is strictly valid, just as it stands, many have some force; they do show some of Spinoza's doctrines being adduced in support of others, and from this we can learn things about how he thinks his system hangs together. A chart I made showing the deductive ancestry and progeny of each proposition has been useful to me, telling me which parts of Spinoza's system are intended to inform which others. (For further discussion of Spinoza's use of the geometrical method, see Shmueli 1978.)

Nietzsche is certainly right in saying that the deductive apparatus masks Spinoza's philosophy. For certain of his deepest and most central doctrines he offers 'demonstrations' that are unsalvageably invalid and of no philosophical use or interest; it is not credible that he accepts those doctrines because he thinks they follow from the premisses of those arguments.

He accepted them, rather, for the reason that sensible people do accept general propositions—because they explain facts and solve problems. If we are to see Spinoza's doctrines as the live, energetic things they were in his own mind, and not as framed parchments hung on an historical wall, we must see them as *hypotheses to solve problems*. Spinoza was temperamentally inclined to dogmatic confidence in his rightness, which shows in some of his formulations and in his treatment of some of his ablest correspondents. But what substantively happens in his work is, nevertheless, hypothetico-deductive. There is more to be said, much of it well said by Parkinson (1990).

A dominant feature of Spinoza's thought is explanatory rationalism—that is, the view that there are no brute facts, because every coherent why-question has a true and explanatory answer. This might have encouraged him to value his 'geometrical' approach, but it does not justify or fully explain it. I shall return to explanatory rationalism in Chapter 9.

44. Spinoza's dualism

We have seen that Descartes was a 'dualist' in two ways. He held both of these:

Property-dualism: There are just *two* basic conceptually non-overlapping ways of being—namely, thought and extension.

Substance-dualism: The smallest number of substances that it takes to instantiate both thought and extension is *two*.

Spinoza accepted the former. He sharply distinguishes truths that pertain to thought from ones that pertain to extension; which puts him on Descartes's rather than Aristotle's side of that fence. He expresses this position of his by saying that thought and extension are both 'attributes', a technical term that he defines thus: By attribute I understand what the intellect perceives of a substance as constituting its essence' (1d4).

In this definition, though not everywhere in the *Ethics*, Spinoza uses 'essence' in roughly the sense Descartes gave it in writing that 'Each substance has one principal property which constitutes its nature and essence, and to which all its other properties are referred' (*PP* 1:53; see also 51 and 56). Descartes here introduces the concept of a *basic* way that a thing can be—a property of which all the thing's other properties are mere special cases. He uses the word 'essence' in this connection, and Spinoza gives it that sense in 1d4 when explaining 'attribute'.

There is a difference. Whereas Descartes says that each substance has *one* basic principal property, Spinoza allows that a single substance might be of several fundamental kinds. In 1d4 'constituting its essence' could as well be 'constituting an essence of it'. This still leaves Spinoza with a broadly Cartesian concept of essence or basic property, which could be expressed by adapting Descartes:

To each substance there belong principal attributes. . . . Each substance has a set S of essences or principal properties which jointly constitute its nature, and to the members of which all its other properties are referred—meaning that every property of the substance outside S is a special case of some one member of S, and no member of S is a special case of any other member of S.

This implies that each principal property has its own subset of other properties that are 'referred to' it: *each* principal property relates to its determinates in the way that Descartes says that *the* principal property relates to all the other properties of the thing.

In both Descartes and Spinoza, the boundary between thought and extension is impermeable to logic: no inference is valid which runs from premises about one to a conclusion about the other. So we have here a dualism not only of properties but also of concepts. This will become crucially important in §63.

The dualism of properties and concepts that one finds in Spinoza seems to have been deeply ingrained in his mind: he never argues for it, any more than Descartes did. We might see 2p1d as an attempt to prove that thought is an attribute, but considered thus the argument does not work. It amounts to this: 'Particular mental events occur within Nature; so Nature must have some attribute within which they fall; therefore thought is an attribute of Nature.' This assumes that all mental events—thoughts—constitute a natural class, and not a mere rag-bag like the class of Christmas gifts or nuisances; and that there are attributes—that is, that the whole notion of a basic way of being is not a mistake. And even with those two assumptions made, we get only that all thoughts fall under *thought*, and that they fall under an attribute; not that thought is an attribute. Perhaps thought and extension are two special cases of something more basic. Spinoza apparently could not entertain this possibility; for him the status of thought and extension as attributes—basic ways of being—was an unexaminable axiom.

All of that is nearly true, and is the best I can do at this stage. In saying it, I have ignored something I shall confront in §65, namely 1d4's implication that an attribute is not really a Cartesian essence or basic property, but merely what 'intellect perceives as' being such.

We shall find Spinoza saying that the world instantiates 'infinite(ly many) attributes', but I join many scholars in giving little weight to his implication that there are more than two (see Kline 1977). There are two reasons for this: one about the meaning of a word, the other about what happens in Spinoza's writings.

(1) In an argument I shall examine in §45, Spinoza takes 'x has infinite attributes' to entail 'x has all attributes', meaning that x exists in every basic way in which it is possible to exist.[1] In your sense and my sense of 'infinite' this entailment does not hold. Infinitely many whole numbers are even, but not all whole numbers are even. So Spinoza does not mean by 'infinite' what we do, and we need to know how different his meaning is from ours. There are reasons why he might use 'infinite' to mean 'all possible'—meaning that and nothing more. Lacking any developed mathematical theory of infinity, he could steer only by the etymological meaning of the word, namely 'unending'; and he could reasonably construe this not as meaning 'going on without end', but merely as 'not reaching a limit or boundary', where a limit is something that *could be* but *is not* surpassed. This would make 'infinite attributes' mean no more than 'every possible attribute'.

In many cases where Spinoza says there are infinite Fs (an infinity of Fs), he does think that no finite set of Fs exhausts them all. His thought of the extended world as infinite is the thought of it as stretching for ever in all directions. But it could still be that his *basic* 'infinity' thought is an 'all possible' one. In many contexts, if all possible Fs are G, then (in our sense) infinitely many Fs are G. For example, until the nineteenth century, everyone thought that space's being in our sense 'infinite' follows from its not having a boundary.

Spinoza holds that there is a single substance which is the *ens realissimum*, the most real being. One might think he commits himself to that substance's having more than two attributes by this: 'The more reality or being each thing has, the more attributes belong to it' (1p9). And perhaps he does. But his only 'demonstration' of this is the laconic absurdity: 'This is evident from 1d4.' Also, 1p9 is idle; its first appearance is its last, though it may be silently at work in the bizarre final argument for God's existence in 1p11d.

(2) Nowhere in the *Ethics* does the thesis that there are more than two attributes do any work. Apart from the phrase 'infinite attributes', the only indication in that work that there are more than two attributes occurs at the end of 2p7s. Spinoza has been explaining that no facts under thought entail any under extension, or vice versa, and cryptically adds: 'I understand the same concerning other

---

[1] For another instance of Spinoza's taking 'infinite' to entail 'all', see 1p16c1. Also 1p17c2s at CS 426: 'infinitely many things in infinitely many modes, i.e. all things'.

attributes.' He rightly holds that if there are any other attributes, they must be conceptually self-contained (so to speak), otherwise they would not be basic ways of being, which is to say that they would not be attributes. But he does not make anything of this, and the passage does not strenuously imply that there are other attributes. Curley's '*the* other attributes' suggests otherwise; but '*the*' is optional, not being enforced by anything in the Latin. I conclude that if Spinoza thought there are at least three attributes, he does not put that belief to work.

The only place where the question comes up in writings that are certainly his is a pair of letters to friends who asked why we know nothing about the other attributes (letters 64 and 66, Wolf 306–8, 310). Spinoza does not say 'There are only two', and I do not contend that he believed that there are only two. He thought there might be more, so he had to tackle the question of why we know only two. His answer to it is feeble and out of line with the doctrines of the *Ethics*; and it may be noteworthy that in these letters only one sentence outright entails that there are more than two attributes.

The apparently Spinozistic *Short Treatise on God, Man and his Well Being* openly treats the doctrine of God's infinite attributes as entailing that God has more than two; but this treatment belongs to a different world from the *Ethics*:

We find in ourselves something which openly indicates to us not only that there are more [than two attributes], but also that there are infinite perfect attributes which must pertain to this perfect being before it can be called perfect.

And where does this Idea of perfection come from? It cannot come from these two, for two gives only two, not infinitely many. From where, then? Certainly not from me, for then I would have had to be able to give what I did not have. From where else, then, than from the infinite attributes themselves, which tell us that they are, though they so far do not tell us what they are. For only of two do we know what they are. (1661a, CS 64n.)

This is miles away from, and below, the severe epistemology of the *Ethics*. I guess that it represents a misunderstanding by a student copyist of things Spinoza said as a mocking echo of Descartes's saying, of the divine attributes of which he has an idea, that 'the more carefully I concentrate on them, the less possible it seems that they could have originated from me alone' (CSM 2:31). This passage in the *Short Treatise* should be not allowed to infect our understanding of the *Ethics*.

So we can reasonably focus on the two attributes that Spinoza tells us about, and keep our minds open to the possibility that he did not seriously think—and did not take himself to have asserted—that there are others. From now on I shall treat Spinoza as an attribute-dualist, like Descartes.

This dualism is reflected in some structural aspects of the *Ethics*. Part 1 presents Spinoza's most basic and general metaphysic. Although it is basic enough to spread across both attributes, it is weighted towards extension, for a reason I shall explain in §61. Part 2 has as its announced topic 'the human mind', which it reaches in stages. The first nine propositions describe how mentality as such fits into the material world. The next four apply this to human minds and bodies, without describing humans in any detail. Those four propositions say, in effect:

'Whatever humans are like in detail, this much must be true of them just because they are thinking and embodied.' Then the theory of mind is interrupted by a 'physical interlude' (as it has been felicitously called), a set of 'lemmas' and other apparatus through which Spinoza presents a dizzyingly abstract physics and, on the basis of that, an equally abstract biology; the 'individuals' of which he writes are best thought of as organisms. After this he moves into his more detailed account of the human mind in 2p14–49. Spinoza explains why he places the physical interlude just there:

To determine what is the difference between the human mind and the others, and how it surpasses them, we have to . . . know the nature of the human body. . . . In proportion as a body is more capable than others of doing many things at once, and being acted on in many ways at once, so its mind is more capable than others of perceiving many things at once. (2p13s)

He says more to the same effect, all of it contending that the route to understanding human psychology runs through biology.

45. Spinoza's monism

Spinoza says explicitly that property-dualism does not entail substance-dualism: 'Although two attributes may be conceived to be really distinct (i.e. one may be conceived without the aid of other), we still cannot infer from that that they [are attributes of] two different substances' (1p10s). Nor does he endorse either of Descartes's arguments for substance-dualism, which indeed could not have carried weight with him. The separability argument (§§29–31) relies on a thought-experiment of a kind that Spinoza never employs; its first-person emphasis makes it quite foreign to his way of thinking. This cuts him off also from the most plausible way of coming to think that the mind has no parts, from which Descartes had launched the indivisibility argument for substance-dualism (§28). Lacking this first-person emphasis, Spinoza can declare that the human mind 'is not simple, but composed of a great many ideas' (2p15), thus rejecting one premiss of the indivisibility argument. (For more on the mind's non-simplicity, see Della Rocca 1996a: 41–3.)

In fact, not only does Spinoza hold that a single substance can instantiate both thought and extension, he also holds the vastly stronger thesis that there is only one substance altogether—Nature—and that the familiar things we encounter (pebbles and galaxies and gusts of wind) are its *modes*. That is, they are properties of it, or ways that it is.

His official 'demonstration' of this extreme monism runs as follows:

There is a substance that has infinite attributes (1p11).
No two substances can have an attribute in common (1p5).
So there is only one substance (1p14).

Assuming that there could not be a substance with no attributes, this argument is valid if—but only if—'has infinite attributes' entails 'has every possible attribute'. Let us so understand it.

Spinoza reaches the first premiss by a route that I shall discuss in §47. The second premiss has embarrassed his supporters, because his argument for it seems to confine it to substances that have only one attribute each; yet he firmly maintains that one substance has all the attributes. Briefly, the argument says that two substances would have to be distinguished from one another either by their 'affections' or by their attributes. ('Affections' are just modes, accidents, states. Do not confuse the word with 'affect', a term Spinoza uses in *Ethics* 3 to cover emotions and also damaging character-traits such as avarice and alcoholism.) Set aside their affections, and then they must be distinguished by their attributes; so their attributes must be different; so the two substances cannot share an attribute. One may challenge the setting aside of the 'affections', but I discuss that in *Study* and shall not go into it here. Even with that conceded, nothing in the argument rules out there being two extended substances of which one thinks while the other does not—as Leibniz crisply noted in some notes on the *Ethics* (L 198–9). The underlying assumption seems to be that a substance can have only one attribute; yet 1p14d conjoins the conclusion of this very argument with his further thesis that one substance has all the attributes!

Of the various attempts that have been made to uncover a real argument here, the most considerable—in my estimation—is that of Curley (1988: 9–30). Though I respect his ingenious and scholarly exercise, I am not convinced by it. I also hope it is not the whole story. The argument that Curley finds in Spinoza's text works *ad hominem* against Descartes: each premiss is to be accepted purely because Descartes could not have rejected it. I hope Spinoza was hunting for bigger game than that, so that he can interest us as philosophers and not merely as antiquarians.

In my next two chapters I shall present an alternative argument for the thesis that there is only one substance. It is better, philosophically speaking, than Spinoza's official argument; it is also more deeply Spinozistic. It arises from the confluence of two streams of thought. One is monism about *extended* substance. Metaphysical problems about extension, I shall show in §§53–4, pushed Spinoza towards the view that *There is only one extended substance*. He also has a powerful reason for maintaining that *Every thinking thing (every subject of mentalistic properties) is also extended*. From those two propositions, and the assumption that thought and extension are the only attributes, it rigorously follows that there is only one extended substance, which is the ultimate subject of all the thinking that gets done. What if there is a third attribute? In that case, Spinoza's reasons for his second premiss would also yield: *Every thinking and extended thing also has the third attribute*, and the argument would go through as before.

46. Spinoza's pantheism

Spinoza gives the one substance two names, 'Nature' and 'God'. His famous phrase *Deus sive Natura* means 'God, or in other words Nature'. Why does he think that 'God' is a good name for Nature—that is, for the world as a whole?

His position looks like a form of pantheism (everything is God), which seems to be at the opposite pole from atheism (nothing is God). Yet the pantheist and the atheist agree in not drawing a line through reality separating the divine from the not-divine; and this agreement is no small thing. Indeed, Spinoza argues for it in a way that might lead one to suspect that he is really an atheist. In his *Descartes's Principles*, he gives an argument for monotheism: there cannot be as many as two Gods (*DP* 1p11, *CS* 254–5). Nothing like this argument occurs in Descartes's *Principles of Philosophy*, so presumably Spinoza included it because he accepted it. Here it is in my words:

If there are two Gods, then either God A knows about God B or he does not. If he does not, he is not omniscient and so is not a God (in the Christian sense). If he does, then he is partly passive—acted upon—because he is in a state of knowledge of God B which must be caused in him by God B—and so again he is not a Christian God.

This relies on the Christian tradition that God is not acted upon—as in Aquinas's doctrine that God is Pure Act. Many biblical episodes suggest the contrary, but Spinoza holds that these tales should be disregarded as detracting from God's dignity, power, and splendour. Aquinas was also committed to not accepting them as literally true, by his doctrine that nothing is predictable univocally of God and man.

In the argument as I have stated it, B's being a God plays no part. It purports to rule out not only *a God and another God*, but also *a God and another reality*, implying that there could not be an omniscient and purely active God and also something else. Descartes had an answer to that:

All sense-perception involves being acted upon, and this involves dependence on something else. Hence it cannot be supposed that God perceives by means of the senses, but only that he understands and wills. And even his understanding and willing are not distinct operations, as they are with us; rather, there is always a single identical and perfectly simple act by means of which he simultaneously understands, wills and accomplishes everything. (*PP* 1:23, *CSM* 1:201, slightly streamlined)

This may give him a basis upon which to accept the argument against polytheism without being swept on into pantheism; but I wonder what it means. Anyway, Spinoza is evidently unwilling to take this line, for in his *Metaphysical Thoughts*—published as an appendix to the Cartesian work—he says not only that 'God's ideas are not determined, as ours are, by objects placed outside God', but more strongly that 'The objects of God's knowledge are not things outside God'; yet he has said, just before that, that 'God is omniscient' (*CS* 327). Those two claims jointly imply that there is only God, and one of them seems to come straight from the supposed monotheism argument that I have just reported.

Most of those who believe in God and a separate world think of God as acting in that world, for his own purposes, which include the bringing of benefit to humans. I shall use 'Intervention' to name the proposition: *God intervenes in the natural order so as to make things go well for human beings.* We learn much about Spinoza's 'theology' when we grasp his three deepest reasons for rejecting this. They can be found in *Ethics* 1 Appendix, though they operate elsewhere in the work as well.

(1) Spinoza rejects with contempt the thesis that God intervenes in the natural order. Whatever is the case could in principle be rigorously explained, he holds, because everything happens in accordance with strict, necessary laws of nature; but if an extramundane God kept stirring things up, the demands of explanatory rationalism could not be met. People think they can explain things in terms of the will of God, but they deceive themselves; they 'take refuge in the will of God, i.e. the sanctuary of ignorance' (1 Appendix, *CS* 443). Now an Interventionist might say: 'Admittedly, we know little about God's purposes, but he does have them, and they do explain what happens when he interferes. So Intervention need not offend against explanatory rationalism.' This brings us to Spinoza's second objection.

(2) Intervention credits God with acting in the furtherance of purposes, and Spinoza denies that this could happen. His only real argument for this denial in *Ethics* 1 Appendix is mistaken. It turns on this claim: 'This doctrine takes away God's perfection. For if God acts for the sake of an end, he necessarily wants something which he lacks.' Locke took this view of teleology, as did Leibniz; but it is wrong, as can be seen from the fact that one's purpose in acting might be to prevent change rather than to produce it (see Bennett 2001b). Anyway, this flawed argument is mainly aimed *ad hominem* at traditional theists, and can hardly be Spinoza's main reason for denying that God has purposes. That denial must owe more to his identification of God with Nature, and still more to his doubts about the whole concept of purpose (§§83–4).

(3) Spinoza holds that many of the qualities traditionally attributed to God require limitation or finitude of some kind, and are therefore theologically inadmissible. He would include in this the attribution to God of the kind of love of humans that Intervention attributes. 'He who loves God', he said memorably, 'will not try to get God to love him back' (5p19). On this topic he engages in mockery, some of it more funny than fair. He says, for example, that people arrive at their views about divine psychology by modelling it on their own, which is why they attribute to their Gods such disgraceful motivations—greed for power and praise, a wish to 'bind men to them and be held by men in the highest honor'. Of the twists and turns one needs to reconcile Intervention with the observed facts, he observes sardonically that they imply that nature and the Gods are as mad as men are. At the core of all this lies the sober conviction that there is no extramundane God—that the belief in an omnipotent, omniscient, omnipresent *person* is an infantile fantasy.

With these negative claims about God, we should ask whether Spinoza's meta-physic really does include a theology. Does he seriously hold that Nature is God, or is he rather a mealy-mouthed atheist or a mocking one? The German poet Novalis famously described him as 'a man drunk with God'; whereas Arnauld called him 'the most impious and most dangerous man of this century'; and Leibniz, reporting this, adds his own view that Spinoza was indeed an atheist in the sense that 'he did not acknowledge any Providence which distributes good fortune and bad according to what is just' (A 2:2:535). That is true. It is also true that in his detailed work in philosophy Spinoza proceeds as an atheist would. At no stage does he pause to change direction because of some consideration regarding what God wants, or what respect we owe to God, or how much more God knows than we do, or anything like that. Yet he sincerely used 'Deus' as a name for the substance which he also called 'Natura'. I shall explain.

The Christian tradition which largely shaped Spinoza's theological thinking, despite his Jewish upbringing, describes God as infinite, eternal, omniscient, omnipotent, not criticizable by any valid standard, and not acted upon by any-thing else; and Spinoza (reading 'omniscient' in a funny way) held that the nat-ural world satisfies all of these, and that nothing else does. So he identified Nature with God. I think also that he actually *felt* about Nature somewhat the way that many Christians feel about God: awe and reverence and fear and a kind of love. (This is well caught in the closing pages of Isaac Bashevis Singer's beau-tiful story 'The Spinoza of Market Street'.) So his use of 'Deus' should be taken seriously and treated with respect.

Still, the item in question is *the natural world*—in no way personal, an 'it' rather than a 'he'. This creates a problem for translators into English—one which does not arise for any other language that I know of. By using 'he', we suggest that God is a person; if we use 'it', we give the impression that Spinoza constantly nudges us with reminders that God is not a person. The personal pronoun mis-represents his doctrine, the impersonal one his practice.

In his official argument for monism, Spinoza is able to describe the one sub-stance as having 'infinite attributes' purely because he calls it 'God' and brings 'infinite attributes' into his definition of that word. There is a traditional theo-logical reason for this, or at least for including 'has all the attributes' in the definition of 'God'. God was often characterized as the *ens realissimum*, the most real being, the being such that no being could possibly be more real; and one can reasonably interpret this as meaning that God exists in every basic way in which anything could exist, which is to say that God has all the attributes. The one sub-stance's being God, however, plays no part in Spinoza's existence proof for it, as I now show.

47. Spinoza's a priori argument for God's existence

Descartes had revived a notorious a priori argument for God's existence—the one Kant infelicitously called the 'ontological argument'—which Spinoza and Leibniz each took over from him, though with variations. Although the argument as a whole is sterile and boring, one feature of Spinoza's version of it is worth noting.

Possible versions of the a priori argument could be ranked in the following way. At the first level, the argument explicitly includes existence in the definition of 'God' or the specification of the concept of God; I cannot recall anyone's ever advancing it in that form. At the second level, the definition includes something that contains existence under one layer of wrapping: at this level we find Descartes's 'having all perfections', Leibniz's 'having all positive properties', and Norman Malcolm's 'existing necessarily' (in one sense of that phrase), each of which is analysed into ingredients that include existence. A third-level version of the argument would define 'God' in terms of something which unpacks into elements one of which unpacks into elements which include existence; I have no examples of this. Spinoza's version of the argument belongs at the *fourth* level. His definition of 'God' includes 'having infinite attributes', and one might expect existence to be extracted directly from that, as from Descartes's 'having all perfections', putting the argument at the second level. But Spinoza does not argue like that, and indeed his metaphysic would collapse if it classified existence as an attribute. Rather, he defines 'God' as 'a substance having infinite attributes', and then proceeds to unwrap 'substance'. For him the term 'substance' means 'item that is its own cause', which he takes to mean 'item whose existence is absolutely necessary', which contains 'item which exists' in its meaning. So he gets from 'God' to 'existent' through the successive removal of four wrappings—not from God's theological glories, but just from his (or its) status as a substance.

The first link from God to substance hardly needs comment, or the fourth from necessary existence to existence. The two intermediate links remain to be discussed: from substance to 'cause of itself,' and from that to necessary existence.

(1) Spinoza follows a long tradition in taking it that a substance must be independent in some way; and like Descartes he takes this to mean that it must not depend on anything else for its existence. In 1p7d he moves *directly* from 'No substance is caused by anything else' to 'Every substance is the cause of itself'. The suppressed premiss, that everything has a cause, is his version of explanatory rationalism, the doctrine that every Why-question has an answer.

(Spinoza defines 'substance' in 1d3 in terms of conceptual independence, which for him is causal independence. Oddly, he does not argue on this basis that a substance cannot be acted upon from outside itself, and instead 'demonstrates' this in 1p6d: causal connection requires a shared attribute, by 1p5 no two substances share an attribute, so no substance causes any other. Why does he take this argumentative detour? I think he has a general strategy, of which this is a part, of bringing out that his principal results can be defended in more than one way. I shall return to substance and independence in §51.)

(2) Secondly, Spinoza defines 'cause of itself' (1d1) in such a way as to equate 'x is cause of itself' with 'x has a nature which cannot be conceived of except as existing'. The latter phrase does not accurately express his meaning. He means to equate x's being cause of itself with its having a nature which cannot be conceived of except as *instantiated*, or with x's nature's being such that x itself cannot be conceived of except as existing. In other words, x is of a kind such that there absolutely must be something of that kind. A thing that is self-caused in that sense must exist; so it does exist; QED.

Like some of his contemporaries, Spinoza thought that he could also express this by saying 'x's essence involves existence'. This formulation, though popular among friends of the a priori argument, is a broken reed. In the only relevant sense of 'essence' that anyone understands, to call a property P 'essential to x' is to say that x has P at every world at which x exists. So *existence belongs to the essence of everything*! It is trivially true that everything—including the fattest unicorn, the fountain of youth, and Zeus—exists at every world at which it exists. So that formulation does not mean what Spinoza wants it to mean. When he says things of the form 'The essence of x contains existence', he means that x is of such a nature that it is necessary that x exists, or x has a nature which must be instantiated.

Spinoza does not merely stipulate this as a meaning for 'x is its own cause'; rather, he offers it as a philosophical proposal for how 'cause of itself' can best be understood. The proposal has this to be said for it: If something were 'cause of itself' in the 1d1 sense, so that its existence really did follow from its concept in some way, that *would* satisfy any rationalistic demands for an explanation of why it exists, so that it would perform the same task as causal explanations do for other things.

In this way of handling 'cause of itself', Spinoza may be taking his lead from Descartes, who debated with Arnauld about how to make sense of 'x is the cause of itself', and gradually *retreated* into something like Spinoza's 1d1. He admitted that this changes the meaning of 'cause', which in its ordinary sense involves temporal priority (Obj and Rep 4, CSM 2:148, 167–8),[2] but he contended that the change is defensible and the only way to make *any* sense of 'cause of itself': 'When we ask whether something can give itself existence, this must be taken to be the same as asking whether the nature or essence of something is such that it does not need an efficient cause in order to exist.' That does not go so far as to equate 'x gives itself existence' with 'x's nature is such that it must be instantiated'; but it does introduce the thought that a self-caused thing might be understood to be a thing whose nature is such that the question of why it exists is either self-answering or else needs no answer. Descartes chose the latter, Spinoza the former; but I suspect that Descartes set him on this path.

---

[2] This implies that the relations among events treated of in loop theory are not causal; I do not know whether Descartes noticed this.

Spinoza has, then, a sober reason for holding that any substance, properly so-called, must be something that absolutely could not have not existed. But it does not follow that there are any substances. At most it follows that if there could be substances in that sense, then there are. But there is no reason to believe that such things are possible; and the standard objections to the a priori argument establish that they are not (§247).

48. Mind-body parallelism

Although Descartes apparently accepts real action of mind on body and only quasi-action of body on mind, this difference matters little in the context of his thought, for three reasons: (1) he has no solid theory about the nature of causation; (2) he has no driving need to explain every non-causal regularity; and (3) he can in any case explain regularities by supposing that God intervenes to make them obtain.

None of those holds for Spinoza: (1) he has a view about what causation is; (2) as an explanatory rationalist he demands an answer to every why-question; and (3) the God he believes in could not intervene in the course of nature. I have already discussed 2 and 3. Let us now turn to (1) Spinoza's views about causation. His explanatory rationalism led him to what I call 'causal rationalism'—that is, the view that causal necessity is absolute necessity, that causation cannot be distinguished from entailment, that an effect follows from its cause with the same necessity as that with which the conclusion follows from the premises in a valid argument.

How does the first kind of rationalism imply or encourage the second? Well, if causal necessity is weaker than logical or absolute necessity, it must be legitimate to ask, with respect to any particular causal transaction, 'Why on this occasion did causal necessity operate?' This has no answer, so explanatory rationalism is infringed (§265).

Spinoza does not explicitly announce causal rationalism, probably because it, like his dualism, went too deep for him to see it as needing defence. But he does explain one consequence or aspect of it. A causal rationalist should maintain that for P's being the case to cause Q to be the case, there must be a suitable conceptual link between P and Q, a conceptual conduit along which the absolute necessity can flow. When in §63 I come to the dramatically important 2p7s, we shall find Spinoza saying this explicitly and relying on it to solve a problem.

Now, add causal rationalism to Spinoza's Cartesian view about the lack of significant conceptual overlap between thought and extension (the two attributes), and you get the result that there cannot be causal action either way between mind and body. Spinoza presents that inference in the *Ethics* when he derives 2p6 from 1p10:

Each attribute is conceived through itself without any other (by 1p10). So the modes of each attribute involve the concept of their own attribute, but not of another one; and so (by 1a4) they have Nature for their cause only insofar as it is considered under the attribute of which they are modes, and not insofar as it is considered under any other.

In less formal terms: the facts about the world are facts about the modes that it instantiates; each mode involves a single attribute; the attributes—because they are absolutely basic—are conceptually self-contained, with no logical flow between them; so there is no such flow between two modes that belong to different attributes. And where there is no logical flow, there is no causal flow. So mentalistic facts can be causally explained only by other mentalistic facts; materialistic only by materialistic.

Still, Spinoza must explain why there seems to be interaction: I jab you with a pin, you feel a pain, and you cry out. It looks as though—using subscripts to mark places in the causal chain—Jab_1 causes $Pain_2$ which causes Cry_3. Someone who denies this owes us a rival account of the episode; if he cannot provide one, thereby 'saving the appearances', he has no claim on our attention. The occasionalists' rival account was anathema to Spinoza because it involves divine interference in the natural order. His own treatment differs greatly from theirs. According to him, in 2p7, two causal chains run in parallel: one goes from Jab_1 to (material event)$_2$ and thence to Cry_3, while the other goes from (mental event)$_1$ to $Pain_2$ and thence to (mental event)$_3$. Of the six events in the two chains, we are familiar with two from one chain and one from the other, and with thoughtless optimism we stitch them together into a single interactionist chain. The latter, however, is metaphysically grotesque, and cannot be the real truth of the matter—so Spinoza thinks.

Why postulate a parallelism? Without it, Spinoza could offer this minimal thesis:

> The jab causes the cry through intervening material events, and the pain has its own mental causes and effects though we are not sure what they are; there are two causal systems here, with no leakage from either to the other. The belief that Jab caused Pain which caused Cry is just a mistake, and there is nothing more to be said about it.

But if he left it at that, Spinoza would not have explained the multifarious *appearances* of interaction between mind and body. If the minimal thesis tells the whole story, then the fact that Jab preceded Pain which preceded Cry is merely a random association of events, like the fact that last Tuesday a dog scratched itself and then someone had a thought and then a triplet of atoms combined to form a water molecule. This would be intolerable. With so much apparent interaction, there must be something systematic behind it. So Spinoza supposes a parallelism.

In his terms, the mental counterpart of x is 'the idea of x', which I call $I(x)$; and the material counterpart of y is 'the object of y', which I call $O(y)$. Thus, the object of the idea of my head is my head, that is, $O(I(x))$ is x. Similarly, $I(O(x))$ is x: let x be my present pain; then $O(x)$ is the correlated bodily event, and $I(O(x))$ is the idea of that—namely, my pain.

Given this parallelism, we can, after all, explain events under one attribute in terms of events under the other. It turns out that there is a followable chain linking Jab to Cry through Pain: it is available to anyone who knows enough about what sorts of material (or mental) events are paired by the parallelism function. Spinoza ought to acknowledge this, and he does not. Had he discussed it, he would have pointed out that these 'explanations' involve a heavily empirical element—we can learn what maps onto what under the parallelism only by looking to see—and so they would be unlike the truly causal explanations that he thinks there can be within the confines of an attribute.

He here offers us the metaphysical hypothesis that there is some function from mental items to material ones and back again, so that for any given item in either domain the function picks out precisely one item in the other domain. What is this function? What are these $I( )$ and $O( )$ relations? Well, I have given you Spinoza's technical terminology for them, and have begun to tell you about his metaphysical system involving them. You want more than that, but Spinoza and I cannot offer it, except for some fragmentary examples. You know what it is like when you feel a pain? Well, when that happens in your mind, a corresponding event occurs in your body; without knowing just what event it is, we can easily believe that there is one. Right? Well, the ordered pair {your pain; that bodily event} is an instance of the cosmos-wide relation that generates the parallelism. We naturally think of the bodily event as cerebral, but Spinoza does not say that.

For Spinoza this parallelism must hold clear across the board: *every* mental event is paralleled by a material one, and vice versa. The 'vice versa' part looks mad: a mental counterpart to the flight of a comet which nobody ever sees? He has a reason to suppose a partial parallelism between human minds and human bodies, but why should he postulate a complete parallelism across the cosmos? Because a partial parallelism would clash with some of his basic principles, as I now explain.

If Spinoza settled for the position that some material events have counterparts under the attribute of thought, while others do not, the question would arise: 'Why does the parallelism hold just where it does, and not elsewhere?' Spinoza's explanatory rationalism demands that this have an answer, but his property- and concept-dualism imply that it could not possibly have one. The limits on the parallelism could not be explained in terms of something that underlies both thought and extension: each is basic, so nothing underlies them. Nor could the limits be explained purely from within either attribute, because Spinoza's extension/thought dualism rules out there being causal or explanatory links between facts under one attribute and facts under the other. There is, therefore, nowhere for answers to come from; so the questions cannot arise; so the parallelism must be total. QED. (I develop this line of thought further in *Study* 133–7.)

Renewed objection: 'Whether or not Spinoza is committed to it, a cosmic parallelism of the mental and the material is too absurd to be taken seriously. We can pretend to give it respect, adopting the tone of voice that one reserves for wild old dead philosophical doctrines; but we cannot see it as a legitimate contender in the public arena in which intelligent adults debate seriously about mind and body.' This natural protest is reasonable on the face of it, and this should not be forgotten. We cannot properly understand this part of Spinoza's thought unless we face up to its appearance of being crazy.

One Spinoza scholar dealt with this by denying that Spinoza has any doctrine about how mind relates to body. According to Albert Balz, when Spinoza says that there is an 'idea' corresponding to every material reality, he is doing logic, not psychology:

Spinoza's problem is not set in terms of the relation of psychical ideas in a spiritual substance to modes of a physical, extended substance. Nor does Spinoza split existence into two halves, things of the mind and things of extension. Idea means for Spinoza what essence had denoted in scholastic philosophy. It is a logical entity, and in explicated form and verbally expressed, it is a definition. (Balz 1917: 30)[3]

Balz sticks by this and develops it forcefully. He holds, for example, that Spinoza's term *anima* (soul, but connected with 'animated') belongs to biology, and *mens* (mind) to logic; and that he has no term to express the notion of what is 'psychic or spiritual'. Some parts of Spinoza's text support this view of his doctrines better than the customary view of them as including a theory of the mental (I mention a few in *Study*, 53–4). But far more of the text does not fit, and I am sure that Spinoza really does espouse a parallelism between the realms of extension and of thought, with these terms taken in roughly Descartes's senses for them.

Curley in his first book on Spinoza (1969) went a good distance in Balz's direction: when Spinoza speaks of 'the idea of' some item in the material world, Curley interprets him as meaning something like *the truth about* that item, and not as referring to a mental counterpart of it. That turns the bold doctrine that states of affairs in the material world map onto *mentalistic states of affairs* into the tame thesis that materialistic states of affairs map onto *true propositions about them*. This cannot be accused of undue temerity.

When it comes to Spinoza's doctrine concerning ideas *of ideas*, however, Curley switches. He has to, because Spinoza explains that there must be ideas of ideas because, 'as soon as someone knows something, he thereby knows that he knows it, and at the same time knows that he knows that he knows, and so on to infinity' (2p21s). Balz ignores this passage; Curley does not, and reasonably thinks that it must belong to psychology rather than to logic. Spinoza, he rightly assumes, could not have used the language of 'knowing that he knows' to make a point merely about propositions about propositions. However, Curley's sensible handling of this bit of Spinozist doctrine dooms his overall interpretation. He

---

[3] A related view is that the mind for Spinoza is the form of the body—a position that goes back to Aristotle and owes nothing to Cartesian dualism. 'The form of the stone . . . is the very soul of the stone to the extent . . . that the form is considered in abstraction from the material components' (Benardete 1980: 66). Benardete is setting forth this view, not endorsing it.

has to regard 'idea of' as ambiguous, meaning one thing in 'idea of a boat' and another in 'idea of an idea', and this contradicts Spinoza's most forthright statement about ideas of ideas. Where x is a material thing, he says that I(I(x)) relates to I(x) in the same way as I(x) relates to x (2p21). In the murk surrounding 'ideas of ideas', that one thing shines out clearly: we are *not* to suppose that 'idea of' works differently in 'idea of an idea' from how it works everywhere else. Yet Curley's interpretation supposes precisely that.

Balz and Curley want to see Spinoza as other than demented in his opinions; so do I. They have achieved this by making him misuse language strangely; but we need not pay such a high price. Spinoza's comprehensive mind–body parallelism, though bold, is, when properly understood, not as wild as it at first seems. It does not say that a window struck by a stone feels pain; the mentalistic counterpart of that collision is not an event in anything that could properly be called a mind. I think Spinoza holds this:

Just as a living human body is made up of simpler material components no one of which is alive, so the correspondingly complex human mind is made up of simpler components no one of which is recognizably mental, though they belong on the mentalistic side of the line because they contribute to what is recognizably mental and have no bearing on the world of matter.

(For an expansion of those remarks, see my *Study* 127–39 and Nagel's important 1979.)

49. Descartes's robot

Spinoza's explanatory rationalism, conjoined with his thesis that no causal explanations run between the attributes, entails that all human behaviour can be explained in purely materialistic terms. Descartes had denied that:

If any such machines had the organs and outward shape of a monkey or of some other animal that lacks reason, we should have no means of knowing that they did not possess entirely the same nature as these animals; whereas if any such machines bore a resemblance to our bodies and imitated our actions as closely as possible for all practical purposes, we should still have two very certain means of recognizing that they were not real men. The first is that they could never use words, or put together other signs, as we do in order to declare our thoughts to others. For although we can certainly conceive of a machine so constructed that it utters words, and even utters words which correspond to bodily actions causing a change in its organs . . . it is not conceivable that such a machine should produce different arrangements of words so as to give an appropriately meaningful answer to whatever is said in its presence, as the dullest of men can do. Secondly, even though such machines might do some things as well as we do them, or perhaps even better, they would inevitably fail in others, which would reveal that they were acting not through understanding but only from the disposition of their organs. For whereas reason is a universal instrument which can be used in all kinds of situations, these organs need some particular disposition for each particular action; hence it is *moralement* impossible for a machine to have enough different organs to make it act in all the contingencies of life in the way in which our reason gets us to act. (*Method* 5, CSM 1:139–40)[4]

Descartes here gives a quantitative reason for holding that some movements that human beings make cannot be explained materialistically. Of no individual human action would he say, 'You could not explain *that* in purely materialistic terms'; but the sheer amount and complexity of human linguistic and other behaviour defeats its being explained in terms of the structure and movements of parts of the body. Because 'these organs need some particular disposition for each particular action', 'it is *moralement* impossible for a machine to have enough different organs to make it act in all the contingencies of life'. The French adverb means that such a machine is ruled out by things that we know for sure—things of which we are *moralement sûrs*. These presumably include facts about how small the average human skull is and how large the smallest organs in the brain.

Descartes thus has no reason to assert that it is absolutely a priori impossible for a mindless creature to speak as humans do. Gilson's statement to this effect is disdained as 'amazing' by Séris (1993: 190 n. 2), but Gilson was right.

Descartes here shows a profound insight into the complexity of human behaviour. Imagine trying to carry out this exercise:

Lay out rules for reasonable conduct by a reasonable person in the form 'In situations of kind K, behave in manner M'. The values of K must be stated in terms of how the various situations affect the sense-organs and brain, and the values of M must be stated in terms of impulses along nerves, contractions of muscles, and so on. Pretend that you have the information you need to do all this, and that you are archangelically fast in thinking and writing. To keep the task within bounds, confine yourself to a set of rules that is full enough to cover everything that some one reasonable person *does* do in the course of ten hours, together with everything that she in particular would have done if the relevant situations had arisen.

If the organs of the body are to be 'disposed' to behave in accordance with these rules, the latter must be purely materialistic; that is why I laid those constraints on K and M.

Contemplating something like that project, Descartes was impressed by how many rules there would have to be. How many *would* there have to be? Certainly they would outnumber the electrons in the visible universe; Descartes could not have given that answer, but he saw enough to be satisfied that one brain could not contain enough separate mechanisms to be disposed to obey all these rules.

Spinoza responds that we should not dogmatize about what purely material causes could achieve until we know more about the submicroscopic structures within organisms. Read his beautiful treatment of the matter in 3p2s, including this:

---

[4] See also CSMK 302–4.

Experience has not yet taught anyone what the body can do from the laws of nature alone, insofar as nature is only considered to be corporeal . . . For no one has yet come to know the structure of the body so accurately that he could explain all its functions—not to mention that many things are observed in the lower animals that far surpass human ingenuity, and that sleepwalkers do a great many things in their sleep that they would not dare to awake. This shows well enough that the body itself, simply from the laws of its own nature, can do many things which its mind wonders at. (3p2s)

In this, as in several other respects, Spinoza, despite the estranging surface of his work, comes closer to the thought of the late twentieth century than do most of his near-contemporaries, including Descartes.

I have not found him facing up to Descartes's quantitative insight. Had he done so, he might have said something about how small bodily mechanisms can be, or tried to meet the problem in some other way. How do *we* deal with Descartes's problem? Most of us think that material events can be explained materialistically, and do not think that sheer smallness and numerousness of 'organs' can do the job. So . . . ? The problem has not yet been solved: questions about the brain 'architecture' underlying our capacity to speak and behave reasonably are still debated by cognitive scientists and philosophers of mind. But we can make a start. If we accept my formulation of Descartes's problem, and claim that all human behaviour can be explained materialistically, we must accept: *Each rule of conduct corresponds to a material disposition. Each material disposition is embodied in a mechanism—a particular, appropriately structured part of the brain. There are trillions of trillions of rules of conduct.* Descartes thought that this trio implies that the brain contains many trillions of distinct, appropriately structured parts, and he thought it too small for that. But he was wrong about what is implied. Given that two rules involve two dispositions, which are grounded in two 'organs' in the brain, it does not follow that the two 'organs' have no material overlap. They might share nearly all their matter. A single neuron may be linked to many others, each linked to many others in turn, and so on; so that the one is a part of millions of physically overlapping mechanisms, each making the organism obedient to one specific input–output conditional.

Descartes must have known that a single chunk of structured matter could be part of several different 'organs' or mechanisms. His own physiology and anatomy repeatedly avails itself of versions of that idea. I can only suppose that he did not clearly see his own procedures in that way, and that this failure blocked him from carrying the 'shared matter' idea over as a solution to his problem about the physical control of human behaviour.

50. 'A queer kind of medium'

A second contrast between Spinoza and Descartes is subtler, deeper, and more important. As well as denying that material mechanisms control all of human bodily behaviour, Descartes says something remarkable about how a mind can do the job. Rather than saying that a mind can produce obedience to all those rules because there is no practical impediment to packing in all the mental mechanisms, as none has any size, he says that 'reason is a universal instrument which can be used in all kinds of situations'. He seems to mean that reason can cover and control many different eventualities without having separate mechanisms (or the mental equivalent of them) for each. This is an interesting thing to say; it has haunted me for years; but I do not know what to do with it. I doubt if Descartes had anything very specific in mind when he said this, beyond merely excusing the mind from having to control behaviour through distinct mechanisms for different movements. This fits with his not taking seriously enough the idea of the mind as a substance with an intrinsic nature which explains its workings (§42).

This performance by Descartes probably falls within the scope of Wittgenstein's mockery of a certain common way of thinking:

Understanding, meaning, interpreting, thinking . . . seem to take place in a queer kind of medium, the mind; and the mechanism of the mind, the nature of which, it seems, we do not quite understand, can bring about effects which no material mechanism could. Thus for example a thought (which is such a mental process) can agree or disagree with reality; I am able to think of a man who is not present; I am able to imagine him, 'mean him' in a remark which I make about him, even if he is thousands of miles away or dead. (1958: 3–4)

A little later, discussing what makes a linguistic expression meaningful—what gives it 'life'—Wittgenstein attacks the perhaps Lockean view that an expression gets a meaning through being associated with a mental image:

If the meaning of the sign is an image built up in our minds when we see or hear the sign, then let us [try] replacing this mental image by some outward object, for example a painted or modelled image. Then why should the written sign plus this painted image be alive if the written sign alone was dead?—In fact, as soon as you think of replacing the mental image by a painted one, and as soon as the image thereby loses its occult character, it ceases to seem to impart any life to the sentence at all. (It was in fact just the occult character of the mental process which you needed for your purposes.)

It would be hard to exaggerate the cleansing power of the observation that we are tempted to tolerate mysteries so long as they occur in the mind, and of the proposal to fight this temptation by refusing to credit minds with any power that one could not also attribute to bodies.

Descartes's remark that reason is 'a universal instrument' lies within range of Wittgenstein's scorn, because it assumes that thought is 'a queer kind of medium' whose mechanisms we do not quite understand. Descartes credits the mind with powers that do not reside in mechanisms as the powers of the brain do, purchasing this comfort at the expense of allowing mysteries and incoherences which would be intolerable if they were not housed in that haven of the occult, the mind.

The contrast with Spinoza could not be more striking. Although Spinoza's *Ethics* strikes the reader as strange, recalcitrant, and hard to connect with the real world and real philosophy, some of its doctrines make it more at home in the late twentieth century than in the seventeenth. One of these is the thesis, implied by 2p3,7, that whatever happens in anyone's mind is matched by something that happens in his or her body.

This would have been rejected by most philosophers in the seventeenth century, when it was usually held that some of the mind's doings could not be modelled in a purely material system. Descartes, for one: he must believe in a radical lack of isomorphism between minds and bodies. Contrast that with Spinoza, a child of his own time but an adoptee of ours, who held that every mental state or event is paralleled by a material state or event. His freedom from the temptation to appeal to the mind's occultness, like many of his best intellectual traits, passed unnoticed through the centuries.

It is a facet of something even more general in his thought, namely naturalism about mankind. He did not think that we are radically special in any way: the whole story about people can be told with concepts that are needed, anyway, to describe other parts of Nature. Not just other organisms; the concept of life itself has no *basic* place in the true story of the universe, and the difference between organic and inorganic is like that between complicated and simple, or orderly and jumbled—a smooth difference of degree with no ultimate significance.

Add to that Spinoza's view that whatever happens in anyone's mind is strictly paralleled by something that happens in her body, and you get a position that is strikingly free of temptations to regard the mind as queer or occult, a haven for the inexplicable.

I should remark that Spinoza's view about what life is lies at the heart of his account of 'individuals' in the physical interlude between 2p13 and 14 (for a good discussion see Van der Hoeven 1973). In characterizing 'individuals'—organisms—in terms of how their constituent particles move, Spinoza is offering a simplified version of the sort of account Locke gave, in his great Identity chapter, of what it is for a part of the world to be alive (§292). He was also in the tradition of the mechanistic biology of Descartes (see MacKenzie 1975).

Chapter 7

One Extended Substance

51. The thing thought and the independence thought

The concept of substance, as employed in philosophy in the seventeenthth and eighteenth centuries, contained two strands: a *thing* thought and an *independence* thought. In contrasting substances and modes, philosophers were at once contrasting things with properties or modes and contrasting independent items with dependent ones. For a firm grip on Spinoza's metaphysic, we need to understand what these two strands are and how they are interrelated.

The 'thing' strand goes back to Aristotle's *Categories*, which launched the understanding of a substance as an item upon which something could be predicated and which could not in its turn be predicated on something else. This expresses the idea that the world is made up of *things* that have *properties*. Although we can also treat a property in a somewhat thing-like way—as when we say 'Generosity is the highest virtue', which grammatically resembles 'Everest is the highest mountain'—the property can be predicated of other things, and is therefore not a 'substance' in Aristotle's sense. The thing thought still dominated the meaning of 'substance' in the seventeenth century. We find it often in Descartes's writings—for example, in a passage quoted earlier, where he says that we have no direct access to substances as such, but 'can come to know a substance by one of its attributes, in virtue of the common notion that nothingness possesses no properties or qualities' (CSM 1:210). This tie of 'substance' to 'thing' is vividly present in Locke's *Essay* (§203). He also connected 'substance' with the independence thought—for example, when writing of properties or 'modes' as 'dependences on or affections of substances' (*Essay* II.xii.40), which apparently makes the thing/property line coincide with the independent/dependent line. The same holds in Descartes's works. Indeed, he actually defines 'substance' in terms of independence as well as of 'thing': 'By *substance* we can understand nothing other than a thing [*rem*] which exists in such a way that it needs no other thing for its existence' (*PP* 1:51).

What exactly is the independence thought? And why is it linked with the thing thought in the meaning of the word 'substance'? These two were not merely conjoined in the concept of substance, as *plane* and *closed* are in the meaning of 'triangle'; they were evidently supposed to be integrally connected. But how?

Well, all this might have started with the idea that properties depend on the things that have them, and not conversely. This implies that substance/property connects with independent/dependent because it entails it. This line of thought is shaky, though. On a Platonist view, properties do not depend in any way on their possessors. An Aristotelian will say that a property cannot exist unless some substance has it; but this form of dependence holds in the other direction too—a substance cannot exist unless it has some property. To get a one-way dependence, it seems, we must think in terms of property-instances, tropes; which amounts to taking our substance/non-substance line as distinguishing between two kinds of *particulars*. If we adopt the majority opinion that a trope must be owned, and cannot be transferred, we can say that any trope depends for its existence on the existence of the particular substance that has it. And the converse does not hold: the thing can exist even if that trope does not—as long as the trope is not essential to the thing. I suspect, though, that most adherents of the idea that properties are dependent beings would say that even an essential trope depends on its owner in a way in which its owner does not depend on it. If so, then the present paragraph does not exhibit the real source for the independence thought; or else it reveals it, and shows it to be mistaken.

By the seventeenth century, anyway, the 'independent' element in the meaning of 'substance' was sometimes understood as causal: x is a substance only if it is impossible for x to be caused to go out of existence. This might have come about through sheer drift, as William Kneale has suggested (1939–40). That would be disappointing, though—a notion of causal independence arrived at through mis-thinking an idea of metaphysical independence that was probably unsound in the first place.

Kant understood the independence thought causally, and sought to show that the other strand in the concept of substance carries this one with it. The two strands as he described them are the thing thought and the thought of guaranteed everlastingness. The latter entails causal independence, because any item which causally depends for its existence on something else could be annihilated by the withdrawal of that external support; so no such item could be guaranteed to last for ever. In his 'First Analogy of Experience', Kant argues that any substance (as defined by the thing thought) must be everlasting; and this, if it succeeded, would tie the two strands together not through history and muddle but through conceptual necessity (*Critique* A 182–9). I cannot see that Kant's argument does succeed, but it is a notable attempt to master the conceptual materials we are now wrestling with. (I analyse and criticize it in my 1966: 181–201.)

After years of struggle with it, I have come to think that causal independence is a blind alley—not that it was not present in some seventeenth-century thinking about 'substance', but that it did little work there. That is certainly the case with Descartes, to whom I now return briefly.

He shows us that he understands the independence of substances to be causal. Having defined 'substance', he proceeds:

There is only one substance which can be understood to depend on no other thing whatsoever, namely God. All other substances . . . can exist only with the help of God's concurrence. Hence the term 'substance' does not apply univocally . . . to God and to other things; that is, there is no distinctly intelligible meaning of the term which is common to God and his creatures. . . . Corporeal substance and mind (or created thinking substance) can be understood to fall under this common concept: things [*res*] that need only the concurrence of God in order to exist. (*PP* 1:51–2, CSM 1:120)

Requiring substances to be causally independent, therefore, Descartes can allow no substance but God. A weaker concept of independence gives him a weaker sense of 'substance', in which the term applies to created minds and bodies.

In the rest of his work, however, his uses of 'substance' are controlled entirely by the thing thought, as in *PP* 1:52, 56. Furthermore, it seems to be the complete, full-strength thing thought: there is no hint that your mind and mine, because they are 'independent' only in a charitably weakened sense of the term, are admitted to the category of *things* by courtesy rather than by right. It would have been hard for Descartes to do otherwise. He divides reality into substances and their properties, qualities, modes; if my mind were a substance only by courtesy, then would it by the strictest standards be a mode or property? Nothing in Descartes's work points that way. Indeed, I can find no evidence that he ever considered bringing together in a single thought the following:

the strong concept of independence,
the tie of independence to 'substance'
the tie of 'substance' to the left-hand side of the thing/property line
the thesis that whatever is not substance is property.

That achievement was left to Spinoza, as we shall see. In Descartes's work the thing thought dominates, and the independence thought quietly drops out of sight, right there in the remainder of *PP* 1:52.

52. Can a Cartesian body be annihilated?

A different kind of independence is at work in the thought of Leibniz, and perhaps of others, concerning substances. A thing that has parts is ontologically dependent on them; given that the parts exist and are related thus and so, the thing exists; so it is an ontological upshot, and thus not independent for existence. By this standard, substances must be *basic* things, items that would appear in the most fundamental inventory of the world's contents. For Leibniz this implies that no material thing can be a substance because every portion of matter is splittable into smaller ones (§187).

One way out of this is to give up the idea of basic *things* and settle for basic *stuff*—to give up substances and settle for substance. This was not Leibniz's solution, but it could have been Descartes's. Had he thought of substances as ontologically independent, and thus been interested in what the world of matter basically contains, he could have said this:

Bodies are the only material things there are; a body is a portion of matter satisfying certain constraints; and as such it cannot be basic, because its parts are ontologically prior to it. So there are no basic material things, only stuff—matter. Count nouns have a ground-floor role on the thinking side of the line, but on the extension side we must rest content with a mass term, *matter*.

This fits Descartes's actual practice fairly well, but he seems not to have thought it out in these terms. A passage in the Synopsis of the *Meditations* has him saying that any human body is destructible through 'a change in the shape of some of its parts', and is thus not a substance in the 'pure' way in which human minds are. This is preceded by the remark that 'body, taken in the general sense, is substance', which points somewhat to the idea that the basic extended reality is not a thing or things, but stuff.

The Latin could be translated instead 'body, taken in the general sense, is a substance', and that count-noun rendering has generated a literature on the question of whether Descartes was really a monist about material substance, holding that there is only one such. This is a pointless debate. If he thought that there is just one material substance, this is little more than a disposition on his part to use the word 'substance' in a certain way. Nobody thinks that anything turns on this in the rest of his work. Above all, if there is just one extended substance, what is the metaphysical status of finite bodies? There is no hint in Descartes of the view to which Spinoza was led, that they are modes of the one substance—that is, that they are adjectival upon it.

I find it more plausible to see Descartes as thinking of material substance as an infinite quantity of stuff, the totality of matter, and to see finite bodies as substantial portions of it. But the texts shed a dim and flickering light on this. Latin has no articles. It is always a judgement call whether an occurrence of *substantia* should be translated as 'a substance' or merely as 'substance'. French has articles, but the French texts do not help. In none of the main ones does the plural 'substances' occur in the CSM translations. The singular 'substance' occurs ten times (setting aside a count use that concerns a thinking substance), and in each of these Descartes uses the word in speaking of 'the substance *of*' something, usually the brain. This is a special use of 'substance' (§207); nobody understands it well, apparently, and it does not help us here. We might look for guidance to plural uses of 'substance' in the Latin. 'Substances' occurs often in CSM, and I am sure that it usually corresponds to the Latin plural *substantiae*. (Not always: at CSM 1:63, 'different species of substances' should be 'different species of substance'.) Few of these occurrences give us any lead, however. In many instances, Descartes is discussing substances in general—distinguishing them from attributes, for example. In others, he contrasts mind and body as distinct 'substances', making a point that would survive if he said instead that my mind is one substance and my body is a distinct *portion of* substance. (For a thorough and helpful examination of all these issues, and many references to the relevant secondary literature, see Stuart 1999.)

The position I tentatively ascribe to Descartes, however, is still not secure and stable, for a reason which Spinoza highlighted and built on. The view in question holds that those portions are distinct realities, metaphysically on a par with the entire material world of which they are parts; but Descartes should find it difficult or impossible to accept this, because of his rejection of container space (§11). If the sub-portions of a given portion of matter are real and really distinct from one another, then—as Descartes insists in one of his arguments for substance-dualism—it is possible that one should go out of existence while the others remain. But Descartes cannot allow this to be possible: his view that container space is absolutely impossible has the effect that the fate of one portion of substance is necessarily tied to the fates of others.

Given container space, there is no problem: a coin is annihilated, leaving behind it a coin-shaped portion of space which was co-located with it and is not now co-located with anything; and this need not affect anything else. Locke saw this, and used it to argue for the possibility of empty container space:

Those who assert the impossibility of space existing without matter must . . . deny a power in God to annihilate any part of matter. No one . . . will deny that God can put an end to all motion that is in matter. . . . Whoever then will allow that God can during such a general rest annihilate this book . . . must necessarily admit the possibility of a vacuum; for it is evident that the space that was filled by the parts of the annihilated body will still remain and be a space without body. (*Essay* II.xiii.21 (*bis*))

This challenge to Descartes is, like much in Locke, deep and instructive. Descartes cannot deny that one portion of matter could go clean out of existence, for he holds that each portion needs God's continual activity to stop it from slipping into nothingness. Let us ask him, then, to tell the full story of what would ensue if that did happen.

Locke seems to be right: Descartes could not say that one portion could be annihilated while nothing moved. He is reported to have said in conversation that if God annihilated the contents of a vessel, its sides would thereby come into contact *without having moved* (AT 4:109; I learned about this from Garber 1992: 342). It is bewilderingly foolish, and I suspect that his companion misunderstood whatever it was that Descartes said. He has in fact no coherent way of allowing for the annihilation of some matter while nothing moves.

What about annihilation without stasis? One might think that Descartes has no problem about that. As the matter goes out of existence, its erstwhile location is synchronously filled with other matter pouring in from neighbouring locations. That cannot be the whole story, though, for the replacing matter must be replaced in its turn by yet other matter, which must be replaced by . . . and so on, *ad infinitum* (§20). The Cartesian account of ordinary movement postulates a finite loop: matter is replaced by matter which is replaced by . . . the matter that was first mentioned. Annihilation cannot be like that, however. The loop cannot be closed, because the initial matter goes out of existence, and so is not available to replace anything.

In response, Descartes might say that the annihilation of some matter would require a synchronous *infinite* movement: the sequence 'which is replaced by some matter which is replaced by . . .' does not end. This is a possible story. It is modelled by a famous story about a hotel with an infinity of rooms, all full; one more traveller arrives, and the hotelier fits him in by giving him room 1 and requiring every other guest to move—in each case from room n to room n + 1. This is mathematically respectable; but it is not clear that an event with this structure could conceivably happen in reality. Even if it could, the application of it to our present problem is intuitively troubling: a small event that God could easily cause to occur would lead to the movement of *an infinite quantity of matter*. That is hard to swallow, and in any case, I doubt if anyone before the nineteenth century was in a position even to contemplate it.

Failing that, Descartes's back is to the wall. He must say that a coin cannot be absolutely annihilated unless at the same time a new portion of matter, of exactly the same size, comes into existence. Had he seen and accepted this, he could have concluded that God's continual conservation is addressed not to the separate portions of matter but to the entire material world. The only material that could be annihilated is *that*; the idea that some part of it might slip out of existence while the rest remains makes no sense.

By a fairly cogent line of reasoning we have brought Descartes to the point where he must say that portions of matter do not ontologically depend on their parts; that the part/whole relation that obtains in the material realm is not, surprisingly, one in which the fate of the whole depends on that of the parts *rather than vice versa*. He may have had some sense of this, but there is no evidence that he got to the bottom of it. He seems nearly always to have thought of portions of matter as distinct realities. If he had come to have doubts about that, Descartes would then have needed what he did not have—a positive account of how portions of matter relate to larger portions that include them, and more generally of how bodies relate to the material world. Spinoza saw that need, and met it with a bold, beautiful metaphysical hypothesis.

53. Spinoza sees the problem

Spinoza rejected container space, as Descartes did, saw that this gave him a problem about how one portion of matter could go out of existence while the rest remained, and concluded that such portions are not really distinct from one another:

If corporeal substance could be so divided that its parts were really distinct, why, then, could one part not be annihilated, the rest remaining connected with one another as before? And why must they all be so fitted together that there is no vacuum? Truly, of things which are really distinct from one another, one can be, and remain in its condition, without the other. Since, therefore, there is no vacuum in nature (discussed elsewhere), but all its parts must so concur that there is no vacuum, it follows also that they cannot be really distinguished, i.e. that corporeal substance, insofar as it is a substance, cannot be divided. (*Ethics* 1p15s)

Locke, we saw, found it obvious that God could annihilate one body while holding all the others still; Spinoza here says that this could not happen, and asks why.
How can the continued existence of one portion of matter be absolutely tied to
that of another? If they are truly *one* and *another*—'really distinct'—their ontological fates should be separable; but they are not; from which Spinoza infers that
the portions are not really one and another.

He discusses the annihilation of some matter while other bodies 'remain connected as before'—that is, not packing in to fill up the gap. He stipulates that the
other bodies do not move, I believe, because that makes it *obvious* that portions
of matter are not ontologically independent of one another. He really thinks that
a portion of matter could not be annihilated while the rest stayed in existence,
whether moving or still.

Although he has a rhetorical reason for focusing on annihilation plus stasis, I
am sorry that he went about things in this way, because it has misled some of his
readers. I have encountered philosophers who believed something like this:

What centrally engages Spinoza's attention in 1p15s is the supposed fact that if one body
were annihilated, others would have to move. They would have to do so because 'There
is no vacuum', meaning that if there is container space, it is all full. The question is: Why
could a vacuum not be created by the annihilation of a body? What sort of metaphysical
rubber bands are at work to hold bodies together, so that if one went out of existence, the
others would crowd into its erstwhile location, ensuring that no vacuum is left? The
answer is that the other bodies are under this constraint because they are not really, basically, ultimately distinct from one another.

The wording is mine, but not the content; I have encountered this interpretation
more than once. In fact, it is incoherent. Saying that individual portions of matter are not 'really distinct' has no appearance of explaining why under certain circumstances they must rush around filling gaps. Spinoza writes of things' having
to 'concur', so that no vacuum occurs between them; the Latin is *concurrere*,
from *con* = 'with', *currere* = 'run'; but this does not show that he is talking here
about gap-filling movement. He and others regularly used the word to express a
general idea of harmony, agreement, interrelatedness, with no suggestion of
movement. Causes are said to 'concur' to produce an effect, God to 'concur' in
things that happen, and so on.

Anyway, this gap-filling interpretation does not square with what Spinoza says
about there being no vacuum. In 1p15s he says only that 'there is no vacuum in
nature (discussed elsewhere)', but that last phrase—*de quo aliàs*—has to refer to
the only other place in his acknowledged writings where vacuum is discussed, *DP*
2p33 (*CS* 268). That work was written as a textbook of Cartesian philosophy, and
Spinoza does not believe it all; but he presumably believes the part he invokes in
Ethics 1p15s. The passage is pure Descartes. 'It is a contradiction that there
should be a vacuum,' Spinoza writes, supporting this by defining 'vacuum' as
'extension without corporeal substance', which he equates with 'body without
body', and thus dismisses as 'absurd'. He also refers the reader to Descartes's

Principles of Philosophy 2:17–18 for details, with this comment: 'The main point there is that bodies between which nothing lies must touch one another, and also that nothing has no properties.' This criticizes the idea of vacuum understood as a *nothing* which is extended, and follows Descartes in ignoring the possibility of a substantial container space some or all of whose portions are co-located with bodies. This is a defect in the passage, but the fact remains that Spinoza here means to be presenting a *conceptual* critique of the idea of extension without extended stuff; the latter is taken to be nonsense; and it would be excessively odd if he thought that something's being nonsense could explain a fact about bodies' having to move.

Spinoza's real point is that if container space is rejected (and along with it compression, expansion, and the co-location of matter with matter), there could not possibly be an annihilation of a portion of matter while the rest remained in existence, whether moving or still. He implies that here: 'If extension consisted of distinct parts, then it would be intelligible that some of its parts might be destroyed even though it remained and was not destroyed by the destruction of some of its parts' (1661a, CS 72). An even more vivid example will be quoted in §55.

In 1p15s Spinoza purports to be giving informal evidence for the truth of something that he has demonstrated abstractly. Unlike my considerations regarding matter, extension and so on, Spinoza's supposedly demonstrated proposition, 1p12, concerns substances and attributes generally: 'No attribute of a substance can be truly conceived from which it follows that the substance can be divided.' Spinoza's demonstration of this relies on the highly suspect 1p5, the no-shared-attribute thesis; and the demonstration of the companion proposition 1p13, 'A substance which is absolutely infinite is indivisible', rests on what seem to be mere mistakes about infinity. It is only when we get to 1p15s and the discussion of the indivisibility of *extended* substance that we find something to get our teeth into.

54. Spinoza's solution and Curley's challenge

So much for the problem. What is Spinoza's solution? What can he say about how restricted portions of matter *do* relate to portions that include them and to the entire material world?[1] He says that finite bodies are *modes* of the material world; they are properties or 'affections' of it, or ways that it is. One element in this is the thesis that necessarily the whole material world is the only extended substance that there is. This may be about the same as adopting 'substance' only as a mass noun: there may be no real difference between 'There is only sub-

---

[1] Woolhouse (1990: 28) argues that 'it is a mistake to identify Spinoza's extended substance with Descartes's extended substance'. My contrary view is supported, I submit, by the explanatory uses that I make of it. Woolhouse's arguments are rigorously criticized in Cover 1999.

stance' and 'Necessarily there is only one substance'. Spinoza himself, though, would reject the mass-term view. It equates his one substance—God—with the totality of material stuff, and he would reject that as demeaning. There is no need to pursue this. Our engagement with Spinoza's metaphysic of materiality will be the same, whether we take him to say that bodies are modes of substance or that they are modes of *the* substance.

In his first book on Spinoza, Curley did a fine thing. He challenged the assumption of Spinoza scholars that they had any notion of how comets and apples and molecules could be 'modes' in the normal sense of being properties of a single substance. Since sense cannot be made of this, he argued, we should stop conspiring in the pretence of understanding it. Rather than walking out on Spinoza, however, Curley conjectured that by 'mode' he meant less than his contemporaries did.

According to Curley (1969: 37), Spinoza divorced 'substance' and 'mode' from the thing/property thought, taking them to convey the independent/dependent thought and nothing more; and he understands this causally. For Curley's Spinoza, therefore, 'There is only one substance' means that only one thing depends on nothing else for its existence; and that is all it means. Calling finite bodies 'modes', therefore, is just saying that they depend causally on other things. Spinoza's monism about extended substance is intelligible on this reading of it. And Curley's Spinoza might have accepted it: everyone's Spinoza believed in the divisibility of all matter, and Curley's might have thought that splitting a body is destroying it; from which he could infer that any body is destructible by some other body.

This conjecture about Spinoza's semantic malpractice had the merit of seeming to yield the best way to make sense of his calling bodies 'modes' of a single substance. Even if it really did that, however, this would hardly suffice to outweigh the drawbacks of this proposal.

(1) Curley's Spinoza misused a pair of standard technical terms for no good reason and without warning. (Curley's evidence that Spinoza misused them is not a reason for Spinoza to misuse them.) Calling it a 'misuse' is putting it mildly. The thing/property element in the meanings of 'substance' and 'mode' is not merely ancient history which we might learn about by revisiting Aristotle; it was active in Spinoza's own intellectual milieu. We there find people connecting 'substance'/'mode' both with thing/property and with independent/dependent; but the former contrast is always dominant. I have already referred to Descartes's *PP* 1:52, 56 in this regard. See also Leibniz's warning to De Volder that if he defines 'mode' purely in terms of dependence, he will have to conclude that only one thing is not a mode, and that this is wrong because modes are properties (L 524). What could have persuaded Spinoza to jettison the core meanings of 'substance' and 'mode', using them with only their outer shell of meaning as 'self-sufficient' and 'dependent', respectively?

(2) Curley offers a reading for 'Finite bodies are modes', but not one for other related things that Spinoza says. For example, the status of bodies as 'modes' does

not imply for Curley's Spinoza that they are not also really distinct parts of the material world; so it does not lock into the argument of 1p15s. None of Spinoza's denials concerning 'distinct parts' receives any light from the modal status of bodies on Curley's interpretation of the latter.

(3) Curley's interpretation can make no sense of Spinoza often saying that bushes and galaxies are modes *of* the one substance under the attribute of extension (or modes of extension, for short). Curley equates 'x is a mode' with 'x is causally vulnerable', which provides no meaning for the dyadic 'x is a mode of y' (thus Leibniz, L 524).

(4) Curley's interpretation gives the lie to Spinoza's own account of what he means by 'mode' in 1d5: 'By *mode* I understand the affections of a substance, or that which is in another through which it is also conceived.' It is beyond question that 'affection' (Latin: *affectio*) means a state or quality. Not only did Spinoza not warn readers about his semantic malpractice, Curley must say, but he positively misled them about it *in a definition*.

As Carriero (1995: 254) remarks, Curley's reading 'disappointingly flattens Spinoza's position'. It turns Spinoza's substance-monism into the mere thesis that all finite bodies are destructible while the material world as a whole is not. If this part of Spinoza's metaphysic was really so small and tame, that would disappoint the hopes of those who had seen him as grappling with the deep question about what there basically is in the world of matter.

So it is good news that Curley's initial challenge has been met. In my *Study* I offered a reading of Spinoza's monism which shows how he could use 'substance' and 'mode' in their full normal senses and still coherently maintain that there is only one extended substance and that finite bodies are modes of it. I shall now tell what I believe to be Spinoza's story, filling in details that he left out.

55. Spinoza on bodies as modes

There is one extended substance, which I call Space. Basically, there are no other extended things; but when we imply that there are—namely, bodies *in* space— what we say is not outright false. It would be false if it were understood to be said at the level of basicness and strictness at which we say that there is only one extended thing; but it need not be understood thus. The main task in developing this monist metaphysic is to provide the rules for reinterpreting familiar statements about 'things in space', showing what they amount to in terms of the basic metaphysic.

To keep things manageable, I shall take a simple extended world—one which we would describe in the shallow vernacular as a Euclidean space containing spheres of matter. Take first a freeze-frame of that world: unmoving spheres suspended in space. At the basic metaphysical level, it comes down to this: *Space has some spherical regions that are thick, while all the rest of Space is thin.* I use 'thick' and 'thin' as mere place-holders for *some* suitable adjectives. I do not know just what ones to use, but that does not matter for the viability of this metaphysical project.

Am I quantifying over regions of space? Have *they* turned out to be the substances—the basic things—in this metaphysic? Not at all. They are not basic things, because they depend for their existence on the existence of Space as a whole. It may seem suspicious that I tell the metaphysical story in a way that *seems* to treat them as its basic things, but the suspicion can be allayed. My need to tell the story in this way is shallow and practical, not deep and theoretical. In principle (though not in practice) I could do it all with adjectives and adverbs, on the model of the replacement of 'There are thick spherical regions' by 'Space is somewhere spherewise thick'. I explain all this more fully in *Study 95–6*.

Now let us introduce movements of spheres which do not alter in either size or shape. I start with the statement *A sphere moves through space*, and explain how this can be true, in its way and at its level, because of facts at the level of the basic monist metaphysic. To do this I need a couple of technical terms.

A *thing-slice* is a pair whose members are a connected region S of Space and a moment T of time, such that at T, S is thick and is surrounded by a region that is not thick.

Using this, I introduce my second technical term:

A *thing-sequence* is a sequence of thing-slices $\{S_1, T_1\}, \{S_2, T_2\}, \ldots, \{S_n, T_n\}$ such that the T-members of the pairs are temporally continuous, and the S-members of the pairs, when taken in temporally continuous order, are spatially continuous.

Remember that any fact about what thing-sequences there are is just a more or less complex fact about how Space is—how thickness and thinness are distributed across it through time.

Now, if the statement 'Something moves during the interval from T_1 to T_n' is true, it is so because

There is a thing-sequence $\{S_1, T_1\}, \ldots, \{S_n, T_n\}$ whose spatial components are not all the same.

The statement that during that interval something moves along an always new track, not retracing or crossing its path, is made true by the fact that

There is a thing-sequence $\{S_1, T_1\}, \ldots, \{S_n, T_n\}$ whose spatial components are all different.

Thus, what we informally call 'movement through space' is, deep down, not the movement of any *thing*, because there is only one thing; rather, it is an alteration in where Space is thick and where it is thin. Compare: 'The thaw moved steadily eastward throughout the day', 'Elvis-mania moved from the USA to Europe'.

More complex statements can be handled similarly. For example, we might want to say at the familiar level that no two bodies are ever co-located. To explain this through the monist metaphysic, I need to be able to count and distinguish thing-sequences, which I do through this rule: For any thing-sequence(s) x and y, x is y just in case x has exactly the same members as y. Then the statement that co-location does not occur is equivalent to: *No thing-slice belongs to two thing-sequences*.

I like many things about this metaphysic, including the help it gives us in seeing that the issue about co-location is contingent. Some philosophers have thought that it stands to reason that co-location does not occur, but careful thinking even at the familiar level can satisfy one that—as Leibniz pointed out—it does not stand to reason (*NE* 124). The monist metaphysic confirms this: there is plainly no conceptual barrier to there being distinct thing-sequences that share some members.

One can fairly easily develop the account to yield a monist statement of what it would be for bodies to be splittable (or not), for there to be a speed limit on movement of bodies (or not), for bodies cleanly to come into or go out of existence (or not); all of these and other things can be expressed in terms of constraints on thing-sequences—that is, in terms of *how Space is*.

The monist metaphysic also helps us to see that an extended world might not be organized as what we ordinarily call 'bodies in space'. For example, reality might consist of *waves* which did not consist of *streams of particles*; and the truth about such a world would be a different set of facts about *how Space is*. The monist metaphysic alerts one to such possibilities. Not that it alerted Spinoza to them: in the physical interlude between 2p13 and 14—his account of the material world at the familiar level, one up from the basic monist metaphysic—there are only particles.

Spinoza's metaphysic can handle statements about bodies' going out of existence: that is what happens when a thing-sequence has a temporally latest member $\{S_n, T_n\}$, with neither S_n nor any region adjoining it being 'thick' at $T_n + 1$. That is the nearest we can get to an annihilation, but for Spinoza it would not be the going out of existence of any *thing*; it would just be the one thing's altering in a certain manner. Suppose we ask him about a real annihilation, not merely something that could be described colloquially as such but really consists in the altering of something that stays in existence. How should he reply? If I have him right, he ought to say: 'You are asking about the annihilation of a region; which makes sense only if you mean the annihilation of the whole of space.' That is exactly what he does say, in Letter 4: 'If a single part of matter were annihilated, the whole of extension would vanish with it.' This stunning pronouncement makes perfect sense—it is exactly right—if Spinoza holds the metaphysic that I attribute to him.

I led us into Spinoza's metaphysic through an episode in 1p15s. There is more in that scholium that fits my interpretation and no other that I know of. For example, he writes there that what we informally call different bodies or portions of matter are really instances of qualitative variety within a single extended reality: 'Matter is everywhere the same, and parts are distinguished in it only insofar as we conceive matter to be affected [= propertied] in different ways, so that its parts are distinguished only modally, but not really' (*CS* 424). That is, the only differentiation is qualitative, and is not a difference between one thing and another. Spinoza continues:

For example, we conceive that water is divided and its parts separated from one another—*qua* water, but not *qua* corporeal substance. For *qua* substance, it is neither separated nor divided. Again, water, *qua* water, is created and annihilated, but *qua* substance it is neither created nor annihilated.

That is, no extended real thing goes out of existence; what one might think of as the annihilation of a bit of matter is really just a region's changing from being thick to being thin.

(In *Study* 94 I said that my understanding of 'bodies are modes' would be undermined if modes were taken to be individual accidents, tropes, and I added my opinion that tropes are 'nonsense'. I have learned a lot since then: tropes are just fine, and my interpretation of Spinoza's monism has nothing to fear from them. For evidence of Spinoza's tolerance of tropes, see Carriero 1995. He uses the evidence primarily to rebut Curley's thinning-out of the meaning of 'mode'; but he also seems to hold that once tropes are admitted, there is no longer a strong case for my interpretation of Spinoza's substance-monism. I cannot imagine why I conceded this; and I am sorry that Carriero took my unreliable word for it.)

56. Objections by Curley

Curley has agreed that my interpretation meets his challenge, but he still rejects it. I have found something that Spinoza *could* have meant while using 'mode' with its full normal meaning, he says, but not something that he *did* mean. Although Curley has not replied to my list of drawbacks in his interpretation, he has offered objections to mine, which I shall discuss.

The difficulties that he finds in my interpretation make it less 'attractive' than his own, he says. Underlying more specific disagreements between us, I think Curley and I may differ in our general picture of what sort of philosopher Spinoza was—or perhaps in what sort we hope he was. Curley seems to want Spinoza's doctrines to be, above all, true. No doubt Spinoza wanted to say only true things; but I see him also as original and bold and deep, and as having a kind of recklessness. It shows in many of his views: that everything has a mental counterpart, that the human condition can be fully described without using teleological explanations, that animal selfishness is a substitution instance in a general metaphysical truth. These and others of his doctrines have a feeling about them of 'Full speed ahead, and damn the torpedoes', which typifies Spinoza's work. It would be in character, therefore, for his substance-monism to be like that too, as it is on my interpretation. Now let us look at the difficulties that are said to confront the latter. (This section relies on Curley 1991 and Bennett 1991*b*.)

(1) Curley rightly says—taking the point from me—that Spinoza, on my interpretation of him, cannot account for genuine reference to particulars. His metaphysical scheme, as developed by me, enables him to analyse only statements of the form 'There is an F particular which stands in relation R_n to particulars of which one is G_1, the second is $G_2 \ldots$' and so on, with each G_i standing for a predicate, a description. The materials that he allows himself do not enable him to make proper sense of statements that pick out a body and say something about *it in particular*. But this has nothing to do with the metaphysic I have attributed to him. To refer to contingently existing particulars, one must use indexicals—paradigmatically in thoughts or phrases of the form 'thing that is F and is within ten feet of where *I* am *now*'. (I shall defend this in §128 in the context of Leibniz's thoughts about individual reference.) Spinoza lacks the resources for a good account of individual reference, because he gives no special privilege to 'I' or to 'now'. His views about substances and modes have nothing to do with this. Curley's interpretation does not liberate Spinoza from the problem; it merely hides it by staying away from the level where it becomes visible, the level where the action is.

(2) Curley rightly says that my interpretation relies on the view—which most commentators share—that Spinoza identified God with the whole of reality. There are difficulties with that, he points out, mostly coming from troubles in Spinoza's handling of temporal concepts. These troubles, like the one about indexicality, are patently there in Spinoza's thought on any interpretation of his theology and/or his substance-monism. If there were good enough reason to back Spinoza off from identifying God with the universe, my interpretation of his material monism could doubtless be adjusted accordingly.

(3) Curley's third point amounts to this: The core meanings of 'substance' and 'mode' do not fit with their shell meanings; if we give enough weight to the latter, while also insisting that we attribute to Spinoza something coherent, then we must throw away the core. Well, I would rather throw away the shell. But actually it is more complicated than that. The shell meaning that Curley finds in the concept of causation is that of mere causal self-sufficiency, and he is certainly right that *that* independence thought is not tightly tied to the thing thought. It is easy to devise a metaphysic in which there are extremely thing-like atoms which can be annihilated by outside influence through normal causal processes.

That, however, reflects a poor understanding of what the independence thought is. For some seventeenth-century purposes, what we most need is the idea of things that are independent in the sense that they are not ontological upshots of anything else—that is, the idea of basic things. In the case of Spinoza, the operative idea is rather that of logical independence, the dependence that untransferable modes (tropes) have on the substances that have them. This comes out when in Spinoza's definition of 'mode' he equates 'the affections of a substance' with 'that which is in another through which it is also conceived'. That conceiving-through is a kind of dependence, and one that weighed heavily in Spinoza's thought. So my interpretation, in which the thing thought predominates, smoothly brings in also the kind of independence thought that Spinoza cared most about. The kind that tends to be left out in the cold is causal independence as this would ordinarily be understood. But that *should* be left out in the cold; it is not a central part of what Spinoza is talking about when he uses the language of independence. Curley has thrown out the core of Spinoza's meaning for 'substance' in order to retain a shell that Spinoza did not give it in the first place.

57. Spinoza's two levels

I have saved until last a fourth complaint of Curley's, which, I shall argue, leads to fresh evidence *for* my interpretation. He writes: 'Bennett seems to me to vacillate about the extent to which we are entitled to read Spinoza as an exponent of' the metaphysic of extension I have been presenting here. This charge must have arisen from a momentary failure to grasp something which Curley usually seems to understand. I attribute to Spinoza a ground-floor metaphysic which describes the extended world in monadic predications on Space, and a second-level physics which describes it in a language quantifying over finite bodies and making them subjects of predication. What Curley calls my 'vacillation' is actually a consistent pair of things, each of which I unwaveringly assert. (1) Spinoza's ground-floor metaphysic makes it prima facie possible for the second level to take any one of countless different forms. (2) In his thinking about the second level, Spinoza did not avail himself of the potential riches that the ground floor offers—did not open his mind to the possibility that the extended world might be organized into something other than particles in space. This is neither vacillation on my part nor positive misconduct on Spinoza's.

Objection: 'If Spinoza believed in this difference in levels, one would expect him to announce it; but he doesn't.' This assumes that if Spinoza had a two-levels account of the extended realm, that would be a special feature of it, marking it off from the work of other metaphysicians. In fact, the work of any interesting metaphysician involves two or more levels. I do not mean levels of reality: the metaphysicians I am talking about do not describe reality as stratified; rather, they stratify their accounts of it. At the basic level of speech, thought, and conceptualization, they express truths in terms that directly reflect the metaphysical situation; at the less basic level, they say things that are still true, but, as stated, are bad pointers to the metaphysical situation, and one needs an account of what their truth amounts to, comes down to, arises from, in terms of facts expressed at the basic level. The non-basic level gets a hearing only because it involves ordinary, familiar ways of saying things.

Consider Descartes on qualitative variety in the material realm: he does not object to our saying that things differ in how hard, heavy, splittable, etc. they are;

but he says that these statements get their truth purely from fundamental facts about how various portions of matter move in relation to their immediate neighbours (§18). And consider Locke on secondary qualities: he allows familiar statements about things being green, warm, and odorous; but he tells us that the underlying reality that makes those statements true is that things are disposed to cause certain kinds of mental states in us (§188). Then there is Hume on the existence of individual minds: he does not rule out familiar statements about a thought's occurring in the very same mind as it occurred in yesterday; but he says that such truth as that contains comes from the existence of a sequence of perceptions that are related causally and in other ways (§307). Consider also Berkeley on extra-mental causation: we are allowed to say (speaking 'with the vulgar') that the fire caused the kettle to boil, but if we want the fundamental reality that gives this such truth as it has, we shall speak 'with the learned' and say things about regularities that obtain because of God's activities in causing ideas in our minds (§212). Reflect also on contemporary metaphysicians who deny that in wearing a new ring composed of old gold you are wearing two things, a ring and a portion of gold; and who propose that, strictly speaking, there are no rings but only portions of gold of which some are annular for a while.

Anyone who thinks he has metaphysical news about the world will distinguish levels of speech about it. Many plain, quotidian statements, he will say, are metaphysically misleading as they stand, though they can be sanitized—rendered acceptable or even interpreted as true—by being understood in terms of corresponding basic truths. This being standard procedure, there is no reason for a metaphysician to trumpet the fact that he is following it.

58. Bodies and motion

The two-level nature of Spinoza's exposition in the *Ethics* makes itself felt in many ways, one of which concerns the notion of *bodies moving*. This belongs at the non-basic level: on the ground floor one does not quantify over bodies or anything else that moves. Nothing moves, because no thing moves, because there is only one thing, and there are no places outside it. Much of the work, however, has to be written in the less fundamental language of moving bodies—for example, when Spinoza writes about how human beings behave towards one another. So, after introducing and defending his metaphysic of matter on the ground floor, he needs to move up to the everyday, familiar level at which one speaks of bodies in motion. That is what he does. Here are the facts.

Part 1 is ground-floor metaphysics all the way, and accordingly it contains no theoretical uses of the concepts of body and of motion.

The word 'body' occurs in three places in part 1. In 1d2 Spinoza tries to explain a very general doctrine of his by pointing to a familiar example which involves 'body'. Here he momentarily reaches up to the non-basic level, for expository purposes. The word also occurs in 1p15s and the Appendix, each time when Spinoza is characterizing the errors of others, not advancing doctrines of his own.

In the Appendix, he refers to 'the motion the nerves receive from objects presented through the eyes', this being part of his subjectivism about aesthetics; but this is general rhetoric. In it, as throughout the Appendix, the severities of the basic metaphysic are relaxed.

No cognate of 'move' occurs before the Appendix. The noun 'motion' occurs only in 1p32c2, where Spinoza prematurely refers to the fundamentals of physics through a phrase that he will not properly introduce until the part 2 physical interlude—namely, 'motion and rest'. There is no doctrinal use of 'motion' here. Spinoza is not presenting his own metaphysic, but merely warning readers against the mistake of believing in freedom of the will. If you allow 'freedom' into psychology, he implies, you will have equally good or bad reasons for allowing it also into physics—or, as he puts it, for allowing 'freedom of motion and rest'.

Spinoza's monism continues to be crucially important early in part 2, especially at 2p7s, where he completes his account of how mentality fits into an extended universe; and it continues to work in the background through pp8–11, where he develops his parallelism, working steadily towards applying it to the specific topic of how human minds relate to human bodies. It is fitting, therefore, that in part 2 no cognate of 'body' or 'move' occurs before 2p12 (except in two axioms and a definition which lie dormant until 2p13). In 2p12 Spinoza explicitly mentions 'the human body': he has his long-distance sights on—among other things—some doctrines in individual and social psychology, involving theses about how people behave towards one another. Moving bodies, then, will be unavoidable. But then his substance-monism will no longer have specific work to do, so he can comfortably move up to the familiar level at which bodies move through space.

This is exactly what happens. Having said in p12 that a certain thing will be the case 'if the object of the idea constituting a human Mind is a body', Spinoza proceeds in 2p13 to affirm that 'the object of the idea constituting a human Mind is a body'; and then he embarks on the physical interlude. In this sketchy physics, topped by an abstract biology, he is trying to get us to think in a certain way about human bodies, because, he says, they will call the tune when we try to think about human minds. The physics is corpuscularian, so it makes copious use—*for the first time in the doctrinal parts of the work*—of the concept of bodies moving in space.

Those who see Spinoza as the broad-brush, impressionistic, mystical philosopher who has charmed many poets and some philosophers will neither see nor care that he gives the concept of motion no positive work to do until he reaches the physical interlude. But if we see him, rather, as a tough-minded analytic metaphysician, then we shall want to know why 'motion' and 'body' appear only in marginal, negative, non-theoretical ways until 2p12 and then torrentially burst into action. My explanation is that this is where Spinoza starts to expound matters that require the familiar language, one level up from basic metaphysics.

In his fundamental metaphysic, the one substance has (at least) two attributes, under each of which there are 'infinite and eternal modes'. Spinoza's label for the one pertaining to extension is 'motion and rest'. This label is not announced until the physical interlude in part 2, and my line of thought in this section suggests a reason why: until that stage in the work, Spinoza operates at the basic level, where the concept of moving body has no place.

Objection: 'Still, you ought to maintain that "motion and rest" is a terrible name for whatever it is supposed to name. Whatever we finally think about infinite and eternal modes, they are certainly an important, load-bearing part of Spinoza's metaphysical structure. Wouldn't it be stupid of him to give one of them a label that is quite inappropriate in the context of his basic metaphysic?' No, it would not, if no good alternative were available. And none is. I did my best by stipulating half-understood meanings for 'thick' and 'thin', but we have no clear, accessible, familiar language in which to state briefly what goes on at the basic level.

I submit that Spinoza knew all this. He knew that in the context of his metaphysic the term 'motion' could only be a place-holder for something that he could not express in idiomatic language. That explains an episode in the *Short Treatise*. Introducing immediate infinite and eternal modes, he writes: 'We know only two of these: Motion in matter, and Intellect in the thinking thing' (1661a, CS 91). There is a footnote—presumably by Spinoza himself, or by his copyist on his behalf—keyed to the word 'motion': 'What is said here of Motion in matter is not said seriously. For the Author still intends to discover its cause, as he has already done, to some extent, a posteriori. But it can stand as it is here, because nothing is built on it, or depends on it.' Curley adds in a puzzled editorial footnote: 'It is unclear what portion of the text Spinoza intends to disavow'; but it is clear to me that Spinoza is disavowing the word 'motion'. What *immediately* follows from the one substance's nature as extended is not motion, but rather something more basic, which shows up as motion at the metaphysical level where bodies move. At the basic level there are shifting patterns of qualitative variation among regions of Space. I call these the metaphysical underlay or source of the movements of bodies; Spinoza calls them the 'cause' of motion. That is standard usage on his part: he is willing to classify as causal just about any kind of dependence.

Chapter 8

Explaining the Parallelism

59. 'Idea of' in Spinoza

Spinoza's parallelism doctrine seeks to reconcile the appearance of mind-body interaction with a metaphysic which sternly forbids any causal flow between attributes. It postulates two parallel causal systems, with a correspondence relation—some metaphysical function—mapping events in one onto events in the other, and causal chains in one onto causal chains in the other. Spinoza expresses the function in two ways: if it links mental item x with extended item y, then x is I(y), the 'idea of' y, and y is O(x), the 'object of' x.

Spinoza first announces the parallelism here: 'In God there is an idea both of God's essence and of everything that necessarily follows from God's essence' (2p3). This needs to be decoded a little. What it means is: 'The universe contains a mental counterpart both of the laws by which the universe works and of all particular events and states of affairs.' Using my shorthand, given any extended thing, state or event y, there is a corresponding mental thing, state, or event I(y). To complete the parallelism doctrine, Spinoza needs to assert that causal chains under one attribute map onto chains under the other, as he does here: 'The order and connection of ideas is the same as the order and connection of things' (2p7).

Think back to the example of Jab–Pain–Cry (§48). The parallelism doctrine cannot serve its intended purpose unless it identifies O(Pain) with something one could plausibly think to be caused by Jab and to be the cause of Cry. So it must be something in the body of the person concerned. Spinoza secures this with a typically bold and sweeping proposition: 'The object of the idea constituting the human mind is the body' (2p13). I tend to think of the parallelism as mapping mental events onto brain events, and mental characteristics onto structural features of brains; but the official doctrine just says that the parallelism maps your mind onto your body.

Onto what does it map the body of an ant, or a pebble, or a jab in the arm with a pin? Do not think that Spinoza could say: 'There is such an item as the idea of a pebble just so long as somebody thinks about or imagines or perceives the pebble.' Obviously, this approach could not secure that at every moment there is an idea of every mode of extension. Less obviously, but more profoundly, the relation between my thought and that pebble when I see or think about the pebble is not the 'idea of' relation that enters into the cosmic parallelism between extension and thought. This parallelism pairs that idea of mine with some state of or event in my body—nothing else. As for the ideas of an ant, a pebble, a jab in the arm with a pin—they need not be recognizably mental, and need only to be capable of generating mentality when they are assembled in the right way into complexes.

The 'idea of' terminology suggests that I(x) represents x. The counterpart relation has little to do with our ordinary notion of mental representation, of the partly introspectible content of what a person believes or knows or is thinking about, because the 'object of' a thought that I have about you is not *you*, but rather some state of my own body. Yet Spinoza does sometimes use the language of representation in describing the parallelism, especially when he infers from 2p7—'The order and connection of ideas is the same as the order and connection of things'—this corollary:

From this it follows that God's power of thinking is equal to his actual power of acting. That is, whatever follows intrinsically [*formaliter*] from God's infinite nature follows representatively [*objectivè*] in God from his idea in the same order and with the same connection.

(For the Latin adverbs, see §34.) So 2p7 says that the material realm is matched, with the same 'order and connection', by a mental realm; and 2p7c adds that the mental realm represents the other.

Perhaps this is not really an addition. Spinoza seems to think it is not, announcing 2p7c as a corollary which follows from 2p7. Even if we read 'follows' a bit loosely, not looking for an outright entailment, the fact remains that Spinoza introduces the concept of representation immediately after 2p7 and long in advance of presenting any detailed philosophical psychology. He evidently regards this concept as obviously and immediately available to him, not one that must first be worked for through a detailed account of what it is. One wonders why.

He cannot be deriving it from the sheer fact of parallelism, working with a thin concept of representation according to which I(x) represents x simply because there is a systematic function mapping one onto the other. For in Spinoza's scheme that function works both ways, but he certainly does not think that x represents I(x). Presumably, then, he sees representativeness as somehow of the essence of the mental: I(x) represents x simply by virtue of being a *mental* or *thinking* counterpart of x. I do not like crediting him with such a hazardous assumption; but I see no way out.

If the only kind of mental representation that Spinoza allowed was that generated by the parallelism, he would be committed to holding that all we ever perceive or think about are states of our own bodies. He is too realistic and reasonable for that. Although somewhat condescending about empirical knowledge of the world around one, Spinoza knows that it occurs, and needs to provide for it. He does so, thus: 'The human mind perceives the nature of a great many bodies together with the nature of its own body' (2p16c1). He has inferred this from the fact that if some external body x causes an event e in my body, my idea *directly* of e will be of a nature that owes something to x. This is a sketch of a causal theory of perception: light bounces off x on to my eyes, causing a change in my brain, which has its mental counterpart. I may think of the latter as a visual image of x, and so it is. But that breaks down into two: it is the mental counterpart of (or: the idea directly of) my brain state, which was caused by an interaction with x; so, in my terminology, it is my idea *indirectly of* x. Spinoza goes on to say, in a second corollary, that this idea indirectly of x contains more information about the state of my body than about x's state.[1]

The indirectly-of relation embodies a causal theory of perception, but not only of that. The 'ideas' that Spinoza speaks of include beliefs as well as perceptions: he seems to regard my idea directly of my body as a richly complex and mostly unconscious belief about my bodily state, and my idea indirectly of you as a skimpier belief about your body (§73).

60. The official arguments for parallelism

Spinoza's arguments for parallelism differ from the motivating reasons that I have offered on his behalf. The latter use only Spinozistic materials, and have more force than his official arguments, which seem to me no better than the argument for substance-monism using the no-shared-attribute thesis. Grudgingly, I give them a section.

According to 2p3, every material item has a mental counterpart: I take this to imply that there is a cosmos-wide function which maps material items onto mental ones, and vice versa, with similarities in one domain being mapped onto similarities in the other. The story of the parallelism would be almost vacuous if it did not include that last clause. For example, the fact that pain regularly follows pin jabs can be explained through the parallelism only if such jabs in general are paired by it with some class of mental events which are about as alike as the jabs are. A further requirement will be discussed in a moment.

Spinoza's argument for 2p3 says, in effect: There could be a mental counterpart for every material item, and whatever could be so, is so. Spinoza expresses this in theological terms: 'Whatever we conceive to be in God's power necessarily exists' (1p35), but the underlying thought is not theological, I think. Spinoza's reasoning from 1p16,c to 1p34 and thence to 1p35 amounts to the following: (1) There is only God; so (2) whatever is the case is caused to be so by God, that is, follows necessarily from God's nature; so (3) if something is not the case, that is

---

[1] A single idea is at once directly of a state of my body and indirectly of something else. We can speak of two mental 'contents' here, understanding a content as a relational property of an idea: the one idea has different representative relations to different items. This position, as offered in *Study*, has been misrepresented by Della Rocca (1996a: 52), who credits me with holding that Spinoza employs 'different senses of representation'. I have said nothing about senses of 'representation' (let alone senses of representation).

because God's nature causally rules it out; so (4) whatever is not the case is causally impossible; so (5) whatever is possible is actual—that is, whatever God could do, God does do. Premiss 1 is Spinoza's substance-monism. The move to 2 is licensed by explanatory rationalism, taken as implying that whatever happens is caused to happen. In Spinoza's universe nothing is uncaused, and causation is always deterministic; neither he nor anyone else had dreamed of probabilistic causation. The further moves to 3, 4, and 5 are all valid, and need no comment.

Given substance-monism and determinism, this argument for 1p35 goes through. It does not, however, enlarge the scope of what is true by saying that *whatever is possible is true*, but rather contracts the scope of possibility by saying that *whatever is false is impossible*. In the light of this, consider the other premiss that Spinoza needs for 2p3: namely, that God can contain an idea of every material item. This now becomes a mere shot in the dark. Spinoza purports to infer it from 1p16, but look for yourself, and you will see that it does not follow.

I should add that if 2p3 did succeed in showing that every material item has a mental counterpart, it could also be turned into an argument showing that every mental item has a material counterpart: God could make the material world as rich as that, so he does make it as rich as that.

Now let us turn to the rest of the parallelism doctrine: namely, the assertion in 2p7 that the mental counterparts of material items are causally organized in the same way as the material items themselves—that is, that the 'idea directly of' relation maps causal chains under one attribute onto causal chains under the other. That is the second constraint that the parallelism must satisfy if it is to do its assigned work.[2]

Now see (again) Spinoza's statement of this, followed by his entire argument for it:

The order and connection of ideas is the same as the order and connection of things. Demonstration: This is clear from 1a4. For the idea of each caused thing depends on the knowledge of the cause of which it is the effect.

Although Spinoza does not say so, 2p3 also lies in the background of this: assuming that every event in the material realm has a mental counterpart, 2p7 merely says how these mental items are causally related to one another. When he talks about 'knowledge' (*cognitio*), here and in 1a4, Spinoza is referring to mental particulars, items of knowledge or thought or belief or the like. He presumably takes 1a4 to say: if x causes y, then a *cognitio* of y is caused by ('depends on and involves') a *cognitio* of x, and inferring from this that corresponding to the material causal chain there is a matching mental one.

This argument fails, because 1a4 has two readings, one of which makes it plausible, while the other makes it support 2p7. No reading gives it both virtues. To

[2] Compare: 'The representation of the present state of the universe in the dog's soul produces in it the representation of the subsequent state of the same universe, just as in the things represented the preceding state actually produces the subsequent state of the world. In a soul, *the representations of causes are the causes of the representations of effects*' (Leibniz, 1697a, FW 200).

connect it with 2p7, we must take 1a4 to say that the mental counterpart of y must be caused by the mental counterpart of the cause of y; and there is no reason to accept that, let alone to treat it as axiomatic. To make 1a4 plausible, we must take it to express the familiar truth that a really complete knowledge of any item requires knowing about its causes. This does not imply 2p7, for two reasons. First, it says that knowledge of the effect *requires for its completion* knowledge of the cause, but not that the former *is caused by* the latter. Second, the knowledge-of that this involves is not the idea 'directly of' that features in 2p7 and parallelism, but rather the 'indirectly of' relation. When understood so as to have some chance of being true, 1a4 involves ordinary familiar 'knowledge of', like my knowledge of the French Revolution, which would be better if I knew more about the Revolution's causes; and the parallelism matches this not with the French Revolution but with some states of and events in my body. In a nutshell, certain thoughts of mine relate in one way to the French Revolution and in another to the state of my body; the believable version of 1a4 concerns the former of these relations, and 2p7 the latter; one cannot validly argue across the chasm.

61. The thing-identity thesis: explaining parallelism

In presenting a solid Spinozistic reason for believing the parallelism doctrine, I said nothing about what might make it true. Spinoza's official arguments for 2p3,7 ought to do both: convince us of the doctrine by deriving it from acceptable axioms, and explain its truth by showing how it follows from basic features of reality. Evidently he did not trust 2p3d,7d to perform the latter task, for in 2p7s he offers a different account of what makes the parallelism true. This account is more interesting and worthy of respect than the official arguments. I now expound it.

   In the great, under-appreciated scholium to 2p7, Spinoza does three striking things in quick succession. Let us look at the first two together. (1) He reminds us that there is only one substance, so that the thinking substance and the extended substance are one and the same. (2) He goes straight on to say that any mode of extension is identical with the idea of it—that is, with the corresponding mode of thought:

[1] The thinking substance and the extended substance are one and the same substance, which is comprehended now under this attribute, now under that. So also [2] a mode of extension and the idea of that mode is one and the same thing, but expressed in two ways. . . . For example, a circle existing in nature and the idea of the existing circle . . . is one and the same thing, which is explained through different attributes. (*CS* 451)

The astonishing thing-identity thesis 2 entails, among other things, that your mind is your body. It pops up out of nowhere: Spinoza does not 'demonstrate' it here, and nothing earlier in the *Ethics* has prepared the way for it. He does not infer it from (1) his substance-monism. He links the two only by the phrase *Sic etiam*: he is conjoining them in a manner implying that they are similar, as indeed they are. *Just as* the worlds of thought and of extension are aspects of a single substance, *so also* the members of any particular mind–matter pair are one and the same thing.

(3) Having asserted 1 and 2, Spinoza says that this is why we shall find the same order and connection of causes under each attribute. (I prefer 'that is why' to Curley's 'therefore' for *ideò*; Spinoza is explaining, not concluding.) So he offers what he has said up to here in the scholium as *explaining* the parallelism that he has asserted in 2p7; and the offering is genuinely explanatory, in a way that the unsound 2p3d and the unhelpful 2p7d are not.

Spinoza's words do not make clear whether 2 alone provides the explanation or whether 1 has a role in it also; but I declare that both are involved. Do not think that parallelism follows from 1 alone. A single substance could fall under two attributes without its history under one mirroring its history under the other. Some philosophers today hold that a person is a substance having material properties and mental ones; they do not hold that some mental feature matches each material feature of a person; and this overall position of theirs seems consistent.

To grasp how 1 and 2 join forces to explain (3) the parallelism, one must get (1) the substance-monism right, which involves seeing that Spinoza uses 'mode' to mean what it normally meant then. Bodies are properties or states of the one substance, so that what we ordinarily call the movement of a thing through space is basically an alteration in which regions of space are 'thick' (so to speak) and which 'thin'. According to this monism, my body is a mode—an 'affection' or state or quality—of the one substance. The whole truth about my body is equivalent to something that would be stated at the most basic level in the form:

The one substance is extended and F,

for some astronomically complex value of F. Here 'F' stands for an aspect of the one substance's nature—it is a complex quality that the substance possesses. It would be convenient to call it a 'mode', but that would be wrong, because for Spinoza each mode *includes* an attribute, whereas I am using 'F' to designate what remains of a certain mode when its attribute—extension—is peeled off. It is the *further detail*, additional to mere extension, that must be true of the one substance for the entire story of my body to be true.

This same story is meant to apply, *mutatis mutandis*, to finite thinking things: Spinoza holds them to be modes of the one substance under the attribute of thought. So far I have not given him any sober reason for stretching the monism of extended substance to embrace thinking substance as well, or tried to make the stretch look independently reasonable or even intelligible. The only support for it—which must also make it intelligible, if anything does—is its role in the present explanation. I offer it as a metaphysical hypothesis whose explanatory power might persuade us to accept it. Now, it says that the whole truth about my mind (the idea of my body) is equivalent to something of the form:

The one substance is thinking and G,

for some complex value of G. Here again, 'G' stands for a complex quality that the one substance possesses.

In the preceding two paragraphs, I have added nothing to what Spinoza says: finite things are modes of the one substance, some under extension, some under thought. Once we get this clear in our minds, we can easily see what he must mean by the doctrine I call 'the thing-identity thesis'. When he implicitly calls my mind and my body 'one and the same thing', he must mean that F is G. The basic facts which, combined with the universe's being extended, make true the story of my body are the very ones which, combined with the universe's being a thinking thing, make true the story of my mind. What it takes for there to be a material object like my body is for there to be an F extended substance, and what it takes for there to be a mind like mine is for there to be an F thinking substance— for the same value of F.

That is my conservatively literal account of what Spinoza means by the thing-identity thesis. Each object–idea pair whose members are matched in the parallelism involves a single qualitative item—a single aspect of the nature of the one substance—which shows up as a pair because it combines with both the attributes, which are different.

This explains the parallelism. Monism says that one substance has all the mental modes and all the material modes, while the thing-identity thesis says that a single underlying nature combines with extension to yield all the material modes, and with thought to yield all the mental ones. Every instantiated mode under either attribute, therefore, is matched by an instantiated mode under the other: if something is F and thinking, then something is F and extended, and vice versa. So we get a parallelism in which material similarities map onto mental ones, and—most important—material causal chains map onto mental ones.

To see this, let us return to (a) the causal sequence from Jab to O(Pain) to Cry, and ask why, if that occurs, there should also be (b) a causal sequence from I(Jab) to Pain to I(Cry). The answer is that the truth about a, stated in basic terms, has the form:

Extended reality is F, which causes it to be G, which causes it to be H.

If the extended thing is also thinking, then it follows from this that:

Thinking reality is F, which causes it to be G, which causes it to be H.

And that is the whole truth about b. The causal details in the first chain come not from the extendedness but from F-G-H, so those must be causally interrelated in the same way when combined with the other attribute. So, necessarily, causal chains map onto causal chains.

I have argued that (3) parallelism does not follow from (1) substance-monism alone. Nor does it follow from (2) the thing-identity thesis alone. To see why, let us suspend judgement on 1 and see how far we can get with 2 alone. We are assuming that the proposition *There is a body which . . . [fill in the entire truth about my actual body]* is equivalent to

E: There is an extended substance which is F;

and the proposition *There is a mind which . . . [fill in the entire truth about my actual mind]* is equivalent to

T: There is a thinking substance which is F.

From 2 we get that the very same value of F occurs in both these propositions. But that is as far as 2 takes us. For all it says to the contrary, it might be that E is true and false, or vice versa. What rules *that* out is the thesis (1) that the only thinking substance is also the only extended substance.

Margaret Wilson (1981) alleged that my interpretation of 2p7s is in trouble because in 1p1 Spinoza says that a substance is prior in nature to its states, which he never says about how a substance relates to its attributes; and Carriero (1994: 641) seems to offer this as his whole reason for rejecting my 'interesting and particularly original treatment'. If there is any real difficulty here, it is too remote and oblique to outweigh the merits of the interpretation. For some argument on the point, see my *Study* 147–8.

62. Trans-attributes qualities

The qualitative items I have designated by 'F' in the above explanation are trans-attributes ones. Note the plural: they spread across both the attributes, combining with each. They are not modes in Spinoza's sense of the term, because he standardly takes modes to include attributes. If truth about my body is the fact that the one substance is extended and F, the property or quality that Spinoza calls the 'mode' that is my body is not F but extension-and-F.

One might say—and in *Study* and elsewhere I have said it—that although that is Spinoza's standard use of 'mode', he must in 2p7s be using the word in a thinned-out sense, making it cover the item that remains if you take a mode (in the ordinary sense) and peel off its attribute. Why just there? Because only there does he have any need for the concept in question: namely, to express the thing-identity thesis. I have even questioned whether Spinoza really does ordinarily think of each mode as involving an attribute, but that was a mistake. When he writes, 'The modes of each attribute involve the concept of their attribute' (2p6d), one hesitates; it seems odd to say that a *mode* involves a *concept*. But I do not think there is anything to be made of this. We had better understand the remark as scholars usually have, as meaning 'The modes of each attribute involve their attribute'.

Spinoza's definition of 'mode' is evidence for this: 'By mode I understand the affections of a substance, or that which is in another through which it is also conceived.' After defining substance as that which is conceived through itself, Spinoza means to define 'mode' in terms of what is conceived through (a) substance. He gives no hint that a mode must also be conceived through an attribute; and this could be because he does not think that it must, which would have to be because he thinks of each mode as involving an attribute.

In 1p15d he writes: 'Except for substances and modes there is nothing.' This seems to leave out the attributes; but it does not do so if they are included in the modes.

Further evidence of Spinoza's thinking of 'modes' as involving attributes is provided by the very sentence in 2p7s which expresses the thing-identity thesis. After characterizing the thinking substance and the extended substance as 'one and the same *substance*', what Spinoza says of a mode of extension and a mode of thought is not that this is 'one and the same *mode*', but rather that it is 'one and the same *thing*'. He seems to keep 'mode' out of that last clause deliberately, presumably because even here he chooses to take modes as intra-attribute rather than as trans-attributes.

It is, then, safer to suppose that in Spinoza's idiolect 'mode' applies only to fattened-up items each of which includes an attribute. Using 'mode' in this way, he cannot consistently identify a mode of extension with a mode of thought. Yet he does pick out a mode of one and a mode of the other and call them 'one and the same thing', and I explain this by taking it to mean that the two modes—which *are* two, because their attributes are different—are identical with respect to everything except their attributes; that is, they come from combining two attributes with one and the same trans-attributes quality.

This use of 'one and the same thing' is not fully satisfactory on my interpretation, but nor can it be on any other. Spinoza maintains that the attributes are different, and that minds and bodies involve their respective attributes; so he cannot outright identify minds with bodies. (For a dissenting view see Della Rocca 1996a: 163–4.) Another reason for this is 2p7, which invites us to see the mental and material realms as running parallel; it takes two to make a parallelism! It is important to grasp that in the thing-identity thesis Spinoza is not identifying mode with mode; the outright identity which that thesis affirms is not of modes but of trans-attributes qualities which are ingredients of modes, the remaining ingredient in each being an attribute. In §67 I shall exhibit the special terminology that Spinoza uses for referring to the trans-attributes nature of the one substance.

63. A difficulty and a suggested solution

Spinoza's thing-identity thesis, on my interpretation of it, might seem to conflict with the doctrine—which he has just affirmed in 2p5,6—that no causes flow across the boundaries between attributes. That would be damaging, because the latter doctrine is vital to many Spinozistic lines of thought, including his view that human physical behaviour is explicable in terms not of psychology but of biology. The threat is as follows. Consider a short causal chain of material events:

A needle enters an arm at T_1, causing neuron N to fire at T_2.

Expressed in a deeper and metaphysically more illuminating way, this is a fact of this form:

Reality is extended and F at T_1, causing it to be extended and G at T_2,

where F and G stand for trans-attributes qualities of the world. Now, suppose that the 'idea of' the firing of N is a stab of pain. The fact that it occurs is the fact that:

Reality is thinking and G at T_2.

We are now threatened with having to allow the causal sequence:

Reality is extended and F at T_1, causing it to be thinking and G at T_2,

meaning that a stab in the arm causes a pain. Given nothing but the perfectly general premiss that reality falls under each attribute, we can run causal explanations freely from the material to the mental and back again. Given a premiss affirming the two attributes of the one substance, we have all we need for sharp, deep, clean causal explanations that run across the boundary between the attributes. Where Spinoza tells us that the boundary is impervious to such logico-causal flow, the thing-identity thesis seems to imply that the flow can occur at a level deeper than that of the attributes, being carried by the one substance's trans-attributes qualities.

This threat assumes that in the jab-firing causal transaction, extension is merely the stage on which this little causal drama is played out, and is not itself an actor. Similarly with all other causal sequences under either attribute. The causal thrust comes from the trans-attributes qualities that make the difference between one item and another within an attribute. This has to be Spinoza's view, for without it, the thing-identity thesis could not explain the parallelism of causal chains.

To get him out of this fix, I have to credit him with accepting a thesis which I call Combine: *No element in the trans-attributes nature of the one substance can be thought of in isolation from any attribute.* Some such element does indeed at T_2 combine with extension to yield the neuronal event and with thought to yield the pain, but, according to Combine, we cannot in our thought isolate that element; our only conceptual grasp of it, beyond the mere thought that *there is* such an item, is in one or other of its combinations—the neuronal event and the pain.

If Spinoza accepts this, he can postulate the entire trans-attributes nature of the one substance while fending off the threat that it will carry causal explanations between the attributes. The threat was that we could causally infer my pain at T_2 from the jab at T_1, through an inference containing this:

Reality is extended and F,
Reality is thinking,

so

Reality is thinking and F.

Combine says that we cannot conduct that inference, because we cannot pull F out from its combination with extension and track it through into its combination with thought. (For further development of this approach, which I first presented in *Study*, see Della Rocca 1996a: 144–51.)

Although Spinoza does not ever assert Combine, I believe that he accepts it. The attribution of it to him solves too many problems to be wrong.

You might well think that it fails with the very problem that I introduced it to solve. It follows from Combine that we cannot conduct a trans-attributes causal explanation, because that would require a kind of abstraction of which we are incapable; but might there not still *be* an explanation—a causal reason—for some fact, even if nobody could think it? In short, my hypothesis reconciles the thing-identity doctrine with there being no *followable explanations* running between attributes, but not, apparently, with there being no *causal flow* between them.

This very difficulty is the next thing that Spinoza tackles in our scholium. At exactly the point where an alert reader—having understood Spinoza in the manner of my interpretation—might detect a whiff of inconsistency, Spinoza explains that *when he says that no causes run between the attributes, he means only that no followable explanations do so.* Here is the passage again (the emphases are mine):

When I said that God is the *cause* of the idea . . . of a circle only insofar as he is a thinking thing, and the *cause* of the circle only insofar as he is an extended thing, this was for no other reason than because the intrinsic being of the idea of the circle can be *perceived* only through another mode of thinking as its proximate cause, and . . . so on to infinity. Hence, so long as things are *considered* as modes of thinking, we have to *explain* the order of the whole of nature, or the connection of causes, through the attribute of Thought alone. And insofar as they are *considered* as modes of Extension, the order of the whole of nature has to be *explained* through the attribute of Extension alone. (*CS* 451–2)

This passage has the form, 'When I said that P, this was for no other reason than because Q', which I take to mean: 'When I said that P, what I meant was Q'. Spinoza states P in terms of 'cause', and Q in terms of 'perceive', 'consider' (twice) and 'explain' (twice), and does not use 'cause' in direct application to the world except in the passing phrase 'connection of causes'. He picks up and psychologizes the doctrine about the causal insulation between the attributes, explaining it in terms of how things must be explained, perceived, considered. This is exactly the right thing for him to be saying just here, if (but only if) he accepts Combine.

64. Five problems solved

My account of 2p7s, as so far presented, solves five problems. Three concern the Spinozistic metaphysic as a whole, the other two the structure and content of 2p7s in particular. Problems A and B are famous; C–E are not.

Problem A   Because of Spinoza's radical dualism of concepts and properties—and especially his denial of causal flow between attributes—some of his readers have wondered what content he can give to (1) the thesis that a single substance has properties of both kinds. What does this thesis say, beyond expressing a preference for a certain wording? We have this extended realm and this mental realm; Spinoza calls them two sides or aspects or attributes of a single world or substance; but so what? This cannot affect our causal story about either realm, and what other difference can it make? When Locke declared that we cannot discover whether your thought is done by an animal body or by an unextended substance associated with it, he came close to implying that the two stories have the same content (§116). Similarly with Spinoza—how can he ward off the threat of vacuity?

Here is the answer. That the two attributes are possessed by one substance rather than by two makes a huge difference; the attributes are held together in a single substance by the latter's trans-attributes nature, the network of qualities which runs across all the attributes, giving the one substance its integrity, its wholeness. There is no threat that Nature, just because its attributes are so disconnected, will conceptually fall apart. Spinoza runs no risk of having to admit that 'two attributes, one substance' differs verbally but not really from 'two attributes, two substances'.

Problem B   The (3) mind–body parallelism is essential to, and structural in, Spinoza's account of the human condition; and his explanatory rationalism is the air he breathes. If he had to postulate the parallelism without being able to explain it, he would be acutely uncomfortable; and if he had to postulate it while thinking that it could not be explained, he would suffocate. My account of 2p7s provides the explanation: the parallelism results from an underlying qualitative sameness on each side of the line. The qualities in question—the trans-attributes ones—are not independently accessible to intellect, so it cannot be proved or helpfully illustrated by examples. But Spinoza asserts that they are *there*. He cannot prove this—nor does he try to, but merely asserts it. Even considered as a postulate or hypothesis, however, it meets his need for something that could explain why the parallelism obtains.

Problem C   Along with problem A, there should have been similar worries about the meaning and content of (2) Spinoza's thesis that a mode of extension and the idea of it are one and the same thing. My interpretation answers this.

Problem D   In 2p7s, Spinoza mentions (1) substance-monism, (2) the thing-identity thesis, and (3) parallelism, this being 2's first appearance in the *Ethics*. Why does it show up just here? What has it to do with the other two? What movement of thought occurs when Spinoza asserts 1, adds that *sic etiam* 2, and moves to *ideò* 3? Spinoza scholars have not worried about this cluster of questions; but for anyone who trusts him to have written deliberately on the basis of careful thought, they press for answers. My interpretation provides them.

Problem E   Another question that ought to have troubled Spinozists down the centuries is, Why does Spinoza recall, at this point in the scholium, his denial of causal flow between attributes? And why, having done so, does he restate it in psychological terms? My interpretation answers both these questions. Spinoza has just finished explaining why the parallelism obtains; the explanation asserts that a common nature runs across the attribute boundary, which seems to collide with his denial of logico-causal flow between attributes; and he needs to explain why it does not. This is the right place for him to recall the 'no causal flow' doctrine, and his psychologizing of the notion of causal prevents the collision.

65. A further problem solved: attribute and essence

A notorious problem in the understanding of the *Ethics*—the subject of great debate and a mountain of literature—is solved by my hypothesis that Spinoza thinks there are qualities that can combine with different attributes but cannot be thought in abstraction from any attribute. The problem concerns 1d4, Spinoza's official definition of 'attribute': 'By attribute I understand what the intellect perceives of a substance as constituting its essence.' The problem is to explain 'what intellect perceives as . . .'. Or '. . . perceives as if'; the difference does not matter, because either way the problem remains. Suppose we ask Spinoza: In your view, does each attribute *really* constitute an essence of the substance that has it? If he answers Yes, then he behaves bizarrely in suppressing this information in his definition of 'attribute', writing about what intellect perceives an attribute as, and thereby giving the impression that his answer is No. If, on the other hand, his answer is indeed No—an attribute does not really constitute an essence of the substance that has it—then three further questions arise: (1) Why is the answer No? What stops an attribute from being an essence? (2) If an attribute is not an essence, why does intellect perceive it as one? (3) Why does Spinoza not define 'attribute' in terms of what attributes really are, rather than of what intellect perceives them as?

My interpretation of the materials in 2p7s implies that Spinoza should answer the original question by saying 'No, an attribute is not really an essence'; and it supplies answers to the three further questions arising out of that. Though 2p7s and 1d4 occupy seemingly remote regions of logical space, one is the key that unlocks the other.

When Spinoza defines the term 'essence' in 2d2 he gives it roughly the meaning we now give it: F-ness belongs to the essence of x if x could not possibly exist without being F; the essential is the absolutely indispensable. But that is not the sense of 'essence' that 1d4 involves, and it does not help to solve our problem. What 1d4 employs is a different sense of 'essence', the one Descartes uses here: 'To each substance there belongs one principal attribute . . . Each substance has one principal property which constitutes its nature and essence, and to which all its others are referred' (PP 1:53). In §44 I showed how to adapt this to the position of someone who, like Spinoza, believes that a single substance can have more than one essence or fundamental nature:

> To each substance there belong principal attributes. Each substance has a set S of essences or principal properties which jointly constitute its nature, and to the members of which all its other properties are referred—meaning that every property of the substance outside S is a special case of some one member of S, and no member of S is a special case of any other member of S.

Now, with 'essence' understood in this way, let us ask Spinoza whether the attributes of the one substance are essences of it? According to my interpretation of 2p7s, Spinoza's answer must be No.

(1) Why is the answer No? An attribute is not an 'essence' in the sense of my adaptation of Descartes's PP 1:53, because not everything that is true of the one substance is either a special case of extension alone or a special case of thought alone. On the contrary, the one substance has a trans-attributes nature every element of which combines both with extension and with thought; the attributes do not relate to the substance as jointly exhaustive and mutually exclusive 'containers' of all the substance's properties, in such a way that each property of the substance falls under just one attribute. A Cartesian essence is the sole container of whatever falls under it; a Spinozistic attribute is not the sole container of anything.

(2) Why does intellect perceive attributes as essences if really they are not? So far as our thought is concerned, extension presents itself as the sole container of whatever falls under it; as a matter of metaphysics, we know that all those items also fall under the other attribute, but we cannot *think* them individually as doing so, because that would require conceptually latching on to them by peeling off one attribute and slapping on the other—which cannot be done. We have to treat the attributes as though they were basic, or were 'principal properties', because the intellectual operation that belies this cannot be performed. That is the force of the thesis I called Combine.

(3) Why does Spinoza not define 'attribute' in terms of what attributes actually are? Because the fact that intellect engages with attributes as though they were Cartesian essences is the most helpfully explanatory thing that can be said about them. At the outset of a work like the *Ethics*, the need to point the reader's mind in the right direction and for the right distance when he encounters the word 'attribute' is met perfectly by the information that attributes are the properties that will figure in his thought as essences in the adapted Cartesian sense. If my interpretation of him is right, Spinoza should think that his explanation is

unbeatably accurate and helpful. That it generated centuries of confusion and speculation is due not to defects in it, but rather to Spinoza's neglecting to declare openly the metaphysical structure that lay behind it.

This is not a mere plea in mitigation. I proclaim 1d4 to be exactly right, the best definition Spinoza could have given for 'attribute'. He *has to* point to the attributes as the predicables which must in all our thought be treated as basic or 'principal' in Descartes's sense; he has no other way to pick them out as a class. And he *ought to* include a warning that they are basic only in our thought, not in reality. 'By attribute I understand what the intellect perceives of a substance as constituting its essence'—perfect! In §44, when expounding Spinoza's property-dualism, I followed the path pointed out by 1d4, introducing the attributes as basic and working with them as such. The metaphysical fact that they are not basic did not trip us up back then, and did not need to be confronted until its time came.

Spinoza provides a clue that 1d4 and 2p7s somehow belong together. Look back at the statement of monism that opens the scholium. Where one might expect Spinoza to write: '*Every attribute* pertains to one substance only', he actually writes: '*Whatever can be perceived by an infinite intellect as constituting an essence of substance* pertains to one substance only.' Instead of two Latin words meaning 'every attribute' he uses the eleven Latin words of his definiens for 'attribute', with 'infinite' thrown in for good measure. Nowhere else in the *Ethics* does Spinoza use that definiens in place of 'attribute' itself. Why here? And why nowhere else?

Because the full force of the definition has work to do here and nowhere else. Throughout the rest of the *Ethics* we can treat the attributes as basic, as Cartesian 'essences'; this is safe—indeed inevitable—because our intellects must perceive them as basic. Only here, where trans-attributes qualities have to be introduced in explaining parallelism, does Spinoza need to admit that, as a matter of sheer metaphysics, the attributes are not really basic.

66. Intellectual limitations?

Many commentators have noticed uneasily that Spinoza's definition of 'attribute' seems to imply that some kind of illusion is at work: intellect perceives attributes as something that they are not. Previous candidates for the intended illusion—that the attributes are illusory, or that the distinction between them is so—conflict with the main lines of Spinoza's philosophy. They are also insensitive to the wording of 1d4, which points to a difference between actuality and what intellect perceives, and locates it in the status of an attribute *as an essence*.

Is Spinoza speaking here only of human intellects, holding that some limitation of ours prevents us from thinking any trans-attributes element except in combination with an attribute? No, because when he repeats the definiens of 1d4 in 2p7s, he expands it to 'whatever can be perceived by an *infinite* intellect'. For him 'infinite' means 'unlimited'; by inserting it into the definiens, he signals that *any* intellect perceives attributes as essences. Not even an unlimited intellect, he implies, can have access to any trans-attributes quality other than in combination with an attribute. This has rightly been urged as a prima-facie difficulty for my interpretation.

An 'infinite' or unlimited intellect should be one that has nothing wrong with it; it should be in all relevant ways omniscient and infallible; and Spinoza does say that an attribute would be 'perceived as' an essence of its substance even by an intellect of that kind. I am unmoved. 'My' Spinoza does not hold that even an unlimited intellect would believe that an attribute is an essence of its substance: that would be absurd, given that Spinoza himself did not believe that attributes are essences. What he does hold—I here stay close to his own words—is that any intellect, finite or infinite, would *perceive an attribute as an essence*. The claim concerns the nature of the mental presentation of the attribute in a mind—any mind, even an unlimited one. In *Study* I wrote that '1d4 implies that there is something in the nature of an illusion or error or lack of intellectual depth or thoroughness in taking an attribute to be a basic property', but I was wrong to include 'error'. Perceiving extension (say) as an essence no more entails error than does seeing a half-submerged stick as bent. Spinoza adds 'infinite' to the definiens so as to warn the reader that his thesis concerns impermeability to intellect as such, not merely to the limited intellects of humans; he is not alleging error against any intellect. His thesis is just that the complex consisting of a trans-attributes quality and its attribute is *inherently* resistant to being conceptually dismembered in a certain way.

There is nothing mysterious about this. Let us work with the example Spinoza uses when, introducing the thing-identity thesis, he identifies a material circular thing with the idea of it. The facts about this dinner plate, stated at the metaphysically basic level, will be a fearfully complex predication on Space; but never mind all that. For present purposes we need only the simple predication *x is circular*. We can split up the meaning of that into:

x has the shape of a closed plane figure, and a point in x is equidistant from every point on its boundary.

We can think each of these in isolation from the other: each could be true of something of which the other was false (squares; spheres). And between them they capture the content of 'x is circular', with one element in that—namely that x is extended—being entailed by each. Now suppose we tried to split up its meaning along a different plane of cleavage:

x is extended, and Fx.

The dummy predicate 'F' stands for what remains of *x is circular* after you delete *x is extended* from it—the differentia that marks off the species of circles from within the genus of extended things. We have no non-tricky way of saying what that differentia is. (The tricky way is to say that F = circular-or-not-extended.) So there we have it: x's being extended is *part but not all* of x's being circular; there is more to the latter than that; but we cannot cleanly express the 'more'. And this seems to be in the nature of the case, and not to result from any stupidity on our part. This example serves to legitimize the notion of a complex that is intrinsically unsplittable along a certain line of cleavage.

What a labour to accommodate a single occurrence of 'infinite'! Still, we had to face it, because it is not negligible as a slip of the pen might be. One might wonder why Spinoza put 'infinite' in, rather than holding that Combine is true of us because of our limitations. Perhaps he thought—as he reasonably could have—that the 'limited intellects' version of Combine would leave him with a fact which cries out for explanation, and that he had no idea of what an explanation of it might be like. As for the 'inherent inextricability' alternative: he might plausibly have regarded that as a logically essential feature of trans-attributes qualities, not needing further explanation.

67. Expressing

When Spinoza writes about the world's causal powers, he ought to be referring to its trans-attributes nature or 'essence', and so he often is:

'Whatever happens does so only through the laws of God's infinite nature and follows from the necessity of his essence' (1p15s, *CS* 424).
'From the necessity of the divine nature there must follow infinitely many things' (1p16).
'. . . the necessity of the divine nature, or (what is the same thing) the laws of God's nature' (1p17d).
'God acts from the laws of his nature alone' (1p17d).
'The modes of the divine nature have followed from it necessarily . . . either insofar as the divine nature is considered absolutely or insofar as it is considered to be determined to act in a certain way' (1p29d).
'All things have been determined from the necessity of the divine nature to exist . . . and to produce effects in a certain way' (1p29d).

The trans-attributes status of God's nature or essence is highlighted also by Spinoza's repeatedly writing of it as *expressed* by the attributes:

'God [has] attributes each of which expresses an eternal and infinite essence' (1d6; also in 1p10s, 1p11, 1p14d, 1p16d).
'Each attribute expresses the reality or being of substance' (1p10s).
'By God's attributes are to be understood what expresses an essence of the Divine substance' (1p19d).
'. . . such attributes of substance as express an eternal and infinite essence' (1p29s; also 1p31d).

These should present an agonizing problem for anyone who holds that, despite 1d4's use of 'what intellect perceives as', Spinoza thinks that an attribute is an essence of the substance that has it. If x expresses y, then x can hardly be y! On my understanding of 1d4, that problem does not arise; but we still have to understand what Spinoza means by attributes' expressing the one substance's essence.

He means that each attribute 'expresses' the trans-attributes nature of God or reality in the sense of letting it through, combining with it so that it becomes accessible to intellect. The system of trans-attributes qualities is like a story written in ink which intellect cannot see, and the attributes tell intellect the story by reading it aloud, *expressing* it. This uses 'express' in roughly the sense of 'give information concerning', as Spinoza often does. Here, for example: 'This [idea] . . . must indicate or express a constitution of the body or of some part of it' (*CS* 542). Similarly in 1p20d, he writes that the attributes display (reveal to view, make clear to the understanding, unfold) God's eternal essence. Those are all good meanings for the Latin *explicant*; they improve upon Curley's 'explain'.

Spinoza also says that modes express God's essence:

'By body I understand a mode that in a certain and determinate way expresses God's essence insofar as he is considered as an extended thing' (2d1).

'The intrinsic being of ideas is a mode of thinking, that is, a mode that expresses in a certain way God's nature insofar as he is a thinking thing' (2p5d2).

'The essence of man . . . is an affection or mode, which expresses God's nature in a certain and determinate way' (2p10cd).

Here, as always, Spinoza thinks of each mode as including an attribute. When we think about a mode, therefore, we do not cleanly latch on to any element in God's trans-attributes nature, but only on to a combination of the latter with some attribute. Those combinations, the modes, speak to us of the fundamental trans-attributes nature, *expressing* the basic truth about God.

(Just once Spinoza writes of modes which 'express God's attributes' (1p25c). I think this was a mere slip—'attributes' for 'nature'. It is supposed to follow from 1d5 and 1p15, neither of which mentions attributes; and in 3p6d, which is its only recurrence, it is taken to have said only that modes 'express God's power', which puts Spinoza back on track.)

I have followed Spinoza in telling one story twice: the two sets of quotations about *expressing* tell from different sides the same metaphysical story about God's trans-attributes nature: it is expressed by the attributes (when they are modified); it is expressed by the modes (understood as including an attribute). As long as the topic is the whole of the one substance, there is no difference between the modified attributes and the attribute-including modes; which is why Spinoza could unambiguously use the one term 'express' in these two sets of passages. In 2p1d he uses it in both ways in nearly adjacent sentences.

The picture I have drawn does not square with three clusters of phrases where Spinoza is writing about 'infinite and eternal modes', which he says

'... follow from [the necessity of] the absolute nature of] an attribute' (1p21,d, five times).

'... follow from the absolute nature of some attribute of God' (1p23,d, twice).

'... [are] produced by [or: follow from] the absolute nature of an attribute of God' (1p28d, five times).

According to my interpretation, each mode follows from an attribute only in conjunction with some element in God's trans-attributes nature; yet here we have Spinoza saying that each infinite mode follows from an attribute alone. This break in the pattern occurs only in the four pages containing these clusters, and at the end of them Spinoza backs off. Having repeatedly alluded in 1p28d to what follows from the absolute nature of an attribute, in 1p28s he drops this in favour of 'produced by God', 'follow from God's absolute nature', and the like. And in 1p29s he outright equates 'whatever follows from the necessity of God's nature' with 'whatever follows from any of God's attributes'. Nowhere else in the *Ethics* do we find Spinoza implying that a mode may follow purely from the nature of an attribute; indeed, nowhere else does any such phrase as 'the nature of an attribute' occur at all. In §70 I shall suggest an explanation for this anomaly.

Spinoza's thinking in this part of his metaphysics is deep, adventurous, and—though it has a certain simplicity at its core—intricate in its details. Philosophical effort and some skill were required simply to *keep up with* it; but the exegetical aspects of this chapter have been plodding, conservative, and uncreative. Finding these doctrines in Spinoza's text has required little more than reading it with care and respect. (1) Spinoza explicitly asserts the thing-identity thesis, which, when construed plainly and literally, and accepting that the item(s) whose identity is in question are modes, entails that there are trans-attributes property-like elements which can combine with each attribute. (2) The claim that substance-monism and the thing-identity thesis explain the obtaining of the parallelism is right there on the page. (3) So is the psychologized explanation of what he means by 'There is no causal flow between the attributes'. (4) The relevance of that explanation to the thing-identity thesis is indicated by one's occurring right after the other. (5) What the 1d4 definiens actually says, plainly means to call into question an attribute's really being an essence of the substance that has it. (6) That the definiens for 'attribute' occurs in 2p7s and nowhere else in the *Ethics* is a plain fact about the text. Spinoza links those two; I merely follow.

Chapter 9

Explanatory Rationalism

68. Causal laws in Spinoza

Spinoza was an explanatory rationalist: he firmly assumed that for every true proposition P there is a sufficient reason why it is the case that P.[1] Unlike Leibniz, he does not announce this as doctrine, but his assumption of it is a powerful force in his philosophy.

It makes him a strict determinist. He could not countenance anything's happening without being deterministically caused to do so. He tends to think in terms of fact-causation—not that event's causing this one, but this state of affairs obtaining because that one did. The repeated occurrence of 'cause or reason' and 'reason or cause' in 1p11d—where 'or' translates *seu*, expressing equivalence—is just one example of Spinoza's viewing causes as satisfying one demand of explanatory rationalism.

The causation he believes in is strictly necessitating: given a cause, the effect absolutely must follow. Causes are to their effects as premises are to conclusions in a valid argument. This too is required by explanatory rationalism, as Hume saw (§265). The world as Spinoza sees it, then, unfolds in accordance with a comprehensive and absolutely necessitating system of causal laws.

A few times he alludes to the 'laws of God's nature' (1p15s, 1p17,d, 1 Appendix), but those laws also show up in his system in a different guise. Spinoza says that there are infinite modes as well as finite ones. The latter include particular things; the former are causal laws. Or so Pollock (1888: 150–4) and Curley (1969: 66–74) have thought, and I follow them in this. Thus, the top-level infinite mode under the attribute of extension—the one that Spinoza calls 'motion and rest'—comprises the most basic laws of physics.

As for the finite modes—'particular things, or things which are finite and have a determinate existence'—Spinoza's most important statement about them is 1p28, which says that each owes its existence and nature to a preceding finite item which caused it . . . and so on backwards to infinity. These links between one finite item and the next take place by virtue of the infinite modes, which are the laws of physics. The same story could in principle be told for the attribute of thought. Remember that the basic laws of physics are not absolutely basic: they result from the intersection of the attribute of extension with the universe's

---

[1] Do not follow Garrett (1997: 35) in using 'explanatory empiricism' to name the contradictory of this. 'Empiricism' concerns the senses, by contrast with *reason*; but in my phrase the 'ratio' element refers not to that faculty but to the existence of *reasons*.

trans-attributes nature or essence. The basic laws of psychology come from the same underlying nature in conjunction with the other attribute.

In Curley's elegant presentation (1969: 68), each event is causally related to God through an infinite chain of finite items (the causally prior particular events), and through a finite chain of infinite items (the sequence of ever more general physical laws, ending soon in 'motion and rest'). Each of these inputs belongs to God: the former is a series of his finite modes, while the latter is an unfolding of some of his infinite modes—that is, an unfolding under one of the attributes of laws governing the trans-attributes nature of the world.

Before moving on with laws and necessity, I add a few words about Spinoza's system of infinite modes. These are universal features of the world; they apply at all times and places. They form a hierarchy, topped by 'the most immediate mode of the attribute', by which Spinoza explains that he means 'the mode which, in order to exist, needs no other mode in the same attribute' (1661a, CS 153 n.). Below that are mediate infinite modes, each of which depends on (presupposes, involves, 'needs in order to exist') a mode above it in the hierarchy. Spinoza does not tell us whether the infinite modes under a given attribute form a single stream or rather a delta. Indeed, he says almost nothing about this mediate/immediate distinction in the *Ethics*, though it can be seen at work in 1p28s. I do not know what prompted the man who wrote to Spinoza about this; but his question and Spinoza's answer are worth looking at.

The questioner asks for 'examples of those things which are immediately produced by God, and of those which are produced by some infinite mediate modification' (letter 63, Wolf 305–6). Spinoza replies that the immediate infinite mode of thought is 'absolutely infinite understanding', and of extension, 'motion and rest'. His only example of a mediate infinite mode is *facies totius universi*—usually translated as 'the face of the whole universe', but Hallett's 'the make of the whole universe' (1957: 12) is better, because it does not suggest that Spinoza is referring only to the world's surface.

Spinoza is usually and rightly taken to mean *facies totius universi* to be a mode under extension only; he cannot mean it to fall under both attributes, for no mode can do that. He offers no mediate infinite mode under the attribute of thought; some have been troubled by this, but it is a non-problem. If you accept *facies totius universi* as a mediate infinite mode under extension, then I can tell you about a corresponding mode under thought: namely, the idea of *facies totius universi*. According to Spinoza's metaphysic, that is a correct and uniquely identifying label for the item in question, and we know exactly how it fits its referent into the system as a whole—namely, as the mental counterpart, under the cosmic parallelism, of the make of the whole universe. That Spinoza has not characterized this item in familiar untechnical language is neither suspicious nor instructive. He has not done so because no suitable language is available. His correspondent did not ask for doctrine; he asked for examples, in which certain metaphysical elements would appear in more familiar terms. Of course Spinoza cannot always do this; there is no news in that.

69. Time and eternity

For Spinoza the concept of eternity includes that of absolute necessity. To understand how it does so, we need to grasp his handling of all the time-related concepts. His careful precision regarding them deserves to be noticed.

In 2d5 he defines 'duration' (Latin *duratio*) as 'an indefinite continuation of existing'. What is indefinite is not the 'continuation' but the statement about it. If you say of something that it lasts through time, without saying for how long, or when in relation to the present, duration is the only temporal concept you are using.

If you say that it lasts for three days, or that it used to exist but does so no longer, you bring in not only duration but also the concept of *tempus*, usually translated as 'time'. Spinoza uses *tempus* only when tenses or temporal measurement are involved. Each of those distinguishes some times from others, subjecting duration to a demarcation or cut. Tenses do this by distinguishing the present moment from some others; measurement does it by singling out moments when processes begin and end. That is the job of *tempus*: to cut into duration in some way. This is pointed up nicely by 5p23d, where Spinoza writes of the conditions under which we 'attribute to the human mind any duration that can be made definite by *tempus*'—that is, any limited or finite duration. Curley has 'defined' rather than 'made definite'. Each is possible for the Latin, but mine makes better Spinozistic sense.

If you say that something exists at all times, you go beyond merely applying duration to it, for you say how long it lasts; but you are not employing the concept of *tempus*. This is the unique special case in which you can say how long something lasts, without cutting into duration, for you say how long precisely by saying that no cut is needed. I shall use 'sempiternal' in its standard meaning: a sempiternal thing exists at all times, lasts for ever. Spinoza did not use the word, but he had the concept.

Like many philosophers before and since, Spinoza distinguishes sempiternity from *eternity*. There are two ways to do this. (1) Sempiternity and eternity are rivals: eternal things do not exist at all times, but rather exist outside time—in an 'eternal now', perhaps. Like Hobbes (1651: ch. 46), I can make little sense of this. (2) There is more to eternity than to sempiternity: to be eternal is to be not merely sempiternal but also . . . something further. Most Spinoza scholars have associated him with 1, which is odd, because there is no textual evidence—not even prima facie evidence—for it in the *Ethics*.[2] His actual view was of the 2 type; and for that there is plenty of evidence.

Here is his official account: 'By eternity I understand existence itself, insofar as it is conceived to follow necessarily from the definition alone of the eternal thing'

---

[2] See the scholars listed in *CS* 429 n. 53. There is one bit of support in Spinoza's *Metaphysical Thoughts* (*CS* 316–17), and Woolhouse (1990: 34–5) builds on that. For a defence of associating Spinoza with 2 rather than 1, see M. Kneale 1969.

(1d8). He means that 'x exists eternally' or 'x is eternal' means that it is absolutely necessary that x exists. For him, therefore, eternity is a modal concept. He reinforces this in an explanatory note added to the definition, saying that the existence of an eternal thing 'cannot be explained by duration or time, not even a duration conceived to be without beginning or end'. Similarly in 5p23s he says that if a thing is eternal, 'the existence it has cannot be explained through duration'. These statements imply that you cannot explain what eternity is purely through the other two temporal concepts (duration and *tempus*), but this could be because there is more to eternity than mere limitless duration or sempiternity; it need not imply that eternity is incompatible with duration.

Spinoza plainly does not regard them as incompatible. He combines tenses with eternity in writing of what 'has been actual from eternity and will remain [so] to eternity' (1p17s, *CS* 426), and remarking of infinite modes that they 'have always had to exist' and, in the same sentence, that they are 'eternal' (1p21).

So we have a conceptual hierarchy in which *duratio* comes at the top. This divides into *existing at some but not all times* (*tempus*) and *existing at all times* (sempiternity). The second of these further divides into contingent (mere sempiternity, so to speak) and necessary (eternity). In all of this there is no basis for the idea that God, Nature, the universe, is not really in time, does not really endure.

In using this concept of eternity, Spinoza implies that there are contingent truths. This is only one of many aspects of his work that would collapse if he took seriously and consistently the thesis that whatever is true is absolutely necessary. Still, he did commit himself to that thesis. Let us look into this matter.

70. Is this the only possible world?

Explanatory rationalism threatens to imply that there are no contingent truths. Supposing the past to be infinite, one might hope that each particular matter of fact could be explained causally through antecedent matters of fact; but this would still leave unexplained the great proposition which conjoins them all; and the rationalist cannot count that as a brute fact with no explanation. He needs, that is, an answer to the question: Why is this world the actual one? Leibniz squarely faced this problem and tried to solve it (§71). Spinoza was unlike Leibniz in not being given to writing things of the sort: 'Because of my doctrine P, I have this terrific problem Q, which I solve thus: R.' But he did have the problem, and did try to solve it—obliquely, leaving us to struggle.

Spinoza really believes it to be necessary that there exists a substance with every possible attribute, and thus necessary that there is an extended world with a mentalistic side or aspect to it. He holds also that the infinite and eternal modes, embodying causal laws under the different attributes, pertain to the world necessarily; but at this point we must pause.

In the part of the *Ethics* that deals with the infinite and eternal modes, they are said to follow from the 'absolute nature of' God's attributes. In §67 I noted that this does not square with Spinoza's central thesis that each mode combines an attribute with some aspect of God's trans-attributes nature; and I pointed out some anomalous aspects of Spinoza's language in that short stretch of the *Ethics*. I now suggest a reason, though not a justification, for this departure.

It is that, without it, Spinoza has no basis on which to assert that the infinite modes necessarily pertain to the world. He is willing to rely on his a priori argument for the thesis that necessarily there is a substance that has every possible attribute (§47), but this does not suffice to give him (for example) an absolutely necessary physics. He knows this. When he wrote in letter 83 that 'Matter is badly defined by Descartes as extension, [and] must necessarily be explained by an attribute which expresses infinite and eternal essence', he meant that to get a physics, you need to supplement the mere attribute of extension with a set of causal powers. This has to be something extra—the powers inherent in God's trans-attributes nature—and not derivable from extension alone. Spinoza can *say* that God has his trans-attributes nature, or the causal laws part of it, necessarily; but he has no basis for this—not even a flimsy seeming-basis such as he has for God's existing and having all the attributes. In this situation, and needing to lock the absolute necessity of causal laws into his system, he indulgently allows himself to imply that the infinite modes follow from the attributes. I cannot make good sense of 1p23d, which purports to prove that this is the only way in which a mode could be necessary; but even without that, the fact remains that Spinoza has no other basis for the necessity of causal laws.

Let us proceed: necessarily God exists and has all the attributes and has the infinite and eternal modes. This still does not get Spinoza to the conclusion that whatever is true is necessary.

Let P be some particular proposition (by which I mean one reporting the existence of a particular thing or the occurrence of an event) that is caused to be true in the manner described in 1p28. Its being thus caused does not make P necessarily true; it only makes it inevitable—that is, necessitated by how the world was up to then. Whether it is necessary depends on whether its causes were necessary, . . . and so on backwards to infinity. Each member of the series is necessitated, but it does not follow that any member is necessary. Spinoza, however, is under pressure to say that each is necessary. If we can direct our thought to the entire infinite series of events and ask 'Why did that occur?', the answer cannot come from within the series; nor can it come from any contingency outside the series, for there are none; so either the question is unanswerable, or it is self-answering. Spinoza's explanatory rationalism will not allow the former alternative, so he is under pressure to give the latter, saying that the obtaining of the whole series is necessary so that its own nature sufficiently explains its existing.

Spinoza evidently did not clearly see this. In one of his letters he wrote:

If someone asked by what cause such a finite body is set in motion, I could reply that it is done by another body, and this body again by another, and so on to infinity. This answer . . . is available because . . . by positing each time another body we assign a sufficient and eternal cause of such motion. (Letter 40, Wolf 233–4)

This is not perfectly explicit, but the phrase 'sufficient and eternal cause' suggests that the demands of explanatory rationalism are met by the determinism of 1p28. They are not.

Spinoza's failure fully to think this through was probably encouraged by, and is certainly manifested in, his holding that *facies totius universi* is necessarily a feature of the universe. His name for it suggests that he thinks of this infinite mode as the totality of particular facts about the extended realm, the make of the universe, or in Pollock's phrase 'the sum of material things'. If this is what the make of the universe is, and if it is necessary, then Spinoza does claim necessity for each particular fact about the world; which implies that this is the only possible world. This supports Samuel Alexander's remark that the infinite modes 'as it were break the fall from Heaven to Earth': they do it as pillows break falls, by being soft. Looked at from above (so to speak), the make of the entire universe is something like *the fact that the material world is laid out somehow*; looked at from below, it is *the great fact about how in detail the material world is laid out*.

In one place Spinoza gives a hard-edged argument for inferring necessitarianism from his kind of determinism. He confronts the objection: 'If it were supposed that God had made another nature of things, or that from eternity he had decreed something else concerning nature and its order, no imperfection in God would follow from that' (1p33s2, *CS* 437). This is a theological version of an argument which, when purified, runs like this: Granted that each particular event is necessitated by earlier events in accordance with necessary laws, the whole series could still have been other than it is. Granted that the series never began, so that each member of it was necessitated by earlier members, there is still no necessity that *this* series rather than some other should have been actual. Spinoza, alas, responds not to the purified argument, but only to the theological version of it, replete with the assumption—which he rejects, but supposes his opponent to accept—that God has intellect and will. I have been unable to extract any respectable philosophy from the theological trappings.

What did Spinoza actually think about whether this is the only possible world? I am not sure. The evidence is equivocal, and his position may not have been consistent. (For details that I cannot go into here, see *Study* 119–24.) A good paper by Don Garrett (1991) contends that Spinoza consistently held that this is the only possible world; Garrett discusses my reasons for thinking that Spinoza was inconsistent about this, and effectively disposes of some of them. Curley and Walski (1999) challenge Garrett's understanding of some of the texts; but they seem to me to take the whole matter too calmly, apparently not feeling the explanatory rationalist tug towards denying that there are any contingent truths. I should mention that as well as the purely rationalist tug, there may well have been a historical push at work, as is argued in scholarly detail by Carriero (1991).

Garrett seems to err in his handling of this: 'All the things which follow from the absolute nature of any of God's attributes have always had to exist and be infinite' (1p21). This, and the considerable development of it in 1p21d, implies that no finite mode—such as a particular event—follows from the absolute nature of any attribute. There is an oddity here, as I have pointed out; but Spinoza is implying that the facts about particular physical events are not, after all, related to God in any way that would make them necessary, as distinct from being inevitable given what preceded them. This is a prime exhibit for those who hold that Spinoza committed himself to there being contingent truths.

Garrett offers 'two alternative replies' to this line of thought. One seems to me a non-starter. The other (1991: 198) is based on this: 'Spinoza nowhere denies that the whole *series* of finite modes follows from the absolute nature of the attributes. His claim is only that no *individual* mode follows from it.' Garrett develops this at length, but does not meet the seemingly obvious objection that the truth about 'the whole series' entails a long conjunction, which cannot be necessary unless each conjunct is so. Huenemann (1999: 230–1) develops this point against Garrett. His own original interpretation of this part of Spinoza's work leads him to agree with Garrett—though not quite for his reasons—that Spinoza is a consistent necessitarian.

However the exegetical argument comes out, let us not forget that it is hard to do good philosophy consistently with the opinion that this is the only possible world. The idea that nothing false is possible stultifies thought as greatly as does the libertine idea that everything false is possible.

71. Leibniz's pursuit of contingency

Leibniz's explanatory rationalism was as strong as Spinoza's, and more openly pronounced—under the label 'the principle of sufficient reason'. This permeates his writings in many different guises, such as the powerful remark that 'Nothing unintelligible happens' (*NE* 381). Leibniz intermittently thought he could prove this, but his attempts fail: they depend upon equating 'All the necessary conditions for P obtain' with 'Sufficient conditions for P obtain', which would be acceptable only to someone who was already an explanatory rationalist (A 6:6: 118). In his mature works he did not try to prove his principle, but he continued to regard it as a necessary truth, or at least as fundamental, indispensable, not seriously in contention. Right at the end of his life, he demanded rhetorically: 'Is this a principle that needs to be proved?' and went on to say that, without it, 'one cannot prove the existence of God or account for many other important truths', and to fire off another rhetorical question: 'Has not everybody made use of this principle on a thousand occasions?' (L 717).

Leibniz is well aware of the intellectual obligation that he incurs by accepting the principle of sufficient reason:

The first question we are entitled to ask will be *Why is there something rather than nothing?* . . . Moreover, even if we assume that things have to exist, we must be able to give a reason *why they have to exist as they are* and not otherwise. (PNG 7, FW 262)

Leibniz finds his answer in God, whom he takes to be outside the world:

The dominant One of the universe not only rules the world but also fashions or creates it; he is above the world and, so to speak, extramundane, and hence he is the ultimate reason for things. (UO, AG 149)

No reason for the world can be found in any one [particular state]; indeed, assuming as many of them as you like will not in any way help you to find a reason; so it is obvious that the reason must be found elsewhere. (Ibid.)

The reasons for the world . . . lie in something extramundane, different from the chain of states or series of things whose aggregate constitutes the world. And so we must pass from physical or hypothetical necessity, which determines later things in the world from earlier ones, to something that has absolute or metaphysical necessity, for which no reason can be given. (Ibid. 150)

Why, then, is this world the actual one? Because it is the one that God chose to actualize, freely choosing it because it is the best possible world. Why did God choose to actualize the best possible world? Because God has all perfections. Why is there a God, and why does he have all perfections? Both of these are absolutely necessary truths, according to Leibniz, who accepts the a priori argument for God's existence which Descartes and Spinoza had also endorsed (Mon 41–5, FW 273–4); so either there is no legitimate question as to why they are true ('no reason can be given'), or there is one, and it is self-answering. The important content of Leibniz's description of God as extramundane is that the facts about his existence and nature are absolutely necessary; this excludes them from the range of contingent facts which Leibniz wants to explain, and which he calls 'the world'.

A threat looms. In this section let 'Alpha' refer to the actual world, being understood as shorthand for 'the world at which . . .' followed by a conjunction of every actually true proposition. Now consider these:

(1) God exists and is perfect.
(2) God always acts for the best.
(3) Alpha is the best possible world.
(4) God creates Alpha.
(5) Every true proposition is absolutely necessary.
(6) God has no choice about what worlds to create (that is, about what propositions to make true).

Because he accepts the a priori argument for God's existence, Leibniz must hold that 1 is absolutely necessary; if it entails 2, then that is also necessary. It is plausible to think (assuming that 3 is true) that 3 is necessary; and 2 and 3 jointly entail 4, which is thus necessary too. But Alpha conjoins all the truths that actually obtain; and so we get 5, which in turn entails 6, which Leibniz abhors. Here is Leibniz describing the threat to Arnauld:

If one wanted totally to reject merely possible things, one would be destroying contingency and liberty; for if nothing were possible except what God in fact creates, what God creates would be necessary, and God, wanting to create something, could create nothing but that, without having freedom of choice. (Mason, 62–3)

Leibniz has two ways of dealing with this, which I shall try to make clear.

In chapter 17, I shall present a thesis of his which threatens to imply that all subject–predicate propositions are absolutely necessary, and shall show him trying to fend off that conclusion by contending that a proposition is contingent if it cannot be proved by a demonstration of finite length. The source of the threat has nothing to do with theology; Leibniz usually writes about these matters as though the question of God's choices is far from his mind. So it should be! The whole truth about Alpha can be expressed in propositions of the form 'There is a substance which . . .', with no use of the subject–predicate form; so threats to contingency from the use of that form are not threats to God's freedom of choice about which existential propositions to make true. (They are threats to human freedom, of which more in §134.)

There is just one exception to this. Proposition 3 above—that Alpha is the best possible world—is of the subject–predicate form, and the argument to necessitarianism which I have outlined assumed that 3 is absolutely necessary. I learn from Sleigh (1990a: 87) that Leibniz faults the argument at that point:

[Leibniz confronts this argument:] It is necessary that if God chooses to create a world, then he chooses the best, but whatever world is the best, is so of necessity. Let that world be A. Then it is necessary that if God chooses to create a world, then God chooses to create A. So God has no choice among worlds . . . Leibniz rejected this argument, asserting that 'this proposition—"A is the best"—is certain, but it is not necessary, because it cannot be demonstrated'.

He means that it cannot be finitely demonstrated; he is invoking his theory about contingent subject–predicate propositions. Where I have said that as long as there are contingent existentials we can let the subject–predicate propositions slide, Leibniz replies in effect that there is just one proposition of the subject–predicate form—namely (3) that Alpha is the best possible world—that entails all the true existentials and thus, if it is necessary, confers its necessity on them. This gives him a reason for wanting to deny that 3 is necessary.

If he is right about 3's contingency, then he really can block the inference to (5) the thesis that all truths are absolutely necessary, and so it blocks *that* route to (6) the thesis that God has no real choice about which world to create. But what of it? There is a route to 6 that does not involve 3's necessity. If 1 and 2 are both absolutely necessary and 3 is *true*, then 6 follows. The absolute necessity of God's creating the best world, together with the sheer *fact* that Alpha is the best, implies that God chooses Alpha through the necessity of his nature and has no choice in the matter.

Leibniz's other response to the threatening argument is better, because it challenges the necessity of (2) the thesis that God acts for the best. That blocks both routes to 6. At one stage he evidently held that God's existence and character absolutely necessitate his behaviour: 'It is impossible for him not to be affected by the most perfect harmony, and thus to be necessitated to do the best' (L 146). In later years, however, he backed off from this, and held rather that God's doing something morally sub-optimal would go against his character, and thus be *morally absurd*, but would not be *absolutely impossible*. Apart from the obscure 'cannot-be-demonstrated' theory which I now set aside, the only entrance for contingency into Leibniz's world is the narrow crack between God's character and his conduct. Because some commentators ignore this element in Leibniz's thought, and others deny its existence,[3] I illustrate it at some length:

Even if the world is not metaphysically necessary, in the sense that its contrary implies a contradiction or logical absurdity, it is nonetheless physically necessary, or determined in such a way that its contrary would imply imperfection or moral absurdity. And just as possibility is the foundation of essence, so perfection . . . is the foundation of existence. This makes it obvious how the Author of the World can be free, even though he does all things determinately because he acts on the principle of wisdom or perfection. (UO, AG 151)

That is the reason for the existence of the best, which God's wisdom brings him to know, his goodness brings him to choose, and his power brings him to produce. (Mon 55, FW 275).

Individuals or contingent things . . . have no necessary connection with God, but were produced freely. God was inclined toward them for a definite reason, but he was not necessitated. (Comments, AG 273)

Spinoza wrongly holds that the world is an effect of the divine nature, even though he almost adds that it was not made by chance. There is a midpoint between what is necessary and what is by chance, namely, that which is free. The world is a voluntary effect of God, but a voluntary effect due to inclining or prevailing reasons. (Ibid. 277)

God chooses freely, even though he is determined to choose the best. (NE 179)

[The proposition that God wills to choose the most perfect is] the first principle concerning existence . . . the first of all propositions of fact, i.e. the origin of all contingent existence. (Quoted in Curley 1976: 95)

When God . . . chooses the best, what he does not choose, and is inferior in perfection, is nevertheless possible. . . . God chooses among possibles, that is, among many ways none of which implies a contradiction. (L 697)

---

[3] Under the leadership of Couturat (1902: 28 n. 23). Russell, who had got Leibniz right on this point in his 1900 book, later adopted Couturat's interpretation (Russell 1903: 377 n. 8). Couturat's lax performance converted Russell from his first understanding of Leibniz to a textually less well-supported one—namely, that for Leibniz all existential propositions are analytic—although he saw that this is 'very inferior' to the doctrine he had rightly attributed to Leibniz in his book. Carriero (1993: 8–9) sides with Couturat, relying heavily on this: 'Leibniz explicitly says [at NE 358] that existence is found in the notion of a subject possessing that predicate.' In fact Leibniz writes only that the notions of existence and of the subject are linked, connected, go together; containment is not implied, let alone 'explicitly' mentioned.

In this way Leibniz tries to admit contingent truths while still excluding brute facts. Although it is not absolutely impossible that God should have acted differently, the excellence of his nature provides us with *an* answer to the question of why he chose to actualize the best possible world. Notice how strongly this commits Leibniz to the idea that there are moral standards that are independent of God's will. He hated Descartes's view that God's will sets the moral standards rather than conforming to them, and we see now that he has more than merely theological reasons for this (§72).

Contingency cannot be reconciled with the principle of sufficient reason, I submit. Leibniz's attempt fails, because it leaves an unanswerable why-question. The necessary truth about God's character implies that it would have been morally absurd for him to create anything worse than the best; but we can still ask: Why did he not do something morally absurd? Leibniz may answer, 'Because he is perfectly good'; but if this explanation is not an absolutely necessitating one, a question still remains. Why does God's conduct mirror his character, rather than there being slippage in the logical gap along the interface between them?

Objection: 'You are inviting Leibniz to worry over a why-question that he has already answered, an action that he has already explained. When asked "Why did God do that?", Leibniz replies that he did it—that is, created the best possible world—because he is morally perfect. This does explain that action; so the case should be closed.' That, however, harbours a mistake. We are not asking Leibniz to explain *an action* but rather *a fact*. Leibniz can explain the action by pointing to how it relates to God's character; but now we are asking why God did something that matched his character in that way; and 'because he is morally perfect' does not answer that. This is a fair demand, for Leibniz's principle of sufficient reason holds that there is an explanation for the truth of every true proposition, the obtaining of every state of affairs. Leibniz confirms this when he writes to Clarke (L 717) that the principle of sufficient reason concerns the existence of 'a sufficient reason for a thing to exist, for an event to happen, for any truth's obtaining'. This *explicitly* takes the principle to cover the explaining of existences, events, and propositions.

A theological tension makes itself felt here. Many Christian philosophers have thought that it derogates from God's goodness to suppose that he *could* act badly; others have thought that it derogates from his power to suppose that he *could not*. Leibniz has a 'could' theology, but occasionally he writes as though he had a 'could not' one. In at least one of his fairly early writings he says that God *could not* have actualized any world other than this one, and hastens to add that, nevertheless, other worlds are possible 'in their nature'. I am suspicious of this as philosophy, because I believe that something which is absolutely ruled out by something absolutely necessary is itself absolutely necessary 'in its nature'. In any case, this approach does little to meet Leibniz's demand for freedom for God. At best, it implies that what prevents God from choosing any other world is internal to him, rather than the external impediment of every alternative's being impossible 'in itself'; but it is still a prevention, a blockage, a lack of freedom.[4]

There is also a tension of another kind. Just before a passage I have quoted, Leibniz writes:

Since something rather than nothing exists, there is a certain urge for existence or (so to speak) a straining toward existence in possible things or in possibility or essence itself; in a word, essence in and of itself strives for existence. . . . All possibles . . . strive with equal right for existence in proportion to the amount of essence or reality or the degree of perfection they contain. (UO, AG 150)

This seems to banish God from the scene, implying that it is, after all, absolutely necessary that the most perfect world should be actual. Here is more of the same:

Everything possible demands that it should exist, and hence will exist unless it is prevented by something else which also demands to exist and is incompatible with the former; and hence it follows that the combination of things always exists by which the greatest possible number of things exists. . . . And hence it is obvious that things exist in the most perfect way. (G 7:194; translation adapted from Russell 1900: 296)

If this was Leibniz's considered position, then he must have been—as Russell said—insincere in affirming that there is contingency stemming from God's free choices. In short, when Leibniz writes, 'We can now understand in a wonderful way how a kind of divine mathematics or metaphysical mechanism is used in the origin of things' (AG 151), we should ask what brings *divine* mathematics into the picture. Why won't a godless metaphysical mechanism do the trick?

No Leibniz scholar today doubts the sincerity of Leibniz's Christianity; nor is it credible that he thought this to be the only possible world. So we need to reconcile the above passages with the doctrine of contingency as stemming from God's free choices. That is easily done. Reading the troublesome passages in context, we find that 'Possibles tend towards actuality in proportion to the amount of perfection they involve' is offered not as basic, but rather as a result of God's character, with the sole exception of a passage at AG 150. The more perfect tend more strongly towards existence *because* their perfection inclines God the more strongly to actualize them. This has been observed by Rescher and others, and the whole case is well laid out by Blumenfeld (1973). Here is a relevant text: 'All beings, in so far as they are involved in the first Being, have, above and beyond bare possibility, a propensity toward existing in proportion to their goodness, and they exist by the will of God unless they are incompatible with more perfect [ones].'[5]

---

[4] For a chronicle of other ambiguities and waverings of Leibniz on this question, see Adams 1994: 36–42. Sleigh (1990a: 82–3) argues against Adams that the 'possible in itself' account of the contingency of God's choices is something that Leibniz dropped in the 1680s rather than holding to it throughout his career. For further discussion, see Carriero 1993: 12–13.

[5] Written by Leibniz in the margin of 'Specimen inventorum de admirandis naturae Generalis arcanis', G 7:309–10. I was led to this by Rescher 1967: 38n.; the translation is Rescher's. Other relevant passages are Mon 54–5, FW 275; 1710: sect. 201, G 6:236; PNG 10, FW 263. In the last, FW's 'put forward their claims to' is correct, unlike L's and AG's too passive 'have a claim to' and Catherine Wilson's too active 'try for' (1989: 280 n. 33).

72. Choices, especially God's

As his theory of contingency illustrates, Leibniz is unwilling to explain anything's arising from an arbitrary decision by God. His demand for reasons—perhaps encouraged by a view about what decision must be—leads him to insist that for every choice of God's there must be a reason. Spinoza also invokes God when trying to satisfy the demands of explanatory rationalism; but his appeal is always to God's nature, not to his choices. Spinoza's God is not 'a man or like a man', has no will, does not make choices or decisions, and *a fortiori* does not act 'for the best'. He (or it) does what he (or it) does from the absolute necessity of his (or its) nature.

Contrast those two with Descartes. Unlike Spinoza, Descartes thinks of God as choosing and deciding, but he does not agree with Leibniz that such decisions are guided by independent standards of value:

It is self-contradictory [*repugnat*] to suppose that the will of God was not indifferent from eternity with respect to everything that has happened or will ever happen; for it is impossible to envisage anything's being thought of in the divine intellect as good . . . , or worthy of . . . action or omission, prior to the decision of the divine will to make it so. . . . For example, God did not will the creation of the world in time because he saw that it would be better this way than if he had created it from eternity . . . On the contrary, it is because he willed to create the world in time that it is better this way. (Rep 6, CSM 2:291)

Then what explains God's actions? According to Descartes, nothing. He is profoundly not an explanatory rationalist: his scheme of things makes abundant room for brute theological facts, truths about God for which there are no reasons.

Leibniz rejects this, never more clearly or sharply than here, writing to Molanus:

Descartes's God . . . is not a God like the one we imagine or hope for, that is, a God just and wise, doing everything possible for the good of creatures. Rather, Descartes's God is something approaching the God of Spinoza, namely, the principle of things and a certain supreme power or primitive nature that sets everything going and does everything that can be done. Descartes's God has no will . . . , since according to Descartes he does not have . . . the good as object of the will. (AG 242)

This is not unreasonable. Descartes says that his God has a will, and he speaks freely of God's choices; but those 'choices' are not made in accordance with any independent standards, so Leibniz is entitled to suggest that they hardly deserve the name. Clearly, explanatory rationalism is at stake in this disagreement, but other things are going on as well. Let us look into them.

For Leibniz it is virtually blasphemous to think that any of God's choices are arbitrary, made for no reason. We see this in some of the many passages where he scolds Locke for allowing that God makes some arbitrary choices, referring, for example, to 'the arbitrary will and good pleasure of the wise architect'. Quite apart from explanatory rationalism, Leibniz sees this as an issue of respect: 'To attribute the origin [of bodies' powers] to God's "good pleasure"—that appears hardly worthy of him who is the supreme reason, and with whom everything is orderly, everything is connected. This good pleasure would indeed be neither good nor pleasure if God's power did not perpetually run parallel to his wisdom' (*NE* 382).

Yet Descartes was partly moved by piety in concluding that *all* God's choices *are* arbitrary. He denied that God could be guided by or measured against any standards that were independent of his will, and in Chapter 24 we shall see how far he took that denial, including his calling it 'blasphemous' to think otherwise. We can see his point, but Leibniz evidently could not; and that was a failure in him. Any believer in a person with the powers and metaphysical status of the God of Christianity should think he faces a dilemma: either God steers by independently valid standards of what is right and reasonable, or he does not; the former implies that some momentous realities exist independently of God, while the latter implies (among other things) that praise of God as 'good' is virtually contentless. Leibniz takes the former option, Descartes the latter. I think that Descartes realized that piety might pull the faithful away from his position, as well as towards it; but Leibniz evidently had no such awareness of the dilemma, no sense of how his own position might seem to derogate from the greatness of God.

(Descartes's voluntarism about value came not only from a religious sense of what is appropriate for God but also from a philosophical view about the metaphysics of value. He opted for voluntarism partly because the going alternative struck him as philosophical rubbish. Many philosophers, of whom I am one, do hold that the idea of objective fact-like values that are somehow just *there* to be consulted, and by which conduct can be judged, is an incoherent superstition; and I think that this was Descartes's view. It is true that in contexts where he is saying that God is not a deceiver, he calls him 'supremely good' (§186); but that need not be read as a value-judgement. Descartes holds that deceit manifests weakness, and I think he means that God is 'supremely good' in not being defective, ill-made, weak. I have not, I confess, found him explicitly condemning the notion of fact-like values that are independent of God, but the parallel diagnosis is certainly right for his voluntarism about modality—his view, namely, that modal truths are made true by God's will. That has some roots in piety, but it also reflects Descartes's view that no other account of modal truth is philosophically acceptable.)

Now let us stand back so as to get our three philosophers within a single frame. Descartes's thesis that God is not guided by independent standards incurred Leibniz's wrath, for at least two reasons. (1) Explanatory rationalism: Descartes allows for absolutely brute facts, while Leibniz does not. (2) Piety: Leibniz thinks that it is impious to credit God with behaviour in which he is not steering by standards of the good that are external to his will. Now, Spinoza agrees with 1, as we have seen; and he rejects 2. His rejection of 2 marks a big difference between him and Leibniz, for whom God is ultimately 'like a man'. Still, their agreement regarding 1 leads Leibniz to favour Spinoza over Descartes in this area. Although it is an error of Spinoza's that he 'does not attribute intellect and will to God', Leibniz writes, 'he correctly denies that God is indifferent and that he decides anything by an absolute [exercise of the] will' (Comments, AG 278). Although Leibniz finds it offensive to subject God to absolutely necessity and to deny him any real will, as Spinoza does, he judges it to be even worse to allow for brute facts such as would obtain if there were arbitrary choices. This goes with Leibniz's reporting that he used to be attracted to Spinozism, something he never said about Cartesianism.

Now consider Spinoza's evaluation of the other two positions. He has shown, he says, 'that things have been produced by God with the highest perfection, since they have followed necessarily from a given most perfect nature'. He realizes that many will object to this 'because they have been accustomed to attribute another freedom to God', namely 'an absolute will'. By this phrase Spinoza means a will that is radically free, acting without any necessitating cause; and he rejects this—as Leibniz was later to do—as 'futile, and a great obstacle to science'. After several paragraphs of mainly theological bickering, Spinoza comes to this:

I confess that this opinion, which subjects all things to a certain indifferent will of God and makes all things depend on his good pleasure, is nearer the truth than that of those who maintain that God does all things for the sake of the good. For they seem to place something outside God, which does not depend on God, to which God attends as a model in what he does, and at which he aims as at a certain goal. This is simply to subject God to fate. (1p33s2, CS 438–9)

Fatum here seems to mean merely something external, something independent of God. So Spinoza's rejection of the idea of standards external to God, by which God might steer and against which God might be judged, weighs more with him than does his explanatory rationalism. He would rather have brute theological facts than believe in a God who is guided by independent standards of goodness, as Leibniz would later do.

Spinoza here declares a position (Leibniz's) which conforms to explanatory rationalism to be further from the truth than Descartes's, which does not. This is initially surprising, because the demand for a 'because' for every 'why?' so dominates Spinoza's thought. Are we to conclude that explanatory rationalism plays a weaker role in Spinoza's thought than in Leibniz's? One possible answer is that Spinoza sees the Leibnizian picture as involving teleology: God 'aims' at something 'as at a goal'; and Spinoza objected to teleology, all teleology, for more than merely theological reasons (§§83–4). Perhaps instead—or as well—he was influenced by the thought that a God acting in accordance with standards would be a person—'a man, or like a man'—which he regards as poisonous metaphysical rubbish, to be avoided at all costs. Objection: 'But that diagnosis is not plausible, because the hated anthropomorphism has already been conceded in

Descartes's view that God chooses and decides, whether or not guided by external standards.' Possible response: 'Not really. Spinoza is relatively tolerant of the
Cartesian position on God's choices, because he thinks that such unguided
choices would not really be choices—the "indifferent will" could not be a genuine will—so what is conceded here is not really anthropomorphic.' I do not
know how to arbitrate this dispute.

Anyway, whatever his reasons, Spinoza implies that while Descartes is wrong
about God's will, Leibniz is even more so. Leibniz explicitly says that Spinoza is
wrong about this, but that Descartes is more so. If Descartes were asked to rank-
order the other two positions, which would he put in the middle and which at
the bottom? That would depend on whether he gave more weight to the 'nothing independent of God' thesis and any scruples he might have about objective
values, or to the idea that God is a person. I think he would give primacy to the
former, thus concluding that in this area Spinoza is wrong, while Leibniz is even
more so.

Chapter 10

Spinoza on Belief and Error

73. Beliefs

Philosophers of mind these days commonly agree in dividing mental phenomena into two classes. (1) There are *intentional* or *representational* states—beliefs that P, desires that P be the case, fears that P may be the case, and so on. (2) There are *phenomenal* states of mind—mental items that feel a certain way; these include pains and itches and sensory experiences, states for which we have the notion of what it is like, on the inside, to have them. The two classes may overlap in occurrent thoughts and mental images, of which it is plausible to say (1) that they have content, and (2) that there is something that it feels like to have them.

Spinoza has little to say about type 2, except for a couple of changes of state that he calls 'pleasure' and 'unpleasure'. I shall not discuss these, and will confine myself to contentful states and, more specifically, to beliefs and desires. It is widely and (I think) correctly held these days that the representational aspects of the mind have belief and desire as their core and essence. Those two concepts can be satisfactorily analysed without help from fear, wonder, etc., but the converse does not hold.

This view of things seems to inform Spinoza's *Ethics* too. In part 3 he has an extensive account of 'Affects'—potentially damaging states of mind and body—each of which he undertakes to explain by first classifying it with respect to pleasure, unpleasure, and desire, and then saying what beliefs are associated with it. See for yourself the definitions of the affects at the end of part 3, and *Study*, chapter 11. That is evidence of the centrality of belief and desire in Spinoza's thinking about the human mind.

It is natural to think that believing that P is something more than non-committally having in mind or 'entertaining' the thought that P (§248). Spinoza seems to reject that. He imagines an opponent claiming that one can have something in mind ('perceive' it) without thereby committing oneself to any proposition, whether true or false:

No one is said to be deceived insofar as he perceives something, but only insofar as he assents or dissents. For instance, someone who mentally constructs a winged horse does not on that account grant that there is a winged horse, i.e. he is not on that account deceived unless at the same time he grants that there is a winged horse. (2p49cs, *CS* 487)

Replying to this, Spinoza concedes that 'the imaginations of the Mind, considered in themselves, involve no error'; I shall discuss this in §75. He continues:

'But I deny that a man affirms nothing insofar as he perceives. For what is perceiving a winged horse other than affirming wings of a horse?' (ibid. 489). This
should be considered alongside these: '[Some people wrongly] think that an idea
is something mute, like a picture on a tablet, and not a mode of thinking, viz. the
very act of understanding' (2p43s, CS 479). 'They look on ideas . . . as mute pictures on a panel, and preoccupied with this prejudice they do not see that an idea,
insofar as it is an idea, involves affirmation or negation' (2p49cs, CS 486). These
three belong together, but what do they mean?

In our delphic trio of statements, I submit, Spinoza is working towards a view
that has been propounded in recent decades by Armstrong (1961) and by others
following him, including Pitcher (1971) and Dennett (1978). It is the theory that
the basic mentally available raw materials that we get in sensory encounters with
the world—and in sense-like hallucinations, etc.—are *beliefs* about our environment or *inclinations to believe*. This theory has a lot going for it. For one thing, it
cuts through a profound difficulty about how empirical beliefs can be based upon
the occurrence of sensory states. Popper presents it in his report on Fries's
trilemma:

J. F. Fries taught that if the statements of science are not to be accepted dogmatically, we
must be able to justify them. If we demand justification by reasoned argument . . . we are
committed to the view that statements can be justified only by statements. The demand
that *all* statements are to be logically justified . . . is therefore bound to lead to an infinite
regress. Now, if we wish to avoid the danger of dogmatism as well as an infinite regress,
then it seems as if we could only have recourse to psychologism, i.e. the doctrine that
statements can be justified not only by statements but also by perceptual experience.
(Popper 1959: 93)

On the Armstrong view, the problem disappears: our rawest sensory intake
consists in dispositions to believe, so that the only basing relation we need is the
basing of beliefs on other beliefs, which is relatively unproblematical, and at least
spares us from having to embrace the view ('psychologism') that some of our non-
doxastic psychological states can play the justificatory role that beliefs also play.

Many people find the theory incredible: they rightly see it as a challenge to the
idea of the introspectible phenomenal *given*, the raw experienced data of the
senses; and they think that this denies something which everyone just *knows* to
be real. I sympathize with this criticism, and with another: the Armstrong theory deprives us of our best chance of analysing the concept of belief. The only
viable kind of analysis I know of is the functionalist one, according to which
beliefs and desires are mental states that mediate between sensory intake and
behavioural output (§77). This requires that sensory input be identifiable independently of any beliefs, and it collapses if that cannot be done.

Is this theory of Armstrong's what Spinoza is getting at in the delphic trio? I
think so. Listen to this:

[1] I deny that a man affirms nothing insofar as he perceives. For what is perceiving a
winged horse other than affirming wings of a horse? Thus [*enim*], [2] if the mind perceived

nothing else except the winged horse, it would regard it as present to itself, and would not have any cause of doubting its existence, or any faculty of dissenting, unless either the imagination of the winged horse was joined to an idea which excluded the existence of that horse or the mind perceived that its idea of a winged horse was inadequate. (2p49cs, CS 489)

The meaning of 2 is plain enough. Spinoza is saying that when the thought that P comes into the mind, it comes as the belief that P unless other beliefs prevent it from doing so (I choose to ignore the second disjunct). He is thinking mainly of sensory intake, claiming that if I have a sensory presentation as of a winged horse, I shall automatically think I am confronted by a winged horse unless I am forearmed with beliefs which count against that. Objection: 'But we don't encounter winged horses through the senses. A winged-horse presentation would be illusory; so why would Spinoza pick that as an example if his point was about sensory intake?' Perhaps he wanted to dramatize his point through an example which we would intuitively feel would not induce us to form the corresponding belief. He wanted us to realize that what shields us from believing we are confronted by a winged horse is our background knowledge about what kinds of horses there are. He offers this, I think, as empirically plausible—something we shall be inclined to concede to him if we think about it a little. And he offers it as illustrating or confirming the theoretical proposition 1.[1]

Someone who thinks that there is a raw phenomenal introspectible given might nevertheless accept 2 as a fact about our psychological workings, a mere fact about what we are apt to do with our data of the senses if nothing prevents us from doing it. But this seems not to be Spinoza's position. If it were, it would not be appropriate for him to keep saying that he is advancing a thesis about what ideas are. 'In the mind there is no . . . affirmation . . . except that which the idea involves insofar as it is an idea' (2p49). 'Singular volitions [= affirmations] and ideas are one and the same' (2p49cd).

The strongest evidence against the Armstrongian interpretation of 1 is Spinoza's use of the abrupt rhetorical question, 'What is perceiving a winged horse other than affirming wings of a horse?' It is as though he expected the reader, once he gets his mind around the question, to see that his answer is obviously right; yet nobody could think this about the Armstrong theory. Well, perhaps Spinoza is bullying the reader a little. He sometimes does.[2]

---

[1] In Curley's translation Spinoza goes from 1 to 2 with the link of 'For . . .', implying that 2 gives a ground or reason for 1. I do not see how it could do so, on any interpretation. According to the Lewis and Short dictionary, the Latin word *enim* can be used 'to corroborate a preceding assertion'. Instead of 'Thus', I could have used 'As witness the fact that'.

[2] For a stimulating further development of something like the view I have taken here of ideas and beliefs, see Matson 1991. He goes further than I am willing to follow, taking Spinoza to a place where his property-dualism fades from sight.

74. Belief and the will

All this occurs in combination with Spinoza's discussion of a seemingly different topic. It starts with Descartes's account in the Fourth Meditation of what happens when he commits an intellectual error, nested within a more general account of what happens when he comes to have any belief:

My errors depend on two concurrent causes, namely on the faculty of knowledge which is in me, and on the faculty of choice or freedom of the will; that is, they depend on both the intellect and the will simultaneously. . . . The will simply consists in our ability to do or not do something (that is, to affirm or deny, to pursue or avoid); or rather, it consists simply in the fact that when the intellect puts something forward for affirmation or denial or for pursuit or avoidance, our inclinations are such that we do not feel we are determined by any external force. (CSM 2:39, 40)

Descartes wants to clear God of responsibility for my errors: they result from my will, which is radically free and not an effect of any cause that can be laid at God's door.[3] For present purposes, forget about the theology and the invocation of radical freedom, and focus on Descartes's seeming to imply that acquiring a belief is something that one does, a voluntary action. Philosophers have denied this ever since, and I agree with them: I cannot get you to believe something just by offering a reward (however lavish) for doing so or a punishment (however dreadful) for not doing so. Descartes is right that I can use my will 'to affirm or deny'; but believing is not affirming.

In saying all this, I have—like Descartes's critics in general—been equating believing that P with assigning a high subjective probability to P. It has been maintained that this is wrong. Suppose it is right, and that to believe that P is to give it at least a 0.95 chance of being true. Then consider a fair lottery with a thousand entrants. What is your subjective probability for 'This entrant will not win the lottery' as applied to each entrant? It had better be 0.999. So, according to the present view, you *believe*, of each entrant, that he or she will not win; you also believe that these are all the entrants; yet it would be unreasonable for you to believe that no one will win. This seems to be a case where it is utterly reasonable to believe that P, which obviously and elementarily entails Q, yet it is utterly unreasonable to believe that Q. That is incredible; so we have a problem. One might respond to it with the thought: 'Do I really believe that Smith will not win? Perhaps I don't. I give him almost no chance of winning, but his not winning is not something I accept, adopt, make my own, stand behind.' This is the thought that belief should be distinguished from high subjective probability, and that it is, or involves, a kind of *acceptance* which may, after all, be voluntary. (For developments of this line of thought, see de Sousa 1971, Kaplan 1981, Maher

---

[3] Descartes's views on freedom are, I confess, much more complex and somewhat more obscure than this suggests. For a helpful recent discussion, with a review of much of the secondary literature, see J. K. Campbell 1999.

1986.) I am not convinced of this; but it merits careful thought, as does the suggestion that it may throw light on what Descartes says about belief and the will. (For a different route to a more sympathetic view of this part of Descartes's thought, see Rosenthal 1986.)

Now, Spinoza in 2p49s addresses himself to this part of Descartes's thought. He rejects the element of radical freedom ('absolute will') in favour of a strict determinism, and I have nothing to say about that. I want to focus on his further rejection of the view that beliefs—here understood as assignments of probabilities—are voluntary. This is separable from his denial of radical undeterministic freedom; even Spinoza would agree that when you walk, you move your legs voluntarily (though not 'freely' in Descartes's sense), and he is denying this kind of voluntariness to your beliefs and withholdings of belief:

I deny that we have a free power of suspending judgment. For when we say that someone suspends judgment, we are saying nothing but that he sees that he does not perceive the thing adequately. Suspension of judgment, therefore, is really a perception, not [an act of] free will. (2p49cs, *CS* 488)

His point, I take it, is that we do not choose our intellectual evaluations of the evidence that comes our way: the assigning of probabilities is not to be compared with voluntary bodily movements.

If that is what Spinoza is getting at, he seems to be right: Whether I believe something or suspend judgement on it depends upon the probability that I assign to it, and this depends not upon my will but upon my epistemic circumstances. In this endorsement of Spinoza's line of thought I am taking it to concern belief or judgement considered as subjective probability, and not any kind of acceptance or commitment that can be voluntary. This, it must be admitted, does not square well with his implication that suspending judgement is refraining from 'affirming [or] denying'. There is evidently much in this part of Spinoza's thought that I do not understand.

75. Error

In 1a6 Spinoza says that if an idea is true, it agrees with its object, but he means this as a biconditional: a belief is true *if and only if* it agrees with its object. Well, then, what relations are expressed by 'agrees with' and 'is the object of'? From Spinoza's handling of these expressions in his arguments, we learn this about agreement:

If x and y are counterparts under the parallelism, then x agrees with y.

And we learn this about the 'object' relation:

If x is y's object, then x and y are counterparts under the parallelism.

These merely explicate what Spinoza means by 'agree' and 'object', making it a trivial, analytic truth that every idea agrees with its object, if it has one. What is not trivial, but is a thesis in Spinoza's metaphysics, is that every idea has an object with which it agrees. So we may understand his account of truth as saying that an idea is true if and only if it has an object with which it agrees. It still follows that every idea is true, but this is now an untrivial consequence of Spinoza's metaphysic.

Still, trivial or not, there it is: *Every idea is true*, so *there cannot be any false beliefs*. Spinoza accepts that argument to that astonishing conclusion (2p32,33). He sometimes writes as though there were 'false ideas', but that is not his considered view, as he pretty well admits in 2p43s, where he writes: 'As regards the difference between a true and a false idea, it is clear from 2p35 that the former is to the latter as being is to non-being'; 2p35 says that 'falsity consists in the privation of knowledge'.

The word 'privation' is a scholastic technical term meaning something like 'lack which is a defect'. A lack of vision, for example, would be called a privation in a man, but not in a tree. Spinoza cannot use the term in that way, however, because in the sternly naturalistic philosophy which he declares in 1 Appendix and abides by throughout most of his work there is no basic place for the concept of defect or of something's not being as it ought to be. In his own words:

Privation is . . . only a being of reason, a mode of thought, which we form when we compare things with one another. We say for example that a blind man is deprived of sight because we easily imagine him as seeing, whether through comparing him with others who see or comparing his present state with his past ability to see. When we consider this man in this way, . . . we say that he is deprived of sight. But when we consider God's decree and his nature, we can no more affirm of that man than of a stone that he is deprived of vision. (Letter 21, CS 377)[4]

In our present context, Spinoza uses 'privation' merely to refer to a certain lack; it is indeed one that would commonly be regarded as a defect; but he is not making anything of that.

In 2p35d he writes something which means this (what follows is not a strict translation):

There is nothing positive in ideas that constitutes the form of falsity (by 2p33). However, falsity cannot consist in mere lack of knowledge; for bodies lack knowledge, yet we do not say that they err or are deceived. Nor does it consist in mere ignorance, for we distinguish ignorance from error. So it consists in the following special kind of lack of knowledge . . .

Let us stop Spinoza here for a moment, while we consider the thesis that error is some kind of lack of knowledge. If P is the case, someone is ignorant about it if *he does not believe that P*; he is in error about it if *he believes that not-P*. When things get complex and tangled, a person can believe something that contradicts

---

[4] See also letter 19, CS 359. For more on this topic, see Carriero 1995: 270–3.

something he knows; so error is not stronger than ignorance, but logically independent of it. Even if I am wrong about this, however, we cannot get a good account of error by starting with ignorance and building on it. Analogously, a good account of the meaning of 'She passionately detests him' would not start with 'Her attitude to him is not one of bored indifference', even though that would be true if the other were.

Aware of the surface implausibility of his view of error, Spinoza goes to unusual lengths to defend it in informal, intuitive ways, trying to win us over. Most of this material is in two scholia, 2p17cs and 2p35s. Here is the relevant part of the former:

> As a start on indicating what error is, I should like you to note that the imaginations of the mind, considered in themselves, contain no error. The mind, that is, does not err merely because it imagines, but only insofar as it is considered to lack an idea that excludes the existence of those things that it imagines to be present to it. For if the mind, while it imagined nonexistent things as present to it, at the same time knew that those things did not exist, it would of course attribute this power of imagining to a virtue of its nature, not to a vice. (2p17cs, *CS* 465)

I think his line of thought is this:

> Suppose I hallucinated a tiger, and for a while thought I was seeing an actual tiger. When the error occurred, my mind *contained* a tigerish bit of imagining, and *lacked* intellectual support for the belief that there were no tigers nearby. But we take error to be something bad, whereas that 'imagining' is perfectly good in itself, an agreeable addition to the rich pattern of my mental life. So the error—the bad part of the initial situation—must consist in my lack of certain beliefs about the local fauna.

This is the best I can do for Spinoza, but it is not good enough. It implies that my lack of knowledge *was* my error about the tiger, but really that lack *caused* the belief. Or, if the 'belief as default' thesis is true, the lack *allowed* the belief to occur. The original situation contained not merely a positive tigerish imagining, but also a false belief based on it, and that false belief, having been caused or allowed partly by ignorance, was dislodged by new information. The same criticism applies to the size-of-the-sun example in 2p35s.

Spinoza's theory is not confined to errors linked with 'imagination'—that is, with the senses. Here is a favourite example of his: 'Men are deceived in thinking themselves free, an opinion which consists only in this, that they are conscious of their actions and ignorant of the causes by which they are determined' (2p35s, *CS* 473). The mistake is obvious. Spinoza was—and knew he was—ignorant of the causes which determined his actions, yet he did not think himself radically free. Some people's ignorance of causes may cause them to believe in freedom, but it is never identical with that belief. Nor can Spinoza rescue his position by replacing 'ignorant of the causes' etc. by 'ignorant of the fact that their actions have determining causes'. He would then no longer be a counter-example to his own theory, but plenty of other people would be: namely, ones who are agnostic both about determinism and about radical freedom. Admittedly Spinoza is not committed to this 'belief in freedom' thesis by his overall view of error; but the thesis illustrates his propensity for being wrongly satisfied with 'species of ignorance' accounts of error.

76. A better account of truth?

Given that Spinoza was aware that his account of error is implausible, why did he not drop it in favour of the simple theory that an error is a belief which is false? Possible answer: 'He could not do so because he had defined "true" in terms of an idea's agreement with its object. A load-bearing part of his metaphysical structure is the doctrine that every idea has an "object" with which it "agrees", that is, with which it is paired in the parallelism; which entails that every idea is true.' Then why did Spinoza not reconsider his account of truth, exploring whether he might identify it with some kind of 'agreement' other than the pairing laid down in 2p3 and 2p7?

Such a reconsideration seems to be called for quite apart from the problem about error. If we find it plausible to say that a true idea is one that 'agrees' with its 'object', this is because we think of a belief's object as the item that the belief is, in the ordinary sense, *about*, and not in terms of the belief's neural underlay. Our ordinary notion of the source of a belief's truth-value is indicated by how we refer to the belief in a phrase of the form 'John's belief that . . .' with a sentence in the gap: my belief that there is an African sculpture on my desk is true because of what stands on my desk, not because of what happens in my skull.

In short, the kind of agreement that we ordinarily associate with truth is something like Spinoza's indirectly-of relation (§59). If Spinoza had analysed truth and error in that way, his account would have been more plausible—among other things in not implying that there are no false beliefs. Why did he not take that way out? Here is a possible answer:

Spinoza deals sketchily with 'indirectly-of' because he thinks of it as a superficial, unimportant, dispensable part of our conceptual armory. He would say of the mental item that I have called 'my belief that there is an African sculpture on my desk' that if we knew enough, we could replace the phrase by a better one of the form 'my belief that . . .' with the gap filled by a description of the corresponding physical state. So he thinks he is addressing himself to the best notion of truth—the one that is geared to the best notion of the content of a belief, the one that brings in correlated bodily states (direct) rather than causally linked external states of affairs (indirect).

If that were Spinoza's position, he would be flagrantly abusing the concepts of 'belief that P' and 'true belief' under the guise of offering superior versions of them. Some of our contemporaries look forward to the day when we shall have a properly scientific treatment of cognitive states, one that attends solely to their neural correlates and ignores their relations to the outer world; and Spinoza seems to sympathize with that project. But the project jettisons the concept of *belief that* P where P is a proposition about the world that is represented in the belief; one of the relevant books is subtitled 'The Case Against Belief'. By moving to a purely neural and internalist view of cognition, therefore, we find a basis not for calling all beliefs true, but rather for dropping the notion of belief considered as a cognitive state with a content and a truth-value.

Anyway, that is not Spinoza's position. His denial that any beliefs are false is not a delicate plant that will grow only in the soil of the directly-of relation. His formal argument for it, relying as it does on the senses of 'agree' and 'object' that come from the parallelism, is conducted purely in terms of that relation; I admit that. But when he illustrates and informally argues for his doctrine in the scholia, he confines the discussion to the indirectly-of relation. When he writes about what the mind imagines 'as present to it' and of the child's naïve belief that the sun is a few hundred feet away, the indirectly-of relation is in question. These beliefs or ideas are thought of as erroneous because of how they relate to something outside the believer's body, and Spinoza is arguing that their error lies in their involving a kind of ignorance of *that outer reality*. He seems to hold that a belief cannot be outright false of either its indirect or its direct object.

Well, perhaps this is a double view of his: his official account of truth implies that no idea can be 'false' in the directly-of sense; and for some other reason he holds that no idea can be 'false' in the indirectly-of way. The 'other reason' is available. If we ask Spinoza, 'How can a belief of mine be about an external state of affairs S?', he answers, 'By being the idea directly of a state of your body that is caused by S' (see 2p16). This is his only provision for a belief about something other than the believer's body; it is his entire theory of the indirectly-of relation. It implies that a belief can have x as its indirect object only by being the mental counterpart of a brain state that is *caused by x*, and it can be the belief that P (where P is not about the believer's body) only by being the mental counterpart of a brain state that is *caused by P's being the case*.

On this theory, an idea in my mind counts as my belief that there is a sculpture on my desk only because its cerebral counterpart—its direct object—is caused by there being a sculpture on my desk; another counts as my belief that the sea is choppy only because its cerebral counterpart is caused by the sea's being choppy; and so on. But obviously my brain state cannot be caused by an absent sculpture or by the choppiness of a smooth sea. So even if we define truth and falsity through the indirectly-of relation, we still get the result that there are no false ideas.

Or almost none. Spinoza points out one class of exceptions in 2p17. My idea indirectly of x will remain unchanged, even after x has altered or moved, for as long as my body does not relevantly alter. So an idea can positively misrepresent its indirect object, but only by being out of date, which covers a minuscule fraction of what we normally think of as false belief.

So Spinoza cannot provide liberally for false indirect beliefs any more than for false direct ones; and he may have been aware of this. Perhaps, then, although he demonstrates his thesis in directly-of terms, and informally defends it in terms of the indirectly-of relation, he really means to be talking throughout about both at once. It would not be out of character for him to demonstrate through one relation a doctrine that he meant to apply also to another; his demonstrations do not always give his real or his best reasons for the conclusions. This is probably because he liked them to be short, and to depend upon his technical terminology; and sometimes his best reasons could not be forced into that mould. So it is in the present case. To attack false belief in terms of the indirectly-of relation would have required more words, and would have been more informal, than he liked. The indirectly-of relation is not part of the system—it occurs mainly in one informal discussion, playing virtually no part in the deductive structure.

For years that was the best explanation I could find for Spinoza's strange performance. But I became dissatisfied with it because I am sceptical about philosophical coincidences. It is not likely—I came to think—that a philosopher would provide bases for two ways for a belief to have content, one relating it to the brain, the other to the external world, and that it should just *happen* that each is unfriendly to the concept of false belief. With as tough and deep a philosopher as Spinoza, one should look for a common source for both halves of the story.

77. A suggested explanation

I now think there is a profound reason, lying deep enough to straddle the gap between 'directly of' and 'indirectly of', why Spinoza should deny that any belief can be false. He does not explicitly present it, but it arises out of views that he did hold. I think it had force in his thinking, even if only subliminally, and that it ultimately explains his holding that false belief is impossible. If I am wrong in attributing it to Spinoza, it is still worth considering as philosophy.

Discussing error in 4p1s, Spinoza alludes to imaginings that might lead their subject astray, and says firmly that 'they are not contrary to the true'. This phrase is suggestive. I think that *Spinoza was grappling with the problem of how something that is real can be contrary to the true*, or how there can be a logical conflict—a relation of P to not-P—between one part of reality and another. The speed of light is finite, and John believes that the speed of light is infinite. John's mind is a natural object, a small chunk of the real, just as his body is, or as the grit in my shoe is. How can a natural object contain something false? Or, to put the problem another way: if some fact about John's mind is ideally described by saying

John believes that the speed of light is infinite,

and if it is also the case that

The speed of light is finite,

then the total true story about the universe includes both 'the speed of light is finite' and 'the speed of light is infinite'. How can this be?

Many philosophers, if asked that question out of the blue, would dismiss it as a cheap trick. That response unpacks into this:

A falsehood can be part of a truth when the latter reports the existence of a false belief. To get 'The speed of light is infinite' into an account of the real world, we need only to find someone who believes that the speed of light is infinite. The mystery vanishes when we recall that some parts of reality are mental representations, for we know that such mental items have that feature of being-about-something which enables them to be at once real and false.

Spinoza would not take that way out unless he could explain how it could be so. He would want some account of what is going on conceptually when a falsehood is nested inside a true report of a belief, and would refuse to be fobbed off with the pseudo-explanation that this is a basic property of the mind. His parallelism debars him from treating any aspect of the mental as 'occult' or 'queer' (§50); and his naturalism debars him from treating anything as occult or inexplicable.

Spinoza's denial that anything real can be untrue is similar in spirit to his denial that anything real can be wrong or defective. Because he thinks that Nature (or God) has no purposes and is subject to no external standards, he denies that there is any pathology of Nature: he pours scorn on certain common attitudes by saying that they imply that 'Nature has gone wrong' (CS 545). A child with leukaemia, Spinoza would say, is a perfect specimen of one kind of natural object, and is not a result of Nature's erring, producing something intrinsically wrong or bad or substandard. A single frame of mind can encourage one to think both that nothing real is intrinsically bad and that nothing real is false. I accept the former doctrine, while rejecting the latter; but I agree with Spinoza that the notions of real pathology and real falsehood are problematic, differing from him only in thinking that the latter problem can be solved.

To solve the problem of how beliefs can be false, Spinoza needed a better account of mental representation: something more than the thin 'idea indirectly of' relation that he gives in the vicinity of 2p16,17. My own preferred candidate for such a better account is the functionalist kind of theory of belief which I mentioned in §73. That is usually seen as part of a programme of comprehensive materialism; Spinoza would have rejected the latter, but functionalism could be put to work without it. Without insisting that mentalistic concepts are reducible to materialistic ones, one might deploy functionalism as an aid to sorting out mentalistic concepts in terms of their relations to the material world. However, even a functionalism that was not a direct affront to Spinoza's property-dualism would have been triply unacceptable to him if he had thought of it.

(1) Functionalism, understood in our present way, tries to understand what beliefs are by seeing what role they play in explaining behaviour. This would repel Spinoza, who rejects all explanations that run from one attribute to another.

(2) Functionalism explains belief while also explaining desire; it runs the two in harness, as collaborators in explaining behaviour. The basic idea behind this is plain enough: your taking an umbrella is explained by your thinking it may rain,

but only if you want not to get wet; it is explained by your not wanting to get wet, but only if you think it may rain. Spinoza's own account of desire would not allow it to play any such role as this (§85).

(3) Functionalism requires a liberal use of statements about the dispositions of things—that is, statements about what would happen if such-and-such were the case. The core of the functionalist account of belief could be expressed skeletally in the equation of 'x believes that P' with:

> x is disposed to behave in a manner which would satisfy x's desires if P were the case.

To attribute a disposition to a thing is to assert a counterfactual conditional about it: 'He is disposed to φ' means something of the form 'If . . . were to happen, he would φ'. So the displayed formula is a counterfactual whose consequent has another counterfactual nested within it. Now, Spinoza uses counterfactuals himself, but I think he was suspicious of them. One bit of evidence occurs in his reply to a correspondent who has asked 'whether by our precaution we can prevent what would otherwise happen to us'. Instead of answering simply, 'Yes; for I might stop safely at the edge of a precipice, whereas *if I had taken another step I would have fallen*', Spinoza writes: 'Since one could ask a hundred such things in an hour without arriving at any conclusion about anything, and since you yourself do not press for an answer, I shall leave your question unanswered' (letter 23, CS 390). The rudeness of this rebuff catches our attention, as does its being longer than a decent answer would have been. I think Spinoza was unwilling to use a counterfactual conditional if he could talk his way out of it. His snub includes a sort of counterfactual, but he probably did not notice this.

His determinism may have made him suspicious of counterfactual conditionals. Many determinists, holding that P's being the case was inevitable from the start of the universe, have inferred that it makes no sense to think about what would have ensued if P *had not* been the case. They are wrong, I think, but their position is not unreasonable. Of contemporary theorists of counterfactuals, the one who has worked hardest and best to reconcile them with determinism is David Lewis, and the feature of his analysis that produces the consistency—a certain use of the concept of *miracle*—has attracted more criticism than any other feature of his work on this topic. Although this criticism has not been intelligent, its sheer volume testifies to there being a prima-facie problem about showing how counterfactuals can be true in a deterministic world.

This third aspect of functionalism, incidentally, helps with the question 'How can a false proposition occur in a true description of reality?', by suggesting the answer:

> (1) A false proposition can be the antecedent or the consequent of a true counterfactual conditional.

This can stand on its own, or it can be adduced to underpin and explain the answer I looked at earlier:

(2) A false proposition can be the content of a false belief that somebody has.

With help from functionalism, we can use 1 to explain why 2 is true, which gives us the benefits of 2 without the threat that in giving that answer we are appealing to the mind's status as a 'queer kind of medium'.

78. Adequate ideas

Back in §75 Spinoza was telling us what he thinks error is. I cut him off at the point where he said that it is a species of ignorance; but now let us hear him on what species it is. He writes: 'Error consists in the privation of knowledge that inadequate knowledge of things, or inadequate and confused ideas, involve' (2p35d). Let us see what he means by 'inadequate ideas'—a topic we also need for another purpose.

The phrase 'adequate idea' is ostensibly defined in 2d4; but that is a left-over from how the term 'adequate' is used in Spinoza's *Emendation of the Intellect*, and it has nothing to do with its use in the *Ethics*. Spinoza does not invoke 2d4 until 4p62d (having used 'adequate' well over a hundred times in parts 2 and 3), and then he misrepresents it, as he does also in his only other mention of it (5p17d). Let us set it aside. The use of 'adequate' in 2p11c is also misleading; for details see *Study* 177–8.

We have to focus on 2p24,d in which Spinoza finally settles on his preferred use of '(in)adequate'. In this use, (in)adequacy is not a property of an idea, but a relation between an idea and a mind that contains it. Most of the ground is covered by this: *For idea I to be inadequate in mind M is for the causes of I to lie at least partly outside M.* Inadequate ideas, in short, are exogenous ones. It obviously follows that plenty of your ideas are inadequate relative to your mind; but such an idea may be adequate relative to some mind of which yours is a part. Your body is a material 'individual' (= organism), which may be part of some larger individual, which may be part of a larger one still—or so Spinoza maintains. He moves from individuals that are 'composed only of the simplest bodies' to the thought of a number of these assembled into a whole whose ability to survive through changes qualifies it as an individual of a second, more complex kind. Then:

If we should further conceive a third kind of individual, composed of many individuals of this second kind, we shall find that it can be affected in many other ways, without any change of its form. And if we proceed in this way to infinity, we shall easily conceive that the whole of nature is one individual, whose parts, i.e. all bodies, vary in infinite ways without any change of the whole individual. (Lemma 7s in the physical interlude, *CS* 462)

This seems to imply that any idea in your mind is also in some more comprehensive mind, and in yet another more capacious still, and so on; and an idea which is inadequate relative to your mind may be adequate relative to many minds of which yours is a part. The limiting case is the mental side of the entire universe—God—relative to which all of your ideas are adequate, because none of them is caused from outside God's mind. Spinoza says this, making it explicitly clear that his concept of inadequacy is relational: 'All ideas insofar as they are related to God are adequate. . . . There are no inadequate ideas except insofar as they are related to the singular mind of someone' (2p36d).

Whenever I speak in a monadic way of an idea as '(in)adequate', without further explanation, it will always be an idea in the mind of some human being, and I will mean that it is (in)adequate relative to that mind. That is determinate, because Spinoza does not think that you and I can be parts of larger human beings.

Once the notion of (in)adequacy is made clear, we hardly need a proof that most of our ideas are inadequate, but Spinoza gives one (2p24d). A human body (he argues) is a physical complex which metabolizes, continuing to exist while changes occur in which particles compose it; so the causes of its state at any time lie mostly outside it (because many of the body's parts have only recently come into it); therefore (by 2p7) the causes of the corresponding ideas lie outside its mind. This proof is sound. Incidentally, in Spinoza's full statement of it, the 'directly-of' relation is treated as representative: the mental counterpart of the parts of a human body is equated with 'the *knowledge of* each part of the individual composing the human body'.

I have been vague on whether the doctrine is that idea I is adequate relative to M only if

(1) the immediate cause of I lies within M,

or

(2) every cause of I lies within M—that is, no causal chain leading to I includes anything that lies outside M.

Spinoza does not address this, but we must choose 1 or something like it; otherwise, no idea is adequate relative to any mind except God's, and that is not his position. A third option is to make adequacy a matter of degree: I is adequate relative to M *to the extent that* its causes lie within M. I have not found Spinoza saying anything along those lines.

79. Mutilation

Given what Spinoza means by '(in)adequate', he is entitled to suppose that inadequate ideas involve a lack of knowledge: if I have an inadequate idea, its cause lies outside my mind, so the object of its cause lies outside my body, so I have no knowledge of (= no idea directly of) that cause. I do have an idea indirectly of the item in question, namely the inadequate idea that we started with; but this does not make up for the lack that Spinoza is talking about, which is strictly tied to the directly-of relation.

Now we are expected to accept that this kind of knowledge-lack is what we familiarly recognize as error. It is incredible, put like that. 'Error is ignorance as such'—absurd! And Spinoza will not have it. 'Error is the special kind of ignorance that inadequate ideas involve'—to my ear, that sounds no better. Any chance that Spinoza has of convincing us of his doctrine of error will have to come from two other adjectives which in 2p35 and elsewhere he runs in harness with 'inadequate': namely, 'mutilated' and 'confused'.

He has a sound reason for calling inadequate ideas 'mutilated'. When other bodies act on my body, and accordingly when my mind is subject to outside influence, there is something arbitrary, ragged, meaningless about where the line falls between what is in me and what is not. The causal sequence that includes this idea of mine is orderly, reasonable, and coherent, but only bleeding chunks of it get into my mind, so that what my mind captures is 'mutilated . . . and without order for the intellect' (2p40s1, CS 477). This is ignorance, a lack, but Spinoza sees it as an especially grievous one.

This analogy may convey some idea of how Spinoza sees mutilation as a cognitive deficit. Imagine looking down on a football game from a roof high above it, through a tube that shows only a circle of three yards radius near the centre of the field, and trying from that alone to understand the game. The crux is the arbitrariness of the confinement to that bit of the field. You could not figure out what was happening if you were allowed to track just the ball, or just the quarterback, but those restrictions would be less arbitrary, meaningless, 'mutilating' than the circle, which is in that respect comparable to the boundaries of a human being.

This analogy is imperfect because it concerns the indirectly-of relation, whereas Spinoza's thesis should involve only directly-of. He is talking about ideas of mine which are inadequate because their causes lie outside my mind; so he ought to hold that all ordinary sensory states are inadequate and thus 'mutilated', and the difference between large and small views of external events such as football games is irrelevant to this doctrine. Still, the analogy may help a little.

Anyway, although Spinoza is committed to rejecting it, he also virtually commits himself to accepting it. His view of mutilation as a cognitive deficit is presumably linked with his view (1a4) that to know something properly, you have to know what caused it; and in that, 'know' can be understood in terms of either directly-of or indirectly-of. In §60 I remarked that the directly-of reading is needed for Spinoza's subsequent use of 1a4, while indirectly-of is needed for the axiom to be plausible. It would not be surprising if that two-faced aspect of 1a4 carried through to Spinoza's concept of mutilation, and there is evidence that it did in a famous passage from his Letter 32:

Imagine a tiny worm living in the blood, capable of distinguishing by sight the particles of the blood and of intelligently observing how in collisions each particle either rebounds or communicates some degree of its motion, and so forth. That worm would be living in the blood as we are living in our part of the universe; it would have no idea as to how all

the parts are modified by the overall nature of the blood and compelled to mutual adaptation as the overall nature of the blood requires, so as to agree with one another in a
definite relation. Since there are many external causes which modify the laws of the
nature of the blood and are reciprocally modified by the blood, it follows that there occur
in the blood other motions and other changes, resulting not solely from the reciprocal
relation of its particles but from the relation between the motion of the blood on the one
hand and external causes on the other. (Wolf 210–11)

This does not speak explicitly of 'mutilation', and it does have a concern (which
I have edited out) with the part/whole relation. Still, nobody could doubt that it
belongs with Spinoza's doctrine about inadequacy and mutilation; and I offer it
as evidence that he thought of the latter partly in terms of the indirectly-of
relation.

I have said that *most* of the ground is covered by a definition that equates 'inadequate' ideas with exogenous ones. Most but not all, because there are two kinds
of exogenous ideas that Spinoza counts as adequate. The only justification I can
find for these exceptions is that ideas of these kinds are not 'mutilated'; which
confirms that mutilation calls the tune in Spinoza's thinking about (in)adequacy.

In 2p38 he writes: 'Whatever is common to all, and is equally in the part and
in the whole, can only be conceived adequately.' What are common to all and are
equally in the part and in the whole are geometrical properties. Spinoza aims to
spare our knowledge of the geometrical aspects of the outside world from the
dyslogistic label 'inadequate'. To him, as to his contemporaries, it seemed clear
that we can have unimpugnable geometrical knowledge of the physical realm, so
he needed to make room for it—perhaps also for knowledge of fundamental
physics; I am not sure about that. Spinoza's demonstration of 2p38 does not
work, but he has some justification for it. If a property is 'common to all, and is
equally in the part and in the whole', he could argue, then even when an idea of
it is caused in my mind from the outside, there must be a qualitative continuity,
a smoothness, across my boundary, so that this idea of mine will not be mutilated.

In 2p39 Spinoza stretches the boundaries of adequacy still further; this time I
am not sure what the stretch consists in, let alone how it is to be justified. It is not
put to work anywhere in the *Ethics*. (For discussion see *Study* 183–4.) But here
again the concept of mutilation seems to be central.

80. Confusion

Now let us turn to the thesis that inadequate ideas are confused. In one place
Spinoza says that a confused idea is just the idea directly of a confused material
thing. He is writing about general terms such as 'man' and 'dog', which he thinks
have meanings in the way Locke thought they do, through being associated with
'ideas' that are formed from sensory encounters with many instances. Such

terms are unfit for use in serious theoretical enterprises, Spinoza holds, because those ideas are bound to be confused. Here is why:

The human body, being limited, is capable of forming distinctly only a certain number of images at the same time (I have explained what an image is in 2p17s). If that number is exceeded, the images will begin to be confused . . . The human mind will be able to imagine distinctly, at the same time, as many bodies as there can be images formed at the same time in its body. But when the images in the body are completely confused, the mind also will imagine all the bodies confusedly. (2p40s1, *CS* 476–7)

This implies that an image—a particular state of a physical thing—can be intrinsically 'confused'. But what can that mean? Spinoza seems to have no basis upon which he can say that any bodily state is inherently confused, and in 1 Appendix (starting at *CS* 444) he says so himself, when he includes 'order' and 'confusion' in his list of notions that people *wrongly* apply to natural things. Something has gone awry here. Presumably it is something tempting, because Leibniz also succumbed to it too when he explained indistinct thoughts in the soul in terms of 'confused and indistinct motions in the brain' (*NE* 117).

Spinoza and Leibniz were presumably thinking of something like this: You ink some rubber stamps and imprint them all on a single sheet of paper; the first comes out nice and clear; the second overlaps the first a bit, the third overlaps both of the other two, and so on until eventually the page is a mess. Is not the final total image a confused 'natural thing'? I say No. The page is a mess, but not an intrinsically confused one. After the eleventh stamp, say, the pattern of black and white on the page is—like every real thing—perfectly exact and precise; it could count as an extremely clear and distinct representation of *something*—for example, of another page just like it. I take that point from Locke's brilliant attack on the idea of intrinsic confusion (*Essay* II.xxix.8).

One might hope to get a better grip on how Spinoza thinks of confusion by seeing why he holds that inadequate ideas are confused. We know why inadequate ideas are mutilated—but why are they confused? Spinoza does not answer. In 2p28d he writes that certain ideas are inadequate, from which he infers that they are mutilated, without order for the intellect, etc.—'like conclusions without premises', he elegantly adds. Then he moves on to infer that the ideas are also confused, assuring us that this consequence is self-evident ('known through itself'). Being told that something follows self-evidently does not help those who cannot see that it follows at all.

Spinoza probably associates confusion with loss of information. That seems to be at the heart of the passage about the piling up of too many images. If that is all there is to Spinoza's concept of confusion, though, it cannot help him with his theory of error. In the hope of making the theory plausible, we have looked for something to *add* to mere ignorance in the account of what error is. If we settle for the thesis that error is the kind of ignorance that occurs when ideas come with loss of information, nothing has been added, and the theory is no better off.

What, then, are we to say about confusion? Here is a poor answer: 'Spinoza and Leibniz are wrong to attribute confusion to non-mental items. The mind's being a queer kind of medium shows in, among other things, its ability to house confusion.' That is un-Spinozistic and bad philosophy. Spinoza's willingness to regard the life of the mind as an non-occult part of the natural world is one of his strengths. Where he went wrong, I suggest, was in thinking of confusion as intrinsic, a monadic feature of anything that has it, whether mental or physical. Really, confusion is relational, as Locke showed in the discussion I have mentioned.

I think that our ordinary concept of confusion involves that of error: to apprehend something confusedly involves apprehending it in a manner that makes one likely to err about it. (This restricts confusion to minds, but for a graspable reason and not because the mind has occult powers.) If I am right, then Spinoza is also right in connecting error with confusion. But the connection, far from rescuing his account of error, makes it circular.

81. Spinoza on reason's infallibility

Spinoza has a special job for his doctrine that error is confined to the province of inadequate ideas. He looks to it for a crucial part of his account of human reason, to which I now turn.

Philosophers down the ages have seen mankind as having a mental faculty called 'reason', which is involved in at least two things:

> Acquiring beliefs on the basis of other beliefs: I come to believe that Q because I already believe that P and I am led by reason to infer Q from it.

> Acquiring modal knowledge: I know through the exercise of reason that nothing can both be and not be at the same time, and that a whole is not smaller than its part.

Without going deeply into how these two are related, we can see why they might be run in one harness. If reason leads me to infer Q from P, then reason informs me that if P is true, then Q must be also.

Traditional thinking about reason has taken it to be a faculty with a built-in guarantee of freedom from error. The senses can deceive—so the story goes—but reason cannot. You may sometimes think you are being led by reason when you are not, and may then fall into error; but genuine reason, properly used, will not do that to you. This is trivial if it is secured by a definition of 'reason' or of 'properly used'; but it has been accepted as the substantive thesis that we have a device that takes us from one belief to another in a manner that is guaranteed not to take us from truth to falsehood.

Believers in infallible reason have not been able to explain what it is or what makes it possible. How could our minds contain a belief-engendering device that has this remarkable property? Many philosophers have not squarely faced this question. While acknowledging that some movements of the mind are to be *causally* explained, which demands a naturalistic, empirical psychology, they have seen a mind's moving *through reason* from one belief state to another as one of those inexplicable activities of that queer medium the mind. Wittgenstein could have included in his ironic list of the mind's 'queer' achievements the fact that the mind can acquire beliefs in two ways—by being caused to acquire them and by having reasons for them.

If we want to resist this, and to describe mental events as part of the natural order of things, we should think of reasoned inferences in causal terms. When we come to believe Q because we already believed P and think it to be a reason for Q, something happens in our minds—a causal transaction which takes place because of how our minds are structured. Why does it tend to be truth-preserving? As Bernard Williams writes:

> People sometimes argue [that] it cannot be the case that in rational thought I arrive at one belief causally because I have another belief, since then it would be a perpetual miracle that the laws of nature worked in such a way that we were caused to have beliefs by rational considerations. Granted . . . that q was evidence for p, does it not seem a happy accident or even miraculous that when I believe that q it comes about that I believe that p? (1972: 143)

Williams's point is that it is not a happy accident. We are so structured that our causally explicable transitions do tend to be truth-preserving, and the reason for this is presumably evolutionary. It is to be expected that we should have evolved minds which are disposed to acquire beliefs which are approximately true. Creatures that persistently err in their reasonings have 'a pathetic but praiseworthy tendency to die before reproducing their kind' (Quine 1969: 126).

It would not be surprising if we had evolved a cognitive faculty which outran anything that has ever been needed for survival. The basis for such a faculty could be tied to features that were needed for survival, so that the faculty was selected without being selected *for*. But an *infallible* faculty? Quite apart from the question of why such a thing might have evolved, there is the question of what it could be. Not, presumably, a causal process in which a mechanism works to take the person from one belief to another: there could not be an infallible mechanism.

That would not trouble Descartes. He sometimes assumed reason's infallibility, but did not think of it as a mechanism; in §50 I quoted his description of reason as 'a universal instrument'. This rules out the naturalistic idea of reason as a causally governed mechanism, without putting anything in its place. Descartes has no positive account of reason. He alludes to 'natural reason', sometimes in contrast to divine revelation, and sometimes in a more favourable contrast to the syllogistic discipline of the Schools; and in his letters he often mentions practical reason; but none of this is backed by theory.

When Descartes accords a high epistemic privilege to reason, he neither justifies nor explains. The full title of the *Method* speaks of 'rightly conducting one's reason and seeking the truth', and in it he reports having resolved to 'devote my whole life to cultivating my reason and advancing in the knowledge of the truth' (CSM 1:124). In this work, as in the earlier *Rules for the Direction of the Mind*, he refers often to the need for 'reason' to be guided by 'rules' and to follow a 'method', but he does not tell us what reason is, or why it should have pride of place among the epistemic faculties—why when 'reason tells me' something, I should listen. He speaks of 'the light of nature', 'the light of reason', and 'the light of the mind', but this is only a metaphor. In the *Discourse on the Method* the term 'reason' seems to act as a cipher, a dummy predicate to which no specific value has been assigned. In the *Meditations* Descartes mentions reason as a faculty on four occasions, in the *Principles of Philosophy* somewhat oftener; but none of these mentions throws any light. We might hope to glean an account of reason from what he writes in the *Discourse on the Method* about 'method' and 'rules'; but those two terms throw no light on anything (§143).

Spinoza, uniquely among philosophers that I know, tries to have it both ways: thoroughly a naturalist about reason, which he openly treats as a causal process, he nevertheless claims it to be infallible and offers to explain why. His explanation fails because it relies on his false theory of error; but it is so ingenious and original that it commands our interest.

It comes in 2p40s, where Spinoza officially distinguishes experience from reason. He calls the former *experientia vaga*, random experience. In disciplined scientific inquiries we presumably have unrandom experience, but Spinoza never mentions that. Anyway, what matters here is how experience—both random and controlled—stands in contrast to reason.

(A third kind of cognitive state or process, supposedly higher than reason, is called 'intuitive knowledge'. I regard this as a source for much that is worst in the *Ethics* and the secondary literature, and for nothing good. (See *Study* 364–9. For a dissenting view, see Norris 1991: 74–7.) Associated with intuitive knowledge is Spinoza's doctrine of the eternity of the mind, which I have—with the backing of solid evidence—called 'rubbish which causes others to write rubbish'. Norris is not the only critic to see this coolly objective, clinically precise, and sadly arrived-at description as evidence of my emotional state; he characterizes it as 'by any standard a remarkable outburst of sheer bad temper'.)

All sensory experience consists in ideas that are caused from outside oneself: one's body is acted on by its surroundings, so one's mind is correspondingly acted on from outside it. The mental transaction generates ideas which, since their immediate causes were outside the mind that has them, are inadequate. Reason is a non-experiential faculty, the exercise of which does not involve input from one's environment; so nothing about it requires ideas that are inadequate. In reasoning one sits and thinks, exploring a priori, so any changes that reasoning causes in one's ideas will be caused purely internally. So they will be adequate ideas.

Now, Spinoza has explained all error as a mental lack coming from inadequate ideas. So a faculty that deals only in adequate ideas cannot involve error. Reason is such a faculty. Therefore, reason is infallible. QED. This purports to protect reason against error by giving news not only about reason, but also about error.

Parts 4 and 5 of the *Ethics* make much of reason as a faculty in the exercise of which we are active, as against the senses in the exercise of which we are passive. This is important to Spinoza because of his view that we cannot be hurt from within, but only from outside causes; so for him activity is the way to health and security, whereas the life of passivity—the life of the senses—exposes us to the risk of harm, and thus puts us at the mercy of the two most enslaving emotions, hope and fear. Taken strictly and literally, Spinoza implies that we shall do better if we pay no attention to the world around us. He cannot believe anything so foolish, but he does not make clear what more limited thesis he means to advocate. The good life that Spinoza has in mind, I submit, needs a large input of experience, both random and controlled; and I do not see how he could admit this without relinquishing much of what he does say.

Chapter 11

Desire in Descartes and Spinoza

82. Descartes on desire

Given Spinoza's determinism, naturalism, and mind–body parallelism, one is not surprised that he is hostile to teleological notions. However, he does not just walk out on them. He attacks them, and tries to find an acceptable gloss on the seemingly teleological things that we say and think. These two endeavours, which have not in general been well understood, are instructive and absorbingly interesting; they will be my topic in four sections of this chapter, after one on Descartes's way of being inhospitable towards teleology.

Descartes is openly hostile to any use of teleological concepts in physics (§4). That in itself does not force them out of psychology, for Descartes is not committed to parallelism between the two domains: he regards human minds as profoundly special, neither modelled by the human body nor continuous with corporeal nature. So he could think it goes without saying that minds can generate final causes, having thoughts about the future which affect bodily conduct.

His relevant psychological work does indeed provide for 'desire', and thus for teleology; but the provision it makes is notably thin and unsatisfying. In *Passions* 53–67 he lists and briefly describes 'all the principal passions'. His list picks out as 'primitive' (69) just six: wonder, love, hatred, desire, joy, and sadness. He proceeds to explain each in more depth, offering us this:

The passion of desire is an agitation of the soul caused by the spirits, which disposes the soul to want in the future the things it represents to itself as agreeable. Thus we desire not only the presence of goods which are absent but also the preservation of those which are present. In addition we desire the absence of evils, both those that already affect us and those we believe we may suffer on some future occasion. (*Passions* 86, CSM 1:358–9)

Later on we learn that Descartes sees desires as the required intermediaries between other passions and action. Voluntary action, it seems, always has desire as a near cause: when the passions 'govern our behaviour', they do so 'by producing desire in us' (*Passions* 143, CSM 1:379).

This does not take us far. Nor does an account that Descartes gives of joy, sadness, and desire. When the soul judges something to be good or 'fitting for itself', he writes, there are three cases:

If the good is present . . . then the movement of the will which accompanies the knowledge that this is good for it is joy; if . . . the good is absent, then the movement of the will which accompanies the knowledge of its lack is sadness; while the movement which accompanies the knowledge that it would be a good thing to acquire it is desire. (CSMK 306)

This lacks any suggestion that the third of these 'movements of the will' connects somehow with behaviour that is apt for getting the 'good thing' in question; so it does not get close to the heart of teleology. (If you are puzzled by the first two 'movements of the will', see *PP* 1:32.)

One aspect of Descartes's work, however, challenges him to deal with teleology more probingly and sceptically than he does. He develops a speculative anatomy and physiology of the human brain, aiming to explain as much behaviour as possible in material terms. He sets no limits to the range of such behaviour. The only reason he ever gives for holding that not all human behaviour can be explained through material causes is quantitative: a normal human being has too many behavioural dispositions for material 'organs' to support them all (§49). He does not hint that some *kinds* of human behaviour would have to be explained mentalistically—for example, that some human behaviour involves a teleological element which outruns the capacities of a bodily mechanism. If there is to be teleology in the mind, therefore, we ought to find it also in Descartes's materialistic account of the human condition. And so in a way we do.

The relevant texts are in parts of the *Treatise on Man*, an unfinished work of 1633. Descartes planned to deal there with the whole human condition, body and mind, but the surviving part of the treatise mostly concerns anatomy and physiology. He says that he is describing fictional men: without claiming that every detail of his account of them also fits actual humans, he aims to show what sorts of materialistic explanations *could* be given for various kinds of human behaviour.

In the course of elaborately describing tubes, spirits, filaments, and so on, Descartes turns aside to sketch the mental states and events that could be involved when someone's hand is burned in a fire:

One of the passages leads spirits into all the nerves which serve to move the limbs in the ways needed to avoid the force of that action [of the fire on a person's hand]: thus, into those that withdraw the hand or the arm or the whole body, and into those that turn the head and the eyes towards the fire in order to see in more detail what one needs to do to protect oneself from it. And through the other [passage] they go into all the nerves which serve to cause internal emotions, similar to those which come to us from pain: thus, into those which constrict the heart, which agitate the liver, and the like. And, as well, even into those which can cause the external movements that indicate it [the emotion]: thus, into those which excite tears, which furrow the brow and the cheeks, and which dispose the voice to cry. (*W*, AT 11:192–3)

This seems to represent the emotion as epiphenomenal, causing neither the movements of the limbs nor the other manifestations. Descartes evidently aims to explain each kind of human behaviour purely through material causes, giving no causal role to the familiar mental accompaniments.

We might expect this text to say how goal-seeking behaviour could be caused. The nearest that Descartes comes to doing this is in the following account of the pursuit of food:

If the nerves of the stomach are agitated in the way that I have said they need to be to cause the feeling of hunger, while nothing that seems fit to eat is presented to any of the senses or to the memory, the spirits that this action makes enter . . . into the brain will make their way to a place where they will find several pores which are equally disposed to conduct them into any of the nerves which can serve for seeking or pursuing some object; so that the only thing that can cause them to go through some rather than others [of these nerves] is the inequalities among their parts. (ibid. 194–5)

The phrase 'nothing that seems fit to eat' is an undefended helping of mentalism, but let that pass. For the rest, Descartes is trying to lay the groundwork for a materialistic account of food-seeking. In this, the brain is poised to guide movements of any kind, and Descartes is careful to say that which movements occur depends not on incursions from the mind but on the sizes of the pores. That is all right in principle; but there remains the hard part, which is needed for Descartes's account of the brain mechanics of food-seeking: namely, an account of how facts about available and edible food connect with changes in the pores in the animal's brain. In the brain of a successful food-seeker, events occur that cause bodily movements that are apt for the acquiring of food; that 'apt for' is the crux; and Descartes passes over it in silence.

83. Does Spinoza reject all teleology?

In the Appendix to part 1 of the *Ethics*, Spinoza inveighs against 'final causes'—that is, against teleology. This polemic is mainly addressed to the idea of divine or cosmic purpose—the attempt to explain events by saying that they fulfil some cosmic design. Spinoza calls this 'the sanctuary of ignorance', in which one purports to explain something without really doing so. Into this mixture he throws one remark that seems to reject *all* uses of teleological notions: 'This doctrine concerning the end turns Nature completely upside down. For what is really a cause it considers as an effect, and conversely. What by nature comes before it puts after' (*CS* 442). This makes sense as a rejection of all teleology:[1] it is of the essence of teleology that an event is explained with help from the mention of some *subsequent* event; Spinoza usually ties explanation to causation; so it is understandable that he should think that teleological explanations get the order of causation backwards. She put bait on the hook in order that the fish should bite it. The baiting precedes the biting, and causes it; yet the 'in order to'

---

[1] And it does not make sense if it is confined to divine teleology, as maintained by Curley (1990) and Garrett (1999).

statement purports to use the biting to explain the baiting. I took that line in *Study*, where I depicted Spinoza as comprehensively rejecting all teleology.

Someone who sees the risk that teleological explanations ('final causes') will turn nature upside down may think that the difficulty can be removed at least for thoughtful teleology. That obtains when someone acts for an envisaged or thought-about purpose: the action is caused or explained by a contemporaneous or earlier *thought about* the desired upshot of the action. This is teleological because it involves an essential reference to the future: the thought has its effect only because it is a thought of that possible future state of affairs rather than some other. But it does not reverse the order of nature, because the action is not said to depend on anything that lies in the future, but only on a present or past thought about the future. (Thus, for example, Braithwaite 1953: 324–5.)

So Spinoza could have respected the order of nature while still allowing that there is *thoughtful* teleology. And one might well think that this was his position, given that in the Appendix to part 1, where he attacks divine or cosmic teleology, he openly says that people do act with purposes or for ends; indeed, he says that they go wrong precisely by projecting on to the rest of Nature the ends for which they act. In *Study* I played down Spinoza's attack on impersonal, cosmic teleology, saying that its target was so large, obvious, and vulnerable as to deprive the attack of most of its interest unless it were accompanied by a rejection of thoughtful teleology in humans. Against this, Curley (1990) has pointed out that in Spinoza's day the attack was substantive and even scandalous. He is right. When I wrote that, I was not thinking historically, as I should have been.[2]

There, then, is the case for seeing Spinoza as rejecting impersonal teleology and accepting thoughtful teleology for human beings. It is slightly better than I allowed in *Study*, and in my response (1990*a*) to Curley's criticisms, I acknowledged having become 'inclined to accept that Spinoza did in a way, and up to a point, and sometimes' think of teleology in that way rather than in the comprehensively rejecting way that I had attributed to him.

84. Spinoza's trouble with thoughtful teleology

I had reasons for those grudging qualifiers. The text does not clearly, explicitly, and consistently go Curley's way. Spinoza never says outright that thoughtful teleology does not reverse the order of nature; and that is one pointer to something that I believed when I wrote my reply to Curley: namely, (1) that Spinoza accepted thoughtful teleology only in a pale and unconvinced manner, and (2) that deep down he wanted to reject all teleology. I now think that 1 concedes too

---

[2] Carriero (forthcoming *a*) holds that my serious historical sin lay elsewhere. He shapes the entire issue of teleology in Spinoza differently from how I do, by relating Spinoza to scholasticism. Even if he is wholly right, I think that my sharper, cleaner approach is *also* needed if one is to penetrate this part of Spinoza's text.

much. Spinoza retained the *language* of thoughtful teleology because he thought he could show that, properly understood, it is not teleological after all, and does not involve the problematic notion of present behaviour's being explained by a thought about a possible future. I still stand by 2: some striking parts of the *Ethics* make best sense, I shall argue, when seen as attempts to avoid genuine thoughtful teleology.

The order and connection of ideas is the same as the order and connection of things: Spinoza held that the physicalistic explanation of why my arm goes up is paralleled by a mentalistic explanation of what happens in my mind when my arm goes up. Now, the mentalistic antecedents may well include a thought of my raised arm's deflecting a stone that I see being thrown at me; that thought cannot cause the physical raising of my arm, because no explanation straddles the divide between the attributes; but it helps to cause the mental counterpart of that physical event, just as the physical counterpart of the thought causes the arm to go up. So it has a causal-explanatory role with respect to what the person does right now, although it involves a representation of something which, if it ever exists, will do so only in the future. This is how thoughtful teleology would have to work in Spinoza's philosophy of mind.

But it will not work. Granted that Spinoza thinks that mentalistic causal chains have a structure that mirrors the structure of physicalistic ones, so that causal explanations under one attribute model those under the other, it is a further question whether that isomorphism brings in any of the *representative* aspects of mental states and events. Now the nearest Spinoza gets to anything we can recognize as genuinely representative mental content is his treatment of the indirectly-of relation between ideas and other things, such as Peter's idea of Paul's body (§59). An idea in Peter's mind counts as an idea of Paul's body only because it (is the idea directly of a state of Peter's body that) was caused by the action of Paul's body. To avoid prolixity, I shall omit the bit I have put in parentheses, and write as though bodily events could cause mental ones.

The causal powers of any item depend purely on its intrinsic nature, not on any of its relational properties—and so, *a fortiori*, not on facts about its origins. If an idea of mine was caused by an interaction with Paul's body, that fact can make a difference to the idea's causal powers only by affecting its intrinsic nature. So Spinoza needs to face this question: When someone has an idea indirectly of some item, to what extent does the intrinsic nature of the idea contain information about its cause? Spinoza should—and I think would—answer: 'To only a small extent'. His statement that Peter's idea indirectly of Paul's body indicates the condition of Peter's body more than of Paul's implies that information is lost.

This is confirmed twice elsewhere in the work. In his treatment of error, Spinoza repeatedly describes inadequate ideas as 'mutilated' (§79). Such ideas, being caused from outside oneself through chance encounters with other things, are torn around the edges, so to speak; they are imperfectly intelligible because they come from an arbitrary cut in the total causal flow, a cut corresponding to the boundary of one's body. This is not a promising platform on which to maintain that such ideas are highly informative about their immediate causes.

Spinoza also gives prominence to the indirectly-of relation in 2p40s1, where he writes about the general ideas that we get from sensory encounters with many instances. He tells a fairly Lockean story about one's general idea of *man* (§80), for instance, and explains what unfits it for use in serious theoretical work. The trouble, he says, is that what one carries away from one's sensory encounters with men will vary according to what sorts of men one has encountered, what thoughts and emotions they have engendered, and so on. Thus my thought of *man* might be intrinsically very unlike yours. So explanations of the form 'He ɸ'd because he wanted . . . and believed——', where the concept *man* comes into the content of the desire or the belief, have no chance of being systematically mappable onto clean physicalistic explanations of the form 'He ɸ'd because a K event occurred in his brain'.

Spinoza ought also to believe that as well as your *man*-involving thoughts' possibly being unlike mine, it could also happen that a thought of yours might have the same intrinsic nature as one of mine, although their contents were different. I shall illustrate this with an example which relies on a view of mental representation which, though thin, is richer than Spinoza's. Where he ties the indirectly-of relation purely to the cause of an idea, the richer theory says that an idea gets its content from what stimuli caused it and what behaviour it causes. Now, consider a pair of animals One and Two, alike molecule for molecule, and living on different parts of the sea-bed in fairly shallow waters. There is a certain kind of contracting movement that each is disposed to make when the amount of light reaching it suddenly decreases. In One's environment the darkening is usually caused by the approach of a predator from above, and the contracting movement serves as a defence (presenting to the predator One's scaly and inedible side); in Two's environment the darkening is usually caused by a certain kind of edible matter falling through the water to the sea-floor, and the contracting movement serves to trap some of this food before the current sweeps it away. So the very same inner state—the one that mediates causally between the sudden lessening of light and the bodily contraction—serves for One as a belief that a predator approaches and for Two as a belief that there is food to be had. (I take the idea of One from Churchland 1979.)

I have been faced with the following objection (I am not quoting):

If representative content is causally inert, Spinoza's reliance on the 'geometrical method' is undermined. That method essentially depends on propositions' entailing other propositions, and for Spinoza this is somehow equivalent to states of affairs causing other states of affairs; the propositions link with one another through *content*—how else?—but according to Bennett, content does no serious causal work.

I reply that Spinoza on his own showing ought not to—and probably does not—think that the geometrical method has serious work to do except on propositions that involve only adequate ideas. Some ideas that are adequate in your mind were caused from outside your mind, but they are ideas only of what is present in the whole and the part—especially ideas of the purely geometrical features of things—and this enables them, despite being exogenous, to escape being 'mutilated'. They make sense (as inadequate ideas do not) because they are ideas of features of things that are instantiated equally by your body and by the rest of the material world; there is no break at the boundary, no mutilation, and thus no objection to *these* ideas being involved in serious arguments and explanations.

For thoughtful teleology to work for him, then, Spinoza needs something that his own philosophy does not permit: namely, many inadequate ideas that are informative enough in the right way about their causes. He also needs something else he does not have—a Spinozistic account of what it is for an idea or belief to be about the future. A teleology that did not mentally reach into the future would not be the real thing. Spinoza might say that my present state can support an idea about my future state because it contains the causally sufficient conditions for my future state, but that kind of futurity is useless to a theory of teleology. For one thing, my intrinsic state hardly ever contains sufficient conditions for my state more than a few seconds hence; nearly always the latter depends also on my environment. Also, if that is the only way a Spinozistic man can think about the future, he is confined to thoughts about what will inevitably come, which is a poor basis for purposive action!

Summing up my argument so far: (1) It is not credible that intrinsic states of mind that are isomorphic with states of the brain should also be systematically connected with the representative content of states of mind. For the latter—the 'of x' and 'that P' aspect of a person's thought—depends upon *relational* features of that state, including the person's past history of being in it, what else was going on at the time, and so on. (2) This truth can be derived from Spinoza's doctrines, and is indicated in his pages clearly enough to make it patronizing and ungenerous to deny him the credit for having seen it himself. (3) To the extent that he did see it, he must have thought that when my arm's going up has a physical cause whose mental counterpart is a mental event that is (among other things) the thought of my arm's deflecting a stone, *that* fact about the mental item has no part in the serious causal explanation of the mental counterpart of my arm's going up. So there was some place in Spinoza's mind for the view that even in thoughtful teleology the notion of the future is causally idle: something is being caused by a thought about the future, but the thought's being about the future—and indeed its entire content, its whole representative nature—is irrelevant to its causal powers. (I agree with Spinoza that a representative content is causally impotent. But I do not reject thoughtful teleology on that account, because I hold that teleological explanations, though genuinely explanatory, are not causal. For supporting argument see Bennett 1991a.) Spinoza had, therefore, solid reason to be dissatisfied even with thoughtful teleology. This encourages me to think that he was not really satisfied with it, despite occasional remarks suggesting the contrary.

That, however, is the weaker part of my case. The stronger is the confirmation it gets from two striking facts about the text of the *Ethics*, facts for which no explanation has been proposed except the hypothesis that Spinoza wanted to exclude all teleology from his system. I give them a section apiece.

85. Spinoza's account of appetite

If he were mainly content with thoughtful teleology, it is clear what Spinoza should say about desire: namely, that a desire is a forward-looking thought whose object (in his technical sense) causes behaviour that is suitably related to the content of the thought. A desire to find gold is a thought of finding gold whose cerebral counterpart causes behaviour which is apt to lead to the finding of gold or which the person thinks is apt for that.

If he did not accept thoughtful teleology, Spinoza would have a problem with desire which he could handle in either of two ways. He could take an eliminative tack: the meaning of 'desire' (as of its relatives 'want', 'intend', 'purpose', etc.) unbreakably ties it to thoughtful teleology; so there are no desires; and the contrary belief is a mere error, like the belief in gremlins. Or he could offer a reductionist programme, showing how 'desire' and related terms could retain most of their ordinary meaning without involving thoughtful teleology.

Significant parts of Spinoza's text look like attempts at reduction, showing what seemingly teleological concepts amount to in non-teleological terms. Nobody can see what they are if they are not that. So they strengthen my case for holding that Spinoza did not seriously and deeply accept thoughtful teleology; for if he did, his reductionist endeavours are pointless.

It may help to glance first at Hobbes. He rejected all teleology, and took the reductionist option:

[The] small beginnings of motion, within the body of man, before they appear in walking, speaking, striking, and other visible actions, are commonly called ENDEAVOUR. This endeavour, when it is toward something which causes it, is called APPETITE, or DESIRE; the latter being the general name; and the other oftentimes restrained to signify the desire of food, namely *hunger* and *thirst*. And when the endeavour is fromward something, it is generally called AVERSION. These words, *appetite* and *aversion*, we have from the Latins; and they both of them signify the motions, one of approaching, the other of retiring. (1651: ch. 6)

According to Hobbes, then, to want something is to move slightly towards it, being caused to do so by the thing itself. This is no doubt meant as a revisionary analysis of the concept of desire—a rescue of as much of it as is consistent with denying teleology. Even considered in that light, it will not do: at most it covers the cases where a person is said to want some object in his environment; it covers 'I want that apple', but not 'I want an apple', let alone 'I want her to speak to me' or 'I want the pain to stop'.

Spinoza's attempt at reduction, though similar in spirit to Hobbes's, differs from it in two ways. It identifies the desire not with a movement, but with the intrinsic state of the person that causes the movement; and it gets the notion of what a desire is *for* out of a likely effect of the desire, rather than out of its actual cause. The latter difference enables Spinoza's account to cover, as Hobbes's cannot, desires for absent objects and for states of affairs.

When Spinoza does all this, his immediate target is often 'appetite' rather than 'desire'. Whereas Hobbes says that appetite is a species of desire (the differentia is: *for food*), Spinoza treats desire as a species of appetite. Desire, he says, 'can be defined as appetite together with consciousness of the appetite' (3p9s). Because the presence of consciousness does not (he holds) affect the outcome, Spinoza makes little of the difference between desire and appetite. But he evidently thinks it important to put 'appetite' first when explaining terms that ordinarily count as teleological: 'The decisions of the mind are nothing but appetites' (3p2s, *CS* 497), and 'By the end for the sake of which we do anything I understand appetite' (4d7). So two apparently teleological terms, 'decision' and 'end', are flatly identified with appetite, and desire is said to be the very same phenomenon with an overlay of consciousness—whatever that is.

The difference between appetite and desire drops out of sight altogether when Spinoza defines 'desire' at the start of the Affect Definitions at the end of part 3:

A desire is a man's very essence, insofar as it is conceived to be determined, by some specific state it is in, to act in some way. (*CS* 531)

This is in line with what he usually says about appetite, as here:

This appetite [for survival] is nothing but the very essence of the man, from whose nature there necessarily follow those things which promote his preservation. And so the man is determined to do those things. (3p9s)

Those two statements give first a general and then a specific version of the same thesis. For someone to want (or have an appetite for) x, Spinoza is saying, is for the person to be in a state such that she is apt to do things that will lead to x. I shall explain how I arrive at that interpretation.

When he connects appetite and desire with a person's 'essence', Spinoza cannot mean 'essence' in the sense of 'basic property' or that of *sine qua non*, each of which would be absurd in this context. His one other meaning for 'essence', one that it carries through most of the *Ethics*, is that of 'intrinsic nature'. A thing's essence is just what it is like in itself. The passages now under scrutiny say that a person's desire or appetite must be understood as some aspect of her *intrinsic* nature. This excludes all the facts about her history and present relations to other things, and thus excludes all the facts about the indirect representative content of her thoughts. I do not see what else can be meant by these definitions of appetite and desire.

The definitions also embody a sketchy suggestion regarding how to take statements that a desire or appetite is *for* such-and-such. A man is said to have an appetite for survival if his intrinsic nature causes him to do things that promote his survival; and, generalizing from that, you are said to have an appetite for x if your intrinsic nature causes you to act in ways that are apt to produce x. Thus, when Spinoza says, 'A desire is a man's very essence, insofar as it is conceived to be determined, by some specific state it is in, to act in some way', I take him to mean: We speak of a person as desiring something if we see him as being causally set on a path towards the achievement of it; and if we want to identify something as *the desire* that he has, it is the aspect of his nature that sets him on that path.

Spinoza's equation of desire or appetite with 'a man's very essence insofar as . . .' etc. occurs about a dozen times; he must have thought it important; so we need to understand it. Well, I have offered a suggested understanding of it. It is faithful to Spinoza's words (except that he sometimes speaks of states not of a man but of his essence, and not of what the man does but of what his essence does), and it credits him with a serious attempt to provide for ordinary talk about wishes and wants without admitting teleology or final causes. His way of doing this, on my interpretation, does not allow that actions might be caused by 'desires' with these understood as mental representations of future states of affairs; on the contrary, the notions of 'essence' (= intrinsic nature) and of causal consequences of that essence (or of the person's having that essence) function precisely to push aside the view that representations of future states of affairs play any role in explaining behaviour. The thesis is that desire is to be understood as causally potent only when construed in intrinsic rather than representational terms, and the only reference to the future that it involves is not

a thought about the future that causes the behaviour,

but rather,

a future state of affairs that is apt to result from the behaviour.

Neither a future state of affairs nor a present thought of one has any role in explaining a present action. All teleology is rejected, including the thoughtful kind; future events come in as effects, but play no part in causes; the 'order of Nature' is restored.

If Spinoza really accepted thoughtful teleology in our ordinary understanding of it, he would not need this quasi-Hobbesian account of appetite and desire. To maintain that thoughtful teleology is a considered part of Spinoza's account of the human condition, one must explain away his repeatedly tying desire to appetite and explaining the latter as he does.

Any representational content of a person's mind at a given moment will super-vene on her intrinsic nature; and in that sense the representational features of ideas are mirrored in their intrinsic features and thus in the intrinsic nature of corresponding bodily states. But because they are mostly relational, the repre-sentational features are not mirrored in a sufficiently full, disciplined and inter-personal way for them to play a part in a causal chain that maps on to the strictly particle-impact physical explanation of what goes on in a person's body. Anyway, if Spinoza does envisage a kind of teleology in which mental representations of the future have a role, what is the point of his repeated emphasis on intrinsic natures? He introduces various words from the teleological repertoire—'decision', 'end', 'desire'—and slams the word 'appetite' up against them; and on about six occasions he explains that an appetite in a person is 'nothing but' that person's intrinsic nature. The phrase 'nothing but' is the battle-cry of the reductionist; it heralds an attempt to get teleology out of the picture. If Spinoza had no such purpose, and was willing on request to explain that the person's intrinsic nature includes the thoughts of the future that teleology needs, this performance of his would be pointless. Why say that appetite is 'nothing but' . . . and then follow that with something that he thinks has nested within it the whole normal teleological story? Garrett (1999: 322–3) offers for Spinoza's account of appetite a reading which, to my eye, is forced and implausible. The account is not intended as reductionist, Garrett says. He does not comment on Spinoza's repeatedly expressing it with help from 'nothing but'.

Spinoza's reductionist attempt, though better than Hobbes's, also fails, for a simple, general reason. The concept of desire is essentially explanatory. It shares this with teleological concepts generally, which are nothing if they are not usable in explanations: the basic use of the concept of desire, say, is not of the form 'When the animal φ'd, it wanted x', but rather of the form 'The animal φ'd because it wanted x'. Aristotle recognized this when he characterized desires and goals in terms of final *causes*; so did Spinoza when he rejected 'this doctrine concerning the end' because it treats effects as though they were causes.

Now, Spinoza's concept of appetite has no explanatory force. An animal's digging a hole cannot be explained by its wanting to dig a hole (or wanting a buried bone), if wanting is understood in terms of Spinozistic 'appetite'. 'It digs a hole because it is in an intrinsic state that leads to its digging a hole'—such an 'explanation' is useless for prediction because it is empty.

Well, then, perhaps we can think up some plausible generalizations that give a working role to Spinoza's concept of appetite and yet could be used for predictions and non-trivial explanations of behaviour. I doubt it, but of course I cannot prove that it is impossible. Anyway, Spinoza himself does not do it. When he gets to the part of the *Ethics* containing doctrine that will enable us to predict and explain various aspects of human behaviour, he quietly abandons his concept of appetite in favour of something else, which I now explain.

86. The 'demonstration' of the *conatus* doctrine

Spinoza has an important doctrine about something called *conatus*—literally 'endeavour' or 'trying'. Roughly and superficially, it says that things have an appetite for their own preservation, with this being understood in his official sense of 'appetite'. This is at the root of a large body of doctrine, presented in

Ethics 3, in which Spinoza purports to describe and explain many aspects of human behaviour. It is the basis for his system of ethics—perhaps properly so-called—in *Ethics* 4, but I shall not explore that here.

The *conatus* doctrine is certainly meant to cover human egoism. It can do so only because Spinoza equates seeking one's own advantage with seeking to stay in existence (see 4p20). He tries in 4p20s to explain away suicide, but the attempt is a dismal affair. Spinoza had a blind spot: he could not see that someone might rationally seek his own advantage by ceasing to exist. This shows up vividly in letter 23, where he writes, concerning a question he has been asked:

> It is as if someone were to ask: if it agreed better with the nature of someone to hang himself, would there be reasons why he should not hang himself? Well, suppose it were possible that there should be such a nature. Then I say . . . that if anyone sees that he can live better on the gallows than at his table, he would act very foolishly if he did not hang himself. (*CS* 390)

The initial question was not about suicide, which Spinoza dragged in, apparently wanting a chance to express an attitude to it, which I think shows a gap in his thinking and feeling. From now on, however, I shall follow him in equating acting for one's own advantage with acting to stay in existence.

Now, Spinoza's doctrine of human egoism is not offered as a thesis specifically about humans. Indeed, the term 'human' could have no place in his philosophy, because our concept of humanity is—he tells us—one of those 'imaginative' ones that differ from person to person according to the accidents of our various histories of engagement with humans, which unfits it for serious theoretical use. Almost certainly the *conatus* doctrine is meant to apply to all organisms ('individuals', as Spinoza calls them in the physical interlude); and he may even intend it as a theory to explain the cohesion of inanimate bodies—that famous problem which was proving so difficult for a physics that allows for repulsive but not attractive forces (§23). His 'demonstration' of the doctrine certainly commits him to giving it the greatest possible generality. The demonstration involves three propositions, of which the first is 'demonstrated' with no numbered premisses, the second is derived from the first, and the third from the first two. Just before demonstrating the third, in 3p6d, Spinoza invokes two propositions from part 1, but they do not enter into the proof. Thus the *conatus* doctrine is meant to arise immediately from considerations that lie so deep that they bypass even the general metaphysic of part 1. Now let us look into the demonstration.[3]

The driving force of the demonstration is 3p4: *No thing can be destroyed except through an external cause.* As well as calling this self-evident, Spinoza deigns to prove it: 'The definition of any thing affirms, and does not deny, the thing's essence . . . So while we attend only to the thing itself, and not to external causes, we shall not be able to find anything in it which can destroy it.' No one will credit that something so short and neat could prove such a tremendous conclusion, but

---

[3] It is discussed in grinding detail in *Study*, ch. 10. For variations on that treatment, see Della Rocca 1996*b*.

let us see what has gone wrong. The demonstration conflates causal with absolute necessity, and neglects temporal differences. A self-destructive thing, Spinoza holds, must have a nature which logically rules out its existing; but this would be a self-contradictory nature, and nothing could have *that*, so there is no such thing, QED. We cannot fix the trouble merely by distinguishing causal from absolute necessity, however, for that still allows this argument: a self-destructive thing must have a nature which causally rules out its existing; that would be a causally impossible nature; nothing could have *that*, so there is no such thing, QED. The larger source of trouble is the neglect of time differences. All that we need is a thing whose nature at T_1 requires its non-existence at T_2, and there is no difficulty about that. Time differences turn impossibilities into mere alterations.

From 3p4 Spinoza derives 3p5: *Things are of a contrary nature, i.e. cannot be in the same subject, insofar as one can destroy the other.* Demonstration: 'For if they could agree with one another, or be in the same subject at once, then there could be something in the same subject which could destroy it, which (by 3p4) is absurd. Therefore, things etc., QED.' This is a trickier tangle than I realized when I wrote *Study*.

For simplicity's sake, I shall take the proposition to be speaking of any *two* things; so it might seem all right to take it as having the form 'If Dest(x,y), then Nonsubj(x,y)'. But what Spinoza actually writes is not an outright conditional, but rather something of the form, 'To the extent that Dest(x,y), to that extent Nonsubj(x,y)'. The Latin is clear about this. Yet the demonstration of 3p5 is devoid of any matter-of-degree concept; and my attempts to extract something reasonable from it have not led me along the 'degree' path. I shall perforce stay with the conditional:

For all x and y, if Dest(x,y) then Nonsubj(x,y).

For convenience and safety, I shall understand 'Dest(x,y)' to mean that each of x and y can destroy the other. The Latin could equally mean merely that x can destroy y; I cannot make this difference affect the worth of the argument.

What are the relata of the Dest and Nonsubj relations—properties or things? The language of 'contrary nature' and being 'in a subject' suggest properties; but the language of 'destruction' seems to belong rather to things, as does Spinoza's mention of 'things' at the start of 3p5. We had better look at 3p5,d under each interpretation separately. On the 'properties' reading, we have this:

(1) If the properties X-ness and Y-ness are mutually antithetical, no thing can have both at the same time.

This is true, but only trivially so. Also, the argument gives 3p4 no real work to do. Spinoza brings it in through the idea that if a subject S had both properties, their antithetical nature would threaten the destruction of S; but this input from 3p4 is not needed, because the argument as I have stated it goes through without it.

On the 'things' reading of 3p5,d, Spinoza offers something like this:

(2) When two things X and Y are mutually destructive, they cannot be parts of a single larger thing.

What can it mean for two things to be mutually destructive? Not that they cannot exist at the same time even a trillion miles apart; some thought of closeness must be involved here. Perhaps: if X and Y were parts of a single thing, that would bring them close enough together for their mutual destructiveness to come into play. This is feeble, though, for nothing has been said about the size of the single thing, which could be as large as you like. Whatever Spinoza has in mind for the role of 'the same subject' in 3p5, the 'individuals' of which he writes in the part 2 physical interlude are presumably among them, and he includes 'the whole of nature' among those (CS 462). So we have to say, after all, that Dest(x,y) holds only if x and y cannot exist at the same time, however widely separated they are. This is so strange and mysterious as to drain the interest out of any doctrine depending on it.

Still, we can see the approximate drift of 3p5,d: If two items are Dest-related, they cannot be absorbed into any one thing; for if they were, that single thing would be intrinsically self-destructive, which 3p4 has declared impossible.

In going from this to 3p6—which is the *conatus* doctrine—Spinoza exploits a feature of 3p4 which I have not commented on so far: namely, his equating 'x and y cannot be in the same subject' with 'x and y are of a contrary nature'. His arguments for 3p5,6 seem to have concerned 'cannot be in the same subject' understood in some normal manner; but in 3p6d the entire weight is thrown on 'are of a contrary nature', with this understood in some quite different way. From 3p5 he infers that each thing 'is opposed to everything which can take its existence away'. This conclusion has not the faintest appearance of following from 'If Dest(x,y) then Nonsubj(x,y)', but if we look to Spinoza's other wording, 'If Dest(x,y), then x and y are of contrary natures', forget the equation of that with 'x and y cannot be in the same subject', and give it some more normal meaning, the inference becomes more plausible. If x and y are 'of contrary natures' in some normal sense, perhaps it follows that x is 'opposed to' y; and we might even stretch this to the point where it implies that x tries to keep y at bay, at a distance, or some such; which Spinoza then interprets so as to imply 3p6, the *conatus* doctrine: *Each thing, as far as it can by its own power, tries to persevere in its being.* The language of 'trying' sounds teleological, as though Spinoza were positioning himself to launch his doctrine of human egoism, bringing 'trying' into the story through the verbal trick that I have exposed in the wording of 3p5.

Spinoza would be innocent of serious malpractice in 3p5 and 3p6d if he were (as has been suggested) working all along with a concept of causation in which causally opposed items *do* 'oppose' one another in some sense that involves trying. That could clear up this little trouble, and indeed destroy my whole story about Spinoza's attitude(s) to teleology. But there is no direct textual evidence for this understanding of Spinoza's position; and it cannot be reconciled with his view that causes relate to effects as premises to conclusions (not as attempts to successes). Those remarks are a comment on a key thesis in Manning 2000. That paper disagrees with my treatment of teleology in Spinoza in other ways too; I recommend it for careful consultation; but I do not retreat.

Now it is true that Spinoza illegitimately introduces teleology in 3p6, as I shall explain; but the word 'try' is not the vehicle for it. He goes straight on to apply his reductive analysis to 'try', depriving it of teleological force: *The trying by which each thing tries to persevere in its being is nothing but the actual essence of the thing* (3p7). The demonstration of this shows that Spinoza means this 'trying' to be understood as an 'appetite' in his technical sense, which he explains in non-teleological terms:

When this trying is related only to the mind, it is called will; but when it is related to the mind and body together, it is called appetite. This appetite, therefore, is nothing but the very essence of the man, from whose nature there necessarily follow those things that promote his preservation. (3p9s)

With 'try' and 'appetite' understood in this reductive manner, *they* no longer import teleology into the story Spinoza is telling. But something else does, as I now explain.

Look back over the 3p4–6 sequence to see what Spinoza can, with some show of justification, carry out of it. The seed out of which everything is supposed to grow is the idea that *self-destruction is impossible*. That yields this:

For any animal A and behaviour x: if A unaided does x, then A's doing x is not destructive to A.

We could understand Spinoza's wanting to strengthen this to '. . . then A's doing x is not harmful to A', which in turn might be strengthened further to '. . . then A's doing x is helpful to A'. He does indeed engage in such strengthenings, but they are applied not to that conditional, but rather to something like its converse. In 3p6 Spinoza purports to have arrived at a generalization to the effect that:

For any animal A and item x: if x is destructive of A, then A resists x,

which has the basic form of a teleological generalization. Later on, Spinoza fattens it up to '. . . if x is harmful to A, then A resists x' and even further to '. . . if x is helpful to A, then A furthers (supports, produces, etc.) x'. Those strengthenings are not fully legitimate, any more than the previous ones were; but my present point is that Spinoza is here working with a general conditional of this form, one saying that if any way of behaving would have such and such an outcome, A will engage in it. This is the form of teleology: it allows one to infer positive conclusions about A's behaviour from premises about what would be harmful or helpful to A; whereas the most that Spinoza's arguments could entitle him to, with a good deal of squeezing and shoving, is the converse conditional, which lets one infer conclusions about what would help or harm A from premises about A's behaviour. Spinoza gets himself to the teleological conditional through malpractice with 'of contrary natures', 'is opposed to', 'strives to', and the rest.

Summing up: From the no-self-destruction starting-point, Spinoza can with some stretching, reach this:

Pseudo-egoism: If A does x, then A's doing x will bring advantage to A.

But he purports to have arrived at this:

Egoism: If A's doing x will bring advantage to A, then A does x.

Of these, only the latter can be used to explain facts about how people do behave (as distinct from facts about how they do not), because it is the only one that has behaviour in the consequent. Explanations using it will be genuinely teleological, because they will explain present behaviour in terms of a fact about the future. But the most that can, without flagrant malpractice, be extracted from the demonstrations leading to 3p6 is Pseudo-egoism. I base this not on delicate subtleties of the wording of those demonstrations, but on their large-scale overall logical shape.

The Egoism implicit in 3p6 lies hidden for a while. Everything in 3p7–11 can be read as involving only Pseudo-egoism, except for one thing that enforces the Egoism reading: 'From a man's nature there necessarily follow those things which are conducive to his preservation' (3p9s). Taken strictly, this means that he does all the helpful things: find something that will bring him advantage, and he will do it. That is Egoism, which then drops out of sight until the end of 3p11d, after which it comes blazingly to the fore:

The Mind, as far as it can, tries to imagine those things that increase or aid the Body's power of acting. (3p12)
When the Mind imagines those things that diminish or restrain the Body's power of acting, it tries, as far as it can, to recollect things that exclude their existence. (3p13)

Again, never mind the teleological word 'try'. My concern is with the teleological form of the conditionals that Spinoza affirms here: each runs from an antecedent about advantage to a consequent about behaviour; and that is the form of Egoism. The same form of conditional is found in a further nine propositions in part 3 that belong to the deductive progeny of 3p12,13.

So, yes, Spinoza does end up with something having approximately the right shape for teleology, thinking that this is all right because he has derived it from innocent raw materials. The derivation, I have shown, is irreparably faulty. The *Ethics* in fact is broken-backed. A concept that is busily at work in the later parts of the work, and is ostensibly rooted in the earlier parts, really has no such roots. Similarly, in the later parts Spinoza tries to connect understanding with survival, and both with happiness, on the basis of theories in part 2 and early part 3 in which these concepts are prominent; and those basings are quite invalid. This is not to dismiss the later parts of the *Ethics* as worthless. Human egoism has support in empirical psychology; it does not collapse merely because it is not a substitution instance of a perfectly general metaphysical hypothesis.

While critical of this performance of Spinoza's, I also admire aspects of it—especially his seeing the prima-facie problem about teleology, and refusing to say 'Teleology is all right so long as it is confined to that queer medium the mind'. But he was wrong to conclude that there is no teleology anywhere. I agree with the now common opinion that events that can be explained in a mechanistic, efficient-cause, pushed-from-behind manner may also be explicable teleologically. Still, we should not contemn Spinoza for his failure to see how to legitimize teleology, and thus the concept of desire. Nobody understood this well until quite recently, and I can find no understanding of it in any of his predecessors or contemporaries. When he rejected the ordinary concept of desire, then, Spinoza was not being stupid or narrow; rather, he had seen something which others had overlooked.

Chapter 12

Leibniz Arrives at Monads

87. Why there are no material substances

Leibniz's philosophy is first and foremost a system of metaphysics: it aims to say what sorts of things there basically are, what they have to do with one another, and how those facts produce the world as we know it. Like every philosopher, he inherited a set of problems that struck him as crucial, and his metaphysic was designed to solve them. The final metaphysic is rich and complex, and Leibniz uses it to 'solve' many problems. Any such apparent success could count as support for the system, but I shall approach his reasons in a more linear fashion, reconstructing a single philosophical path along which Leibniz could have walked towards his metaphysic, looking at the reasons that he could have given at each stage along the way. There is philosophy to be learned from this procedure, which—I shall show—pretty closely follows the intellectual path that Leibniz actually trod.

Let us start with his reason for denying that material things can be substances. What disqualifies them, he holds, is their being divisible, their having parts, their not being 'simple' in his technical sense—'simple, that is, without parts' (Mon 1, FW 268; see also PNG 1, FW 258–9). How is an item's having parts supposed to debar it from being a substance?

One possible answer relies on the idea that a substance must be causally independent for its existence. It is not clear how causal independence relates to the original notion of substance as what lies on the left of the thing/property line; and I am not sure that this idea about substantiality had much currency in the seventeenth century. In §51 we saw it in Descartes's *PP* 1:51, but the latter is notoriously irrelevant to the rest of his work.

Still, let us pick up causal independence and run with it for a little way. It yields this argument for Leibniz's conclusion:

> Whatever is material (1) is extended, and thus (2) has parts, and thus (3) is split-
> table, and thus (4) is destructible, and thus (5) is not a substance.

I used to think that Leibniz argued in this way, and in one place he does write to Arnauld that 'Substantial unity requires a complete indivisible being, which is indestructible by natural means' (FW 118). But I cannot find him or anyone else at that period clearly adducing the above argument, and its move from 3 to 4 was not popular. Gassendi, for example, wrote: 'Supposing you are some corporeal . . . substance, you would not be said to vanish wholly at your death or to pass into nothingness; you would be said to subsist by means of your dispersed parts' (Obj 5, CSM 2:238). Descartes does not comment on this, but he agreed with it (see Rep 2, CSM 2:109). Having paraded the splittability argument in previous work, I now recant: I do not think it throws light on Leibniz's denial that material things can be substances.

A second argument relies on the idea that a substance must be ontologically independent, not any kind of upshot of anything else, something that would appear in a basic inventory of the world's contents. By that standard, no thing that has parts is a substance, because the facts about it—that it exists, and what it is like—are non-causal upshots of facts about what its parts are like and how they are interrelated. A fundamental inventory will not include armies, for instance, because soldiers and weapons are more basic—they can exist without the army, but not vice versa—and when you have completed the facts about their qualities and interrelations, you have already told the whole story about the army.

So this argument runs as follows:

Whatever is material (1) is extended, and thus (2) has parts, and thus (3) is an ontological result of the existence and natures and interrelations of its parts, and so (4) is not a basic or ontologically independent thing, and so (5) is not a substance.

This applies to every portion of matter, because dividing any portion yields smaller ones to which the argument reapplies. There are no substances anywhere along the infinite series of ever finer divisions into parts; so no substance can be a material thing.

Given the infinite divisibility of all matter, this is a pretty good argument, and I think it was what primarily led Leibniz to conclude that no material thing is a substance. What he wrote to Arnauld about this, however, suggests a different line of thought.

This third argument dives down, through the levels where causal and ontological dependence are at work, to the fundamental and original notion of substance as what lies on the left of the thing/property line. Arnauld challenged Leibniz at that level, accusing him of having wilfully changed the meaning of the word 'substance'. To accept that nothing divisible is a substance, Arnauld wrote,

one would first have to define 'substance' and 'substantial' in the following terms: *I call 'substance' and 'substantial' that which has a true unity.* But . . . this definition has not yet been accepted, and . . . [one is] as entitled to say: *I call 'substance' that which is not modality or state,* and [to] maintain that it is paradoxical to say that there is nothing substantial in a block of marble, since this block of marble is not the state of being of another substance. (Mason 107–8)

Leibniz replies that he has not changed any meaning, and that he can show that no unsimple thing—nothing that owes its existence to the 'aggregation' of its parts—can be a substance in the traditional sense of that word. 'What constitutes the essence of a being through aggregation', he writes, 'is only the way of being of the things that make it up. For example, what constitutes the essence of an army is just the way of being of the men who make it up' (FW 124). The fundamental thing/property line is in play here, but not satisfactorily.

If Leibniz were saying that an army is not a substance, because it is a relational property of the soldiers—and is thus adjectival upon them, as a blush is upon a face—he would be wrong. Granted that all the facts about the army are facts about how the soldiers are interrelated, that still does not make it a relation among (a 'state of being of') the soldiers. A general cannot lead a state of being; a quartermaster cannot feed a polyadic relation. To treat the army as a relation among the soldiers is to disregard their status as parts of it.

However, what Leibniz actually says to be adjectival on the soldiers is not the army but 'what constitutes its essence'. That is true: the army's essence does lie on the right of the thing/property line. But so does every essence! A thing's essence is a privileged subset of its properties, so the property-like status of the army's essence teaches us nothing about the status of the army.

No Leibniz scholar today thinks that in this part of his work Leibniz was just floundering. We are all sure that he was on to something, and it has to be the argument which assumes that substances must be ontologically independent and thus without parts. In a later writing (quoted at Sleigh 1990a: 123) Leibniz spells it out: the whole truth about an army can be told without any mention or thought of the army as such.

Why did he not state this properly when debating with Arnauld? Well, Arnauld based his challenge on the assumption that the thing thought is the whole of the concept of substance, and I think Leibniz wanted to respond without seeming to give ground. 'You want to tie "substance" to thing/property? Very well, consider it so tied; and then consider the fact that an army—well, anyway, the essence of an army—is not a thing but a relational property.' What he needed to say was less short, sharp, and intransigent: namely, 'You are right: when I deny that a thing with parts cannot be a substance, I am loading "substance" with more than the mere thing thought. But what I am adding was not invented by me; it is almost bound to be added by any serious metaphysician for whom "substance" is a significant technical term; I mean the addition of the notion of a basic or underived or ontologically independent thing.' That would be better in every way except rhetorically.

Leibniz rejected atomism (§23), and there is a question about the relevance of that to our present topic. Atomism would obviously destroy the splittability argument, but its bearing on the ontological dependence argument is less sure. A spherical atom has parts—an innermost spherical three-quarters and a rind surrounding that—although they cannot be pulled apart from one another. Should the entire sphere be mentioned in a *basic* ontology?

Negative: The sphere's existence is an ontological result of the existence of that core and that rind thus interrelated; and a resultant is not basic. Causation does not come into it.

Positive: An item whose parts are bound together by causal necessity counts as a basic thing. To set causation aside is to misunderstand the notion of basicness that we ought to be using here.

I favour the positive view. If I were sure that reality must consist in countable substances, and believed in atoms and the void, my concept of 'what there basically is', niggardly though it is, would allow that material atoms are substances. Where Leibniz would stand on this, I do not know. The firmness of his anti-atomism left him with no reason to pronounce on the question.

88. Why there are immaterial substances

Arnauld, although he criticized Leibniz's terms of debate, evidently felt the force of the demand to know what is basic in the material world. His proposed response to it was spectacularly indefensible, a case of leading with his jaw, as Sleigh has remarked. 'In the whole of corporeal nature', he suggests, 'perhaps there are only aggregates of substances, because of none of these parts can one say, accurately speaking, that it is a single substance' (Mason 108). Leibniz must have enjoyed nailing that down: 'Being is one thing, and beings another; but the plural presupposes the singular, and where there is no being, still less will there be many beings' (FW 124). That is plainly right. It is self-contradictory to say that there is no such thing as a substance, but there are substances. However, we may see Arnauld as groping for the idea that there are no material substances, only material substance—the idea I have tentatively attributed to Descartes (§52). This may be what is hinted at when, on the same page, he writes: 'It may be of the essence of matter not to have true unity.'

This is an inviting response to the conclusion that there are no material substances: the most fundamental material reality consists of matter, stuff, *substance* which is not an aggregate of *substances*. I have not found Leibniz discussing that way out. All I find are remarks like this: 'Just as number presupposes things numbered, extension presupposes things which are repeated' (Comments, AG 274), which assumes without argument that the ontological ground floor contains things rather than stuff. Catherine Wilson (1989: 74–5) implies that Leibniz conducted such an argument. He was battling with the question of whether the mathematical treatment of infinity could be carried over into nature, Wilson reports, and she continues: 'The problem with this . . . was that it was necessary to begin with something continuous—a quantity of matter, a line segment . . . How did that continuous substance arise in the first place? If all *extensa* were infinitely divisible, what were they made of?' If Leibniz argues like this, he does not succeed. The question of how the continuous stuff 'arose', or what it is 'made of', seems to assume that stuff cannot be basic; but that was the point at issue.

However, we know of something deep in Leibniz's thought that would have sufficed to drive him away from allowing continuous stuff to be basic. An original, learned, and philosophically penetrating treatment of this topic can be found in Levey 1998. I offer only a partial sketch.

Leibniz uses the phrase 'the labyrinth of the continuum' many dozens—perhaps hundreds—of times, and this points to a concern which could explain his tacit rejection of basic, infinitely divisible stuff. He was an important, original mathematician, who knew a great deal about the mathematics of continuity, and something of what continuity implies regarding infinity and infinitesimals. He was perturbed by problems such as that of 'the angle of the tangent': this is the angle made by a straight line and a circle to which it is a tangent. It is greater than $0°$ because the two lines diverge; yet it is smaller than any angle between two straight lines; worse still, it becomes even smaller as the circle enlarges. This is one of many things that Leibniz accepted as mathematics, but thought could not be true of anything real. His way of dealing with 'the strange difficulties over the composition of the continuum', he wrote to Arnauld, was to conclude that the real world cannot be composed of continuous stuff (FW 119). All continuity pertains to space and time, and to lines and periods, and so on, and these are not real but 'ideal'. Leibniz wrote to De Volder:

In actual things there is only discrete quantity, that is, a multitude of . . . simple substances, though in any sensible aggregate or one corresponding to phenomena this may be greater than any given number. But a continuous quantity is something ideal, which pertains to possibles and to actual things considered as possible. The continuum has indeterminate parts, but nothing is indefinite in actual things, in which every division that can be made has been made. . . . When we seek actual parts in the order of possibles and indeterminate parts in aggregates of actual things, we confuse ideal things with real substances and entangle ourselves in the labyrinth of the continuum and inexplicable contradictions. (AG 185)

A ground-floor ontology, therefore, cannot include continuous stuff; it must be occupied by individual substances; and since they cannot be material, they must be immaterial.

Here is the argument again, shaped a little differently. It has three premisses which Leibniz is convinced are true:

(1) There is a basic inventory of discrete things that the world contains.
(2) No aggregate of things is a basic thing.
(3) Every portion of matter is an aggregate of its parts, which are also portions of matter.

From 1 and 2 it follows that reality is made up substances that are simple, have no parts. From that and 3 it further follows that none of those substances is a material thing. On the ontological ground floor, then, there is no matter, but there are simple unextended substances which I shall call *monads*, the name Leibniz gave them in the last twenty years of his life (see AG 155, editorial note).

A terminological note: I have often used 'monadic' in its standard logical sense, to mean 'one-place' in contrast to 'relational', 'dyadic', etc. From now on I shall *also* sometimes use it as the adjective cognate to Leibniz's 'monad'. I cannot easily dispense with either use of this word; but contextual clues will prevent troubles from ambiguity.

89. How bodies relate to monads

Having gone this far, Leibniz has to explain the metaphysical status of matter. Unwilling to write off the material world as nothing, he has to fit it into his metaphysic somehow. He does this by saying that the material world is the appearance to us of the monads: although nothing is really extended, certain aggregates of monads appear to us as extended by appearing to us as bodies. Leibniz expressed this by calling material things 'phenomena'.

So Leibniz's metaphysical scheme has three levels: what are basically *real* are immaterial substances; material things are appearances of those substances and constitute a *phenomenal* level of reality; and space and time are *ideal*—they are purely mental constructs. (For a good exposition of this matter, see Hartz and Cover 1988.)

Why did Leibniz relate matter to monads by appearance/reality rather than by some other relation? He has an answer to this, which relies on his view that fundamental reality consists in things that are not aggregates, so that *being* is inseparable from *unity*. Consider now any aggregate that we think of as a single thing—an army, for instance, or the body of a man, or a boulder. What is the source of the seeming or semi- or quasi- or pseudo-unity of such an item? It comes, Leibniz answers when writing to Arnauld, from the unifying thought of some mind:

What is not truly *a* being is not truly a *being* either. It has always been thought that unity and being are interchangeable. . . . I therefore believed that I would be allowed to distinguish beings by aggregation from substances, since these beings have their unity in our mind only. (AG 86)

This is the thesis about mind-based unity that Kant used to such good effect in his criticism of Descartes's view that minds are simple (§28). It takes Leibniz to the conclusion that matter is an appearance by a short, sharp argument: An aggregate gets its unity from a unifying mind, so it gets its being from a mind, so it is an appearance. (This argument is helpfully stated and attributed to Leibniz in Adams 1994: 246–7.)

Most of us will be unconvinced by it. When we speak of *an* army, *a* corpse, *a* boulder (we shall protest), we may be saying something that has some objective truth to it because the army or boulder actually has a certain unity, or at least pseudo-unity. This is not all 'in our mind'; it comes from facts about how the aggregated items (the soldiers, etc., or the particles of granite) are related to one another. Leibniz indeed admits this to Arnauld, right in the heart of his 'unifying thought' doctrine: '. . . since these beings have their unity in our mind only, a unity founded on the relations or modes of true substances' (AG 86). (For a good treatment of all this, see Hartz 1992.)

Furthermore, even if Leibniz had shown that bodies have their being purely in minds, it is a big step from this to the conclusion that they are appearances of something else. Leibniz takes this step without justifying or even noticing it.

Fortunately, we can supply a sturdier basis for the thesis that the material world is the appearance to us of monads. It is the *faute de mieux* one: bodies will have to be how monads appear to us, because there is no other way to admit them into the scheme of things while reserving the metaphysical ground floor for monads.

Monads are ultimately real, then, and some aggregates of them appear to us as bodies. They are not parts of bodies, Leibniz insists: they have no size, and by merely juxtaposing sizeless things you do not get a thing that has size; n times 0 = 0, however large n is. Yet he often skates dangerously close to saying just that. Material things are 'composed' of monads and 'contain' them, he says, and conversely he describes monads as 'constituents' of bodies. All this sounds unhappily like a part/whole relation. Leibniz tries to block this impression, and to explain that the part/whole account is not entailed by the others, by using the analogy of a line and its constituent points:

> Although the aggregate of these substances constitutes body, they do not constitute it as parts, just as points are not parts of lines, since a part is always of the same sort as the whole. . . . Just as there is no portion of a line in which there is not an infinite number of points, there is no portion of matter which does not contain an infinite number of substances. But just as a point is not a part of a line, though a line in which there is a point is such a part, so also a [monad] is not a part of matter. (Notes on Fardella, AG 105)

This seems all right. We do think of a line as containing points, though we also know better than to say that it is composed of points as a whole is of its parts. This shows that 'contains' need not be thought of in whole/part terms, but still it does not help us much. A relation that holds between ideal lines and ideal points cannot illuminate the relation between phenomenal bodies and real monads.

What drew Leibniz into the dangerous language of 'constituting' and the like was presumably the following. A given body is, according to his metaphysic, the appearance to us of one unique aggregate of monads; so we can point to a particular nail and speak of 'the monads which appear to us as *that*'; and one is tempted to think of them as *in* the nail in some way. Similarly, although Leibniz does not hold that monads are spatially organized (§111), we can make a derivative sense for 'where monad x is' by borrowing the location of the body which is the appearance of an aggregate including x. This requires the assumption that no monad does double duty, contributing to the appearance of two distinct bodies (§102).

It would have been better for Leibniz to avoid any suggestion that monads are parts of bodies. Sometimes he does: 'Accurately speaking, matter is not composed of these constitutive unities, but results from them . . . Substantial unities are not really parts but foundations of phenomena' (L 536). The word 'results' has a generic meaning of which causal resulting is only one species; another is ontological resulting, as wholes from parts. Leibniz here employs a third: bodies result from monads in the sense that they are appearances of them. Each species could be stated in terms of inference: we can infer the facts about a body from

the facts about its cause, together with causal laws;
the facts about its parts, together with geometrical principles;
the facts about certain monads, together with whatever principles govern how reality relates to appearance.

In at least one place he writes of monads—here called 'indivisible forms or natures'—as 'the causes of appearances', but that was never his considered doctrine (DM 18, FW 72).

Leibniz calls the material world a 'well-founded' phenomenon—not a crazy dream, but the orderly appearance of a reality. It is integral to his metaphysical view that there are systematic rules governing what monadic states of affairs appear as what kinds of extended-world situations. He does not try to state them, or to explain why or how monads appear to us thus rather than so. Obviously he could not explain this through a familiarizing model, because any such model must be drawn from the level of appearance. An account of how surface textures relate to seen colours, for example, would not help, because both relata belong at the phenomenal level. Leibniz uses such analogies, nevertheless, when he writes that the 'very being' of material things is 'in a way mental, or phenomenal, like that of a rainbow' (NE 146); but he presumably knew how little they achieve. That does not condemn his metaphysic, and it does not clash with the principle of sufficient reason: it allows that there is a reason why a given aggregation of monads should appear to us thus rather than so, and is merely silent about what the reason is.

Having escaped from the 'labyrinth of the continuum', Leibniz is clear and definite in saying that monads are not continuous, and that space is so; the discrete / continuous line coincides with the real / ideal one. But what about the middle or phenomenal level? Given that matter is infinitely divisible, it seems to follow that it is continuous.[1] On the other hand, he might be uncomfortable with that, given that matter is rooted in the real. Here is Adams on the question:

Continuity . . . is 'an ideal thing', not a creature of the ultimately real. It might still be thought a feature of bodies, if bodies are only phenomena; and Leibniz can be quoted on both sides of the question whether bodies *are* continuous or only *appear* to be

---

[1] The difference between the cardinality of the real numbers and that of the rationals was not known until the nineteenthth century, and is irrelevant to the concerns of this work; so I use 'continuous' throughout to mean 'continuous or at least dense in the mathematical sense'.

continuous. An important text of 1702 classifies body as continuous (AG 251). The other answer is given in texts of 1705, at least as regards 'matter': 'In fact matter is not a continuum, but is something discrete, actually divided to infinity' (G 2:278). 'Matter appears to us [to be] a continuum, but it only appears so' (G 7:564). . . . I think Leibniz probably ought to hold that bodies only *appear* to be continuous. (1994: 233)

Although there is some difficulty in the idea of something that is infinitely divisible yet not continuous, I agree with Adams about what Leibniz ought to say, and I am not swayed by the 1702 text that he mentions. Leibniz does say there that matter is continuous; but his central concern is with something else, and the continuity remark may reflect mere carelessness in wording.

I have presented Leibniz as arriving at his metaphysic of monads by combining the infinite divisibility of matter with the conviction that reality must be made up of basic (non-resultant, non-dependent, partless) things. In his early years he also wrestled with a different set of problems about the divisibility of matter—problems having to do with whether and how far the properties of a mathematical series could be modelled by a physical reality. For a stimulating introduction to the whole issue, see Levey 1999.

90. Divisibility and substances: some options

For Leibniz nothing is extended at the most basic level, and one step up from there—at the level of appearance—there are bodies. This takes him towards Plato, as he knew. Towards the end of his life he wrote, of the view that 'material things are only phenomena, though well founded and well connected', that 'Plato had caught some glimpses of this' (L 655). It also takes him away from his immediate philosophical forebears—Descartes, Locke, and Spinoza. Each of those three confronted a wholly real extended world whose secrets and surprises are just those of small portions of extended matter: the entire story is on one ontological level. How did those three avoid travelling Leibniz's route?

I shall answer this for Locke in §187. The answer for Descartes we already know: if he was able to reconcile substantiality with infinite divisibility, it was by moving from 'substances' to the mass concept 'substance'; and that was anathema to Leibniz.

Spinoza had a different solution, which did not require him to relinquish substance as a count (rather than mass) concept. It led him a good distance down the road with Leibniz, as Leibniz saw:

Spinoza says that no substance, not even corporeal substance, is divisible. This is not a remarkable thing for him to say, since for him there is only one substance. But it is true for me as well, even though I admit an infinity of substances, since in my view all of them are indivisible, that is, are monads. (Comments, AG 274)

In effect, Spinoza holds that rocks and galaxies are not substances because they are too small, whereas Leibniz says that they are not substances because they are too big. Spinoza's position lets him still treat rocks as fully real—not as *things*, but as *real* in the way most of us think that blushes and shortages are real—whereas Leibniz's implies that material things are not real but are appearances. Now, Leibniz eventually came to have many objections to Spinoza's philosophy, but they are not available as challenges to the initial Spinozist metaphysic of matter. Let us think of Leibniz as walking through the divisibility problem and reaching the fork in the road which leads in one direction to Spinoza's monism and in the other to his monadic theory. What reasons could he give *at that point* for preferring his direction? This is about all we get from him: 'If there were no monads, Spinoza would be right. Then everything other than God would be transitory and would vanish into simple accidents or modifications, since there would be no base of substances in things, which consists in the existence of monads' (L 663; see also AG 274). This shows that Leibniz sees himself and Spinoza as offering the best two ways of solving a single problem. Considered as support for his solution, however, it is disappointing. For the point about transitoriness to be cogent, Leibniz would need grounds independent of his monadic metaphysic for holding that some things other than God are not 'transitory'. What grounds could he have? The apparently durable things that we encounter in everyday life are indeed transitory in Spinoza's system, but that is a reasonable thing to believe; and indeed Leibniz himself believes it. For him ordinary 'things' are aggregates that can easily pass out of existence through dissipation (or, according to his other account, through no longer being thought of as unities).

As well as saying little about why we should prefer monadism to substance-monism, Leibniz never mentions a reason that some of us have for choosing the other way: namely, that his is an appearance/reality metaphysic, while Spinoza's is not. Spinoza held that by thinking about pebbles and rivers in the right way, we shall see that they—the very pebbles we throw and the rivers we swim in—are modes of the one substance. He sees this as the right way to conceptualize the given world, *not* as implying that it is an appearance of some underlying reality. Leibniz would probably count this against Spinoza's metaphysic. Having sketched his monadism in the *New Essays*, he continues excitedly: 'If one also bears in mind what constitutes the nature of those real unities, namely perception and its consequences, one is transported into another world, so to speak: from having existed entirely amongst the phenomena of the senses, one comes to occupy the intelligible world of substances' (*NE* 378). One can hear a liking or preference at work here—something conative rather than cognitive. My own preference goes the other way.

Even if there are no deep Leibnizian reasons against Spinoza's metaphysic of matter, Leibniz's preference for monadism is not puzzling. Once he got this metaphysic under way, he was able to do—to his own satisfaction—an astonishing amount in terms of it; he must have seen its supposed explanatory power as strong evidence of its truth.

91. Why monads are mind-like

The initial thrust towards monadism, I have said, comes from Leibniz's need to get the count-concept of *substance* to grip on to a world in which every extended thing is an aggregate. I stand by that as intellectual biography. Leibniz writes:

At first, after freeing myself from bondage to Aristotle, I accepted the void and atoms, for it is these that best satisfy the imagination. But thinking again about this, after much meditation I saw that it is impossible to find *the principles of a real unity* in matter alone or in what is merely passive, since this is nothing but a collection or aggregation of parts ad infinitum. Now, a multiplicity can derive its reality only from *true unities* . . . etc. (NS, FW 145)

But Leibniz was confirmed in his adherence to this theory by other things he could do with it; and because of these further applications we should not dismiss the monadic metaphysic as resulting purely from a refusal to countenance basic stuff as against basic things.

Much of the work that Leibniz makes his monadism do relies on his view that monads are mind-like—are on a continuum with minds strictly so-called, differing from them only in degree. This requires a fresh input of philosophical reasons, beyond anything I have so far reported.

Carriero (forthcoming *b*) holds that if Leibniz came to his monadism from the problem of unity in matter, it must have been by taking a single 'momentous leap' to the view that 'substantiality ultimately resides exclusively in mental things'. Naturally finding this to be extravagant, Carriero seeks the root of Leibniz's monadism not in the unity-in-matter problem, but rather in scholastic views connecting substance with activity and teleology, which bring mentality with them. That emphasis is indeed present in Leibniz's thought, but I think it constitutes flowers, not root. In the account I favour, there is no one momentous leap, but only two controlled steps.

The best way to understand Leibniz's second step, to the view that all monads are mind-like, is to break it into two sub-steps. One takes us to the thesis that (1) minds properly so-called are all monads or simple substances. The second takes us from this to the thesis that (2) all monads that are not minds are on a qualitative continuum with ones that are. Leibniz's reasons for these two are different.

(1) So far, the only meaning we have for 'monad' is 'simple substance', meaning 'substance that has no parts'. At this early stage in the buildup of Leibniz's thought, the thesis that minds are monads is just the thesis that they are simple, have no parts. He was as sure of that as Descartes was, and we should consider why. Do not say: 'He thought that minds are simple because he thought they are monads.' I want reasons for minds' simplicity that might support the view that they are monads. The fact—pointed out by Parkinson (1965: 163)—is that Leibniz does not ever present any. Still, I think he has one, as follows.

I have sketched and endorsed Kant's analysis of the view that we can tell a priori that minds are simple (§28). That analysis, which I applied to Descartes, also fits Leibniz; indeed, Margaret Wilson (1974) argued persuasively that Leibniz is a better source for Kant's Second Paralogism than Descartes. According to Kant, the view that minds are simple grows out of the first-person, present-tense psychological stance of methodological solipsism. This fits Descartes, who adopts that stance in his First Meditation; but not Spinoza, for whom the I–now thought has no special role. It does seem to have figured in Leibniz's thoughts about substances as simple, non-composite, not aggregates: 'I saw that these forms and these souls must be indivisible, like our minds'; 'By means of the soul or form there is a true unity which corresponds to what is called "I" in us' (NS, FW 148*). In the first draft of the same work, Leibniz wrote: 'When I say "I" (*moi*), I refer to a single substance . . . Setting aside souls and other such principles of unity, we could never find any corporeal mass or portion of matter which would count as a genuine substance' (G 4:473). (For other examples, see FW 118 and L 578.)

It is striking that Leibniz should proceed in this first-person manner when the simplicity of substances is in question, for it is not his customary way of thinking. He does not usually adopt the Cartesian first-person stance; in particular, he does not use himself as a touchstone for his whole doctrine about substances—for example, appealing to introspection, as Berkeley did, to support his claim that substances are active. Yet, when expounding the simplicity of substances, he conspicuously resorts to the first person singular. Evidently he found the simplicity of the soul to be especially obvious in his own case, and expected you to find it especially obvious in yours, and me in mine. This explains why he was irresistibly drawn to think that minds are monads, *ipso facto* bringing himself within the scope of Kant's critique.

(2) Leibniz was not one to tolerate sharp, deep lines through reality; for him, differences of degree are paramount. The things of which the world is composed are discrete: the world is ontologically granular. But the continuity that Leibniz resists in ontology dominates his thoughts about how things differ qualitatively: the quality space with which he operates is not granular. He frequently announces this as doctrine—saying, for instance, that 'The nature of things is uniform'. We find it at greater length in the *New Essays*, at a point where he implies that every part of the universe is 'just like here', and continues: 'Not in every respect, since the kinds and degrees of perfection vary infinitely, but as regards the foundations of things. The foundations are everywhere the same; this is a fundamental maxim for me, which governs my whole philosophy' (*NE* 490). This implies that the deepest differences amongst things are ones of degree; no things are marked off from the rest by a fundamental difference of kind. He wrote to Queen Sophie Charlotte: 'My great principle, as regards natural things, is . . . that it is at every time and every place in every thing and every way just like here. [*C'est tousjours et partout en toutes choses tout comme icy.*] That is to say that nature is basically uniform, though it varies as to more and less, and in degrees of perfection' (G 3:343). He does acknowledge—indeed proclaim—just one difference that is 'of kind, not of degree'. That is the difference between our works

and God's, between 'the least productions and mechanisms of divine wisdom and the greatest masterpieces produced by the skill of a limited mind' (NS, FW 148). This does not compromise the gradualism which is my theme.

Given gradualism, and the thesis that minds are monads, it follows that all monads are qualitatively continuous with minds. Leibniz argues in just that manner. He has been discussing 'primitive force' in physics (§105), says that it is rooted in a 'principle of action' in the monads that appear as matter, and continues: 'In this principle of action there is something analogous to what is in us, namely perception and appetite. For the nature of things is uniform, and our nature cannot differ altogether [Latin: *infinite*] from the other simple substances of which the whole universe consists' (L 537).

Another reason that Leibniz gives is moral-theological. We all know that some animal bodies (including our own) are in some way dominated by minds, but those bodies constitute only a tiny proportion of the material world. Leibniz does not believe that mentality occurs only in those few peculiar pockets of the universe. That it should do so, he writes, 'is consistent with neither order nor with the beauty or reasonableness of things'. 'And there is no reason', he continues, 'why souls or things analogous to souls should not be everywhere, even if dominant and hence intelligent souls like ours cannot' (NI 12, FW 218). This line of thought does not compete with the preceding one.

92. An aside on Leibniz's gradualism

What grounds does Leibniz have for his 'fundamental maxim' or 'great principle'? He might defend it on moral-theological grounds: It is better that the world should be qualitatively continuous, and we can trust God to have created the best possible world. But I have not found him saying just this, and I think that qualitative gradualism lies even deeper in Leibniz's mind than his theology. It connects somehow with his explanatory rationalism, though not directly: I do not think he holds that there could be no deep reason for the lines that he refuses to draw. However, he writes to De Volder: 'I do not believe that any reason can be given *a priori* against a leap from place to place which is not also effective against a leap from state to state' (L 515). He has just explained that what rules out the former, apart from empirical evidence, is the principle that 'the more we analyse things, the more they satisfy our intellect'.

Leibniz's gradualism implies that only differences of degree separate animals from monads that are lower on the intellectual scale. He tends to reserve 'mind' (and sometimes, but not always, 'soul') for the relatively high-level kind of monad that constitutes an animal mind, while letting 'monad' range over all simple substances. In one place he writes that 'the best' monads are souls, and that the best souls are minds (PAB, AG 319); but he does not keep to this throughout his writings.

Leibniz credits all monads with perceptions and appetites, as we shall see, but he wants a distinction to be made, reserving 'soul' for 'those substances whose perceptions are more distinct and are accompanied by memory' (Mon 19, FW 270; see also Mon 24). We animals, he writes here, have 'something more than' the equipment that all monads share, and he characterizes it in terms of distinctness of perceptions and of memory. Whatever distinctness is (§§124–5), 'more distinct' must mark a difference of degree. The same probably holds for 'accompanied by memory'. Leibniz holds that every monad retains traces of its entire past, and his only idea about what it takes for such a trace to count as a memory is that memories are more 'distinct' than other traces; which makes the having of memory, too, a matter of degree (§113).

Leibniz's gradualism promises a smooth run not only from animals to other monads, but also from humans to other animals. This is what we find in Spinoza, who has no reason to regard humans as categorially special, and cites 'man' as one of those general terms that is not fit for serious theoretical work (§80). Hume's naturalism also led him to think of humanity as continuous with the rest of the animal kingdom (§285). But it is *not* what we actually find in Leibniz. His gradualism is prima facie in tension with his religious conviction that humans are special amongst the monads that we know. When he writes about how humans relate to God, his gradualism drops out of sight. It appears briefly when he writes that 'rational souls . . . have incomparably more perfection than' monads in general (NS, FW 146); but it disappears when he writes that any rational soul is 'an image of the divinity', and is 'like a little divinity in its own sphere' (PNG 14, FW 264; Mon 83, FW 280). I cannot find him saying what difference of degree marks off monads that are images of the divinity, or ones that have reason, from the rest; and there are indications that at this point Leibniz means the gradualism to be suspended. He writes to Bernoulli: 'When I spoke about the origin of the soul or the changes in an animal, I clearly declared that I said nothing definite about the origin and state of the rational soul, and that the Kingdom of Grace has special laws, laws besides those by which the Kingdom of Nature is governed' (AG 170). In the next letter he writes: 'Rational souls, that is, intelligences like ours, created in a special sense in the image of God, are governed by laws far different from those by which those lacking intellect are governed', describing the latter as 'subject only to natural laws' (AG 171; see also NS, FW 147).

93. Further evidence that monads are mind-like

I have been looking for reasons that Leibniz could have adduced when first developing his metaphysic of monads. He gets further reasons for it down the line, when he can look back with satisfaction at all the uses to which the metaphysic has been put, regarding them as confirming its rightness. Starting with the bare assertion that the world is composed of simple mind-like substances, Leibniz uses this to provide metaphysical underpinnings for various facts about the phenomenal world of matter; this requires him to make certain specific claims about the natures of monads; and he regards those claims as best, or even as only, explicable in terms of monads' mind-likeness. In this section I shall present one example of this pattern, starting with Leibniz's contending that the concept of force must have a place in physics, and must be grounded in mental substances. 'I found then that their nature consists in force, and that from this there follows something analogous to sensation and appetite' (NS, FW 145).

This involves an aspect of Leibniz's thought which goes back to views that he held at the time when he accepted material substances and even atoms. He thought then that any material substance must be associated with—informed by—a mind, and about this he never changed his mind. A good exposition of it can be found in a relatively late writing (NI 13, FW 218–20). For an excellent exposition of this matter, which I shall treat only briefly, see Mercer and Sleigh 1995.

Descartes and other Cartesians did not endow matter with any intrinsic force or impetus or anything like that; their matter is wholly passive, so that when a body moves, the cause of that movement does not lie in the body itself but in the intervention of God. Leibniz found this incredible, was sure that there must be real forces at work in matter, and inferred from this that matter must be infused by mind. The assumption that minds are inherently active, while unthinking matter is passive, goes back long before Leibniz, and was shared by many other philosophers. In his earlier years, it was embodied in the theory that matter is ultimately real and is pervaded by mentality; later, matter is demoted to the rank of well-founded appearance, but Leibniz continues to think that mentality must pervade it. There are forces present in matter, he still holds; they are the appearance to us of forces at work within the underlying monads; and in regarding monads as centres of force one *ipso facto* credits them with something like mentality.

In §18 we saw a special reason that Leibniz adduced for postulating forces in matter. Descartes tried to get qualitative variety out of differences of movement, in matter that is otherwise perfectly uniform, and Leibniz convincingly argued that it cannot be done. In the Cartesian scheme of things, he argued, nothing is ever moving at any given moment, so that at any instant the universe is qualitatively homogeneous. Here is how he proposes to remedy this:

At any moment of its motion, not only is a body in a place with the same size and shape as itself, but it also has a tendency or strives to change that place, so that its next state follows from its present one, by the force of its nature. If this were not so then at . . . any moment a moving body would in no way be different from a body at rest. (NI 13, FW 218–19)

A homogeneous extended realm cannot achieve qualitative variety just from motion amongst its parts. If it is to be variegated, something more is needed, and within the limits that Descartes and Leibniz set for themselves it looks as though it has to be *forces* that are real and operative at instants as well as across time. However, this is not a weighty part of Leibniz's case for forces in matter, because it is an *ad hominem* argument: it gives a reason why a Cartesian should postulate forces, but to some others, including Leibniz himself, it does not apply. He does not maintain that all variety in matter supervenes on differences of movement, so he is not under pressure from this source to fatten up movement by putting force into it.

For various reasons, then, Leibniz espoused a sort of panpsychism—a belief that mentality pervades the universe. Does this make him like Berkeley? Adams thinks so, and calls Leibniz an 'idealist' in the title of his book (1994); Margaret Wilson resolutely resisted this (1987). Leibniz's explicit remarks about Berkeley do not settle the issue. On the one hand, late in his life he wrote to Des Bosses: 'The Irishman who attacks the reality of bodies does not seem to bring forward suitable reasons or to explain himself sufficiently. I suspect that he belongs to the class of men who want to be known for their paradoxes' (AG 306). Yet that same winter he wrote in his own copy of Berkeley's *Principles of Human Knowledge*: 'There is much here that is correct and close to my own view. But it is expressed paradoxically' (AG 307). He goes on with some proposed revisions of Berkeley's metaphysic, which drain most of the content from his expression of agreement; but this note does not bring us to the heart of the issue between Adams and Wilson.

Adams is right in maintaining that Berkeley and Leibniz share a core metaphysical thesis: namely, that there are only mind-like entities. But they differ *toto coelo* in their reasons for this. Berkeley starts from the certainty of his own mind, and argues for the incoherence of the notion of matter, contending that we cannot have any idea of it, and that even if we had such an idea matter could not be what we perceive (see Chapter 28). Leibniz's route to panpsychism is not like that. This difference is well expressed by Adams:

One reason why the idealistic character of Leibniz's philosophy may be less than obvious to us is that we expect idealism to be rooted primarily in the philosophy of perception, whereas for the mature Leibniz it is motivated largely by worries about the *unity* of bodies. [Perception did have a role back in the 1670s, but later on] the thesis of the phenomenality of bodies rests heavily on the argument that aggregates, by virtue of their disunity, are only phenomena. (1994: 245)

This seems to me—as to Lopston (1999: 367)—a pretty good reason for not calling Leibniz an idealist and likening him to Berkeley.

Chapter 13

Causation and Perception in Leibniz

94. The rejection of inter-substance causation

Leibniz holds that no created substance could possibly act causally upon any other: there is no transeunt (= going-across) causation in which causal influence passes between substances, but only immanent (= staying-inside) causation, in which a single substance causes changes of state in itself. Immanent causation serves Leibniz's turn in several ways: he gets metaphysical mileage out of the thesis that each substance develops under the influence of nothing but its own nature. Still, there was stick as well as carrot in his denial of transeunt causation: he found something deeply problematic in the idea of one substance's acting on another. Let us see why.

Like some of his contemporaries, Leibniz held that transeunt causation properly so-called involves the transfer of tropes or 'individual accidents' from one substance to another (§35). He regards this as absurd, nonsensical, or at least impossible. 'Nothing ever enters into our mind naturally from the outside,' Leibniz writes, 'and it is a bad habit of ours to think of our soul as receiving messenger species [accidents, tropes], or as if it had doors and windows' (*DM* 26, FW 78). And again: 'Two different subjects . . . cannot have precisely the same individual affection, it being impossible that the same individual accident should be in two subjects or pass from one subject to another' (L 704). This does not lead him to reconsider his view about what transeunt causation would be; rather, he infers that such causation does not happen.

The popular thesis that minds and bodies cannot interact, Leibniz holds, is based on a view of causation which really implies that no substance can act on another. Responding to De Volder's view that 'nothing prevents substances of the same nature from acting on each other', Leibniz wrote back: 'What prevents substances of diverse natures from acting on each other? When you have explained that, you will see that all finite substances are prevented from mutually influencing each other' (L 534). Sleigh calls this passage 'gallingly enigmatic' (1990*a*: 166), but it seems to me plain enough. The popular view held that minds cannot interact with bodies, because the former have no motion to give and the latter no thoughts to give; and Leibniz holds that the notion of *giving* that is at work here—namely, that of the transfer of accidents—is inherently cankered, so that a substance can no more give what it has than give what it lacks.

An aside: in one place Leibniz seems not to pin everything on the passage of accidents from one substance to another, but to say that transeunt causation would have to consist in *either* that *or* the passage of a substance from one sub-stance to another, and then to contend that neither is possible:

There is no way in which it could make sense for a monad to be altered or changed inter-nally by any other created thing, because [1] there is nothing to rearrange within a monad, and there is no conceivable internal motion in it which could be excited, directed, increased, or diminished within it, as can happen in a composite, where there is change among the parts. [2] Monads have no windows through which anything could enter or leave. Accidents cannot be detached, nor can they stroll about outside of substances, as the sensible species of the Scholastics used to do. So [3] neither substance nor accident can enter a monad from without. (Mon 7, FW 268)

It is natural to think that Leibniz is saying in 3 that neither (1) substance nor (2) accidents can pass from one monad to another, these being the only candidates for how transeunt causation could happen. And indeed 2 addresses itself to the 'accident' part of this; no problem there. But 1 does not fit. If it had said that a monad does not contain substantial parts *which can leave it and enter another monad*, Leibniz would be saying that you cannot act on a monad by adding to or subtracting from its parts, like shooting an animal or pruning a tree. But in 1 he says, rather, that a monad does not contain substantial parts *which can be trans-posed in it*. I cannot explain this.

Who had ever said that transeunt causation does consist in the passage of sub-stances? Perhaps nobody, and that might somewhat justify Eileen O'Neill's star-tling conclusion that 'Leibniz is the originator of the system of *influxus physicus*', that being one of his phrases for what transeunt causation would involve (1993: 29). I attach no special weight to that phrase, or to the odd feature I have noted in Mon 7. Of course Leibniz did not originate the doctrine that transeunt causa-tion involves trope transfer, rightly thinking he had found it in the works of many predecessors, including Locke (NE 224). Incidentally, the objection that accidents cannot 'stroll about' outside any substance seems misplaced. A trope-transfer theorist could reject action at a distance, as Leibniz himself does, and thus avoid such strolling. Now back to the main thread.

There is still no consensus among philosophers about what causation is. Probably the most popular single view is the 'humean' thesis that one event causes another if the two relate in the right way to a causal law—that is, to *a true universally quantified proposition whose antecedent has vastly many instances and . . .* with some further constraints to meet certain well-known difficulties. The friends of that thesis believe, with Hume, that we have no coherent notion of *causal necessity* that is weaker than *absolute necessity* but stronger than *being implied by a true universally quantified proposition whose antecedent . . . etc.* In their view, causal laws are just the most general and basic contingent truths about how the world goes.

Leibniz held that this relation does indeed hold between events in one monad and events in another: the histories of the individual monads are systematically correlated; the world unrolls in an order which is expressible in universal truths

of the form 'When a substance that is F does A, any substance that is G does B';
but this does not involve causing because it cannot involve the passage of accidents. This order exists in the world because God puts it there, Leibniz adds. It is
a *harmony* amongst the histories of the individual monads; and God set them up
in such a way that it would always obtain, so it was *pre-established*. As Ishiguro has
emphasized (1977), Leibniz's famous pre-established harmony is a theologically
underpinned account of what Hume, but not Leibniz, called 'causation'. In the
context of Leibniz (as of Descartes) we should call it 'quasi-causation'.

Leibniz differs from contemporary 'humeans' more than merely verbally.
Unlike them, he holds that *within* individual substances there is a real connection—a really effective making—between earlier and later states, and that this is
causation properly so-called. He sees God as establishing the harmony by selecting the initial states of the individual monads and the laws according to which
each will develop, doing this in such a way that the separate histories will harmonize (§109).

Rejecting transeunt causation amongst created substances, Leibniz allows it
between God and his creatures: 'Some have believed that something or other
passes from the soul to the body and vice versa—that is the hypothesis of real
influx. . . . [But in fact] with the exception of the dependence of creatures on God,
no real influx from one to the other is intelligible' (quoted in Sleigh 1990a: 143).
Leibniz has to make this exception; for if God's action on the world were not
transeunt, the world would be (part of) God, which would lead to Spinozism. I
do not see how trope transfer can be possible from God to a created substance,
yet *unintelligible* as between one finite substance and another. A little more mildly,
Leibniz says elsewhere that the flowing of a trope from one substance to another
is 'impossible . . . except through Divine omnipotence' (NS, FW 150). This backs
off from 'unintelligible', raising the question of what Leibniz really has against
'real influx' between created substances. Perhaps he really did find it unintelligible, and accepted it as between God and creatures out of theological deference
rather than considered philosophical opinion.

95. Leibniz against occasionalism

Leibniz's objection to transeunt causation does not hold against immanent causation, which, because it involves only one substance, raises no problem of double ownership of tropes. So he is free to allow immanent causation, which he
positively wants for several purposes, one being to fend off occasionalism.

The theory of 'occasional causes', as Leibniz understands it, goes as follows.
What happens in any substance is caused by God alone, but we get the appearance of causal relations between created substances because God lets an event in
one substance be the 'occasion'—the prompt—for him to cause a change in
another. Some Cartesians used this theory to explain why minds seem to act

upon bodies, and vice versa: there is no action in either direction, they held, but God makes it seem as though there is by letting events in one category be his occasion for causing events in the other.

Leibniz agrees with the occasionalists' denial of transeunt causation, but hates the positive part of their account. They 'did get to the heart of the difficulty by pointing to something that could not possibly be true', he writes, but they failed to 'remove it by saying something that actually is true' (NS, FW 149; see also PT, AG 33). Their way of bringing in God, Leibniz protests, is an appeal to a *Deus ex machina*. It is not perfectly clear what his objection is. Writing to Arnauld, in the context of mind–body interaction rather than transeunt causation generally, he alludes to 'the hypothesis of occasional causes . . . according to which God, on the occasion of something's happening in the body, arouses thoughts in the soul which change the course it would have taken without this intervention' (AG 76*). Arnauld defends occasionalism against what he takes to be Leibniz's charge: namely, that it makes God bustle around causing events to occur in certain patterns. It need not do that, says Arnauld:

Those who claim that my will is the occasional cause of the movement of my arm and that God is the real cause of it . . . do not claim that God does this in time through a new act of will which he exercises each time I wish to raise my arm; but by that single act of the eternal will, whereby he has wished to do everything he has foreseen it would be necessary to do. (Mason 105–6)

Leibniz's reply to this changes the subject. He has earlier objected that 'The hypothesis of occasional causes . . . introduces a sort of continual miracle, as though God were constantly changing the laws of bodies on the occasion of the thoughts of minds, or . . . etc.' (FW 113); and here he writes as though Arnauld had been defending occasionalism against that, saying that the occasionalist could suppose that God interferes in a regular, law-like manner. Against that imagined response, Leibniz counter-attacks: '[The occasionalists] introduce a miracle which is no less miraculous for being continual. For it seems to me that the notion of miracle does not consist in rarity' (AG 82). The position that Leibniz here wrongly implies to be Arnauld's was in fact that of Malebranche. When the latter speaks of 'God's acting by general volitions', he means that he acts (by particular volitions) 'in consequence of general laws that he has established' (quoted in Sleigh 1990b: 164). Leibniz's views about miracles are complicated, shifting, unclear, and philosophically unrewarding; but all we need in this context is plain enough: 'Properly speaking, God performs a miracle when he does something that surpasses the forces he has given to creatures and conserves in them' (AG 83). Occasionalism, then, is objectionable not because it represents God as unruly, or as continually busy, but just because it implies that some events in a thing are not upshots of 'the forces God has given to it'. This amounts to objecting to occasionalism because it conflicts with Leibniz's view that things develop through the immanent forces that are in them—a thought which cannot play any part in an *argument* for the 'immanent causation' view as against occasionalism.

Oddly, if Leibniz had not changed the subject—under the noxious attraction of the concept of miracle—he could have answered Arnauld's defence quite well, on the basis of something which he certainly believed a decade later and probably did back in 1687. He held that God would not bring it about that x becomes G at T_2 merely by ordaining at T_1 that it shall do so. That would involve action at a temporal distance, which Leibniz rejects, though not in those words. He says, rather, that if it were to happen, x would become G at T_2 merely because it had an 'external denomination'—the bare relational property of *having once been ordained to become G at this time*—without this being reflected in any present intrinsic property of x:

[Sturm contends] that the motions which take place now come about as the result of an eternal law which God has set up, a law which he then calls a volition and a command; and also that no new command or volition is then necessary, far less a new effort or laborious process. . . . I ask, has this volition or command—or if you will this previously laid-down divine law—bestowed on things merely an external denomination? Or has it really produced some permanent impression in things themselves . . . ? The former appears to be the doctrine of the authors of the system of occasional causes . . . The latter is the usual view and, I believe, the true one.

For since this earlier command does not now exist, it cannot now do anything unless it left behind some continuing effect which still endures and operates. . . . If what is distant in time and place could operate here and now without an intermediary, then anything could be said to follow from anything else equally well. (NI 5–6, FW 212–13)

In flatly rejecting the former view, Leibniz puts himself in a reasonable position to hold that, absent transeunt causation, there are only two choices: his own theory and a form of occasionalism that does imply that God is continuously busy making particular events happen.

According to Leibniz's metaphysic, God gives to each separate monad a *basic nature* (as I shall call it) from which its entire history inevitably flows according to causal laws which God also confers on the monad. He chooses these histories (by choosing the natures that produce them) in such a way that there will be a harmony, and there is no need for him to interfere after that. Leibniz writes: 'God initially created [every monad] in such a way that everything in it must arise from its own nature by a perfect *spontaneity* with regard to itself, yet by a perfect *conformity* to things without' (NS, FW 150). The entire harmony is God's doing, but he did it by what he 'originally created'—that is, by his choice of 'the first constitution' of each thing. Thus Leibniz can credit God with producing the order among events, without supposing him to be improperly busy or to use action at a temporal distance.

96. God's conservation of his creatures

Leibniz himself credits God with constantly acting on the created world, not causing the changes in it, but causing it to stay in existence: 'Created substances depend on God who conserves them and indeed produces them continually by a kind of emanation, just as we produce our thoughts' (*DM* 14, FW 66). Elsewhere when expounding a Thomist doctrine, he seems to endorse its thesis that God 'operates immediately on all created things, continually producing them' (*NE* 222). Also, 'In strict metaphysical truth there is no external cause that acts on us except God alone and he alone communicates himself to us immediately by virtue of our continual dependence' (*DM* 28, FW 79).

This doctrine of Leibniz's seems to be a bit of unconsidered piety for which he has no positive reasons and which does not fit well with his best reason for rejecting occasionalism—namely, that it keeps God at work rather than crediting him with being able to set things up properly from the outset. It is understandable that the astute Bernard Williams (1963: 349d), presenting Descartes's 'picture of created things tending constantly to slip out of existence if it were not for God's sustaining activity', says that this stands 'in contrast . . . with the outlook of Leibniz'. It doesn't, but it should.

What kind of causation is involved in God's sustaining activity? One might say: 'Leibniz cannot answer that acceptably. He says that any action of one substance on another involves the passage of accidents, which he says is impossible.' But that is wrong. He is committed to the passage of accidents only for transeunt *alteration*, in which one substance changes the properties of another. He need not extend this to transeunt *bringing into existence* or (our present topic) *keeping in existence*.

Still, has he any other account of what such causation is like? I have quoted him as saying that God produces created substances continually 'by a kind of emanation', and 'emanate' recurs in that same paragraph. (It is rooted in some ancient and medieval thought. For some of the facts, see Cover and O'Leary-Hawthorne 1999: 263 n. 18.) The corresponding French seems to mean merely that God is the productive cause of other substances; it offers no detail about *how* this might be. However, Leibniz there and again in *DM* 32 goes further by comparing this activity of God's with something familiar: 'God . . . produces them continually by a kind of emanation, just as we produce our thoughts'; 'All other substances depend on God, in the same way as thoughts emanate from our substance.' This is astonishing. When we 'produce our thoughts', we cause some alteration in ourselves; that is, our thoughts 'emanate from our substance' only because the substance *has* the thoughts, just as faces have blushes, bowls have shapes, and so on. Leibniz's comparison implies that God's conserving us is his causing himself to be in some state, which then implies that we are not separate substances, but rather states or modes of God. Leibniz would reject that, calling it 'Spinozism'. I do not understand his offering a comparison which so obviously implies it.

Lacking any acceptable account of how God might act on any other substance, Leibniz could still stand firm, saying that although we cannot conceive *how* God does it, we understand the proposition *that* he does it. (That is what Descartes says to Burman about a related divine activity at CSMK 347.) For something as deep, all-encompassing, and *sui generis* as God's upholding of his creation—Leibniz might say—we cannot expect to have any idea of how it happens; this lack of ours is neither surprising nor troubling.

Alternatively, he could retreat a little, reducing God's preservation of the world to a mere non-interfering consent: we depend on God only in the sense that at any given moment he could annihilate us. This may be all that Christian piety demands, and it creates no special problems for Leibniz. How would God annihilate a creature? Leibniz could reply that it is the reverse, so to speak, of creation, and leads to no problem that does not face every Christian philosopher. But this really would be a retreat, for it does not imply that God continually 'produces' his creatures.

Taking that word seriously, we might understand Leibniz as following Descartes in his view that God really does create us anew at each moment. But that is not open to him, for it pulls the rug out from under his thesis that each monad develops through immanent causation, with each of its temporary states arising causally from its preceding state.

God's sustaining activity, I contend, is grit in the cogs which we should flush out and then forget.

97. How monads develop

According to Leibniz's metaphysic, each monad's entire history inevitably flows from its God-given basic nature according to causal laws which God also confers on the monad. He chooses these histories (by choosing the natures that produce them) in such a way that there will be a harmony, and there is no need for him to interfere after that: 'God initially created [every monad] in such a way that everything in it must arise from its own nature by a perfect *spontaneity* with regard to itself, yet by a perfect *conformity* to things without' (FW 150). The entire harmony is God's doing, but he did it by what he 'originally created'—that is, by his choice of 'the first constitution' of each thing.

When a monad causes itself to undergo a change of state, it does so according to laws imposed upon it by God. But what does it do? What does Leibniz say or think about the nature of such immanent causation? We cannot answer that the causing state absolutely or 'metaphysically' necessitates the caused state. Leibniz writes that each substance in its unfolding 'follows only its own laws, laws which it received with its being' (AG 148); whereas an absolutely necessary law would not hold for every monad, and would not have to be given by God. When we find Leibniz apparently implying—as he sometimes does—that the historical development within a monad is absolutely necessary, this is because of a tremendous mistake of his which I shall expound in §133—one from which he eventually recovered.

Except when making that mistake, Leibniz seems to hold that God's giving laws to a monad consists in his conferring upon it some kind of real causal efficacy—'a real though subordinate and derived power', in Hume's phrase. But he has no account of what such a power is, or of what happens in its exercise. He certainly does not suppose that in immanent causation an accident or trope passes from an earlier to a later stage of the monad. That could not apply to a monad's causing itself to acquire at T_2 a property which it lacks at T_1.

The causation that is in question is strictly deterministic: every temporary state of a monad follows inevitably from its preceding state. This gave Leibniz a prima-facie problem about human freedom, which he tried to solve in various ways that I do not much admire and shall not discuss. For a brief, enjoyable treatment of the problem in the context of Locke's similar view, see *NE* 175–83, 196–8. For a good discussion of the issue as it arises in the context of Leibniz's own metaphysic, with useful references to the secondary literature, see Sotnak 1999.

(I have handled all this as though temporality were basic in Leibniz's metaphysic, and I am inclined to agree with Arthur (1985) in thinking that it is. But an impressive case has been made by Cover (1997) for attributing to Leibniz the view that causal order is really basic and that temporal order supervenes on that. Nothing in the present work depends on the choice between these two views.)

Some of Leibniz's views on causation and quasi-causation are intertwined with his views about the mentalistic aspects of monads—specifically their perceptions and their appetites. I turn to these now.

98. Perception: the account

Perception, according to Leibniz, is a species of the genus *expression*. For a (change of) state S_x in one thing x to 'express' a (change of) state S_y in another thing y, what is needed is this:

> There are reliable general principles about how states of x-like things correlate with states of y-like things, so that someone who knew those principles and knew that x was in state S_x could infer that y was in state S_y.

A state of one thing, then, expresses a state of another if the former contains the information that the latter occurs—as tree rings do about past droughts, and specks on a photographic negative do about galaxies. In those two examples, one thing contains information about another because it was caused by it, or so we think; but Leibniz would not say that, because it implies that there is transeunt causation. All he claims for expression is a system of dependable correlating general principles; they need not be causal.

Here is Leibniz's account of expression in his own words:

One thing is said to express another if the one has properties which correspond to those of the other. . . . The model of a machine expresses the machine itself, . . . speech expresses thoughts and truths, numerals express numbers . . . What is common to all these expressions is that we can pass from a consideration of the properties in the expressing item to a knowledge of the corresponding qualities of the thing expressed. Hence it is clearly not necessary for that which expresses to be similar to the thing expressed, as long as a certain analogy is maintained. (1678, L 207*)

So 'x expresses y' means just that x contains information about y; and x can be a cloud in the sky, the rings of a tree, the spots on someone's face, or the state of a monad.

For Leibniz, to say that x perceives y is just to say that *some state of x expresses a state of y, and x is a monad*. As he wrote to Arnauld:

Expression is common to all the [monads] and is a genus of which natural perception, animal feeling, and intellectual knowledge are species. In natural perception and feeling it suffices that what is divisible and material and is found dispersed among several beings should be expressed or represented in a single indivisible being or in a substance that is endowed with a true unity. (L 339)

So expression is correlation, and perception is expression by monads. 'Natural' perception is perception of 'divisible and material' things—shoes and ships—that are represented within a single substance. Drop 'natural', and you include also the perception of other monads. Or so I believe Leibniz intended, and so he is generally understood. In at least one place (G 2:311) he explains 'perception' as 'nothing other than the expression of many things in one', which equates the word with the phrase 'natural perception', and implies that the states of one monad, though correlated with the states of another, are not perceptions of it. I think this was carelessness on Leibniz's part, and that in such formulations he was thinking of sense perception, 'natural perception', and neglecting to make this clear. For a different way out of the difficulty, and a scrupulous inquest into it, see Kulstad 1978.

Sleigh (1990a: 174) shows that Leibniz sometimes writes as though there were more to perception than I have allowed; but he does not deny that the sparse account reported above is all that Leibniz explicitly offers. Mates remarks on how thinly formal it is:

Leibniz holds a very abstract view of perception. . . . For him, x perceives y (where x is a monad and y is a monad or an aggregate of monads) if and only if the state of x expresses that of y. And the relation of expression . . . is very abstract and general. . . . All that is required is that from the nature of the perception it should be possible to infer, via some law or laws, corresponding features of what is perceived. (1986: 199)

One might feel that the account is so abstract that 'perception' is a misnomer. There is something in that; but more is at stake here than a mere issue of terminology.

Catherine Wilson (1999) has argued that with such an abstract notion of perception it is 'arbitrary' what perceives what. For a usable, non-arbitrary perception concept, she argues, there must be means or mechanisms of perception, and this takes us from mere monads to the organisms or embodied monads about which Leibniz also theorizes (§120). She contends that Leibniz's overall philosophical plans and assumptions required him to waver between monads and organisms, that the elements in his thought cannot be harmonized, and that his supposed 'system' is therefore 'illusory'. Not being fully persuaded of her view regarding arbitrariness, I would not embrace her conclusion as boldly as she does. She is right that Leibniz does sometimes waver between monads and organisms (§111), but I am not convinced that he is committed to doing so by his deepest assumptions and aims. Still, Wilson's powerful paper richly repays careful study, and her 'hermeneutics of suspicion' is justified: Leibniz does indeed confront difficulties which he seems to have no prospect of solving, and some of which he seems not to have recognized.

Some of them concern perception, as I shall explain (§100) after a needed preliminary.

99. Bottom-up versus top-down

Everyone agrees that Leibniz held that human minds are monads, and that many facts about minds can be explained or clarified by setting them into the context of the monadic metaphysic. What about explanations running in the opposite direction? Leibniz thinks we can be helped to get the hang of his monadic metaphysic by thinking of it in terms of our experience of our own minds; I have quoted him writing of 'a soul or substantial form, on the model of what is called "I"'. However, despite those mild attempts to familiarize the metaphysic by relating it to our experience, I see Leibniz's theory-building as proceeding strictly in an upwards direction. He aims to develop his metaphysic in an austere way, allowing himself the concepts of logic and mathematics, and of *substance*, *quality*, *time*, *correlation*, and little else, not availing himself of concepts from familiar human psychology with no warrant except their familiarity. For him, I contend, our psychological concepts are to be clarified and justified by being developed out of the parsimonious initial stock. That is the 'purely bottom-up' account of Leibniz as a theory-builder.

A 'partly top-down' account would say that he is sometimes willing to import into his monadic metaphysic some concepts that he takes unanalysed from armchair psychology. This makes it possible to hold that Leibniz means to explain 'perception' not purely through the abstract concept of expression but also partly through the idea that perceptions have something *cognitive* about them—with the notion of cognition being taken on board, unanalysed, on the strength of its quotidian familiarity to us. If this were right, Leibniz might say: 'In monadic perception there is reliable correlation; but it is accompanied by a further *je ne sais quoi*; to get a sense of that extra element, think about perception as you experience it in your own life.'

At a later stage we shall wrestle with Leibniz's distinction between clear and confused perceptions. Here is Broad on that topic:

A monad is confused in so far as its total state at any moment contains modifications which it fails to recognize and distinguish. Leibniz used certain well-known psychological facts to show that the total state of any human mind . . . contains factors which it fails to discriminate. If so, there is no difficulty in believing that monads below the level of human minds are habitually much more confused than human minds. (1975: 97)

This concerns the evidence for monadic confusion, rather than the analysis of the concept. But it looks as though Broad sees Leibniz as engaging in a partly top-down endeavour, in which our grasp on monadic confusion is to come from our experience of confusion and unawareness in ourselves. I oppose this view of Leibniz's project.

As regards the concept of perception, at least, the record favours the bottom-up view: the texts confirm the account I have given, which is why Mates affirms it so confidently. Most strikingly, after giving his minimal accounts of perception and appetite in a letter that he drafted but did not send to Remond in 1714, Leibniz continues: 'It is inconceivable that there should be anything else in simple substances or, therefore, in the whole of nature' (G 3:622). This intensely bottom-up remark would be stupid from someone engaged in a partly top-down project. There is further confirmation all through Leibniz's writings. I am glad about this. If I became convinced that he was a partly top-down philosopher, I would lose much of my interest in him. I cannot see the point of constructing a metaphysic in terms that, instead of being cleanly defined, are explained partly through analogies with our unanalysed experience.

If Leibniz is moving from the bottom up, he has formidable problems which vanish if he allows himself to reach up into everyday psychology and pull concepts from there down into his metaphysic. This is not surprising, for a potentially illuminating project is likely to meet more obstacles than a duller one. Nor is it very regrettable, for some of our best learning from a philosopher such as Leibniz comes from seeing him try to make bricks without straw, and thereby learning about the right way to make bricks.

Leibniz can pursue his bottom-up project while still saying that one may be helped intuitively to grasp certain elements in his metaphysic by bearing in mind what familiar facts they are the grounding for. That is all he is doing when, replying to De Volder's complaint that he has almost no understanding of primitive forces, he writes: 'This principle of action is most intelligible, since in it there is something analogous to what there is in us, namely perception and appetite' (AG 180). Perhaps the same is true of his writing elsewhere that monads 'must be understood along the lines of our notion of souls', though to my eye this looks like a regrettable break in the bottom-up pattern (NS, FW 145).

100. Perception: the short-fall

Leibniz's concept of perception is his only metaphysical grounding for the whole cognitive side of the human condition—not only perceptions narrowly so-called, but also beliefs, and indeed any informative relation to items other than oneself. We have seen him counting 'intellectual knowledge' as a species of expression (and, I think, of perception).

So he ought to build up the abstract account of monadic perception into something full enough to capture the main features of cognition as we have and know it. Leibniz hardly even tries to do this, and there is much to be learned from thinking about the obstacles to his succeeding had he tried.

The little that he says on the topic is ostensibly addressed to something different—not to the question 'What marks off a human belief from a run-of-the-mill monadic perception?', but rather, 'What marks off a high-level monad from a run-of-the-mill one?' Answering the latter, Leibniz says that the higher intellectual status of humans consists in the special quality of their perceptions; so really he is answering the former question as well.

The differentia is a perception's degree of distinctness. That is Leibniz's point here:

If we wish to call *soul* everything that has perceptions and appetites in the general sense I have just explained, then all **partless** substances or created monads can be called souls. But since belief is something more than a **mere** perception, I think that the general name of 'monad' . . . is sufficient for **low-grade** substances, which have only that [= have mere perceptions, with nothing special about them], and that we should reserve 'souls' for substances whose perception is more distinct and accompanied by memory. (Mon 19, FW 270*)

Leibniz wrote this clumsily: each of the three words I have put in bold type translates the one French word *simple*! I use 'belief' to render the French word *sentiment*, which could mean 'sensation', 'feeling', 'belief', or various other things. Leibniz here means it to stand for a high-grade mental possession that typifies 'minds' strictly so-called. FW has 'feeling', AG has 'sensation', and L has 'sentiment'; I prefer 'belief', but I may be wrong.

To satisfy us of that account of what marks off souls from low-grade monads, Leibniz needs to explain memory and distinctness. It will turn out that he cannot. His sketchy account of memory depends on the concept of distinctness and not on anything else; so the whole weight falls on distinctness; and we shall later find a profound difficulty in the way of his explaining that acceptably (§124).

Even if they were well explained, however, distinctness and memory could not do the job. A decent account of human minds must involve a treatment of belief, and Leibniz is committed to developing that out of his account of monadic perception generally. The view that a theory of belief should build upon the bare idea of a mental state that is informative about something else is plausible and promising. But the building is hard to do, and Leibniz does not even try, perhaps because he had some sense of the difficulties he would face. Here are four of them.

(1) Leibniz needs to provide for beliefs as long-term possessions, rather than discrete episodes. He can probably do this, with help from the concept of disposition.

(2) His account of perception in general makes it a relation between an episodic state of a monad and some other particular state of affairs. It seems not to provide for a monad's having a perception of such contingent general truths as that unimpeded bodies travel in a straight line. Leibniz can credit a monad with perceiving that x is G for each x such that x is F, but that is not perceiving that every F is G. He is well aware of the difference between these; it looms large when he contrasts humans with lower animals (§285).

(3) I do not see how Leibniz could bring conditional, negative, and disjunctive beliefs within the compass of his theory of perception. To give a robust account of the place in the human psyche of general beliefs and beliefs that are in other ways complex, one probably has to bring language into the story. In one place Leibniz writes that although language was developed for communication, it also 'enables man to reason to himself' (*NE* 275); that approaches my point, but does not quite get there; and anyway he says it in a context where his bottom-up project is not in sight. I am not optimistic about a Leibnizian solution to this difficulty.

(4) Beliefs can be false. Like nearly everyone else at the time, Leibniz did not see the concept of belief as challenging or problematic, and did not confront the question of how something false can get into a mind. To answer it, I believe, one needs a richer conceptual base than he allows himself; one needs to develop the concept of belief in tandem with that of desire; and he must fail, because his metaphysic does not attribute to monads anything that could serve as an underpinning for desire. The nearest thing he offers is *appetite*, and that is not near enough, as I now show.

101. Appetite

Leibniz's account of appetite is, at least on the surface, straightforward: 'The action of the internal principle which brings about change, or the passage from one perception to another, can be called appetition' (Mon 15, FW 269). 'The internal qualities and actions of a monad can be nothing but its perceptions (that is, representations of the composite, or external, in the simple) and its appetitions (that is, its tendencies to go from one perception to another) which are the principles of change' (PNG 2, FW 259). So, whereas a perception is a short-lived intrinsic state which carries information, an appetite is an endogenous tendency to alter. A monad's perception is the signal it carries that such-and-such is the case outside it; its appetite is its self-generated tendency to move from one state to another. Notice that appetite is causal, as perception is not.

Immediately after giving his minimalist explanation of appetite as 'the tendency to go from one perception to another', in the letter for Remond, Leibniz goes on to say that in the case of humans (in whom 'perception is an understanding') appetite is called 'will'. He is exploiting the entrenched idea that what makes an action voluntary—and thus a product of the agent's will—is its being caused from within the agent rather than imposed from without. That is a good start, but Leibniz is not well placed to move on from there.

A good account of the will must provide for attempts that fail, acts of the will that do not lead to whatever was being willed. I do not mean failing to ignite the kindling wood, which is caused by external circumstances. My topic is internal failure—to remember the Alamo, or to stop thinking about Istanbul. Leibniz tries to provide for that:

The action of the internal principle which brings about change, or the passage from one perception to another, can be called appetition. In fact appetite cannot always completely reach the whole perception toward which it tends, but it always obtains some part of it, and attains new perceptions. (Mon 15, FW 269)

This relies on the notion of *tendency*: an appetite may tend towards something that it does not actually reach; and this is to be a basis for the idea of a goal that an organism pursues but does not achieve. Well, what is it for a monad to have an unrealized tendency to change?

If Leibniz had worked on that question, he would have found that his account of monadic appetite does not justify his restatements of it in teleological terms: 'Souls act according to the laws of final causes, through appetitions, ends, and means' (Mon 79, AG 223). 'The laws of appetites [are] the laws of the final causes of good and evil' (PNG 3, FW 259). He has provided no basis for 'final cause' or 'ends and means'. His fundamental theory says only that the individual monad runs through its history in accordance with laws given to it by God, laws which embody the efficient causality of its unfolding. I agree with Adams:

The language of 'appetite' and 'ends and means' may be somewhat misleading. It suggests the pursuit of a desired future state of affairs, but the action of a Leibnizian substantial form is more like what is sometimes called 'acting on principle'. In Leibniz's view, the 'internal principle' governing 'the passage [of a substance] from one perception to another' is not based on the desirability of the later perception in itself, but rather on the following of certain laws of nature. (1994: 318)

Even when Leibniz tries to preserve freedom by saying that the forces leading the monad from one state to another 'incline but do not necessitate', he still treats them as belonging to efficient causation. There seems to be no route from his basic metaphysic to the reality of a person who does something for the sake of some end, let alone the more fully teleological notion of a person who does something because he thinks it will lead to a certain end. (For more on this see Bennett 2001b.)

This difficulty might disappear if Leibniz were using familiar facts about ourselves to explain key concepts in his metaphysical system, for then he could say: 'A substance gets from state S_1 to state S_2 through an exercise of a force, or the instantiation of a causal tendency. I call this an instance of appetition. If you want to know more about it, I can tell you that it is as though the substance in its S_1 state *wanted* to become S_2.' To the extent that Leibniz explains things in that top-down direction, using vague, intuitive, everyday knowledge to elucidate the fundamental terms of his metaphysical system, the latter is drained of serious interest. Fortunately, he does not do this often, and I shall continue to hold him to the sterner standard set by the bottom-up direction.

102. Quasi-activity and -passivity

Now I can return to causation, starting with a point about how bodies relate to monads. This rock in my hand is the appearance of an aggregate of monads, and so is the water in that pond. From there Leibniz could go either of two ways. (1) He could hold that the two aggregates do not overlap: each body is the appearance of a determinate aggregate of monads, none of which contribute to the appearance of any other body. (2) Or he could hold that some monads may contribute to the appearances of several distinct bodies.

The difference is of great moment. If 1 is correct, then Leibniz by rejecting transeunt causation between monads implicitly rejects it also between bodies. On the other hand, if 2 is right, then one body might genuinely act upon another. When I throw the rock into the pond, apparently causing ripples on its surface, this seeming influence might be the appearance of the truly (immanently) causal development of monads belonging to both aggregates.

Although he never says so, nobody could doubt that Leibniz assumes 1 throughout. This shows in many ways, not least in his holding that there is no transeunt causation between bodies any more than there is between monads.

Our everyday causal thought and talk, Leibniz holds, reflects a genuine metaphysical underlay, namely the harmony amongst the monads; so genuine truths underlie the strictly false things we say about bodies' interacting. Some of these falsehoods involve the notion of causal direction: we say that the ingot's entering the water caused it to become cooler, not the converse. Not wanting to declare all such talk to be unsalvageable rubbish, Leibniz needs to describe the proprieties that govern it.

Really, there are two tasks here. One is to lay out the criteria by which we steer when we use the language of transeunt causal direction. This, however, might be regarded as a Lockean or English problem, rather than a Leibnizian or Continental one, and I cannot find that Leibniz addresses it.

He does undertake the other task, which is to say what the underlying metaphysical reality is in a case where (as I shall say, for short) one thing quasi-acts on another. Leibniz holds that all seeming truths—all propositions that it is all right for us to accept—at the phenomenal level are grounded in facts about monads. So he is committed to holding that the respectable things we say in the language of transeunt causation correctly report the appearance to us of some underlying reality; and he needs an account of the latter.

One might have expected him to appeal to time order to solve this problem. If S_x contains the information that S_y occurs at some time, the former counts as quasi-caused by the latter if it is *later* than it. For a reason I shall give in §112, this would imply that each monadic state quasi-causes everything that happens later; but the extravagance of that would not deter Leibniz from saying it, as we shall soon see. Yet he does not base quasi-causal direction on temporal order; I am not sure why. It could be because he held that monads are not basically temporally organized, though I have doubts about that (§97).

Leibniz offers three accounts of quasi-causal direction. Here is one, which he gives several times:

When a change occurs which affects several substances . . . I believe we may say that the substance which thereby immediately passes to a higher degree of perfection or to a more perfect expression exercises its power and *acts*, and the one which passes to a lower degree shows its weakness and *is acted upon*. (DM 15, FW 68)

Notice the phrase 'we may say'. Earlier in the section Leibniz has said that the purpose of this bit of theory is 'to reconcile the language of metaphysics with practice'—that is, to give the metaphysical grounding of permissible though not strictly true things that we say.

The phrase 'degree of expression' makes it sound as though Leibniz thinks that some monads express more than others do. That is not so: he holds that each monad expresses everything (§112). The 'degrees' he speaks of are degrees of *distinctness* of expression or perception, with distinctness understood as the opposite of confusion. We shall come to this concept in §124, along with the equation of degrees of distinctness with degrees of perfection. In the meantime, set all of that aside. What Leibniz says here is problematic just because of its form. Taking it that events e_x and e_y occur in different substances, Leibniz tells us that judgements of quasi-causal direction are grounded thus:

e_x quasi-caused e_y ≡ in e_x x changed to a higher degree of perfection and in e_y y changed to a lower.

This has the abstract form:

e_x caused e_y ≡ F(x) and G(y).

That cannot be right, because the left-hand side is relational while the right is not. Nothing in the right-hand conjunction provides for the notion of this monad's quasi-acting *on that one*; yet Leibniz has said that he is dealing with 'the action of one finite substance on another'. The problem is pointed to by an aside which I suppressed when quoting from him. Leibniz wrote: 'When a change takes place by which several substances are affected (*in fact every change affects all of them*), I believe one may say that . . .', etc. The clause I have italicized gives the game away; Leibniz cannot focus sharply and accurately on the question of what makes it the case that *this* monad quasi-acts upon *that* one. Similarly in PT, AG 33.

Nearly three decades later, Leibniz offered—cheek by jowl—two other accounts of quasi-causal direction. One openly confines itself to the monadic 'x is active' and 'y is passive', rather than the dyadic 'x acts upon y':

A created thing is said to *act* externally insofar as it is perfect, and to *be acted on* by another insofar as it is imperfect. Thus we attribute *activity* to a monad insofar as it has distinct perceptions, and *passivity* insofar as it has confused ones. (Mon 49, FW 274)

Whereas in the earlier account Leibniz grounds 'active'/'passive' in rising/falling degrees of distinctness, now he grounds it in distinctness/confusion of perceptions. The difference is enormous. Leibniz holds that monads fall along a continuum from the lowliest substances up through humans to superhuman 'spirits', and that a monad's place on this continuum is fixed *solely* by how distinct its perceptions are. Combine this with the account of quasi-causal direction quoted above, and you get the result that monads are 'active' (as we wrongly but permissibly say) exactly in proportion to how high they are on the cosmic scale. The account in the *Discourse on Metaphysics* has no such implication: it allows for a low-ranked substance to be 'active' whenever it comes to perceive more distinctly for a moment. The extra baggage that the later account carries is a further defect in it, I submit, in addition to its neglect of the relational 'x quasi-acts *on* y'.

A page later, purporting to follow out the consequences of this, Leibniz tells a different tale:

Among created things, action in one thing is accompanied by passion in another, and vice versa. For God, considering two simple substances together, finds in each reasons that require him to adjust the other to it; and consequently, what is active in some respects is passive when considered in another way: active insofar as what can be clearly understood in it serves to explain what happens in the other; and passive insofar as the explanation for what happens in it is to be found in what is known distinctly in the other. (Mon 52, FW 275*)

Here at last Leibniz offers something that is relational not only in its explanandum but also in its explanans: x quasi-acts on y (in particular) because something that happens in x is needed to explain something that happens in y (in particular). Furthermore, it captures the intuitively plausible idea that causes explain their effects, and not vice versa. Although the topic is only the direction of *quasi-causation*, Leibniz offers a deep grounding in the relation 'God has reason to adjust y so that it accords with x'. This can only be a stab in the dark. Given how seriously Leibniz takes the idea of God's infinite intellectual power, the notion of his making one choice in the light of another is suspect; it makes better Leibnizian theological sense, I suggest, to see God as simply thinking the best possible world in a single act of the intellect, and choosing it through a single act of the will. When Leibniz postulates dependencies among God's choices and aligns them with the direction of quasi-causation, this looks like a triumph of hope over piety.

Chapter 14

Leibniz's Physics

103. The grounding principle

Given that the material world is only the appearance to us of an underlying monadic reality, one might expect Leibniz to be flexible and open-minded about it. He cannot explain in detail how monads appear to us as matter, so his convictions about them do not constrain what he thinks about the material world. Or so one might suppose (Jolley 1986: 50; C. Wilson 1989: 194); but what we find in the texts is a philosopher who—early and late—holds fierce opinions about many aspects of the world of appearance. As well as discovering what some of these are, we should ask why Leibniz thinks he is entitled to them.

Let us start with his denial that bodies exert attractive forces on one another. In §23 I reported Locke's reluctant concession that there may be such forces, because bodies may have powers that are 'above what can be derived from our idea of body', or—he adds—'can be explained by what we know of matter'. For Leibniz it is a matter of high principle—I call it his 'grounding principle'—not to concede that anything can have powers that are not explained by its nature:

Whenever we find some quality in a subject, we ought to believe that if we understood the nature of both the subject and the quality we would conceive how the quality could arise from it. So within the order of nature (miracles apart) it is not at God's arbitrary discretion to attach this or that quality haphazardly to substances. He will never give them any that are not natural to them, that is, that cannot arise from their nature in an explainable way. (*NE* 66; see also 378–82)

Leibniz must be taking it that each thing has a basic nature, a set of properties that do not arise from any deeper facts about the thing; and he is urging us to expect that any of the thing's *other* properties will be grounded in this basic nature. Without the latter, the grounding principle would imply an infinite regress.

In protecting it from that, however, have I not trivialized it? Does it not merely say that apart from the ungrounded properties of a thing, all its properties are grounded? That is indeed all it says, but it is not trivial because the thesis that each thing does have a basic nature is a substantive one. It also seems to be a reasonable thing to believe. For it to support Leibniz in rejecting traction, however, a further premiss is needed: namely, that if a thing is material, then that is its *basic* nature. Otherwise, its materiality and its power to attract other things might both be upshots of some property lying deeper in the thing.

Sometimes Leibniz thinks it worthwhile to assert a weak consequence of the grounding principle: namely, that all of a thing's dispositional properties supervene upon—are grounded in—its intrinsic properties. Dispensing with this, he holds, leads to bad philosophical practice:

> If God gave things accidental powers which were not rooted in their natures and were therefore out of reach of reason in general, that would be a back door through which to re-admit 'over-occult qualities' which no mind can understand, along with inexplicable 'faculties' (those little goblins) . . . helpful goblins which come forward like gods on the stage . . . to do on demand anything that a philosopher wants of them, without ways or means. (*NE* 382)

We may well sympathize with this. We would not, for instance, be willing to countenance two kinds of stuff which were exactly alike in all respects, at all levels, except that one was soluble in water while the other was not.

But Leibniz needs more than this out of the grounding principle. To support him in rejecting attractive forces, for example, it must demand that any powers a body has—such as a power to attract other bodies—must supervene upon its intrinsic qualities in a manner that is intelligible, makes sense, in some degree 'stands to reason'. In §23 I sketched how this demand is satisfied by bodies' powers to repel one another and not by a power to attract. (In all this, of course, the topic is quasi-powers, to go with the quasi-causation between bodies.)

The frame of mind which generates this strong version of the grounding principle makes itself felt often in Leibniz's thought. Against Locke's view that it is arbitrary—a result of God's good pleasure—that surface texture of kind T produces colour ideas of kind C, Leibniz writes: 'It is not God's way to act in such an unruly and unreasoned fashion. I would say, rather, that there is a resemblance of a kind' between the ideas and their material causes (*NE* 131). In his next paragraph he continues: 'It is thoroughly reasonable that the effect should correspond to the cause; and how could one ever be sure that it does not, since we have no distinct knowledge either of the sensation of blue (for instance) or of the motions which produce it?' Here Leibniz's unflagging demand that everything be reasonable leads him to speculate that if we could take in enough detail in our colour sensations, and knew enough about their physical correlates in our bodies, we would see an isomorphism between the two. He is probably right about this. C. L. Hardin in his classic work on colour (1988: 133) argues convincingly that 'qualitative similarities and differences amongst sensory states amount, in the final analysis, to similarities and differences in . . . neural processing'.

Returning now to attraction: Leibniz takes it that the basic nature of any body includes its antitypy, that is, its occupying a region of space to the exclusion of other bodies; and he thinks that this naturally and intelligibly leads to bodies tending to repel one another, whereas there is no such basis for their tending to attract one another. That line of thought goes through smoothly if bodies are fundamentally real—as it did for Locke and Descartes, for instance—but what if the material world is only an appearance? The answer, it seems, is that the argument still stands: Leibniz applies his grounding principle, and the underlying principle of sufficient reason, just as vigorously to appearances as to real substances. If challenged on this, he would say that the principle of sufficient reason implies that whatever God chooses to make real *or apparent* will be reasonable, so that even at the phenomenal level we will find only things whose properties are explicable in terms of their basic natures.

What could the 'basic nature' of matter be for Leibniz? One might think he could look to physics for it, like this:

As we learn more and more about the fine structures of things, we shall eventually get down to a level where there is just fundamental matter, with a few simple properties from which all the rest flow. It is true that such matter is an appearance of an underlying reality which is infinitely qualitatively complex; but all that lies on the far side of the divide between appearance and reality, and we shall never encounter it in our empirical scientific inquiries. All the latter will bring us to is simple essentially uniform matter.

But Leibniz does not believe that. There is, he writes, 'never anything in nature with perfectly uniform parts' (L 544). He believes that we would never reach a qualitative plateau which we could deem to give us the 'basic nature' of matter (§122). So far as I can see, for him the 'basic nature' of matter will have to come purely from the concept of matter. This might be a sufficient basis for some of his views about physics, notably the view that there are no attractive forces; but others of his a priori pronouncements about the physical world are less easy to justify. They all purport to concern how bodies interact; but, according to Leibniz they never do interact, for that would be transeunt causation. Seen in this light, some of his most confident pronouncements look peculiar.

104. Some principles of Leibnizian physics

A striking example is Leibniz's emphatic contention that any bodily event can be explained purely in terms of 'mechanism', which for him means impact mechanics, the laws governing collisions. This is a compendium of several theses, which we should examine separately. I shall silently take it as understood that the scientific explanations that are in question here are only quasi-causal.

(1) Leibniz is refusing to explain any particular events in terms of Aristotelian 'forms'—the kind of explanation that appeals to 'the form of oak' to explain why an acorn develops as it does. In this he aligns himself with the Galilean revolution (§1), which he sees has come to stay—'the great light of our age', he calls it. This is less a philosophical opinion than a reading of where science is moving, and above all the upshot of seeing that after two millennia of stasis science at last *is* moving. 'Galileo, . . . Descartes [and others] have quite clearly purged inexplicable chimeras from physics' (PAB, AG 319). Leibniz writes of having proved that

they are right about this, but he has not. What he is doing is mounting the only scientific bandwagon that is going anywhere.

(2) Leibniz's endorsement of 'mechanism' is also fed by his denial that any material event can be explained through a mental one. The Galilean revolution does not entail this. Descartes was a prime revolutionary who firmly rejected the earlier Aristotelian paradigm; yet he held that human behaviour cannot all be explained in terms of physical mechanisms and must partly result from the influence of the mind (§49).

Leibniz rejects this. 'I attribute to mechanism everything which takes place in the bodies of plants and animals except their initial formation', he writes. 'Thus I agree that the movements of what are called "sensitive" plants result from mechanism, and I do not approve of bringing in the soul when plant and animal phenomena have to be explained in detail' (*NE* 139). This holds for humans too: 'Nothing is so wonderful that it could not be produced by nature's mechanism' (*NE* 220). I have not found him discussing Descartes's reason for the contrary view: namely, that a human head is too small to contain all the needed mechanisms; but it is obvious what he should say. Leibniz's metaphysic does not limit how small a mechanism can be or, therefore, how many mechanisms can be comfortably housed in one skull. He is in fact committed to there being nano-mechanisms as small as you like (§122).

Anyway, he is encouraged in his faith in the powers of mechanism by his conviction—largely based on theology, it seems—that this is a wonderfully good world whose goodness consists at least in part in how rich it is in phenomena and how simple in the quasi-causal principles that govern them:

We could not exaggerate nature's liberality; she goes beyond anything that we can devise . . . Philosophers used to have two axioms: the realist one seemed to make nature profligate and the nominalist one seemed to declare her to be stingy. [In fact,] nature is like a good housekeeper who is sparing when necessary in order to be lavish at the right time and place. She is lavish in her effects and thrifty in the means she employs. (*NE* 323–4)

Though Leibniz expresses the point there in terms of the excellence of 'nature', his real topic is God, who is 'the reason for the greatness or power in the mechanism of the universe as now constituted' (UO, AG 152).

(3) Given that physical events are to be explained physically (2), and that this is to be done without help from Aristotelian forms (1), it follows that the whole of physics must conform to the outlines of the Galilean programme. This is not to say that all its explanations must appeal only to how bodies push one another. It is one thing to say that true total physics is a matter of micro-structures and a few basic physical principles; it is another to confine the latter to impact mechanics. We have seen Leibniz's reason for taking that further step.

He also rules out action at a distance, for reasons that are not clear to me. Writing to him, Clarke gave this reason: 'That one body should attract another [from a distance] without any intermediate means is indeed not a miracle, but a contradiction; for it is supposing something to act where it is not' (Alexander 53). Leibniz does not challenge this argument; and at *NE* 130 he tacitly endorses Locke's version of it as sufficing to rule out action at a distance. But Leibniz is not entitled to argue like that, because he holds that a body cannot act where it *is*, either. When one body collides with another whose movement is thereby altered, he contends, it does not act upon the other; the two are merely correlated within the overall 'harmony'. There is nothing wrong with correlation across a distance—especially for a philosopher who holds that distances are even further from being real than are bodies and transeunt causation. Perhaps Leibniz uncritically carried his hostility to action at a distance over from his realist days when he was in a position to argue as Locke and Clarke did.

Leibniz hates the various rivals to a physics of bodily impact. In a ferocious anti-Newton piece he attacks many approaches, condemning those 'who fabricate miracles, or who fabricate incorporeal principles that . . . regulate . . . bodies, who put forward the four elements or the four primary qualities as if they contained the ultimate explanation of things, or who—uninterested in understanding the particular force by which we evacuate with pumps . . .—postulate in nature a primitive, essential, and insuperable quality which makes it abhor, as it were, a vacuum' (PAB, AG 317). In such polemics he often appeals to *the times*, the modern age which has brought such benefits that are now under threat from a fashion for non-Galilean fantasies:

In the time of Mr. Boyle . . . nobody would have ventured to publish such chimerical notions. I hope that happy time will return . . . Mr. Boyle made it his chief business to inculcate that everything was done mechanically in natural philosophy. But it is men's misfortune to become disgusted with reason itself and weary of light. Chimeras begin to appear again. (AG 344)

A similar note is struck in 'A Physicist against Barbarism', where Leibniz rails against 'crude philosophers' who 'bring forth attractive, retentive, repulsive, directive, expansive, and contractive faculties'. He gives them a historical setting:

This can be forgiven in [people who wrote when] the clear foundation for philosophizing was either not yet known or not yet fully appreciated. But what person of understanding would now bring forward these chimerical qualities . . .? It is permissible to recognize magnetic, elastic, and other sorts of forces, but only insofar as we understand that they are not primitive or incapable of being explained, but arise from motions and shapes. However, the new patrons of such things do not want this. (PAB, AG 313)

Leibniz's nose for where physics was likely to progress, though it led him into the Galilean camp, was not unerring. He was wrong to reject traction; also, he complains against 'the new patrons of such things' that 'these people . . . now go further and find fault with the idea that the flow of the light of the stars is instantaneously diffused through the medium' (PAB, AG 318).

105. Forces in Leibniz's physics

In maintaining that only repulsive forces can be intelligibly grounded in 'the idea of body', Leibniz is not saying that true physics can be deduced from the premiss that each body has a location from which it excludes others. To get true physics, he says, the occupants of space must be credited with exerting forces and not just impenetrably sitting there (NI 11, FW 216–17; compare Kant, *Critique* B 321). If you have antitypy but no forces, Leibniz says, you get the wrong physics (AG 245–56); I say that you get no physics; but either way, something more is needed—and he says that the need is for forces.

The exact status of these in his thinking is peculiar. Start with Leibniz's criticisms of Descartes's view that all qualitative variety in matter supervenes purely on differences in how portions of matter move (§18). One criticism focuses on Descartes's view that the fact that something moves is just a complex fact about where it is at different times. This entails that at an instant there is nothing in the universe to indicate whether and how various things are moving; from which Leibniz infers trouble for Descartes's theory about qualitative variety. His remedy is to postulate that matter contains real forces that are operative at instants as well as across time. 'In the present moment of its motion,' he writes, 'not only is a body in a place with the same size and shape as itself, but it also has a conatus or nisus for changing its place, so that the state following from the present one results per se from the force of its nature' (NI 13, FW 218). A moving body is, at an instant, 'in a place with the same size and shape as itself'; but so is a motionless body, which is why the Cartesian philosophy cannot distinguish the two. Leibniz repairs this by supposing that even at an instant the moving body is the locus of a force-for-moving (a 'conatus or nisus') which it would not have if it were not on the move.

If Descartes took that over, it would solve his problem regarding qualitative variety; but Leibniz cannot use this as an independent argument for his view about forces, because he does not have the other half of Descartes's problem—I mean the thesis that apart from motion (or forces) matter is all qualitatively uniform. Leibniz did not accept anything like that (§122).

So we are still looking for reasons why he might believe that all matter is permeated by forces which are real even at an instant. I cannot find any that are consistent with his mature metaphysics. He makes these forces sound energetic and effective, and any argument for them must depend on that; but the mature metaphysic cannot allow them any efficacy, because they interrelate different substances (or, more exactly, appearances of aggregates of different substances). Leibniz's insistence on forces in matter seems to be an incautious hold-over from earlier days when he was a realist about matter and thought that a portion of matter informed by a force is a true substance.

I do not mean that he merely retained some verbal habits. He really did go on believing in these forces. Here he is in 1695 contending that matter's antitypy is due to 'passive force' which also explains its inertia:

The primitive force of being acted upon or of resisting . . . is what explains why bodies cannot interpenetrate, but present an obstacle to one another, and also why they have a certain laziness, so to speak, or a reluctance to move, and will not allow themselves to be put into motion without lessening to some extent the force of any body that is acting on them. (SD, FW 156)

I have not found any text in which Leibniz, after saying something like this, comments on the tension between it and the theses that matter is an appearance and that transeunt causation does not happen.

His earlier work on these issues, before monads, is subtle, complex, and hard to grasp. Fortunately, we now have a fine exposition of it on which I gratefully rely (Mercer and Sleigh 1995: 73–89; also helpful is M. D. Wilson 1976). There are two crucial points. (1) Leibniz wanted a concept of body or material substance according to which bodies *act*—they *do* things—and this must come from within the substance itself. 'A substance is a being which subsists in itself, [and therefore] has a principle of action within itself' (L 115). On this view, matter such as Descartes believed in—which changes only by moving, every movement being caused by God—is not substantial at all. (2) For matter to be a subject of active forces, Leibniz held, it must be infused or informed or directed by something like mind. He was sure that any account of the material world must include on its ground floor some such notion as that of force or *nisus*, and that this could come only through supposing that something like mentality infuses all of matter (force = 'conatus' = trying or endeavour). The belief that minds are inherently active, while matter is not, went back long before Leibniz and was shared by many others. (See Mercer and Sleigh 1995: 75.) Locke is one of those who connected mind with activity (*Essay* II.xxi.4); Berkeley is another (§221).

In those early years, therefore, Leibniz espoused a kind of panpsychism: he thought that mentality permeates the entire material world, while viewing matter in a realist manner. After about 1686 that realism fell away, and Leibniz came to regard matter as merely the appearance of simple immaterial substances. From then on he had a different kind of panpsychism: not real matter informed by mind, but matter as an appearance of mind-like substances. He may be entitled to go on uttering some of the same sentences, but he ought to be—and to make us—aware that he now means something different by them. What actually happens, it seems, is that he goes on believing some of the original story. When in his later years he thinks about the material world, having concluded that it is only a well-founded phenomenon, he still feels entitled to be sure that matter is infused with forces: they are no longer needed to explain why bodies act upon one another, but they are a vehicle for a panpsychism that Leibniz still believes in, though now it is utterly transformed. We can see both bases for panpsychism at work in 'On Nature Itself'.

106. Activity and passivity within the monad

Leibniz's early views about matter, mind, and activity arose from his conviction that a complete substance must have both a passive and an active aspect, except for God, who is purely active. As applied to monads, this is an unadmirable piece of philosophy that Leibniz expressed in deplorable terminology. I offer an account of it as prophylaxis against being confused by some of the texts; I can get no profit from it. The terminology created for me a blank wall of incomprehension until I found it explained in Adams 1994, on which I rely heavily here.

I repeat: Leibniz holds that any individual monad has a passive as well as an active aspect. The unfolding of its successive states, though caused purely from within, is to be thought of as action or activity which is brought to bear *on* something—some aspect of the monad—which is therefore passive. Before looking into the philosophy of this, such as it is, let us confront the terminology as Leibniz gave it to De Volder: 'I distinguish: (1) the primitive entelechy or soul; (2) the matter, namely, the primary matter or primitive passive power; (3) the monad completed by these two' (L 530–1; Adams's translation). Here is Adams's explanation of this baffling passage (1994: 265):

The monad (3) is 'a simple substance . . . ; *simple*, that is to say without parts'. The primitive entelechy (1) and primary matter (2) must not, therefore, be conceived as *parts* that compose the monad, but rather as aspects or properties of the monad. . . . 'Entelechy' is sometimes used by Leibniz . . . as a synonym for 'monad' or 'simple substance'; but here the entelechy clearly is not the complete monad, but a property or aspect of it. Since it goes together with primitive passive power to form the monad, the entelechy here is presumably the monad's primitive active power. . . . It is striking that the 'soul' is not identified here with the monad, but with an aspect of it, and is presumably not a substance but something that can be considered as an entity only by abstraction from a complete substance or monad.

Adams's interpretation convicts Leibniz of serious ambiguity in his uses of 'entelechy' and 'soul', and of 'matter'. He scrupulously treats the interpretation as speculative, but I am sure it is right. It stops the quoted passages from colliding head-on with Leibniz's principal philosophical doctrines, and it throws light on other texts where Leibniz also uses 'soul' to stand for the monad's active aspect and 'matter' for its passive aspect. Here is one: 'This substantial principle itself is what is called the soul in living things and a substantial form in other things; and insofar as *together with matter* it constitutes a substance that is truly one, . . . it makes up what I call a monad' (NI 11, FW 217; my emphasis). A mere page later Leibniz seems to return to the familiar doctrine of the monads that we know and love: 'Spirit is to be understood . . . as a soul or as a form analogous to a soul, . . . something constitutive, substantial, enduring, what I usually call a monad, in which there is something like perception and appetite.' Here monads are identified with souls, and are not said to result from combining soul with matter.

So much for the terminology. Now for the philosophy of the thesis that every substance has a passive and an active aspect. It is not obvious how Leibniz could justify this. Ordinarily one thinks of a thing's passivity in terms of other things acting upon it, that is, in terms of transeunt causation; but in that sense a monad is purely active, with nothing acting upon it (unless we bring in God, in which case the created monad is purely passive). So Leibniz is doing something else with 'active' and 'passive', but I have not found him clearly explaining what it is.

The thesis that every non-divine substance has a passive as well as an active aspect presumably has a long and convoluted history, but I do not know it. Looked at philosophically, the thesis has little to recommend it, especially when it is divorced from transeunt causation. After that divorce, we are left with the idea that a created thing's activity must be exercised within a context (or against a grain) of passivity: 'Although God does not need a passive element through which to act, created mind does' (Mercer and Sleigh 1995: 79). Perhaps part of the thought is that a being which was active and in no way passive would be divine.

Another possibility is that in his earlier years Leibniz became accustomed to insisting that bodies must be loci of passive and active powers, this being needed to explain their interactions, and that he carried this over into the immaterial non-interacting substances that he later believed in, without properly thinking it through. This is like an explanation I suggested for his denial of action at a distance.

Or perhaps, as well or instead, Leibniz was encouraged by his wish to have a metaphysical grounding for his views about active and passive forces in matter (§102). For a fuller discussion of this see Rutherford 1995a: 253–7. In the following passage Leibniz starts with activity and passivity as they are dealt with in physics, and then seeks to ground them in aspects of monads, ending up with a use—already quoted above—of the deplorable terminology:

It is in this very passive force of resisting . . . that I locate the notion of primary matter or bulk, which is everywhere the same in all bodies and proportional to their size. . . . And just as matter has a natural inertia which is opposed to motion, so in a body itself, indeed in every substance, there is a natural constancy which is opposed to change. . . . A first entelechy or first subject of activity must be recognized in corporeal substance; that is, a primitive motive force . . . which always acts but which in collisions between bodies is modified in various ways through conatus and impetus. And it is this substantial principle which is called the soul in living things and a substantial form in other things; and insofar as together with matter it constitutes a substance that is truly one, or one per se, it makes what I call a monad. (NI 11, FW 216–17)

The phrase 'in a body itself, indeed in every substance' shows Leibniz believing that this aspect of his physics can be metaphysically grounded in a direct and simple way. The activity and passivity found in matter are themselves present in the monads of which matter is an appearance. No argument is given for this. The phenomenal supposed facts that are to be grounded are suspect, because they involve transeunt causation; and even if they were legitimate, and had to be metaphysically grounded, why should it be through the reappearance of the very same concepts down at the monadic level?

The vexatious terminology comes from the same source. Theorizing about physics, Leibniz holds that its subject-matter must involve active and passive forces, and he associates activity with soul, entelechy, and form, and associates passivity with matter. This is primary matter—that is, matter considered merely as an undifferentiated lump that fills space, not the richly endowed secondary matter which is what physics is about. In each of these associations he is encouraged by the scholasticism which throbs audibly in the background of all his thought, especially the link between form/matter and active/passive. The time-honoured terminology makes a kind of sense when applied to the phenomenal material world, but a voice in his ear should have warned Leibniz not to carry it down, unchanged, to the monadic level.

He has an account of what monadic passivity is. It relies on the traditional view that activity is a perfection, passivity an imperfection; so that a monad is passive to the extent that it is imperfect or is moving downwards on the value scale, and active in so far as it is moving up. (In §102 we saw this at work in connection with quasi-causal direction.) If we ask Leibniz how we can tell more from less perfect, the only help he offers is the thesis that perceiving distinctly is better than perceiving confusedly. The upshot of all this is that the passive aspect of the monad consists in all the facts about how its perceptions are confused, while its active aspect consists in the facts about how its perceptions are distinct. The more distinct they are overall, the greater is its active-to-passive ratio.

The active/perfect equation, though historically unsurprising, has no claim on our philosophical respect. As for the perfect/distinct equation, Leibniz does not even try to defend it. He carries the *language* of active/passive down to the monadic level, and stipulates that it is to carry meanings having to do with perfect/imperfect and thus with distinct/confused. Even if he had a good account of the latter, tying it to the terminology of 'active' and 'passive' would not enable it to serve honestly as the causal underlay of the phenomenal facts about forces and resistance to them.

The only attempt that I know of to improve on this is proposed by Rutherford (1995a: 140–1). The monad is *on course towards the good*, or *has the good as its goal* in some way; so its active aspect is to be thought of in teleological terms—the monad moves up the perfection scale because it is trying to do so. What would impede this upward movement? Only confused perceptions, which are poor knowledge states which limit the monad's grasp of what is or would be good. Perhaps Leibniz had some such idea as that, though I know of no direct evidence for it.

107. Leibniz on teleological explanation

Although he gives mechanism an even wider scope than Descartes did, Leibniz also makes a place for teleology in biology and physics. Descartes rejected teleological explanations on the grounds that if they had a place, it would involve knowledge of God's purposes, which we cannot have (Med 4, CSM 2:38–9; *PP* 1:28). Nor do we need it for science. Principles of a purely mechanistic efficient-causal sort are all we need to 'explain all natural phenomena' (*PP* 2:64). Leibniz agrees that no events in the material world have to be explained teleologically; we have seen him saying that 'mechanism' can do all the work. Yet he also finds room for teleology. There are four parts to this story.

(1) Even if we completed a perfect total physics, Leibniz holds, we could, and should, still ask: Why are *these* the basic principles of physics? Sometimes he parades this question in order to make the point that the fundamentals of physics are underpinned by substances that are not material:

We must consider how these mechanical principles and general laws of nature themselves arise from higher principles and cannot be explained by quantitative and geometrical considerations alone; that there is rather something metaphysical in them . . . which is to be referred to a substance devoid of extension. (CT, L 409)

Often, however, his point is that the basic laws of physics are contingent, so that the explanation for their obtaining must be that they were chosen by God:

By a consideration of efficient causes alone . . . we cannot give the reason for the laws of motion. For I have found that we have to bring in final causes, and that these laws do not depend on the principle of necessity, as logical, arithmetical, and geometrical truths do, but upon the principle of fitness, that is, upon the choice of wisdom. (PNG 11, FW 263)

Everything in nature can indeed be explained mechanically, but the principles of mechanics themselves depend on metaphysical and, in a sense, moral principles, that is, on the contemplation of an efficient and final cause, namely God, the most perfectly effective cause, and cannot in any way be deduced from the blind composition of motions. (1691, AG 245)

This doctrine of Leibniz's is fairly plain sailing. Within physics narrowly construed, all we need is mechanism, but that cannot answer the question: Why are the basic laws of physics as they are? The answer is that they are contingent, cannot be strictly deduced from geometry or from the essence of matter; so we must explain them by supposing that God, for his own good reasons, chose that they should be operative. This explanation, because it refers to someone's reasons or purposes, could be accounted teleological.

Leibniz valued this reason for thinking that teleological considerations are relevant 'even in physics and mathematics', because it serves 'to clear the mechanical philosophy of the impiety with which it is charged' (*DM* 23, FW 75). It provides, he writes elsewhere, 'one of the most successful and most evident proofs of the existence of God' for 'anyone who looks deeply into things' (PNG

11, FW 263). It is, he says in a third place, a part of what 'cured' him of 'the
Spinozist view which allows God infinite power only, not granting him either
perfection or wisdom, and which dismisses the search for final causes and
explains everything through brute necessity' (NE 73; see also NI 3, FW 211).
Philosophically speaking, this is simple, thin stuff: it does not require us to think
hard about what teleology is, or to consider whether it can enter into any sort of
interplay with mechanism, as distinct from providing a metaphysical platform
upon which untrammelled mechanism can operate.

(2) Teleological notions have a place in biology, Leibniz holds. He seems to
have two views about how. (a) Like biologists today, he sees that biology has use
for the concept of *function*. Without denying that every biological event can be
explained in terms of its efficient causes, we think better about organisms if we
realize that various parts and aspects of an organism have a function in its life—
something that they are *for*. Leibniz ties this to God's purposes, and uses it
against Descartes, maintaining that biological structures give us evidence about
God's purposes: 'The reasons for what was created by an understanding are the
final causes or plans of the understanding that made them. These are apparent in
their use and function, which is why considering the use parts have is so helpful
in anatomy' (AG 242). I have not found Leibniz exploring the concept of biological function—for example, considering whether it could stand on its own feet
without theological help. His own treatment of it is always theological; for
instance DM 22, FW 74–5. (b) Just once that I know of, Leibniz brings teleology
into biology in a different way. I have already quoted it: 'I attribute to mechanism
everything which takes place in the bodies of plants and animals *except their
initial formation*' (NE 139; my emphasis). This gives up on the 'reconciling'
endeavour, and backs off from the thesis that mechanism can explain every material event. Leibniz implies here that although the life and procreation of an organism can be mechanistically explained, given that the organism exists, its existence
cannot be explained without reference to God's purposes. I do not know how
serious he was about this. Perhaps he thought of 'their initial formation' as part
of the creation of the world, and thus as not an exception to universal mechanism
in the world.

(3) Leibniz is also willing to invoke notions that he thinks are teleological in
the thick of doing physics, and not merely in thinking about why its basic principles are true. He acknowledges that 'the [mechanistic] way of efficient causes
is deeper and in some sense more immediate and *a priori*'.[1] As against those merits in mechanistic or efficient-cause explanations, Leibniz remarks:

The way of final causes is easier, and yet is frequently of use in discovering important and
useful truths which it would take a long time to find by the other, more physical route.
Anatomy can provide significant examples of this. I also believe that Snell, who first

---

[1] For Leibniz and his predecessors, an a priori explanation of P explains why P is true, whereas an a posteriori one merely provides reason for thinking that P is true. Leibniz also came to use 'a priori' in the
sense of 'non-empirical'—the Kantian sense which is also ours, which he seems to have helped to create.
For a good exposition see Adams 1994: 109–10.

discovered the rules of refraction, would have been a long time in discovering them if he had first tried to find out how light is formed. But he apparently followed the method . . . of final causes. (*DM* 22, FW 75; see also SD, FW 163–4)

Snell's law says that when light passes from one translucent medium into another, there is—for any given pair of mediums—a constant relation between the sine of the angle of incidence and the sine of the angle of refraction. Leibniz says that this has the effect that light passing between different mediums always follows 'the easiest' or anyway the 'most determinate' way to pass from a given point in one medium to a given point in the other (1696, L 479). His long explanation of this has not helped me to see what Snell's law has to do with light's following the —est path from point A to point B, however the blank is filled. But an explanation by Feynman *et al.* (1963: 26.4) does seem to show that if light has different speeds in the two media, and if it always travels by the quickest route from a point in one to a point in the other, then its angle as it passes between them will conform to Snell's law (which Feynman attributes to Fermat).

   Snell offered his law in a paper which does not survive, and which Leibniz did not see. Leibniz published a supposed demonstration that Snell's law could be reached by asking 'What path for a light ray would be the easiest to get from A to B?', and he conjectured that Snell had arrived at it in that way. The ratio-of-sines principle was first published by Descartes, who sought to derive it mechanistically from a *mélange* of different points and principles, using a model involving tennis-balls, blankets, and more. Leibniz suspected that Descartes took the law from Snell without acknowledgement; and this accusation—the justice of which I cannot estimate—is relevant to his thesis about the usefulness of teleological thinking in physics. 'The demonstration Descartes attempted to give of this same theorem by way of efficient causes is not nearly as good' as the final-cause grounding for it, Leibniz writes (*DM* 22, FW 75); and he thinks it unlikely that the 'theorem' could have been discovered in any way but his:

Descartes's way of explaining the law of refraction by efficient causes . . . is extremely forced and too hard to understand. . . . It can easily be seen to be an afterthought adjusted somehow to the conclusion, and was not discovered by the method he gives. So we may well believe that we should not have had this beautiful discovery so soon without the method of final causes. (1696, L 480)

Leibniz is not here merely repeating his point that patterns in nature bring in teleology because they reveal God's purposes. He says that asking a teleological question could help one to *discover* Snell's law. Every time he reiterates that teleology can ('frequently') help one to do physics, he adduces this one example.

   Notice that the Leibnizian treatments of teleology that we have been looking at do not propose teleological explanations for individual events. One urges the physicist to remember his Maker; one says that animal structure is often hard to explain without reference to ends; and the third recommends thoughts about purposes as convenient—and perhaps practically essential—means to certain discoveries in physics. All these are consistent with Leibniz's reiterated view that everything that happens in the world of matter can be explained mechanistically. The only exception is the sentence about the first formation of animals.

(4) Leibniz's cherished formula—there are only monads, and in them there is only perception and appetite—implies that whatever happens in an individual monad is to be explained teleologically. If not, then the term 'appetite' is culpably idle and misleading. But Leibniz does not make good on this (§101), and indeed describes the successive unfolding of a monad's states in terms that seem to belong purely to efficient causation—that is, to 'mechanism' broadly conceived.

There is an intellectual debt here which Leibniz does not, and in my opinion could not, pay. When he is theorizing down at the basic monadic level, he does not loudly proclaim his commitment to final causes in the individual monad; but he does proclaim this sometimes when he is attending to the phenomenal level at which there are material bodies. In a doctrine which I shall examine more fully in §§120–1, Leibniz holds that each organic body is a 'machine' which gets a special kind of unity from its association with a single 'dominant monad'; so when he thinks about animals, he is attending at once to the phenomenal world of spatially extended matter and to the fundamentally real world of monads. Keeping these two in play together, he says that the former is to be explained in terms of efficient causes (mechanism), the latter in terms of final causes (teleology). So the scholastics were right in 'holding to indivisible forms' and to the teleology that goes with them, but they were wrong to invoke them to explain things that should be explained by mechanism:

Nature has, as it were, an empire within an empire, a double kingdom of reason and necessity—that is, of forms and of material particles—for just as all things are full of souls, they are also full of organic bodies. These kingdoms are governed each by its own law, with no confusion between them, and the cause of perception and appetite is no more to be sought in the modes of extension than is the cause of nutrition and other organic functions to be sought in the forms or souls. But [God] brings it about that two very different series in the same corporeal substance respond to each other and perfectly harmonize with each other. (CT, L 409–10)

Elsewhere Leibniz explicitly connects this with mechanism versus teleology: 'Souls act according to the laws of final causes, through appetition, ends and means. Bodies act according to the laws of efficient causes, or of motions. And these two realms, that of efficient causes and that of final causes, are in harmony' (Mon 79, FW 279).

Some philosophers today believe that some events can legitimately be explained both mechanistically and teleologically.[2] Leibniz sometimes sounds as though he agreed with this, but he does not. He wants to explain bodily events mechanistically and mental ones teleologically, so his position is irrelevant to the desire some of us have to explain a person's physical behaviour teleologically—

---

[2] See, e.g., Davidson 1963 and Dennett 1971. For an exploration of *how* the two sorts of explanation might both be valid for a single event, see Bennett 1976: 72–8 and 1991a.

that is, in terms of what he wanted to bring about. All Leibniz has is his faith in the 'harmony', according to which at the very moment when I (my soul) performs a want-an-apple act of the will, my hand is mechanistically caused to go out and close itself on an apple. For a close examination of this 'two realms' doctrine, in which it is shown to be tricky and dangerous, see Bennett 2001*b*.

108. An old myth about teleology

Let us accept that Snell's law is equivalent to the proposition that light passing between different mediums always follows the easiest path from A to B. Why should this 'easiest path' principle be accounted teleological? A similar question arises about a high-level thesis in Descartes's physics, affirmed by him in a letter to Clerselier and labelled by Garber as 'the principle of least modal change' (PLMC): 'When two bodies having incompatible modes collide . . . the change they undergo is always the least possible, that is, if they can become compatible by changing a certain quantity of these modes, a greater quantity of them will not be changed' (CSMK 247). Garber remarks that this 'is an obviously teleological principle' (1992: 247). This presumably stands or falls with the characterization of the 'easiest path' version of Snell's law as teleological. My question about the latter could equally be raised about the PLMC.

Returning to this thesis later in his book, Garber implicitly answers my question: 'It is often emphasized in the literature that the PLMC is a kind of teleological principle, that to justify using it in physics would force us to speculate about God's ends in creating the world, and attribute to God a desire to minimize certain physical magnitudes. That it would' (1992: 292). By parity of reasoning, I suppose, Leibniz's form of Snell's law is supposed to force us to attribute to God a desire to maximize the 'easiness' of the paths of light rays.

Well, the teleological nature of the PLMC may be 'often emphasized in the literature', but it is illusory. We can choose to treat the PLMC as showing God's desire to minimize certain magnitudes, but by that standard we can treat any law of physics as showing what God wants. Newton's gravitational law, for example, may show that God wants to bring it about that the relative acceleration between two otherwise isolated bodies varies inversely with the square of the distance between them; but it is not a teleological law, and does not 'force us' to attribute anything to God. Objection: 'Newton's law does not involve a superlative, but the other two do. Leibniz's version of Snell's law entails that the light takes the *easiest* path, and the PLMC says that colliding bodies change in the *least* possible way.' Yes, there is that difference, but what is teleological about superlatives?

Perhaps, then, the idea is that Snell's law and the PLMC each speaks of bodies' behaving in such a way that the resultant situation is thus-and-so. If the body dependably behaves *now* in a manner that leads to the obtaining of a certain state of affairs *later*, some kind of forward-lookingness seems to be involved; and this might seem to smack of teleology. But if this is teleology or an appearance of it, the ordinary behaviour of poured water also invites a teleological interpretation: water is poured into one end of a pool, someone draws a bucket of water out of the other end, and a beaver swims across the middle; millions of water molecules variously move in such ways that the *final state* of the pool's surface is a smooth plane at right angles to the line of gravity. Yet nobody, so far as I know, has claimed to detect a teleological pattern here.

Chapter 15

Harmony

109. The pre-established harmony

Which changes in a monad are 'perceived' by which other monads? Leibniz boldly replies that each monad at each moment perceives the entire universe, meaning that it perceives every state—and thus every change of state—of each other monad. This may seem madly excessive. Given his commitment to a basic metaphysic of monads and his rejection of transeunt causation, he needs to postulate *some* correlations between states of different monads, so as to account for the fact that fires seem to make kettles boil, bodies to change each others' velocities in collisions, and so on. But he is not called upon to postulate a universal pattern of correlation; the fire which boils my kettle does not seem to affect everything else in the universe. Similarly with perception as we ordinarily understand it: most things seem to perceive nothing, and even you and I seem to perceive only a tiny fragment of what is the case. Why, then, does Leibniz go so far?

It is because of his gradualism (§92). A limited harmony among the monads would require that lines be drawable between the monads that are, and those that are not, 'harmoniously' related to a particular monadic change; and that would be anathema to Leibniz, because of his metaphysical vision of a world which at bottom is qualitatively smooth. The gradualism which leads him to hold that all monads are on a continuum with minds also leads him to contend that any change in any monad is reflected in—expressed by—changes in every other: 'Every individual created substance exerts physical action and passion on all the others. From a change made in one, some corresponding change follows in all the others' (PT, AG 33). The term 'follows' is meant quasi-causally: 'In metaphysical rigor, what we call causes are only concurrent requisites.'

Leibniz's cast of mind does not allow him a cut-off point between monadic states that are and ones that are not reflected in a given monad. He is a gradualist not only about how the world varies qualitatively, but also about what happens in it. 'Every natural change happens by degrees', he writes (Mon 13, FW 269). In a charming passage, he admits seemingly discontinuous happenings: 'The beauty of nature, which insists upon perceptions which stand out from one another, asks for the appearance of jumps and for musical cadences (so to speak) amongst phenomena' (NE 473). But that is only appearance, he assures us. In reality: 'In nature everything happens by degrees, and nothing by jumps; and this rule about change is one part of my law of continuity.'

Because of this 'law of continuity', Leibniz holds that a change in one monad which produces a change in another will produce some change in every monad. (Throughout this discussion, 'produce', 'effect', etc. are all to be understood in their 'quasi-' senses.) In the radiating out of effects from this change, there cannot be a cut-off point with some effects on this side of it and none on the other. Leibniz thinks that this fits with things we believe—or ought to believe—independently of his metaphysic. Shortly after a passage recently quoted, Leibniz writes: 'This is in agreement with our experience of nature. For in a vessel filled with a liquid (and the whole universe is just such a vessel) motion made in the middle is propagated to the edges, although it is rendered more and more insensible the more it recedes from its origin' (AG 33). In the material world, he is saying, experience shows us that each event produces changes throughout the rest of the universe, and that is the appearance to us of the underlying fact that every change in any monad is reflected in every other.

Does our experience of nature show us that? We may agree about the ripples in a bowl of liquid, but when we are told that the whole universe is an example of this, we should pause. Leibniz, however, evidently expects us to come to agree with him when we have reflected on our experience. He thinks (I conjecture) that we shall be led his way by the likes of this:

> If you drop a stone into the middle of the Atlantic Ocean, it will make an easily visible ripple for a few inches out, a barely visible one for a bit further, and the further you get from the stone the smaller and thus less perceptible will be the change it makes. As the distance increases, the size of the effect will lessen proportionately. It follows that even at the African shore that dropping of the stone makes *some* difference, though that far away it will be really tiny. At even greater distances, on a distant star for example, it will be smaller still. But it makes sense to suppose that there is always some difference. There would be something arbitrary and not fully intelligible if there were, at some point in the journey out from where the stone was dropped, a change from some difference to none rather than from a tiny difference to a still tinier one.

That is all in terms of 'distances', and thus it pertains to the level of appearance. But the appearance is 'well founded'—that is, based on something at the monadic level—and Leibniz thinks that it must be based on the principle of monads' universal, unconstrained 'perception' of one another.

In one respect, (1) the underlying monadic thesis is not a snug fit with (2) the thesis that effects may gradually lessen but never fade away to nothing. According to 1, every monad's state is correlated with the *synchronous* states of all the other monads, whereas the natural way to take 2 is as saying that any change in one thing *eventually* makes a difference in each other thing.

In another respect, 1 is vastly stronger than it needs to be to underpin 2. Although 2 entails that when I snap my fingers, that event will make a difference to what goes on at certain place 1,500 miles away—it does not entail that the difference could not have come about in any other way; so it does not entail that a study of that place, by someone with archangelic keenness of perception and knowledge of science, would reveal that I have snapped my fingers. My gesture made a difference there, but so did every other part of the universe, and the piling up of those differences could easily obliterate some of the signs. This contrasts starkly with (1) the thesis that every monad perceives every other. According to this, each monad underlying the contents of the distant place I am talking about is in some state from which all the contemporaneous facts about all the monads underlying my finger-snap could in principle be read off by someone knowing the general principles that govern the 'harmony'. That is what Leibniz means when he says that each of the former set of monads *perceives* each of the latter set.

Consider the following possible-world story. Though not Leibnizian, it makes my general point that 'Everything that happens affects everything else' does not entail that the way each thing is contains reliable signs of how everything else is:

> There is a universe consisting of atoms floating in a Euclidean container space, and subject to Newton's gravitational law in an analogue way: the further the difference, the smaller the gravitational tug; and there are no minima, so that every movement of every body makes *some* difference to every other, however distant. However remote body B_2 is from body B_1, if B_1 had not moved as it did (and everything else had been just the same), B_2 would not have moved exactly as it did.

This satisfies (2) the condition of universality of causal influence. But this could be a universe in which huge amounts of information are lost. Suppose we know that at a certain moment B_2 slowed down slightly while continuing to move along a certain determinate straight line: although this was the precise result of movements by some other body or bodies, there need be no indications in B_2 of what bodies or how they moved. The events in B_2 encode information about the resultant at the place of B_2 of their various gravitational forces, but those events do not select any one out of the countless ways of producing that resultant.

110. The mirror and collapse problems

According to Leibniz, each quality of a monad is a perception: the entire history of a monad can in principle be told by recounting its perceptual state at each time. This has led some Leibniz scholars to think that he is confronted by what I call the 'mirror' problem. Here is how Lotze stated it a century ago:

Perception . . . is the general activity of all monads; but *what* do they perceive? You will hardly find an answer in Leibniz; the monads, each of them from its own point of view, mirror the universe, but the universe itself consists only of other monads. . . . Therefore, what each monad can reflect is only the way in which it itself is reflected in others and these are reflected in one another; there would be *no independent state of affairs or content in the universe* to serve as grist for this process of reflection. (Quoted in Mates 1986: 79)

Mark Brown tells me that apparently consistent set theories have been developed in which two sets can be members of one another. This might provide a model for a solution of the mirror problem; it seems more promising than the elaborate one offered by Mates (1986: 78–83). But there is a less drastic way out than either of these.

The 'problem' assumes that when a monad has perception P, the whole fact of the matter consists in the representative content of P. But that is not Leibniz's view. P is a perception of x, he holds, if P is a *monadic* (= non-relational) state which is correlated with some state of x through dependable general regularities in events. These regularities must be statable (in principle) in non-representative terms: they correlate the intrinsic, non-relational states of one monad with those of another; the representative content of these states results from the correlations, and so cannot be what is correlated in the first place.

So the mirror problem is too easily solvable to count as a genuine problem. Leibniz's ontological ground floor contains monads that have clusters of intrinsic qualities; these count as perceptions only because of how they correlate with one another; so their status as perceptions is derivative, not basic. The basic story—the 'content in the universe' that Lotze demanded—is the totality of facts about the intrinsic states of the individual monads.

In one place, Leibniz seems to undercut my defence of him on this point. Making the point that a substance can have no parts yet many qualities, he throws in the remark that the qualities 'must consist in the variety of its relations to things outside it' (PNG 2, FW 259). That is ominous, and it becomes worse when he adds: 'like the way in which in a centre, or a point, although it is completely simple, there is an infinity of angles formed by the lines which meet in it'. This suggests that we shall get a better grasp of how a simple substance can be qualitatively complex if we grasp that the qualities in question are all relations to other things—like the angles at a point.

This makes the qualitative complexity of a monad depend upon the multitude of other things that it perceives, which reverses the account I have given, and revives the mirror problem. It is an odd performance, because Leibniz could have made his point about the qualitative complexity of a simple substance without mentioning representation; all he need do is to distinguish parts from qualities—no parts, many qualities—like Descartes saying that the mind has no parts, many faculties (§28). Anyway, the passage is an aberration, a slip. By making a monad's modifications supervene on its relations to other things, Leibniz contradicts his own doctrine that all relational truths are made true by conjunctions of underlying monadic truths (§135); he contradicts his statement that 'every soul is like a world apart, independent of every other thing except God' (AG 76), and he contradicts his own account of what he means by 'expression' and 'perception' (§98).

Leibniz's metaphysic is thought by some to be confronted also by what I call the collapse problem, which I now explain. Obviously, the metaphysic would be useless if it did not allow that some monads are qualitatively unlike some others. Indeed, given Leibniz's acceptance of the principle of discernibility of the diverse (§142), every monad must be unlike every other. But then there is thought to be trouble (I am not quoting):

According to Leibniz, there is nothing to any monad except its perceptions of other monads. Furthermore, each monad represents *all* the other monads. So the representative story that one tells is exactly the same as the representative story that each other tells; the stories are the same; so the monads are indiscernible; so there is only one monad.

The problem, in short, is to find a way for Leibniz to prevent the monads from being indistinguishable from one another and thus—by the identity of indiscernibles—collapsing into one.

What solves the mirror problem also dissolves the collapse problem. Suppose that some state of x's is a perception of some item z, and that a state of y's is also a perception of z. It does not follow that these are the same state. They might be profoundly different, having in common only that each is correlated with z in such a way as to count as a perception of it—just as certain facts about local droughts and floods might be encoded in tree-rings, mud deposits, and a diary. The crucial point, which also served to (dis)solve the mirror problem, is that the states of the monads are *basically intrinsic,* and *only derivatively representational.*

111. The points of view of monads

Leibniz's own solution for the collapse problem includes that one, but enriches it with further detail. When two monads perceive a third, he says, they will be unalike in how distinctly they perceive it. That is one way for them to be intrinsically unalike, and Leibniz seems for some reason to put all his eggs in that basket.

This solution has been espoused by many Leibniz scholars. For it to succeed, the concept of distinctness of perception must be defended in Leibnizian terms. I postpone that until §124, so that I can first display most of the load that Leibniz makes this concept carry. But there is no need to delay discussing a neighbouring concept: namely, that of a monad's points of view:

Just as the same town when seen from different sides will seem quite different and is as it were multiplied perspectivally, in the same way it happens that, because of the infinite multitude of simple substances, it is as if there were as many different universes; but they are all perspectives on the same one, according to the different points of view of each monad. (Mon 57, FW 275)[1]

----

[1] See also *DM* 9, FW 61.

Each monad has points of view at different times, but I shall limit the discussion to some one time, assigning to each monad a single point of view.

The concept of 'point of view' makes the metaphysical picture easier to grasp, in two ways. (1) The theory is that each monad represents the entire universe, but no monad is just like any other; and we get intuitive help with that from the thought of seeing one thing variously from different angles. (2) The totality of facts about the states of the monads is the ground-floor reality which appears to us as (among other things) a spatially organized material world; for this to be so, one might think, the world of monads must include something isomorphic to a spatial structure; and Leibniz provides this by assigning each monad its own unique point of view:

Because of the plenitude of the world everything is linked, and every body acts to a greater or lesser extent on every other body according to its distance, and is affected by it in return. It therefore follows that every monad is a living mirror . . . which represents the universe in accordance with its own point of view and is as orderly as the universe itself. (PNG 3, FW 259)

What is a monad's point of view? Leibniz does not think that monads are literally at distances from one another, because he assigns all spatiality to the level of 'well-founded appearance' or to the even less basic level of the 'ideal' (AG 338). So a monad's point of view is not a point in space. Leibniz writes to Arnauld that 'each individual substance expresses the entire universe in its own way and according to a certain relation, or, so to speak, in accordance with the point of view from which it regards it' (FW 112). The phrase 'so to speak' proclaims that 'point of view' is a metaphor.

Then what are points of view if they are not literally points? All we know so far is that a monad's point of view is linked with how distinctly x perceives this or that part of the universe. I believe Leibniz means this link to be conceptual: a monad's point of view is a logical construct out of the distinctness of its perceptions, not a further differentiating fact about it. 'Point of view emerges as an end product of perception, and is to be explained as a structural feature of the entire perceptual field of the monad' (Earman 1977: 227). This spares Leibniz two problems that would arise if Rescher (for instance) were right in holding that for Leibniz monads are distinguished from one another in two ways: by differences in point of view and by differences in distinctness of perception. (See Rescher 1967: 63; also Broad 1975: 98–9.) This would require him to explain what points of view are if they are logically independent of facts about distinctness of perceptions, and to explain what correlates them with patterns of distinctness and confusedness of perceptions. Leibniz ignores both 'problems', I suggest, because they do not exist.

I conclude that when Leibniz is theorizing about monads, terms such as 'closest' and 'point of view' are metaphors, and do not stand for anything that can explain facts about distinctness of perceptions. (For a strong case for most of this, see Cover and Hartz 1994.) This fits Leibniz's 'so to speak' way of introducing the phrase to Arnauld, and with his always writing of a monad as perceiving things 'according to' and never 'from' its point of view. In contexts that are clearly spatial, as in seeing a town from different viewpoints, he uses 'from' (French *de*, Latin *ex*); but for monadic points of view he always uses the French *suivant* or *selon*, or the Latin *secundum*. The many passages in AG and L (and three in FW) which conflict with this are all mistranslations.

When we plunge into the deep chilly waters of 'distinctness', we shall at least not have to be wary of a shark called 'point of view'.

My interpretation does not fit well with Leibniz's writing that a given monad's perceptions 'can be distinct . . . only for things that are either the closest or the largest in relation to' the monad in question (Mon 60, FW 276). This seems to separate distinctness logically from closeness and thus, presumably, from 'point of view'; and that is awkward for the account I have given. However, although at this point in 'Monadology' Leibniz's topic is monads, I conjecture that he is already looking ahead to the material things which he explicitly introduces in his next section. If I am right, and he is thinking of a monad's perceptions not only of other monads but of bodies, then he is operating partly at the phenomenal level at which closeness is literal, spatial. What else could make sense of a perceived thing's being 'large'? The notion of a thing's being 'large in relation to [a] monad' is peculiar, but not only on my interpretation.

In a formidable paper, Catherine Wilson (1999: 379–80) offers that 'closest or largest' passage as a ground for attributing to Leibniz the view that the distance between two bodies is inversely proportional to how distinctly the grounding monads of each perceive those of the other. (Her other evidence is weaker: it is Leibniz's saying that each soul perceives the body which it dominates 'more immediately' than it does anything else.) She shows that Leibniz is in deep trouble if he correlates distance simply with distinctness; for one thing, this would imply that higher monads are spatially close to many things, while low-grade ones are distant from everything! It seems reasonable, though, to see Leibniz as not meaning as a matter of doctrine to relate distinctness to distance in that simple way, and to have held merely that the phenomenal distance between two bodies is grounded *somehow* in facts about the distinctness of the perceptions of the monads of which they are appearances.

112. Forward signs and traces

Leibniz holds that someone who knew all the general principles of the pre-established harmony and the whole truth about the present state of one monad could infer the whole truth about the present state of every other monad. As if that were not enough, he strengthens it in two ways which I shall introduce separately, though he usually fuses them.

(1) As an explanatory rationalist, Leibniz had to be a determinist, holding that whatever happens at a given time is deterministically caused to happen by

preceding states, events, and processes. Add to that his restriction of causation to the immanent variety, and you get the result that each episode in the history of any monad is an inevitable upshot of previous episodes, which in their turn were . . . and so on. So the state of any monad at a given moment causally determines the whole of its subsequent history: if you knew the relevant causal laws, and knew exactly what the monad's state is now, you could 'read off' its entire future history. 'Since every present state of a simple substance is a natural consequence of its preceding state, the present is big with the future' (Mon 22, FW 271; see also *DM* 14, FW 67).

Laplace said that a perfectly equipped observer could predict the future of the universe if he knew enough about its present state. He had to take the universe as a whole, because he thought that things interact. Leibniz reached Laplace's conclusion by way of something stronger. According to him, the Laplacean predictor could foretell the whole future of any substance within the universe by attending only to it, having no need to attend to other substances, because they are powerless to affect that one. Add to this the universal synchronous harmony, and you get the result that the predictor could foretell the whole future of the universe by attending to only one substance; its state at T carries the information about every other monad's state at T, and standard determinism takes it from there.

(2) While Leibniz's determinism committed him to this doctrine of perfectly informative forward signs, there is no such obvious source for a second thesis which he often ran in harness with that one; namely, that every event in a substance's history leaves 'legible' traces in it for ever after. From a monad's state at any given time, he held, its past history can be read off:

> 'Each soul retains all its previous impressions . . . Within each substance there is a perfect bond between the future and the past' (*NE* 114).
> 'In my view, every individual substance always contains traces of everything that has ever happened to it and marks of what will ever happen to it' (AG 71).
> 'Every soul . . . holds in its substance traces of everything that happens to it' (AG 76).

This is the temporal dual of the preceding doctrine. Leibniz commonly offers the two as a pair, as in a passage just quoted and another to come in a moment.

Often, indeed, when he writes of how each monad mirrors the whole universe, Leibniz seems to be combining the three doctrines—synchronous mirroring, forward signs, and traces. This triad entails that the complete state of any one monad at any moment contains the whole news about the entire present, future, and past history of the universe. Although he is not explicit about it, I think this is what Leibniz means here: 'The present is big with the future and burdened with the past, all things harmonize, and eyes as piercing as God's could read in the lowliest substance the universe's whole sequence of events' (*NE* 55; see also FW 119). He sees this as a strength in his philosophical system. He seems to think it an obvious defect in the Democritean metaphysic that atoms could not be big with the past and future of the world.

We understand the synchronous harmony and the determinism, but why the doctrine of indelible traces? Determinism does not imply it, and Leibniz's confidence about it needs to be explained. The explanatory rationalist frame of mind that turns philosophers into determinists has no tendency to imply the temporal converse of determinism. Some systems of physics, perhaps including Leibniz's, are in some way temporally symmetrical, and I do not know what to make of this fact; but I do not believe that decently informed determinist physicists in the seventeenth century would or should have believed that *it is causally impossible for information to be lost from the universe*. In §109 I sketched a Newtonian universe which is strictly deterministic but which loses information all the time. That was to show that deterministic causal influence can spread throughout the universe without each thing's being informed about each other; but it also secures my present point that causation could be deterministic without each substance's retaining indelible traces of its whole past. At an abstract enough level these are the same point.

Perhaps Leibniz thought his doctrine of traces to be inseparable from his doctrine of forward signs: 'Since every ordered series involves a rule for continuing, or a law of progression, God, by examining any part of the series whatsoever, sees in it everything that precedes and everything that follows' (AG 102). Presumably he means that God can do this by looking at one 'part of the series' and knowing the rule of progression. This is right so far as continuing the series is concerned ('everything that follows'): knowing the rule is knowing how to go forward from any given place in the series. That in turn involves knowing some way of getting to where you are, but must there be only one way of getting there ('everything that precedes')? John O'Leary-Hawthorne has given me this rule for generating a number series, which is which is determinate in the forward but not the backward direction:

If x = 20 or less, x's successor = x + 2
If x > 20, x's successor = x + 1.

Start at 2 and that rule gives: 2, 4, 6, 8, 10, 12, 14, 16, 18, 20, 22, 23, 24, . . .
Start at 3 and the rule gives: 3, 5, 7, 9, 11, 13, 15, 17, 19, 21, 22, 23, 24, . . .
It would be nice to have one that is backward-indeterminate at every locus; but this example suffices to make my general point.

Here is another suggestion. Leibniz needs a lot of (nearly) synchronous harmony to underpin transeunt quasi-causation at the phenomenal level; similarly, he needs some monads sometimes to contain traces of some of their past states, to underpin traces and quasi-traces at the phenomenal level. And, just as the synchronous harmony had to be total because Leibniz would not draw any line that would limit it, so too the traces must be universal: every monad must at all times contain traces of all its past states, because there is no reasonable way of stopping short of that. I find this use of gradualism less persuasive than the other. Without drawing any fundamental lines, one would think, Leibniz could allow that as a monad's history unfolds, its successive states tend to erase traces of some of its earlier ones. Still, this may be one cause of his belief in perfect traces.

113. Why Leibniz needs insensible perceptions

Leibniz intended his doctrine of traces to underpin, among other things, memory. (In treating our memories as causal upshots of our previous states, he anticipated the causal theory of memory which seems not to have become common property until it was fully developed in Deutscher and Martin 1966.) A conspicuous fact about human memory is how much we forget, and Leibniz needs to reconcile this with his doctrine that each monad at each moment contains traces of every fact about its past. He does this by maintaining that we are not aware of all our mental states; my mind contains a trace of my first experience of eating a grape or rolling on grass, but I have forgotten those episodes—I have no memory 'strictly so called' of them—because I am not consciously aware of the traces of them which I carry:

> Memory is sometimes not possible, because of the multitude of past and present impressions which jointly contribute to our present thoughts; for I believe that each of a man's thoughts has some effect, if only a confused one, or leaves some trace which mingles with the thoughts which follow it. One may forget many things, but one could also retrieve them, much later, if one were brought back to them in the right way. (*NE* 114–15)[2]

This brings us to Leibniz's belief in 'insensible' mental states: that is, ones whose owner is unaware of them.

The difference between sensible and insensible perceptions is one of degree, and primarily—as the above passage hints—of degree of distinctness/confusion. Leibniz holds that although my complete past is perceived in my present state, many of those perceptions are too confused for me to be consciously aware of them; others are distinct enough for me to be sharply aware of them; and these two groups shade into each other. Gradualism still reigns. The distinct/confused continuum will be discussed in §§124–5. In the mean time, get used to the association of 'confused' with 'insensible' or not subject to conscious awareness.

Leibniz's belief in unconscious mental contents marks him off from all his approximate contemporaries, especially Descartes, for whom the mind's transparency to itself was definitive of mentality (§26). Locke came close to this in a comment on the suggestion that a mind might have content of which it is not aware (does not 'perceive'): 'It seem[s] to me near a contradiction to say that there are truths imprinted on the soul which it perceives or understands not; imprinting, if it signify anything, being nothing else but the making certain truths to be perceived' (*Essay* I.ii.5). Something akin to the Descartes–Locke

---

[2] For memory 'strictly so called', see *NE* 107.

position on the mind's transparency was fairly common currency until the time of Freud; but Leibniz was an exception.

Conscious awareness is what the secondary literature usually calls 'apperception', but the use of this word is historically and linguistically insensitive, and orthographically comic. In Leibniz's day the verb phrase *s'apercevoir de* meant 'to be aware of', as it still does, but French had no cognate noun. Nor did English, which acquired 'awareness' two centuries later. Wanting such a noun, Leibniz coined *aperception*—except that at that time it was given two p's, like many other French words that now have only one. Retaining the second is like writing 'specifick' when discussing Locke's views about specific names and ideas. But we do not need this French word at all; there was nothing technical, obscure, or specialized about it; its form and meaning were tied to a familiar everyday phrase; and the correct English translation is 'awareness'.[3] Now down to business.

Without the doctrine of 'insensible perceptions', Leibniz's metaphysic would be refuted by plain facts of experience. I have mentioned its role in reconciling his extreme doctrine of traces with the weakness of our memories; and it performs a similar service for his theories about the scope of the synchronous 'harmony' and of forward signs. Insensible perceptions save Leibniz's metaphysic from implying that every mind is plainly omniscient. If all perceptions were within reach of our awareness, he writes, 'every monad would be divine' (Mon 60, FW 276). Each monad stretches to infinity through what it represents, but is brought back to finitude by the facts about what it is aware of: 'Monads are limited not in what objects they know but in how they know them. Monads all reach confusedly to infinity, to everything; but they are limited and differentiated by their level of distinct perception' (ibid.).

The thesis that a monad can have perceptions of which it is not aware is needed for another reason as well. Set aside the problems regarding the scope of the synchronous harmony, the determinism, and the doctrine of indelible traces, and Leibniz is still forced into insensible perceptions by his thesis that the material world is the appearance of monads whose states are perceptions. The key in my hand is the appearance to me of an infinity of substances each of which has an infinity of perceptions. So most of those perceptions are ones of which their owners are unaware, the alternative being an intolerably extreme panpsychism, implying that the tiniest portion of mud is the appearance of an infinity of beings each of which is aware of its condition and ongoing history.

Spinoza, incidentally, also needs there to be unconscious mental events, for a reason that overlaps Leibniz's. Though he does not cram into finite minds as much information as Leibniz does, Spinoza does say that your mind has

---

[3] This view of the word's origin is endorsed by Kulstad (1991: 22–3), though he retains the archaic barbarism 'apperception' in his title and text. His book offers a learned discussion of the place of awareness and self-awareness in the work of Leibniz and of Locke. McRae (1976: 32) holds that Leibniz was doing more than merely coining a noun; but that is because he thinks that *s'apercevoir de* means the same as *apercevoir*, 'to perceive'. Gennaro (1999: 358) sticks to 'apperception', without mentioning the etymological case against it, because he thinks that 'awareness' does not fit smoothly enough into a theory of his about what the phenomenon is.

complexities which mirror all the events in your body. That is more than you are aware of, therefore . . . etc. But Spinoza makes no provision for meeting this theoretical need of his, and seems not to be properly aware that he has it.

114. How Leibniz recommends insensible perceptions

Leibniz is strikingly unapologetic in contending that there are insensible perceptions. Apparently he did not feel the tug of the other view. He seems somehow to have escaped, right from the start of his philosophical career, approaching mentality in the manner of Descartes and Locke—that is, starting with the thought of his own mind as immediately *given* to him, the afterthought being: given whole and entire. He seems to have thought of minds rather in an external or third-person manner, taking them as substances endowed with certain powers and properties. Nothing in this conception of the mind enforces self-awareness. This difference of stance appears dramatically when, silently taking it for granted that plenty of things can exist when nobody is aware of them, Leibniz says that Locke needs to show that 'thought in particular' cannot (*NE* 113).

In any case, he maintains, there is abundant empirical evidence that human minds have insensible perceptions. It is partly scientific: 'Insensible perceptions are as important to pneumatology [= psychology] as insensible corpuscles are to natural science, and it is just as unreasonable to reject the one as the other on the pretext that they are beyond the reach of our senses' (*NE* 56). 'Hundreds of indications lead us to conclude that at every moment there is in us an infinity of perceptions . . . of which we are unaware because they are either too minute and too numerous, or else too unvarying, so that they are not sufficiently distinctive on their own' (*NE* 53). Later on, Leibniz confronts Locke's challenge to the view that some mental states are not noticed, saying scornfully: 'It is as though someone were to ask, these days, how we know about insensible particles' (*NE* 117).

Just before that put-down, Leibniz objects to the dogmatism of those who 'deny that anything happens in the soul of which we are not aware', and brings a reason against them: 'Anything which is noticeable must be made up of parts which are not: nothing, whether thought or motion, can come into existence suddenly.' So he invokes his event-gradualism as an aid to his view that the scientific smart money is on unconscious mental states. Here it is again:

Nothing takes place suddenly, and it is one of my great and best confirmed maxims that nature never makes leaps . . . [which] implies that any change from small to large, or vice versa, passes through something which is intermediate in respect of degrees as well as of parts; and that no motion ever springs immediately from a state of rest, or passes into one except through a lesser motion . . . All of which supports the judgment that noticeable perceptions arise by degrees from ones which are too minute to be noticed. (*NE* 56–7)

How is gradualism supposed to help the case for perceptions of which one is not aware? The answer can be gathered from Leibniz's discussion of hearing the roar of the sea:

To hear this noise as we do, we must hear the parts which make up this whole, that is the noise of each wave, although each of these little noises makes itself known only when combined confusedly with all the others, and would not be noticed if the wave which made it were by itself. We must be affected slightly by the motion of this wave, and have some perception of each of these noises, however faint they may be; otherwise there would be no perception of a hundred thousand waves, since a hundred thousand nothings cannot make something. (*NE* 54)

I have more respect for this argument than I used to, though it does require the gradualism, which I do not believe.

Leibniz also argues for insensible perceptions with help from his Spinozist thesis that the events in anyone's mind must mirror all the events in his body:

There is always a perfect correspondence between the body and the soul . . . I even maintain that something happens in the soul corresponding to the circulation of the blood and to every internal movement of the viscera, although one is unaware of such happenings . . . If during sleep or waking there were impressions in the body which did not touch or affect the soul in any way at all, there would have to be limits to the union of body and soul, as though bodily impressions needed a certain shape or size if the soul was to be able to feel them. And that is indefensible if the soul is incorporeal, for there is no relation of proportion between an incorporeal substance and this or that modification of matter. (*NE* 116)

Notice that Leibniz does not here say that every event in my body is mirrored by one in my mind because my mind is a monad and therefore reflects everything that happens anywhere. Rather, he starts from what he thinks to be a commonplace of our experience: we know quite well that some bodily events are echoed in our minds; well, if some are, they all must be, because there is no proportionality between bodies and minds, which means that there is no *reasonable* basis upon which God could draw a line separating bodily events which have mental echoes from ones which do not.

With that in hand, Leibniz argues afresh for insensible perceptions: 'There is always a perfect correspondence between the body and the soul, and I use bodily impressions of which one is not aware, whether in sleep or waking states, to prove that there are similar impressions in the soul.'

Chapter 16

Animals that Think

115. Leibniz against thinking matter

Leibniz was passionately concerned to discredit the thesis that some material things think. Locke, silently snubbing Descartes's two arguments purporting to prove the contrary, recommends agnosticism on the question. Indeed, 'Can material things think?' is his favourite example of a seemingly simple question to which we probably cannot know the answer. Leibniz disliked this attitude, and told friends that his main purpose in writing the *New Essays* was to oppose Locke's tolerance of thinking matter. Nicholas Jolley (1984) has used this as an organizing idea in understanding that work as a whole. His interpretations are always interesting and helpful, and he makes a surprisingly strong case for the view that the *New Essays* is driven by this one concern. Yet I am not convinced: I cannot overcome the fact that Locke has only one rather agnostic section on the topic, and Leibniz offers only a page or two of response to it. I do not know what to make of Leibniz's own testimony about his purposes. Anyway, there is plenty of evidence that he hated the thesis that matter thinks. That antipathy is my present topic.

Why did he care? In the background is the common view that if the soul—the thing that thinks—is material, then it can have no guarantee of immortality; for any material system can be destroyed through natural processes, by being dissipated, dismantled into smaller parts. We find this in Descartes's *Discourse on the Method*, where he alludes to 'the arguments which prove that our soul is of a nature entirely independent of the body, and consequently that it is not bound to die with it'. He does not treat this as a proof of immortality, saying merely that 'since we cannot see any other causes which destroy the soul, we are naturally led to conclude that it is immortal' (*Method* 5, CSM 1:141). This theme turns up again in the Synopsis to the *Meditations*, where Descartes writes that in the ensuing work he lays the foundations for arguments about the immortality of the soul. His account of what can be inferred is suitably modest: 'These arguments are enough to show that the decay of the body does not imply the destruction of the mind, and are hence enough to give mortals the hope of an after-life' (CSM 2:10). To take the further step to the conclusion that 'the mind is immortal by its very nature', he continues, 'we need to know that absolutely all substances . . . are by their nature incorruptible and cannot ever cease to exist unless they are reduced to nothingness by God's denying his concurrence to them'. He does not deny that God could—as Mersenne suggested—'endow the mind with just so much strength and existence as to ensure that it came to an end with the death of the body' (Obj 2, CSM 2:91). 'I admit that I cannot refute what you say,' Descartes replied, because he was not willing to use human reason to limit what God could do. Still, he went on, 'We have no convincing evidence . . . that any substance can perish; and this entitles us to conclude that the mind, in so far as it can be known by natural philosophy, is immortal' (Rep 2, CSM 2:109).

Leibniz announces a similar stand. The annihilation of a mind or monad is not absolutely impossible, according to him, but it would be miraculous: 'I believe that the immortality of the soul would be very improbable if one destroyed its immateriality, and if sensation could be produced and destroyed in matter as one of its modifications. After that it would need a miracle to make it subsist or revive' (quoted in Jolley 1984: 22). Leibniz's complex attitude to miracles, and his shifting standards for what counts as miraculous, create a mysterious and boring maze which I decline to enter.[1] I focus on the part of his position that he shares with Descartes: any structured material thing can be destroyed by being dissipated or deprived of structure through the ordinary movements of material particles; and there is no comparable scenario for the destruction of a thing that has no parts.

Actually, Leibniz holds that animal bodies are not naturally destroyed (§122). He alludes to 'the preservation of the soul—or rather, on my view, of the animal', and writes that the Cartesians gave themselves avoidable troubles because they 'failed to hit on the idea of the preservation of the animal in miniature' (NE 58, 67). However, in his metaphysic the continuing existence of an organism requires the continuation of its dominant monad (§121); and the indestructibility of that depends on its not being material.

116. The grounding principle again

The issue over thinking matter can be expressed as a pair of options about what it is to be a thinking animal like you and me. According to Descartes and Leibniz,

(1) A thinking animal is a material body specially associated with an immaterial mind which is a distinct substance.

According to the believer in thinking matter,

A thinking animal is a wholly material thing which thinks.

Leibniz argues for 1 by arguing against the latter thesis, which he does by splitting it into two sub-cases and disputing them separately:

---

[1] For a guide through the tangle, see Adams 1994: 81–102. For a resolute inquest into how Leibniz's tolerance of miracles complicates—and, I think, damages—his philosophy, see Kulstad 1993.

(2) A thinking animal is wholly material, and its thoughts have been simply added to it by God without arising from the rest of its nature.

(3) A thinking animal is wholly material, and its thoughts result in a natural way from the interplay of some or all of its parts.

So the argumentative structure is a trilemma: there are three rival stories about what thinking animals are; 2 and 3 are refuted, so 1 carries the day. The structure of the argument emerges when Leibniz, after dispatching 3, writes: 'So sense and thought are not something which is natural to matter, and there are only two ways in which they could occur in it: [1] through God's combining it with a substance to which thought is natural, or [2] through his putting thought into it by a miracle' (*NE* 67). In this section I shall discuss Leibniz's case against (2) the view that thought is brute-factually added to the animal's material nature.

To get a handle on this, let us look briefly at Locke's agnosticism about whether any matter thinks. Locke worked with a substantialist picture in which a bare substance can support properties of any kind, and a property-dualist picture in which properties fall into two sorts, pertaining to mind and matter respectively, with no logical commerce between the two. So, he thought, nothing could make it absolutely impossible that matter should think; for matter to think is just for a thing to have a bunch of properties of one kind and a further bunch of a quite unrelated kind.[2] So the question 'Does any matter think?' is not like 'Are any cannibals carnivorous?' or 'Are any cannibals vegetarians?'—which can be answered just by thinking about them—but rather like 'Are any cannibals short-sighted?' Except that the last can be settled empirically, whereas Locke could think of no evidence that would decide between 'A human is or has an immaterial thinking substance' and 'A human is a material thing which thinks'.

So he writes: 'We know not . . . to what sort of substances the Almighty has been pleased to give that power [of thinking], which cannot be in any created thing but merely by the good pleasure and bounty of the creator' (*Essay* 541:5). He thinks of this 'good pleasure' as a perfectly free choice, unconstrained by reasons. Later on he calls it arbitrary: 'The original rules and communication of motion being such wherein we can discover no natural connexion with any ideas we have, we cannot but ascribe them to the arbitrary will and good pleasure of the wise architect' (560:1). In his day, 'arbitrary' could be used merely to express dependency on someone's choice, without implying that the choice is groundless or capricious; and Locke's phrase 'the wise architect' suggests that he meant it in that way. The French *arbitraire*, on the other hand, carried an unavoidable implication of groundlessness; and that is how Leibniz understood Locke.

In §72 I quoted Leibniz saying that this 'good pleasure' of the creator 'would indeed be neither good nor pleasure if God's power did not perpetually run par-

---

[2] That is how Leibniz understood Locke's position, and I am inclined to agree with M. D. Wilson (1979b, 1982)—against Ayers (1981; 1991: ii.144–5)—that Leibniz got it right. See Stuart 1998 for a case for siding with Wilson about this aspect of Locke's thought, while not agreeing with her that this put Locke in conflict with a mechanism to which he was also deeply committed.

allel to his wisdom'—that is, if there were not reasons for God's choices. The suggestion that God might act without a reason is not only impious, he thinks, but is also objectionable at an even deeper level, conflicting with Leibniz's confident belief that there is a true and explanatory answer to every why-question. Perhaps the deepest difference between the two men is that Locke countenances absolutely brute facts, whereas Leibniz hates the thought of them.

Recall Leibniz's grounding principle (§103): 'Whenever we find some quality in a subject, we ought to believe that if we understood the nature of both the subject and the quality we would conceive how the quality could arise from it. . . . God will never give to substances any qualities that . . . cannot arise from their nature as explicable modifications' (NE 66). Of the many tasks that this performs for Leibniz, I reported two: it supports his rejection of attractive forces, and leads him to speculate that our sensory qualia have unnoticed features which are isomorphic to movements within our bodies. Now we meet a third: the grounding principle dislodges Locke's view of God as giving things a material nature and then arbitrarily loading them with mentalistic properties as well.

A wrinkle should be ironed out. The grounding principle must say that all the non-basic properties of a thing must be explicable through its *basic* properties, the latter being ungrounded. Well, given that a thing's basic nature includes its being material, why should it not *also* include its being mental? Granted the property-dualist assumption that neither is reducible to the other, could not a single thing have both? Leibniz would reply that it would be disorderly and unreasonable for God to give a substance two basic natures connected only by belonging to a single substance. What is intolerable in Locke's position, he would say, is its supposing that a thing might be both material and thinking without these two being interrelated in any of their details; and this is not made better by the plea that each of these natures of the thing is basic in it. (Spinoza holds that thought and extension are sort-of-basic in the one substance—are 'perceived by intellect as' basic—but he also holds that in their details they are perfectly isomorphic with one another (§65). In this part of his philosophy he is not in conflict with Leibniz.)

117. Leibniz's 'mill' thought-experiment

Setting aside as bad philosophy and insulting theology the thesis (2) that in a thinking animal thought is brute-factually added to some matter, Leibniz sees his only remaining target as the thesis (3) that a thinking animal has thoughts which explicably arise from the interplay of its parts. He prefers this to 2, seeing it as less deeply wrong; but he thinks he can show that 3 is also false; from which he infers (1) that all thinking is done by immaterial substances.

To evaluate this work, we need to understand what kind of relation Leibniz has in mind when he speaks of thought as explained by, or arising naturally from, a thing's material nature. The question of what causal relations bodies have to minds, and why and how, was a dominant problem of the age. Leibniz sliced through this knot with his thesis that nothing except God can act causally on anything else. Still, he allows for explanatory relations that are not causal; a collision, he holds, can *explain*, even though it cannot *cause*, a particle's starting to move. All the explanations of physics are like that: they rest upon the true, contingent, non-causal generalizations that express the 'harmony'.

In §104 we saw Leibniz asserting that we should never adduce mental events to explain, even non-causally, material events. He bases this on the self-sufficiency of a purely materialist physics. Such a physics is possible; no facts about the world defeat it; so we should stay with that way of explaining the facts about bodies, not dragging in unneeded considerations about what goes on in minds. As for whether the mental realm provides the resources for such explanations, Leibniz is silent about that, and has no need to address it.

He also urgently denies that any explanatory relation—even a weak, non-causal one—runs from facts about bodies to a certain kind of fact about minds. This body-to-mind denial differs in two connected ways from the converse mind-to-body one. First, it does not rest on any thesis about the self-sufficiency of psychology; it does not have the form 'We can explain every mentalistic fact in mentalistic terms, so we ought not to drag in facts from the material realm'. Rather than saying that facts about bodies are not *needed* to explain certain facts about minds, it says that they *cannot* explain them. Secondly, it does not say that no facts about minds can legitimately be explained by facts about bodies; it applies only to the small though crucial subset of mentalistic facts that are at stake in 3, and thus in the case against thinking matter.

We have seen that Leibniz's hatred of arbitrariness leads him to hold that the intrinsic features of perceptions are isomorphic with the physical events which explain them: 'There is always a perfect correspondence between the body and the soul' (*NE* 116). 'Pain does not resemble the movement of a pin; but it might thoroughly resemble the motions which the pin causes in our body, and might represent them in the soul; and I have not the least doubt that it does' (*NE* 131–2). Such an isomorphism would have to support a weak explanatory relation: the pain is *thus* because the bodily particles are running *so*. Even apart from this special isomorphism doctrine, Leibniz's whole account of perception opens the door to body-to-mind explanations. At this moment, I see a blue heron; my state counts as a perception of the heron because it and the bird are suitably correlated under principles of the universal harmony. This approach to perception warmly invites the idea that our perceptual states can be non-causally explained through the material states of affairs that they represent.

What cannot be materialistically explained, Leibniz seems to hold, is mentality as such. Given that a state of yours is a perceptual (and thus a mental) one, its detailed intrinsic nature may be non-causally explained by some facts about your own body or bodies in your environment; but no such facts could explain the state's being perceptual, because none could explain its being a mental state.

'Perception', Leibniz writes, 'cannot be explained by any mechanism whatsoever' (AG 192). He is denying that it could be explained even in the weak, non-causal, non-logical sense that we have been considering.

Leibniz says and defends this over and over again. Here are two examples:

Material particles, however small they might be, could not be combined or modified so as to produce perception; seeing that large particles could not do so (as is obvious), and that in small particles everything is proportional to what can occur in large ones. (*NE* 440)

Perception . . . cannot be explained on mechanical principles, i.e. by shapes and movements. If we pretend that there is a machine whose structure makes it think, sense, and have perception, then we can conceive it enlarged, but keeping to the same proportions, so that we might go inside it as into a mill. Suppose that we do: then if we inspect the interior we shall find there nothing but parts that push one another, and never anything that would explain a perception. Thus perception must be sought in simple substances, not in what is composite or in machines. (Mon 17, FW 270)

These passages are from 1705 and later; I do not know whether Leibniz used anything like this line of argument earlier. (I have no date for a vivid example in G 7:328–9.) What is going on in these passages? Without agreeing, we at least *understand* Leibniz's assuming that macroscopic physics is permanently confined to 'mechanical principles, i.e. shapes and movements', and his confidence that 'in small particles everything is proportional to what can occur in large ones'. So we know what lies behind his maintaining that if any physical array could produce a thought, then a large, clunking, push-mechanism such as a mill could do so. But where is the argument that it could not?

At the level of 'well-founded appearance' where material things appear, Leibniz is a Cartesian sort of concept-dualist, who finds it obvious that no facts involving only materialistic concepts could outright entail any mentalistic ones; but that is not his point in the above passages, in which he is denying that materialistic events could even weakly, non-causally, explain mentality as such. Some writers have credited Leibniz with merely denying that facts about pushes and pulls could lead with absolute necessity to conclusions about mentality; but this does not square with the language in which he expresses the grounding principle. My examples come from the *New Essays*, because that is where Leibniz has the most need to emphasize this aspect of his thought:

'He will never give them any [qualities] that are not natural to them, that is, that cannot arise from their nature in an explainable way' (66).

'It is not God's way to act in such an unruly and unreasoned fashion. I would say, rather, that there is a resemblance of a kind . . . It is thoroughly reasonable that the effect should correspond to the cause' (131).

'God produces and conserves in things only what is suitable to them and can be explained through their natures' (381).

'If God gave things accidental powers which were not rooted in their natures and were therefore out of reach of reason in general . . .' (382).

'God's power perpetually runs parallel to his wisdom' (382).

When Leibniz chooses the language of natural, explainable, rooted, resemblance, parallel, and correspond, I see him as carefully avoiding the idea of absolute necessitation. Similarly with the 'mill' passages, which are couched in terms of producing, of ways of arising, and—above all—of explaining. It is not credible that all of this means something about absolute necessitation. As for 'deduce', in seventeenth-century English it did not generally mean 'derive with logical rigor', the word for that being 'demonstrate'; and I imagine that the same is true of its French and Latin equivalents.

Whatever Leibniz's point is about big machines, he evidently thinks he need not argue for it. When we have conducted his 'enter the mill' thought-experiment, he says, we shall find it 'obvious' that the system we have entered could not even weakly—non-logically, non-causally—explain a perception. The thought-experiment is meant to elicit intuitive agreement from us; it is (in Dennett's phrase) an 'intuition pump', like some similar ones that Searle (1980) has offered in recent years. Without being puzzled by Leibniz's calm confidence that the intuitions will be forthcoming, we should still ask what is supposed to justify them. Here are two suggestions, neither of them satisfactory.

Perhaps Leibniz is thinking of perception in a dyadic manner in the 'mill' passages: to know that *perceptions* are involved, we must look beyond the mill to things with which its states are dependably correlated, whereas the thought-experiment confines us to the mill. But that has nothing to do with relations between material mechanism and mind; it purely concerns the difference between intrinsic and relational facts about a thing. It yields only a triviality, like the fact that by inspecting a nuclear family you could not see anything you could identify as a cousin.

Or he might be claiming, as do some contemporary philosophers, a deep categorial difference between any possible facts about matter (such as brains) and the given, experienced nature of sensory qualia. I doubt that, however. Leibniz's words do not suggest a concern with qualia; the mentalistic word he uses most is 'perception'. The intrinsic nature of the phenomenally given is not much of a topic with him in any context. When he does mention it, his point is the *likeness* between qualia and their material accompaniments (§103).

I cannot find good support for Leibniz's intuition about the mill, but I can offer a reason for being suspicious of it. If we walked into a material structure, we would 'find there nothing . . . which would explain a perception', Leibniz assures us; but he does not say what we might find that would 'explain a perception' if we inspected an immaterial substance. I suspect that *any* thought-experiment in which one observes events which are supposed to combine to produce thought would lead him to conclude 'There is nothing here that can explain thought'. Leibniz might agree with that, and still stand firm. He could maintain that nothing could explain perceptions because the mentalistic properties of a thing must be basic to it, and not the upshots of anything deeper— unlike a thing's biological properties, which result from processes which, taken severally, have nothing biological about them. That is a possible view, but one would like to see it supported by more than a single recurring thought-experiment.

118. Locke's God argument

This section is an aside. Locke uses an argument that is all of a piece with Leibniz's 'mill' thought-experiment:

Matter, incogitative matter and motion, whatever changes it might produce of figure and bulk, could never produce thought . . . Divide matter into as minute parts as you will (which we are apt to imagine a sort of spiritualizing, or making a thinking thing of it), vary the figure and motion of it as much as you please; a globe, cube, cone, prism, cylinder, &c. whose diameters are [as small as you like] will operate no otherwise upon other bodies of proportionable bulk than those of an inch or foot diameter; and you may as rationally expect to produce sense, thought, and knowledge by putting together in a certain figure and motion gross particles of matter, as by those that are the very minutest that do anywhere exist. They knock, impel, and resist one another just as the greater do; and that is all they can do. (*Essay* IV.x.10)

This is vulnerable in exactly the way that Leibniz's versions of it are, and I have no more to say about that.

However, Locke has another and better argument. It is still defective, I believe (because I think that matter can cause thought); but it does not rest on dogmatism about the future of physics or about relations between large and small. It is mentioned in passing in the discussion of thinking matter in *Essay* IV, where Locke considers whether matter could, unaided, produce thought, and says emphatically that it could not. Matter could think, he says, but only if there were already a thinking being that enabled it to do so. In a world lacking it, mentality could not come into existence through a change in the physical arrangements. This is contended in IV.iii.6, where Locke also claims, oddly, to 'have proved' it in a later chapter.

That is IV.x, where he seeks to prove that there is a god. (For a detailed exposition of this remarkable chapter, see Bennett 2001*a*.) Without spending long on this 'proof', I should say a few words about its tremendous invalidity. Using 't' to range over past times and 'x' over presently existing non-eternal things, Locke adduces premisses from which he reasonably infers this:

$(x)(t)(\exists y)((y \text{ exists at } t) \ \& \ (y \text{ caused } x \text{ to exist}))$.

Given any present object and any past time, there existed something at that time which caused the existence of that object. He then invalidly strengthens this to:

$(x)(\exists y)(t)((y \text{ exists at } t) \ \& \ (y \text{ caused } x \text{ to exist}))$.

Given any present object, there is some other thing which existed at every past time and caused the existence of the object. Then, by a further invalid move, he strengthens this to

$(\exists y)(x)(t)((y$ exists at t) & (y caused x to exist)).

There is something which existed at every past time and caused the existence of every present object. In short, Locke makes the existential quantifier march out to the head of the line. The first formula yields no eternal thing at all; the second says that each non-eternal thing has an eternal thing in its causal ancestry; the third says that one eternal thing is in the causal ancestry of every non-eternal thing. At *NE* 436 Leibniz precisely nails both shifts of the quantifier.

Having argued (invalidly) that there has from all eternity been a thing that caused the existence of every non-eternal object, and contending that the universal cause must be a thinking thing, because otherwise it could not have caused you and me, Locke proceeds to consider whether this eternal thinking being could be material. After discarding (with reasons) several versions of that possibility, he reaches the one that concerns us: 'It only remains that it is some certain system of matter duly put together that is this thinking eternal being' (627:3). This is the hypothesis that the universe contains thought because, and only because, the structure and mode of operation of a certain material system make it a thinker. The structure must be understood physicalistically, and the mode of operation must be mechanistic, with nothing happening in it because of the intentions of any designer or guardian. Locke is right to exclude designers, etc., because we are discussing a theory about the origin of all mentality in the universe: if there are any designers or guardians, they must result from the workings of the material system we are now discussing, and so they cannot help the system to work in the first place.

The topic is the production of thought 'when before there was no such thing as thought, or an intelligent being existing' (623:31). That clause occurs in the middle of Locke's 'knock, impel' argument (his version of the 'mill' argument), but it has no role in it: that argument simply appeals to our intuitions about what can be caused by knocking and impelling, without reference to whether there is thought anywhere else in the universe. But the latter idea is crucial in Locke's deeper and more interesting argument:

If it be the motion of its parts on which its thinking depends, all the thoughts there must be unavoidably accidental and limited; since all the particles that by motion cause thought, being each of them in itself without any thought, cannot regulate its own motions, much less be regulated by the thought of the whole, since that thought is not the cause of the motion (for then it must be antecedent to it, and so without it), but the consequence of it, whereby freedom, power, choice, and all rational and wise thinking or acting will be quite taken away. So that such a thinking being will be no better nor wiser than pure blind matter; since to resolve all into the accidental unguided motions of blind matter, or into thought depending on unguided motions of blind matter, is the same thing; not to mention the narrowness of such thoughts and knowledge that must depend on the motion of such parts. (*Essay* IV.x.17)

I love this beautifully deep and abstract argument. Going deeper than Leibniz's mill, it does not assume that seventeenth-century mechanism must be the final truth in physics, or that the laws governing the very small must be the same as those governing the large. Let us now see how it works.

The argument can be seen as saying that there is some kind of regularity or orderliness such that:

thought that is worthy of the name must have it,
something that has it cannot be caused by something that lacks it, and
no movements of bits of matter can have it unless they are guided by thought.

I say 'there is some kind of regularity . . .' because if the argument were stated in terms of regularity as such, it would be fatuously wrong. For then it would imply that the movements of particles that are not guided by thought must be a mere chaotic jumble, like the Brownian motion of tiny particles in a liquid. We know better, and so did Locke. He knew that a pendulum clock has orderly, regular, patterned movements that result purely from an underlying physical structure.

What, then, was he talking about? He might say: 'My topic is a certain very high *degree* of ordered complexity that is required for "thought", properly so called. Pendulum clocks are too simple to be relevant.' But that would be a risky line to take. Given that a simply structured clock can exhibit simple patterns of behaviour, could not more complex patterns—up to any level you like—be achieved by physical things that were suitably complex in their structures? I hope Locke would answer Yes.

Some would say that a material system could not become complex enough unless some thinking being designed it that way; but that was not Locke's opinion. Here is what he says on the topic:

Whether it be probable that a promiscuous jumble of printing letters should often fall into a method and order which should stamp on a paper a coherent discourse, or that a blind fortuitous concourse of atoms, not guided by an understanding agent, should frequently constitute the bodies of any species of animals: in these and the like cases, I think, nobody that considers them can be one jot at a stand which side to take. (*Essay* IV.xx.15)

See how carefully he avoids the routine natural-theology line of thought! He says that without something like divine intervention it is not *probable* that animals should *frequently* come into existence. That is too weak to support his God argument. Its use of 'frequently' weakens it, because the God argument concerns a singularity, namely the question of whether one particular thinker could be a material system; and its use of 'probable' weakens it still further, because the God argument is supposed to establish the outright impossibility that God should be made of matter (see 541:12 and 620:32).

How, then, is the God argument supposed to work? Faced with my point about the orderliness of the behaviour of a clock, Locke would have replied (I believe) that the clock's movements are wrong not in degree of ordered complexity but rather in kind. What kind might he be referring to? The only plausible candidate is the kind *teleological*. Then the argument would run as follows. (a) Mentality essentially involves teleology: it is because the mind reaches out to possible futures that it leads people to do things so as to bring about various upshots, thus endowing them with 'freedom, power, choice'; the teleological nature of mentality is the source of the possibility of 'rational and wise thinking [and] acting'. (b) Teleology cannot be conferred upon a system by causes that do not themselves manifest teleology. (c) There cannot be anything goal-oriented about the movements of matter that is not guided by thoughts, the 'accidental unguided motions of blind matter'. Therefore (d) no such movements could cause mentality.

In stating the argument I have brought in some phrases of Locke's that suggest that he was thinking of teleology. From now on, I shall assume that he was; I have no further defence of the purely exegetical point.

The argument is valid, and I think its premiss a is true and important. The best way to get mentalistic concepts rooted in the physical world is through teleology: we get mentality launched through theories about how animals do things that they think will lead to certain upshots. (I defend this at length in my 1976.) But b is suspect and c, I contend, is false. Although work remains to be done on this question, it is widely and rightly believed these days that there can be goal-pursuing behaviour that is mechanistically explicable, or—what comes to the same thing, that some behaviour can be at once mechanistically and teleologically explainable (see my 1976: 72–8 or 2001b).

This argument of Locke's, incidentally, implies that thought cannot, in the unaided course of nature, be the upshot of any kind of complex underlying procedure; so that what fundamentally explains the occurrence of some thought cannot be that it results from a complex event made up of simpler events no one of which in itself involves mentality. Suppose otherwise. Suppose that the occurrence of events $e_1, \ldots, e_n$ in certain relations to one another have as an upshot the occurrence of thought, this happening through processes that would operate even if this were the first thought in the universe. According to Locke's God argument, this cannot happen, because what goes on in each separate e_i would be accidental, unguided, and blind. Such events could not give rise to something as guided and unblind as thought. The argument does not rely on supposing that the separate events are movements of bodies. In offering it, indeed, Locke has committed himself to denying that thought as such can have natural causes. I think he might accept that if it were put to him.

119. How thinking matter relates to Leibniz's metaphysic

Descartes's confidence that no material thing thinks, like Locke's official agnosticism about this, was framed by robust realism about matter: an item's being a portion of matter, both philosophers thought, is a basic fact about it. When Leibniz joins in this debate, he too writes like a realist—a mind–matter *dualist*, which is indeed what Lopston (1999) thinks him to be. When he argues (1) that

thinking is done by an immaterial mind, through his use of the grounding principle to attack (2) brute-fact addition of thought to matter, and the 'mill' story to
attack (3) mentality arising naturally out of a thing's material nature, he does not
hint that any portion of matter is just the appearance to us of an infinitely numerous aggregate of mind-like monads. Matter figures here as it does in the related
passages of Locke's *Essay*.

The trilemma that gives this issue its shape can survive being combined with
Leibniz's monadic metaphysic. In that context, each horn of the trilemma starts
by saying that *a thinking animal is the appearance of an infinite aggregate of mind-like
monads*. Then they part company:

(1) One privileged member of the aggregate has all the thoughts that are
attributed to the animal as a whole. They count as belonging to the whole
because of how its other members relate to this privileged one.

(2) This appearance has thoughts which do not belong to any member of the
aggregate, and are not explicable in terms of any of the appearance's other
properties.

(3) This appearance has thoughts which do not belong to any member of the
aggregate, and can be explained in terms of the interplay of some or all of
the appearance's parts.

Option 1 belongs comfortably within the monadic metaphysic, whereas 2 and 3
are less at ease there, because they stretch up into the level of well-founded
appearance. Still, each makes sense, and Leibniz would be willing to argue
against each in pretty much the way that he argues in his realist-sounding treatments of the issue.

Why does he always argue this issue in a realist-sounding manner? I have no
evidence about Leibniz's frame of mind when engaged in this debate, but we can
consider what strategy he could reasonably be following. In Chapter 12 I presented his monadism as coming in two stages: first, the case for regarding matter
as an appearance of real simple substances; second, the case for holding that
minds are substances of this kind. It would make sense for Leibniz to hold fast to
the first stage, while regarding the second as prima facie at risk in the debate over
thinking matter. Thus, if he could not show that no matter thinks, he would lose
an important part of his case for holding that any of the simple substances which
he postulates are minds—the part which says that there is nothing else for minds
to be, given that portions of matter never think. The loss of this would undermine his position about the immortality of the soul or mind, but not his metaphysic of matter.

The remainder of the story was the view that minds are simple. If they are,
then no minds are bodies, no matter ever thinks. I do not know why Leibniz
when he is controverting thinking matter does not mention simplicity—why he
does not argue, as Descartes did, that material things cannot be minds because
they have parts. Perhaps he has not consciously articulated his reasons for

confidence that minds are simple, and is thus deterred from using their simplicity as a premiss in a further argument.

120. 'Substantial forms' and the unity of organisms

For Leibniz, then, an embodied human or other thoughtful animal is an organic body which is specially associated with a high-grade monad, a mind. The familiar correlations between events in the body and events in the mind are to be explained not causally but through the 'harmony': God has wound up a certain infinity of monads in such a way that when one of them has a want-an-apple appetition, the others so behave that at the phenomenal level your hand goes out and picks up an apple; and so on for all the rest. But your mind relates to your body in another way as well, and this is the one that Leibniz writes about most. I shall explain it now.

I have several times quoted him using the phrase 'substantial form', which I now explain. He applies it to his simple substances, especially before adopting 'monad', but also quite often in the *New Essays*, perhaps stimulated by Locke's sneers at 'substantial forms' as philosophers' nonsense. Leibniz's use of the phrase comes from his doctrine that any organism, though not strictly a substance (according to his later views), is substance-like in various ways, and it gets this status from its relation to a single *dominant monad*. That is the special role of your mind: it is a dominant monad which confers a quasi-substantial unity upon your body.

Such a monad is called a 'substantial form' because of its role in the organism, but *how* that role justifies that label is not quite what one might expect. Leibniz brings in 'form' in order to liken the role he assigns to the dominant monad in the organism to the role of a 'form' in the philosophy of Aristotle; and the adjective 'substantial' is there not because the item is a substance but because it confers a quasi-substantial unity on the organism.

This doctrine was important to Leibniz because of his attachment to the notion of *single thing* and his concern to know what items in the world can be taken to be single things on a basis other than mere convention, or arbitrarily. (For an exceptionally good brief sketch of this matter, see Sleigh 1990a: 121.) Absent a substantial form, he held, no serious use can be made of the concept of a single thing that has parts or is an aggregate. We *can* view an aggregate as a single thing, Leibniz concedes, but if we are strict about this, we shall admit that such 'things' are evanescent: 'An army accurately considered is not the same thing even for a moment. . . . Since its entire nature consists in number, figure, appearance and similar things, when these change it is not the same thing' (quoted, ibid. 123). An army goes out of existence and is replaced by a new one, according to this, not only if one soldier joins or leaves, it but also if a soldier gets promoted or polishes his boots. We have standards for sameness of army that are looser than this; but Leibniz presumably saw these as arbitrary from a meta-physical point of view, expressing our needs and interests, but not reflecting real joints in the world.

As well as being inconveniently short-lived, arbitrary individuals are also embarrassingly plentiful:

If many things are posited, then by that very fact it is understood that some single thing is immediately assumed. The former are said to be the parts, the latter, the whole. It is not necessary that they exist at the same time or in the same place; it is sufficient that they be considered at the same time. Thus, from all the Roman emperors together we con-struct a single aggregate. (Quoted, ibid. 124)

Leibniz goes on to make again the point that really 'no entity that is truly one is composed of parts', and that entities which have no dominant monad 'are no more a single entity than a pile of sticks' and 'do not remain the same more than a moment'.

So we have a couple of reasons for being, as metaphysicians, not interested in such pseudo-things as armies and hats, and for according focused respect to monads. Between these, however, there are *organisms*. In the passage from which I have just quoted, Leibniz also writes: 'From these considerations the ancient philosophers correctly attributed substantial forms, such as minds, souls or primary entelechies, to those things that they said made up a *Unum per se*.' The view that he is here applauding is not that 'minds, souls or primary ent-elechies' are genuinely single things (though of course they are), but that a bit of the world may count as a genuinely single thing because it *has* a mind, soul, or entelechy.

An animal is indeed more really a single enduring thing than is a shawl (say). We may decide to count a shawl as the same after a few fibres are lost to it, but it is more than merely our decision that enables the same animal still to exist after losing some hairs. Organic unity, then, is real. But does it require a dominant monad or entelechy? Locke answered No, in his wonderful account of organic unity as resulting from relations amongst corpuscles, culminating in this:

That being then one plant which has such an organization of parts in one coherent body partaking of one common life, it continues to be the same plant as long as it partakes of the same life, though that life be communicated to new particles of matter vitally united to the living plant, in a like continued organization conformable to that sort of plants. (*Essay* II.xxvii.4)

This shows how an organism can get its diachronic unity just from how it is orga-nized, rather than having unity conferred upon it by a soul or substantial form.

Presenting this in the *New Essays*, Leibniz allows Locke's spokesman to say only this: 'What constitutes the unity (identity) of a single plant is having such an organization of parts in one body, partaking of one common life, which lasts as long as the plant exists, even though it changes its parts' (*NE* 231). Truncated though this is, it contains Locke's central thought. Leibniz confronts this on its own terms, keeping out of sight his view that matter is only an appearance, and writing like a realist about matter. In that vein, he rejects outright the Lockean view of organic unity:

Organization or configuration alone, without an enduring principle of life which I call *monad*, would not suffice to make something remain . . . the same individual. . . . When an iron horse-shoe changes to copper in a certain mineral water from Hungary, the same kind of shape remains but not the same individual: the iron dissolves, and the copper, with which the water is impregnated, is precipitated and imperceptibly replaces it. . . . We must acknowledge that organic bodies as well as others remain 'the same' only in appearance, and not strictly speaking. . . . But as for substances which possess in themselves a genuine, real, substantial unity, . . . and as for substantial beings which are sustained by a single indivisible spirit: one can rightly say that they remain perfectly 'the same individual' in virtue of this soul or spirit which makes the *I* in substances which think. (*NE* 231–2)

Unless a unifying substance is involved, Leibniz is saying, the seeming sameness of the organism is like that of any inanimate object, such as a horseshoe in which all the molecules are gradually replaced. While agreeing that one story is more complex than the other, he would put the two on a par, metaphysically speaking. As he says a little later: 'An organic body does not remain the same for more than a moment; it only remains equivalent. And if no reference is made to the soul, there will not be the same life, nor a "vital" unity, either. So the identity in that case would be merely apparent' (*NE* 232).

One might naturally take Leibniz to mean something like this:

The empirically given, familiar facts about how organisms hang together cannot be explained purely through the physics of particles of matter. You say that the 'life' of the organism consists in facts about the behaviour of particles, facts that can be explained in terms of impact mechanics and minute structures; but in fact it is not so. The behaviour that we call 'life' requires also a dominant monad.

Leibniz's actual position is nothing like that. He refuses to explain anything that happens in an organism by appealing to its dominant monad. All the particular facts, he keeps saying, can be explained purely mechanistically: 'All particular natural phenomena can be explained mathematically or mechanically by those who understand them,' he writes in a passage which also introduces 'indivisible forms or natures' (*DM* 18, FW 72). In bringing both of these into his account, Leibniz claims to be 'reconciling the mechanical philosophy of the moderns with the caution of some intelligent and well-intentioned persons' who think that mechanism cannot be the whole story. (See also FW 119.)

121. How dominant monads create organic unity

Let us be clear about this. Material mechanisms suffice to explain all the biological facts—all the facts about structures and events in organisms—but in so doing they still leave out the facts about which organic configurations have 'strictly genuine' unity. It follows that genuine unity, such as only a uniting soul or monad can provide, *is additional to all the biological facts*; which seems to imply that there cannot be conclusive empirical evidence that any actual organism has such unity. Any case for believing that strictly genuine unity exists must come from meta-physical considerations rather than from biology. (Leibniz evidently did not believe this in 1678 when, writing to Conring, he expressed the Cartesian opinion that 'we cannot assert with certainty that there is a sentient soul in beasts unless phenomena are exhibited which cannot be explained mechanically' (L 190). I do not know when he came to be sure that all the biological facts can be explained mechanically and that nevertheless animals have souls.)

Leibniz was challenged about this by Arnauld. Conceding that the unity we confer on 'a heap of gold, a star, a planet' is superficial and conventional, Arnauld maintained that we rightly 'ascribe more unity to those bodies whose parts work together towards one and the same end, like a house or watch'. The most vivid examples of the latter kind of unity, he said, are 'organic bodies, that is animals and plants', to which we attribute unity 'without any need on that account to bestow souls on them' (Mason 110). Leibniz's long reply, after traversing a wide stretch of profitable and entertaining territory, circles around this point of Arnauld's and finally alights on it: 'If parts which work together towards the same end are more suited to composing a genuine substance than ones which are [merely] in contact, then all the officers of the Dutch East Indies Company will form a real substance, much better than a heap of stones' (FW 127). That is evasive. Leibniz has no doubt that a rabbit is substantial enough to qualify for a dominant monad, and that the Company is not; his basis for this must lie in empirically findable differences between the two; and those should be conceded to Arnauld as a basis for making his point that the dominant monad seems to have no work to do in this story.

'Could it not still be needed as the *producer* of the material facts that lead us to think of rabbits and cabbages as unified organisms?' Sleigh seems to imply that Leibniz would answer 'Yes, but I do not know how'. Sleigh has a vigorous passage (1990a: 107) on Leibniz's failure, when challenged by Arnauld, to say how 'a soul or substantial form (or entelechy) produces a true unity from ingredients, some of which are divisible entities'. He merely says that we know that this does happen somehow in our case, knowing this 'from the inside out, so to speak', so that 'there must be an acceptable account' of *how* it happens. The text Sleigh is relying on seems to me not to say quite this; but if it does, then Leibniz is bluffing. The alleged experiences do not, and probably could not, occur: nothing, it seems, could count as experiencing the non-causal production by one's own mind of the organic unity of one's body.

Leibniz's real answer, I believe, is not 'Yes, but I don't know how', but rather a resounding No. He denies not only that the dominant monad in an organism *causes* any changes in it, but also that it *explains* any of its changes in the way that some facts about movements of corpuscles help to explain others. So the question remains: with all that denied, what significance can the dominant monad have?

Agreeing with Rutherford (1995*a*: 272–3), I hold that Leibniz must assign to the dominant monad a logical rather than an executive role. He needs a clear, metaphysically basic statement of the criteria governing identity-judgements about organisms: this paw and that are parts of a single cat; this cat is the one I fed yesterday. If this can be done in terms that are objective and metaphysically acceptable, not relying on convention or what it would be intuitively plausible to say, then Leibniz can say that organisms have an identity or unity which is real in a way in which the 'unity' of pebbles, armies, and shawls is not. And if the criteria that do this job essentially involve the concept of an organism's 'dominant monad', then the latter has a role in the organism's unity—a logical role in the criteria for unity.

I have not found Leibniz himself saying all that, but I think it must be his view. How would it go in detail?

It must be done at the level of monads. I shall speak of a monad as being 'in' a given portion of matter M if it is one of the monads of which M is the appearance to us. By an obvious extension, a monad is 'in' an organism O at time T if it is one of the monads whose appearance to us is the matter composing O at T. Then the first part of our Leibnizian story will set out the criteria for two monads to be in a single organism at a single time.

Leibniz tells us that an organism's dominant monad perceives all its other monads more distinctly than it perceives any that are not in that organism. Let us optimistically take that as a promise that for any dominant monad D and any time T, there is a unique set of other monads—defined somehow by how distinctly D perceives its members—which contains all and only the monads that are in a certain organism at that time. That could generate a grounded, non-conventional account of the truth conditions for the synchronic unity of organisms. What makes it true that this paw and that whisker are now parts of a single animal? The fact that a single dominant monad D has within its unique D-now set all the monads that are in this paw and all the ones that are in that whisker.

With this in hand, Leibniz could move on to diachronic unity. What makes it the case that the cat I fed at dawn is the one I stroked at noon? Answer: there is a single monad D whose D-at-dawn set appears as the cat I fed at dawn and whose D-at-noon set appears as the cat I stroked at noon. This allows for organisms to metabolize—to undergo a turnover in the monads that are in them. Up at the level where there is matter, an organism corresponds to *a function from times to portions of matter*: no one portion of matter can be identified with this rabbit, because matter comes and goes in it; but at every moment there is a portion which *then* constitutes the rabbit. (I here borrow from Grandy 1975.) Similarly, a Leibnizian organism also corresponds to a function from times to aggregates of monads; the aggregates differ from time to time, but at each moment the D-at-T relation links the dominant monad to one determinate aggregate.

This completes the truth conditions for synchronic and diachronic statements about organisms, conferring upon them a unity that is more real and grounded than that of artefacts or piles of sticks. Or rather, it would do so if we could fit it up with something solid to replace the mushy 'a unique set of other monads—defined *somehow* by how distinctly D perceives its members'. I have not been able to make this more precise. It is not easy, as you will discover if you try.

Anyway, it does not matter much. Leibniz's account of organic unity, however we polish its abstract surfaces and tighten its logical joints, still faces a problem that seems insoluble. There is no reason why the items that count as organisms by his criteria should be organisms as ordinarily understood. Why should a Leibnizian organism—defined by any such account as I have been discussing—be like the rabbits or cabbages that we are familiar with?

A barely possible way out of the difficulty may be provided by Hartz's speculation that 'this unifying process . . . must be a sort of teleological superharmony between the dominant and subordinate monads that God notices when he surveys possibilia' (1996: 79–80). As I understand this, it would still give the dominant monad a logical or criterial, rather than an executive, role: the idea would be that a material system counts as organically unified if the events that it undergoes tend to satisfy the desires of some one monad. And now Leibniz might solve the evidence problem thus: it is reasonable to attribute organic unity to a rabbit because the events that it undergoes have the right pattern to be satisfactions of the desires of a single monad. This works less well for a cabbage than for a rabbit. Worse, it requires Leibniz to rest important weight on something which he has constructed flimsily, if at all: namely, the notion of teleology showing up in the world of matter (see Bennett 2001*b*).

Leibniz's entire response to Locke on this topic is unsatisfactory, in my opinion. One does have an intuitive sense that organisms are strongly unified in an objective, non-conventional way; but that intuition is based on the biological facts; it is a résumé of our empirical evidence about how things go in organisms. It can stand on its own feet, without any of the trappings of dominant monads. It does stand on its own feet in the work of van Inwagen (1990: 98), who defends a basic ontology containing nothing but fundamental physical particles and organisms. Leibniz, however, when Locke and Arnauld confront him with rabbits and cabbages, trashes them. If you omit the dominant monad, he says, all you have here is on a par with a horseshoe in Hungarian water or the officers in a corporation. He does not face the question 'What is your evidence that rabbits and cabbages do have dominant monads while horseshoes and corporations do not?'

122. The scope of the organic realm

I now present a trio of Leibnizian doctrines about organisms, in increasing order of logical strength. The weakest is still strong enough to startle.

Animals into Animals   Leibniz holds that every organic body is composed of organisms; which implies that organisms are infinitely divisible *into organisms*.

'Each living body has a dominant entelechy, which in an animal is its soul; but the parts of that living body are full of other living things—plants, animals—each of which also has its entelechy or dominant soul' (Mon 70, FW 278). In using 'animals' in my label for this doctrine, I am adopting Leibniz's carelessness about the difference between 'animal' and 'organism'.

One of his reasons for 'Animals into Animals' involves a problem that he and his contemporaries had about procreation. A question that had puzzled Aristotle was still unanswered: how do plants and animals manage to breed true, producing offspring of their own rather than of some other kind? In the early modern period, little was known about procreation—even the relative roles of sperm and ovum were still a topic of debate. (See the Glossary note on Leeuwenhoek in the Remnant–Bennett edition of *NE*.) Getting that straightened out, however, would still leave a problem. Buffon, the great eighteenth-century biologist, likened procreation to an animal's stamping its own likeness on to other animals, as though it were a metal mould used to create clay copies; except that in the case of the animal the mould is internal (Jacob 1974: 79). He was not in a position to make good sense of *un moule intérieur*; but the reality, he thought, must be something that could be so described. In this he was right, as we now know; but this knowledge came through discoveries that were far beyond the reach of anyone in his century or earlier ones.

One theory of generation held that the relevant part of one parent (the sperm or the ovum) contains tiny replicas of the parent: a fox's sperm contains invisibly small foxes, which enlarge in the vixen's womb. That seems like a desperate solution when one asks about the status of the original fox's grandchildren: did the invisibly small fox in the sperm contain yet smaller foxes, which, . . . ? Leibniz answered Yes. He accepted this solution of the 'breeding true' problem, including what it implies about an infinity of foxes:

There are small animals in the seeds of large ones, which through conception assume new vestments that they make their own, and which give them the means to feed and to grow in order to pass on to a larger stage and so propagate the larger animal. . . . Spermatic animals themselves grow from other, smaller, spermatic animals, in relation to which they count as large; for in nature everything goes on to infinity. (PNG 6, FW 261–2)[3]

That view of procreation gave Leibniz one argument for the thesis that not only souls but their animal bodies are immortal:

Just as animals do not entirely come into being with their conception or generation, so they do not entirely go out of existence in what we call their death; for it is only reasonable that what does not begin naturally should have no end in the order of nature either. And so, throwing off their mask or their tattered clothing, they merely return to a smaller stage on which nevertheless they can be just as orderly and as capable of sensing as they were on the larger one. (PNG 6, FW 261*)

---

[3] See also the 'pleasant though very silly example' at *NE* 329.

Leibniz was confident in, and excited by, his doctrine that animals last for ever. 'The machines of nature are as imperishable as souls themselves,' he writes, 'and the animal together with its soul persists for ever' (*NE* 329). Later in the same work he proudly lists some of the jewels in his doctrinal crown, culminating in 'the preservation after death of souls and even of animals' (*NE* 383). Why is it a strength in a metaphysic to imply the preservation of animals? This was presumably in part a residue of Leibniz's earlier Aristotelianism, in which the mind or soul is the form of the body, and thus cannot naturally exist without a body. The Christian doctrine of the resurrection of the body no doubt comes into it also; but I am neither expert nor interested in these matters, and shall not explore them.

Bodies into Animals   Leibniz went further, holding not merely that every organism but that every portion of matter can be decomposed into organisms. Successive divisions of a piece of flint will eventually bring one to organic bodies, he wrote to Bernoulli, though he did not know how far one would have to go for this (L 512). 'Animals into Animals' is just a special case of 'Bodies into Animals', but I took the former separately so as to exhibit some explanatory work that it does without help from its stronger parent.

I can find no separate explanatory work for the latter. The only Leibnizian reasons I can find for 'Bodies into Animals' come from its being entailed by a stronger doctrine yet, the third in the trio.

Pan-domination   This is the doctrine that every monad is the dominant monad of some organism. I think that is what Leibniz is saying in the last clause of this:

There is no part of matter which . . . does not contain organic bodies, there are souls everywhere as there are bodies everywhere, the souls and even the animals subsist always, organic bodies are never without souls, and souls are never separated from organic bodies. (1705*a*, L 590)

That final clause expresses Pan-domination if (but only if) it is using 'soul' as equivalent to 'monad'—which Leibniz does sometimes but not always. Pan-domination seems to be presupposed at the end of the Preface to the *New Essays*. Some people have trouble conceiving immaterial substances because they think of them as 'separated from matter', Leibniz says there; but they need not be thought of like that, he continues, 'and indeed I do not believe that such [separated] substances ever occur naturally among created things'. This implies that no substance (not merely no high-grade substance or soul) is 'separated from matter', which seems to mean that every substance dominates some animal body. This extraordinary doctrine sits uneasily with the thesis that every body is the appearance of a colony of monads, but contradiction can be avoided by invoking an infinite regress.

Why should Leibniz accept this madly extravagant doctrine? Well, his metaphysic is motivated partly by a desire to explain the appearance of mind–body interaction in the human case, so he starts from certain facts about a few organisms on one tiny planet. Indeed, where else could he start? But his meta-physical story is apt to spread further: by affirming that all basic differences are ones of degree, thus abolishing walls and moats in his metaphysic, Leibniz is not well placed to assert that this unity-conferring role is confined to humans or ter-restrial mammals—or indeed confined to anything. For this reason, I conjecture, he lets it roam across all the monads, holding that each is the dominant monad of some organic body. That is why he applies the label 'substantial forms' to mon-ads generally, not just to some privileged subset of them.

I have found one text that flatly contradicts Pan-domination. In it, Leibniz distinguishes, as a subset of all monads, 'dominant and hence intelligent souls, like human souls' and says that they 'cannot be everywhere' (NI 12, FW 218). Furthermore, the direct textual evidence for his acceptance of Pan-domination is rather thin. Still, his use of 'substantial form' as equivalent to 'monad' strongly supports it; so does his acceptance of 'Bodies into Animals', which seems to have no Leibnizian thrust behind it apart from its being entailed by Pan-domination.

123. Corporeal substances

In §120 I wrote of the *quasi*-substantial unity of organisms, crediting Leibniz with holding that organisms are metaphysically intermediate between inorganic aggregates and monads. According to Garber and some other Leibniz scholars, however, Leibniz in his middle period regarded organisms as corporeal sub-stances—full-fledged, with nothing 'quasi' about their substantial status—and this seems to have shown itself at least occasionally in his work until a quite late stage. See Garber 1985, which Adams (1994) calls 'the most powerful and inter-esting presentation to date' of this view of Leibniz's thought, while remarking that it goes back to Broad 1975, which was actually written in the 1950s. The tex-tual support for Broad and Garber is confusing, as Sleigh has pointed out:

Consider . . . the analysis of the components of a substance that Leibniz presented in a let-ter to De Volder of 20 June 1703. The analysis ends with 'the animal, i.e. corporeal sub-stance, which is made one by the monad dominating the machine' [AG 177]. Yet three letters later, with no doctrinal change intervening, Leibniz wrote to De Volder (13 June 1704): 'Accurately speaking, however, matter is not composed of constitutive unities, but results from them, since matter, i.e. extended mass, is nothing but a phenomenon grounded in things, like the rainbow or mock sun, and all reality belongs to unities alone' [AG 179]. It is clear that the unities mentioned in this passage are monads, not corporeal substances. In the same vein, consider the famous ontological chart that supplements Leibniz's letter to Des Bosses of 19 August 1715 [Loemker, p. 617]. There, under the rubric 'Unum per se, complete being', we find two types of substance mentioned—sim-ple substances (that is, monads), and composite substances (such as animals)—much as we do in the 'Monadology' itself. Yet writing to Des Bosses three years earlier, Leibniz had put his metaphysical cards on the table: 'All that I consider useful in fundamental explanations of all phenomena are the agreements amongst the perceptions of monads; corporeal substances do not come into it.' (Sleigh 1990a: 110)[4]

There is an instability here, and scholars do not agree about what Leibniz really thought. Adams (1994: 268–72) helpfully sorts out the different things that could be going on in the texts where Leibniz seems to count organisms as genuine substances; I shall not repeat them here. For a powerful further discussion of this matter, see Cover and O'Leary-Hawthorne 1999: 52–4.

There is in any case a crushing objection—which Leibniz could hardly have overlooked—to conjoining monadism with a belief in corporeal substances strictly so-called. The monadism conjunct entails that inorganic matter is a well-founded appearance, and not fundamentally real; the corporeal-substance conjunct says that organisms are fundamentally real. How can these two be reconciled with the plain fact that inorganic matter enters and leaves organisms? This would require that when a bit of inorganic matter is—as Locke might say— caught up in the life of an organism, its metaphysical status changes radically. There is no chance of Leibniz's making that credible.

For that and other reasons, I agree with Adams that there is little profit to be gained in this area. He defends at length his conclusion: 'The Aristotelian [corporeal-substance] elements that are undeniably present in Leibniz's thought are not inconsistent with his monadological theories, but are part of them; there is no major change from his middle to his later years on this point' (Adams 1994: 308–40). I would add that if there is a change, is seems merely to involve Leibniz's preferences for the use of the word 'substance', not his views about what there basically is.

124. Distinctness of perceptions

The concept of the distinctness/confusion of perceptions has been busily with us for a long time. It

>   provides the differentia marking off minds or 'souls' from within the class of monads generally (§91),
>   generates Leibniz's account of the direction of quasi-causation (§102),
>   lies at the heart of his solution of the collapse problem (§110),
>   gives him a basis for saying that we are unaware of most of our perceptions, without which limitation 'each monad would be a divinity' (§113), and
>   plays a central, if obscure, role in his account of the unity of organisms (§121).

Leibniz makes no other concept carry such a heavy and various load; so it is a special pity that he has a probably fatal problem with validating this concept of

---

[4] I have modified Sleigh's translation of the last quoted sentence, hoping to make it clearer. For references to some secondary literature on this matter, see Mercer and Sleigh 1995: 123 n. 54; Hartz 1996; FW 12n.

distinctness. It comes from a pair of aspects of his thought. One is his view that *every fact about* each monad is represented in every other. The other is his wanting his account of genuine mental representation to arise out of his more general doctrine about correlations amongst states of monads; so he has to explain distinct/confused in terms of that more general doctrine. The alternative would be to introduce expression generally, and then to add something about distinct/confused, this being a radically extra feature of the world. Leibniz's desire for uniformity of theory gives him a reason for not proceeding in the second manner; and anyway he has made no provision for any such extra feature. He really does hope to get a complete theory of mind out of his abstract theory about a world of correlated unextended substances. Or so I say, believing that Leibniz has an upward-moving strategy which does not allow him to explain distinct/confused by borrowing from our intuitive sense of what distinctness and confusion are in our own thoughts (§99).

Even if I am wrong in this general thesis, and Leibniz does sometimes deliberately move from the top down in his explanations, he had better not accept Broad's invitation (§99) to try to explain the confused/distinct polarity for monads on the basis of mental confusion as we know it. Our intellectual confusions are presumably incomparable with anything that happens in very low-level monads; and anyway, our confusion essentially involves error. That comparison would sink if it were thrown into the monadic waters. Leibniz is clear about that: 'Our perceptions are always true; it is our judgments . . . in which we go wrong' (*DM* 14, FW 66). He has no proper account of what judgements are, but that is another story. One might try a top-down account of monadic confusion by appealing to blurred vision, indistinct hearing, and the like. But those essentially involve loss of information: my view of something cannot be blurred if every qualitative difference across the thing's surface corresponds to a qualitative difference in my visual field in so far as I am aware of it. But every monad contains all the information there is; nothing is lost.

I conclude that even if Leibniz means to allow himself some downward-moving explanations in his monadic metaphysics, none can help him to explain the distinctness and confusion of monadic perceptions. As for upward-moving ones, I have encountered only one proposal worth discussing.

125. Brandom's interpretation

It is in a good paper by Brandom (1981). In the first part, Brandom sets the scene, explains the problem, and valuably makes it clear that in Leibniz's phrases 'distinct perception' and 'distinct idea' the adjective has different senses. (For more help with this see M. D. Wilson 1977: 125.) He sees that Leibniz has a problem explaining what distinctness or confusion of perceptions is, and undertakes to solve it for him in a bottom-up manner, without borrowing from armchair human psychology.

His initial clue is the fact—which we have already noted in passing (§§102, 106)—that Leibniz sometimes connects how distinctly a monad perceives with how perfect it is. I think that when Leibniz writes thus about the perfection of monads, he is thinking of how close they are to God's perfection, especially how great their activity-to-passivity ratio is, God's being infinity-to-zero. Brandom, however, tries a different tack, suggesting that Leibniz may have thought of the perfection of monads on the model of the perfection of worlds: 'God has chosen the most perfect world, that is, the one which is simultaneously the simplest in hypotheses and the richest in phenomena—as would be a geometrical line whose construction was easy yet whose properties and effects are very admirable and far-reaching' (DM 6, FW 58). Brandom looks for something analogous to this as an account of the perfection of monads, and thus of the distinctness of their perceptions.

He finds it in the thought that although each monad perceives everything that is the case, monads may differ in how economically they do so. With 'simplest in hypotheses and richest in phenomena' in the background, Brandom writes:

One substance is more perfect than another if from fewer premises about it, more about its world can be deduced than is the case for the other. The 'hypotheses' will be statements reporting the occurrence of a perception in some monad, and the 'phenomena' deducible from them will be statements reporting on the inherence of an accident in some subject. Thus higher degrees of perfection of expression correspond to more inclusive sets of expressed (inferable) accidents. (1981: 463)

Although what monad x expresses at a given moment must be exactly what monad y expresses then—namely, everything—it may be that some single perceptions of x's each express what it takes several of y's perceptions to express, and not conversely. If the total number of perceptions in y is finite, it will follow that x uses fewer perceptions than y to do its expressing; but even if each monad had an infinity of perceptions at the time in question, there is still a plain sense in which x can be said to achieve the same overall result as y in a manner that is 'simpler in hypotheses'.

Brandom holds that the more that is expressed by the average one of x's perceptions, the more perfect an expresser or perceiver x is. I gather that he holds, further, that the more a perception expresses, the more distinct it is. This account of distinctness (and, by implication, of confusion) does not ascribe ignorance or error to any monad; nor does it lean on informal concepts imported from folk psychology. It is truly responsive to Leibniz's problem of explicating distinct/confused in a bottom-up manner.

How are we to count and individuate perceptions? These are just *states* of the substance that has them—parts of the story about how it is—and they count as perceptual only because they correlate with facts about other things. Brandom's theory requires this 'story about how the substance is' to be divisible into atoms; it demands that there be an objectively right way of breaking it down into minima, each corresponding to just one perception. I do not see how to do this.

Brandom has no suggestions either, but he suspects (he tells me) that Leibniz thought it could be done. Let us see.

(1) Leibniz mainly explains our unawareness of certain perceptions by saying that they are too small or inconspicuous; in just two places that I know of, he attributes our unawareness of some perceptions to how 'numerous' they are (NE 53, L 294). This requires that the perceptions be numerable, so there is support for Brandom here, but it is not strong. In each case, 'numerous' is conjoined with 'small' in a manner that is consistent with Leibniz's having no considered view about the countability of perceptions.

(2) The only other possible support I can find for Brandom's interpretation is Leibniz's writing that 'each distinct perception of the soul includes an infinity of confused perceptions which embrace the whole universe' (PNG 13, FW 264), and alluding to 'confused perceptions, infinitely many of which are contained in each distinct perception' (AG 229*). I shall not now explore the reasons for this puzzling thesis—my only attempts to make sense of it have not satisfied or interested me. At present what matters is this: the proposition that each distinct perception *includes* an infinity of confused ones apparently implies that each distinct perception *has the same expressive (informative) content as* infinitely many confused ones; and this seems to yield Brandom's result that a distinct perception is one that does the job more economically—with fewer perceptions for a given amount of expressed content—than confused ones do. There is, however, a reason for doubting this whole line of thought.

Leibniz takes distinct/confused to be a continuum, with differences of degree all along it. And if the remarks about perceptions that are confused because they are so numerous are to be part of the story, the numerousness has to be thought of in finite terms: I was not conscious of my perception of the falling of that one drop of water because it was accompanied in my mind by tens of thousands of similar ones. But now we have Leibniz saying flatly that each single distinct perception includes an infinity of confused ones: there is no room here for a difference of degree, and humdrum hundreds-of-thousands numerousness has no place either. This failure of fit looks serious.

I doubt that Leibniz saw clearly how big a problem he had with the concept of distinctness of perceptions. I do not think it can be solved satisfactorily in his upward-moving terms; nor is he in better shape with top-down help. Either way, the problem is insoluble by him, and the strategic situation shows why. In his metaphysic every substance at every moment contains all the information there is; yet that metaphysic must underlie, support, and explain facts about the human condition including these:

> that we are aware of some (but not all) the facts about our environments,
> that we remember some (but not all) of our pasts,
> that we are aware of some (but not all) that goes on in our minds,
> that some (but not all) of the occupants of our world strike us as mind-like.

In Leibniz's basic metaphysic, 'some but not all' does not occur; the system is made up of wall-to-wall universal generalizations, as he proclaims. So the differences marked by 'some but not all' must be ones of degree; and Leibniz chooses degree of distinctness to do nearly all the work. No honest concept could bear such a burden.

Chapter 17

Leibniz's Contained-Predicate Doctrine

126. Leibniz's contained-predicate doctrine

Leibniz expressed his contained-predicate doctrine (CPD for short) in a letter to Arnauld:

In every true affirmative proposition, whether necessary or contingent, universal or particular, the notion of the predicate is in some way included in that of the subject. (FW 111–12)

The terms 'subject' and 'predicate' refer here not to linguistic expressions, or to components of abstract propositions, but rather to the *thing* that is spoken about and the *property* that is attributed to it. So Leibniz implies that if Socrates is wise, then the concept of Socrates includes the concept of wisdom.

Like any substance, Socrates falls under countless concepts; but Leibniz uses the singular '*the* concept of Socrates' to refer to the unique complete concept of Socrates. In the relevant texts the phrase 'complete notion' keeps turning up; also the only concept of Socrates that could deserve the label '*the* notion of Socrates' is his complete concept; and, thirdly, if 'the notion of the subject' that Leibniz alludes to were anything less than the thing's complete concept, the CPD would be too obviously false.

It should be uncontroversial to say that each thing *has* a complete concept. Of the infinity of concepts under which Julius Caesar falls, some contain others and some do not; and one unique one includes all the others—the concept of being-F-and-G-and-H-and . . . and so on through everything that is ever true of Julius Caesar. This concept picks out a complete life history, down to the least turn of a finger and lift of an eyebrow; if it were laid out for us, we could read off from it the whole of Julius Caesar's life story. Leibniz carefully explains to Arnauld that the notion of a complete concept is clean, harmless, and defensible without recourse to theology (AG 74).

Every item in whatever category has a complete concept, and in one place Leibniz says so (G 2:131). Yet he also tends to associate complete concepts with substances in particular. Sleigh explains this as arising from Leibniz's associating complete concepts with substantives, and thinking that in an ideal language the only substantives would name substances—terms like 'squareness' and 'wisdom' would not occur (Sleigh 1990a: 54–5). That is persuasive, but it does not allow Leibniz to use his complete-concept concept to help mark off substances from other categories of being, and in particular to mark it off from 'accidents' (which in this context are individual accidents, tropes). Yet Leibniz evidently purports to do just that:

The nature of an individual substance or of a complete being is to have [1] a notion so complete that it is sufficient to contain and to allow us to deduce from it all the predicates of the subject to which this notion is attributed. An accident, on the other hand, is a being [2] whose notion does not include everything that can be attributed to the subject to which the notion is attributed. (*DM* 8, FW 60)

What 2 means, and needs to mean if the passage is to distinguish substances from accidents, is that

> An accident is a being whose notion does not include everything that can be attributed to the accident.

Leibniz gives no reason to believe this, and it seems plainly false. To take an example of his, the kinghood of Alexander the Great

> is an instance of a political/social quality,
> is more general than Alexander's personhood and
> is less general than Alexander's conquering-kinghood.

So it falls under a concept that involves those three properties of it; and also under ever richer concepts, until we reach the complete concept of Alexander's kinghood, which involves all the properties of that trope. Why not?

Here is what Leibniz says next:

Thus the quality of King which belongs to Alexander the Great, in abstraction from the subject, is not sufficiently determined for an individual, and does not include the other qualities of the same subject, nor all that the notion of this Prince comprises.

That ought to defend 2, but it does not. Whereas 2 implies that that notion does not include everything that can be attributed to *Alexander's kinghood*, Leibniz's back-up says only that the (complete) notion of Alexander's kinghood does not include everything that can be attributed to *Alexander*. The two passages could be harmonized if in the former of them we replaced (2) 'the subject to which the notion is attributed' by (2*) 'the subject to which the subject of the notion is attributed', meaning 'the subject of the accident whose notion is being discussed here'. But then the passage as a whole would be presenting a skewed contrast: what 1 asserts of the substance is not what 2* denies of the accident.

I cannot see how this can be anything but a blunder. *A fortiori*, I cannot see that it has anything to teach us. Mercifully, Leibniz's writings contain little of this line of thought, and I shall say no more about it.

'In a true subject-predicate proposition the concept of the predicate is contained in the complete concept of the subject'—that is trivial. What 'complete concept of x' means is just 'concept that contains the whole truth about x'. But Leibniz, although he sometimes writes that 'all philosophers' have committed themselves to the CPD, sees it as substantive—as posing threats, inviting misunderstandings, and throwing light. The triviality that a thing's complete concept contains the whole truth about it has no such power.

So the CPD must say something non-trivial *about* the complete concept of each substance. The non-trivial element in the CPD, I submit, is this:

> *Semantic Thesis*   The only way in which thoughts or words can latch on to an individual substance is through its complete concept.

Leibniz does not quite say this in so many words, but it must be his view. He has solid reasons for accepting it, as we shall see. Also, nothing else could justify his use of '*the* notion of the subject' to refer to its complete concept. Finally, nothing else would support a threat which he sees posed by the CPD: namely, that every subject–predicate proposition will turn out to be absolutely necessary. Let S* be a concept of Socrates that differs from (S) his complete concept in not including the concept of wisdom. If I can refer to Socrates through S*, then I can formulate a proposition *Socrates is wise* with the help of S*, and the CPD—which concerns S alone, and not S*—would have no appearance of implying that this proposition is necessary.

According to the Semantic Thesis, the meaning of each of an individual's names includes its complete concept: 'The subject term . . . means the totality of predicates possessed by the item denoted by the subject' (Hacking 1976: 138). Thus, the true proposition—using 'T' as shorthand for 'the morning of 14 March 44 BCE'—that

> Caesar has no premonition of death at T

is equivalent to a proposition of the form:

> The person who F and G and H and has no premonition of death at T and J and K and . . . etc. had no premonition of death at T.

The threat of absolute necessity is easy to see.

Extravagant as that sounds, Leibniz really does say it, often. Here for example:

The predicate . . . is always in the subject . . . . The connection and inclusion of the predicate in the subject is explicit in identities, but in all other propositions it is implicit and must be shown through the analysis of notions; *a priori* demonstration rests on this. (PT, AG 31)

'Identities' are statements of the form 'A is A' or 'Whatever is F and G is F', or the like. Leibniz is saying that subject–predicate truths that are *not* explicitly like this can be shown to be true 'through the analysis of concepts', which he equates with 'demonstration'—meaning rigorous, knock-down proof.

Although he writes much about 'the complete notion' of Julius Caesar, Leibniz does not explicitly speak of 'the meaning of "Julius Caesar"'. But the CPD really does rest on the Semantic Thesis, which implies something about meanings. Leibniz would have agreed. He wrote: 'The subject term must always include the predicate term in such a way that anyone who understands perfectly the concept of the subject will also know that the predicate pertains to it' (*DM* 8, FW 59–60).

Leibniz sometimes says that the CPD has been common property. He implies this just before the passage last quoted, and again here:

When I say that the individual concept of Adam contains everything that will ever happen to him I mean only what all philosophers mean when they say that the predicate is included in the subject of a true proposition. It is true that the consequences of a doctrine so evident are paradoxical, but the fault lies with the philosophers, who do not sufficiently pursue the clearest notions. (AG 73–4)

He never explains why he thinks that the CPD follows from something commonly accepted and 'evident'. Faced with the flat denials of Arnauld and others, he merely asserts that they have not thought well enough. Later in the correspondence, Arnauld seems to accept the core of the CPD, without having been given good reason to do so. This has led some to think that he really accepted it all along, which somewhat supports Leibniz's claim that it has been common property; but I agree with Sleigh (1990*a*: 41–2) in rejecting both parts of that.

Probably the view that all philosophers are committed to the CPD connects with Leibniz's frequent assertion that the CPD explains what it is for a subject–predicate proposition to be true. Immediately after the sentence I quoted at the start of this chapter, Leibniz adds: '*Praedicatum inest subjecto*; or I do not know what truth is.' Shortly thereafter: 'There must always be some foundation for the connection between the terms of a proposition, and this must be found in their concepts.' Enlarging a little another of my quotations: 'The predicate . . . is always in the subject . . . , and the nature of truth in general or the connection between the terms of a statement consists in this very thing.' Also: 'What is it to say that the predicate is in the subject, except that the notion of the predicate is in some way included in the notion of the subject?' (AG 73*).

To say that the predicate is in the subject (one wants to reply) is to say that the property is possessed by the thing—that Socrates is wise, that Caesar has no premonition of death at T. We have no need to bring 'concepts' or 'notions' into the story, and nobody has satisfactorily explained Leibniz's thinking that they obviously belong there. Granted, *S is P* is true just in case the complete concept of S contains the concept of P; but if that explains anything, it is the meaning of 'complete concept', not the nature of truth. As Leibniz writes, my complete concept contains the whole truth about me, because 'this concept is structured precisely so that one can deduce from it everything that is the case about me' (AG 76).[1]

This is a dead end. I now turn away from the 'nature of truth' idea about the CPD, and look instead at the Semantic Thesis.

---

[1] I offer 'structured precisely so that . . .' to render *fabriquée exprès en sorte que* . . .; the Petit Robert dictionary equates *fait exprès* with *parfaitement adapté*. AG's 'constructed explicitly so that . . .', whatever that means, cannot be right. Mason, whose translation of Leibniz's correspondence with Arnauld is almost flawless, has 'purposely created in such a way that . . .', which cannot be right either, because Leibniz did not think that concepts are created.

127. God's proper names

The thought of an individual thing must include the thought of everything that is true of it. Why should Leibniz believe this? Part of the answer lies in his view that God's practical thoughts about creation must involve the complete concepts of things. When God creates a particular thing, Leibniz holds, his creative intent embraces all the thing's details, rather than aiming at certain broad features and leaving the rest to subcontractors such as chance: 'My supposition is not simply that God wished to create an Adam of whom the concept is vague and incomplete, but that God wished to create a particular Adam sufficiently determinate for an individual' (AG 69). This makes sense in a theology like Leibniz's, where there are no subcontractors. Humans have freedom, but Leibniz does not allow that it fills gaps in God's creative intent.

In the above quotation the phrase *assez determiné à un individu* contains a hint of trouble. It suggests that God, by using Adam's complete concept in advance of creating him, has a thought not merely about a substance which is F and G and H . . . , but about *him*, Adam, that individual. Sellars evidently understood Leibniz in that way:

This individual concept of a substance [is] the sense of God's proper name for that individual; thus, the individual concept of Julius Caesar is the sense of the divine name for this individual substance we refer to as Julius Caesar. (1965: 30)

Most of what Leibniz says about God's thoughts about individual substances occurs in the context of God's creative intent, and thus concerns thoughts about substances that do not yet exist. Did he think that God has a use for proper names of mere possible individuals? Apparently he did. Writing to Arnauld about his having earlier spoken of God's 'creating a particular Adam, . . . chosen from among an infinite number of possible [men]', he explains:

[We may conceive] a certain person conceived of in general terms, in circumstances which seem to us to determine Adam as an individual, . . . as when one understands by Adam the first man that God places in a garden of pleasure which he leaves because of sin . . . But all that is not sufficiently determining; there would be many disjunctively possible Adams or many individuals whom all that would fit. That is true, whatever finite number of predicates incapable of determining all the rest one may take, but what determines a certain Adam must contain absolutely all his predicates, and it is this complete concept that determines generality in such a way that the individual is reached. (FW 110)[2]

Leibniz here envisages God's pre-creation thought as latching on to Adam, that individual, and not merely on to a complete schema-for-an-individual which fits the actual Adam.

---

[2] The final clause renders Leibniz's French–Latin phrase *qui determine rationem generalitatis ad individuum* (G 2:54), meaning 'which determines the general terms to the individual' or, informally, 'employs the general terms to pin down an individual'.

Prima facie these differ; and they really differ if two substances could fall under a single complete concept. Compare:

(1) Two complete concepts never apply to one actual thing;

(2) One complete concept never applies to two actual things.

1 is an innocent truth of logic; 2 is the thesis of the discernibility of the diverse (§142). Leibniz accepted it, and had reasons for doing so; but it is controversial. Nobody should be willing to settle the controversy by inferring 2 from the premiss that a complete-concept thought is an individually referring one. Yet that inference is valid; so we should deny its premiss.

Further trouble arises from the next part of the position that Sellars attributes to Leibniz:

Although Leibniz insists that we have a confused grasp of [the complete concept], which consists of our *petites perceptions* in so far as they represent Julius Caesar, this confused grasp of the concept is not, of course, *our* concept of Julius Caesar. For the sense of the term 'Julius Caesar', as we use it, is not, strictly speaking, an individual concept at all but—one is tempted to say—a peculiar kind of general concept.

That is right too, I believe. Leibniz seems to draw a conclusion about what we need for reference to actual substances from his premiss about what God needs for reference to possible ones. That is a suspect inference. Suppose that God's creative intent really does involve a thought which picks out a possible substance through its complete concept, and that this is genuine reference. Why should this constrain our references to actual substances? For God to pick out Caesar in advance of creating him (as I am briefly supposing he does), he must select him from an infinity of possible things; but we face no such task. For most and perhaps all of our purposes, we need only pick out Caesar from all the actual things that there are; and this confinement to actuality might give us help that would not be available in reference to non-actual individuals.

128. Referring to bodies

It might, and indeed it certainly does. Our success in referring to contingently existing individuals depends essentially on the fact that in each case we are trying to select the referent from among all the actuals only, not from among all the possibles. This success, however, does not come through our simply dumping actuality into our individual concepts. If it did, then things would stand thus:

We take a suitable incomplete concept of Caesar—express it by 'F'—and refer to Caesar as 'actual thing that is F'. Although 'F' unaided embraces many possible people, it applies to only one actual one, and so 'actual F' does the job.

That procedure, however, faces a difficulty. Consider a proposition about the Lincoln Memorial: how do we get our minds or words fixed on that object to the exclusion of all others? Let us try to do this through a description expressed in purely general terms, with no indexicals—no uses of 'I' or 'this' or 'here' or 'now'. We are to suppose, then, that 'the Lincoln Memorial' stands for something of the form 'thing which is F', where 'F' stands for a description of size and shape and texture, etc. Take it that F does not include 'made of marble', then consider how we are to understand the proposition:

L: The Lincoln Memorial is made of marble.

We have three options, each with actuality built into it:

L1: Some F thing is made of marble.
L2: Every F thing is made of marble.
L3: There is just one F thing, and every F thing is made of marble.

None of these is equivalent to L. I think L is true, but it could be false even if L1 were true. It could be that the Lincoln Memorial is made of white granite, but that the universe contains somewhere an F object—nearly a duplicate of the Lincoln Memorial—that is made of marble. So L1 is too weak, too easy to make true, to be equivalent to L. Similar reasoning easily shows that L2 and L3 are too strong. However improbable it may be that L is true and L3 false because a second F object lurks somewhere, it is possible. When you and I think that the Lincoln Memorial is made of marble, we do not commit ourselves to any view about whether the Memorial has a near-duplicate a thousand light-years away; so L3 is not equivalent to L. We are still looking for an understanding of what thought L is.

It does not help to bring in relational properties of the Lincoln Memorial. Let F stand for something of the form 'object with this shape, that size, this color, that texture, in this relation to an object which [description of the Washington Monument], in that relation to [description of the White House], . . .' and so on. It remains epistemically *possible* that L should be false and L1 true, and that L should be true and L2 and L3 false. Enlarge the relational picture further still, and the point remains. If F includes 'in this relation to *the Washington Monument*', that pins it down to only one possible referent. But we have no interest in a purported account of how we refer to the Lincoln Memorial which helps itself to a reference to the Washington Monument!

I have been resorting to the notion of 'massive reduplication' of chunks of the world, which was canvassed by Strawson (1959) for a purpose like my present one. As we enlarge the initial relational description to include relations to the city, the country, the planet, the galaxy, and so on, the idea of its fitting two actual items becomes ever more fanciful; but that is irrelevant to the logical or semantic point. We refer to the Lincoln Memorial without implying anything about distant galaxies; so what we say or think cannot be verified or falsified by facts about those. What, then, *do* we say or think? When you said 'The Lincoln Memorial is made of marble' and I chattered on about near-duplicates which may exist at remote times and places, you irritably thought this to be irrelevant to what you meant. So it was; but how did your meaning exclude it?

By the use of indexicals. My thought of the Lincoln Memorial is the thought of a large stone structure at one end of a long mall with a tall needle-like structure half-way along it and a domed building at the other end, in a capital city in *a country immediately to the south of where I am now*—the basic indexicals being 'I' and 'now'. If I were to replace the italicized phrase by 'a country which is K', where 'K' stands for a long general description of the United States, the resultant thought might capture other things as well as the Lincoln Memorial. But this just shows that the phrase is not short for a description of the country in question; just as I do not use 'I' and 'now' as shorthand for descriptions of myself and of the present.

Leibniz here, more clearly than anywhere else that I know of, writes about reference to individuals and the threat to it from reduplication:

Paradoxical as it may seem, it is impossible for us to know individuals or to find any way of precisely determining the individuality of any thing except by keeping hold of the thing itself. For any set of circumstances could recur, with tiny differences which we would not take in; and place and time, far from being determinants by themselves, must themselves be determined by the things they contain. The most important point in this is that individuality involves infinity, and only someone who is capable of grasping the infinite could know the principle of individuation of a given thing. (*NE* 289–90)

This raises Strawson's and my problem, and declines to solve it in our way. Leibniz here relies on his view that we can identify a place only in terms of how its contents relate to other physical things. That view is right, with one small exception: anyone can at any moment identify one place without interrelating bodies, namely by picking it out as 'the place where I am now' (for short: 'here'). Leibniz denies this: 'All propositions into which existence and time enter have as an ingredient the whole series of things. And "now" and "here" can be understood only in relation to other things' (1686*b*, PM 98–9). He is wrong about this, because 'now' and 'I'—and therefore 'here' as well—are given to our thought in an immediate way which lies deeper than any interrelating of events or of bodies. That is how we can secure unique reference among the actuals.

What is spatially related to oneself must be actual, which is why God cannot use this procedure to select a particular non-actual individual from a range of possibles. Nor can he use any other procedure. The whole idea of individual reference to non-actuals—unlike the idea of a completely saturated creative intent—is nonsensical.

Even in referring to actual monads, God is not spatio-temporally related to them; so he cannot refer to them in that way. There are also questions—and a philosophical literature—about whether he has any use for the indexical thought of *now*; but I shall not explore that here.

In a discussion of individual reference and re-identification in a 1672–3 work, Leibniz has a proposal which silently relies on indexicals (A 6:3: 147). That he turned away from this later may be explained by his coming to believe—as we have just seen—that his relationalism about *place* applied to *here*. Cover and

O'Leary-Hawthorne (1999) hold that Leibniz went on being content with index-icals. They agree that the CPD comes from a view about what is needed for ref-erence to an individual substance, but trace this need to a different source. They attribute to Leibniz the view that the (loosely speaking) law governing the unfolding of a thing's successive states is, strictly speaking, the thing (§311). And because each substance is a law, referring to a substance is referring to a law. Of course, any cognitive grip on the law—that law and no other—requires a thought which contains or entails the law's entire content. Getting a cognitive hold on an individual substance, they remark, is like grasping 'a mathematical function' (Cover and O'Leary-Hawthorne 1999: 182).[3]

Indeed, this would seem to follow from that view of substances. Problems arise about how to relate this conclusion to any facts about whether and how we creatures can refer to substances; but Cover and O'Leary-Hawthorne do not go into that. Nor does Leibniz. He did in about 1698 arrive at something like the view of substances with which these authors credit him, though I am not con-vinced that it went as far as theirs does towards turning substances into purely abstract entities. Even if it did, it can hardly be what motivated the CPD, which had disappeared from Leibniz's writings about a decade earlier.

129. Reference and causality

Starting with a question about individual reference ('How can I refer to an indi-vidual?'), I moved across to one about guaranteed uniqueness of a description ('How can a thought or phrase of mine be guaranteed to apply to at most one thing?'). The two questions are linked: a descriptive thought or phrase which *could* apply to more than one thing thereby fails to secure individual reference. Still, the questions are not equivalent: a thought or phrase which does apply to one thing and could not apply to more is not thereby certified as referring to that one thing. There is more to reference than mere guaranteed uniqueness of appli-cation.

Suppose that someone who has never heard of the Lincoln Memorial plays around with the fantasy of there being a structure which . . .—and her fantasy fills in details which fit the actual structure. They include a *present* spatial relation to *herself*, which guarantees that her fantasy cannot fit more than one thing. Suppose further that she has undergone a psychotic episode and confidently regards her fantasy as a memory. Does all this make it the case that she is think-ing about the Lincoln Memorial? Obviously not. Her thought cannot fit two things, and happens to fit one; but it is not about that one.

For it to be so, her thought must be causally related to the Lincoln Memorial in an appropriate way. What enables my thought to be about that particular

---

[3] In much of this they were anticipated by Beck 1969: 221–3, and even more by Fleming 1987.

thing is its being a remote causal consequence of an interaction between the Lincoln Memorial and something else—presumably my sense-organs or those of people who have told me about it, or told others who have told me, or have told others who have drawn pictures which I have seen, or . . . there are countless ways to do the job. But a causal chain there must be.

It is widely accepted these days that a *de re* thought—that is, a thought in which an individual is referred to—requires a causal connection; and the popularity of the view owes much to Kripke (1972). It was anticipated by Kant in his thesis that intuition (= the capacity for having thoughts about particulars) is in humans a sensible (= passive) faculty. Strawson's fine 'Monads' chapter does not bring in the causal requirement for reference, presumably because Strawson was not aware of it. He wrote that chapter before getting far in his work on Kant, and long before Kripke wrote.

Anyone who understands the causal-chain point can see that a uniquely applicable description need not be even a part of individual reference. I can refer to Praxiteles while knowing virtually nothing for sure about him, let alone being sure of some description that does apply to him and could not apply to two people—unless of course I bring into the description something causal and indexical, like 'carved *this* statue'.

This crucial ingredient in individual reference, properly understood, was not available to Leibniz because of his deeply entrenched view that no finite thing acts on anything else.

130. Essences

Leibniz's contained-predicate doctrine seems to imply that any truth of the form 'S is P' generates a corresponding truth of the form 'S could not possibly have not been P', which means that every property of a thing is essential to it. Objection: 'If the CPD concerns the meanings of subject terms, it may be relevant to essences *de dicto*, but it cannot have any bearing on essences *de re*.' Though plausible, this is wrong. The doctrine implies that if Adam sinned, then it is part of the meaning of 'Adam' that its bearer sinned, and thus that it is of the essence of Adam *qua* bearer-of-the-name-'Adam' that he sinned. That looks like a merely *de dicto* essence, but the CPD goes further, implying that if Adam sinned, then it is part of the meaning of *every* possible expression referring to Adam that its bearer sinned. Because this concerns every possible way of referring to Adam, it asserts a *de re* essence. This line of thought slopes down into some deep water, which I shall enter in §134. I am unmoved by the reason that Cover and O'Leary-Hawthorne (1999: 151n.) give for opposing it.

Some writers deny that Leibniz infers from the CPD that all of an individual's properties are essential to it. His only conclusion, they say, is weaker than that. Let us look into this. The heading of *DM* 30 includes this: 'We do not have the right to complain, and we must not ask why Judas sins . . . but only why Judas the sinner is admitted to existence.' In the body of the section Leibniz writes:

Why is it that this man will assuredly commit this sin? The reply is easy: otherwise it would not be this man. For God sees from all time that there will be a certain Judas whose notion or idea (which God has) contains this future free action. Therefore only this question remains, why does such a Judas, the traitor, who in God's idea is merely possible, actually exist? (DM 30, FW 81*)

Let us linger on 'otherwise it would not be this man', which is short for 'someone who did not commit this sin would not be this man'. At least three English versions have 'otherwise *he* would not be this man', which implies that if Judas had not sinned, he would not have been self-identical. (The impeccable edition of Lucas and Grint gets it right.) If this were what Leibniz meant by *autrement ce ne serait pas cet homme*, he would certainly be implying the absolute necessity of Judas's sinning: any counterfactual of the form 'If P had been the case, then Q would have been the case', where Q is logically impossible, entails that P is impossible too. Arnauld did at one point wish that view on Leibniz, who did not reject it; but it is not what he said (Mason 33).

His words mean something weaker, namely: 'Judas sinned thus. Anyone who did not sin thus would not be Judas.' Now, if this means 'Anyone at any possible world who does not sin in this way is not Judas', then it follows that Judas commits the sin at every world at which he exists, and thus that it is absolutely necessary that he committed this sin. But plenty of counterfactual conditionals fall short of being statements of absolute necessity. If it had rained yesterday, we would have cancelled the picnic—that is true because of people's wishes, what other dates were available, the lack of shelters, etc. At some possible worlds many of those other conditions are different too, and at some of those we hold a picnic in the rain. Or, in technical terms, we cancel the picnic at the closest worlds where it rains yesterday, but not at every such world.

Perhaps such a weaker reading can be given for Leibniz's 'otherwise it would not be this man'. If that is answerable only to the 'closest' worlds at which some fairly Judas-like person does not sin thus and so, then perhaps at some more 'remote' world Judas himself does not sin in that manner.[4] But I cannot put flesh on those bones. Sleigh (1990a: 71–2) notes that Leibniz does not say outright that each of a substance's properties is essential to it, and believes that Leibniz did not believe this. He conjectures that this may be reconcilable with the thesis that, for every F such that Fx, if anything had not been F, it would not have been x; but he has no detailed suggestions for what the 'off-beat notion' might be through which the trick was worked. For a detailed and toughly argued case against Sleigh on this matter, see Mondadori 1993: 155–65.

---

[4] I am not here 'forcing the systems of Stalnaker or Lewis . . . on Leibniz' (Sleigh 1990a: 71), but merely relying on what the conditional in question means for me and presumably also for Leibniz, even if he did not have the Stalnaker–Lewis way of making that meaning clear.

Setting counterfactuals aside, another problem confronts the position that Sleigh attributes to Leibniz. The complete concept of Judas cannot be different at some worlds from how it is at Alpha (the actual world): no sense attaches to the idea that a concept might have been different from how it actually is. So Sleigh's Leibniz must say that at some worlds Judas has a different complete concept from the one he has at Alpha. But according to the CPD there is no way to say or think this. Objection: 'Yes there is. I can easily think *Judas sins at Alpha and Judas does not sin at W*, using two different concepts of Judas.' Reply: 'That is not to our purpose unless it includes the thought that the two are concepts of *one man*; and that brings us back to where we started, wanting to have a thought that Sleigh's Leibniz will not allow us.'

Leibniz does maintain that some subject–predicate propositions are contingent. Here is one of his many statements of how:

In contingent truths . . . , though the predicate inheres in the subject, we can never demonstrate this, nor can the proposition ever be reduced to an equation or an identity, but the analysis proceeds to infinity, only God being able to see (not the end of the analysis, indeed, for there is no end, but) the nexus of terms or the inclusion of the predicate in the subject, since he sees everything that is in the series. (1679, L 265)

That the 'infinite analysis' story has no bearing on contingency as we understand it has often been pointed out—for example by Russell (1900: 61–2), Nason (1942: 27), Curley (1976: 92–3), Mates (1986: 112–17). Nor has the story anything to do with essences or what obtains at all possible worlds—notions that are conspicuously absent from the account. It is perhaps a little odd that this should be so. It will seem most odd to those who think that Leibniz explained necessity as truth at all possible worlds; but in fact he did not ever do so. Most of what he says about necessity belongs to formal logic or to epistemology; and when he ventures briefly into the metaphysics of necessity, he does so in terms not of possible worlds but of relations amongst ideas in the mind of God.

Mates credits Leibniz with holding that every property of a substance is essential to it, and suggests that he could have found this attractive because he could not see how to divide a thing's properties into the essential and the accidental:

Leibniz . . . could make no sense of essentialism, the doctrine that some attributes of an individual are essential and others are accidental. From the beginning to the end of his intellectual career . . . he considered that in this respect all of an individual's attributes are on a par; and since the alternative to taking all of them as accidental (which would require us to say, for example, that Adam could have had all the attributes of Bucephalus) was clearly unacceptable, he was driven to the other alternative of declaring them all equally essential. (1986: 43)

This is plausible as exegesis. Leibniz writes to Arnauld: 'If in the life of some person, or even in the universe as a whole, some event were to occur in a different way from how it actually does, nothing would prevent us from saying that this would be another person or another possible universe which God has chosen' (FW 109). The curious turn of phrase 'nothing would prevent us from saying . . .'

seems to confirm Mates's view: the thought is that we are free to say that all the properties are essential, because no solid barrier separates essence from accident. Contrast Locke's view in *Essay* III.vi.4, that because there is no barrier we should say that all the properties are accidental. (When at *NE* 305 Leibniz asserts that some of a thing's properties are essential to it and others accidental, he may be merely making the best comment he can on some doctrines of Locke's, short of digging deeply into his own philosophy.) Margaret Wilson (1979*a*: 729) has challenged Leibniz's right to go his way rather than Locke's; Cover and O'Leary-Hawthorne (1999: 195–9) defend him. I decline to arbitrate.

There are indeed problems about drawing an objective and justified line through the properties of an individual, with the essential on one side and the accidental on the other. Of course we have intuitions about essence and accident, as did Arnauld, who protested that his priestly celibacy was not of his essence and that he might have married (Mason 30). Leibniz replied that conclusions about possibility should not be based on such casual thought-experiments, which he explains away as products of thinking about individuals through merely partial concepts of them. He did not comment on a fine irony which I missed too until it was pointed out by Yablo (1990: 161–2). Forty-six years earlier Arnauld (Rep 4, CSM 2:139–43) had objected to Descartes's claim that he could exist even if there were no matter, implying that Descartes was putting too little into his essence on the basis of a casual thought-experiment! Incidentally, Arnauld was right both times: if I have an essence, it is richer than Descartes thinks and poorer than Leibniz thinks.

A second possible attraction of the CPD is theological. As Margaret Wilson pointed out, Leibniz seems to want the CPD 'as a basis for denying that God is responsible for a created individual's misfortunes or bad choices, since *that individual* could not have existed unless he made those choices', etc. Even if I believe that the world would have been better if it had not contained someone who failed as I did at time T, I cannot say that it would have been better if *I* had not failed at T; so I cannot complain that God has dealt a poor hand *to me*. This chips away at one corner of the theodicy problem (see also C. Wilson 1989: 94–5).

The thesis that all of a substance's properties are essential to it does not entail that a substance could not possibly have existed at a different world. For this substance, falling under this complete concept, to share a world with substances other than the ones it actually coexists with, would be contrary to God's wisdom but not absolutely impossible. On this question I agree with Cover and O'Leary-Hawthorne 1999: 89–110 against, among others, Mondadori 1975. In taking this position I am assuming that the basic properties of any monad are all logically monadic—that is, not relational (§135).

131. Infinite analysis: why?

If the CPD is true, how can any subject–predicate proposition be contingent? In Leibniz's own words: 'If at any particular time the concept of the predicate inheres in the concept of the subject, how can the predicate ever be denied of the subject without contradiction and impossibility?' (1679, L 264). We have seen him answer that this can be so if the predicate-concept is not extractable from the subject-concept through a finite analysis. Before examining this doctrine, let us consider why Leibniz cares. What, for him, would be so bad about allowing that every subject–predicate proposition is absolutely necessary?

He abhors Spinoza's philosophy because it implies that whatever is true is absolutely necessary, against which Leibniz asserts that there are contingent truths which were selected by God to be true out of a larger array of possibles: 'The world is a voluntary effect of God . . . Even if we imagine it to be perpetual, it would still not be necessary. For God could either have not created anything or have created the world otherwise; but this was something he did not do' (Comments, AG 277). This gives Leibniz a need for contingent existential propositions—a need which he tries to satisfy (§71)—but he is under no theological pressure to make room for contingent subject–predicate ones. He does not need to credit God with choosing whether or not Judas will sin, so long as he can credit him with choosing whether Judas will exist. The whole truth about the actual world can be expressed in propositions of the form 'There is a substance which . . .', with no use of the subject–predicate form. Once God has chosen which existentials are to be true, his plan for creation is complete. So threats to contingency from the use of the subject–predicate form do not threaten God's freedom of choice. I am still taking it for granted that 'existent' is not a predicate.

In §71 I presented Leibniz's one attempt to connect the two themes of God's choices and subject–predicate contingency, and argued that it fails. It is a rather recherché affair, anyway, and I cannot believe that it sits near the centre of his thought. So the problem of motivating his search for subject–predicate contingency still stands.

Perhaps Leibniz was motivated by a desire to answer the following question:

According to the CPD, every subject–predicate proposition is absolutely necessary (because each is 'analytic' in Kant's sense of that word). But we all have strong intuitions that some of these are necessary, others contingent, and we tend to agree about where the line falls. Presumably we are drawing some distinction, even if it is not strictly that between 'necessary' and 'contingent'. What distinction is it?

We might see Leibniz as adducing his 'infinite analysis' story in answer to this question. The cases where P can be extracted from S only through an infinite analysis, he might be saying, are just the ones where 'S is P' strikes us as contingent.

I have little enthusiasm for this as exegesis, or as philosophy. I doubt that Leibniz ever did cleanly isolate and confront the minor problem of explaining human intuitions of contingency. If he had, he would have done better to say rather that the cases in which 'S is P' strikes us as contingent are just the ones where what we are aware of in the concept of S does not include the concept of P. Each of us has folded into his being all that is needed for complete individual concepts, Leibniz believes, but he must think that most of it consists in fuzzy little perceptions of which we are not aware; so when we seem to ourselves to refer to individuals, our would-be referring thought has some content of which we are aware; and if that does not include the predicate of our proposition, the latter will strike us as contingent.

132. Infinite analysis: how?

Does the infinite analysis account work? Whether or not it engages with anything else, is it a wheel that turns? On the face of it, the answer is No. If the concept of Caesar includes 'has no premonition of death on the morning of 14 March 44 BCE', how could it possibly *need* an infinite analysis to extract this predicate-concept from it? The infinite analysis serially unpacks the content of the subject-concept; in such an unpacking some items must be laid bare early on, thus being extracted from the subject-concept through an analysis which is not merely finite but downright short. Yet, will not plenty of those be values of P such that we would ordinarily say that 'S is P' is contingent? Adams (1994: 34) calls this the 'Lucky Proof' objection to Leibniz's notion of infinite analysis, as applied to the proposition that Peter denied Jesus: 'Why couldn't we begin to analyze Peter's concept by saying "Peter is a denier of Jesus and . . ."? Presumably [this] must be ruled out by some sort of restriction on what counts as a step in an analysis of an individual concept, but so far as I know, Leibniz does not explain how this is to be done.'

I cannot conceive of how one might relevantly restrict 'what counts as a step in an analysis'. A more promising move is to concede that the Lucky Proof objection is irresistible if the subject-concept contains the other in a simple conjunctive way, and to claim that that is not how it is structured. Two suggestions have been made for how this might be.[5]

The All Worlds structure   According to this, the concept of Judas (say) is the concept of *being that has the J-role at the best possible world*, where 'the J-role' stands for a complex, largely relational predicate which picks out Judas and nobody else at the actual world and never applies to two things at any world. For a thing x to have the J-role at a world w is for x to exist at w and to cut a Judas-like figure at w—to fit into w in the kind of way in which Judas fits into the actual world.

---

[5] There is a third in Hacking 1978: 191. I do not know what to say about it. Carriero (1993: 20–6) has a fourth. It is subtle and interesting, and does much better justice than any of the others to Leibniz's likening of this matter to such infinite procedures as the progressive decimal expansion of π. But it is not really about the analysis of notions, and thus has no connection with the CPD.

Somehow—heaven knows how—the J-role has to be so understood that its meaning does not include any of the properties that we think of as possessed contingently by Judas; so having the J-role must not analytically involve sinning or betraying one's master or the like. If Leibniz could avail himself of this notion and use it in assigning to the concept of Judas the structure I have proposed, he might get the result he wants: an unpacking of the concept which reveals that Judas sinned must discover whether sinning is contained in the concept of *having the J role at the best possible world*; this involves finding out which possible world is the best one; and that may be feasible only through an infinite process of pairwise comparisons of worlds.

Is not this view of the structure of complete individual concepts too complex, *ad hoc*, and rickety for Leibniz to have accepted it? Apparently not. After remarking that 'propositions into which existence and time enter . . . do not admit of demonstrations, i.e. of terminable resolution by which their truth may appear', Leibniz continues: 'Indeed, even if someone could know the whole series of the universe, he still could not give a reason for it, unless he compared it with all other possibles. From this it is evident why no demonstration can be found, however far the resolution of notions is continued' (1686b, PM 99). This, it seems, does not adequately separate what it takes to analyse the concept of Judas from what it takes to explain fully why Judas exists. But the former question is present, and seems to be answered in terms of the All Worlds structure.

This account of how individual complete concepts are structured has no claim on our philosophical respect. The structure it attributes to each concept is fabricated just to ward off the Lucky Proof objection. Also, it takes us right away from Leibniz's serious reason for holding that individuals can be referred to only through their complete concepts. Imagine arguing that individual reference is possible only through concepts with the All Worlds structure!

The Start and Law structure   A different account of the structure of the subject-concept may also be at work in the passage last quoted. Leibniz may sometimes have thought of the complete concept as explicitly containing only (a) the monad's initial total state and (b) its law of development. An analysis which uncovers something contained in this concept must start from those base materials and work out from them that Judas sinned or Caesar crossed the Rubicon; and this might not be a finite process. How could it not be finite? There are two possible answers to this.

(1) The series of the monad's states is continuous, so that no total temporary state of the monad has immediate neighbours—between any two such states an infinity of others intervenes. Leibniz could hardly take this way out, because it asserts that something real is continuous, whereas he puts continuity two levels away from reality, in the 'ideal'. Also, it threatens to make virtually every *S is P* proposition contingent, whereas we are supposed to be explaining a line between those that are contingent and those that are not. There is no decent chance of avoiding this last difficulty by supposing that while some parts of the sequence of events are continuous, others are discrete.

(2) A more promising answer to our question has been defended by O'Leary-Hawthorne and Cover (forthcoming). A substance's complete concept, they hold, represents, and is isomorphic with, its law of development; such a law guarantees the substance's performing a certain action at a given time on the basis of its *total* state at the preceding time; that total state consists in an infinity of tiny inclinations and tendencies, and the resultant of all of them leads to Judas's sinning. In this account, it takes an infinite analysis to arrive at P from any earlier state of the substance, initial or not; the relevant infinity is that of separate aspects of the monad's state *at any given moment*; and the account does not require that time be continuous. A finite subset of those aspects of a monad at T_1 will lead by law to some of its aspects at T_2; but (these authors suggest) such a subset will never lead to large-scale 'actions' at T_2 or—more generally—to any facts about the monad that would appear in the P position of an S–P proposition that is a good candidate for the 'contingent' label.

This gets rid of the continuity problem; it fits with things Leibniz says about the causal antecedents of large-scale 'actions'; and the authors argue that it fits well with Leibniz's repeated comparison of his 'infinite analysis' idea with some mathematical issues regarding incommensurability. I know nothing about this last matter; but the other two make this account of where the infinity comes from superior to the preceding one.

Still, I do not accept it. It is true, as Cover and O'Leary-Hawthorne say, that the whole truth about Adam includes a law and not a mere ordered list of temporary states; so in thinking of Adam, God has to think of a law (§312). These authors believe that such a law can apply to only one set of states, so that when you know the law, you potentially know all the states: in their account, the 'Start and Law structure' of a substance's concept gives way to a 'Law structure'. Either way, according to their Leibniz, God thinks of Adam purely through his law or through that and one initial state, not bringing the remaining individual states into his referential thought, because they would be redundant there. But that goes against Leibniz's emphatic view that God's greatness shines especially brightly in his feat of harmonizing the created monads by attending to all their particular temporary states:

Each of these souls . . . has to draw up [its states] from the depths of its own nature; and so necessarily each soul must have received this nature . . . from a universal cause, upon which all of these beings depend and which brings it about that each of them perfectly agrees with and corresponds to the others. That could not occur without infinite knowledge and power. (*NE* 440)[6]

This cherished and often-repeated theme of Leibniz's conflicts with the idea that God thinks of his creatures purely in the '(Start and) Law' manner.

Even if I am mistaken about this, and Leibniz can hold that God thinks about individuals only by thinking of their laws of development, what connects this with the semantic views that launched the CPD in the first place, or with the

---

[6] See also Mon 56–9, FW 275–6.

problems that are supposed to arise from it? What can a mere fact about how God *does* proceed have to do with threats to freedom and to contingency? The only threat to freedom here comes from the determinism of the monad's law of unfolding; and that is sheer metaphysics, owing nothing to any thesis about a substance's complete concept. Prospects might be brighter if the thesis were that God *must* think of the substance by thinking of its law (and perhaps its initial state) and not the rest of its particular states, but how could that be defended? Leibniz cannot say that thinking enumeratively of all the states would be too hard for God.

Nobody has made respectable sense of what Leibniz says about finite and infinite analysis of subject-concepts. Furthermore, even if he did succeed in that, nobody thinks the result would have anything to do with contingency as we understand it, or, therefore, that it could satisfy Leibniz's need to defend contingency (in our sense) so that God has real choices to make. We should drop the matter. It is too late in the day to expect the mystery to be cleared up, and I guess that if Leibniz or scholarship did remove the veil, we would conclude that the search had not been worth our trouble. I mean: worth our trouble as philosophers. It is different for antiquarians.

133. The contained-predicate doctrine construed as causal

The contained-predicate doctrine has a certain surface likeness to the doctrine of immanent causation, and Leibniz sometimes runs them in a single harness, as here: '[1] The concept of this particle of matter . . . involves all the changes it has undergone and will one day undergo. And in my view [2] every individual substance always contains traces of what has ever happened to it and marks of what will ever happen to it' (AG 70–1). He seems to offer 1 as less disputable than 2 ('in my view'), which suggests that he does not regard 1 as entailing 2. But quite often he *does* imply that 1 entails 2, or even that they are equivalent. Consider this, written to Arnauld:

It is not so easy to judge whether the journey I intend to make is contained in the concept of me; otherwise it would be as easy for us to be prophets as to be geometers. I am not sure whether I shall take the journey . . . These things appear to us to be undetermined only because the foreshadowings or marks of them in our substance are not recognisable by us. (AG 75)

Here a difficulty in determining whether P belongs to Leibniz's individual concept is set alongside a difficulty in determining, at a particular time, whether his state *then* contains signs that P will later be true of him. Leibniz does not equate the two, implying merely that removing the second difficulty would remove the first; but he seems not to be sharply aware of how different they are. This is reinforced in a subsequent letter which he drafted but did not send to Arnauld, in which he wrote: 'Extension is an attribute which cannot make up a complete entity, no action or change can be deduced from it, it expresses only a present state, not at all the future and past as the concept of a substance must do' (FW 116). In fact, the richness of a thing's complete concept has nothing to do with the informative richness or poverty of its temporal stages; the two are wholly different. The semantic CPD says that the concept of Leibniz contains the whole truth about him; whereas the causal doctrine says that each temporal stage of Leibniz contains the marks of his past and future stages. The former could be true and the latter false. Consider these two:

(1) Despite current orthodoxy, one cannot refer to any particular except through descriptions. Because of the reduplication problem, it takes a complete description to do this.

(2) Determinism is false. Some events in the history of a monad are neither fully explicable in terms of its preceding states nor in theory predictable from them.

These jointly entail that no thing can be securely referred to—even by Laplace's predictor—until it has run its course. Grasping this entailment helps one to see that 1 is consistent with 2. In fact, 2 on its own has no bearing on the semantics of individual reference or, therefore, on the CPD.

The converse holds too. I have good reasons to reject the CPD: other substances do act upon me, and I have immediate conceptual access to *myself*; so I can refer to other substances without using complete concepts of them (§§128–9). That *obviously* leaves me free to hold the immanent causation doctrine about every other substance in the universe; and also to accept its temporal dual: namely, the thesis that each state of a substance contains all the news about its past as well as future states. Leibniz's extravagant doctrine about signs and traces has no bearing on any issues about individual reference.

Leibniz thinks otherwise:

God, seeing Alexander's individual notion or haecceity, sees in it at the same time the basis and reason for all the predicates which can be said truly of him . . . ; he even knows a priori (and not by experience) whether he died a natural death or whether he was poisoned, something we can know only through history. Thus when we consider carefully the connection of things, we can say that from all time in Alexander's soul there are vestiges of everything that has happened to him and marks of everything that will happen to him and even traces of everything that happens in the universe, even though God alone could recognize them all. (DM 8, FW 60; see also AG 76)

This opens with contained predicate and closes with immanent causation and its temporal dual, without acknowledging the change of topic. The two are run together even more fiercely in an earlier work where Leibniz uses the CPD as a reason for denying that substances act on one another: 'No created substance exerts a metaphysical action or influence on any other thing. For . . . we have already shown that from the notion of each thing follows all of its future states'

(PT, AG 33; see also *DM* 14, FW 66–7). And in the next paragraph he writes about what follows 'from the first *constitution or notion* of a thing'. In fact, 'constitution' belongs to the immanent causation doctrine, while 'notion' belongs to the CPD.

There is a hint of the same trouble when Leibniz, having introduced the CPD to Arnauld, writes: 'This is my great principle, with which I believe all philosophers should agree, and one of whose corollaries is the commonly held axiom that nothing happens without a reason, which can always be given, why the thing has happened as it did rather than in another way' (FW 112). Leibniz here takes the CPD to entail the principle of sufficient reason as applied to events that occur in the course of a substance's lifetime. In a way, it does. The CPD entails that there is an answer to each question of the form 'Why is it the case that S does X?', where 'S' refers to an individual substance, and 'X' refers to an action or event. But the only answers it guarantees are ones of the form 'S does X because the concept of doing-X is contained in the concept of S'. That does not answer the why-question that Leibniz seems to and ought to have in mind. When he asks 'why the thing has happened as it did rather than in another way', he points us to questions of this form:

Why is it that a monad which is in state S_1 at time T_1 will move to being in partial state S_2 at T_2?

This is a legitimate why-question, which can be answered by appealing to the causal principles that govern monads. The fact to be explained does not identify any one monad, so it provides no excuse for bringing in any complete concept, which means that the CPD cannot get a finger-hold.

(Loeb (1981: 277–91) discusses whether a monad's complete concept entails that its unfolding is governed by deterministic immanent causation; he rightly says that it does so only if being-thus-governed is crammed into the concept; which means that the CPD does not provide any independent reason for accepting Leibniz's view about causation in monads. I agree; but my concern is with Leibniz's more insidious tendency to conflate the causation doctrine with the CPD, not merely to infer one from the other.)

Leibniz has made a mistake here. Some, such as Adams, defend him on the grounds that what he meant by 'concept' was something causally active, a locus of force or the like. I doubt this; but even if he did, it remains true that he launched a doctrine in semantics—aiming to tell the truth about what *truth* is—and then treated it as metaphysics, smudging the line between conceptual containment and natural causation. Fleming (1987: 86–7) endorses this part of Leibniz's thought, writing that 'there is . . . no room for any created substance to affect or be affected by any other created substance' because 'Everything that happens to a monad follows from the notion or the law of the series of that monad'. He concedes this to Leibniz by allowing him 'a shift in terminology [whereby] the law of the series becomes the notion of the subject'. My point is that this is a shift in more than terminology.

I suspect that Leibniz came to see for himself that the two doctrines—immanent determinism and the CPD—are unrelated. Catherine Wilson summarizes the historical picture:

Having dropped the subject-predicate logic as a basis for a theory of substance, Leibniz has turned to other models: to the stored-up potential and released energy of seemingly inanimate objects, to the physical development of a living creature, and to the production of thoughts in the mind. This shift is already apparent by 1690. To Fardella, Leibniz explains that it is from the nature of substances or their 'primitive power' (not their concepts!) that their 'series of operations' follows. In effect, notions which are peripheral in the *Discourse*, better elaborated in the Arnauld correspondence of 1686–7, assume center-stage from 1690 onwards. (1989: 160)

Broad (1975: 24–5) also grasped this trouble in Leibniz as Wilson does. By the time of 'Monadology' (1714), Wilson notes, 'logical content has been expunged'—that is, the CPD has dropped from sight. Nor does it appear in the *New Essays*, written about a decade before that. In the anthologies of Ariew–Garber, Francks–Woolhouse, and Loemker I can find no sign of the CPD later than 1690.

I cannot find Leibniz disowning the contained-predicate doctrine. Nor does he in his mature years liberate himself from the need for it, by allowing indexicality and transeunt causation for finite creatures, and/or by relinquishing the fancy that God can think *de re* about individuals in advance of creating them. Furthermore, we have found in the *New Essays*, written within a dozen years of Leibniz's death, the passage about individual reference that does most to support and explain the CPD (§128). However, if he went on believing this doctrine, why did he fall silent about it? Probably because he stopped having any reason to parade it in his writings, especially the bad 'reason' that came from conflating it with his doctrine about the causal organization of each monad. He seems eventually to have realized that that is indeed a conflation, a mistake.

134. Freedom and the contained-predicate doctrine

Sometimes Leibniz associates his project of showing how some subject–predicate propositions can be contingent with that of rescuing human freedom. If it is necessary that Judas sins (so the thought goes), then his sinning is not a free act, and he ought not to be blamed or punished for it. When Leibniz has that 'problem' in mind, he says that the subject-concept contains the concept of the person's acting thus-or-so *freely*. I have quoted him writing that Judas has 'a notion or idea [which] contains this *free action*' (my emphasis).

The mere thesis that every individual *has* a complete concept poses no threat to freedom. If an act of mine is 'free' in your favourite sense, then this fact belongs to my total story, so the concept of it is part of my complete concept. There is no tension here.

Objection: 'Yes there is. If at T_1 it is laid down in my concept that I shall start walking at time T_2, then at T_1 it is already settled that I shall walk at T_2; and that does conflict with the act's being "free" in any sense which implies that it was not in principle predictable, or that the question of whether it would be performed was genuinely open.' Reply: Who said that it was settled at T_1? An infinity of complete concepts all fit my history up to and including T_1; some are concepts of people who start to walk at T_2, and some are not. The concepts are laid up in the third realm or the divine intellect—they are fixed in advance, frozen, untouchable by human hand. My doings cannot affect a concept, but they can ruin its chances of finally turning out to be the concept of me. (That, I hope, is what Leibniz means when he writes (FW 108) that if he behaved differently in a certain way, 'that would destroy the individual or complete concept of me'.) Every time I act, a pack of complete concepts falls by the wayside, having lost their chance of being *my* individual concept. As I draw my last breath, a single competitor remains, the winner, the concept that captures the total story of me.

Leibniz seems to agree with this when, addressing an intermediary about Arnauld's charge that the CPD removes human freedom, he writes scornfully that mere facts about concepts cannot affect the situation of the person on the ground:

I had said . . . that the individual concept of each person contains once for all everything that will ever happen to him; from this [Arnauld] deduces the consequence that every-thing that happens to a person . . . must happen through a more than fatal necessity. As though concepts or previsions made things necessary, and a free action could not be included in the perfect concept or view that God has of the person to whom it will belong. (FW 98)

That brings in a new theme: namely, God's knowledge in advance of how I shall act at T_2. Leibniz seems content with the idea that God knows in advance that I shall *freely start to walk at T_2*. I choose not to add to the literature on the question of what kinds of freedom are consistent with what kinds of foreknowledge.

For the rest, Leibniz is right: the doctrine that there is a complete concept of each of us is irrelevant to who we are, how we live, what possibilities are open to us. Had he kept this more steadily in mind, he would not have confused the CPD with the thesis of immanent deterministic causation.

However, this smooth surface is ruffled when we add in the false thesis that a substance can be referred to only through its complete concept. In this section I have assumed the falsity of that. I wrote of all the complete concepts which, at T_1, still have a chance of being *mine*, purporting to refer to myself other than through my complete concept.

Perhaps, then, radical freedom is threatened by Leibniz's full-strength thesis that no substance can be referred to except through its complete concept. Objection: 'How could it do so? Your personal freedom could not be affected by semantic facts about what it takes to refer to an individual.' Yes, it could, in two ways.

Although the CPD as I understand it is a semantic doctrine, it implies something about *de re* essences (§130). According to it, *betraying Jesus* is essential to Judas *qua* F for *every* F that enables us to refer to Judas (that is, for the only F that enables us to do this, namely the one expressing his complete concept). So we can drop the *qua*, and say that betraying Jesus is essential to Judas, period. So we can say of Judas that *he could not have done otherwise*, meaning this in a strong sense; and that seems to conflict with his betraying Jesus freely, on any reasonable account of freedom and even on some unreasonable ones. Leibniz's tussles with this problem are various and slippery and, in my experience, not philosophically instructive.

Anyway, that threat to freedom from the CPD is a relatively shallow affair. Here is a more dangerous and more interesting one. When I have a practical problem, I ask myself 'What am I to do?' We have seen the CPD seeming to imply that my answer is always absolutely necessary; but now we come to the fact that the CPD, as I understand it, implies that I cannot even ask the question.

For me to have any thought—interrogative or affirmative, worried or confident, accepting or sceptical—about whether at this moment to stand or to sit, I need a thought that latches on to *me*, this individual, in advance of settling whether I shall stand or sit. Each of us, in fact, can mentally or linguistically refer to him- or herself without going through any descriptive concept, let alone a complete one. That is why someone who has total amnesia can wonder *what to do* by wondering 'What shall I do?' That is a special case; but in more ordinary ways this *I*-thought, unassisted by descriptions (and *a fortiori* not propped up by complete ones), is essential to how we make sense of the human condition. If Leibniz's theory of reference were correct, a sentence such as 'In a moment from now, I may stand or I may instead sit' is either an absurdity or else a masquerade, something that purports to refer to an individual when really it does not.

It is an understatement to say that Leibniz's theory of reference poses a threat to human freedom. If the theory were true, and we did not have at our disposal the indexical use of 'I', we could not think coherently about ourselves at all.

Chapter 18

Leibniz and Relations

135. Relations

Leibniz held that there are no basic relational truths, and that the entire fundamental truth about the world could be told in attributions of monadic predicates
to monads; where Fx is a monadic truth if neither it nor its contradictory entails
the existence of any individual other than x.[1] This doctrine of Leibniz's means
that relational truths supervene on monadic ones, in this sense:

> For any individuals x and y and any dyadic relation R, if it is true that R(x,y),
> then there are monadic predicates F_1 and F_2 such that:
>
> F_1x and F_2y, and
> (F_1x and F_2y) entails R(x,y).

For example, the truth of 'Arnold is taller than Danny' is entailed by two monadic
truths assigning heights individually to the two men. I have stated this for dyadic
relations; it is easy to see how to complicate it so that it covers n-adic relations for
any n.

A further complication is needed also. As John O'Leary-Hawthorne has
pointed out to me, the dyadic fact that at a certain time *x quasi-acted upon y* is
made to obtain not merely by a conjunction of monadic propositions about x and
y, but also by an endless conjunction of such propositions about all the other
monads—the conjunction that expresses the cosmic harmony. I shall spare us the
labour of revising the formula so as to take this into account.

In my idiolect, a monadic predicate is used to attribute to a thing a monadic
property; Leibniz's favoured term for the latter is 'intrinsic denomination'. In this
phrase 'intrinsic' means 'monadic', one-place, pertaining only to the one subject
and not involving any other. A 'denomination' is often a name or other linguistic expression, but in these contexts it is not a linguistic item, but rather a property, something for which a linguistic predicate can stand. This is explained and
defended by Mates (1986: 218–19), to whom I am much indebted in this chapter.
For further good discussion see Cover 1989, and Cover and O'Leary-Hawthorne
1999: ch. 2.

---

[1] The phrase 'nor its contradictory' is crucial, for without it the predicate '. . . is the only thing that
exists' would count as monadic, which it plainly is not. For further help, see Langton and Lewis 1998.

Leibniz is often said to believe in the 'reducibility' of all relations, and that word may have encouraged critics to credit him with the opinion that each relational proposition is equivalent to some conjunction of monadic ones. That opinion is clearly false; Sidgwick's being abler than Moore is not equivalent to any conjunction of facts about how able each is. Nor did Leibniz think it is. He grounds relational facts in monadic ones not by equivalence but by *supervenience*. Many explanatory or derivation relations have been brought under the term 'supervenience', but all we need is entailment: every relational truth is a logical consequence of a conjunction of monadic truths. These monadic truths make the relational truth hold; with them included in our story, the relational truth adds nothing. The relevant inferences go through on the strength of logical principles some of which are relational (that 3 > 2, for instance), but only a shallow critic could think that this is a difficulty for Leibniz's supervenience thesis.

The texts in which Leibniz says that relational truths supervene on monadic ones are plentiful but unclear. Here are some typical ones:

Relations and orderings are to some extent 'beings of reason', although they have their foundations in things. (*NE* 227)

The unity that collections have is merely a respect or relation, whose foundation lies in what is the case within each of the individual substances taken alone. So the only perfect unity that these entities by aggregation have is a mental one. (*NE* 146)

A relation, since it results from a state of things, never comes into being or disappears unless some change is made in its foundation. (Quoted from Mates 1986: 223))

While it can happen that a relation involves in its essence the existence of several things, it involves the one differently from how it involves the other; thus paternity involves the two individuals David and Solomon, but differently in the two cases. (Ibid. 223–4)

Relations are not produced per se, but result when other things are produced, and have reality in our intellect. Indeed, they are there when nobody is thinking; for they get that reality from the divine intellect, without which nothing would be true. (Ibid. 224)

A relation is an accident which is in several subjects and is only a result or supervenes with no change made on their part if several things are thought of at once; it is *concogitabilitas* [= a thinking-together]. (Ibid. 224)

There are also others.

Leibniz sometimes writes that there are no purely extrinsic denominations. This is often thought to express his supervenience thesis, but it does not: its source lies elsewhere in his system. His example of a man who remains in India while his wife dies in Europe (L 365) is an awkward basis for discussing this matter, so I substitute another. For some years, Arnold is taller than Danny; then around time T it becomes the case that Danny is taller than Arnold. The supervenience thesis, if wrenched away from the metaphysical ground floor and naïvely applied at the level of appearance where people have heights, implies that this new relational fact is entailed by a conjunction of monadic facts about the two men. For Danny to become taller than Arnold, a monadic change must occur in at least one of them; but that is all that the supervenience thesis demands, and it does not imply that both must alter. For all it says to the contrary, the relational change could occur purely through Danny's growing taller; in which case Arnold would become shorter than Danny with this being a purely extrinsic denomination—a relational property acquired wholly through a change in something else. When Leibniz says that this cannot happen, and that if one man becomes taller than another, there is a monadic alteration in each, he is relying on his doctrine that every alteration in a substance is reflected in ('perceived by') every other substance (§109). This implies that if Danny alters at T, then so does Arnold—and so do you and I and the mayor of Paraparaumu. This has nothing to do with the supervenience thesis. Here I disagree with Hintikka 1976: 164–5.

136. Why Leibniz accepted the supervenience thesis

The supervenience thesis seems plainly false. It holds for the likes of 'John is taller than James' and 'Mary has the same-coloured hair as Helen', and so on; but it seems not to hold for these:

David is father to Solomon.
Socrates is uneasy about Xanthippe.
Bowen Bay is close to Pasley Island.

These seem not to supervene on underlying conjunctions of monadic propositions, which means that they look like counter-examples to Leibniz's general supervenience thesis. There are plenty more where they came from. Why does Leibniz's overall metaphysical project require that the thesis be true? And why does he find it believable when it strikes us as clearly false? I shall take these in order.

Leibniz did his metaphysical thinking in terms of substances and 'accidents'. The latter term often occurs in a contrast between essential and accidental; but in all the passages touching on the supervenience thesis, 'accident' just means something on the right of the thing/property divide. For Leibniz, accidents are not universals; they are abstract particulars, tropes, each being individuated by the substance that possesses it. The whiteness of one page is a distinct accident from the whiteness of another, even if the two are perfectly alike. A striking example of how wedded Leibniz is to this view of accidents ('affections', 'properties') as particulars occurs in his fifth letter to Clarke:

If space is the property or affection of the substance which is in space, the same space will sometimes be the affection of one body, sometimes of another body, sometimes of an immaterial substance, and sometimes perhaps of God himself . . . But this is a strange property or affection, which passes from one subject to another. Thus subjects will leave off their accidents like clothes, that other subjects may put them on. At this rate how shall we distinguish accidents from substances? (L 702)

A further example comes, as we have seen, from Leibniz's view about what transeunt causation would have to be (§94).

So we are confronted by an ontology of substances and accidents, with each accident essentially belonging to whatever substance possesses it. This helps us to understand Leibniz's discomfort over relations. The last of my series of quotations in §135 speaks of a relation as 'an accident which is in several subjects', but Leibniz's real view is that if there basically were relations, that is what they would have to be—which proves that basically there are none. He writes to Des Bosses:

Relations which join two monads are not in one monad or the other, but equally well in both at the same time, i.e. really in neither but in the mind alone. . . . I do not believe that you have established the existence of an accident that can, at the same time, be in two subjects and has one foot in one, so to speak, and one foot in the other. (AG 203)[2]

More examples will surface in due course. It is easy to mock the picture of a relation as standing astride two substances with a foot in each; but it is only a picture. Leibniz is wrestling here with a serious metaphysic of substance and accident, and he is right in thinking that relations do not fit.

He has another reason for needing relational truths to supervene on monadic ones. His account of how God goes about creating a world, which is central to his philosophy, requires that the basic world story lacks relational propositions. According to the account, God selects initial states of monads, and confers on each a law of development governing the successive unfolding of all its later states; and that is the whole story. The pre-established harmony comes about through God's taking note of which conjunctions of monadic propositions are true at the different possible worlds: at one of them, for example, monad x is F at time T *and* monad y is G at time T; an infinity of such conjunctions will embody the truth about the pattern of harmony at the world in question. Propositions in which one monad is related to another could play only a destructive role in this account. Admit them, and Leibniz's basic account of God-and-world crumbles.

Writing to Arnauld, Leibniz flirts with the destructive idea that God in creating Adam settled everything, because Adam's individual concept 'encloses' the whole history of the human race; but he immediately backs off from that into the story that he resolutely tells all through his mature work, in which Adam's history is correlated with yours and mine because 'Each individual substance expresses the whole universe of which it is a part according to a certain relationship, through the connection which it has to all things by virtue of the coherence of the decisions or purposes of God' (L 333–4). The same picture is forcefully drawn here:

Each substance is like a world apart, independent of all other things, except for God; thus all our phenomena, that is, all the things that can ever happen to us, are only consequences of our being. . . . And God alone . . . is the cause of this correspondence of

---

[2] See also NE 216.

[substances'] phenomena and brings it about that that which is particular to one of them is public to all ; otherwise, there would be no interconnection. (*DM* 14, FW 66–7)[3]

It is the essential core of this doctrine that God creates the substances *separately*. The harmony amongst their states is due to his selecting them appropriately. This, for Leibniz, is the most striking evidence we have of God's greatness:

These beings have received their nature . . . from a universal and supreme cause; for otherwise . . . their mutual independence would have made it impossible for them ever to have produced this order, this harmony, this beauty that we find in nature. But this argument, which appears to have only moral certainty, is brought to a state of absolute metaphysical necessity by the new kind of harmony which I have introduced, namely the pre-established harmony. For each of these souls . . . has to draw up [its states] from the depths of its own nature; and so necessarily each soul must have received this nature—this inner source of the expressions of what lies without—from a universal cause, upon which all of these beings depend and which brings it about that each of them perfectly agrees with and corresponds to the others. That could not occur without infinite knowledge and power. (*NE* 440)

Notice that this gives Leibniz a need to banish from the ground floor any statements relating substances to other substances. He has no need to banish other relational statements, which is just as well because he needs some of them—for example, the statement that a monad's momentary state is *caused by* its preceding state (thus Broad 1975: 39).

The second question was: Why does Leibniz find his supervenience doctrine believable? Consider the examples I gave of relational truths that seem not to supervene on monadic ones: David is father to Solomon; Socrates is uneasy about Xanthippe; Bowen Bay is close to Pasley Island. The recalcitrance of these comes from three sources: (1) causal relations, as in that of father to son; (2) intentional relations (one person's beliefs about or desires regarding another), as in the 'uneasy about' relation; (3) spatial relations, as in my third example. These three are involved, in complex ways, in other relations that also refuse to supervene on monadic truths. All three are probably involved in the fact that Socrates is married to Xanthippe. I conjecture, though I cannot prove, that when any relational fact about substances fails to supervene on monadic ones, it is because it involves one or more members of that trio. They certainly cover much of the territory.

None of the three makes trouble for Leibniz in his basic ontology. (1) He steadfastly rejects transeunt causation, denying that any truths relate one substance causally to another. He allows for quasi-causation, but that supervenes on monadic truths (§94). (2) His fundamental account of the world includes something like intentional relations—each monad 'perceives' all the states of all the others—but Leibniz's careful account of perception shows that it too supervenes on monadic facts (§98). When the whole truth is in about each monad's monadic state at each instant, the whole truth about what is a perception of what flows

---

[3] See also L 711.

logically from that, with no further factual input. Leibniz's theory regarding 'appetition' is also supposed to involve intentionality; but this does not give rise to trouble because appetition, for him, does not relate one substance to another (§101). (3) His monads are not spatially related to one another. He does say that each monad perceives the others 'according to its point of view', but the point of view is not a spatial position; rather, it is a logical construct out of facts about how distinctly or confusedly the monad perceives the universe (§111); and Leibniz probably thinks that not merely perception, but also its degrees of distinctness, can be brought within the scope of the supervenience thesis. I argued in §125 that he cannot have a decent account of distinctness, but that difficulty owes nothing to his rejection of basic relations.

In an unpublished note Leibniz proposes that 'Paris loves Helen' is equivalent to 'Paris loves, and by that fact [*eo ipso*] Helen is loved' (Couturat 287). This is not in the spirit of the supervenience thesis, because it asserts an equivalence. Also, the highly suspect *eo ipso* indicates that the unwanted kind of relational statement is not being got rid of: it cannot be a monadic fact about Helen that she is beloved by virtue of Paris's being a lover. The right thing for Leibniz to say is that the truth of 'Paris loves Helen' results from the truth of some monadic propositions about Paris's intrinsic state, including emotions, beliefs, and so on, and other monadic propositions about Helen by virtue of which some of Paris's states count as perceptions of or thoughts about Helen. Carry this out thoroughly enough, and I conjecture that you will think you have captured the whole truth in 'Paris loves Helen' except for the idea that Paris's state is in some measure caused by Helen; but that is the ingredient that we know Leibniz will not allow.

So Leibniz needs the supervenience thesis, and his basic metaphysic permits it to him.

137. Temporal relations

As well as causal, intentional, and spatial relations, there are temporal ones: x is F *before* it is G, and *while* y is H. Those are equivalent to the explicitly relational statements: x's being F *precedes* its being G, and *is synchronous with* y's being H.

One of Leibniz's two reasons for rejecting basic relations had to do with God's way of creating the harmony: the splendour of his feat of getting all the monadic histories to correlate in orderly ways requires the histories to be logically independent of one another; and that bars inter-substance relations from the basic metaphysic. But this does not apply to temporal relations. Temporal order among the episodes in a monad's history, and public-time synchronicity between the episodes of different monads, are vital to Leibniz's metaphysic. Far from impeding his account of how God plans the harmony, they integrally belong to it. If God did not think of monadic states as temporally ordered within each monad and as held in a public time that embraces them all, he would have no harmonic project.

Leibniz's other reason for the supervenience of all relational truths came from his resisting the notion of an accident that stretches between two relata. 'Correction! Leibniz had a problem with an accident's having one foot in each of two *substances*; the relata of temporal relations are not substances but events or states of affairs; so they are not problematic for him.' That may be right, but let us not accept it uncritically. I did formulate the problem in terms of relations between substances; but perhaps that was too narrow to capture the difficulty that Leibniz was wrestling with. If temporal relations really are ultimate in, and irremovable from, his metaphysical scheme, we need to know whether he ought to regard this as a defect in it, and if not, why not. And I cannot answer this.

One might argue that these relational statements fit Leibniz's supervenience thesis, because the fact that x's becoming F *pre-dates* y's becoming G is the logical upshot of a conjunction of monadic propositions of the form 'x becomes F at T_1 and y becomes G at T_2'. But are those monadic? On the face of it, 'x becomes F at T_1' relates an event to a time. I believe that to be wrong, but cannot say why.

If it is all right to regard 'x becomes F at T_1' as monadic, there remains a further possible threat. We have the monadic propositions that x becomes F at T_1 and y becomes G at T_2, but to get from that to the openly relational statement that one event pre-dates the other, we need also the proposition that T_1 pre-dates T_2—and isn't that relational? One might respond on Leibniz's behalf that T_1 and T_2 are times, and thus neither real nor phenomenal, but merely ideal. Interrelating them is all right, just as is the interrelating of numbers. I am not sure about that either. The interrelating of numbers was judged to be acceptable for Leibniz not because numbers are ideal, but because the relational statements in question are part of logic (broadly construed): they are used to get from the basic story to the supervenient one, and are not themselves part of the story. When I try to consider whether temporal relations between times have that same status, I get lost. This section is a confession of failures.

138. Relational properties

I have said nothing about the requirement that all basic truths be of the subject–predicate form. Some writers have seen that as leading Leibniz to reject basic relations, others as an immediate consequence of his doing so. Each view may seem to open the door to the idea—which has been advanced by Ishiguro (1972: 88–93), Hintikka (1976: 165–6), and others—that although Leibniz needs to banish from his fundamental metaphysic any truths of the form R(x,y) he can allow ones of the form Fx where F is a relational predicate. On this account of his position, Leibniz rejects the relational proposition that David is father to Solomon, considered as asserting that a certain dyadic accident links the two men, but he allows the subject–predicate proposition that David is father-to-Solomon.

There is prima-facie support for this in a few texts, as when Leibniz writes to Des Bosses: 'You will not, I believe, admit an accident which is in two subjects at once. Thus I hold, as regards relations, that paternity in David is one thing, and sonship in Solomon is another, but the relation common to both is a merely mental thing, of which the modifications of singulars are the foundation' (L 609). The statement that paternity in David is one thing, and sonship in Solomon is another, might seem to mean that being-father-to-Solomon is a basic property of David and that being-a-son-of-David is a basic property of Solomon. Again, Leibniz writes to Clarke about three ways of conceiving the ratio between a line L and a shorter line M. He allows each of these two:

(1) a ratio of the greater L to the lesser M, (2) a ratio of the lesser M to the greater L.

But he strenuously rejects:

(3) the ratio between L and M without considering which is the subject and which the object.

In each of 1 and 2, Leibniz writes, we know which line 'is the subject of that accident which philosophers call "relation"', but in 3 we are at a loss:

It cannot be said that both of them, L and M together, are the subject of such an accident; for then we should have an accident in two subjects, with one leg in one and the other in the other, which is contrary to the notion of accidents. Therefore, we must say that this relation, in this third way of considering it, is indeed out of the subjects; but being neither a substance nor an accident, it must be a mere ideal thing, the consideration of which is nevertheless useful. (AG 339)

It is easy to read Leibniz as permitting the statements (1) that L is longer-than-M and (2) that M is shorter-than-L, each attributing a relational predicate to a subject.

I have no confident alternative reading of the passages, but this one cannot be right because it represents Leibniz as incompetent.[4] One reason for saying this has been decisively argued by Mates. How does the proposition that David is father to Solomon differ from the proposition that David is father-to-Solomon? We can devise ways of distinguishing the two sentences, Mates says, but they will not express two propositions. If Leibniz really were to hold that items of the form $R(x,y)$ are to be excluded and ones of the form Fx included, with the values of F

---

[4] Cover and O'Leary-Hawthorne (1999: 72 n.) characterize the former passage as 'a healthy first step' towards Leibniz's full-scale rejection of basic relations and relational predicates. Their subsequent treatment of it, however, underestimates the passage's recalcitrance. 'There are many things that can make it true that David has paternity,' they write. 'David's having paternity entails none of them, but all of them entail David's having paternity' (82). Leibniz, though, wrote not of the proposition that David has paternity, but of 'paternity in David'; that ought to be a trope, which opens the door to those who hold that it must be a relational trope.

including the likes of begets-Solomon and exceeds-M, that would be an idle spin-
ning of verbal wheels (Mates 1986: 213–15).

To put flesh on the bones of this argument of Mates's, recall Leibniz's two
main sources of unease about relations. (1) A basic (unsupervenient) relation
between two substances would be an accident that is in two substances at the
same time, which Leibniz thinks is metaphysical rubbish. (2) If there were basic
relations between distinct substances, Leibniz would lose his account of God's
creation of the world. Each of these troubles would remain, in full strength, if
he admitted basic relational predicates. (1) What could he say about the semantics and metaphysics of such a predicate? He would have to say that the accident
(trope, individual quality-as-possessed) for which it stands somehow includes or
involves a substance other than the one that possesses it. He would be trading
in

> Paternity is a two-legged accident with one foot in David and the other in
> Solomon

for this:

> Being-father-to-Solomon is a one-legged accident whose only foot is in David,
> while Solomon has both feet in that accident.

A poor trade! Leibniz would rightly regard the second item as no less trashy
than the first. (2) The account of God's creation of the world would still be in
ruins, for God's determining of the life's course of any one monad would logically include the determining of the future history of the entire universe. The
supposed shift from relations to relational properties does not avert that
calamity.

I do not know why Leibniz wrote those two passages and some others like
them. Notice, though, that the David–Solomon passage involves a relational
statement which would not occur—even as a candidate for elimination—in
Leibniz's fundamental ontology. What underpins the (apparent) fact that one
man fathered another is an infinitely complex fragment of the pre-established
harmony; and that supervenes on the whole monadic truth about all the monads. The lines L and M are even further from the ground floor: in Leibniz's
scheme lines are 'ideal' things, mental constructs that are not even appearances
of substances (§89). Those two observations, while not explaining the passages,
warn us not to treat them as clear pointers to basic Leibnizian metaphysics.

139. Compossibility

Those who hold that Leibniz was tolerant of basic relational properties have one
last card in their hand. It involves his notion of compossibility, which I shall
expound also for its own sake.

Let F stand for a partial or complete specification of a beautiful and useful possible person, but not of any actual person; and let us ask why no F person ever
exists. Leibniz may answer: because there being an F substance is ruled out by the
substances that are actual. In his terminology, an F substance is not 'compossible'
with the substances that actually exist. 'The universe is not the collection of all possibles,' he wrote to Bourguet, because 'not all possibles are compossible' (L 662).
When at NE 265 he writes (in effect) of accidents as being 'compossible' within a
single substance, this is an aberration. I shall follow his normal usage, restricting
'compossible' to a relation between possible substances.

Here are three questions about Leibniz's concept of compossibility:

(1) What concept is it? That is, what kind of modality is involved in the 'possible' part of 'compossible'?

(2) Do Leibniz's other doctrines permit him to say that two severally possible
substances are not jointly compossible?

(3) Does his compossibility concept do work for him that cannot be done otherwise?

The answer to 1 must be either that the possibility in question is absolute (logical, conceptual), the concept that is involved in 'possible substance'; or that it is
some non-absolute kind of possibility, so that A may be incompossible with B
without its being absolutely impossible that both should exist. (These accounts
of compossibility are called, respectively, 'logical' and 'lawful' in Margaret
Wilson's interesting 1993a.) I shall argue that the 'absolute' answer to 1 implies
that the answer to 2 is No; while a 'non-absolute' answer to 1 implies that the
answer to 3 is No. In short, the thesis that two possible substances might be
incompossible is either inconsistent with the rest of Leibniz's system or else idle
within it. This result accords with the scrappy, casual, conflicting ways in which
the notion of compossibility turns up in the texts. I shall start with the 'absolute'
answer to 1, which implies the negative answer to 2.

In one place Leibniz writes: 'The compossible is that which, with another,
does not imply a contradiction' (Grua 325; quoted in Mates 1986: 75 n. 36). That
gives the 'absolute' answer to 1, implying that the modality involved in 'S$_1$ and S$_2$
are compossible substances' is the very one involved in 'S$_1$ is a possible substance'. This may not be Leibniz's lasting opinion about compossibility, however;
I can find no other text in which he explicitly makes compossibility as weak as
this or incompossibility so strong.

The absolute account of compossibility puts it out of business in Leibniz's philosophy, because of his thesis that the basic truth of the world contains no propositions in which substances are related to others. The whole truth about one
substance cannot logically clash with the whole truth about another unless one
of these logically involves propositions about the other substance; and that lets
in relations—or relational properties; the difference is trivial. Rescher (1967)
relies on it, using relational properties to rescue compossibility (16), while maintaining (71–3) that for Leibniz all relations are 'reducible'.

Those who maintain that Leibniz did mean to let in relations or relational properties may here play their last card:

If we are wrong, and relational properties are out, then every individually possible substance is compossible—with this understood in the 'absolute' way—with the totality of actual substances. In that case, incompossibility cannot explain anything. This is evidence that we are right (see Brown 1987).

I reply that the single text in which Leibniz openly endorses the absolute account of compossibility cannot outweigh his philosophical reasons for rejecting relational properties. Anyway, if he employs incompossibility in this way, it draws wages, but does no work. On the proposed view, the proposition that *There is no F substance because there being one is absolutely incompossible with the substances that are actual* owes its truth to relational properties of actual substances. One such property of one substance will suffice: substance x has the relational property *does not coexist with any F substance*. That absolutely rules out there being an F substance; but the very ease of the victory shows that nothing has been *explained*. The supposed explanation has no more content than this: 'There is no F substance. That is because there being one is absolutely incompatible with the fact that there is no F substance.' The initial why-question still stands, only now we have to rephrase it: 'Why did God not actualize an F substance and adjust the relational properties of the other substances accordingly?'

Let us now look into compossibility with its modality taken as less than absolute. Three alternatives suggest themselves. Given the question 'Why did God not *also* create an F substance?', the answer 'Because that is incompossible with the substances already existing' might mean that if an F substance were added to the world's contents, the resulting world

(a) would be worse than the actual world, or
(b) would not conform to the natural laws that actually prevail, or
(c) would conform to no possible set of natural laws.

If *a* were right, incompossibility would have no role of its own, serving merely to re-express Leibniz's familiar view that God always acts for the best. The same presumably holds for *b*. Suppose that the addition of an F substance would result in a world whose laws were different from those that actually obtain, how would that explain God's not adding one? It could only be that the new laws would be worse than the old; which again throws the explanation back into the lap of Leibnizian optimism. More abstractly, version *b* of compossibility cannot explain any of God's choices, because, according to Leibniz, the natural laws of any world are themselves chosen by God. (This point is made by D'Agostino 1976: 94–5.)

One might think that the same holds for *c*: God could choose to create a world that did not perfectly conform to any set of general laws; he does not actually do this, because such a world would not be the best. However, in one place Leibniz says that every possible world conforms to general laws, taking this out of the scope of God's choices; and this points to a version of *c* that does not, like *b*, really belong in (1) the 'value' approach to compossibility. It is in fact another version of the 'absolute' approach, but this is the handiest place to discuss it.

The interpretation in question was defended by Russell, who has been followed in this by Hacking (1976) and others. He cites this passage in which Leibniz, writing to Arnauld, affirms the premiss for it:

I think there is an infinity of possible ways in which to create the world, according to the different designs that God could form, and that each possible world depends on certain principal designs or purposes of God which are distinctive of it, i.e. certain . . . *laws* of the *general order* of this possible universe with which they are in accord and whose concept they determine, as well as the concepts of all the individual substances which must enter into this same universe. (FW 107)

Russell comments (1900: 67): 'This passage proves quite definitely that all possible worlds have general laws, which determine the connection of contingents.' From this he derives interpretation *c* of compossibility: 'Without the need for *some* general laws, any two possibles would be compossible, since they cannot contradict one another. Possibles cease to be compossible only when there is no general law whatever to which both conform.'

The premiss is there in Leibniz's own words: Every possible world conforms to general laws. But the inference from that to a concept of incompossibility is Russell's; there is no textual evidence of Leibniz drawing it. Objection: 'But it is a valid inference; so Russell is entitled to hold Leibniz to that concept of incompossibility.' Reply: It is not; and he is not. The only reason Leibniz ever gives for the premiss blocks the inference from it to Russell's conclusion:

Nothing completely irregular occurs in the world, and one cannot even feign such a thing. . . . Suppose that someone jots down a number of points at random on a piece of paper . . . I maintain that it is possible to find a geometric line whose notion is constant and uniform, following a certain rule, such that this line passes through all the points in the same order in which they were jotted down. (*DM* 6, FW 58)

Leibniz says here that we cannot even fake a fiction about a set of particulars that conform to no rule. This seems to be offered as absolutely necessary, and Leibniz may believe it about any possible set of particulars, however large. If so, that supports the premiss: every possible world conforms to general laws, because every set of possible substances does so. But it destroys the inference to Russell's account of incompossibility; for if *that* is why only law-governed worlds are possible, there can never be a threat that by adding F to a given world God would end up with something not law-governed. That is probably why Leibniz himself never draws the inference. (In this critique of Russell, I agree with Brown 1987: 179–80 and with M. D. Wilson 1993*a*: 129.)

Why does Leibniz want incompossibility? Apparently it is to explain the nonexistence of certain possible substances. When we ask why such explanations are wanted, however, the primary texts and the secondary literature are unclear and uncertain. Two general ideas seem to be at work.

Some views of Leibniz's to the effect that *ceteris paribus* existence is better than non-existence lead him sometimes to say that God will not leave any possible substance unactualized if it is compossible with those he has actualized: 'What is not, never has been, and never will be is not possible, if we take *possible* in the sense of the *compossible*,' Leibniz writes to Bourguet (L 661). I can make nothing of this, and decline to hold him to it. Indeed, he drifts away from it on the next page. To be true to himself, Leibniz must leave some room for God to decline to actualize some possible substance on the grounds that its existing would make the world worse than it would otherwise be. Occasionally he writes as though all it means to call one world better than another is that the former contains more substances (or more substances and fewer or simpler basic laws), but I am sure that this is not his fundamental conviction about value.

There remains the question with which I opened this section, of why God did not improve this world by adding to it one more superb substance. Leibniz might be tempted to plead incompossibility in answering this, but the pressure cannot be great. Having to defend the thesis that this is the best possible world against persuasive evidence that it is not, he frequently argues that some goods derive some of their value from sharing a universe with evils; and, realizing that this seems too weak to explain most actual evil, he adds that our impressions about this are worthless because we know so little of the world—are so far from seeing the whole picture—that we are not entitled to make judgements about what would make it overall better. Such moves are standard in Christian theodicies, and Leibniz freely avails himself of them. Why should they not do all the work that might otherwise be assigned to incompossibility? For a clear indication that Leibniz thinks they do not, we need to find him saying that although it would be *better* if an F substance were added to the world's contents, God cannot add it because it is not compossible with what actually exists. Nobody has found anything like that in the corpus.

Apart from the mysteries surrounding compossibility that pour forth in the letter to Bourguet from which I have twice quoted briefly, most of Leibniz's uses of the concept serve only to express his well-known views about existence and value, summed up in the embarrassing doctrine that this is the best possible world. (See, for example, *NE* 307.)

In one passage which Gerhardt (G 7:41) seems to date to around 1677, Leibniz wrote: 'It is as yet unknown to men [a] whence arises the incompossibility of diverse things; or [b] how it can happen that diverse essences are opposed to each other, seeing that all purely positive terms seem to be compatible with one another.' Problem *b* concerns how any proposed specification for an individual substance, if stated in purely positive terms, can be incapable of being actualized. Leibniz eventually reached his answer to that: namely, it cannot. A purely positive specification, he held, would specify God, this being his consistency proof for the concept involved in the a priori argument for God's existence; the nature of every other substance is partly negative. This has nothing to do with the problem (a) of the compossibility of one substance with another, though Leibniz has misled some commentators into thinking otherwise.[5] Regarding problem *a*, Leibniz never had a solution to announce. Now back to relations.

140. Everything leads to everything else

Relational concepts permeate our ordinary ways of thinking and talking about the material world—the world of appearance—and often we cannot dispense with them at that level. Through most of the *New Essays* Leibniz politely joins Locke in the world of appearance without reminding us that that is all it is; and in that framework he writes: 'There is no term which is so absolute or so detached that it does not involve relations and is not such that a complete analysis of it would lead to other things and indeed to all other things' (*NE* 228). The example he has just given, of a relation that does not immediately spring to mind but has to be dug out, is the thought of 'black' which involves—but not immediately—the thought of 'its cause'. This is tied to the level of appearance; and it seems also to use 'analysis' to refer to something other than the kind of analysis that spreads out the contents of a concept.

That last point stands out even more sharply in another place, where Leibniz again writes, this time to De Volder, that everything leads to everything else:

There is nothing in the whole created universe which does not need, for its perfect concept, the concept of everything else in the universality of things, since everything flows into every other thing in such a way that if anything is removed or changed, everything in the world will be different from what it is now. (L 524–5)

Notice the phrase 'need, for its perfect concept'. Immediately before this remark, Leibniz wrote: 'To be "contained in" . . . is more than to need something else.' He is thus explicitly divorcing this 'everything leads to everything' passage from any implications about analysis as you and I understand it: namely, as a laying bare of what a concept *contains*.

With that in mind, Mates arrives at this reading of the two 'everything leads to everything' passages:

I interpret the passages in question to mean only that, ultimately, every individual concept needs every other, and not to be in any way inconsistent with Leibniz's denial of the reality of relations or to imply that any 'relational properties' are included in such concepts. (1986: 220)

If this is right (as I think it is), those passages imply nothing about the status of relations or relational properties. If they did, it would be something absurdly strong: namely, that according to Leibniz *all* properties of monads are relational. The existence of a paper defending exactly that is, Mates says sardonically (219 n.

---

[5] Notably Ishiguro (1972: 47–8). Her translation of the passage is misleading: she puts 'Until now nobody has known . . .', but the Latin means only 'So far nobody has known . . .'.

36), 'a testimonial to the infinite possibilities of scholarship'. My discussion has been heavily indebted to Mates's chapter on Leibniz's views about relations—both to its philosophical points and to its leads to crucial texts.

141. Space as a system of relations

Although he refused to allow inter-substance relations in his basic metaphysic, Leibniz is famous for having defended the view that space is a system of relations. There is no inconsistency in this, because everything pertaining to space belongs at the phenomenal or ideal levels, not at that of basic reality. Still, I choose this as my place for some comments on Leibniz's relationalism about space.

Leibniz thought that if there were such a thing as space, it would be continuous; he was sure that nothing real is continuous (§88); so he needed to maintain that there is no such real thing as space. He could have based this on his general metaphysic, which says that spatial concepts come into play only at the phenomenal and ideal levels. That would free him to allow that there is such a pseudo-thing (phenomenal rather than real) as space. He could have viewed talk of space as an infinite extended thing as he did talk about bodies' acting on one another—namely, as permissible, though not strictly and basically true.

He could have, but he did not. Even while taking the phenomenal level on its own terms—writing like a realist about matter—Leibniz insists that space is not a thing, but rather a system of relations. He has a reason for this which can be found at the phenomenal level; it does not engage his worries about the labyrinth of the continuum. We can handle this entire matter, as Leibniz does, on the basis of an actual or pretended realism about matter.

In §13 we saw Descartes demanding to know what remains between the sides of a flask after all the air has been removed from it. If there is nothing between them, he said, then they touch, so the flask has collapsed. As I pointed out, Descartes has overlooked a possibility: namely, that *Side S_1 is apart from side S_2* is a basic dyadic fact about the two sides, and not a consequence of a triadic fact that *Some thing is between S_1 and S_2*. That is essentially the position that Leibniz defended in his correspondence with Clarke.

As I said in §12, the relational view of space should not be confused with a relational view of place. (I shall call these 'R-space' and 'R-place', for short.) Locke was officially agnostic about whether space is a substance or a system of relations, but he openly held that the concept of *where* a body is can only be the concept of how it spatially relates to other bodies. Even Descartes, who held that space is a substance (which he called 'matter') accepted a peculiar version of R-place (§15). Neither philosopher was led into inconsistency by that combination of views.

Leibniz in his third letter to Clarke argues for R-space. His argument might seem to involve R-place, but really it does not. Here it is:

Space is absolutely uniform, and without the things placed in it one point of space absolutely does not differ in anything from another. Now, from hence it follows (supposing space to be something in itself, besides the order of bodies among themselves) that it is impossible there should be a reason why God, preserving the same situations of bodies among themselves, should have placed them in space after one certain particular manner and not otherwise—why everything was not placed the quite contrary way, for instance, by changing east into west. But if space is nothing else but this order or relation, and is nothing at all without bodies but the possibility of placing them, then those two states, the one such as it is now, the other supposed to be the quite contrary way, would not at all differ from one another. . . . Consequently there is no room to inquire after a reason for the preference of the one to the other. (AG 325)

This is best seen as a *reductio ad absurdum*. Start with the hypothesis that space is an infinitely extended thing, accept the premiss that this thing is 'absolutely uniform', and Leibniz will lead you from that to the conclusion that space is not a thing after all.

Now, the uniformity premiss implies *R-place for humans*: we humans cannot distinguish any place from any other except in terms of the bodies that are in them. From that premiss we cannot infer *R-place for God*. If space were an infinitely extended substance, it would have distinct regions which God could refer to and re-identify, even if they were perfectly alike. We do not know how; but in Christian philosophical theology God is standardly credited with knowings and doings of which he is capable *absolutely* rather than through the exercise of ways and means. It would be odd to deny him such powers in this context, and Leibniz does not do so. It is no part of his argument that if space were a uniform thing, God could not tell one region of it from another. He has the premiss

(1) Space is absolutely uniform,

which implies

(2) R-place for humans.

Leibniz argues from 1 to

(3) R-space,

but he does not get there via 2. Here is how the argument works.
    Start with one hypothesis and one premiss:

(a) Space is an infinite extended thing.
(b) Space is perfectly uniform.

From hypothesis *a* it follows that

(c) Space is composed of distinct regions whose identity does not depend on any facts about their contents,

which implies

(d) There is a fact of the matter about where in space the material world is.

From *d* together with Leibniz's theology we can infer

(e) God chose to put the world in one location rather than another.

From premiss *a*, however, it follows that

(f) There can be no reason for God to prefer one location for the world to another.

From *e* conjoined with *f* we get

(g) God made a choice for which he had no reason.

This Leibniz regards as absurd, and so something has to give; and in his view what must give is (a) the hypothesis of the argument.

I have not found Leibniz discussing the credentials of (b) the premiss that space is perfectly uniform. The other weakness in the argument is the extravagantly rationalistic rejection of *g*. Leibniz's rationalism leads him to maintain, frequently, that not even God could think: 'I want it to be the case that either P or Q obtains, but not both; there is no reason for preferring either; I choose Q.' Few have agreed with him about this.

142. The discernibility of the diverse

Leibniz holds that no two individual things can be intrinsically exactly alike. This is at work in his view that a complete concept suffices to pick out one individual (§127), and in some other parts of his thought. Having mentioned various possible contributors to this thesis of the discernibility of the diverse, I am now placed to discuss the thesis itself. It is usually called 'the identity of indiscernibles', but the final 's' in that is a logical solecism, and not always a harmless one.

Here is a reason for holding that no two monads can be exactly alike. Our only way of making at least preliminary or prima-facie sense of the idea of two indiscernible things involves our being able to *locate* them differently, assign them different positions in some system of ordering that does not supervene on their intrinsic natures. Without such a locational difference, there is nothing for the thought of 'this one rather than that' to grip on to. Now, the obvious candidate for such an ordering is space: we think we can conceive of two indiscernible atoms that are never spatially co-located. That is not available for monads, however, because they are not spatially organized. Their system of points of view is isomorphic to a spatial system, but it cannot serve here, because it supervenes on intrinsic differences amongst the monads (§111).

As well as space, there is time. We can conceive of two indiscernible atoms which have exactly the same spatial trajectory throughout their lifetimes. Each comes into existence, follows that trajectory, and goes out of existence a year later, and the two lifetimes do not overlap. I cannot see that Leibniz has any deep reason to reject the monadic analogue of that: one monad goes through a finite history and is then annihilated, being replaced by a different monad that goes through exactly the same history. I doubt if he considered this possibility, and I shall say no more about it. My main interest, like his, is in the discernibility of the diverse as applied to synchronous things.

Time is irrelevant to that, and space is not available. There could in principle be some third organizational structure—some third system of as-it-were locations—which would enable two indiscernible monads to be differently located though intrinsically alike. But Leibniz does not provide for any such *tertium*, and I have no suggestions for what might serve in this role. From here on, I shall take it for granted that the discernibility of the diverse holds for monads.

I agree with Parkinson (1981: 309–10) that the discernibility of the diverse for monads does not imply it for bodies; yet Leibniz asserts it in the latter application, writing that 'In fact, every body differs in itself from every other', and adducing empirical evidence for this:

I remember a great princess . . . saying one day while walking in her garden that she did not believe there were two leaves perfectly alike. A clever gentleman who was walking with her believed that it would be easy to find some, but search as he might he became convinced by his own eyes that a difference could always be found. (*NE* 231)

The thesis that no two *leaves* are alike is a timidly tiny step towards the thesis that no two bodies are exactly alike, and one wonders how seriously Leibniz is taking all this. Still, he liked this story, and repeated it to Clarke, adding: 'Two drops of water or milk, viewed with a microscope, will appear distinguishable from each other. This is an argument against atoms, which are confuted, as well as the void, by the principles of true metaphysics' (AG 328). It is not much of an argument against atoms. Still, Leibniz is entitled to adduce empirical evidence for the unalikeness of diverse bodies, and to hold that this accords with the richness he attributes to the world on theological grounds. However, he goes further, maintaining that the existence of two indiscernible bodies is 'confuted by the principles of true metaphysics', is 'not possible' (ibid.), and is 'contrary to the greatest principles of reason' (*NE* 231). Why?

One argument, which I have found only once in his writings, is directed against the thought of two indiscernible bodies' being in different places. It comes just after he has acknowledged that 'time and place . . . do distinguish for us things which we could not easily tell apart by reference to themselves alone', but has gone on to say that 'things are nevertheless distinguishable in themselves, so that time and place do not constitute the core of identity and diversity' (*NE* 230).[6] He then proceeds to say why this must be so—that is, why location alone could not do the job:

To which it can be added that it is by means of things that we must distinguish one time or place from another, rather than vice versa; for times and places are in themselves perfectly alike, and in any case they are not substances or complete realities.

---

[6] The next sentence is wrongly translated in the first edition of the Remnant–Bennett translation.

Their alikeness does not offend against the discernibility of the diverse because they are ideal entities, not fundamentally real and not well-founded phenomena either. (Their not being 'substances or complete realities' is not enough, for bodies are not substances either, yet the discernibility of the diverse is supposed to hold for them.)

There is something wrong here. The relational view of place, which we and Leibniz accept, implies that ultimately our working notion of where a thing is at T is the notion of how it is spatially related to other things; but it does not follow that we cannot distinguish things by where they are located. Borrowing a formulation that Leibniz uses later, the fact that 'place and time must themselves be determined by the things they contain' does not entail that they cannot serve as 'determinants' of the identity and diversity of bodies (*NE* 289).

If this argument of Leibniz's were right, it could not be true (as he rightly says it is) that 'time and place distinguish for us things which we could not [otherwise] easily tell apart'. Also, if the argument were right, it alone would prove that there could not be a world of several Democritean atoms all with the same size and shape. Leibniz seems to regard it as having that power, but that is incredible. We can distinguish a world with two indiscernible atoms circling around one another from one with three such atoms; and if there are lurking reasons why this distinction is incoherent, they cannot come from the harmless relational account of place. Take a three-atom world: R-place implies that we have no use for the notion of where atom x is at T except that of how it is spatially related to atoms y and z; but that leaves us with the thought that the world contains atom x and *another* atom y and *a third* atom z. This is merely the thought of a certain configuration of matter in space; it does include the thought that at any given time there are three atoms which are *differently* located. But that thinly negative locational thought is not challenged by R-place.

A second argument seems to be at work when Leibniz writes, about Democritean atoms:

They could have the same size and shape and would then be indistinguishable in themselves and discernible only by means of external denominations with no internal foundation; which is contrary to the greatest principles of reason. In fact, every body . . . differs in itself from every other. (*NE* 230–1)

This appeals to Leibniz's doctrine that all relations between things supervene on intrinsic monadic properties of the things. The appeal is weak. The thesis of the supervenience of relations looks wrong for spatial relations; and when I made that point in §136 I defended Leibniz by taking the supervenience thesis to be meant only at the monadic level, where spatial concepts get no purchase. If he chooses to apply it to bodies—and to infer from it the discernibility of diverse bodies and thus the falsity of atomism—he ought to defend it at that level. There seems to be no way for him to do this.

Objection: 'But if diverse monads must be indiscernible, then so must diverse bodies, because they are appearances of aggregates of monads.' Let us look into this. It argues:

> (1) Every monad must be somewhat unlike every other. So (2) every aggregate of monads must be somewhat unlike every other. So (3) every body (being the appearance of one such aggregate) must be somewhat unlike every other body (being the appearance of another). This is equivalent to (4) the discernibility of diverse bodies.

This argument seems to be at work in Saw 1954: 55. We are granting its premiss 1, which certainly entails 2. The move to 3 assumes that every monadic difference shows up at the level of appearance, so that in the transition from reality to appearance no information is lost. Leibniz probably believed this, though he has no deep reason for it, as he has for the converse thesis that every apparent difference has a real one underlying it. Let us grant it, and thus allow the inference to 3. The big trouble comes in the final claim that 3 is equivalent to 4. It is not, because 3 is satisfied as long as each pair of bodies differs in *some* way, but the difference might consist merely in where they are. There is no metaphysical obstacle to the locational difference's being the appearance of *all* the differences between the underlying aggregates of monads. The latter might be entirely 'used up' by the bodies' being in different places.

Chapter 19

Descartes's Search for Security

143. What the search was about

These days Descartes is famous mainly for one fragment of his work: namely, a thought-experiment that he conducted in the *Meditations*. In this he challenges his own beliefs as radically as he can, wanting to discover which of them can survive the challenge and be accepted as secure. Many books have been dedicated to this, and it seems often to be the sole topic in undergraduate teaching about Descartes. I agree with Margaret Wilson (1978: 221–3; 1992: 202–3) that the secondary literature has made too much of it at the expense of other aspects of Descartes's work.

Still, it is not without interest, and there is philosophy to be learned and exercised in wrestling with it; so I shall devote most of this chapter to Descartes's attempt to establish some propositions as secure against doubt or challenge. In this I shall follow most scholars in supposing that he wants beliefs that are *normatively* secure—that is, ones that he is *entitled* to retain in the face of all challenges and doubts. In my next chapter I shall present a different thread that runs through these texts. It shows Descartes to be pursuing a goal that is not normative, aiming not at entitlement but rather at stability—a system of beliefs that will stay put, and not be subject to constant revisions. He connects this with the notion of beliefs that one cannot doubt, this being a matter not of (normative) entitlement to believe, but merely of (factual) inability to call into question. This strand in Descartes's thinking was not properly noticed until Louis Loeb and I independently saw it; but it is there, and a grasp of it helps to make sense of texts that are otherwise bewildering.

I place these two chapters here because they link Descartes much less with Spinoza and Leibniz than with Locke, Berkeley, and Hume.

In the *Meditations* Descartes reaches some conclusions about proper intellectual conduct. His normative project seems to convince him that one would be behaving badly in accepting anything that was not logically secure against any possible doubt; his factual project suggests, rather, that one ought to accept only what one cannot call into question. Nobody could live by either constraint, and in Descartes's subsequent work he does not try. He announces at the outset that he aims to establish standards by which to live the rest of his intellectual life, but we cannot take this seriously, given that no such thing happens. His typical style is dogmatic and confident; he often implies that there is no significant chance of his being wrong about the matter in hand; but no one could think that in his later works—the Replies to Objections, the *Principles of Philosophy*, the *Passions of the Soul*, and the voluminous correspondence—he was usually guided by the rule that only what is certain or indubitable should be accepted. In his other writings—apart from the re-run of the *Meditations* in *PP* 1—no such standard is even mentioned.

Although the all-in security project appears first in the *Meditations*, it was described four years earlier in Descartes's *Discourse on the Method*. Do not call it 'Discourse on Method', for that is a solecism; the full title is 'Discourse on the method of rightly conducting one's reason and seeking the truth in the sciences'. One might expect 'the method' in question to involve obedience to the security standard which was to be explored more fully in the *Meditations*, but that turns out to be wrong. The only 'method' described in the *Discourse* has nothing to do with the themes of the *Meditations*, and arises from a set of notably jejune rules (CSM 1:120), which Leibniz unkindly, but not unfairly, summarized as: 'Take what you need, treat it as you need to, and you will get what you want' (G 4:329). Anyway, it is not clear that they define 'the method' of the title. Descartes's many claims about this have left a strange situation where scholars disagree about whether he thought he had one method or several, and about what any of them are (Weber 1972, Curley 1978, Schuster 1993, Garber 1993a). There is no profit here.

I do not know what led Descartes into his security project. As for what can be taken out of it: we can have a good time with the project because we are interested in seeing where you can get to if you look for doxastic security, starting where Descartes did; his pages help us to think about indubitability, normative justification, and so on. But their chief philosophical significance lies in the framework of assumptions within which Descartes sets up and tackles his security problem.

Let us focus on his arrival at First Base: I mean the episode in which he accepts without question the proposition *Cogito*, 'I think', and infers from it the proposition *Sum*, 'I exist'. The latter is secure, he declares, even if an omnipotent and malevolent deceiver is at work: 'Let him deceive me as much as he can, he will never bring it about that I am nothing so long as I think that I am something.' Because of his way of establishing his own existence, Descartes thinks he can securely accept that, whatever else he may be, he is at least a thinking thing; and with this in hand he reiterates his previous position that he still has no secure beliefs about the existence of any material bodies, even his own head and torso and limbs. This leads him to his remarkable 'separability argument' (§§29–31), whose premiss is that he can be in an unmuddled frame of mind while being sure that he exists yet questioning whether there are any bodies. The conclusion is that he, his mind, is not a body.

Substance-dualism carries through into Descartes's other works, if only by encouraging him to keep psychology from intruding into physics. On the strength of it he claims to have a physics which takes account of the whole nature of matter, which he could not do if matter had psychological properties. And we have Descartes's word for it that substance-dualism is the main output of his security project, or at least of the crucial First Base part of it. Someone wrote to him remarking that his *Cogito* argument was reminiscent of this by Augustine (*City of God*, bk. 11, ch. 26):

> We exist, and we know that we exist, and we love both our existing and our knowledge of it. In these three things at least there is no possibility of deception. . . . In these truths I have no fear of the Academicians' arguments when they say, 'What if you are mistaken?' If I am mistaken, I still exist. He who does not exist cannot be mistaken; so I still exist, even if I am mistaken.

Here is nearly the whole philosophical part of Descartes's reply to his correspondent:

> I am obliged to you for advising me of the passage of St Augustine to which *I think, so I am* is somehow related. I read it today in the library of this town [Leyde], and I find that it is indeed used to prove the certainty of our being and then to show that there is in us an image of the Trinity in that we exist, we know that we exist . . . [etc.]; whereas I use it to show that this *I* which thinks is *an immaterial substance* and not at all corporeal. These are two very different things. It is so simple and natural to infer that one is from the fact that one doubts that anyone at all might have written it; but still I am glad to have converged on St Augustine, if only to hush the little minds who have tried to find fault with the principle. (CSMK 159)

This reflects Descartes's distaste for being likened to earlier philosophers (§5). But presumably he meant what he wrote: namely, that he valued the *Cogito* episode chiefly or only for its role in helping him to establish that he is an immaterial substance.

Nobody today thinks that Descartes succeeded in proving substance-dualism; but that does not exhaust the interest that his First Base position holds for us. In that position, he takes as given all that he is immediately aware of in himself—the existence of certain thoughts, feelings, and so on—and questions everything else. That is, he raises the question: What, if anything, entitles me to believe that there is a material world outside my mind? Nobody has been moved by the reassurances that Descartes eventually gives himself about this, and it seems clear that a comforting answer to the question cannot meet the standards of certainty and proof against error that he sets. As Frege wrote centuries later, 'By the step with which I secure an environment for myself I expose myself to the risk of error. . . . We find certainty in the inner world while doubt never altogether leaves us in our excursions into the outer world' (1918: 34).

In posing his question, Descartes was adopting the stance of methodological solipsism (§26). Spinoza and Leibniz did not seriously engage with the outer-world question in anything like Descartes's way, neither of them being given to solipsism as a philosophical method. Locke had enough sympathy with it to want to attend somewhat to the outer-world question, though it did not exercise him greatly. Berkeley found it profoundly troubling, passionately rejected

Locke's answers, and built a philosophy out of his attempt to do better. Hume also rejected Locke's position, found Berkeley's to be unbelievable, and was sure that there is no third way: 'This sceptical doubt with respect to . . . the senses is a malady which can never be radically cured . . . Carelessness and inattention alone can afford us any remedy' (*Treatise* 218).

The interesting form of methodological solipsism draws the line between oneself and the rest of the world in Descartes's way, starting with nothing but the immediate deliverances of one's conscious awareness. What Descartes treated as secure was *himself*, considered as the subject of states given to him in immediate awareness. He knew about these directly, he held, without reliance on any intermediary which might introduce falsity or even doubt. According to Burnyeat (1982), this was new. Nobody had formulated scepticism in Descartes's way before him; nobody took his own thoughts as known for sure, while questioning the existence of his own body. It is perhaps a mark of Descartes's influence on us that it is hard for us today to see what could be philosophically going on when someone claimed to be sure of the existence of himself—including flesh and bones as well as pleasures and thoughts—while challenging his entitlement to believe in anything else.

144. Getting to the omnipotent Deceiver

The object of Descartes's exercise is to acquire a normatively secure hold on the truth. I have such a hold on P if I could not have any good reason to question whether P or doubt that P.

The opening shot in the campaign is this: 'Whatever I have up to now accepted as most true I have acquired either from the senses or through the senses. But from time to time I have found that the senses deceive, and it is prudent never to trust completely those who have deceived us even once' (CSM 2:12; throughout this chapter and the next unadorned numerical references are to pages in CSM 2). How can Descartes know that 'the senses deceive'? He has found that they do: once he saw a tower that looked cylindrical but turned out to be square. How did that happen? Well, he saw that it was square, and even touched its walls and felt the corners. This story involves a trust in the senses; quite generally, any specific anecdote about how the senses have misled one will also partly rely on them. Still, Descartes can say: 'Well, the senses have told me conflicting stories, so that at least some of what they have told me is false.'

He suggests that perhaps distrust of the senses can be confined to a relatively small subset of beliefs about the environment, excluding ones about large, obvious, near-at-hand matters, about which it would be crazy to have doubts. That paragraph is a set-up, for Descartes proceeds to laugh at himself for writing it, and to destroy it by suggesting that perhaps right now he is dreaming. Evidently some of his dreams were more life-like than any of mine, but other people say they find his accounts plausible. Anyway, all he needs is that, for all he knows to the contrary, he *could* be dreaming—perhaps having the first vivid and detailed dream of his life. Descartes puts it well in the Sixth Meditation: 'Every sensory experience I have ever thought I was having while awake I can also think of myself as sometimes having while asleep' (53); he does not say that it happens, just that for all he knows to the contrary, it happens.

This sceptical argument is really too good. Descartes tries to draw its sting in the final paragraph of the *Meditations*, now relying on the existence of a veracious God:

When I distinctly see where things come from and where and when they come to me, and when I can connect my perceptions of them with the whole of the rest of my life without a break, then I am quite certain that when I encounter these things I am not asleep but awake. And I ought not to have even the slightest doubt of their reality if, after calling upon all the senses as well as my memory and my intellect in order to check them, I receive no conflicting reports from any of these sources. (62)

God's veracity is the reason why he ought not to doubt under those conditions; we shall come to that later. My present concern is with his belief that sometimes the conditions are satisfied. What entitles him to that? This is what Hobbes asks in the Third Objections, when he points out that someone might dream that his present experience fits in with his past life. Descartes agrees, but adds: 'But after- wards, when he wakes up, he will easily recognize his mistake' (137). What good does that do? How does that help him to decide whether, right now, he is dream- ing? Even as he has an experience of waking up out of a dream, how does he know that he is not waking from a dream within a dream into a simple dream?

Near the end of *Method* 4, Descartes refuses to defend himself against the sug- gestion that he is dreaming. Dreams can at most mislead us concerning the states of affairs that we might learn about through the senses, he says, and error about those 'does not matter' because the senses are unreliable anyway. 'Whether we are awake or asleep, we ought never to let ourselves be convinced except by the evidence of our reason.' If reason *did* present us with something clear and distinct in a dream, it would be as valid as if we were awake. That strengthens the defence against scepticism by shortening the line, reducing the area to be defended. Descartes is not entitled to this stratagem, however, because in the later parts of the *Meditations* he explicitly claims to have secured his central, general beliefs about the material world; these involve a cautious reliance on the senses, and are thus vulnerable to the suspicion that he might be dreaming.

The next three paragraphs of the *Meditations* propose that the simplest ele- ments of what one experiences in a dream 'are real and exist'. These include 'cor- poreal nature in general, and its extension; the shape of extended things; the quantity, or size and number of these things; the place in which they may exist, the time through which they may endure, and so on'. That leads to this sugges- tion: 'Arithmetic, geometry and other subjects of this kind, which deal only with the simplest and most general things, regardless of whether they really exist in nature or not, contain something certain and indubitable.' It does not matter exactly what Descartes means by this. What does matter is how he uses it: just as 'The senses do not deceive us about big close-up things' prompted him to bring in dreams, so here 'The simplest elements of experience are real and exist' prompts him to ratchet up the scepticism still further by bringing in the possibility of an all-powerful Deceiver.

The last four paragraphs of the First Meditation introduce the catch-all possibility that Descartes is the victim of an omnipotent and malevolent being who has set out to deceive him completely, including leading him to believe that two and three make five when really they do not. The move towards this through the idea of a deceiving God is a playful intellectual dance, not solemn philosophy.

For a helpful summary of the stages in which doubts have been induced, see the paragraph at 53–4. Recently, some philosophers have revived something like the Deceiver move, asking whether and how I can know that I am not a brain in a vat, with neural inputs provided by a power-mad scientist. There are differences; the thought 'Perhaps I am a brain in a vat' is not part of the thought 'Perhaps there is no material world'.

145. The Deceiver's scope: arithmetic and memory

We have seen Descartes introducing the Deceiver to create doubts about whether two and three make five, and whether squares have four sides. Even for this, though, he does not rely heavily on the supposition of a Deceiver, because he has a more prosaic reason for doubt: 'Since I sometimes believe that others go astray in cases where they think they have the most perfect knowledge, may I not similarly go wrong every time I add two and three or count the sides of a square, or even in some simpler matter, if that is imaginable?' (14). So as well as the indiscriminate, block-busting thought 'Perhaps *somehow* I am being misled when I think that 2 + 3 = 5', there is the slightly more specific one: 'When I think that 2 + 3 = 5, perhaps I am making one of those elementary mistakes that I have sometimes seen others make.' In any case, one way or another Descartes is calling into question his elementary arithmetical beliefs.

Does he mean to extend this to the whole of logic? If not, his procedure seems arbitrary. His Deceiver hypothesis, and his observation about how 'I sometimes believe that others go astray', apply to logic as well as to arithmetic. And he seems not to mean to draw the line there, for he says 'or even in some simpler matter, if that is imaginable'. With elementary logic in question, however, we are suddenly caught in quicksand. For now it seems that Descartes has called into question all his logical beliefs, but plans to reclaim them by *arguing* from some foundation. Trust in those arguments should not be greater than trust in the logical conditionals that are their principles of inference; so the procedure must beg the question. One cannot reason one's way out of scepticism about reason.

Frankfurt (1970: 61–3) contends that in the First Meditation Descartes intended to cast doubt only on the arithmetical beliefs of the ordinary untutored sense-bound person who has not yet learned to perceive things clearly and distinctly. Descartes's doubts, he holds, do not extend to the logic that he actually uses early in the Second Meditation, because that involves only logical truths that are 'distinctly' perceived. Frankfurt makes a persuasive case for this, but if he is right about how Descartes means to be arguing, then there is an unsolved problem. When using logic early in the Second Meditation, before arguing for a special status for what is 'distinctly' perceived, what ought Descartes to think—right then—about the logic he is using? I shall return to this shortly.

Early in the Second Meditation we find: 'I will suppose, then, that everything I see is spurious. I will believe that my memory tells me lies'—this is the only place in the work where the reliability of memory is put into question. Various parts of Descartes's attempt to vanquish scepticism rest upon trust in memory, but nowhere does he offer to justify that.

His only recorded pronouncement about the reliability of memory (so far as I know) was made to Burman. Remarking that at a certain point Descartes is confident that he once did so-and-so because he remembers doing it, Burman points out that 'I may think I remember something which I do not in fact remember'. He reports Descartes as replying: 'I have nothing to say on the subject of memory. Everyone should test himself to see whether he is good at remembering. If he has any doubts about that, then he should make use of written notes and so forth to help him' (CSMK 334). This is highly vulnerable. A note does not inform me about my past unless I know things about who wrote it and what it means, and those ultimately rely on memory. There is no way around this difficulty, I believe: the problem is insoluble.

From now on, I shall discuss Descartes's struggles with scepticism on the assumption—which he practically adopts—that elementary logic and memory-beliefs are not on the table, are not under challenge, and thus do not need to be defended.

146. Defeating the Deceiver

Early in the Second Meditation Descartes reaches the foundation he has been digging for: his own existence. This, he says, is guaranteed by the fact that he thinks—we have here the famous inference of *Sum* from *Cogito*. Descartes rightly says (*PP* 1:10) that this rests upon a principle of inference—a little bit of logic that validates the move from premiss to conclusion—though he insists that one can make the move without explicitly applying this principle of inference (100; see also CSMK 333).

What is the principle of the inference? The passages I have just cited include 'It is impossible that that which thinks should not exist', 'Everything which thinks is, or exists . . . It is impossible that he should think without existing', and 'Whatever thinks exists'. Descartes seems to have faced himself with a scepticism radical enough to question even that, but I shall bypass that in the meantime, and instead ask what entitles him to the premiss 'I think'.

When Descartes uses the phrase 'deducing existence from thought'(100), he suggests that 'I think' or its cousin 'Something thinks' is to be derived from the still more basic premiss 'There is a thought'. That derivation might rely on this:

We cannot initially become aware of a substance merely through its being an existing thing, since this alone does not of itself have any effect on us. We can, however, easily come to know a substance by one of its attributes, in virtue of the common notion [= self-evident truth] that nothingness possesses no attributes . . . Thus, if we perceive the presence of some attribute, we can infer that there must also be present an existing thing or substance to which it may be attributed. (PP 1:52, CSM 1:210)

If Descartes thinks that a thought is a property or attribute of the mind in which it occurs, then this passage provides a basis for inferring that there is a thinker because there is a thought. It also implies that in the *Cogito* passage he *ought* to be arguing in that manner, treating the proposition *Cogito* as inferred, rather than directly given to his awareness. But then the inference—from 'There is a thought' to 'There is a thinker'—relies on a principle which he cannot plausibly claim to be proof against doubt. Either way, he is in trouble. I shall say no more about this, however. From here on, the argument can be taken as starting either from 'There is a thought' or from 'I think'.

Is Descartes entitled to the argument (construed either way) at this stage in his inquiry? He has envisaged an omnipotent and malignant Deceiver, to serve as a virtually universal doubt-caster or question-raiser. For a while this doubt seemed to extend to the most elementary truths of logic; and Descartes encouraged this impression. A page or so back he asked 'So what remains true?', answering wryly, 'Perhaps just the one fact that nothing is certain' (16). What has now happened to rescue him?

He deploys a special little argument that he thinks will hold the Deceiver at bay:

If I convinced myself of something then I certainly existed. But there is a deceiver of supreme power and cunning who is deliberately and constantly deceiving me. In that case also I undoubtedly exist, if he is deceiving me; and let him deceive me as much as he can, he will never bring it about that I am nothing so long as I think that I am something. (17)

This seems to be an attempt to employ the form: *If P, then not-P; therefore not-P.* This is valid: if something's falsehood follows from the supposition of its truth, then it is false. Thus Descartes. Let P be the supposition that I falsely believe that I exist. If P is true, then I falsely believe something, so I believe something, so I think, so I exist, so P is false.

This argument really does prove (1) *It is not the case that I falsely believe that I exist.* This, however, does not entail that (2) *I exist.* It could be that 1 is true and 2 false because I do not believe anything. It is not the case that Berlioz now falsely believes he exists, but not because he now truly believes he exists. Descartes's argument against the Deceiver, in short, requires the premiss 'I think that I exist' or, anyway, 'I think'. The working role of this premiss in the argument gets masked by his pushing scepticism not in the form 'Perhaps not-P', but rather in the form 'Perhaps I am wrong in thinking that P'; and this effect is increased by the hypothesis that a *deceiver* is at work. The speculation about someone who brings it about that Descartes's beliefs are false is designed to leave unchallenged the premiss that he does have beliefs: the possibility that he confronts is not *Perhaps I do not exist*, but rather *Perhaps I am wrong in thinking that I exist*, which puts 'I think' out of the zone of combat.

Objection: 'How could it be in the zone? If Descartes did not invoke a possible deceiver—a creator of false beliefs—he would have to tackle the thought "Perhaps some malign but powerful being has brought it about that I do not exist" or "that I do not think" or "that no thoughts occur"; but there is nothing he could do with such a thought, and indeed it does not clearly make sense to suppose that he could even have it.' I agree. My complaint is not with how Descartes conducts himself at this point in his intellectual adventure, but only with his not explaining and justifying his undefended acceptance of the proposition that he thinks.

How could he defend it? Curley (1978: 93, 95) has offered this answer: 'The premise of the *cogito* argument can be represented as being supplied by the opposition, as being a necessary ingredient in any skeptical hypothesis which would provide a reasonable ground of doubt. . . . Descartes need not claim to know that premise, which is supplied by the skeptical opposition.' But this is not a debating society; we are not observing a game, or even a battle, which Descartes aims to win under agreed rules with permitted weapons. He tells us what is going on—one man sits alone by the fire trying to refound his belief system. The fact that some challenger hands him a premiss ought to be irrelevant to this project, which is intellectual and solitary rather than political and communal. Descartes declares this. In introducing the Deceiver, he told Burman, he means to 'raise not only the customary difficulties of the sceptics but every difficulty that can possibly be raised' (CSMK 333).

The only other thing Descartes might say to defend his acceptance of *Cogito* is that he could not call it into question—that is, that it is 'indubitable' in the correct sense of that word. That, however, seems to have nothing to do with the normative project of finding a system of beliefs that are known for sure or absolutely justified. As Margaret Wilson wrote: 'The crucial issue is whether we can *know* certain propositions prior to proving God; the observation that there are certain moments when we cannot for the moment doubt is epistemically irrelevant' (1978: 133). For a decent understanding of Descartes's treatment of scepticism, the main thing we have to do is to understand how it relates indubitability to justification and other normative concepts. In order to get a clear run at this, however, I need to introduce some concepts and sweep away some clutter; and that will take the rest of this chapter.

147. The non-theological derivation of the truth-rule

We have to face up to Descartes's 'truth-rule', as it is sometimes called. He derives or defends this in three ways, the first of which is my present topic. It is a philosophically boring disaster, which it would be pleasant to ignore. Still, I shall work through it—partly for the aerobic exercise that this will involve, and partly to ensure that it does not trip us up when we are attending to graver matters. Here it is, from early in the Third Meditation:

I am certain that I am a thinking thing. Do I not therefore also know what is required for my being certain about anything? In this first item of knowledge there is simply a clear and distinct perception of what I am asserting; this would not be enough to make me certain of the truth of the matter if it could ever turn out that something which I perceived with such clarity and distinctness was false. So now I seem to be able to lay it down as a general rule that whatever I perceive very clearly and distinctly is true. (24)

Let us first try to understand the conclusion of this. Descartes explains 'clear' and 'distinct' only once:

I call a perception 'clear' when it is present and open to the attentive mind—just as we say that we see something clearly when it is present to the eye's gaze and stimulates it with a sufficient degree of strength and openness. I call a perception 'distinct' if, as well as being clear, it is so sharply separated from all other perceptions that it contains within itself only what is clear. (PP 1:45)

Although I shall retain them, 'clear' and 'distinct' are poor translations for Descartes's Latin and French. The word translated 'clear' really means 'vivid': witness his writing that intense pains are 'very clear' (PP 1:46), and such facts as that the French phrase lumière claire means 'bright light'. As for 'distinct', what that means is closer to what we would ordinarily mean by 'clear'. That is not evident from Descartes's official definition (above), but it is supported by his actual usage, in which a 'distinct' idea is one all of whose inner detail is luminously present to the person who has the idea, one in which there is nothing hidden. And we can drop 'clear', because Descartes's definitions make 'clear and distinct' pleonastic, like 'rectangular and square'.

A distinct thought, then, bears every possible internal mark of not involving confusion, conceptual opacity, muddle, or the like. This makes Descartes's 'rule'—that 'whatever I perceive very distinctly is true'—obviously false. One can easily have a controlled, unmuddled, transparent apprehension of a false proposition. The truth-rule as stated cannot be rescued from either obvious falsity or else triviality. Bernard Williams (1978: 183) saves it from falsity by taking 'perceiving P distinctly' to mean 'seeing P to be true', but that leads to triviality. Margaret Wilson (1978: 141–2) found clear water between those two by taking 'perceiving P distinctly' to be seeing the contradictoriness of not-P. That still leaves the 'truth-rule' close to triviality, and it does not fit Descartes's text, for it does not allow that he could perceive distinctly that *I am a thinking thing*.

I shall contend in §148 that Descartes did have in mind something he could reasonably think to be substantive and true, and that he misstated it.

There is fatal trouble with how the rule is derived. This is the argument's form:

(1) *I am a thinking thing* had a certain virtue V lacked by many other propositions that had been considered.

(2) It must have been made to have V by some other feature that it had.

(3) The only feature of it that all the others lacked, apart from V itself, is CD. Therefore,

(4) What gives V to the proposition *I am a thinking thing* must be its having CD. Therefore,

(5) CD must be in general sufficient for V: any proposition that has CD has V.[1]

(6) Whatever has V is true. Therefore, from 5 and 6,

(7) Whatever has CD is true.

What is V? Perhaps it is indubitability-by-Descartes: the proposition *I am a thinking thing* is special in that Descartes cannot doubt it. He does indeed emphasize indubitability, and advises readers of the *Meditations* not to accept anything 'unless it has been so clearly and distinctly perceived that we cannot but assent to it' (Rep 2, 112). Observe also the start of the truth-rule passage: 'I am certain that I am a thinking thing. Do I not therefore also know what is required for my being certain about anything?' On that account of what V is, Descartes has some troubles with moves 2–5, which would have to concern the causes for Descartes's inability to doubt; but they pale beside the obvious fact that on this account of V, 6 is unsupported, so Descartes has not derived a *truth*-rule.

Well, then, can V be understood normatively? When Descartes writes 'I am certain that I am a thinking being', does he mean something that entails 'I am rightly confident that I am a thinking being'? If so, then premisses 2–5 could concern the reason that justifies Descartes in his confidence, and he could infer that since it justifies confidence in that case, (5) it must do so wherever it occurs. For 6 to be all right on this reading, V must be a truth-entailing warrant for accepting the proposition that has it, for otherwise 6 will again be left dangling. But then what right has Descartes to assert 1? Indeed, what right does he think he has? I suppose he would claim that his Deceiver-foiling argument gave him the warrant he needed to launch the truth-rule argument; but that is fatal to the latter. If the argument against the Deceiver had succeeded, line 3 in the truth-rule argument would be false: what established *I am a thinking thing* for Descartes, on this supposition, was not his distinctly thinking it, but his having a sound argument for it.

Construed normatively or otherwise, therefore, the argument from 1 to 6 fails. Also (a separate fact) its conclusion is a disaster. There is no solution to this problem for Descartes; the argument is beyond repair.

---

[1] Descartes writes: 'what is *required* for my being certain about anything', but that must be a slip. The conclusion is about what suffices, not what is needed.

Fortunately, we need not take seriously his claim to be deriving a rule at this point in the *Meditations*. Later in the work he offers two things that are meant to justify the truth-rule, and neither owes anything to the argument in the Third Meditation. One comes late in the Fourth (43), the other in the Fifth (48). Descartes gives primacy to the former in his Synopsis, where he says that 'In the Fourth Meditation it is proved that everything we clearly and distinctly perceive is true' (11), making no such claim for the Fifth. The Fourth Meditation's theological treatment of the truth-rule is obscure, but at least we can see that it stands on its own feet, rather than building on the argument at 24. Descartes does not suggest that the earlier derivation of the truth-rule might collaborate with his theology and his theory of error to yield some doctrinal treasure that neither could yield on its own. Nor does he explicitly invoke the rule in the pages between those two discussions of it. When he says that he sees 'clearly' that P, or announces Q as 'clear and distinct', these are mere assertions, and not inferences to something's truth from its being distinctly perceived.

The same holds for the seeming defence of the truth-rule in the Fifth Meditation (48). It also brings in God; and despite its not being described in this manner in the Synopsis, it does have the form of a defence of the truth-rule: 'Now I have perceived that God exists [etc.], and I have drawn the conclusion that everything which I clearly and distinctly perceive is of necessity true.' Again Descartes does not here rely on the defence at 24 in the Third Meditation.

In the latter Descartes writes only that 'I *seem* to be able to lay it down as a general rule'. Although he does not explain this tentativeness, it is perhaps a hint that he is not claiming here to make a solid addition to his body of doctrine. Perhaps he intends only to get the truth-rule on the table—to get us accustomed to it as something it would be good to be assured of—in preparation for the later theological defence which is supposed to give that assurance.

148. God's role

To grasp the theological defence of the truth-rule, we need first to get clearer about what the rule is. It claims truth for any proposition that one relates to in a certain favoured manner; and the texts show this to be a complex involving two simpler relations: having P in mind distinctly, and being absolutely sure of P's truth (or unable to doubt that P). How are these supposed to be interrelated?

Sometimes Descartes says or implies that one always brings the other with it, so that a sure-fire way to become unable to doubt P is to 'perceive' P distinctly: 'My nature is such that so long as I perceive something very clearly and distinctly I cannot but believe it to be true' (48). This cannot be right as a general thesis. If we can perceive P distinctly, then we can do the same to its contradictory; yet they cannot both be indubitable. I can find no way of fine-tuning 'perceive distinctly' so as to avoid this result. (For a resolute attempt to do so, see Bonnen and Flage 1999.)

To get anywhere with this part of Descartes's thought, we must take his topic to be situations where we have something distinctly in mind *while* being unable to doubt it. The idea of distinctness as banishing doubt is a red herring; what he needs is the sheerly conjunctive idea of *combining* distinctness with indubitability. Needing shorthand, I shall express the meaning of 'x has P distinctly in mind while being entirely unable to doubt or question it' in the form *x Distinguishes P*. And I contend that the best way to understand the truth-rule (though it is not what Descartes actually says) is as saying: *For any P, if I Distinguish P, then P is true*. This gives him a chance of steering between triviality and falsehood; and it paves the way for a coherent theological defence.

Descartes may hold that the only propositions that can be Distinguished are ones which cannot be held distinctly in mind without being found indubitable. He is certainly interested in such propositions: 'Some things are so transparently clear and at the same time so simple that we cannot ever think of them without believing them to be true' (Rep 2, 104). His most acute interpreter, Spinoza, built that idea into the truth-rule, which he said Descartes meant to apply to 'the things to which we must necessarily assent when we perceive them distinctly' (DP 1p14s; CS 256). If that is Descartes's position, he will presumably think that in *these* cases the distinctness of conception produces the inability to doubt; and that might help to explain why he sometimes slips into saying that distinctly conceiving *any* proposition makes one unable to doubt it.

Anyway, this extra detail does not affect the strategic situation. We are confronted by two possible readings of the truth-rule, Spinoza's:

> If someone perceives P distinctly and is thereby caused to be unable to doubt it, then P is true;

and mine:

> If someone perceives P distinctly and at the same time cannot doubt it, then P is true.

Mine has the weaker antecedent, so it is stronger, and could therefore be harder to defend. But Descartes's theological defence, which I shall now present, counts as well for the strong rule as for the weak one.

He wants God as a guarantor of the truth of any proposition that anyone Distinguishes—that is, finds indubitable while having it distinctly in mind. His account of how God does this, at the end of the Fourth Meditation (42–3), includes some peculiar stuff about a distinct perception's being 'something'; I shall not go into that.

My concern is with the truth-rule's being embedded in a more general discussion in which Descartes clears God from responsibility for our intellectual errors on the grounds that we err only because we sometimes *choose* to assent without being fully entitled to do so. This might seem to fail if we sometimes err not by choice but by compulsion, finding a falsehood to be indubitable by us. Even then, however, we might fight against the indubitability, saying to ourselves: 'I cannot doubt that P; but I should work on this, trying to find a basis for questioning it.' That would be the right thing to say in cases where our mental grasp of P is insecure—there is an unclarity or fuzziness about it, a cloud within which error may lurk. In such cases, we are still free—not immediately to withhold assent, but to look around, think harder, try to get the matter into sharper focus. However, when I Distinguish a proposition, there is nothing more I can do: the proposition is presented with all the internal marks of being present in my mind with all its detail on view, nothing hidden, no smoke-screen, no backyard, *and* I cannot doubt it. If I were then in error in believing P, God would in effect be a liar. But he is not, so there are no such cases, which is to say that any proposition which anyone ever Distinguishes is true.[2]

149. Why is there no circle?

This defence of the truth-rule is only as good as its premiss that there is an omnipotent and veracious God. Before getting to the philosophically worthwhile questions arising out of that, I reluctantly spend a section on the accusation—which is as old as the Objections to the *Meditations*—that Descartes's defence of the truth-rule is viciously circular. He needs his truth-rule to establish anything beyond the limited confines of the *Cogito*; he establishes his right to it through his theology; but the latter goes far beyond the *Cogito*, therefore cannot be argued for without reliance on the truth-rule. So goes the charge.

For much of this century English writers tried to meet it through what I call 'the memory defence' (for example, Stout 1929 and Doney 1955). According to this, there is no circularity because God is invoked not to defend the truth-rule, but only to help us to apply it in some cases. The reliability of 'If I ever Distinguish P, then P' is assured without theological support, but God comes to my aid at a time when I am not Distinguishing P, but seem to recall having done so earlier: I want to know whether I can trust my memory about this, and Descartes says that I can if (but only if) I am assured that I am in the hands of a non-deceiving God.

The memory defence is dead now, and I am puzzled that it ever lived. There are no texts in its favour, and several that go against it.[3] The little that Descartes ever says about memory is complacent, thin, and miles removed from the truth-rule.

A different defence against the charge of circularity has turned up at intervals down the years, never gaining ascendancy, but never quite dying out either. I shall call it 'the Bréhier view', after its inventor. Wrong as I believe it to be, it has

---

[2] The account of this part of Descartes's thought in Newman 1999: 580 has interesting points of similarity with, and of difference from, mine.

[3] The most influential statement of the case against it is Frankfurt 1962. It is also rejected in Curley 1978: 77–8; B. Williams 1963: 191–8; Kenny 1968: 187–8; and in many other places.

kept good company, being affirmed by Kemp Smith (1952: 273–7) and Etchemendy (1981), treated with respect by Hacking (1973: 181) and hinted at by Margaret Wilson (1978: 128). According to the Bréhier view, the truth-rule serves at a given time to establish the truth of P *at that time*, and God's existence and nature assure us that P will continue to be true *thereafter*. 'The only problem is to know how I can foresee with certainty that . . . what is intuited will continue to be true' (Bréhier 1937: 201). Most of the propositions that we are initially assured of by the truth-rule are necessary truths; so the Bréhier view of God's role requires that even those be at risk, capable of being made false through the will of God. Descartes did indeed hold that view (§180); so the Bréhier view can get over that hurdle.

However, it has no textual support. When Descartes in truth-rule contexts makes use of 'was'/'is' and 'then'/'later', he is contrasting an inability at one time to doubt P with a later ability to doubt it, not contrasting P's truth at one time with its falsehood later. Consider also the terms in which he announces in the Fifth Meditation that the truth-rule needs help from theology:

My nature is such that so long as I perceive something very clearly and distinctly I cannot but believe it to be true. But my nature is also such that I cannot fix my mental vision continually on the same thing, so as to keep perceiving it clearly; and often the memory of a previously made judgment may come back, when I am no longer attending to the arguments that led me to make it. And so other arguments can now occur to me which might easily undermine my opinion, if I did not possess knowledge of God. (48)[4]

This counts decisively against the Bréhier view. If Descartes's concern were that a once true proposition might have become false, his repeated emphasis on 'my nature' would be pointless, as would his contrast between two intellectual states that I may be in. He goes on to introduce the thought that 'there have been frequent cases where I have regarded things as true and certain, but have later been led by other arguments to judge them to be false'. This creates the worry which a belief in a veracious God will supposedly vanquish; and it is the thought that on the past occasion I *was* wrong—that is, that the proposition in question *was* false. The Bréhier view is a non-starter.

For a fresh start on meeting the charge of circularity, let us go to near the end of the Fifth Meditation:

So long as I perceive something very clearly and distinctly I cannot but believe it to be true. But my nature is also such that I cannot fix my mental vision continually on the same thing, so as to keep perceiving it clearly; and often the memory of a previously made judgment may come back, when I am no longer attending to the arguments which led me to make it. And so other arguments can now occur to me which might easily undermine my opinion, if I did not possess knowledge of God; and I should thus never have true and certain knowledge about anything, but only shifting and changeable opinions. For example, when I consider the nature of a triangle, it appears most evident to me . . . that its three angles are equal to two right angles; and so long as I attend to the proof

---

[4] See also *PP* 1:13.

I cannot but believe this to be true. But as soon as I turn my mind's eye away from the proof, then in spite of still remembering that I perceived it very clearly, I can easily fall into doubt about its truth if I am without knowledge of God. For I can convince myself that I have a natural disposition to go wrong from time to time in matters which I think I perceive as evidently as can be. (48*)

The previous judgement *was* made, the supporting arguments *were* employed, the mental apprehension *was* clear (distinct?), and so on. Memory, in short, is trusted without question; so there is no support here for the 'memory defence'.

In this long passage Descartes commits himself to something with the form:

While I Distinguish P, I have an epistemic advantage with respect to P even if I know nothing of God; but after I have stopped Distinguishing P, I no longer have that advantage, though I can regain it if I know that God is good and veracious, and also know that I did earlier Distinguish P.

The knowledge of God is supposed to re-establish the epistemic advantage, because it is supposed to imply the truth-rule, which confers the advantage if I know that I earlier Distinguished P.

So the story goes as follows. Carefully and intelligently deploying every doubt-inducer he could think of, Descartes ran up against propositions that he Distinguished—that is, was unable to doubt while having them distinctly in mind. While that lasted for a given P, it put an end to his sceptical troubles over P: he could not withhold his assent, and could find no leverage for the thought that his inability to do so was pathological. But when he looks back to earlier episodes of that kind, he can then raise the sceptical questions again, saying in effect: 'I was unable to doubt that P while thinking hard and sharply about it, but perhaps that was just my pathology and not a reflection of a secure status in P itself.' The veracity of God assures him that this is not so.

This can work only if Descartes has the epistemic advantage with respect to God's existence and veracity, without getting it through the truth-rule. For this, he needs to Distinguish an argument proving there is a veracious God. While he has that in his mind in that way, he is epistemically advantaged with respect to its conclusion, which he can thus use to validate the truth-rule and thus get epistemic leverage on other propositions which he does not currently Distinguish.

So the case for God's existence and veracity must be gone through in a single intellectual sweep, held before the mind all at once so as to be Distinguished all at once. If it needed a protracted demonstration, that would require Descartes to accept something on the grounds that he remembers finding it indubitable a few minutes before; and that would bring the truth-rule back into play, closing the circle.

The need for an intuitive proof of God's existence and veracity is an overlap between my account of Descartes's position and the memory defence. The latter also requires that such a proof be gone through in a single specious present, a psychological moment, so that it can be known without reliance on memory for its earlier stages. Bernard Williams (1978: 197) has questioned whether

Descartes relies on any such event, and even whether he regards it as possible; but there are two pieces of evidence that go against him.

In the *Rules*, Descartes stresses the importance of getting arguments into a form in which one can take them in by a single movement of the mind. 'Every single thing relating to our undertaking must be surveyed in a continuous and wholly uninterrupted sweep of thought', he writes there (*Rules* 7, CSM 1:25). He expands this by saying that one must 'learn to pass from the first to the last [proposition] so swiftly that memory is left with practically no role to play, and one seems to intuit the whole thing at once'. His reason for this is not like his reason in the *Meditations*, for the *Rules* does not work from a first-person sceptical baseline. Its concerns are more practical: the rules are advice for reducing the chances of error and confusion, and not stern imperatives for the seeker after epistemic purity. The two works belong to different intellectual worlds, and we should not expect the earlier to throw much light on the later. Still, they are by the same man, and reflect some of the same preoccupations; and both show Descartes to have a 'thing' about the superiority of (one-step) intuition over (multi-step) demonstration. It would be in character for him to invoke it to defend himself against the charge of circularity.

Even more conclusive is a part of Descartes's conversation with Burman (CSMK 334–5). His interlocutor says: 'It seems there is a circle. For in the Third Meditation the author uses axioms to prove the existence of God, even though he is not yet certain of not being deceived about these.' Descartes's reply includes this: 'He does use such axioms in the proof, but he knows that he is not deceived with regard to them, since he is actually paying attention to them.' Burman: 'But our mind can think of only one thing at a time, whereas the proof in question is a fairly long one involving several axioms. . . . So one will not be able to keep the attention on all the axioms.' Descartes: 'It is just not true that the mind can think of only one thing at a time. . . . It is clear that we are able to grasp the proof of God's existence in its entirety. As long as we are engaged in this process, we are certain that we are not being deceived, and every difficulty is removed.' If Williams were right, Descartes would not have said this.

Descartes's argument for God's existence and perfection in the Third Meditation may seem—as it did to Burman—too lengthy to be compressed into a single intuition; but its prolixity is due to externals, side-issues, corrections of possible misunderstandings, and so on; the core *argument* is not so long. Anyway, Descartes also had at his disposal the a priori argument for God's existence which he took from Anselm. This led him to write: 'As regards God, if I were not overwhelmed by preconceived opinions, and if the images of things perceived by the senses did not besiege my thought on every side, I would certainly acknowledge him sooner and more easily than anything else. For what is more self-evident than the fact that the supreme being exists?' (47; see also 37).

Even if one could get the proof of God's existence and veracity into a single intuition, and become assured of the truth-rule on that basis, this assurance would last only as long as one was Distinguishing the proof of God (thus Garns

1988). That puts our philosophy and physics on an intermittently shaky basis, unless we have a one-step or intuitive grasp of God's existence which we can bring to mind at will, or perhaps one that is always present in our thinking. The entire story is becoming fanciful, is it not? Ought not Descartes to be embarrassed by being committed to such a burdensome demand as that a satisfactory body of knowledge requires that a veracious God be there in one's thinking—complete with a proof of his existence—all the time? Perhaps; but that raises a larger question which I postpone until Chapter 20.

Three remarks by Descartes seem at first to undermine my account, but they do not. Here is one: 'If we did not know that everything real and true within us comes from a perfect and infinite being, then, however clear and distinct our ideas were, we would have no reason to be sure that they had the perfection of being true' (*Method* 4, CSM 1:130). When asked by Burman about this passage, Descartes explained that he had overstated his position: 'If we did not know that all truth has its origin in God, then however clear our ideas were, we would not know that they were true, or that we were not mistaken—I mean, of course, when we were not paying attention to them, and when we merely remembered that we had clearly and distinctly perceived them' (CSMK 353).

The second: 'If I do not know [that God is not a deceiver], it seems that I can never be quite certain about anything else' (25). Descartes explained to Mersenne that this too was an overstatement: 'When I said that we can know nothing for certain until we are aware that God exists, I expressly declared that I was speaking only of a knowledge of those conclusions which can be recalled when we are no longer attending to arguments by means of which we deduced them' (Rep 2, 100). In fact, he did not expressly declare it until two Meditations later, but the interpretation still stands.

Here is the third: 'The certainty and truth of all knowledge depends uniquely on my knowledge of the true God, to such an extent that I could not perfectly know anything else until I knew him' (49). Here again the circle seems to threaten; but the shadow disappears in the light of facts about the Latin. The noun *scientia* and verb *scire* stand for permanent, highly organized knowledge—stable, complex, interconnected, high-level theory, such as we could not build without reliance on previously established results. The noun *cognitio* and verb *noscere* can refer more humbly to any secure epistemic intake, however fragmentary. Now go through the passage again: 'The certainty and truth of all knowledge [*scientia*] depends uniquely on my knowledge [*cognitio*] of the true God, to such an extent that I could not perfectly know [*scire*] anything else until I knew [*noscere*] him.' Descartes is saying that for any *scientia* we need a *cognitio* of God; there is no circle here.

For further textual evidence for my account of Descartes's position, see his Second Replies (104–5) and Fourth Replies (171).

I have been agreeing with what most Descartes scholars now believe, to this extent: my knowledge of God is supposed to give me—through the truth-rule—an epistemic advantage with respect to P at a time when I do not have a special relation R to P; and I can have this advantage, without help from God, at times when I do have R to P. This is the view of Curley (1978: 192–3), Tlumak (1978), Gewirth (1941: 371–3), Van Cleve (1979: 66–71), Frankfurt (1965), Cottingham (1986: 66–70), and others. Less prevalent in the literature is the value I assign to R: namely, thinking P distinctly *while* finding it indubitable. In my next chapter I enter territory where I have less company still.

Chapter 20

Descartes's Stability Project

150. Indubitability

Picking up the thread from the end of §146: what could justify Descartes in accepting the proposition *Cogito*? I have been pretending to know the answer, writing freely of the 'epistemic advantage' that we are supposed to have with respect to P at a time when we Distinguish it; but I have not said what advantage it is. All Descartes tells us concerning the *Cogito* (premiss and inference) is that he 'recognizes this as self-evident by a simple intuition of the mind'; but we ought not to be satisfied with that. The question is crucial for his strategy, because the advantage—whatever it is—has to give him his theology independently of the truth-rule.

It is not puzzling that he does accept *Cogito* and the inference to *Sum*. While he is Distinguishing a proposition, he has no problem with it. He is perfectly confident of its truth, and cannot genuinely question it. He cannot even pretend to question it: the proposition is distinct in his mind, so he cannot explore it for lurking confusion or error. That unproblematic status is a kind of privilege that a proposition can have before the truth-rule has been established. However, this is a factual and psychological way of not having a problem, not a normative or logical one. Granted that Descartes has no problem about P at this time because he Distinguishes it, it does not follow that he is entitled to be sure of P, still less that P is true. He cannot raise a problem about P, but there may be one for all that.

So Descartes could not coherently announce his project like this: 'I aim to have only true beliefs, achieving this by refusing to believe anything that I can doubt.' When embarking on his project and contemplating finding propositions that he cannot doubt, he should think that this inability may show his limitations rather than the propositions' truth. While in the throes of factual indubitability, he will talk truth and think truth, but before and after he has to admit that indubitability does not automatically guarantee truth.

Nevertheless, Distinguishing is Descartes's bedrock. The edifice he aims to build is based on propositions that he accepts because he must—because they are not dubitable by him while he has them distinctly in mind. He virtually admits this in the long passage quoted fairly early in §149: without his belief in a veracious God, he writes there, 'I can easily fall into doubt' about a previously established position—as though freedom from doubt were the object of the exercise. Note also that the First Meditation is labelled 'Concerning those things that can be called into doubt', not '. . . things that one is entitled to call into doubt'. How, then, does Descartes relate this to the project of acquiring beliefs that are justified and/or true? How does he expect to erect a structure of such beliefs on a foundation of mere inability to call P into question? I shall look at four answers to this.

(1) Perhaps Descartes was in a muddle, and systematically failed to distinguish factual indubitability from normative certainty. We certainly saw him get them tangled in the non-theological argument for the truth-rule (§147). In passages I have quoted he uses the phrases

> I cannot but believe it to be true,
> I can never be quite certain,
> we would have no reason to be sure they were true,
> he knows that he is not deceived,

as though they were on a par, whereas really two are factual and two normative. He may have been in trouble with the word 'certain', and in any case we should be wary of it. In careful usage, 'I am certain that P' is psychological and factual, while 'It is certain that P' is normative. Some of Descartes's uses of 'certain' are plainly factual:

> Some . . . perceptions are so transparently clear and at the same time so simple that we cannot ever think of them without believing them to be true. That I exist so long as I am thinking, or that what is done cannot be undone, and the like—of these we manifestly possess this kind of certainty. (Rep 2, 104★)[1]

Other uses of the word are at least dubious. For example: 'I should hold back my assent from opinions which are not completely certain and indubitable' (12). For other possible waverings, see what Descartes says to Burman at CSMK 334 and 353; also *PP* 1:13 and *Method* 4, CSM 1:126–7. However, for reasons that will appear, I do not believe that the 'muddle' diagnosis covers much of the ground.

(2) It is perhaps true that if someone realizes that P is normatively certain, 'it is only reasonable that he should be unable to withhold his belief, because he has the best possible basis for assenting' (Frankfurt 1970: 164). That might help in getting indubitability from justification, but my topic runs in the opposite direction; it is Descartes's apparent wish to get justification out of indubitability.

(3) Etchemendy (1981: 17) credits Descartes with doing it like this: 'When we have "a conviction so strong that nothing can remove it", we can be assured that the world conforms to our conception, at least to the extent that our conception is complete. If it did not so conform, then our conviction could easily be removed—simply through a brute encounter with the world.' This is too empiricist to be Cartesian or to be sensitive to the shape of Descartes's struggle with scepticism. Etchemendy allows Descartes to help himself to the thesis that false beliefs will be exposed as such by the world; but this amounts to assuming that most of the sceptical problem has been solved.

---

[1] In this chapter, unadorned numerical references are to pages in CSM 2.

(4) I used to think that Descartes could start with factual indubitability and work with it alone until he established the theological defence of the truth-rule, which would then carry him across the gap to normative justification and indeed to truth. The idea was as follows. Descartes accepts a series of propositions, starting with *Cogito*, because he has no choice about them. Along this chain of certainties, he encounters a veracious-God theology and some elementary logic; and these yield an argument for the conclusion that those propositions which he could not doubt, given that they were distinct in his mind, must be true. So the chasm is crossed.

Gareth Matthews helped me to see that this is wrong. If there is a chasm between Distinguishing on the one hand and guaranteed truth on the other, someone who starts on the near side of it will find no bridge to the far side. I shall explain.

When he casts his mind back to a proposition that he did once Distinguish, Descartes's theology will give him the reassuring thought: 'God would not allow me to Distinguish a proposition unless it was true.' So he will be carried from a premiss about a past indubitability to a conclusion about truth. But that will not take him across the chasm, because his hold on the conclusion about truth cannot be essentially different from his hold on the optimistic theology from which he derives it. It thus leaves him on the indubitability side: it encourages him to speak in the idiom of the other side, but it does not take him there. The difference is invisible to him while he is Distinguishing his theology and the truth-rule, but it is obvious enough to us as observers of his performance. When in a certain frame of mind, Descartes will declare his theology and the truth-rule to be true, but we bystanders—who are careful and attentive, and know all there is to know about Descartes's frame of mind while not actually being *in* it—can still be sceptical:

That is just conviction and not necessarily truth. If there were an objective guarantee of the soundness of the defence of the truth-rule, then the rule itself would be guaranteed and so would all the beliefs arrived at by applying it. But the concept of an objective guarantee, though it may figure in Descartes's hopes and aspirations, has no working role in his philosophy. All he has by way of support for the theology and the truth-rule is indubitability accompanied by distinctness. So he cannot cross the chasm.

We observers of Descartes's intellectual performance can think this, and he should agree with us at any time when he is not performing—that is, when he is not actually Distinguishing his theology and the argument for it. So he ought to agree that he cannot get across.

151. The stability project

This is not the whole story, though. Up to here I have pretended that Descartes is mainly trying to acquire true beliefs by achieving beliefs that are justified; and I now question that. Although the *Meditations* is famous for its anti-sceptical pursuit of justification, good reasons, and truth, these normative notions actually play a small part in the work, most of which concerns intellectual stability, tranquility, peace in the doxastic kingdom—a system of beliefs that will stay put. I shall now examine the evidence for this. I argued for this position in my 1990b. A similar view is expressed by Loeb (1990). It was adumbrated by Kim (1988: 219), and we were all beaten to it by Smyth (1986).

The first step is to grasp how much of the *Meditations* is in the psychological rather than the normative camp. In the second paragraph of the work we find this: 'Reason now persuades me that I should hold back my assent from opinions which are not completely certain and indubitable . . . So, for the purpose of rejecting all my opinions, it will be enough if I find in each at least some reason for doubt' (12). The first sentence credits 'reason' with persuading Descartes (he does not say how) of a certain normative judgement. But in what follows the work is done not by *that normative judgement* but by *the fact that Descartes has been persuaded of it* and will behave accordingly. This episode, in short, employs the normative concept only under the 'I believe that . . .' operator.

This illustrates a general point: Descartes can mention reasons without being concerned with them in a normative way; he may instead be treating them merely as items one's awareness of which will cause changes in one's beliefs. He certainly does often treat reasons as causes or compellers of states of mind, as here: 'No counter-argument can be adduced to make me doubt it' (48).

A normative attitude to reasons might seem to be suggested when Descartes remarks that 'There is not one of my former beliefs about which a doubt may not properly be raised; and this is not a flippant or ill-considered conclusion, but is based on powerful and well thought-out reasons' (14–15). But when an objector writes that 'powerful and well thought-out reasons' ought to meet standards that Descartes's do not, he replies: 'There may be reasons that are strong enough to compel us to doubt, even though these reasons are themselves doubtful, and hence are not to be retained later on . . . The reasons are strong so long as we have no others which produce certainty by removing the doubt' (Rep 7, 319). This roundly says that what counts is not the (normative) worth of the reason but merely its (factual) power to cause doubt. See Tlumak 1978 for more evidence that Descartes did not confine himself to doubts based on good reasons. One example occurs on 25, where he writes that the hypothesis of a deceiving God is a 'very slight and, so to speak, metaphysical' reason for doubt, yet treats it seriously because it blocks complete confidence. In short, Descartes is concerned with reasons, arguments, considerations, etc. in their role as causes, not as justifiers, of doubt or confidence. Factual (in)dubitability seems to be independently interesting to Descartes, and not merely an interloper that got in through confusion with normative certainty.

He heralds his stability project in the opening sentences of the *Meditations*:

Some years ago I was struck by the large number of falsehoods that I had accepted as true in my childhood, and by the highly doubtful nature of the whole edifice that I had subsequently based on them. I realized that it was necessary, once in the course of my life, to demolish everything completely and start again right from the foundations if I wanted to establish anything at all in the sciences that was stable and likely to last.

Writing and thinking in this vein, Descartes looks merely for psychological certainty, indubitability; he thinks of something that he cannot doubt as bedrock, a stable starting-point. Stable, not true. He says more to the same effect in the Seventh Replies:

When an architect wants to build a house which is stable on ground where there is a sandy topsoil over underlying rock or clay or some other firm base, he begins by digging out a set of trenches from which he removes the sand and anything resting on or mixed in with the sand, so that he can lay his foundations on firm soil. In the same way, I began by taking everything that was doubtful and throwing it out, like sand; and then, when I noticed that it is impossible to doubt that a doubting or thinking substance exists, I took this as the bedrock on which I could lay the foundations of my philosophy. (Rep 7, 366)

The 'bedrock' metaphor is slightly off-centre for *truth*, but perfect for *stability*, the achievement of beliefs that one will not later be forced to give up. Similarly, Descartes's finding it 'impossible to doubt' that P relates him to P psychologically; in logical space it is a neighbour of 'My belief that P is stable', not of 'P is true'.

Objection: 'Why must we choose? Descartes could be pursuing both truth and stability, as elements in a single, cleanly conceived project—namely, to establish a system of beliefs that will be true and therefore stable, the idea being that true beliefs are less likely than false ones to be dislodged by reality.' There could indeed be such a project, motivated in either of two ways: (1) Descartes sought truth as his main goal, but valued stability as one of its incidental benefits; or (2) he had stability as his main goal and valued truth as a means to it. Most scholars would favour 1; but when Descartes's repeated emphasis on stability is brought to their attention, they might settle for 2. That could be an eirenic proposal: I get stability as Descartes's ultimate aim, others get truth as his immediate focus.

Combatively, I demand more. I shall argue that much of the *Meditations* does not fit into any kind of truth project, and shows Descartes to have a concern with stability taken as intrinsically valuable, and as reachable without reference to truth. He does not interrelate his truth and stability projects in any controlled way, and seems not to be fully aware that he has both. But the stability project is there, running alongside the other and sometimes taking over from it. In the long passage that I quoted from 48, for example, Descartes says that my Distinguishing P gives me the advantage that 'I cannot but believe it to be true'; the loss I suffer by no longer Distinguishing it is that 'other arguments can now occur to me which might easily undermine my opinion'. Again, whereas earlier 'it appears most evident to me [that P]' and 'I cannot but believe this to be true', when I stop Distinguishing P, 'I can easily fall into doubt about its truth'.

With stability as his only goal, Descartes can still tell a coherent story about what his belief in God's veracity does for him. While I Distinguish P, my intellectual behaviour must be that of someone who has no problem regarding P's truth. But when my mental spotlight moves off P, my situation changes: granted that an hour ago I did Distinguish P, what good does that do me now that I can look back on my earlier assurance and wonder whether it was pathological? At this point my theology comes to the rescue. I run my mind over the argument for it and Distinguish it; so right now it has a perfectly secure status in my mind, as has the truth-rule that I infer from it; the truth-rule in its turn, when combined with my uncritical assurance that I did Distinguish P, makes P secure as well, even now when I am not focusing on it. My theology, then, greatly increases the range of propositions about which I have security at any given moment—a security that at first could come only from intense mental focus, but can now attend any proposition which anyone has ever Distinguished. This advantage, however, is available to me only while I am actually Distinguishing my theology.

On this account, my theology rescues me from a state of doubt, or lack of confidence; and Descartes sometimes takes this view of it. He derives the truth-rule from his theology in the long passage quoted in §149, employing the concept of truth five times. Four of those, however, occur inside the psychological context 'believe . . . to be true'. The fifth is not thus sheltered—it occurs in a description of the drawback from which the theology is to save us—but even there Descartes contrasts truth not with falsity but with instability: 'I should never have true and certain knowledge about anything but only shifting and changeable opinions.'

The stability theme looms large in his scornful account of the atheist's predicament:

The kind of knowledge [*scientia*] possessed by the atheist . . . is not unchanging and certain. . . . The less power the atheist attributes to the author of his being, the more reason he will have to suspect that his nature may be so imperfect as to allow him to be deceived even in matters that seem utterly evident to him. And he will never be able to be free of this doubt until he admits that he has been created by a true God to whom deception is foreign. (Rep 6, 289*)

The concept of truth serves here as an ingredient in two concepts: knowledge and deception. The 'knowledge' in question cannot involve truth that only our theology puts in our hands, because Descartes attributes it to the atheist. The concept of deception occurs only embedded in psychological contexts: 'suspect that [he is] deceived', 'admits that deception is foreign to God'.[2] What Descartes threatens the atheist with, therefore, are not false or unjustified beliefs, but turmoil and intellectual paranoia.

In writing of the atheist's 'reason to suspect' that he is in error, and not only of his actually suspecting this, Descartes implies that he regards as deplorable the unconscious, innocent plight of someone who would be troubled about stability if he thought hard enough. This comes to the surface in the Second Replies. Discussing the atheist who is 'clearly aware that the three angles of a triangle are

---

[2] I use 'admits' to render *agnoscat*. CSM uses 'recognizes', which is truth-entailing. Either is possible, but mine fits better.

equal to two right angles', Descartes remarks in passing—and in contradiction to 289—that 'this awareness of his is not true knowledge [*scientia*], since no act of awareness that can be rendered doubtful seems fit to be called knowledge'. Then he proceeds to his main point:

[This] atheist cannot be certain that he is not being deceived on matters which seem to him to be very evident . . . And although this doubt may not occur to him, it can still crop up if someone else raises the point or if he looks into the matter himself. So he will never be free of this doubt until he acknowledges that God exists. (Rep 2, 101)

The seemingly odd notion of freedom from a non-actual doubt is really quite all right. At level 1 is the thoughtlessly confident atheist, at 2 the thoughtful worried atheist, and at 3 the thoughtfully secure Cartesian. Somebody at 1 can be brought to 2 through a mere intervention by someone else, but cannot work through to 3 without a radical change in theological belief. So the badness of 2 carries over to 1.

The stability project appears dramatically in the Second Replies:

As soon as we think that we correctly perceive something, we are spontaneously convinced that it is true. Now if this conviction is so firm that it is impossible for us ever to have any cause for doubting what we are convinced of, then there are no further questions for us to ask: we have everything that we could reasonably want. What is it to us that someone may make out that the perception whose truth we are so firmly convinced of may appear false to God or an angel, so that it is, absolutely speaking, false? What do we care about this alleged absolute falsity, since we neither believe in it nor have even the smallest suspicion of it? For the supposition which we are making here is of a conviction so firm that it is quite incapable of being destroyed; and such a conviction is clearly the same as the most perfect certainty. (Rep 2, 103*)

A page or two later, the same line of thought appears even more vividly: 'It is . . . no objection for someone to make out that these might appear false to God or to an angel. For the evident clarity of our perceptions does not allow us to listen to anyone who makes up this kind of story' (104*). This reads like someone who is capable, at least sometimes, of turning away from the pursuit of truth towards psychological stability.

The gap between 'indubitable' and 'stable' must be acknowledged. If I cannot doubt P, this does not automatically ensure that it has come to stay; I might be unable to doubt it at one time and then, through some change in me, come to question or even reject it later. Descartes knows of one way for that to happen: at T_1 I concentrate on P and cannot doubt it; at T_2 I no longer focus directly on P, and then I can doubt it. He assumes, however, that if at T_3 I again focus hard upon P, I shall again find it indubitable as I did at T_1, thus assuming constancy of my intellectual character. This seems to be an assumption for which he can give no reasons that are proof against any of the forms of scepticism against which he is battling. That Descartes makes it is a plain fact, right there in the text; it is not purely a requirement of—and thus a weak point in—the stability interpretation.

152. Protests

Objection: 'The pursuit of intellectual peace and stability *per se* cannot be a significant part, even a small one, of Descartes's concerns. (1) The causes of doubt or of confidence that he entertains are all logical, rational, normative: doubt spreads through his belief system carried by the virus of his recognition of reasons why various beliefs might be false. If he is seriously interested in doubt as such, why does he not also consider other possible sources of it? (2) Suppose he learned that he could get his belief system calmed down by taking a pill, he would not at any level of his mind settle for that. Such a "solution" would either bore or disgust him.'

I am not sure how to reply to 1. Perhaps Descartes saw reasons as the most potent and corrosive cause of doubt. 'Vanquish the sceptical reasons,' he may have thought, 'and other causes of doubt will be child's play.' Or perhaps he thought that he could not defend himself against other causes of doubt: 'I defend where defence is possible.' I do not greatly like either suggestion, but have no other. I still maintain, though, that Descartes was interested in causes of doubt generally. Suppose we confronted him with this nasty thought: 'There might be a cause that made you doubt the foundations of the intellectual edifice you hope to build and was not vanquished by your awareness that there are good reasons for confidence and none against it. This would cause you to lack confidence while knowing that you were intellectually entitled to it.' Descartes, as I see him, would regard this as an alarming prospect, and would want to protect himself against it.

In reply to 2, I agree that if it were put to Descartes in that direct fashion, he would probably recoil, protesting that nothing would satisfy him but the truth. But that response would show that he was not in touch with his own thinking, and passages I have quoted are evidence for this. Further evidence will be provided in Chapter 24, where I shall expound his metaphysic of necessary truths.

Second objection: 'It is not credible that Descartes should ever turn his back on the pursuit of securely held truth in favour of mere confidence or tranquility. The Descartes you depict simply is not the one we know.' He is indeed not the one we have thought we knew, but I am urging that we look again at what he wrote, seeing directly, and not through the distorting lenses of biased commentaries and inaccurate translations.

Still, granted that there is evidence that he often did turn his back on the truth project, we ought to ask why. I suggest this tentative answer. Descartes may sometimes have suspected that the search for an utterly secure grasp of the truth is incoherent. This suspicion might grow from the insight that someone who Distinguishes P must behave exactly as he would if he had (and knew that he had) the most secure objective guarantee of P's truth. The important fact that the psychological notion of Distinguishing P is practically equivalent to the epistemological notion of knowing that one has an absolute guarantee that P is true has been persuasively stated by Panayot Butchvarov:

What could be so much *like* the possession of truth without *being* the possession of truth? I suggest that it can only be the unthinkability, inconceivability, unintelligibility of one's not possessing truth; the unthinkability of one's being mistaken in believing such a truth. I suggest that in the case of primary knowledge the phrase 'having the truth' is a natural but misleading description of the unthinkability of mistake. For even if there were a genuine notion of literal possession of truth, it would function, in life and in thought, in the way in which the notion of unthinkability of mistake does. For if I cannot think how my belief may be false, then the question whether it is false can play no role for me. (1970: 84)

This goes beyond the point about practical equivalence which I have made. The equivalence *would* hold, Butchvarov says, 'even if there *were* a genuine notion of literal possession of truth'. He implies that there is really no such notion; and I am inclined to agree. This needs more defence than I know how to give, but for a start consider these three:

(1) I have an absolute guarantee of the truth of P.
(2) I am not open to even the faintest criticism if I accept P.
(3) I cannot reject P or get myself into a condition in which I can reject P.

The only real content I can give to 1 is that of 2, which is true if 3 is, because 'ought' implies 'can', even in epistemology. So we can link indubitability with normative certainty after all, when we understand the latter in the only way in which it really makes sense to us. Indubitability in the presence of distinctness is not merely the best we can get, but is all we can make sense of, and thus all we can seek or demand, because the rival concept, knowing absolutely for sure that P, is empty. Perhaps Descartes had some sense of this, and was intermittently encouraged by that to let the stability project take over.

153. Interrelating the two projects

I suspect that the stability project was always present in Descartes's mind at some level. I also think that it represents the better side of his treatment of scepticism: the hardest cruces in the text—the acceptance of *Cogito* and the non-theological derivation of the truth-rule—look better if we take truth out of them and interpret them purely in terms of stability or confidence. This should not surprise us if the truth project, conceived as Descartes conceived it and conducted by the standards he has set up, cannot possibly be carried through, and may not even be fully intelligible.

How did the two projects interrelate in Descartes's own mind? My best guess is that he had before him the goal, involving both subjective and objective elements, of arriving at beliefs about which he could not be wrong, perhaps mediated by the concept of perfectly justified beliefs; by his standards the goal cannot be attained, and this fact impressed itself subliminally upon his mind; he kept it out of conscious awareness partly by settling for inadequate arguments; but he stayed optimistic about his pursuit of justification and truth because, under the surface, he was engaged in the more promising stability project, which is structurally enough like the other to substitute for it.

If the last part of this is wrong, then I cannot explain the facts about the strength and relative purity of the subjectivist strand running through Descartes's treatment of scepticism, or the badness of some of his main attempts to execute the truth project. Facts so clear and clamorous should not be written off as an accident with no deep significance for the understanding of what Descartes wrote.

Many commentators have tried to fend off the last two of my theses. They have sought to attribute to Descartes some one line of thought which intelligibly relates factual indubitability to justification and/or to truth. They have usually admitted that the line of thought, whatever it may be, is flawed; but the aim has been to find it—to point to some prima-facie plausible set of considerations and to say, 'Descartes thought he could interrelate the subjectivist and objectivist strands in his thinking like *that*'. Attempts to present Descartes in this light have all failed. They had to. His writings do not contain the needed interrelating structure or any plausible simulacrum of it.

My account of how the two projects came to be entwined is more charitable to Descartes than what seems to be the only alternative: namely, that he simply failed—not seeing clearly how normative certainty and truth differ from indubitability, he regularly conflated the *fact* of confidence with *entitlement* to it. I prefer to see him in my way, as engaged in developing—without fully getting it into focus—a complex, subtle, new line of thought according to which the entitlement is to be explained in terms of the fact.

Louis Loeb, who independently arrived at an understanding of Descartes's stability project, does not share my view that Descartes also pursues the truth project without having the relation between the two firmly under control. He tries to nest the epistemic 'truth' project within the psychological 'stability' one. 'We can think of passages suggestive of the epistemic interpretation as implicitly embedded within the propositional attitude "I irresistibly believe that . . ." or as reports of what can be irresistibly believed' (1992: 224). We can think of them that way, but I see no good evidence that Descartes meant them thus. I am sure that in his texts the factual or psychological concerns keep company with the normative and epistemic ones, with each sometimes standing on its own feet.

Bibliography

Adams, Robert Merrihew (1994). *Leibniz: Determinist, Theist, Idealist*. New York: Oxford University Press.

Aristotle. *Categories*.

——. *On the Heavens*.

——. *On the Soul*.

——. *Physics*.

Armstrong, David M. (1961). *Perception and the Physical World*. London: Routledge.

——(1980). 'Identity through Time', in P. van Inwagen (ed.), *Time and Cause*. Dordrecht: Reidel, 67–78.

Arnauld, Antoine (1640). Objections to Descartes's *Meditations*, in CSM 2:138–53.

——(1686–7). Correspondence with Leibniz, in Mason.

Arthur, Richard (1985). 'Leibniz and Time', in Okruhlik and Brown 1985: 263–313.

Augustine, Bishop of Hippo. *The City of God*.

Ayers, M. R. (1981). 'Mechanism, Superaddition, and the Proof of God's Existence in Locke's *Essay*'. *Philosophical Review*, 90: 210–51.

——(1991). *Locke*. London: Routledge.

Baier, Annette C. (1981). 'Cartesian Persons'. *Philosophia*, 10: 169–88.

Balz, Albert G. A. (1917). *Idea and Essence in the Philosophies of Hobbes and Spinoza*, reissued New York: AMS Press, 1976.

Beck, Lewis White (1969). *Early German Philosophy*. Cambridge, Mass.: Harvard University Press.

Benardete, José (1980). 'Spinozistic Anomalies', in R. Kennington (ed.), *The Philosophy of Baruch Spinoza*. Washington, D.C.: Catholic University of America Press, 53–71.

Bennett, Jonathan (1966). *Kant's Analytic*. Cambridge University Press.

——(1974). *Kant's Dialectic*. Cambridge University Press.

——(1976). *Linguistic Behaviour*, reissued Indianapolis: Hackett, 1990.

——(1986). 'Spinoza on Error', in *Philosophical Papers*, 15: 59–73.

——(1990a). 'Spinoza and Teleology: A Reply to Curley', in Curley and Moreau 1990: 53–7.

——(1990b). 'Truth and Stability in Descartes's Treatment of Scepticism,' *Canadian Journal of Philosophy*, suppl. vol. 16: 75–108.

——(1991a). 'Folk-Psychological Explanations', in John D. Greenwood (ed.), *The Future of Folk Psychology*. Cambridge University Press, 176–95.

——(1991b). 'Spinoza's Monism: A Reply to Curley', in Yovel 1991: 53–9.

——(1994). 'Descartes's Theory of Modality'. *Philosophical Review*, 103: 639–67.

——(1996). 'What Events Are', in A. Varzi and R. Casati (eds.), *Events*. Aldershot: Dartmouth, 137–51.

——(2001a). 'God and Matter in Locke: An Exposition of *Essay* IV.x', in C. Mercer and E. O'Neill (eds.), *The History of Early Modern Philosophy: Essays in Honor of Margaret D. Wilson*. Oxford: Blackwell.

Bennett, Jonathan (2001b). 'Leibniz's Two Realms', in J. A. Cover and D. Rutherford (eds.), *Leibniz, Nature and Freedom*. New York: Oxford University Press.

Berkeley, George (1713). *Three Dialogues between Hylas and Philonous*, in LJ 2:163–263.

Blackburn, Simon (1990). 'Hume and Thick Connexions'. *Philosophy and Phenomenological Research*, 50 suppl.: 237–50.

Blumenfeld, David (1973). 'Leibniz's Theory of the Striving Possibles', repr. in Woolhouse 1981: 77–88.

Bonnen, Clarence, and Flage, Daniel (1999). 'Distinctness', in GH 285–95.

Boyle, Robert (1666). 'The Origin of Forms and Qualities According to the Corpuscular Philosophy', repr. in M. A. Stewart (ed.), *Selected Philosophical Papers of Robert Boyle*. Manchester University Press, 1–96.

Braithwaite, R. B. (1953). *Scientific Explanation*. Cambridge University Press.

Brandom, Robert B. (1981). 'Leibniz and Degrees of Perception'. *Journal of the History of Philosophy*, 19: 447–79.

Bréhier, Emile (1937). *The History of Philosophy: The Seventeenth Century*, trans. Wade Baskin. University of Chicago Press, 1966.

Broad, C. D. (1975). *Leibniz: An Introduction*. Cambridge University Press.

Brown, Gregory (1987). 'Compossibility, Harmony, and Perfection in Leibniz'. *Philosophical Review*, 96: 173–203.

Burnyeat, M. F. (1982). 'Idealism and Greek Philosophy: What Descartes Saw and Berkeley Missed'. *Philosophical Review*, 91: 1–40.

Butchvarov, Panayot (1970). *The Concept of Knowledge*. Evanston, Ill.: Northwestern University Press.

Campbell, Joseph Keim (1999). 'Descartes on Spontaneity, Indifference, and Alternatives', in GH 179–99.

Campbell, Keith (1981). 'The Metaphysics of Abstract Particulars'. *Midwest Studies in Philosophy*, 4: 477–88.

Carnap, Rudolf (1967). *The Logical Structure of the World*. Berkeley: University of California Press.

Carriero, John (1991). 'Spinoza's Views on Necessity in Historical Perspective'. *Philosophical Topics*, 19: 47–96.

——(1993). 'Leibniz on Infinite Resolution and Intra-mundane Contingency. Part One'. *Studia Leibnitiana*, 25: 1–26.

——(1994). 'On the Theological Roots of Spinoza's Argument for Monism'. *Faith and Philosophy*, 11: 626–44.

——(1995). 'On the Relationship between Mode and Substance in Spinoza's Metaphysics'. *Journal of the History of Philosophy*, 33: 245–73.

——(forthcoming a). 'Spinoza on Teleology and Agency'.

——(forthcoming b). 'Substance and Teleology in Leibniz'.

Castañeda, Hector-Neri (1984). 'Causes, Causity, and Energy'. *Midwest Studies in Philosophy*, 9: 17–27.

Caterus, Johannes (1640). Objections to Descartes's *Meditations*, in CSM 2:66–73.

Churchland, Paul (1979). *Scientific Realism and the Plasticity of Mind*. Cambridge University Press.

——(1984). *Matter and Consciousness*. Cambridge, Mass.: MIT Press.

Copleston, Frederick (1946). *A History of Philosophy*, vol. 1. London: Burns Oates & Washbourne.

Cottingham, John (1976) (ed.). *Descartes's Conversation with Burman*. Oxford University Press.

——(1986). *Descartes*. Oxford: Blackwell.

——(1993), *A Descartes Dictionary*. Oxford: Blackwell.

——(1994) (ed.). *Reason, Will and Sensation: Studies in Descartes's Metaphysics*. Oxford University Press.

Couturat, Louis (1902). 'On Leibniz's Metaphysics', repr. in Frankfurt 1976: 19–45.

Cover, J. A. (1989). 'Relations and Reducibility in Leibniz'. *Pacific Philosophical Quarterly*, 70: 185–211.

——(1997). 'Non-Basic Time and Reductive Strategies: Leibniz's Theory of Time'. *Studies in the History and Philosophy of Science*, 28: 289–318.

——(1999). 'Spinoza's Extended Substance: Cartesian and Leibnizian Reflections', in GH 105–33.

——and Hartz, Glenn A. (1994). 'Are Leibnizian Monads Spatial?' *History of Philosophy Quarterly*, 11: 295–316.

——and Kulstad, M. (1990) (eds.). *Central Themes in Early Modern Philosophy*. Indianapolis: Hackett.

——and O'Leary-Hawthorne, John (1999). *Substance and Individuation in Leibniz*. Cambridge University Press.

Curley, Edwin M. (1969). *Spinoza's Metaphysics: An Essay in Interpretation*. Cambridge, Mass.: Harvard University Press.

——(1976). 'The Root of Contingency', in Frankfurt 1976: 69–97.

——(1978). *Descartes Against the Skeptics*. Cambridge, Mass.: Harvard University Press.

——(1988). *Behind the Geometrical Method: A Reading of Spinoza's Ethics*. Princeton University Press.

——(1990). 'On Bennett's Spinoza: The Issue of Teleology', in Curley and Moreau 1990: 39–52.

——(1991). 'On Bennett's Interpretation of Spinoza's Monism', in Yovel 1991: 35–51.

——and Moreau, P.-F. (1990) (eds.). *Spinoza: Issues and Directions*. Leiden: Brill.

——and Walski, Gregory (1999). 'Spinoza's Necessitarianism Reconsidered', in GH 241–62.

D'Agostino, Fred (1976). 'Compossibility and Relational Predicates', repr. in Woolhouse 1981: 89–103.

Davidson, Donald (1963). 'Actions, Reasons, and Causes', repr. in his *Essays on Actions and Events*. Oxford University Press, 3–19.

Della Rocca, Michael (1996*a*). *Representation and the Mind–Body Problem in Spinoza*. New York: Oxford University Press.

——(1996*b*). 'Spinoza's Metaphysical Psychology', in Garrett 1996: 192–266.

——(1999). '"If a Body Meet a Body": Descartes on Body–Body Causation', in GH 48–81.

Denkel, Arda (1997). 'On the Compresence of Tropes'. *Philosophy and Phenomenological Research*, 57: 599–606.

Dennett, Daniel C. (1971). 'Intentional Systems', repr. in his *Brainstorms: Philosophical Essays on Mind and Psychology*. Montgomery, Vt.: Bradford Books, 3–22.

——(1978). 'Toward a Cognitive Theory of Consciousness', repr. in ibid. 149–73.

Descartes, René (1628). *Rules for the Direction of the Mind*, in CSM 1:9–76.

——(1633). *The World* and *Treatise on Man*, excerpts in CSM 1:81–108, complete in AT 11:1–202.

Descartes, René (1637a). *Discourse on the Method of Rightly Conducting One's Reason and Seeking the Truth in the Sciences*, in CSM 1:111–51.

——(1637b). *Optics*, excerpts in CSM 1:152–75, complete in AT 6:81–228.

——(1641). *Meditations on First Philosophy* and *Replies to Objections*, in CSM 2:3–385.

——(1644). *Principles of Philosophy*, mostly in CSM 1:179–404, complete in MM.

——(1648a). 'Comments on a Certain Broadsheet', in CSM 1:294–311.

——(1648b). *Conversation with Burman*, in Cottingham 1976; partly in CSMK 332–54.

——(1648c). *Description of the Human Body*, in AT 11:223–86.

——(1649). *The Passions of the Soul*, in CSM 1:328–404, and in (a better translation) S. Voss (ed.), *The Passions of the Soul* (Indianapolis: Hackett, 1989).

de Sousa, Ronald B. (1971). 'How to Give a Piece of Your Mind: or, The Logic of Belief and Assent'. *Review of Metaphysics*, 25: 52–79.

Deutscher, Max, and Martin, C. B. (1966). 'Remembering'. *Philosophical Review*, 75: 161–96.

Dijksterhuis, E. J. (1961). *The Mechanization of the World Picture*, trans. C. Dikshoorn. Oxford University Press.

Doney, Willis (1955). 'The Cartesian Circle'. *Journal of the History of Ideas*, 16: 324–38.

Earman, John (1977). 'Perceptions and Relations in the Monadology'. *Studia Leibnitiana*, 9: 212–30.

Edwards, Paul (1963) (ed.). *Encyclopedia of Philosophy*. New York: Macmillan.

Etchemendy, John (1981). 'The Cartesian Circle: *Circulus ex tempore*'. *Studia Cartesiana*, 2: 5–42.

Feynman, Richard, et al. (1963). *The Feynman Lectures on Physics: Mainly Mechanics, Radiation, and Heat*. Reading, Mass.: Addison-Wesley.

Fleming, Noel (1987). 'On Leibniz on Subject and Substance'. *Philosophical Review*, 96: 69–95.

Frankfurt, Harry G. (1962). 'Memory and the Cartesian Circle'. *Philosophical Review*, 71: 504–11.

——(1965). 'Descartes's Validation of Reason'. *American Philosophical Quarterly*, 2: 149–56.

——(1970). *Demons, Dreamers and Madmen*. Indianapolis: Bobbs Merrill.

——(1976) (ed.). *Leibniz: a Collection of Critical Essays*. University of Notre Dame Press.

Frege, Gottlob (1918). 'The Thought', repr. in P. F. Strawson (ed.), *Philosophical Logic*. Oxford University Press, 1967: 1–38.

Garber, Daniel (1985). 'Leibniz and the Foundations of Physics: The Middle Years', in Okruhlik and Brown 1985: 27–130.

——(1992). *Descartes' Metaphysical Physics*. University of Chicago Press.

——(1993a). 'Descartes and Experiment in the *Discourse* and *Essays*', in Voss 1993: 288–310.

——(1993b). 'Descartes and Occasionalism', in Nadler 1993, 9–26.

Garns, Rudy (1988). 'Descartes and Indubitability'. *Southern Journal of Philosophy*, 26: 83–100.

Garrett, Don (1991). 'Spinoza's Necessitarianism', in Yovel 1991: 191–218.

——(1996) (ed.). *The Cambridge Companion to Spinoza*. Cambridge University Press.

——(1997). *Cognition and Commitment in Hume's Philosophy*. New York: Oxford University Press.

——(1999). 'Teleology in Spinoza and Early Modern Rationalism', in GH 310–35.

Gassendi, Pierre (1641). Objections to Descartes's *Meditations*, in CSM 2:179–240.

Gaukroger, Stephen (1995). *Descartes: An Intellectual Biography.* Oxford University Press.

Gennaro, Rocco J. (1999). 'Leibniz on Consciousness and Self-Consciousness', in GH 353–71.

Gewirth, Alan (1941). 'The Cartesian Circle'. *Philosophical Review*, 50: 368–95.

Gilson, Étienne (1951). *Études sur le role de la pensée médiévale dans la formation du système cartésien.* Paris: Vrin.

Gorham, Geoffrey (1999). 'Causation and Similarity in Descartes', in GH 296–309.

Grandy, Richard (1975). 'Stuff and Things', repr. in F. J. Pelletier (ed.), *Mass Terms: Some Philosophical Problems.* Dordrecht: Reidel, 1979, 219–25.

Grant, Edward (1981). *Much Ado About Nothing: Theories of Space and Vacuum in the Middle Ages to the Scientific Revolution.* Cambridge University Press.

Grice, H. P. (1986). 'Reply to Richards', in R. E. Grandy and R. Warner (eds.), *Philosophical Grounds of Rationality: Intentions, Categories, Ends.* Oxford University Press, 45–106.

Grosholz, Emily R. (1980). 'Descartes' Unification of Algebra and Geometry', in S. Gaukroger (ed.), *Descartes: Philosophy, Mathematics and Physics.* Brighton: Harvester Press, 156–68.

Hacking, Ian (1973). 'Leibniz and Descartes: Proof and Eternal Truths'. *Proceedings of the British Academy*, 59: 175–88.

——(1976). 'Individual Substance', in Frankfurt 1976: 137–53.

——(1978). 'A Leibnizian Theory of Truth', in Hooker 1978: 185–95.

Hall, A. R. (1954). *The Scientific Revolution 1500–1800: The Formation of the Modern Scientific Attitude.* London: Longmans.

Hallett, H. F. (1957). *Benedict de Spinoza: The Elements of His Philosophy.* London: Athlone Press.

Hardin, C. L. (1988). *Color for Philosophers: Unweaving the Rainbow.* Indianapolis: Hackett.

Hartz, Glenn A. (1989). 'Leibniz on Why Descartes' Metaphysic of Body is Necessarily False', in N. Rescher (ed.), *Leibnizian Inquiries: A Group of Essays.* Lanham, Md.: University Press of America, 21–36.

——(1992). 'Leibniz's Phenomenalisms'. *Philosophical Review*, 101: 511–49.

——(1996). 'Exactly How are Leibnizian Substances Related to Extension?', in R. S. Woolhouse (ed.), *Leibniz's 'New System".* Florence: Olschki, 63–81.

——and Cover, J. A. (1988). 'Space and Time in the Leibnizian Metaphysic'. *Nous*, 22: 493–519.

Hintikka, Jaakko (1976). 'Leibniz on Plenitude, Relations, and the "Reign of Law"', in Frankfurt 1976: 155–90.

Hobbes, Thomas (1640). Objections to Descartes's *Meditations*, in CSM 2:121–37.

——(1651). *Leviathan.*

Hoffman, Paul (1986). 'The Unity of Descartes's Man'. *Philosophical Review*, 95: 339–70.

Hofstadter, Douglas R. (1979). *Gödel, Escher, Bach: An Eternal Golden Braid.* New York: Basic Books.

Hooker, Michael (1978) (ed.). *Leibniz: Critical and Interpretive Essays.* Baltimore: The Johns Hopkins University Press.

Huenemann, Charles (1999). 'The Necessity of Finite Modes and Geometrical Containment in Spinoza's Metaphysics', in GH 224–40.

Hume, David (1739). *A Treatise of Human Nature*, ed. L. A. Selby-Bigge. Oxford University Press, 1964.

——(1748). *An Enquiry Concerning Human Understanding*, ed. L. A. Selby-Bigge. Oxford University Press, 1955.

Ishiguro, Hidé (1972). *Leibniz's Philosophy of Logic and Language*. London: Duckworth.

——(1977). 'Pre-established Harmony *versus* Constant Conjunction'. *Proceedings of the British Academy*, 63: 239–63.

Jacob, François (1974). *The Logic of Life*, trans. B. E. Spillman. New York: Pantheon Books.

Jolley, Nicholas (1984). *Locke and Leibniz: A Study of the New Essays on Human Understanding*. Oxford University Press.

——(1986). 'Leibniz and Phenomenalism'. *Studia Leibnitiana*, 18: 38–51.

——(1995) (ed.). *The Cambridge Companion to Leibniz*. Cambridge University Press.

Kant, Immanuel (1786). *Metaphysical Foundations of Natural Science*, trans. J. Ellington. Indianapolis: Bobbs-Merrill, 1970.

Kaplan, Mark (1981). 'Rational Acceptance'. *Philosophical Studies*, 40: 129–45.

Kemp Smith, Norman (1952). *New Studies in the Philosophy of Descartes*. London: Macmillan. See also Smith.

Kenny, Anthony (1968). *Descartes: A Study of his Philosophy*. New York: Random House.

Kim, Jaegwon (1988). 'What is Naturalized Epistemology?', repr. in his *Supervenience and Mind*. Cambridge University Press, 1993, 216–36.

Kline, George L. (1977). 'On the Infinity of Spinoza's Attributes', in S. Hessing (ed.), *Speculum Spinozanum*. London: Routledge, 342–6.

Kneale, Martha (1969). 'Eternity and Sempiternity', repr. in M. Grene (ed.), *Spinoza: A Collection of Critical Essays*. Garden City, NY: Doubleday, 1973, 227–40.

Kneale, William C. (1939–40). 'The Notion of a Substance'. *Proceedings of the Aristotelian Society*, 40: 103–34.

Kripke, Saul (1972). 'Naming and Necessity', in D. Davidson and G. Harman (eds.), *Semantics of Natural Language*. Dordrecht: Reidel, 253–355.

Kulstad, Mark (1978). 'Some Difficulties in Leibniz's Definition of Perception', in Hooker 1978: 65–78.

——(1991). *Leibniz on Apperception, Consciousness, and Reflection*. Munich: Philosophia Verlag.

——(1993). 'Two Interpretations of the Pre-established Harmony in the Philosophy of Leibniz'. *Synthese*, 96: 477–504.

Langton, Rae, and Lewis, David (1998). 'Defining "Intrinsic"'. *Philosophy and Phenomenological Research*, 58: 333–45.

Leibniz, G. W. (1677). 'Two Sects of Naturalists', in G 7:332–6, and in AG.

——(1678). 'What is an Idea?', in G 7:263–4, and in L.

——(1679). 'On Freedom', in F. de C. 178–85, and in L.

——(1686a). *Discourse on Metaphysics*, in G 2:427–63, and in FW, AG, PM, and L.

——(1686b). 'Necessary and Contingent Truths', in Couturat 16–24, and in PM.

——(1686c). 'Primary Truths', in Grua 302–6, and in AG, PM, and L.

——(1690). Correspondence with Arnauld, in G 2:11–138, and in Mason, excerpts in FW, AG, PM, and L.

——(1691). 'On the Nature of Body and the Laws of Motion', in G 7:280–3, and in AG.

——(1692). 'Critical Thoughts on the General Part of the *Principles* of Descartes', in G 4:354–92, and in L.

——(1695a). 'New System of the Nature of Substances and their Communication', in G 4:477–87, and in FW, AG, PM, and L.

——(1695b). 'A Specimen of Dynamics', in GM 6:235–54, and in FW, AG, and L.

——(1696). 'Tentamen Anagogicum', in G 7:270–9, and in L.

——(1697a). Comment on Bayle's Note H, in G 4:524–33, and in FW.

——(1697b). 'On the Ultimate Origin of Things', in G 7:302–8, and in AG, PM, and L.

——(1698). 'On Nature Itself', in G 4:504–16, and in FW, AG, and L.

——(1699–1706). Corrrespondence with De Volder, in G 2:148–283, excerpts in L and AG.

——(1705a). 'Considerations on Vital Principles and Plastic Natures', in G 6:539–46, and in L.

——(1705b). New Essays on Human Understanding, ed. P. Remnant and J. Bennett. Cambridge University Press, 1981.

——(1709–15). Correspondence with Des Bosses, in G 2:291–521, excerpts in AG and L.

——(1707). 'Comments on Spinoza's Philosophy', in A. Foucher de Careil (ed.), Réfutation inédite de Spinoza. Paris, 1854, 22–70. Excerpt in AG.

——(1710). Theodicy, in G 6.

——(1714a). 'Monadology', in G 6:608–23, and in FW, AG, PM, and L.

——(1714b). 'Principles of Nature and Grace, Based on Reason', in G 6:598–606, and in FW, AG, PM, and L.

——(1716a). Correspondence with Clarke, in G 7:352–440, and in Alexander, excerpts in AG, PM, and L.

——(1716b). 'A Physicist against Barbarism', in G 7:337–44, and in AG.

Levey, Samuel (1998). 'Leibniz on Mathematics and the Actually Infinite Division of Matter'. Philosophical Review, 107: 49–96.

——(1999). 'Leibniz's Constructivism and Infinitely Folded Matter', in GH 134–62.

Lindberg, David C. (1976). Theories of Vision from Al-Kindi to Kepler. University of Chicago Press.

Lloyd, G. E. R. (1963). 'Leucippus and Democritus', in Edwards 1963.

Locke, John (1690). An Essay Concerning Human Understanding, ed. P. Nidditch. Oxford University Press, 1975.

——(1698). Second Reply to the Bishop of Worcester, repr. in The Works of John Locke in Ten Volumes. London: Johnson, 1801, 4: 195–498.

Loeb, Louis E. (1981). From Descartes to Hume. Ithaca, NY: Cornell University Press.

——(1990). 'The Priority of Reason in Descartes'. Philosophical Review, 99: 3–43.

——(1992). 'The Cartesian Circle', in J. Cottingham (ed.), The Cambridge Companion to Descartes. Cambridge University Press.

Lopston, Peter (1999). 'Was Leibniz an Idealist?' Philosophy, 74: 361–85.

Lucas, Peter G., and Grint, Leslie (1953). Translation of Leibniz, Discourse on Metaphysics. Manchester University Press.

MacKenzie, Ann Wilbur (1975). 'A Word about Descartes's Mechanistic Conception of Life'. Journal of the History of Biology, 8: 1–13.

McRae, Robert (1976). Leibniz: Perception, Apperception, and Thought. University of Toronto Press.

Maher, Patrick (1986). 'The Irrelevance of Belief to Rational Action'. Erkenntnis, 24: 363–84.

Manning, Richard (2000). 'Spinoza, Thoughtful Teleology, and the Causal Significance of Content', in J. Biro and O. Koistenen (eds.), New Essays on Spinoza. Oxford University Press.

Marks, Charles E. (1981). Commissurotomy, Consciousness, and Unity of Mind. Cambridge, Mass.: MIT Press.

Mates, Benson (1986). The Philosophy of Leibniz: Metaphysics and Language. New York: Oxford University Press.

Matson, Wallace I. (1991). 'Spinoza on Beliefs', in Y. Yovel (ed.), *Spinoza on Knowledge and the Human Mind*. Leiden: Brill, 67–81.

Mercer, Christia, and Sleigh, R. C., Jr. (1995). 'Metaphysics: The Early Period to the *Discourse on Metaphysics*', in Jolley 1995: 67–123.

Milhaud, Gaston (1921). *Descartes savant*. Paris: Félix Alcan.

Mondadori, Fabrizio (1975). 'Leibniz and the Doctrine of Inter-World Identity'. *Studia Leibnitiana*, 7: 21–57.

——(1993). 'On Some Disputed Questions in Leibniz's Metaphysics'. *Studia Leibnitiana*, 25: 153–73.

Nadler, Stephen (1993) (ed.). *Causation in Early Modern Philosophy*. University Park, Pa.: Pennsylvania State University Press.

Nagel, Thomas (1971). 'Brain Bisection and the Unity of Consciousness' (1971), repr. in his *Mortal Questions*. Cambridge University Press, 1979, 147–64.

——(1979). 'Panpsychism', in ibid. 181–95.

Nason, John W. (1942). 'Leibniz and the Logical Argument for Individual Substances', repr. in Woolhouse 1981: 11–29.

Newman, Lex (1999). 'The Fourth Meditation'. *Philosophy and Phenomenological Research*, 59: 559–91.

Nietzsche, Friedrich (1886). *Beyond Good and Evil*, trans. R. J. Hollingdale. London: Penguin, 1973.

Norris, Christopher (1991). *Spinoza and the Origins of Modern Critical Theory*. Oxford: Blackwell.

Okruhlik K., and Brown, J. R. (1985) (eds.). *The Natural Philosophy of Leibniz*. Dordrecht: Reidel.

O'Leary-Hawthorne, John (1995). 'The Bundle Theory of Substance and the Identity of Indiscernibles'. *Analysis*, 55: 191–6.

——and Cover, Jan A. (forthcoming). 'Infinite Analysis and the Problem of the Lucky Proof'.

O'Neill, Eileen (1993). '*Influxus Physicus*', in Nadler 1993: 27–55.

Palmer, Eric (1999). 'Descartes on Nothing in Particular', in GH 26–47.

Parkinson, G. H. R. (1965). *Logic and Reality in Leibniz's Metaphysics*. Oxford University Press.

——(1981). 'Kant as a Critic of Leibniz'. *Revue internationale de philosophie*, 136–7: 302–14.

——(1990). 'Definition, Essence, and Understanding in Spinoza', in Cover and Kulstad 1990: 49–67.

Pears, David (1990). *Hume's System*. Oxford University Press.

Pitcher, George (1971). *A Theory of Perception*. Princeton University Press.

Pollock, Frederick (1888). *Spinoza: His Life and Philosophy*, reissued Dubuque, Ia.: Reprint Library, n.d.

Popper, Karl R. (1959). *The Logic of Scientific Discovery*. London: Hutchinson.

Quine, W. V. (1969). 'Natural Kinds', in his *Ontological Relativity and Other Essays*. New York: Columbia University Press, 114–38.

Remnant, Peter (1979). 'Descartes: Body and Soul'. *Canadian Journal of Philosophy*, 9: 377–86.

Rescher, Nicholas (1967). *The Philosophy of Leibniz*. Englewood Cliffs, NJ: Prentice-Hall.

Rosenthal, David M. (1986). 'Will and the Theory of Judgment', in A. O. Rorty (ed.), *Essays on Descartes's Meditations*. Berkeley: University of California Press, 405–34.

Russell, Bertrand (1900). *A Critical Exposition of the Philosophy of Leibniz*, 2nd edn. London: Allen & Unwin, 1937.

——(1903). 'Recent Work on the Philosophy of Leibniz', repr. in Frankfurt 1976: 365–400.

Rutherford, Donald (1995*a*). *Leibniz and the Rational Order of Nature*. Cambridge University Press.

——(1995*b*). 'Metaphysics: The Late Period', in Jolley 1995: 224–69.

Saw, Ruth Lydia (1954). *Leibniz*. Harmondsworth: Penguin Books.

Schuster, John A. (1993). 'Whatever Should We Do with Cartesian Method? Reclaiming Descartes for the History of Science', in Voss 1993: 195–223.

Searle, John R. (1980). 'Minds, Brains, and Programs'. *Behavioral and Brain Sciences*, 3: 417–24.

Secada, J. E. K. (1990). 'Descartes on Time and Causality'. *Philosophical Review*, 99: 45–72.

Sellars, Wilfrid. (1965). '*Méditations Leibniziennes*', repr. in Woolhouse 1981: 30–54.

Séris, J.-P. (1993). 'Language and Machine in the Philosophy of Descartes', in Voss 1993: 177–92.

Shmueli, Efraim (1978). 'The Geometrical Method, Personal Caution, and the Idea of Tolerance', in R. W. Shahan and J. I. Biro (eds.), *Spinoza: New Perspectives*. Norman, Okla.: University of Oklahoma Press, 197–215.

Simons, Peter (1994). 'Particulars in Particular Clothing: Three Trope Theories of Substance'. *Philosophy and Phenomenological Research*, 54: 553–75.

Sleigh, Robert C., Jr. (1990*a*). *Leibniz and Arnauld: A Commentary on their Correspondence*. New Haven: Yale University Press.

——(1990*b*). 'Leibniz on Malebranche on Causality', in Cover and Kulstad 1990: 161–93.

Slowik, Edward (1999). 'Descartes, Spacetime, and Relational Motion'. *Philosophy of Science*, 66: 117–39.

Smith, Norman (1902). *Studies in the Cartesian Philosophy*, reissued New York: Russell & Russell, 1962. See also Kemp Smith.

Smyth, Richard (1986). 'A Metaphysical Reading of the First Meditation'. *Philosophical Quarterly*, 36: 483–503.

Sotnak, Eric (1999). 'The Range of Leibnizian Compatibilism', in GH 200–23.

Spinoza, Benedict (1661*a*). *Short Treatise on God, Man, and His Well-Being*, in CS 53–156.

——(1661*b*). *Treatise on the Emendation of the Intellect*, in CS 6–45.

——(1663). *Parts I and II of Descartes's 'Principles of Philosophy'*, in CS 224–346.

——(1675?). *Ethics Demonstrated in Geometrical Order*, in CS 408–617.

—— Correspondence, much in CS, complete in Wolf.

Stout, A. K. (1929). 'The Basis of Knowledge in Descartes', partly repr. in W. Doney (ed.), *Descartes: A Collection of Critical Essays*. University of Notre Dame Press, 1967, 167–91.

Stout, G. F. (1921). 'The Nature of Universals and Propositions'. *Proceedings of the British Academy*, 7: 157–72.

Strawson, P. F. (1959). *Individuals: An Essay in Descriptive Metaphysics*. London: Methuen.

Stuart, Matthew (1998). 'Locke on Superaddition and Mechanism'. *British Journal for the History of Philosophy*, 6: 351–79.

——(1999). 'Descartes's Extended Substances', in GH 82–133.

Tachau, Katherine H. (1988). *Vision and Certitude in the Age of Ockham*. Leiden: Brill.

Taton, René (1958) (ed.). *Histoire générale des sciences*. Paris: Presses Universitaires de France.

Tlumak, Jeffrey (1978). 'Certainty and Cartesian Method', in Hooker 1978: 40–73.

Truesdell, C. (1955). 'Experience, Theory and Experiment', repr. in his *An Idiot's Fugitive Essays on Science*. New York: Springer, 1984, 3–20.

——(1978). 'Our Debt to the French Tradition: "Catastrophes" and Our Search for Structure Today', repr. in ibid. 80–94.

Turnbull, Robert G. (1988). 'Aristotle and Philosophy Now: Some Critical Reflections', in P. H. Hare (ed.), *Doing Philosophy Historically*. Buffalo: Prometheus Books, 117–26.

Van Cleve, James (1979). 'Foundationalism, Epistemic Principles, and the Cartesian Circle'. *Philosophical Review*, 88: 55–91.

Van der Hoeven, P. (1973). 'The Significance of Cartesian Physics for Spinoza's Theory of Knowledge', repr. in J. G. Van der Bend (ed.), *Spinoza on Knowing, Being and Freedom*. Assen: van Gorcum, 1974, 114–25.

Van Gulick, Robert (1988). 'A Functionalist Plea for Self-Consciousness'. *Philosophical Review*, 97: 149–81.

van Inwagen, Peter (1990). *Material Beings*. Ithaca, NY: Cornell University Press.

Voss, Stephen (1993) (ed.). *Essays on the Philosophy and Science of René Descartes*. New York: Oxford University Press.

——(1994). 'Descartes: The End of Anthropology', in Cottingham 1994: 273–306.

——(1999). 'A Spectator at the Theater of the World', in GH 265–84.

Weber, Jean-Paul (1972). 'La Méthode de Descartes d'après les Regulae'. *Archives de Philosophie*, 35: 51–60.

Wedin, Michael (1988). *Mind and Imagination in Aristotle*. New Haven: Yale University Press.

Whiteside, D. T. (1974). Introduction to *The Mathematical Papers of Isaac Newton*, vol. 6, ed. D. T. Whiteside. Cambridge University Press.

Williams, Bernard (1963). 'Descartes', in Edwards 1963.

——(1972). 'Deciding to Believe', in his *Problems of the Self*. Cambridge University Press, 136–51.

——(1978). *Descartes: The Project of Pure Inquiry*. Harmondsworth: Penguin Books.

Williams, Donald C. (1953). 'The Elements of Being', repr. in his *Principles of Empirical Realism*. Springfield, Ill.: C. C. Thomas, 1966, 109–74.

Wilson, Catherine (1989). *Leibniz's Metaphysics: A Historical and Comparative Study*. Princeton University Press.

——(1999). 'The Illusory Nature of Leibniz's System', GH 372–88.

Wilson, Margaret D. (1974). 'Leibniz and Materialism'. *Canadian Journal of Philosophy*, 4: 495–513.

——(1976). 'Leibniz's Dynamics and Contingency in Nature', repr. in Woolhouse 1981: 119–38.

——(1977). 'Confused Ideas'. *Rice University Studies*, 63: 123–37.

——(1978). *Descartes*. London: Routledge.

——(1979a). 'Possible Gods'. *Review of Metaphysics*, 32: 717–33.

——(1979b). 'Superadded Properties: The Limits of Mechanism in Locke'. *American Philosophical Quarterly*, 16: 143–50.

——(1981). 'Notes on Modes and Attributes'. *Journal of Philosophy*, 78: 584–6.

——(1982). 'Superadded Properties: A Reply to Ayers'. *American Philosophical Quarterly*, 19: 247–52.

——(1987). 'Leibniz and Berkeley', in E. Sosa (ed.), *Essays on the Philosophy of George Berkeley*. Dordrecht: Reidel, 3–22.

——(1992). 'History of Philosophy in Philosophy Today; and the Case of the Sensible Qualities'. *Philosophical Review*, 101: 101–243.

——(1993*a*). 'Compossibility and Law', in Nadler 1993: 119–33.

——(1993*b*). 'Descartes on the Perception of Primary Qualities', in Voss 1993: 162–76.

——(1994). 'Descartes on Sense and "Resemblance"', in Cottingham 1994: 209–28.

Wittgenstein, Ludwig (1958). *The Blue and Brown Books*. Oxford: Blackwell.

Wolf-Devine, Celia (1993). *Descartes on Seeing*. Carbondale, Ill: University of Illinois Press.

Woolhouse, R. S. (1981) (ed.). *Leibniz: Metaphysics and Philosophy of Science*. Oxford University Press.

——(1990). 'Spinoza and Descartes and the Existence of Extended Substance', in Cover and Kulstad 1990: 23–48.

——(1993). *Descartes, Spinoza, Leibniz: The Concept of Substance in Seventeenth Century Metaphysics*. London: Routledge.

Yablo, Stephen (1990). 'The Real Distinction Between Mind and Body'. *Canadian Journal of Philosophy*, suppl. vol.: 149–201.

Yovel, Y. (1991) (ed.). *God and Nature in Spinoza's Metaphysics*. Leiden: Brill.

Index of Persons

Index of Subjects